Sunset
Recipe Annual

2001 EDITION

Pear Cream Pie (front, page 202) and
Pear Crumble Pie (rear, page 203)

By the Editors of Sunset Magazine
and Sunset Books

Sunset Publishing Corporation ■ **Menlo Park, California**

SUNSET
BOOKS

VP, General Manager
Richard A. Smeby

VP, Editorial Director
Bob Doyle

Production Director
Lory Day

Art Director
Vasken Guiragossian

STAFF FOR THIS BOOK
Managing Editor
Cornelia Fogle

Production Coordinator
Patricia S. Williams

SUNSET PUBLISHING
CORPORATION

Senior Vice President
Kevin Lynch

VP, Publisher
Christopher D. Kevorkian

VP, Manufacturing Director
Lorinda Reichert

VP, Editor-in-Chief, Sunset Magazine
Rosalie Muller Wright

Consumer Marketing Director
Christina Olsen

Managing Editor
Carol Hoffman

Art Director
James H. McCann

Senior Editor, Food & Entertaining
Jerry Anne Di Vecchio

Designers, Food & Entertaining
Dennis W. Leong,
Keith Whitney

Orange-Ginger Skirt Steak with Onions (page 165)

Welcome to the 14th edition of the *Sunset Recipe Annual*, a compilation of recipes and food features from the past year's issues of *Sunset Magazine*.

This year we sent our writers and reporters on a great taco hunt to find the West's outstanding tacos; we list the best taco restaurants and provide recipes for you to build your own creations. You'll visit Basque festivals and sample traditional dishes. Farmers' markets offer the freshest produce; you'll find a list of our favorites—and dishes to show them off. And you'll find the prize-winning recipes from our barbecue cook-off, along with all our regular monthly features.

Several casual parties put guests to work—the host plans the menu, then assigns easy tasks to teams. We offer casual taco- and pizza-making parties, and feasts inspired by farmers' market produce and Northwest seafood. More formal gatherings range from a fondue party to holiday dinners and buffets.

We think this was a great year. We hope you'll agree.

Cover: Halibut with sake clam broth (page 9). Cover design: Vasken Guiragossian. Photographer: Tucker & Hossler.

Back cover photographers: (top and center) James Carrier; (bottom) Tucker & Hossler.

First printing November 2000
Copyright © 2000 Sunset Publishing Corporation, Menlo Park, CA 94025. First edition. All rights reserved, including the right of reproduction in whole or in part in any form.

ISBN 0-376-02707-X (hardcover)
ISBN 0-376-02708-8 (softcover)
ISSN 0896-2170
Printed in the United States

Material in this book originally appeared in the 2000 issues of *Sunset Magazine*. All of the recipes were developed and tested in the *Sunset* test kitchens. If you have comments or suggestions, please let us hear from you. Write us at Sunset Books, Cookbook Editorial, 80 Willow Road, Menlo Park, CA 94025.

Contents

A Letter from Sunset

DEAR READER,

Not too long ago, among the many e-mail messages I receive daily, there was a complaint. A reader couldn't find an ingredient listed in one of our recipes. As I responded to him, I realized my comments affect you, too.

In this, our 14th *Sunset Recipe Annual,* and in each of the preceding annuals, our food writers have worked hard to keep you up to speed about the latest developments in what's available in supermarkets, farmers' markets (see page 250), ethnic markets, and specialty shops such as natural foods stores. We identify what's new or not well known (see "Citrus Surprises," page 40) and explain the basics: what it is, where to find it, how to use it. Our objective is to keep you informed so that as you plan, shop, and cook for family and friends you can take full advantage of today's market bounty. Still, in any recipe that may require special shopping, we always suggest a reliable supermarket alternative.

Oh, yes. What was it that reader wanted? A fresh chili that's available everywhere. He just hadn't noticed it.

While we're talking about shopping is a good time to acknowledge the web. In recent research I learned that more than 75 percent of *Sunset Magazine* readers use it. This opens the door to a much wider world. In my monthly *Food Guide* I frequently give websites as well as telephone or mail sources for discoveries that are new or hard to find, such as the microplane grater (page 149), telescopic campfire fork (page 205), egg-top cutter (page 234), and Celebration dates (page 321).

But what about the subjects you've come to expect in this book?

Entertaining? It runs a gamut. A creative pizza party (page 18) comes from restaurant designer Pat Kuleto and his wife, Shannon; they invite their guests to build their own pizzas from a lavish selection of toppings. Another participatory party (page 162) has a similar spirit: the guests themselves prepare the dinner, following a team game plan. Mark Peel and Nancy Silverton, a two-chef family, offer a delicious but simple summer supper (page 226) to share with friends. In these parties and others, including holiday meals (a harvest feast, page 308; an Italian-American Thanksgiving, page 320; and festive buffets, page 340), menus are realistically geared for you to manage in your own kitchen.

Tools and techniques are explored in our article on fondue's revival (page 36), with recipes for en-

THE WRITING TEAM: (left to right, seated) Linda Anusasananan, senior writer; Jerry Anne Di Vecchio, senior food and entertaining editor; (left to right, standing) Elaine Johnson, senior writer; Andrew Baker, writer; and Sara Schneider, senior editor.

THE SUPPORT TEAM: (left to right, seated) Dennis W. Leong, associate art director; Linda Haderer, retester; Bernadette Hart, editorial services and test kitchen manager; (left to right, standing) Eligio Hernandez, editorial services; Allene Russell and Dorothy Decker, retesters; James Carrier, staff photographer; and Sarah Epstein, retester. Off scene: Keith Whitney, associate art director; and retesters Angela Brassinga, Bill Hickey, Odette Morais, Cathy O'Brien, Jean Strain, and Linda Tebbin.

tertaining. Slow cooking with the electric crock gets a contemporary update on page 288. Stir-frying goes Indian-style (page 173) in *The Quick Cook,* a regular feature with recipes that take 30 minutes or less. The casseroles ideas beginning on page 104 trim fat from make-ahead favorites; in fact, our *Low-Fat Cook* regularly offers healthy choices such as "luscious cakes with no guilt" (page 50). For savvy beverage selections, our *Wine Guide* overflows with possibilities.

Our "great taco hunt" (page 62), a joint effort by *Sunset* and its readers, was a great hit. Readers voted enthusiastically for their favorite *taquerias,* and editors coaxed forth the recipes, then listed the winners. This was only one of the ways readers contributed this year. *Kitchen Cabinet,* a feature started in 1929, always consists of recipes submitted by readers; this year, we gave awards for holiday pies (page 334). The biggest reader-participation event, however, was our Barbecue Cook-Off 2000 contest (page 188). From hundreds of entries, 75 recipes were prepared and rated in our test kitchens; eventually, 15 finalists came to our headquarters and grilled their creations for a panel of expert judges.

As you leaf through this book, you may notice that our graphic design is undergoing an evolution, aimed at making information more clearly presented and reading easier. To learn more about our magazine, visit our website (www.sunset.com); click on "magazine" to preview the current issue or "subscribe" to become a regular reader. If you are already a subscriber, enter your password and user i.d. (new each month in the *From the Editor* column) to access the previous two years of the magazine.

And if you can't find an ingredient or have a cooking question or suggestion, just e-mail me directly at divecchioj@sunset.com. I'd love to hear from you.

Jerry Di Vecchio

Jerry Di Vecchio
Senior Editor, Food and Entertaining

TO USE OUR NUTRITIONAL INFORMATION

The most current data from the USDA is used for our recipes: calorie count; fat calories; grams of protein, total and saturated fat, carbohydrates, and fiber; and milligrams of sodium and cholesterol.

This analysis is usually given for a single serving, based on the largest number of servings listed. Or it's for a specific amount, such as per tablespoon (for sauces); or by unit, as per cookie.

Optional ingredients are not included, nor are those for which no specific amount is stated (salt added to taste, for example). If an ingredient is listed with an alternative, calculations are based on the first choice listed. Likewise, if a range is given for the amount of an ingredient (such as ½ to 1 cup milk), values are figured on the first, lower amount.

Recipes using broth are calculated on the sodium content of salt-free broth, homemade or canned. If you use canned salted chicken broth, the sodium content will be higher.

Halibut with Sake Clam Broth (recipe on page 9) is one of 25 homemade winter soups and stews to soothe the stressed-out soul.

January

Comfort in a bowl

Paella Soup

Homemade stews and soups to soothe the stressed-out soul

BY LINDA LAU ANUSASANANAN

PHOTOGRAPHS BY JAMES CARRIER

■ WHEN I WAS GROWING UP—AT THE DAWN OF CONVENIENCE foods—the highlight of grocery shopping for me was choosing my favorite soups in those familiar red-and-white cans: beef and barley, bean and bacon, chicken and noodles. To my young taste buds, they were everything the TV ads promised: "M'm! M'm! Good!"

I've never tired of soup or its thicker, chunkier cousin, stew. But I've graduated from cans to pots on the stove. Homemade versions often are just as fast and always taste better, and I can tailor the recipes to my nutrition objectives.

The one-bowl meals here provide all the flavor of slow-simmered dishes, but quickly and with little fat. Some are bright and brash, with worldly flavors. Others have the comforting taste and heft of yesteryear. Some make use of today's high-quality convenience products, such as heat-and-serve cooked beef or quick-cooking grains. You can even choose vegetables for their cooking speed—fresh, frozen, or canned (judiciously used). All of these stews and soups, however, bring an old-fashioned degree of satisfaction.

SEAFOOD

Paella Soup

PREP AND COOK TIME: About 45 minutes

NOTES: A flavored rice mix gives this company-worthy soup a head start.

MAKES: 6 servings

- 2 **red bell peppers** (1½ lb. total)
- 1 teaspoon **olive oil**
- 1 cup cubed (½ in.) **cooked ham** or Canadian bacon (4 oz.)
- 2 packages (5 to 6 oz. each) **Spanish-style seasoned rice mix**
- 1½ quarts fat-skimmed **chicken broth**
- ¼ teaspoon **saffron threads** (optional)
- 1½ pounds (21 to 30 per lb.) **frozen shelled, deveined shrimp**
- 1 cup **frozen petite peas**

1. Rinse, stem, seed, and chop bell peppers. In a 5- to 6-quart nonstick pan over high heat, stir 1½ cups chopped red peppers with the oil and ham until peppers are limp, about 5 minutes. Add rice, water (as specified on package), and seasoning packets. Bring to a boil, cover, reduce heat, and simmer until rice is tender to bite, 18 to 20 minutes, stirring occasionally.

2. About 8 minutes before rice is done, in a 4- to 5-quart pan over high heat, bring broth and saffron to a boil. Stir in shrimp, cover, and return to a boil. Reduce heat and simmer until shrimp is opaque in center of thickest part (cut to test), about 5 minutes. With a slotted spoon, transfer shrimp to a small bowl. Return broth to a boil over high heat.

3. Stir peas into rice mixture and cook until they're hot, about 2 minutes.

4. Mound hot rice mixture equally in the center of 6 wide soup bowls, spoon shrimp around rice, sprinkle with remaining chopped red peppers, and ladle broth around rice.

Per serving: 375 cal., 13% (47 cal.) from fat; 41 g protein; 5.2 g fat (1.2 g sat.); 39 g carbo (3.4 g fiber); 1,405 mg sodium; 184 mg chol.

Halibut with
Sake Clam Broth

Halibut with Sake Clam Broth

PREP AND COOK TIME: About 40 minutes

NOTES: This dish was inspired by Michael Mina, executive chef at Aqua in San Francisco. Look for miso paste and sake in Japanese markets or fine supermarkets.

MAKES: 4 servings

 1 **carrot** (¼ lb.)

12 **clams** (about 1½ in. wide), suitable for steaming

 1 cup **cherry tomatoes**

 1 pound **boned, skinned halibut** or other firm white-flesh fish (¾ to 1 in. thick)

¼ cup **aka miso** (Japanese brown soy bean paste) or purchased teriyaki sauce

 1 tablespoon **sugar**

 1 cup **sake**

 2 cups fat-skimmed **chicken broth**

⅓ cup **dried orzo pasta**

 1 **baby bok choy** (4 to 5 oz.)

 1 cup **frozen petite peas**

⅓ cup finely slivered **green onions**

1. Peel carrot and thinly slice diagonally. Scrub clams. Rinse and stem cherry tomatoes; cut in half.

2. Rinse fish and pat dry. Cut into 4 equal pieces. Mix miso, sugar, and 1 tablespoon sake. Coat fish with miso mixture and set pieces slightly apart in an oiled 9-inch-wide pan.

3. Bake fish in a 450° oven until barely opaque and still very moist-looking in center of thickest part (cut to test), 8 to 10 minutes.

4. As fish bakes, in a 3- to 4-quart pan over high heat, bring broth and remaining sake to a boil. Add orzo, carrot, and clams; cover and cook until clams pop open, 5 to 10 minutes. With a slotted spoon, transfer open clams to a small bowl; discard any that don't open.

5. Meanwhile, trim and discard stem end from bok choy. Pull leaves off stems; rinse and drain both. Cut stems and leaves diagonally into 1-inch lengths.

6. When orzo is just tender to bite, in about 10 minutes total, stir bok choy and peas into broth. Return to a boil.

7. Set a piece of fish in the center of each wide soup bowl. Surround with equal portions of clams and tomatoes. Ladle orzo and broth mixture around fish and sprinkle fish with green onions.

Per serving: 370 cal., 11% (41 cal.) from fat; 41 g protein; 4.6 g fat (0.6 g sat.); 31 g carbo (5.6 g fiber); 846 mg sodium; 52 mg chol.

Chinese Fish and Lettuce Soup

PREP AND COOK TIME: About 35 minutes
NOTES: To easily slice fish very thin, freeze the piece until it's firm when pressed, about 30 minutes, then cut. For drama, bring the boiling broth to the table and ladle it into bowls over the raw fish, lettuce, and noodles—the fish cooks in seconds. Look for wiry bean thread noodles in the international section of well-stocked supermarkets or in Asian markets.
MAKES: 4 servings

- 4 ounces **dried bean thread noodles** (*saifun* or *harusame*)
- 6 ounces (about 6 cups) **green-leaf lettuce**
- 6 cups fat-skimmed **chicken broth**
- 2 tablespoons finely shredded **fresh ginger**
- 1 pound **boned, skinned firm white-flesh fish** such as halibut
- ½ cup **fresh cilantro** leaves, rinsed
- ⅓ cup thinly sliced **green onions** (including tops)
- **Salt** and **white pepper**

1. Put bean threads in a bowl and add enough hot water to cover. Soak until soft to bite, about 10 minutes.

2. Meanwhile, rinse and drain lettuce. Stack 3 or 4 leaves, roll up lengthwise, and cut crosswise into ¼-inch-wide strips. Repeat to cut remaining leaves. Place equal portions of lettuce in wide soup bowls, or all of the lettuce in a 3- to 4-quart tureen.

3. In a 3- to 4-quart pan over high heat, bring broth and ginger to a boil.

4. Meanwhile, cut fish across the grain into paper-thin slices (see notes).

Chinese Fish and Lettuce Soup

Drain noodles; if desired, snip with scissors into 6- to 8-inch lengths. Mound noodles and fish on lettuce; sprinkle with cilantro and green onions.

5. To serve, pour boiling broth over fish in bowls or tureen (see notes); stir to cook fish evenly. If fish does not turn opaque, cover bowls or tureen tightly and let stand 2 to 3 minutes. Add salt and white pepper to taste.

Per serving: 290 cal., 8.6% (25 cal.) from fat; 36 g protein; 2.8 g fat (0.4 g sat.); 27 g carbo (1.3 g fiber); 183 mg sodium; 36 mg chol.

Brazilian Fish and Shrimp Stew

PREP AND COOK TIME: About 25 minutes
NOTES: Anne McGinley of Eugene, Oregon, shares this dish, which makes a fine party entrée, particularly if accompanied by chopped roasted peanuts and additional dried coconut, with chopped fresh cilantro to add to taste. For less heat, seed and devein the jalapeño chilies before mincing.
MAKES: 8 servings

- 2 **onions** (6 oz. each)
- 3 cloves **garlic**
- 1 teaspoon **olive oil**
- 5 to 7 tablespoons minced **fresh jalapeño chilies**
- 3 tablespoons minced **fresh ginger**
- 4 cups fat-skimmed **chicken broth**
- 2 cans (15 oz. each) **tomato sauce**
- 1 can (14½ oz.) **stewed tomatoes**
- ¼ cup **sweetened shredded dried coconut**
- 3 tablespoons **chunky peanut butter**
- 2 pounds (41 to 50 per lb.) **frozen shelled, deveined shrimp**
- 1 pound **boned, skinned firm white-flesh fish** such as halibut
- ½ cup chopped **fresh cilantro**
- **Salt** and **pepper**
- **Cilantro sprigs**, rinsed

1. Peel onions and garlic; mince. In a 5- to 6-quart nonstick pan over high heat, stir onions, garlic, oil, jalapeños, and ginger often until onions are limp, about 10 minutes.

2. Stir in broth, tomato sauce, stewed tomatoes (including juices; break tomatoes into chunks with a spoon), coconut, and peanut butter.

3. When mixture is simmering, stir in shrimp. Cover and cook over medium-low heat 4 minutes. Meanwhile, rinse fish and cut into 1-inch chunks.

4. Stir fish into sauce, cover pan, and cook until fish and shrimp are opaque but still moist-looking in center of thickest part (cut to test), 3 to 4 minutes. Stir in chopped cilantro and add salt and pepper to taste.

5. Ladle into soup bowls. Garnish with cilantro sprigs.

Per serving: 318 cal., 22% (71 cal.) from fat; 43 g protein; 7.9 g fat (1.9 g sat.); 19 g carbo (3.4 g fiber); 1,030 mg sodium; 191 mg chol.

Shrimp and Corn Soup with Mint

PREP AND COOK TIME: About 30 minutes
NOTES: Nicole Perzik, a private chef in Los Angeles, developed this soup for a client who wanted interesting, refreshing dishes while on a low-fat diet. Look for canned ears of baby corn in the international or fancy-food section of a well-stocked supermarket or in an Asian market.

MAKES: 6 servings

6 cups fat-skimmed **chicken broth**

1 tablespoon minced **fresh ginger**

½ pound **banana** or hubbard **squash**

1 can (15 oz.) **whole baby corn,** drained

1 pound (51 to 60 per lb.) **frozen shelled, deveined shrimp**

½ teaspoon finely shredded **orange** peel

½ cup **orange juice**

½ cup chopped **fresh mint** leaves

Asian fish sauce (*nuoc mam* or *nam pla*) or salt

1. In a 3- to 4-quart pan over high heat, bring broth and ginger to a boil.

2. Meanwhile, peel squash and cut into ½-inch cubes. Add to broth, reduce heat, cover, and simmer until squash is tender when mashed, 12 to 15 minutes.

3. Add corn and shrimp; cover and cook over high heat until shrimp is opaque but still moist-looking in center of thickest part (cut to test), 4 to 5 minutes.

4. Stir in orange peel, orange juice, mint, and fish sauce to taste. Ladle into soup bowls.

Per serving: 154 cal., 12% (18 cal.) from fat; 25 g protein; 2 g fat (0.3 g sat.); 7.9 g carbo (2.5 g fiber); 201 mg sodium; 115 mg chol.

POULTRY

Chicken Pot-au-Feu

PREP AND COOK TIME: About 25 minutes
NOTES: This dish is hearty enough that you'll want a knife and fork in addition to a spoon.

MAKES: 4 servings

4 **boned, skinned chicken breast halves** (5 to 6 oz. each)

½ teaspoon **olive oil**

3 cups **fat-skimmed chicken broth**

1 cup **dry white wine**

1 teaspoon **dried thyme**

12 **red thin-skinned potatoes** (1 in. wide)

Put some mussel in it

Thai Hot and Sour Mussel Soup

PREP AND COOK TIME: About 30 minutes
NOTES: Instead of fish sauce, you can add salt to taste.

MAKES: 4 servings

1½ cups **jasmine** or long-grain white **rice**

4 dozen **mussels in shells** (about 2 lb. total)

4 cups fat-skimmed **chicken broth**

3 or 4 **dried hot chilies** (2 to 3 in. long)

6 slices (quarter-size) peeled **fresh ginger**

1 can (7 oz.) **corn kernels with bell peppers,** drained

½ cup chopped **Roma tomatoes**

⅓ cup **lemon juice**

¼ cup chopped **fresh cilantro**

About 1 tablespoon **Asian fish sauce** (*nuoc mam* or *nam pla;* see notes)

1. In a 2- to 3-quart pan, mix rice and 2¾ cups water. Bring to a boil over high heat, cover pan, and cook until most of the water is absorbed, 7 to 10 minutes. Turn heat to low and simmer until rice is tender to bite, 10 to 15 minutes longer.

2. Meanwhile, scrub mussels and pull off and discard beards. In a 5- to 6-quart pan over high heat, bring broth, chilies, and ginger to a boil. Add mussels, cover, and cook until shells pop open, about 5 minutes. Discard any mussels that don't open.

3. Stir corn into hot rice. Mound equal portions of cooked rice in 4 wide soup bowls. With a slotted spoon, discard ginger and dried chilies from mussels, and transfer mussels to bowls.

4. To broth, add tomatoes, lemon juice, cilantro, and fish sauce to taste. Ladle equally into bowls.

Per serving: 405 cal., 7.2% (29 cal.) from fat; 26 g protein; 3.2 g fat (0.6 g sat.); 68 g carbo (0.8 g fiber); 678 mg sodium; 27 mg chol.

8 **baby carrots** (4 in. long)

4 **baby bok choy** (4 to 5 oz. each)

⅓ cup **nonfat sour cream**

1 tablespoon **Dijon mustard**

2 tablespoons chopped **shallots**

1 tablespoon drained **capers**

   Salt and **pepper**

1. Rinse chicken and pat dry. Pour oil into a 5- to 6-quart nonstick pan over high heat. Add chicken and turn as needed to brown lightly on all sides, 4 to 5 minutes total. Transfer chicken to a bowl. To pan, add broth, wine, and thyme; cover and bring to a boil.

2. Meanwhile, scrub or peel potatoes. When broth is boiling, add potatoes. Cover, return to a boil, reduce heat, and simmer for 5 minutes.

3. As potatoes cook, peel carrots. Cut bok choy in half lengthwise; rinse well.

4. Add carrots to pan and arrange chicken in a single layer on vegetables. Cover and cook over medium heat for 10 minutes. Lay bok choy on chicken; cover and simmer until chicken is white in center of thickest part (cut to test), about 5 minutes longer.

5. In a small bowl, mix sour cream, mustard, shallots, and capers.

6. With a slotted spoon, transfer equal portions of chicken and vegetables to wide soup bowls. Ladle hot broth equally into bowls and add sour cream sauce, salt, and pepper to taste.

Per serving: 356 cal., 7% (25 cal.) from fat; 44 g protein; 2.8 g fat (0.6 g sat.); 27 g carbo (3.6 g fiber); 444 mg sodium; 84 mg chol.

Chicken-Avocado Tortilla Soup

PREP AND COOK TIME: About 30 minutes

NOTES: The thinly sliced corn tortillas that Audrey Thibodeau of Gilbert, Arizona, adds to this dish thicken the soup as they dissolve.

MAKES: 6 servings

⅓ cup chopped **onion**

3 cloves **garlic,** peeled and chopped

¾ teaspoon **ground cumin**

¾ teaspoon **dried oregano**

¼ teaspoon **chili powder**

¼ teaspoon **pepper**

8 cups fat-skimmed **chicken broth**

1 can (14 oz.) **diced tomatoes**

1 can (4 oz.) **diced green chilies**

10 **corn tortillas** (6 in. wide)

1½ pounds **boned, skinned chicken breasts**

1 **firm-ripe avocado** (½ lb.)

2 tablespoons chopped **fresh cilantro**

   Salt

   About ½ cup **shredded reduced-fat sharp cheddar cheese**

1. In a 5- to 6-quart nonstick pan over medium heat, stir onion, garlic, cumin, oregano, chili powder, and pepper until spices are fragrant, about 1 minute. Add broth, tomatoes (including juice), and green chilies. Cover and bring to a boil over high heat.

2. Meanwhile, stack tortillas and cut into ⅛-inch-wide strips. Add to boiling broth. Reduce heat, cover, and simmer for 15 minutes, stirring occasionally.

3. Rinse chicken and cut into ½-inch pieces. Peel the avocado, pit, and thinly slice.

4. Add chicken to broth and return to a boil over high heat. Reduce heat, cover, and simmer until chicken is white in center (cut to test), about 5 minutes. Stir in cilantro and salt to taste. Ladle into soup bowls, garnish with avocado, and add cheese to taste.

Per serving: 361 cal., 21% (77 cal.) from fat; 44 g protein; 8.6 g fat (2.4 g sat.); 27 g carbo (3.7 g fiber); 542 mg sodium; 72 mg chol.

Chicken-Avocado Tortilla Soup

Chicken and Leek Stew

PREP AND COOK TIME: About 30 minutes

NOTES: This sturdy stew also calls for knives and forks.

MAKES: 4 servings

6 **leeks** (each about 1½ in. wide)

4 **boned, skinned chicken breast halves** (5 to 6 oz. each)

½ pound **red thin-skinned potatoes**

1 teaspoon **butter** or margarine

2 cups fat-skimmed **chicken broth**

1 cup **dry vermouth** or white wine

1 tablespoon chopped **fresh basil** leaves or 1 teaspoon dried basil

1 teaspoon grated **lemon** peel

1½ cups **frozen petite peas**

2 tablespoons **cornstarch**

   Salt and **pepper**

   Thin **lemon** slices

   Basil sprigs, rinsed (optional)

1. Trim off and discard root ends and tough green tops of leeks. Cut leeks in half lengthwise and rinse well, then cut crosswise into ½-inch-thick slices. Rinse chicken and pat dry. Scrub potatoes and cut into ½-inch cubes.

2. In a 5- to 6-quart nonstick pan over medium-high heat, melt butter. Add chicken and turn as needed to brown lightly on all sides, 4 to 5 minutes total; transfer to a small bowl.

3. Add leeks to pan; stir until limp, 3 to 4 minutes. Add broth, vermouth, chopped basil, lemon peel, and potatoes; cover and bring to a boil over high heat. Reduce heat and simmer 10 minutes. Lay chicken on vegetables in pan; cover and simmer until potatoes are tender when pierced and chicken is white in center of thickest part (cut to test), 10 to 16 minutes longer.

4. With a slotted spoon, return chicken to the small bowl. Add peas to leek mixture. In another small bowl, blend cornstarch and ¼ cup water until smooth. Stir into pan and bring to a boil over high heat, stirring. Add salt and pepper to taste.

5. Spoon equal portions of the leek mixture into wide soup bowls. Top each mound of leeks with a piece of chicken

In a stew

Chicken and Vegetable Stew

PREP AND COOK TIME: About 45 minutes

MAKES: 4 or 5 servings

- 1 pound **boned, skinned chicken breasts**
- 8 **red thin-skinned potatoes** (1 in. wide)
- 2 **carrots** (6 oz. total)
- 4 **shallots** (1 in. wide)
- ½ pound **green beans**
- 1 cup **cherry tomatoes**
- 1 teaspoon **salad oil**
- 2 cups **fat-skimmed chicken broth**
- 2 teaspoons minced **fresh tarragon** leaves or 1 teaspoon dried tarragon
- 2 tablespoons **cornstarch**
- **Salt** and **pepper**

1. Rinse chicken, pat dry, and cut into 1-inch chunks. Scrub potatoes. Peel carrots and cut diagonally into ½-inch-thick slices. Peel shallots and cut in half lengthwise. Rinse green beans and cut off and discard stem ends. Cut beans into 1½-inch lengths. Rinse tomatoes, discard stems, and cut in half.

2. In a 5- to 6-quart nonstick pan over high heat, stir chicken in oil often until chicken is lightly browned, 8 to 10 minutes. Transfer chicken to a bowl.

3. To pan, add broth, potatoes, carrots, shallots, and tarragon. Cover and bring to a boil over high heat. Reduce heat to low and simmer for 5 minutes. Add chicken and beans. Cover and simmer until chicken is white in center of thickest part (cut to test) and potatoes are tender when pierced, about 8 minutes longer.

4. In a small bowl, mix cornstarch and ¼ cup water until smooth. Turn heat under stew to high, stir in cornstarch mixture, and continue to stir until boiling. Add tomatoes, mix, and season to taste with salt and pepper. Ladle into wide soup bowls.

Per serving: 208 cal., 10% (21 cal.) from fat; 27 g protein; 2.3 g fat (0.4 g sat.); 20 g carbo (2.9 g fiber); 109 mg sodium; 53 mg chol.

(if desired, cut breasts crosswise into ½-inch-thick slices). Garnish with lemon slices and basil sprigs.

Per serving: 412 cal., 7.8% (32 cal.) from fat; 44 g protein; 3.5 g fat (1.2 g sat.); 51 g carbo (6.9 g fiber); 273 mg sodium; 85 mg chol.

Chinese Chicken and Corn Soup

PREP AND COOK TIME: About 30 minutes

NOTES: This soup made Eric Lai, now from Saratoga, California, popular with his roommates at the University of California at San Diego.

MAKES: 5 or 6 servings

- 1 **boned, skinned chicken breast half** (5 to 6 oz.)
- 2 tablespoons **Chinese rice wine** or dry sherry
- 1½ teaspoons **Asian (toasted) sesame oil**
- 3 tablespoons **cornstarch**
- 1 clove **garlic**
- 1 tablespoon thinly shredded **fresh ginger**
- 4 cups **fat-skimmed chicken broth**

- 1 carton (12.3 oz.) **shelf-stable silken-style firm tofu**
- 1½ cups **frozen corn kernels**
- 1 **large egg**
- ½ cup thinly sliced **green onions** (including tops)
- **Salt** and **white pepper**

1. Rinse chicken and pat dry. Slice breast crosswise into ⅛-inch-thick strips. In a small bowl, mix chicken with wine, ½ teaspoon sesame oil, and 1 tablespoon cornstarch.

2. Peel garlic and mince or press. In a 3- to 4-quart nonstick pan over high heat, stir the garlic and ginger in ½ teaspoon sesame oil for 10 seconds. Add chicken and stir until meat is no longer pink on the surface, about 2 minutes. Add broth, cover pan, and bring to a boil.

3. Cut tofu into ½-inch cubes. Add tofu and corn to broth and return mixture to a simmer.

4. In a small bowl, blend remaining 2 tablespoons cornstarch and ¼ cup water until smooth; add to soup, and stir until mixture boils. In the same small bowl, beat egg to blend, then pour into soup, stirring to form thin

strands, about 30 seconds. Add remaining ½ teaspoon sesame oil, the green onions, and salt and pepper to taste. Ladle into soup bowls.

Per serving: 219 cal., 31% (68 cal.) from fat; 22 g protein; 7.6 g fat (1.3 g sat.); 16 g carbo (1.1 g fiber); 88 mg sodium; 49 mg chol.

Mexican Chicken Stew

PREP AND COOK TIME: About 50 minutes

NOTES: Chuck Allen of Cathedral City, California, serves this soup for family fiesta dinners.

MAKES: 8 or 9 servings

- 1 **onion** (¾ lb.)
- 4 cloves **garlic**
- ½ teaspoon **salad oil**
- 1 teaspoon **chili powder**
- 1 teaspoon **ground cumin**
- 1 teaspoon **ground cinnamon**
- 7 cups **fat-skimmed chicken broth**
- 1 can (14½ oz.) **Mexican-style stewed tomatoes**
- 3 cups diced (½ in.) **zucchini**
- 1½ cups **frozen corn kernels**

1 to 1½ tablespoons minced **pickled jalapeño chilies** (jalapeños en escabeche) or fresh jalapeño chilies

½ teaspoon **dried oregano**

1½ pounds **boned, skinned chicken breasts**

Salt and **pepper**

About ¾ cup **shredded reduced-fat cheddar** or jack **cheese**

1. Peel onion and cut lengthwise into thin slivers. Peel and chop garlic. In a 6- to 8-quart pan over medium-high heat, stir onion, garlic, and oil until onion is limp, about 5 minutes. Add chili powder, cumin, and cinnamon; stir until spices are fragrant, about 1 minute.

2. Add broth, tomatoes (including juice), zucchini, corn, jalapeños, and oregano. Bring to a boil over high heat. Cover pan, reduce heat, and simmer for 5 minutes.

3. Meanwhile, rinse chicken and cut into ½-inch pieces. Add chicken to broth mixture. Return to a boil over high heat; cover pan, reduce heat, and simmer until chicken is white in center (cut to test), 2 to 3 minutes.

4. Ladle into soup bowls. Add salt, pepper, and cheese to taste.

Per serving: 200 cal., 15% (29 cal.) from fat; 29 g protein; 3.2 g fat (1.5 g sat.); 14 g carbo (2.2 g fiber); 346 mg sodium; 51 mg chol.

Turkey Rice Stew

PREP AND COOK TIME: About 45 minutes

NOTES: Turkey meatballs stay light by poaching in this rice-thickened stew instead of browning in fat.

MAKES: 6 servings

6 cups fat-skimmed **chicken broth**

1 cup chopped **onion**

⅔ cup **long-grain white rice**

½ cup chopped **carrot**

½ cup chopped **celery**

1 pound **ground turkey breast**

¼ cup **fine dried bread crumbs**

¼ cup chopped **parsley**

1 **large egg**

1 teaspoon **dried thyme**

About ½ teaspoon **salt**

¼ teaspoon **white pepper**

1 cup **frozen petite peas**

1. In a 4- to 5-quart pan over high heat, combine the broth, onion, rice, carrot, and celery. Cover and bring to a boil. Reduce heat and simmer broth mixture 10 minutes.

2. Meanwhile, in a bowl, mix turkey, bread crumbs, parsley, egg, thyme, ½ teaspoon salt, and pepper.

3. Increase heat under broth mixture to high and drop turkey mixture, 1 tablespoon at a time, into the pan. Bring the soup to a boil again, reduce heat to low, cover pan, and simmer until meatballs are no longer pink in the center (cut to test) and rice is just tender to bite, 8 to 10 minutes longer. Add peas and stir until hot, about 2 minutes. Add salt to taste. Ladle into soup bowls.

Per serving: 263 cal., 6.5% (17 cal.) from fat; 32 g protein; 1.9 g fat (0.5 g sat.); 28 g carbo (3.2 g fiber); 411 mg sodium; 82 mg chol.

BEEF

Speedy Beef and Barley Soup

PREP AND COOK TIME: About 30 minutes

NOTES: Quick-cooking barley and purchased cooked pot roast significantly abbreviate the cooking time for this old-fashioned favorite. Choose a good-quality pot roast from the meat section of your supermarket.

MAKES: 6 servings

2 **carrots** (6 oz. total)

1 **onion** (½ lb.)

1 cup chopped **celery**

4 cups fat-skimmed **beef broth**

1 cup **quick-cooking barley**

1 pound **heat-and-serve cooked beef pot roast**

1. Peel and chop carrots and onion. In a 4- to 5-quart pan over high heat, combine carrots, onion, celery, broth, barley, and 2 cups water; cover pan and bring to a boil. Reduce heat and simmer until carrots and barley are tender to bite, 15 to 20 minutes.

2. Discard any solidified fat from pot roast and sauce. Scrape sauce from meat into pan. Cut beef into ½-inch pieces and add them to pan. Simmer, covered, until hot, about 3 minutes. Ladle into soup bowls.

Per serving: 252 cal., 25% (62 cal.) from fat; 20 g protein; 6.9 g fat (2.7 g sat.); 26 g carbo (4.2 g fiber); 452 mg sodium; 41 mg chol.

Beef and Winter Vegetable Borscht

PREP AND COOK TIME: About 45 minutes

NOTES: A variety of vegetables makes this borscht particularly light and fresh.

MAKES: 10 servings

1 **onion** (½ lb.)

2 **carrots** (6 oz. total)

2 **russet potatoes** (1 lb. total)

2 cups chopped **red cabbage**

1 **dried bay leaf**

6 cups fat-skimmed **beef broth**

1 can (15 oz.) **pinto beans**

1 pound **heat-and-serve cooked beef pot roast**

1 can (14½ oz.) **diced tomatoes**

1 can (15 oz.) **julienne-cut beets**

2 tablespoons **lemon juice**

Salt and **pepper**

Nonfat sour cream

1. Peel onion and chop. Peel carrots and slice ¼ inch thick. Peel potatoes and cut into ½-inch cubes. In a 5- to 6-quart pan over high heat, combine onion, carrots, potatoes, cabbage, bay leaf, and broth. Cover pan and bring to a boil; reduce heat and simmer until potatoes are tender when pierced, about 15 minutes.

2. Drain and rinse beans; add to pan. Discard any solidified fat from pot roast and sauce. Scrape sauce from meat into pan. Cut beef into ½-inch pieces.

3. Add beef and tomatoes (including juice) to pan. Return to a boil.

4. Stir in beets (including liquid) and lemon juice, and add salt and pepper to taste. Ladle into soup bowls. Add sour cream to taste.

Per serving: 184 cal., 21% (38 cal.) from fat; 15 g protein; 4.2 g fat (1.6 g sat.); 21 g carbo (3.7 g fiber); 528 mg sodium; 24 mg chol.

Hungarian Paprika Beef and Noodle Stew

PREP AND COOK TIME: About 30 minutes

MAKES: 4 servings

1 **onion** (½ lb.)

1 teaspoon **salad oil**

2 tablespoons **Hungarian** or domestic **paprika**

1 teaspoon **caraway seed**

4 cups fat-skimmed **beef broth**

½ pound **dried wide egg noodles**

1 pound **heat-and-serve cooked beef pot roast**

Salt and **pepper**

Nonfat sour cream

1. Peel onion and chop. In a 4- to 5-quart nonstick pan over medium-high heat, stir onion and oil until onion is limp, about 7 minutes. Add paprika and caraway seed; stir until spices are fragrant, about 30 seconds. Add broth, cover pan, and bring to a boil.

2. Stir noodles into broth, cover, and return to a boil. Reduce heat and simmer until noodles are barely tender to bite, 6 to 8 minutes.

3. Meanwhile, discard any solidified fat from pot roast and sauce. Scrape sauce from meat into broth. Cut beef into ½-inch cubes and stir into broth. Cover and simmer over medium heat until beef is hot, about 4 minutes, stirring occasionally. Ladle into soup bowls. Add salt, pepper, and sour cream to taste.

Per serving: 467 cal., 27% (126 cal.) from fat; 34 g protein; 14 g fat (4.8 g sat.); 48 g carbo (2.6 g fiber); 652 mg sodium; 115 mg chol.

Pot Roast and Vegetable Stew

PREP AND COOK TIME: About 40 minutes

NOTES: For a beautiful presentation, use whole baby carrots, 4 inches long.

MAKES: 4 servings

3 cups fat-skimmed **beef broth**

1 **dried bay leaf**

8 **black peppercorns**

½ to ¾ pound **carrots**

8 **red thin-skinned potatoes** (2 in. wide)

4 **leeks** (about 1½ in. wide)

1 pound **heat-and-serve cooked beef pot roast**

Dijon mustard

Prepared horseradish

1. In a 5- to 6-quart pan over high heat, combine broth, bay leaf, and peppercorns; cover and bring to a boil.

2. Meanwhile, peel carrots and cut diagonally into 2- to 4-inch lengths; scrub potatoes. When broth is boiling, add

Pot Roast and Vegetable Stew

carrots and potatoes. Return to a boil, cover, reduce heat to medium-low, and simmer 10 minutes.

3. Meanwhile, trim and discard root ends and tough green tops of leeks. Cut leeks in half lengthwise and rinse well. Tie each pair of leek halves together with cotton string. Lay leeks on potatoes. Cover and simmer 5 minutes.

4. Discard any solidified fat from pot roast and sauce. Scrape sauce from meat and add to broth. Cut meat across the grain into ¼-inch-thick slices and lay on leeks.

5. Cover and simmer until vegetables are tender when pierced, 7 to 10 minutes longer.

6. With a slotted spoon, transfer equal portions of vegetables and meat to wide soup bowls and arrange attractively. Ladle hot broth equally into bowls. Accompany with mustard and horseradish to add to taste.

Per serving: 397 cal., 23% (90 cal.) from fat; 29 g protein; 10 g fat (4.1 g sat.); 45 g carbo (5.6 g fiber); 676 mg sodium; 61 mg chol.

Arizona Albóndigas Soup

PREP AND COOK TIME: About 35 minutes

NOTES: John Schroeder of Scottsdale, Arizona, likes this quick version of the classic Mexican soup.

MAKES: 4 servings

4 cups fat-skimmed **beef broth**

1 can (14 oz.) **diced tomatoes**

1 teaspoon **dried oregano**

½ teaspoon **ground cumin**

½ teaspoon **garlic powder**

½ teaspoon **pepper**

¾ pound **ground lean beef**

¼ cup **precooked dried white rice**

1 **large egg**

½ teaspoon **salt**

½ cup thinly sliced **green onions**

¼ cup chopped **fresh cilantro**

1. In a 5- to 6-quart pan over high heat, combine broth, tomatoes (including juice), ½ teaspoon oregano, and ¼ teaspoon *each* cumin, garlic powder, and pepper; cover pan and bring to a boil.

2. Meanwhile, in a bowl, mix beef, rice, egg, salt, and the remaining oregano, cumin, garlic powder, and pepper.

3. When broth is boiling, drop beef mixture in 1-inch balls into broth. Cover pan, reduce heat, and simmer until rice in meatballs is tender to bite, about 10 minutes. Stir in green onions and cilantro. Ladle into soup bowls.

Per serving: 217 cal., 31% (68 cal.) from fat; 26 g protein; 7.6 g fat (2.7 g sat.); 11 g carbo (1.3 g fiber); 593 mg sodium; 102 mg chol.

VEGETABLE

Southwest Black Bean Soup

PREP AND COOK TIME: About 45 minutes

NOTES: Rice gives this spicy soup a velvety texture and rich body.

MAKES: 7 or 8 servings

1 **onion** (½ lb.)

2 cloves **garlic**

½ teaspoon **olive oil**

2 tablespoons **ground cumin**

1 tablespoon **ground coriander**

¼ to ½ teaspoon **cayenne**

3 cans (14½ oz. each) **black beans**

6 cups fat-skimmed **beef broth** or vegetable broth

3 cups chopped **carrots**

½ cup **long-grain rice**

¼ cup **dry sherry** (optional)

Salt and **pepper**

1 **firm-ripe avocado** (8 oz.)

Rib-sticking veggies

Spicy Pork and Winter Vegetable Stew

PREP AND COOK TIME: About 45 minutes

NOTES: By cutting pork into small chunks, Claudia Martin of Flagstaff, Arizona, cooks a stick-to-your-ribs stew in less than 1 hour.

MAKES: 6 or 7 servings

- 1 pound fat-trimmed **pork loin**
- 2 **onions** (1/2 lb. each)
- 1 **sweet potato** (1/2 lb.)
- 2 **carrots** (1/2 lb. total)
- 1/2 pound **banana** or hubbard **squash**
- 2 **parsnips** (1/2 lb. total)
- 1 clove **garlic**
- 1 **red bell pepper** (1/2 lb.)

  About 2 cups fat-skimmed **chicken broth**
- 1 can (8 oz.) **tomato sauce**
- 2 tablespoons **lime juice**
- 1/8 to 1/4 teaspoon **cayenne**
- 1 package (10 oz.) **petite frozen peas**

  Salt and **pepper**

  Cilantro sprigs, rinsed, or thinly sliced green onions

1. Rinse pork and pat dry. Cut into 3/4-inch chunks.

2. In a 5- to 6-quart nonstick pan over high heat, stir pork often until browned, 6 to 8 minutes.

3. Meanwhile, peel onions and cut into 1/2-inch-thick wedges. Peel the sweet potato, carrots, squash, and parsnips; cut into 3/4-inch pieces. Peel and mince or press garlic. Rinse bell pepper; stem, seed, and cut into 1/2-inch-wide strips.

4. To pan, add onions, sweet potato, carrots, squash, parsnips, garlic, and 1 cup broth. Cover pan and cook 10 minutes, stirring occasionally; add a few tablespoons of water if mixture begins sticking to pan.

5. Add 1 more cup broth, along with the bell pepper, tomato sauce, lime juice, and cayenne to taste. Return to a boil, reduce heat, and simmer, covered, until meat and vegetables are tender when pierced, about 12 to 15 minutes longer. If stew sticks to pan or gets thicker than desired, add more broth as needed.

6. Add peas and stir occasionally until hot, about 2 minutes. Add salt and pepper to taste. Ladle into soup bowls and garnish with cilantro.

Per serving: 242 cal., 16% (39 cal.) from fat; 21 g protein; 4.3 g fat (1.3 g sat.); 30 g carbo (6.7 g fiber); 317 mg sodium; 38 mg chol.

Nonfat sour cream

Cilantro sprigs, rinsed

1. Peel and chop onion and garlic. In a 5- to 6-quart nonstick pan over medium-high heat, stir oil, onion, and garlic until onion is limp, about 5 minutes. Add cumin, coriander, and cayenne; stir until spices are fragrant, about 30 seconds.

2. Drain and rinse beans. Add 2 cans to pan along with broth, carrots, and rice. Cover and bring to a boil. Reduce heat and simmer until carrots and rice are tender to bite, 15 to 20 minutes.

3. In a blender, purée soup, a portion at a time, until smooth. Return soup to pan, add sherry and remaining beans, and stir over medium heat until hot, about 2 minutes. Add salt and pepper to taste.

4. Peel, pit, and slice avocado. Ladle soup into bowls. Garnish with avocado slices, sour cream, and cilantro.

Per serving: 213 cal., 20% (42 cal.) from fat; 12 g protein; 4.7 g fat (0.6 g sat.); 32 g carbo (6.6 g fiber); 322 mg sodium; 0 mg chol.

White Bean and Pasta Soup

PREP AND COOK TIME: About 40 minutes

NOTES: Christine Datian of Las Vegas cooks a big batch of this vegetable soup on weekends, then reheats it to serve on weeknights.

MAKES: 6 servings

- 2 **carrots** (1/2 lb. total)
- 1 **onion** (1/2 lb.)
- 3 cloves **garlic**
- 1 can (15 oz.) **small white beans**
- 1 cup chopped **celery**
- 3 cups **low-sodium tomato juice**
- 2 cups fat-skimmed **low-sodium chicken broth** or vegetable broth
- 1 teaspoon **dried basil**
- 1 teaspoon **dried thyme**
- 1/2 teaspoon **dried rosemary**
- 1 **leek** (1 1/2 in. wide)
- 1/2 cup **dried small pasta shells**
- 2 cups (1/4 lb.) chopped rinsed **spinach**

  Salt and **pepper**

  About 1/2 cup **crumbled feta cheese** or grated parmesan cheese

1. Peel and chop carrots, onion, and garlic. Drain and rinse beans. In a 4- to 5-quart pan over high heat, combine carrots, onion, garlic, beans, celery, tomato juice, broth, basil, thyme, and rosemary. Cover pan and bring to a boil.

2. Meanwhile, trim and discard root end and tough green leaves of leek. Split leek in half lengthwise; rinse well. Thinly slice leek crosswise and add to broth mixture.

3. When soup is boiling, reduce heat, cover, and simmer until carrots are tender when pierced, about 10 minutes.

4. Stir in pasta; simmer, covered, until pasta is just tender to bite, about 10 minutes. Add spinach and stir until wilted, about 1 minute. (If soup is thicker than you like, stir in a little water.) Add salt and pepper to taste. Ladle into soup bowls. Add cheese to taste.

Per serving: 180 cal., 16% (29 cal.) from fat; 11 g protein; 3.2 g fat (1.8 g sat.); 29 g carbo (4.8 g fiber); 327 mg sodium; 10 mg chol.

Split Pea and Potato Soup

PREP AND COOK TIME: About 45 minutes

NOTES: This satisfying soup comes from Joe Race of Seattle.

MAKES: 4 servings

- 1 **onion** (6 oz.)
- ¾ cup **dried green** or yellow **split peas**
- 2 **potatoes** (1 lb. total)
- 2 teaspoons **olive oil**
- 4⅓ cups **vegetable broth** or fat-skimmed beef broth
- ¼ teaspoon **black pepper**
- 2 cloves **garlic**, peeled and minced
- 1½ cups ½-inch cubes **French bread**
  Salt and **hot sauce**

1. Peel and chop onion. Sort peas for debris; discard debris and rinse peas. Peel potatoes and cut into 1-inch chunks.

2. In a 3- to 4-quart pan over medium-high heat, stir 1 teaspoon oil and the onion until onion is limp, about 5 minutes. Add peas, potatoes, and broth. Bring to a boil, cover pan, reduce heat, and simmer until potatoes and peas are tender to bite, 20 to 30 minutes.

3. Meanwhile, in a 9- or 10-inch-wide pan, mix remaining 1 teaspoon oil with pepper, garlic, and bread cubes.

4. Bake bread mixture in a 375° oven until crisp and lightly browned, 20 to 25 minutes (10 to 15 minutes in a convection oven).

5. In a blender or food processor, whirl broth mixture, a portion at a time, until smooth. Return to pan. If soup is thicker than you like, thin with a little water. Add salt and hot sauce to taste. Stir over high heat until steaming. Ladle into soup bowls and garnish with croutons.

Per serving: 308 cal., 11% (33 cal.) from fat; 14 g protein; 3.7 g fat (0.5 g sat.); 57 g carbo (4.5 g fiber); 181 mg sodium; 0 mg chol.

Velvety Potato and Broccoli Bisque

PREP AND COOK TIME: About 35 minutes

NOTES: This authoritatively flavored vegetable bisque comes from Grace Kirschenbaum of Los Angeles.

MAKES: 4 or 5 servings

- 3 **russet potatoes** (1½ lb. total)
- 2 cloves **garlic**
- 1 **fresh serrano chili** (¼ oz.)
- 6 cups fat-skimmed **chicken broth** or vegetable broth
- 1 pound **broccoli**
  About 1 tablespoon **Asian fish sauce** (*nuoc mam* or *nam pla*)
  Reduced-fat sour cream or plain nonfat yogurt (optional)

1. Peel potatoes and cut into ½-inch cubes. Peel and mince or press garlic. Rinse chili; stem, seed (if desired, for less heat), and thinly slice.

2. In a 3- to 4-quart pan over high heat, combine potatoes, garlic, chili, and broth. Cover pan and bring to a boil. Reduce heat and simmer 10 minutes.

3. Meanwhile, rinse and coarsely chop broccoli. Add to broth mixture and return to a boil over high heat. Reduce heat and simmer, uncovered, until potatoes and broccoli are tender when pierced, about 5 minutes longer.

4. In a blender, purée soup in batches. Return to pan. Add fish sauce to taste. Stir often over high heat until steaming.

5. Ladle into soup bowls. Garnish with dollops of sour cream.

Per serving: 176 cal., 4.6% (8.1 cal.) from fat; 15 g protein; 0.9 g fat (0.1 g sat.); 28 g carbo (4.6 g fiber); 243 mg sodium; 0 mg chol.

Squash and Chestnut Bisque

PREP AND COOK TIME: About 45 minutes

NOTES: For Grace Reade's family in Longview, Washington, this golden bisque is a firmly entrenched favorite.

MAKES: 8 servings

- 1 **butternut squash** (3 lb.)
- 1 **onion** (6 oz.)
- 1 cup chopped **celery**
- 1 teaspoon **butter** or margarine
  About ½ cup chopped **water-** or vacuum-**packed canned cooked and peeled chestnuts**, or chopped **pecans**
- 6 cups **fat-skimmed chicken broth** or vegetable broth
- 1 cup **low-fat milk**
  Salt

1. Peel and seed squash; cut squash into ¾-inch chunks. Peel onion and chop.

2. In a 5- to 6-quart nonstick pan over medium-high heat, stir onion, celery,

and butter until onion is limp, about 6 minutes. Add ½ cup chestnuts and stir until lightly browned, 3 to 4 minutes.

3. Add squash and broth. Cover pan and bring to a boil over high heat. Reduce heat and simmer, uncovered, until squash mashes easily when pressed, 20 to 25 minutes. Add milk.

4. In a blender, whirl soup, a portion at a time, until smooth. Return soup to pan, add salt to taste, and, if needed, stir over medium heat until steaming. Ladle into soup bowls and garnish with more chopped chestnuts, if desired.

Per serving: 130 cal., 6.9% (9 cal.) from fat; 8.9 g protein; 1 g fat (0.5 g sat.); 23 g carbo (3.5 g fiber); 98 mg sodium; 2.5 mg chol.

Mushroom-Cauliflower Soup

PREP AND COOK TIME: About 35 minutes

NOTES: Mushrooms provide the dominant flavor, cauliflower the body, of this remarkably rich-tasting soup made by Shannon Kuleto of St. Helena, California.

MAKES: 6 servings

- 1 pound **mushrooms** (chanterelles, shiitakes, and/or common)
- 1 **onion** (½ lb.)
- 1 tablespoon **butter** or olive oil
- 2 tablespoons **all-purpose flour**
- 3 cans (10½ oz. each) **condensed beef consommé**
- 1 cup **dry sherry**
- 2 cups chopped **cauliflower**

1. Rinse mushrooms well; drain. Trim off and discard tough and discolored stem ends, debris, and bruises. Chop mushrooms. Peel and chop onion.

2. In a 3- to 4-quart pan over high heat, stir mushrooms, onion, and butter often until mushrooms begin to brown, 12 to 15 minutes.

3. Add flour and mix well.

4. Remove from heat and stir consommé, sherry, and 1 cup water into pan. Add cauliflower. Return to high heat and bring to a boil; cover pan and simmer until cauliflower is tender when pierced, about 5 minutes.

5. In a blender, purée soup, a portion at a time, until smooth. Return to pan and stir over high heat until steaming. Ladle into soup bowls.

Per serving: 152 cal., 14% (22 cal.) from fat; 9.4 g protein; 2.4 g fat (1.3 g sat.); 14 g carbo (2.4 g fiber); 806 mg sodium; 5.2 mg chol. ◆

Pizza at Villa Cucina

A welcoming kitchen inspires guests to craft their own gourmet rounds
with toppers from sausage to homemade gravlax

BY LINDA LAU ANUSASANANAN • PHOTOGRAPHS BY JUST LOOMIS • FOOD STYLING BY BASIL FREEDMAN

■ The kitchen throbs with activity at the heart of Villa Cucina (Italian for *kitchen house*), perched on a hill in the Napa Valley. This generously scaled, wood-beamed great room, with its wood-burning pizza oven, professional range, antique chopping block island, huge refrigerator, and spacious dining area, rivals many restaurants. It's a fitting focus for a couple whose business revolves around food. Indeed, Pat Kuleto, renowned restaurateur and designer (with such San Francisco credits as Postrio and Boulevard to his name), and his wife, Shannon, make it their business to spend as much

EVERYONE COOKS! From top left on facing page: Shaping pizza dough into floury mounds, spinning it into rounds, anointing it with garlic oil, and adding toppings to taste. Pat Kuleto slides assembled pizza into the wood-burning oven. Above, Pat and his wife, Shannon, join their guests in a toast while the first of many pizzas bakes.

time as possible in this room, putting the ingredients they grow on their 800-acre ranch and vineyard to good use in the cause of entertaining.

With their facilities and restaurant expertise, you might think the results would be fancy. However, as Shannon puts it, "I've learned from restaurant chefs, but I don't try to copy their recipes—that's why you go to restaurants." Instead, her menus are casual, fresh, and hearty—and often involve guest participation. It's a party concept that translates beautifully for any cook to any kitchen, modest or magnificent.

Kuletos'
pizza
party
for 10 to 12

- While-You-Work Appetizer Platter
- While-You-Wait Salad Bar
- Tailor-Made Party Pizzas
- Sangiovese Granita
- Brownies or Chocolate Wafers
- Kuleto Villa Sangiovese and Chardonnay

THE GLOW FROM IVORY CANDLES assembled in Shannon Kuleto's eclectic collection of holders, or stabilized by melted wax, warms the great room and illuminates the 12-foot-long dining table, fashioned from a walnut tree cut on the property.

Guests at a Kuleto party often find themselves in the kitchen chopping vegetables for a combined salad and pizza-topping bar. Shannon provides fuel for their labor in the form of a big platter of appetizers such as deviled eggs, gravlax, fruit, cheeses, crackers, olives, pickles, fresh vegetables, and smoked trout.

When the guests have exercised their creativity assembling the veggies on crusts, the first two pizzas go into the oven and everyone sits down with salads of their own design. Shannon explains, "It's important to the feel of the evening that everyone has this common beginning, the dig-in ritual. And the pizza chef must leave the pizzas in the oven long enough, or you lose the pleasure of anticipation, not to mention digestion."

When the pizzas emerge, crusty and brown, from the oven, everyone shares creation after creation in an evening of deliciously sociable adventure.

Deviled Eggs with Bacon

PREP AND COOK TIME: About 30 minutes

NOTES: If making up to 1 day ahead, arrange filled eggs in a single layer; cover and chill. Wrap bacon and parsley separately and chill.

MAKES: 12 servings

- 6 **large eggs**
- 2 slices **bacon** (1½ oz. total), coarsely chopped
- ¼ cup **sour cream**
- 1 tablespoon **Dijon mustard**
- **Hot sauce**
- **Salt**
- Chopped **parsley**

1. Place eggs in a 3- to 4-quart pan and add enough cold water to cover by 1 inch. Bring to a simmer over high heat, then reduce heat so bubbles break sur-face only occasionally. Cook 15 minutes. Drain eggs, cover with cold water, and let stand until cool, about 10 minutes.

2. Meanwhile, in an 8- to 10-inch frying pan over medium-high heat, stir bacon until crisp and brown, about 3 minutes. With a slotted spoon, transfer bacon to towels to drain. Crumble when cool. Discard all but 1 tablespoon bacon fat from pan.

3. Shell eggs and cut in half lengthwise. Remove yolks and put in a small bowl. Mash yolks with a fork, blending in the reserved 1 tablespoon bacon fat, the sour cream, and the mustard. Add hot sauce and salt to taste.

4. Mound yolk mixture equally in egg white cavities. Sprinkle with bacon and parsley just before serving.

Per serving: 62 cal., 69% (43 cal.) from fat; 3.6 g protein; 4.8 g fat (1.8 g sat.); 0.5 g carbo (0 g fiber); 85 mg sodium; 110 mg chol.

Salad Bar

PREP TIME: About 45 minutes

NOTES: The olives, capers, and salmon are also used on pizzas; arrange them near the pizza toppers. Shannon makes her favorite French dressing ahead, but guests can also create their own dressings from a selection of oils and vinegars at the salad end of the bar. Good olives to offer include pitted niçoise, calamata, Spanish-style, salt-cured, and flavored (with garlic or citrus, for instance).

MAKES: 10 to 12 servings

- 2 tablespoons **lemon juice**
- 1 **apple** (½ lb.)
- 2 **carrots** (½ lb. total)
- 3 **firm-ripe tomatoes** (6 oz. each)
- 1 **red onion** (6 oz.)
- 1 cup **nasturtium blossoms** (pesticide-free; optional)

1½ cups thinly sliced **fresh fennel**

2 quarts (7 oz.) **salad mix**, rinsed and crisped

2 quarts (7 oz.) **baby spinach leaves**, rinsed and crisped

1 quart (7 oz.) **arugula** leaves, rinsed and crisped

1 jar (1 lb.) sliced **pickled beets**, drained

1 cup **pitted olives** (1 kind or an assortment; see notes)

½ cup drained **capers**

Kuletos' gravlax and **poached lemon-thyme salmon** (recipes follow)

Mom's French dressing (recipe follows)

Vinaigrette dressing (recipe follows)

Salt and fresh-ground **pepper**

1. In a small bowl, mix lemon juice with 2 cups water. Rinse apple, core, and cut into matchstick-size slivers; immerse in lemon water.

2. Peel carrots and cut into matchstick-size slivers. Rinse tomatoes, core, and thinly slice. Peel onion and thinly slice.

3. Rinse nasturtium blossoms gently; drain on towels. Drain apple.

4. On platters or in wide bowls, arrange in separate mounds the apple, carrots, tomatoes, red onion, nasturtium blossoms, fennel, salad mix, spinach, arugula, beets, olives, capers, gravlax, and poached salmon. Place Mom's French dressing and the vinaigrette dressing in separate bowls along-side, as well as salt and pepper. Let guests assemble their own salads.

Per serving without dressing: 84 cal., 17% (14 cal.) from fat; 2 g protein; 1.5 g fat (0.2 g sat.); 17 g carbo (2.8 g fiber); 528 mg sodium; 0 mg chol.

Kuletos' Gravlax

PREP TIME: About 20 minutes, plus at least 24 hours to cure

NOTES: Buy salmon that has been frozen, or freeze fresh salmon for at least 72 hours at -4° or lower to destroy parasites before making gravlax. Cure salmon at least 24 hours or up to 2 days. To store cured salmon 2 days longer, discard brine and dill, pat fish dry, cover airtight, and chill. If desired, serve with sour cream laced with chopped fresh dill.

MAKES: About 4 cups; 10 to 12 servings as a topper for salad and pizza

1 **whole** (or piece; 2 lb.) **boned unskinned salmon fillet**

2 tablespoons **salad oil**

⅓ cup **sugar**

⅓ cup **salt**

1 tablespoon **black peppercorns**, coarsely crushed

1 tablespoon **juniper berries**, coarsely crushed

2 cups lightly packed **dill sprigs**, rinsed

¼ cup **gin** (optional)

Lemon wedges

1. Rinse salmon, pat dry, and rub with oil. Mix sugar, salt, peppercorns, and juniper berries; rub mixture onto all sides of fish. Put ¾ cup dill in a 9- by 13-inch pan. Lay fish, skin down, on dill and cover with ¾ cup more dill. Sprinkle with gin. Cover tightly.

2. Refrigerate for at least 24 hours or up to 2 days, turning fish over about every 12 hours.

3. Discard brine and dill. Pat salmon dry and cut across grain into paper-thin, slanted slices. Garnish with lemon wedges and remaining dill sprigs.

Per serving: 111 cal., 39% (43 cal.) from fat; 14 g protein; 4.8 g fat (0.7 g sat.); 1.7 g carbo (0 g fiber); 962 mg sodium; 40 mg chol.

NIBBLE WHILE YOU WORK: While making pizzas, guests enjoy Shannon Kuleto's favorite deviled eggs (above) and gravlax wrapped around tiny scoops of mascarpone cheese (below right). At the table, the first course is make-it-yourself salad.

CHEF IN TRAINING? From left: Three-year-old Daniel Kuleto gives rising dough a poke. Portabella mushrooms, dried oregan

Poached Lemon-Thyme Salmon

PREP AND COOK TIME: About 50 minutes

NOTES: Shannon reserves vegetable trimmings from the salad and pizza bar to add to the broth. Up to 1 day ahead, poach fish; cool, cover, and chill.

MAKES: About 5 cups; 10 to 12 servings as a topper for salad and pizza

1 **whole** (or piece; 2 lb.) **boned unskinned salmon fillet**

2 cloves **garlic,** peeled and pressed

1 tablespoon **fresh thyme** leaves or dried thyme

2 teaspoons grated **lemon** peel

1 quart **fish broth** (made from bouillon cubes and water) or water

2 cups **dry white wine**

2 cups sliced **vegetables** (celery, fennel, carrots, and/or onions; any combination)

1. Rinse salmon and pat dry. Mix garlic, thyme, and lemon peel. Rub onto flesh side of fish. Lay fish in a 9- by 13-inch pan, cover, and chill at least 2 hours or up to 1 day.

2. In a 5- to 6-quart pan over high heat, bring broth, wine, and vegetables to a boil; reduce heat, cover, and simmer 10 to 15 minutes.

3. Meanwhile, cut salmon into 3-inch-wide pieces. Add to simmering broth and return to a simmer. Cover pan and remove from heat; let stand 15 minutes. Lift out a piece of fish and cut to test whether it is opaque but still moist-

looking in center of thickest part. If it's not, return to pan and let stand 3 to 5 minutes longer. If fish still isn't done, return pan to low heat for about 3 minutes, or until it is.

4. With a slotted spatula, lift salmon from broth and place in a single layer on a flat plate. Discard broth or reserve for other uses. When fish is cool, remove and discard any skin and bones. Break salmon into 1-inch chunks.

Per serving: 102 cal., 40% (41 cal.) from fat; 14 g protein; 4.6 g fat (0.7 g sat.); 0.1 g carbo (0 g fiber); 32 mg sodium; 40 mg chol.

Mom's French Dressing

PREP TIME: About 5 minutes

NOTES: "It seared my taste buds with delight," Shannon remembers about her first taste of her mom's old-fashioned French dressing. If making up to 1 day ahead, cover and chill.

MAKES: 2$\frac{1}{3}$ cups

In a blender, combine $\frac{1}{3}$ cup chopped **onion,** 1 cup **salad oil,** $\frac{1}{2}$ cup **catsup,** $\frac{1}{2}$ cup **sugar,** $\frac{1}{2}$ cup **cider vinegar,** 2 tablespoons **lemon juice,** 1 teaspoon **pepper,** and $\frac{1}{2}$ teaspoon **salt.** Whirl until smooth.

Per tablespoon: 67 cal., 79% (53 cal.) from fat; 0.1 g protein; 5.9 g fat (0.7 g sat.); 4 g carbo (0.1 g fiber); 70 mg sodium; 0 mg chol.

Vinaigrette Dressing

PREP TIME: About 5 minutes

NOTES: Add your choice of seasonings to the basic vinaigrette. One of the

Kuletos' secret weapons is a pepper grinder filled with coriander seed. Freshly ground, it adds a warm, spicy fragrance. If making vinaigrette up to 1 day ahead, cover and chill.

MAKES: 1 cup

In a bowl, whisk together $\frac{2}{3}$ cup **extra-virgin olive oil,** $\frac{1}{3}$ cup **seasoned rice** or red wine **vinegar,** 1 minced clove **garlic,** 1$\frac{1}{2}$ teaspoons **ground coriander** (or dry mustard, or 1 tablespoon minced fresh ginger), 1 teaspoon **sugar,** and $\frac{1}{4}$ teaspoon **salt.**

Per tablespoon: 82 cal., 100% (82 cal.) from fat; 0 g protein; 9.1 g fat (1.3 g sat.); 0.3 g carbo (0 g fiber); 36 mg sodium; 0 mg chol.

Party Pizzas

PREP AND COOK TIME: About 2 hours

NOTES: The Kuletos bake their pizzas in a wood-fired pizza oven. For crisp-crusted results in a regular oven, bake pizzas on baking sheets on the bottom rack. If using a pizza stone, heat on bottom rack of a 500° oven at least 30 minutes before using. To transfer pizzas to stone, assemble them on cornmeal-coated 12- by 15-inch baking sheets that have at least 1 edge without a rim, or on a wood pizza peel. Put edge of pan or peel over stone, about 2 inches from far edge, then slide pizza off pan onto stone. Let guests choose their own toppings from this recipe, or try the Kuletos' favorite combinations, given in the recipes that follow.

MAKES: 4 pizzas; 10 to 12 servings

...eeses, and other toppings are ready to embellish sauced dough. Just baked, crisp-crusted pizza glistens with melted cheese.

4 **unbaked** or prebaked **pizza crusts** (recipes follow)

Garlic oil (recipe follows)

2 to 3 cups **marinara** or pizza **sauce,** purchased or homemade

Caramelized onions (recipe follows; optional)

2 to 4 cups **fish** or **meat** (choose several: Kuletos' gravlax on page 21; poached lemon-thyme salmon on page 22; cooked crumbled Italian sausage; thinly sliced coppa or pepperoni; sliced mousse-style pâté)

6 to 8 cups sliced **vegetables** (choose several: red onions, tomatoes, roasted red peppers, fresh fennel, mushrooms)

1 cup **sliced** or whole **pitted olives** (choose several: niçoise, calamata, ripe, Spanish-style)

½ cup drained **capers**

1 to 2 cups **fresh basil** leaves or basil pesto (purchased or homemade), or 2 to 3 tablespoons dried basil or oregano

2 to 3 pounds **cheese** (choose several: crumbled gorgonzola, crumbled feta, sliced brie, shredded jack and/or mozzarella, grated parmesan)

Salt and **pepper**

1. Place each pizza crust on a 12-inch pizza pan or 12- by 15-inch baking sheet (see notes).

2. To assemble each pizza, brush crust with about 1 tablespoon garlic oil, then

"The pizza chef must leave the pizzas in the oven long enough, or you lose the pleasure of anticipation."
—*Shannon Kuleto*

spread $\frac{1}{2}$ to $\frac{3}{4}$ cup marinara sauce to within $\frac{1}{2}$ inch of edge.

3. Over marinara sauce, scatter $\frac{1}{4}$ to $\frac{1}{2}$ cup caramelized onions, $\frac{1}{2}$ to 1 cup fish or meat, $1\frac{1}{2}$ to 2 cups sliced vegetables, 2 tablespoons olives, 2 tablespoons capers, $\frac{1}{4}$ to $\frac{1}{2}$ cup fresh basil leaves or pesto or 1 to 2 teaspoons dried herbs, and about 2 cups cheese.

4. Bake pizzas on the lowest rack of a 500° oven until crusts are well browned on the bottom, 10 to 15 minutes for unbaked crusts, 7 to 12 minutes for prebaked crusts. Cut into wedges. Add salt and pepper to taste.

Per serving ($\frac{1}{3}$ pizza): 563 cal., 59% (333 cal.) from fat; 26 g protein; 37 g fat (18 g sat.); 34 g carbo (3.8 g fiber); 2,177 mg sodium; 98 mg chol.

Unbaked Pizza Crusts

PREP TIME: About 15 minutes, plus 45 minutes for rising and resting

NOTES: To make dough up to 1 day ahead, cover bowl with plastic wrap in step 3, and chill. For a shortcut, instead of making dough, buy and thaw 4 loaves (1 lb. each) frozen bread dough. Use 1 loaf for each crust.

MAKES: 4 pizza crusts

  2 packages **active dry yeast**
  1 teaspoon **salt**
  2 tablespoons **extra-virgin olive oil**
  1 cup **rye** or whole-wheat **flour**
  6 to 6$\frac{1}{2}$ cups **all-purpose flour**
     About $\frac{1}{4}$ cup **cornmeal**

1. In a large bowl, sprinkle yeast over 3 cups warm (110°) water. Let stand until yeast is softened, about 5 minutes. Stir in salt and olive oil. Add rye flour and 3 cups all-purpose flour. Beat with a mixer until dough is elastic and stretchy, 6 to 8 minutes. Stir in 3 more cups all-purpose flour.

2. *If using a dough hook,* beat on high speed until dough no longer feels sticky and pulls cleanly from bowl, 5 to 7 minutes. If dough is still sticky, beat in more all-purpose flour, 1 tablespoon at a time. *If kneading by hand,* scrape dough onto a lightly floured board. Knead until smooth, springy, and no longer sticky, 15 to 20 minutes; add flour as required to prevent sticking. Place dough in an oiled bowl; turn dough over to coat top.

3. Cover dough with plastic wrap. Let rise in a warm place until doubled, 35 to 45 minutes. Punch dough down and knead lightly on a floured board to expel air.

4. Cut dough into 4 equal pieces. Place pieces on a floured board and cover

with plastic wrap to prevent drying.

5. On floured board, roll or stretch 1 piece at a time into an 11- to 12-inch round. Place round on a cornmeal-dusted 12-inch pizza pan or 12- by 15-inch baking sheet; stretch dough, if needed, to reshape.

Per $\frac{1}{12}$ crust: 73 cal., 9.9% (7.2 cal.) from fat; 2 g protein; 0.8 g fat (0.1 g sat.); 14 g carbo (0.8 g fiber); 49 mg sodium; 0 mg chol.

Prebaked Pizza Crusts

PREP AND COOK TIME: About 45 minutes

NOTES: In the Kuletos' wood-fired oven, pizza cooks fast. To speed up the process in a regular oven, start with prebaked crusts. If making crusts up to 1 day ahead, cool on racks, cover, and store at room temperature.

MAKES: 4 pizza crusts

  4 loaves (1 lb. each) thawed **frozen bread dough**, at room temperature
     About $\frac{1}{4}$ cup **cornmeal**

1. On a lightly floured board, roll 1 loaf of dough into an 8- to 10-inch round. Place on an oiled, cornmeal-dusted 12-inch pizza pan or 12- by 15-inch baking sheet. Let rest about 5 minutes. Stretch dough into an even 12-inch round.

2. Bake on the bottom rack of a 500°

ICY CRYSTALS of Sangiovese wine granita cap the evening.

Sangiovese Granita

PREP TIME: **5 minutes**, plus at least 8 hours to freeze

NOTES: If making up to 1 week ahead, cover airtight and freeze. For the fluffiest texture, scrape the slushy mixture shortly before serving, or ask guests to help with this quick, easy process, as Shannon does. Or, up to 3 days ahead, scrape granita, cover, and freeze, then scoop into glasses. Serve with brownies or thin chocolate wafers.

MAKES: 12 servings

  6 cups **Sangiovese wine**
  1 cup **sugar**

1. In a 9- by 13-inch pan, mix wine and sugar until sugar is dissolved. Cover airtight.

2. Freeze until mixture is solid, at least 8 hours or up to 1 week. Scrape quickly with a fork to break into small clumps.

3. Scoop granita into wine or sherbet glasses that have been chilled in the freezer.

Per serving: 149 cal., 0% (0 cal.) from fat; 0.2 g protein; 0 g fat; 19 g carbo (0 g fiber); 6 mg sodium; 0 mg chol.

oven until crust is pale golden brown, 4 to 6 minutes.

3. Slide pizza crust onto a rack to cool. Repeat to shape and bake remaining loaves of dough.

Per $\frac{1}{12}$ crust: 105 cal., 16% (17 cal.) from fat; 2.9 g protein; 1.9 g fat (0.4 g sat.); 19 g carbo (0.8 g fiber); 182 mg sodium; 1.9 mg chol.

Garlic Oil

PREP TIME: About 5 minutes

NOTES: If making up to 1 day ahead, cover and chill.

MAKES: 5 to 6 tablespoons, enough for 4 pizzas

Mix $\frac{1}{4}$ cup **olive oil** and 1 to 2 tablespoons minced or pressed **garlic.**

Per tablespoon: 85 cal., 95% (81 cal.) from fat; 0.2 g protein; 9 g fat (1.2 g sat.); 1.1 g carbo (0.1 g fiber); 0.6 mg sodium; 0 mg chol.

Caramelized Onions

PREP AND COOK TIME: About 25 minutes

NOTES: If making up to 1 day ahead, cover and chill.

MAKES: About 1$\frac{1}{2}$ cups

In a 5- to 6-quart pan over medium-high heat, stir 1 tablespoon **butter** or margarine and 4 cups thinly sliced **onions** until butter is melted. Cover pan and stir occasionally until onions are limp, about 10 minutes. Uncover and stir often until onions are tinged with brown, about 7 minutes longer.

Per 2 tablespoons: 29 cal., 31% (9 cal.) from fat; 0.6 g protein; 1 g fat (0.6 g sat.); 4.6 g carbo (0.9 g fiber); 11 mg sodium; 2.6 mg chol.

Greek Veggie Pizza

Place 1 **unbaked** or prebaked **pizza crust** on a 12-inch pizza pan or 12- by 15-inch baking sheet (see notes for party pizzas, page 22). Spread with about 1 tablespoon **garlic oil** (page 24). Top with ½ cup **caramelized onions** (preceding), ⅓ cup sliced **red onion**, ⅓ cup thinly sliced **fresh fennel**, ⅓ cup coarsely chopped **tomato**, ⅓ cup sliced **mushrooms**, ⅓ cup sliced **canned roasted red peppers**, 1 tablespoon drained **capers**, 2 tablespoons **pitted calamata olives**, 2 teaspoons **fresh oregano** leaves or ½ teaspoon dried oregano, and ¾ cup **crumbled feta cheese**. Bake as directed for party pizzas (step 4).

Per ½₂ pizza: 122 cal., 30% (36 cal.) from fat; 3.6 g protein; 4 g fat (1.7 g sat.); 18 g carbo (1.3 g fiber); 215 mg sodium; 8.4 mg chol.

Italian Molta Carne Pizza

Place 1 **unbaked** or prebaked **pizza crust** on a 12-inch pizza pan or 12- by 15-inch baking sheet (see notes for party pizzas, page 22). Spread with 1 tablespoon **garlic oil** (page 24). Top with ½ cup **marinara sauce**, 1 cup **shredded mozzarella cheese**, ½ cup *each* sliced **mushrooms** and sliced **onion**, ¼ cup **sliced pepperoni**, ¼ cup **thin-sliced prosciutto**, ½ cup cooked crumbled **Italian sausage**, and ½ cup **shredded jack cheese**. Bake as directed for party pizzas (step 4).

Per ½₂ pizza: 179 cal., 44% (78 cal.) from fat; 8.6 g protein; 8.7 g fat (3.4 g sat.); 16 g carbo (1.1 g fiber); 387 mg sodium; 24 mg chol.

Pizza di Mare

Place 1 **unbaked** or prebaked **pizza crust** on a 12-inch pizza pan or 12- by 15-inch baking sheet (see notes for party pizzas, page 22). Spread with 1 tablespoon **garlic oil** (page 24). Evenly distribute ½ cup **caramelized onions** (page 24) and ½ cup **pesto** over crust. Top evenly with 1 cup **poached lemon-thyme salmon** chunks (page 22). Bake as directed for party pizzas (step 4).

Per ½₂ pizza: 154 cal., 44% (68 cal.) from fat; 5.9 g protein; 7.5 g fat (1.2 g sat.); 16 g carbo (0.9 g fiber); 130 mg sodium; 9.8 mg chol.

Gravlax and Gorgonzola Pizza

Place 1 **unbaked** or prebaked **pizza crust** on a 12-inch pizza pan or 12- by 15-inch baking sheet (see notes for party pizzas, page 22). Spread with 1 tablespoon **garlic oil** (page 24). Top with ⅓ cup thinly sliced **Kuletos' gravlax** (page 21), 1 cup thinly sliced **red onion**, ¾ cup **gorgonzola cheese** chunks, and 1 tablespoon drained **capers**. Bake as directed for party pizzas (step 4). Remove from oven and evenly distribute another ⅓ cup thinly sliced **Kuletos' gravlax** over pizza.

Per ½₂ pizza: 129 cal., 32% (41 cal.) from fat; 6.1 g protein; 4.6 g fat (1.8 g sat.); 16 g carbo (1.1 g fiber); 340 mg sodium; 13 mg chol.

Pat's Well-Maybe-It's-a-Little-Rich Brie and Pâté Pizza

Place 1 **unbaked** or prebaked **pizza crust** on a 12-inch pizza pan or 12- by 15-inch baking sheet (see notes for party pizzas, page 22). Spread with 1 tablespoon **garlic oil** (page 24). Top with ½ pound thinly sliced **brie cheese** and ¼ pound thinly sliced **mousse-style chicken**, duck, or pork **pâté**. Bake as directed for party pizzas (step 4).

Per ½₂ pizza: 176 cal., 43% (76 cal.) from fat; 6.9 g protein; 8.4 g fat (1.5 g sat.); 14 g carbo (0.9 g fiber); 220 mg sodium; 33 mg chol. ◆

PAT KULETO and longtime friend Brian Heslip acknowledge a job well done.

foodguide

BY JERRY ANNE DI VECCHIO

Santa Fe diversions

On the trail of the rogue avocado

■ In the Southwest, it's a rare avocado that doesn't end up in guacamole. But wandering along gallery-lined Canyon Road in Santa Fe, I found the exception. Just as my appetite for art was squelched by weary feet and a grumbling stomach, fate brought me face-to-face with the menu posted outside the Apple Hat Bistro's relaxed dining terrace. A promise of simple chicken salad with avocados and oranges was enough to divert me from cultural pursuits. What chef Lester Cisneros delivered was a refreshing surprise: The chicken was lightly smoked; the avocado chunked, not mashed, and flavored with dill; and the whole dressed with, in Cisneros's words, an "orange wash." Simple, satisfying, and easily duplicated.

Orange and Avocado Chicken Salad

PREP TIME: About 40 minutes

NOTES: Garnish salads with dill sprigs and minced fresh jalapeño chilies.

MAKES: 4 servings

4 **oranges** (about ½ lb. each)

3 **firm-ripe avocados** (about ½ lb. each)

½ cup **orange juice**

6 tablespoons **lime juice**

1 tablespoon chopped **fresh dill** or dried dill weed

½ teaspoon **sugar**

Salt

2 cups (10 to 12 oz.) diced or sliced **skinned, boned smoked** or cooked **chicken breast** or turkey breast

About ½ cup very thinly sliced **red onion**

1. With a small, sharp knife, cut peel and white membrane from oranges. Thinly slice oranges crosswise.

2. Peel and pit 2 avocados. On a flat plate, use a fork to coarsely chunk peeled avocados, adding 3 tablespoons orange juice, 2 tablespoons lime juice, dill, sugar, and salt to taste.

3. Mound chunked avocado equally on plates. Top equally with chicken.

4. Peel and pit remaining avocado and thinly slice lengthwise. Separate onion slices into rings. Mix remaining orange juice and lime juice.

5. Arrange orange slices, avocado slices, and onion rings equally on plates, then moisten with orange-lime juice mixture. Add salt to taste.

Per serving: 503 cal., 41% (207 cal.) from fat; 27 g protein; 23 g fat (3.9 g sat.); 55 g carbo (11 g fiber); 71 mg sodium; 60 mg chol.

Jam session

■ Last summer I joined sisters Janet Pendergrass and Linda Strand to survey Columbia Empire Farms, a half-hour drive south of Portland, where sweet Totem strawberries, Meeker raspberries, and marionberries grow. All three are destined for one of the company's newest product lines, Doodleberry seedless jams. The jams are designed with kids in mind: They come in 16-ounce plastic bottles topped with a tiny dispensing hole that performs neatly. Squeeze out the jam, then release the pressure, and the last sticky drop is whooped back inside. Doodleberry jams, which cost about $2.50, are widely available in the Northwest now, and are moving south fast. Watch for them (or order them at 503/554-9060 or www. doodleberry.com).

My grandsons, who have always considered thin crêpes a grand treat for breakfast (a tradition my daughter preserves from the days when I was struggling to be the perfect mom), like them even better "doodled."

RICK MARIANI (4)

Crêpes

PREP AND COOK TIME: About 25 minutes

NOTES: If making up to 3 days ahead, stack crêpes between sheets of waxed paper, wrap airtight, and chill; freeze to store longer.

MAKES: 11 or 12 crêpes

- ½ cup **all-purpose flour**
- 2 **large eggs**
- ¾ cup **nonfat** or whole **milk**

About 3 teaspoons **butter** or margarine

1. In a blender or food processor, whirl flour, eggs, and milk until smooth, scraping container sides as needed. (Or in a bowl, whisk mixture until smooth.)
2. Place a 6-inch-wide non-stick frying pan (measure across the bottom) or crêpe pan over medium-high heat. When pan is hot, add about ¼ teaspoon butter and swirl until melted. All at once, add 2 tablespoons batter and tilt pan to coat bottom evenly (see box at right). Cook until crêpe is dry-looking on top and browned on the bottom, about 1 minute. Turn with a wide spatula and cook until other side is lightly speckled with brown, about 30 seconds. Invert pan over a flat plate and drop crêpe onto it. Repeat to cook remaining crêpes.

Per crêpe: 45 cal., 38% (17 cal.) from fat; 2.1 g protein; 1.9 g fat (0.9 g sat.); 4.8 g carbo (0.1 g fiber); 28 mg sodium; 38 mg chol.

Jam Crêpes

PREP AND COOK TIME: 8 to 10 minutes

MAKES: 4 servings

1. One at a time, lay 1 recipe's worth of **crêpes** (preceding) light brown side up. Spoon (or squirt; see "Jam Session" at left) 1 to 2 teaspoons (¼ to ½ cup total) **seedless berry jam** down the center of each crêpe, then roll to enclose jam. Lay crêpes side by side, seams down, in a shallow 8- by 12-inch casserole.
2. Bake in a 350° oven until crêpes are warm, 5 to 7 minutes. Or heat in a microwave-safe container in a microwave oven at full power (100%) for 2 to 3 minutes.
3. Dust crêpes with 2 tablespoons **powdered sugar,** and squeeze juice from 1 **lemon** (2 to 3 tablespoons) over them. If desired, also moisten crêpes with 2 to 3 tablespoons **orange-flavor liqueur.**

Per serving: 201 cal., 25% (50 cal.) from fat; 6.5 g protein; 5.6 g fat (2.6 g sat.); 32 g carbo (0.5 g fiber); 93 mg sodium; 115 mg chol.

QUICK TIP

For uniform crêpes, pour measured amount of batter into hot pan and tilt in a circular motion to coat bottom. Cook until surface is dry, then turn with a wide spatula.

Better basics

■ No matter how sophisticated the world becomes, skillfully mingled potatoes and onions hold their own. Chef Alex Scrimgeour serves these little luxurious-tasting but simple-to-make onion and potato tarts with his beef and game dishes at Saddle Peak Lodge in the hills of Calabasas, California.

Caramelized Onion and Potato Tarts

RICK MARIANI

PREP AND COOK TIME: About 1 hour

NOTES: Up to 1 day ahead, cook the onion mixture, cover, and chill; up to 4 hours ahead, assemble ramekins, cover, and chill, then uncover to bake.

MAKES: 6 servings

- 1 **russet potato** (about 5 in. long, ³⁄₄ lb. total)
- 1¹⁄₂ pounds **onions,** peeled and thinly sliced
- ¹⁄₂ cup fat-skimmed **chicken broth**
- ¹⁄₄ cup **whipping cream**
- 2 tablespoons **butter** or olive oil
- ¹⁄₂ cup chopped **parsley**
- ¹⁄₂ teaspoon fresh-ground **pepper**
  Salt

1. Peel potato and, using a vegetable slicer or a mandoline, cut lengthwise into even slices no more than ¹⁄₁₆ inch thick; they must be flexible enough to bend without breaking. Bring about 2 quarts water to a boil in a 5- to 6-quart pan.

Add potato, stir to separate slices, and cook about 1 minute. Drain potato and immerse in cold water, rubbing gently to separate slices and remove sticky starch coating. Drain and immerse again in cold water to keep pieces from sticking.

2. Put onions, broth, and cream in pan. Place over high heat, cover, and bring to a boil, stirring occasionally. Reduce heat and simmer until onions are limp, about 7 minutes, stirring often. Uncover, turn heat to

high, and stir often until onions are golden brown and taste sweet, about 20 minutes. If mixture sticks to pan, add water, 1 tablespoon at a time, and stir to release browned bits.

3. Meanwhile, melt butter. Brush interiors of 6 ramekins or soufflé cups (²⁄₃-cup size) generously with melted butter. Drain potato. Line ramekins equally with the largest potato slices, overlapping to cover container interiors, with ends of potato slices extending over ramekin rims by at least 1¹⁄₂ inches.

4. Mix onions with parsley, pepper, and salt to taste. Spoon mixture equally into potato-lined ramekins. Fold extended edges of potatoes over filling and pat level. Brush tops with remaining melted butter.

5. Bake in a 375° oven until potato slices are well browned, 40 to 50 minutes (45 to 55 minutes if chilled). Run a knife between tarts and sides of ramekins; invert tarts onto plates.

Per serving: 148 cal., 44% (65 cal.) from fat; 3.2 g protein; 7.2 g fat (4.3 g sat.); 19 g carbo (2.7 g fiber); 58 mg sodium; 21 mg chol.

A trio of titles

■ Several recent books tackle—with pleasant intensity—the real crux of the issue: Which wines and foods are terrific together, which ones go to war on the palate, and, most important, why?

Mary Evely, executive chef at Simi Winery, deals with the nuts and bolts of flavor affinities in *The Vintner's Table Cookbook: Recipes from a Winery Chef* (Simi Winery, Healdsburg, CA, 1999; $29.95; 707/433-6981). She starts with the wine, adds foods and recipes that complement it, and gives guidelines for venturing on your own.

Carolyn Wente, president of Wente

Vineyards—the oldest continuously operated family-owned winery in California—and Kimball Jones, executive chef at the Wente Vineyards Restaurant, cover slightly different vinous territory, including the winery's history, in *Sharing the Vineyard Table: A Celebration of Wine and Food from the Wente Vineyards Restaurant* (Ten Speed Press, Berkeley, 1999; $29.95; 800/841-2665).

Sid Goldstein, vice president of Fetzer Vineyards, zeros in, with unintimidating technicality, on the behavior of flavors in food and wine in *The Wine Lover's Cookbook: Great Meals for the Perfect Glass of Wine* (Chronicle Books, San Francisco, 1999; $22.95; 800/722-6657). ◆

JAMES CARRIER

The Wine Guide

BY KAREN MacNEIL-FIFE

RICK MARIANI

Does vintage matter?

■ Let's say you're in a restaurant. You scan the wine list and decide on a bottle of the Chateau St. Jean Merlot 1996. The waiter goes to retrieve it, only to come back with an apology: "We no longer have the 1996. The vintage has just changed, and we'll be updating our wine list soon. Would you like the 1997?"

How many people do you think say no? In my experience, not many. Most people who are in the mood for a 1996 Chateau St. Jean Merlot—or want to try it for the first time—are willing to take a chance on the 1997.

Which brings us to the question, Just how much do vintages matter anyway? Lots of us have a vintage chart crumpled up in our wallet somewhere that we rarely—if ever—use. Should we pull it out more often?

At the risk of seeming sacrilegious, I say no. Though traditional wine wisdom has it that vintages are something to be concerned about, current reality suggests otherwise.

Consider the reason behind vintage labeling in the first place. The premise

> ### SUNSET'S STEAL OF THE MONTH
> **Hogue Cellars Pinot Gris 1998 (Columbia Valley, WA),** $8.
> Bold and peachy.
> A refreshing change from Chardonnay.
> — KAREN MacNEIL-FIFE

was that, as a rule, the weather was not on a grape vine's side. Historically, in certain years bad weather led to wines that were disappointingly thin, and listing the vintage was a way of alerting consumers. Such wines would generally be less expensively priced. People would drink the poor vintage until a better one came along, but no one would buy up cases and cellar them away to age.

The winemaker played a very small role in this yearly drama. No matter how talented he or she was, nature had the upper hand, the final say. From both the winemaker's and the wine drinker's standpoint, vintages had to be accepted for what they were. Some were poor, some were good, most were somewhere in between.

In the last 20 years, however, the picture has changed. Winemaking technology and viticultural science have advanced to such a degree that talented winemakers can sometimes turn out fairly delicious wines even when nature is working against them.

This is not to say that wines taste the same every year. They clearly do not. But vintage variations are often differences of character, not quality. For example, in a hot year, many wines will be packed with big, jammy fruit flavors. In a cool year, they will be more austere, lighter-bodied, and possibly more elegant. Are any of these qualities terrible? Isn't it theoretically possible to like both kinds of wine?

Unfortunately, the press routinely assumes that for all wines and all wine drinkers, greatness comes in one form: bigness. But that is simply not true.

There is another problem. A vintage is evaluated and categorized by the media when the new wine is tasted in the spring, six months or so after the harvest. Wine, however, changes over time. Often a vintage is deemed magnificent at first, only later to be declared not as good as originally thought. So what is the point of memorizing the pluses and minuses of vintages if the pluses and minuses change?

A NEW YEAR'S RESOLUTION

The best way to learn nothing about wine is to drink only the wine you already know you like. Why not start off the year (the century!) by discovering something new?

WHITES

■ **Joseph Phelps Vin du Mistral "Pastiche White" 1997 (California),** $10. Some of the world's most intriguing wines are highly aromatic—like this one. Ripe pear, tangerine, and floral aromas waft out of the glass. It has good body, with a shimmering streak of acidity. Great with spicy Asian dishes.

■ **Lake Chalice Sauvignon Blanc 1999 (Marlborough, New Zealand),** $15. Dozens of sassy, no-holds-barred New Zealand Sauvignon Blancs are just now coming to the United States. This one's tightly focused, with fresh-squeezed lime and passion fruit flavors. Very dramatic.

REDS

■ **Arzuaga Crianza 1996 (Ribera del Duero, Spain),** $26. An up-and-coming wine from the rugged plateau north of Madrid (also famous for roast lamb)—concentrated and lush, with big menthol, grenadine, and boysenberry flavors.

■ **Zaca Mesa Z Cuvee 1997 (Santa Barbara County),** $16. If you haven't tasted many Rhône-inspired blends, this is the one to try. Rustic, juicy, meaty, and plump with cherry fruit, this wine—made mostly from Grenache and Mourvèdre—has grip.

The only sensible approach, then, is to have an open mind. Take the vintage charts with a big grain of salt. Remember that wines evolve, and one-shot vintage proclamations are entirely too superficial. A talented winemaker can surprise us even when nature has challenged him or her.

When we recommend wines at *Sunset,* we do list the vintage dates, and the brief descriptions of the wines reflect the vintages named. However, if you can't find the vintage listed, by all means try another one. An enormous part of the joy of wine is in the discovery. ◆

FRESH-COOKED CRAB is easier than you might think to clean and crack, and devilishly good dunked in garlic butter.

Two-for-one crab

Take the plunge one night for a cracked-crab feast, and save the shells for a rich-flavored soup the next day

BY ELAINE JOHNSON • PHOTOGRAPHS BY JAMES CARRIER

If you love crab, don't settle for market-cooked. Plunging the live crustaceans into boiling water yourself is breath-catching, to be sure, but once you've tasted incredibly sweet, succulent home-cooked meat, there will be no going back. By doing it yourself, you have total control over two quality factors: how long the crabs cook and how salty they are.

You can double the return on your labor investment by saving the shells to make an intensely flavored broth for a lively soup.

Classic Cracked Crab

PREP AND COOK TIME: About 1½ hours

NOTES: Buy live crabs on the day you'll be cooking them, and keep in the refrigerator, loosely wrapped, until ready to add to boiling water. If you don't have a pan large enough, cook crabs in sequence. If any crab meat remains after the first meal, reserve for Asian asparagus and crab soup (recipe at right).

MAKES: 4 servings

1. Purchase 4 **live Dungeness crabs** (2 to 2½ lb. each; see notes). Pour about 12 quarts **water** into a 16- to 20-quart pan. Cover and bring to a boil over high heat, about 45 minutes.

Grasp each crab from the back, between the legs, and plunge it headfirst into water. Use tongs to immerse crabs completely. Cover pan, reduce heat, and simmer 15 minutes.

2. Drain crabs and let stand until cool enough to handle, about 15 minutes.

3. To clean and crack each crab, pull off the triangular flap from the belly side. Pull body away from back shell. Pour juices from back into a bowl; also scoop the soft white crab fat and yellow butter from shell into bowl. Discard stomach sack.

4. Pull off and discard red membrane and soft gills from body, and scoop yellow crab butter into bowl. Pull off bony mouth paddles and add to shells. Separately cover and chill crab butter mixture and all shells.

5. Rinse crab bodies under cool running water. With a nutcracker or mallet, crack the shell of each leg and claw section, hitting on the narrow edges. With a knife, cut bodies into quarters.

6. Serve crabs warm or cool, plain or with **deviled garlic butter** for dipping. Use the leg tips to extract meat from shells. Save shells for crab broth (recipe follows); cover and chill.

Per serving without butter: 187 cal., 10% (19 cal.) from fat; 38 g protein; 2.1 g fat (0.3 g sat.); 1.6 g carbo (0 g fiber); 641 mg sodium; 128 mg chol.

Deviled garlic butter. In a 1- to 2-quart pan over low heat, frequently stir ½ cup (¼ lb.) **butter** or margarine, 2 tablespoons minced **garlic,** and ½ teaspoon **cayenne** until garlic is limp, 5 to 8 minutes. Stir in ¼ cup **lemon juice.** Serve warm. Makes about ¾ cup.

Per tablespoon: 72 cal., 96% (69 cal.) from fat; 0.2 g protein; 7.7 g fat (4.8 g sat.); 0.9 g carbo (0 g fiber); 79 mg sodium; 21 mg chol.

Crab Broth

PREP AND COOK TIME: About 1½ hours

MAKES: About 2 quarts

> **Shells from 4 cooked Dungeness crabs** (reserved from classic cracked crab, preceding)
>
> 3 tablespoons **olive oil**
> 1 quart chopped **onions**
> 1 tablespoon minced **garlic**
> ¼ teaspoon **black peppercorns**
> **Crab fat, crab butter, and juices** (reserved from classic cracked crab, preceding)
> 2 quarts fat-skimmed **chicken broth**
> 2 cups **dry white wine**

1. With a mallet, break crab back shells into 2-inch pieces.

2. Put all of the crab shells into an 8- to 10-quart pan; add oil. Stir frequently over medium-high heat until shell edges begin to brown, 12 to 15 minutes.

3. Add onions, garlic, and peppercorns; stir often over medium heat until onions are limp, about 10 minutes.

4. Stir in crab fat, crab butter, and juices, broth, and wine. Cover and bring to a boil over high heat, then reduce heat and simmer until reduced to 2 quarts, about 1 hour.

5. Pour broth through a fine strainer set over a bowl. Discard shells and seasonings. Use broth warm or cool. If making up to 1 day ahead, chill airtight; freeze to store longer.

Per cup: 99 cal., 46% (46 cal.) from fat; 8.6 g protein; 5.1 g fat (0.7 g sat.); 4.3 g carbo (0.7 g fiber); 95 mg sodium; 0 mg chol.

Asian Asparagus and Crab Soup

PREP AND COOK TIME: About 25 minutes

NOTES: Susan Romaine of Santa Barbara shares this recipe. Instead of the Chinese five spice, you can use equal parts ground cinnamon, ground cloves, ground ginger, and anise seed—¼ teaspoon total. To break rice sticks into bite-size lengths, place in a plastic food bag.

MAKES: About 3 quarts; 6 servings

- 2 quarts **crab broth** (preceding)
- 2 tablespoons minced **fresh ginger**
- 1 tablespoon **oyster sauce**
- ¼ teaspoon **Chinese five spice** (see notes)
- 4 ounces **Chinese rice sticks** (*mai fun*) or capellini pasta, broken into bite-size lengths
- 2 cups diagonally sliced 1-inch pieces **asparagus**
- ¼ pound **oyster** or common **mushrooms,** rinsed, tough ends trimmed, and thinly sliced
- ¼ cup chopped **fresh cilantro**
- 1 cup (6 oz.) **shelled cooked crab** or rinsed shelled cooked tiny shrimp
- 1 tablespoon **lemon juice**
- ¼ to ½ teaspoon **hot sauce**

1. In a 5- to 6-quart pan over high heat, bring broth, ginger, oyster sauce, and five spice to a boil. Add rice sticks, cover, reduce heat to medium, and cook for 3 minutes (1 minute for capellini).

2. Stir in asparagus, mushrooms, and cilantro. Cook until asparagus is tender-crisp to bite, about 3 minutes. Stir in crab and lemon juice. Add hot sauce to taste; cook until crab is hot, about 1 minute.

3. Ladle into bowls.

Per serving: 245 cal., 28% (68 cal.) from fat; 19 g protein; 7.5 g fat (1 g sat.); 25 g carbo (1.6 g fiber); 367 mg sodium; 28 mg chol. ◆

ASPARAGUS, NOODLES, AND SEAFOOD soak up flavor from a broth made with fresh-cooked crab shells.

DRAMATIC BAR offers a romantic atmosphere at Southpark Seafood Grill.

Move over, martini
Wine bars are springing up all over Portland

Wine, if you haven't yet noticed, is making a comeback, and cocktails, from cosmopolitans to Manhattans, are making room for Merlots, Pinot Noirs, and other fruits of the vine. If you're interested in broadening your enological horizons, you're in luck: Wine bars serving a wide range of vintages by the glass have been proliferating in Portland, and the city now has quite a few classy hangouts devoted exclusively to wine.

Want to get to know some of the very best Oregon wines? Spend some time at **Oregon Wines on Broadway** (515 S.W. Broadway; 503/228-4655), a combination tasting room and wine bar devoted exclusively to Oregon's best. Of the 36 red wines available here on any given night, 30 will be Oregon Pinot Noirs.

For an utterly romantic experience, drop by **Southpark Seafood Grill and Winebar** (901 S.W. Salmon St.; 326-1300). Adopting a sort of Mediterranean decor, this wine bar is a perfect pre- or post-theater spot.

In ever-trendy northwest Portland, **Blue Tango Bistro & Wine Bar** (930 N.W. 23rd Ave.; 221-1466) is an intimate and romantic venue for sampling vintages from California, Oregon, and Washington. With a few tables in front of the fireplace, it's also a great place to sip Chardonnay on a cold winter night.

Not far away is **Serratto** (2112 N.W. Kearney St.; 221-1195), which many people still think of as the old Delphina's. A makeover in early 1999 gave this space a rustic Italian farmhouse feel. In the vineria, Italian wines are the focus.

In southeast Portland, the **Empire Room Wine Bar** (4260 S.E. Hawthorne Blvd.; 231-9225) is a more bohemian spot, just what you'd expect from its location in the Hawthorne neighborhood. European wines are the specialty here, and there's live music almost every night.

— *Karl Samson*◆

A TANGY ORANGE RUB makes salmon and potatoes a lively dinner pair.

Oven-roasted Salmon Steaks with Red Potatoes

Betty Jean Nichols, Eugene, Oregon

"I'm always experimenting with new ways to prepare seafood," says Betty Jean Nichols. Here's a quick way with salmon—creatively seasoned and paired with little potatoes—ideal for a winter dinner.

PREP AND COOK TIME: About 40 minutes

MAKES: 4 servings

- 1 pound **red thin-skinned potatoes** (about 1 1/2 in. wide)
- 4 teaspoons **olive** or salad **oil**
- 1 **orange** (about 1/2 lb.), rinsed
- 1 teaspoon *each* **dried oregano, ground cumin,** and **chili powder**
- 1 tablespoon chopped **fresh cilantro**
- 1/2 teaspoon **pepper**
- 4 **salmon steaks** (3/4 in. thick, 5 to 6 oz. each)
- **Cilantro sprigs**
- **Salt**

1. Scrub potatoes and cut each in half. In a 9- by 13-inch pan, mix potatoes with 2 teaspoons oil, then turn potatoes cut side up.

2. Bake in a 425° oven for 10 minutes. Turn potatoes cut side down and bake until barely tender when pierced, about 10 minutes longer.

3. Meanwhile, with a vegetable peeler, pare peel (orange part only) from orange. Mince peel. In a small bowl, combine peel, remaining 2 teaspoons oil, oregano, cumin, chili powder, chopped cilantro, and pepper.

4. Rinse salmon and pat dry. Rub seasoning mixture on cut sides of fish.

5. Push potatoes to sides of pan. Set salmon steaks in a single layer in the center of the pan. Bake until salmon is opaque but still moist-looking in the center of the thickest part (cut to test), 8 to 10 minutes.

6. As salmon bakes, use a small, sharp knife to cut membrane from orange; discard. Cut between membranes to release fruit segments; discard any seeds.

7. Transfer salmon steaks to warm plates, and add equal portions of potatoes. Garnish with orange segments and cilantro sprigs. Add salt to taste.

Per serving: 386 cal., 44% (171 cal.) from fat; 28 g protein; 19 g fat (3.3 g sat.); 26 g carbo (3.2 g fiber); 90 mg sodium; 74 mg chol.

Root Vegetable Salad

Elinore Johnson, Atwater, California

Elinore Johnson likes the challenge of finding new ways to combine the vegetables she has on hand. This salad was a recent favorite experiment. The escarole lends a pungent bite; for milder flavor but similar texture, use romaine lettuce.

PREP AND COOK TIME: About 55 minutes

MAKES: 6 to 8 servings

- 3 **beets** (2 to 2 1/2 in. wide; about 1 lb. total), tops trimmed
- 2 **parsnips** (3/4 lb. total)
- 1 tablespoon **olive** or salad **oil**
- 1/4 cup **cider vinegar**
- 2 tablespoons minced **fresh tarragon** leaves or 2 teaspoons dried tarragon
- 1 **Golden Delicious apple** (1/2 lb.)
- 1/2 cup **chopped walnuts**
- 2 cups lightly packed slivered **escarole** or romaine lettuce leaves
- **Salt** and **pepper**

1. Scrub beets and parsnips. Put beets in a 4- to 5-quart pan and add 2 quarts water. Cover pan and bring to a boil over high heat; reduce heat and simmer for 10 minutes. Add parsnips, cover, and continue to cook until vegetables are tender when pierced, about 30 minutes longer. Drain vegetables and let stand until cool enough to touch, about 5 minutes.

2. Meanwhile, in a large bowl, mix oil, vinegar, and tarragon.

3. Pull skin from beets; discard. Peel parsnips. Trim stem and root ends from vegetables; discard. Cut vegetables into 1/2-inch chunks and add to bowl.

4. Peel and core apple; cut into ½-inch chunks and add to bowl. Add walnuts and escarole. Mix salad, adding salt and pepper to taste.

Per serving: 128 cal., 46% (59 cal.) from fat; 2.4 g protein; 6.6 g fat (0.7 g sat.); 17 g carbo (3.3 g fiber); 37 mg sodium; 0 mg chol.

Washington Lemon Pudding

Elizabeth Farquhar, Randle, Washington

Elizabeth Farquhar uses lemon slices, with peel, to give this dessert a slightly bitter but pleasant edge. Instead of the five spice, use equal parts ground cinnamon, ginger, cloves, and anise seed to make 1½ teaspoons. If making up to 1 day ahead, cool, cover, and chill.

PREP AND COOK TIME: About 50 minutes

MAKES: 6 servings

   1 cup tightly packed thin **lemon** slices, seeds discarded

1¼ cups **sugar**

   3 tablespoons **quick-cooking rice cereal**

   3 large **eggs**

1½ teaspoons **vanilla**

1½ teaspoons **Chinese five spice** (see above)

  ¼ teaspoon **salt**

  ¼ cup (⅛ lb.) melted **butter** or margarine

1. In a blender or food processor, whirl lemon slices, sugar, rice cereal, eggs,

CHINESE FIVE SPICE permeates this lemon pudding.

vanilla, five spice, and salt until lemons are minced. Add butter; whirl to mix.

2. Pour mixture equally into 6 ramekins (about ⅔-cup size) or a shallow 6- by 9-inch (1- to 1½-qt.) casserole. Set ramekins or casserole in a 9- by 13-inch pan.

3. Set pan with puddings in a 350° oven. Pour enough boiling water into pan to come halfway up sides of ramekins or casserole.

4. Bake until puddings are browned and feel firm when lightly touched in the center, 30 to 35 minutes for ramekins, 35 to 45 minutes for casserole. Serve hot, cool, or chilled.

Per serving: 300 cal., 33% (99 cal.) from fat; 4 g protein; 11 g fat (5.7 g sat.); 50 g carbo (0.1 g fiber); 210 mg sodium; 128 mg chol.

Super Supper Casserole

Candace Barnhart, Hollywood

When she and her husband were newlyweds, Candace Barnhart invented casseroles to fit their small budget and large appetites. "Even though we have a few dollars more now," she says, "we still like the basics we made years ago."

PREP AND COOK TIME: About 1¼ hours

MAKES: 6 servings

   2 **onions** (about 1 lb. total), peeled and chopped

   1 clove **garlic,** minced or pressed

   1 pound **ground lean beef**

   1 tablespoon **chili powder**

   1 can (8 oz.) **tomato sauce**

   2 cups fat-skimmed **chicken broth**

   8 ounces **dried egg noodles**

   1 can (14 to 15 oz.) **cream-style corn**

   1 can (2¼ oz.) **sliced pitted black ripe olives,** drained

   1 cup (¼ lb.) **shredded cheddar cheese**

     Salt and **pepper**

1. In a 4- to 5-quart pan over high heat, stir onions, garlic, and beef frequently until meat is crumbled and browned, about 15 minutes.

2. Add chili powder, tomato sauce, broth, and noodles. Stirring often, bring mixture to a boil, then reduce heat and simmer until noodles are barely tender to bite, 10 to 12 minutes. Add corn and olives; mix well.

3. Scrape mixture into a 9- by 13-inch casserole, pushing noodles into sauce.

4. Bake, covered, in a 350° oven for 40 minutes. Uncover, sprinkle with cheese, and bake until cheese is melted and mixture bubbles at edges, about 3 minutes longer. Add salt and pepper to taste.

Per serving: 489 cal., 39% (189 cal.) from fat; 29 g protein; 21 g fat (8.7 g sat.); 49 g carbo (4.3 g fiber); 758 mg sodium; 102 mg chol.

Banana-Nut Oat Bran Muffins

Joan Stucey, Klamath Falls, Oregon

Joan Stucey often treats her co-workers to homemade muffins; they voted these the best.

PREP AND COOK TIME: About 40 minutes

MAKES: 12 muffins

     About 2 tablespoons **salad oil**

   2 **oranges** (about 1 lb. total), rinsed

   2 large **eggs**

   1 cup mashed **ripe bananas** (about 2, each 5 oz.)

  ¼ cup **honey**

  ¼ cup firmly packed **brown sugar**

   2 cups **quick-cooking oat bran cereal**

   2 teaspoons **baking powder**

  ½ teaspoon **salt**

  ½ cup chopped **walnuts**

1. Oil 12 muffin cups (2½ in. wide), or line with paper baking cups.

2. Grate 1 tablespoon peel (orange part only) from orange. Cut oranges in half and ream juice. Measure ½ cup juice; save remainder for other uses.

3. In a large bowl, combine orange peel, orange juice, 2 tablespoons oil, eggs, bananas, honey, and brown sugar. Stir to mix well.

4. In a small bowl, mix cereal, baking powder, salt, and walnuts. Add to egg mixture and stir until evenly moistened. Spoon batter equally into muffin cups.

5. Bake muffins in a 400° oven until golden brown, 20 to 25 minutes. Run a knife between muffins and cup sides, invert pan to remove muffins, and set muffins upright on a rack. Serve hot, warm, or at room temperature.

Per muffin: 196 cal., 39% (77 cal.) from fat; 4.8 g protein; 8.5 g fat (1.1 g sat.); 30 g carbo (3.3 g fiber); 192 mg sodium; 35 mg chol. ◆

Bed-and-breakfast treat: A stack of spiced pancakes awaits a shower of tangy fresh lemon sauce. Recipes begin on page 48.

February

fondue revival

From cheese to caramel, dunk-and-dine meal makes a splashy comeback

BY LINDA LAU ANUSASANANAN • PHOTOGRAPHS BY JAMES CARRIER

FOOD STYLING BY VALERIE AIKMAN-SMITH

■ Flower children, baby boomers: Remember those fondue parties of the '60s and '70s? The nights we bonded around melted cheese bubbling away in a fondue pan over an alcohol flame, spearing chunks of bread, washing down hot bites with chilled jug chablis, while Bob Dylan sang "The Times They Are A-Changin'" in the background?

Well, fondue is making a big comeback. Sleek new fondue sets and beautifully revived traditional units are gracing the shelves and websites of cookware stores. Generation X is discovering, as I did back then, that fondue is a great vehicle for intimate, easy entertaining.

Today's take on fondue brings more choices. Swiss cheese is the classic, but, with a Latin variation, fondue bubbles to a new beat. The old-time meat fondue, beef chunks sizzling in hot oil, returns in a safer, fresher version that uses broth instead of oil. And an updated palate of foods to swish through the simmering broth, then into a bright array of dipping sauces, gives both French and Asian touches to fondue. For dessert, caramel-rich dulce de leche moves beyond routine chocolate fondue to another mantle for fruit and cake.

Fondue starts with a pan and a heating element (see "What's New in Fondue," page 39). The contents of the pan determine the foods to use for dunking or cooking, as well as the peripheral collection of sauces, if any. A single setup best suits a party of two to six—so all have ready access to the action. Multiply the scale of the event simply by duplicating the fondue arrangement at other tables. Long fondue forks or skewers serve as cooking and eating utensils. Each person needs a plate for collecting tidbits, and plenty of napkins.

As a fondue vet, let me share why I still like these parties: I do the shopping and chopping, my guests do the cooking and serving. Now that's easy.

Bouillabaisse Fondue

PREP AND COOK TIME: About 30 minutes

NOTES: Use a cooking pan, metal chafing dish without the water bath jacket, a metal fondue pan, or an electric fondue pan with heat turned to high.

MAKES: 4 to 6 servings

- 12 to 18 **red thin-skinned potatoes** ($1\frac{1}{2}$ in. wide), scrubbed
- $\frac{1}{2}$ pound **boned, skinned firm-flesh fish** such as halibut
- $\frac{1}{2}$ pound **sea scallops**
- $\frac{1}{2}$ pound **shrimp** (31 to 40 per lb.), shelled and deveined
   Bouillabaisse broth (recipe follows)
   Rouille (recipe follows)
   Croutons (recipe follows)

1. In a 3- to 4-quart pan over high heat, bring about 1 quart water to a boil. Add potatoes. Cover and simmer until potatoes are tender when pierced, 15 to 20 minutes. Drain; keep warm.

2. Meanwhile, rinse fish, scallops, and shrimp; pat dry. Cut fish into $\frac{1}{4}$-inch-thick slices about 2 inches long. Cut scallops crosswise into $\frac{1}{4}$-inch-thick slices. Cut shrimp in half lengthwise. Arrange fish, scallops, and shrimp on a flat dish.

3. In a 3-quart metal chafing dish or pan over high heat, bring all the broth to a boil. If using a 2-quart fondue pan, fill it halfway with boiling broth (keep remaining broth hot; cover and set over lowest heat on a range).

4. Set container over an ignited alcohol or canned solid-fuel flame. Adjust for maximum heat. Place potatoes, seafood, rouille, and croutons alongside.

5. Spear potatoes or seafood, 1 piece at a time, on fondue forks or thin skewers (metal or wood) and immerse in broth. Cook potatoes until warm or hot, and seafood until barely opaque in thickest part, 30 seconds to 1 minute. Dip hot foods into rouille to taste, or spread rouille onto croutons to eat. If broth stops simmering, return to high heat on a range burner until boiling. Return to fondue burner. As broth in 2-quart pan evaporates, add remaining broth.

6. When potatoes and seafood are consumed, ladle cooking broth into bowls. Spread any remaining croutons with remaining rouille; eat while sipping broth.

Per serving: 511 cal., 28% (144 cal.) from fat; 33 g protein; 16 g fat (2.6 g sat.); 49 g carbo (2.7 g fiber); 781 mg sodium; 72 mg chol.

FONDUE BOUILLABAISSE awaits final touches. Fish, scallops, shrimp, and potatoes are cut into small bites to quick-cook in simmering saffron-scented broth.

Bouillabaisse Broth

PREP AND COOK TIME: About 30 minutes

NOTES: If making up to 1 day ahead, cover and chill.

MAKES: About 6 cups; 4 to 6 servings

In a 2½- to 3-quart pan over medium-high heat, frequently stir 1 teaspoon **olive oil**, 1 cup chopped **onion**, 1 cup chopped **fennel**, and 3 peeled, pressed cloves **garlic** until onion is limp, about 5 minutes. Add 5 cups fat-skimmed **chicken broth**, 1 cup **dry white wine**, 1 tablespoon **tomato paste**, ½ teaspoon **dried thyme**, and ¹/₁₆ teaspoon **powdered saffron** or ¼ teaspoon ground turmeric; bring to a boil. Reduce heat, cover, and simmer until vegetables are soft when pressed, about 15 minutes. Measure broth; if less than 6 cups, add more fat-skimmed chicken broth or water.

Per serving: 73 cal., 9.9% (7.2 cal.) from fat; 7.1 g protein; 0.8 g fat (0.1 g sat.); 2.5 g carbo (0 g fiber); 96 mg sodium; 0 mg chol.

Rouille

PREP TIME: About 5 minutes

NOTES: If making up to 1 day ahead, cover and chill.

MAKES: About 1 cup

In a small bowl, mix 1 cup **reduced-fat** or regular **mayonnaise**, 1 tablespoon minced **garlic**, 1 tablespoon **lemon juice**, and ½ teaspoon **cayenne**.

Per tablespoon: 41 cal., 66% (27 cal.) from fat; 0 g protein; 3 g fat (0.5 g sat.); 3.3 g carbo (0 g fiber); 120 mg sodium; 0 mg chol.

Croutons

PREP AND COOK TIME: About 25 minutes

NOTES: If making up to 1 day ahead,

store airtight at room temperature.

MAKES: 4 to 6 servings

Slice 1 **baguette** (½ lb.) diagonally ¼ inch thick. Arrange slices in a single layer on a 12- by 15-inch baking sheet. Brush with 2 tablespoons **extra-virgin olive oil**. Bake in a 400° oven until crisp and golden, 8 to 10 minutes. Serve warm or cool.

Per serving: 144 cal., 36% (52 cal.) from fat; 3.3 g protein; 5.8 g fat (0.9 g sat.); 20 g carbo (1 g fiber); 230 mg sodium; 0 mg chol.

Swiss Cheese Fondue

PREP AND COOK TIME: About 25 minutes

NOTES: If you use an electric fondue pan, turn heat to medium while mixing and melting fondue, then turn to lowest setting while serving.

MAKES: About 2½ cups; 8 appetizer or 3 or 4 main-dish servings

- 1 to 1¼ cups **dry white wine**
- ½ pound **Swiss (emmenthal) cheese**, shredded
- ½ pound **gruyère cheese**, shredded
- 4 teaspoons **cornstarch**
- 1 teaspoon **dry mustard**
- 2 tablespoons **kirsch** (optional)
  Fresh-ground **nutmeg** and **pepper**
- 1 **baguette** (½ lb.), cut into ¾-inch cubes

1. In a 1½- to 2-quart fondue pan (flame-proof ceramic or porcelain-glazed cast-iron) or heavy-bottom metal pan over medium heat, warm 1 cup wine until bubbles form and slowly rise to surface, about 6 minutes.

2. In a bowl, mix Swiss cheese, gruyère cheese, cornstarch, and mustard.

3. Add cheese mixture, a handful at a time, to hot wine, stirring until fondue is smoothly melted and beginning to bubble. Add kirsch and sprinkle fondue with nutmeg and pepper.

4. Set pan over an ignited alcohol or canned solid-fuel flame (if pan is ceramic, place a heat diffuser between it and heat source). Adjust heat so fondue bubbles very slowly. Check occasionally to be sure fondue is not scorching; if it is too hot, reduce or turn off the heat, then resume heating when mixture begins to cool.

5. Spear bread cubes, 1 at a time, with fondue forks or thin skewers (metal or wood) and swirl through fondue (stir across bottom frequently to prevent scorching); lift out and let drip briefly over pan, then eat. If fondue gets too thick for easy dipping, stir in more heated wine, a few tablespoons at a time. After fondue is consumed, scrape

DUNK CRUSTY BREAD chunks into classic Swiss cheese fondue. The flame under porcelain-glazed iron pan keeps fondue steaming.

the cheese crust from pan to divide and eat; it's considered a special treat.

Per main-dish serving: 656 cal., 49% (324 cal.) from fat; 38 g protein; 36 g fat (21 g sat.); 35 g carbo (1.6 g fiber); 687 mg sodium; 115 mg chol.

Chili-Cheese Fondue

PREP AND COOK TIME: About 25 minutes

NOTES: For an entrée, you can also dip these foods into the sauce: 3 to 4 cups bite-size vegetable pieces (choose 1 to 4—canned baby corn, cauliflower florets, cherry tomatoes, red bell pepper strips, zucchini slices) and 3 to 4 cups bite-size pieces cooked meat (choose 1 to 3—chicken, meatballs, shrimp, sausage).

MAKES: About 2⅔ cups; 8 appetizer or 3 or 4 main-dish servings

Follow recipe for **Swiss cheese fondue** (page 37), but omit wine and use **milk;** omit Swiss cheese and use **jack cheese** or chili-flavored jack cheese; omit gruyère cheese and use **sharp cheddar cheese;** increase **cornstarch** to 2 tablespoons; and omit mustard and use crushed **cumin seed.** After cheeses are melted, stir in 1 can (4 oz.) **diced green chilies.** Omit kirsch, nutmeg, and pepper. Serve with **baguette**

cubes or 6 to 9 ounces tortilla chips.

Per main-dish serving: 657 cal., 55% (360 cal.) from fat; 35 g protein; 40 g fat (24 g sat.); 39 g carbo (1.9 g fiber); 1,206 mg sodium; 128 mg chol.

Bubbling Asian Fondue

PREP AND COOK TIME: About 1 hour

NOTES: If cooking vegetables up to 1 day ahead, cover and chill. Let vegetables warm to room temperature before serving.

MAKES: 4 to 6 servings

- 4 to 6 cups bite-size **vegetable** pieces (choose 2 or 3—asparagus, broccoli, green beans)
- ½ pound boned, skinned **firm-flesh fish** such as halibut
- ½ pound **sea scallops**
- ½ pound **shrimp** (31 to 40 per lb.), shelled and deveined

    Asian broth (recipe follows)

    Sauces (choose 3 or 4—chutney yogurt, cilantro mustard, ginger-soy, wasabi cream; recipes follow)
- 2 to 3 cups cooked **rice**

1. In 5- to 6-quart pan over high heat, bring 2 to 3 quarts water to a boil. Add vegetables. Cook until they turn bright green, 2 to 4 minutes. Drain; immerse in ice water until cool; drain again.

2. Rinse fish, scallops, and shrimp; pat dry. Cut fish into ¼-inch-thick slices, about 2 inches long. Cut scallops crosswise into ¼-inch-thick slices. Cut shrimp in half lengthwise. Arrange fish, scallops, and shrimp on a flat dish.

3. In a 3-quart metal chafing dish or pan over high heat, bring all Asian broth to a boil. If using a 2-quart fondue pan, fill halfway with boiling broth (keep remaining broth hot; cover, and set over lowest heat on a range).

4. Set container on an alcohol or canned solid-fuel flame or an electric burner set on high heat. Arrange vegetables, seafood, sauces, and rice near pan.

5. Spear foods, 1 piece at a time, with fondue forks or thin skewers (metal or wood) and immerse in broth. Cook vegetables until they are hot, and seafood until barely opaque in thickest part, 30 seconds to 1 minute. Dip hot foods into sauces and eat. As liquid evaporates in pan, add more boiling broth, using all.

6. After vegetables and seafood are consumed, ladle remaining broth into bowls and add rice to each portion. Eat with spoons.

Per serving: 235 cal., 7.7% (18 cal.) from fat; 32 g protein; 2 g fat (0.3 g sat.); 21 g carbo (1.5 g fiber); 212 mg sodium; 72 mg chol.

Asian Broth

PREP AND COOK TIME: About 25 minutes

NOTES: If making up to 1 day ahead, cover and chill.

MAKES: 6 cups

In a 2½- to 3-quart pan over high heat, bring to a boil 6 cups fat-skimmed **chicken broth,** ½ cup thinly sliced **green onions,** 6 slices **fresh ginger** (quarter size), 1 or 2 **dried hot red chilies,** and 2 cloves **garlic,** peeled and pressed. Reduce heat, cover, and simmer 15 to 20 minutes. With a slotted spoon, lift out and discard ginger and chilies.

Per cup: 39 cal., 0% (0 cal.) from fat; 8.2 g protein; 0 g fat; 0.9 g carbo (0 g fiber); 77 mg sodium; 0 mg chol.

Chutney Yogurt

PREP TIME: About 5 minutes

NOTES: If making up to 1 day ahead, cover and chill.

MAKES: About ¾ cup

In a small bowl, mix ¼ cup finely chopped **mango chutney** with ½ cup **plain nonfat yogurt.**

Per tablespoon: 25 cal., 0% (0 cal.) from fat; 0.5 g protein; 0 g fat; 5.4 g carbo (0 g fiber); 64 mg sodium; 0.2 mg chol.

Cilantro Mustard

PREP TIME: About 5 minutes

NOTES: If making up to 1 day ahead, cover and chill.

MAKES: About ½ cup

In a small bowl, mix ½ cup **reduced-fat** or regular **mayonnaise,** 2 tablespoons finely chopped **fresh cilantro,** 1 tablespoon **Dijon mustard,** and ½ teaspoon **Asian** (toasted) **sesame oil.**

Per tablespoon: 44 cal., 68% (30 cal.) from fat; 0 g protein; 3.3 g fat (0.5 g sat.); 3 g carbo (0 g fiber); 165 mg sodium; 0 mg chol.

Ginger-Soy

PREP TIME: About 10 minutes

NOTES: If making up to 1 day ahead, cover and chill.

MAKES: About ½ cup

In a small bowl, mix ½ cup **soy sauce,** 2 tablespoons **dry sherry,** 2 tablespoons minced **fresh ginger,** 4 teaspoons **sugar,** and 2 teaspoons minced **garlic.**

Per tablespoon: 25 cal., 0% (0 cal.) from fat; 1 g protein; 0 g fat; 4.3 g carbo (0 g fiber); 1,029 mg sodium; 0 mg chol.

Wasabi Cream

PREP TIME: About 5 minutes

NOTES: If making up to 1 day ahead, cover and chill.

DULCE DE LECHE, a thick caramel, clings sweetly to bits of cake and fruit. A candle under the porcelain-lined copper pan maintains gentle heat.

2. In the same pan over high heat, shake and tilt sugar often until melted and amber-colored, about 3 minutes; take care not to scorch.

3. Remove from heat and add whipping cream and rum (mixture foams). Return pan to medium heat and stir until caramel is dissolved and smooth; boil vigorously, stirring occasionally, until mixture thickly coats a spoon, about 10 minutes.

4. Pour into a 1½- to 2-cup ceramic fondue pan, other heavy metal pan, or metal chafing dish in a water bath jacket. Set over a votive candle or ignited alcohol or canned solid-fuel flame. Adjust heat to lowest setting under fondue pan, to medium under chafing dish.

5. Spear fruit or cake, 1 piece at a time, on fondue forks or thin skewers (metal or wood) and swirl through dulce de leche fondue (stir across bottom frequently to prevent scorching), lift out, and let drip briefly over pan. Sprinkle bites with a few nuts, as desired.

Per serving: 336 cal., 51% (171 cal.) from fat; 2.1 g protein; 19 g fat (12 g sat.); 43 g carbo (2 g fiber); 22 mg sodium; 66 mg chol.

MAKES: About ½ cup

In a small bowl, mix 1 tablespoon **wasabi powder** with 2 teaspoons **water** until smooth. Add ½ cup **sour cream** and 1 tablespoon minced **chives** or green onions; mix well. Add **salt** to taste.

Per tablespoon: 31 cal., 87% (27 cal.) from fat; 0.5 g protein; 3 g fat (1.9 g sat.); 0.6 g carbo (0 g fiber); 7.6 mg sodium; 6.3 mg chol.

Dulce de Leche Fondue

PREP AND COOK TIME: About ½ hour

NOTES: If making up to 1 day ahead, cover and chill; reheat to serve. This fondue is inclined to scorch, so keep heat low. Porcelain-glazed cast-iron and ceramic pans used with a heat diffuser, and pans nested in hot water, maintain the most even temperature.

Choose 2 to 4 kinds of fruit—apples, ba-

nanas, dried apricots, firm-ripe pears, grapes, pineapples, strawberries. Cut fruits that discolor readily just before serving, such as apples, bananas, and pears, and brush pieces with lemon juice.

MAKES: About 1 cup; 4 servings

½ cup finely **chopped pecans** (optional)

½ cup **sugar**

1 cup **whipping cream**

2 to 4 tablespoons **rum** (optional)

3 to 4 cups bite-size pieces **fruit** (see notes)

1½ cups ¾-inch chunks **angel food** or pound **cake** (optional)

1. In a 10- to 12-inch nonstick frying pan over medium heat, frequently stir pecans until lightly toasted, 4 to 5 minutes; pour into a small bowl.

WHAT'S NEW IN FONDUE

Long associated with cheese fondue, thick ceramic pans now come in several sizes and colors, as well as the established earthen tones. These containers sit on denatured alcohol or canned solid-fuel burners, or over votive candles, and work well with cheese and dessert fondues, which need low to moderate heat. Some sets come with heat diffusers that provide better control and protect the ceramic from breaking. Prices for a 1- to 2-quart ceramic fondue set range from $60 to $150.

For broth and the traditional oil fondues, you need a metal container that can take high heat. Some units have electric burners with adjustable controls. Prices for these fondue sets range from $20 to about $300.

Porcelain-glazed cast-iron pans work for all types of fondues. Metal chafing dishes, with or without their water bath jackets, also make suitable containers for fondue. Or you can improvise with pans over portable burners; just be sure the setup is stable enough to be safe. ◆

Citrus surprises

Flavor and color treats are hiding inside
these familiar-looking fruits. Here's how to use them

BY ANDREW BAKER

PHOTOGRAPHS BY RICHARD JUNG

pummelo

Cara Cara
navel

blood
orange

Melogold

Cara Cara
navel

■ Sometimes, things are not what they seem.

A casual glance at the citrus at left doesn't reveal their true identities. Cara Cara navel oranges present no surface evidence that their segments are a rosy color. The pummelo resembles an oversize grapefruit, but beneath its thick peel, the segments are sweet and mild—without a trace of grapefruit bitterness. Melogolds and Oroblancos, both grapefruit ringers, taste sweet. And blood oranges hint at their uniqueness only occasionally, when their skin is blushed red.

These and other less familiar citrus varieties are at their seasonal peak now. They are as versatile as their less exotic counterparts, but each brings a bonus of flavor, color, or textural nuances. Make use of these extras in the recipes that follow: Create a blood orange filling for a tart to show off the individuality of the fruit. Lay mild pummelo and sweet Melogold segments onto tender green herbs for a vibrant salad. Or enjoy a refreshing spritzer cooled by citrus juice ice cubes.

Choose these citrus fruits as you would any other. The fruit should feel heavy for its size, be firm (no soft spots), and show no signs of spoilage (such as mold). Blood oranges, Cara Cara navels, Melogolds, and Oroblancos usually contain few or no seeds; pummeloes usually have seeds.

TARTS get a double burst of citrus— in pastry cream and fruit topping.

Citrus Tarts

PREP AND COOK TIME: About 50 minutes
NOTES: If making crust up to 1 day ahead, bake, cool, wrap airtight, and let stand at room temperature; freeze to store longer. Thaw unwrapped, then fill.
MAKES: 6 servings

1⅓ cups **all-purpose flour**

¼ cup **sugar**

½ cup (¼ lb.) **butter** or margarine

1 **large egg** yolk

1 **Melogold** or white grapefruit (about 1 lb.)

2 **blood oranges** or navel oranges (about 10 oz. total)

2 **Cara Cara navel** or regular navel **oranges** (about 1 lb. total)

1 recipe's worth **citrus pastry cream** (recipe follows)

Mint sprigs

1. In a food processor or a bowl, combine flour and sugar. Add butter, cut into small pieces. Whirl or rub with your fingers until fine crumbs form. Add egg yolk; whirl or mix with a fork until dough holds together. Pat dough into a ball.

2. Divide dough into 6 equal portions. Firmly press each portion over bottom and sides of a 4½-inch tart pan with removable rim.

3. Bake in a 300° oven until pale gold, about 25 minutes; let cool.

4. Meanwhile, peel and segment Melogold, blood oranges, and navel oranges as directed on page 42.

5. Spread pastry cream equally in baked crusts. Drain citrus segments; save juice for other uses. Arrange an equal portion of Melogold, blood orange, and navel orange segments decoratively on each filled pastry. Garnish with mint sprigs. Serve or cover and chill up to 1 hour.

Per serving: 442 cal., 35% (153 cal.) from fat; 5.3 g protein; 17 g fat (10 g sat.); 68 g carbo (3 g fiber); 161 mg sodium; 112 mg chol.

Citrus Pastry Cream

PREP AND COOK TIME: About 20 minutes, plus at least 15 minutes to chill
NOTES: If making up to 1 day ahead, cover and chill the cooked mixture. For the most vibrant color, use blood oranges or ruby grapefruit. Other citrus juices that work well include Cara Cara navel orange, Melogold, pummelo, tangelo, and navel or juice orange. Use

GETTING TO KNOW UNUSUAL CITRUS

•Blood oranges are named for their red juice. The peel may be plain orange or tinged with a red blush: Coloration is characteristic of some varieties or may be due to environment; it's also affected by the season. The flesh may be ruby-red, an orange and red mix, or hardly red at all—for the same reasons. Generally, the flavor of blood oranges is tarter than that of regular juice or navel oranges. The most common variety, Moro, usually has the reddest flesh; others are Sanguinelli and Tarocco. Blood oranges are available from early December to mid-May.

•Cara Cara navel oranges, a natural mutation of the navel orange, have been grown in California and Florida since the late 1980s. The peel is orange, the flesh is pinkish to rosy orange, and the flavor is a little sweeter than that of the regular navel. These oranges are available from early December to April.

•Melogolds and Oroblancos are different hybrids from pummelo

and grapefruit parents. The fruit is harvested at its flavor prime, which may be while the peel is still green (but it will turn yellow). Melogolds are larger, heavier, and thinner-skinned than Oroblancos. While neither has the bitter bite of grapefruit, Oroblancos are juicier and sweeter than Melogolds. They are available from December to mid-April.

•Pummeloes are a citrus variety often mistaken for grapefruit, but the fruit can be much, much larger, and either is round or has a peaked top. Under the peel, pale to medium yellow, is a very thick layer of white pith. The fruit segments, encased in papery membranes, are firm, pale yellow or slightly pink, and composed of distinct large juice sacs (vesicles) that can be gently separated. Extracting the segments requires some patience. The fruit's refreshing flavor has no bitterness, and it can be sweeter than that of grapefruit. Pummeloes are available from mid-November to March.

pummeloes

1 With a sharp knife, cut thick peel and white membrane from each end of a pummelo, exposing fruit. Set fruit on 1 end and, with knife, cut and discard peel and membrane from sides of the fruit.

2 Grasping fruit in both hands, pull from center with equal pressure to split pummelo in half.

3 With segments still attached, cut off the thick center membrane ridge at the tapered end of each piece.

4 Starting at a narrow edge, carefully pull segment away from membrane; avoid breaking fruit. Discard membrane.

other citrus

1 With a sharp knife, cut and discard peel and white membrane from citrus fruit.

2 Over a bowl, cut between membranes and fruit to release fruit segments into bowl. Squeeze juice from membrane into bowl. Discard membrane.

peel from your fruit choice to flavor the pastry cream. Fill tarts (page 41) with the pastry cream or, for a quick dessert, spread the cream thickly onto short-bread cookies.

MAKES: 1½ cups

- ½ cup **sugar**
- 2 tablespoons **cornstarch**
- 1 tablespoon thinly shredded **citrus** peel (see notes)
- 1⅓ cups **citrus juice** (see notes)
- 1 **large egg** yolk

1. In a 1½- to 2-quart pan, mix sugar, cornstarch, peel, juice, and egg yolk. Stir over high heat until boiling, about 5 minutes.

2. Nest pan in ice water and stir occasionally until cool, about 10 minutes. Or cover and chill until cold, about 2 hours. Stir before using.

Per tablespoon: 28 cal., 6.4% (1.8 cal.) from fat; 0.2 g protein; 0.2 g fat (0.1 g sat.); 6.3 g carbo (0 g fiber); 0.5 mg sodium; 8.9 mg chol.

Sichuan Orange Chicken

PREP AND COOK TIME: About 20 minutes
MAKES: 4 servings

- 1 pound **boned, skinned chicken breasts**
- ½ teaspoon **salad oil**
  Blood orange sauce (recipe follows)
- 4 cups hot cooked **white rice**
- ¼ cup chopped **green onions** (including tops)
  Soy sauce

1. Rinse chicken, pat dry, and cut into ½-inch chunks.

2. In a 12-inch nonstick frying pan or a 5- to 6-quart nonstick pan over high heat, stir chicken in oil until lightly browned and no longer pink in center of thickest part (cut to test), 4 to 5 minutes.

3. Add blood orange sauce and stir until boiling, 1 to 2 minutes.

4. Spoon chicken and sauce onto rice. Sprinkle with green onions and season to taste with soy sauce.

Per serving: 479 cal., 4.8% (23 cal.) from fat; 31 g protein; 2.6 g fat (0.6 g sat.); 80 g carbo (0.9 g fiber); 78 mg sodium; 66 mg chol.

Blood Orange Sauce

PREP AND COOK TIME: About 20 minutes
NOTES: If making sauce up to 2 days ahead, cover and chill. It also makes a

refreshing dressing for a green salad or grapefruit segments.

MAKES: About 1 cup

- 1½ cups **blood orange** juice or regular orange juice
- ½ cup **sugar**
- 1½ teaspoons minced or pressed **garlic**
- 1 tablespoon minced **fresh ginger**
- ¼ to ½ teaspoon **hot chili flakes**

In a 10- to 12-inch nonstick frying pan over high heat, mix orange juice, sugar, garlic, ginger, and chili flakes to taste. Boil until reduced to 1 cup, about 10 minutes; stir often. Use hot or cold.

Per tablespoon: 35 cal., 0% (0 cal.) from fat; 0.2 g protein; 0 g fat; 8.8 g carbo (0 g fiber); 0.4 mg sodium; 0 mg chol.

Meyer Lemon–Blood Orange Marmalade

PREP AND COOK TIME: About 1¼ hours

NOTES: Theresa Liu of Alameda, California, says her "harshest food critics"—her sons—give "a big thumbs-up" to this sweet-tart marmalade she created.

MAKES: 7 to 8 jars, 1 cup each

- ½ pound **Meyer lemons**
  About 8 pounds **blood oranges**
- 1 package (1.75 oz.) **low-sugar powdered pectin**
- 4 cups **sugar**

1. Rinse lemons and oranges. Using a vegetable peeler, cut colored part only from 2 of the lemons and 4 of the oranges. Finely chop peel. Put 2 tablespoons lemon peel, 6 tablespoons orange peel, and 1 cup water in a 6- to 8-quart pan; discard remaining peel.

2. With a sharp knife, cut and discard remaining peel and membrane from the lemons and 10 of the oranges. Cut fruit into chunks, discarding seeds.

3. In a blender or food processor, whirl lemons, then oranges, a portion at a time, until you have 2 cups that are smoothly puréed. Pour purée into pan.

4. Whirl remaining fruit, rub juice through a strainer into a bowl, and measure. Squeeze enough juice from remaining oranges to make a total of 4 cups; add juice to pan.

5. Place pan over high heat and bring to a boil, stirring often. Continue to boil, stirring often, until reduced to 5 cups, about 8 minutes.

6. In a small bowl, mix pectin and ¼

cup sugar. Add pectin mixture to pan. Stir over high heat until mixture returns to a rolling boil. Add remaining sugar and stir until mixture returns to a rolling boil. Stir and boil exactly 1 minute. Remove from heat.

7. At once, ladle marmalade mixture into clean canning jars (1-cup size) to within ⅛ inch of top. Wipe jar rims clean. Set a new flat canning lid on each jar. Screw on bands.

8. Protecting hands with pot holders, invert filled jars on a towel for 5 minutes, then turn lid side up. Let marmalade cool at least 24 hours. Check seals by pressing firmly on centers of the lids. If a lid pops back, it's not sealed; store unsealed marmalade in the refrigerator.

Per tablespoon: 37 cal., 0% (0 cal.) from fat; 0.2 g protein; 0 g fat; 9.5 g carbo (0.5 g fiber); 5.6 mg sodium; 0 mg chol.

PUMMELO, Oroblanco, and herbs complement skewered lamb.

Citrus Herb Salad

PREP AND COOK TIME: About 30 minutes

NOTES: The bold flavors of this whole-leaf salad go well with grilled foods, such as skewered lamb, beef steaks, or salmon.

MAKES: 4 servings

- 1 **pummelo** (about 1¾ lb.) or pink grapefruit
- 1 **Melogold** (about 1¼ lb.) or white grapefruit
- ½ cup **fresh mint** leaves
- 1 cup **fresh tarragon** leaves
- ⅔ cup **fresh chervil** leaves or ¼ cup parsley sprigs

- ½ cup **fresh basil** leaves
- 3 tablespoons minced **fresh chives**
- 1½ tablespoons **olive oil**
  Salt and **pepper**

1. Peel and segment pummelo as directed on page 42.

2. Peel and segment Melogold as directed on page 42. Reserve 3 tablespoons juice; save the remainder for other uses.

3. Rinse mint, tarragon, chervil, and basil; gently pat dry. Stack basil leaves and cut crosswise into thin strips. Mix herb leaves, cut basil, and chives. Mound herb mixture equally on plates.

4. In a small bowl, mix reserved 3 tablespoons Melogold juice and oil. Drizzle half the dressing evenly over herbs.

5. Arrange pummelo and Melogold segments on herbs. Drizzle segments equally with remaining dressing. Add salt and pepper to taste.

Per serving: 142 cal., 36% (51 cal.) from fat; 3.5 g protein; 5.7 g fat (0.7 g sat.); 23 g carbo (1.7 g fiber); 9.3 mg sodium; 0 mg chol.

Citrus Spritzer

PREP AND COOK TIME: About 20 minutes, plus 2 hours to freeze

MAKES: 4 servings

- 1¼ cups **blood orange** juice or regular orange juice
- 2 cups **Melogold** or white grapefruit juice
- 1 cup **sugar**
- 2 cups **club soda**
- 4 **blood orange** or regular orange slices

1. Pour blood orange juice into ice cube trays to just below divider rims. Freeze until solid, at least 2 hours.

2. Meanwhile, in a 1½- to 2-quart pan over high heat, stir 1 cup Melogold juice and sugar until mixture boils and sugar is dissolved, about 5 minutes. Let cool, then cover and chill, at least 2 hours. Or nest pan in ice water and stir often until cold, about 10 minutes.

3. Remove frozen juice cubes from trays and divide cubes equally among glasses (about 2 cups each). Pour equal portions of Melogold juice and the chilled fruit juice syrup into each glass, then fill to rim with club soda. Garnish with blood orange slices.

Per serving: 285 cal., 0.9% (2.7 cal.) from fat; 1.3 g protein; 0.3 g fat (0 g sat.); 72 g carbo (0.6 g fiber); 27 mg sodium; 0 mg chol. ◆

food guide

BY JERRY ANNE DI VECCHIO

PHOTOGRAPHS BY JAMES CARRIER

"Mole" means sauce

Out of the Aztec empire to modern-day Las Vegas

■ The pages of my favorite reference for Mexican foods, *The Mexican Cook Book for American Homes,* are yellowed with age and stained with use. Josefina Velazquez de Leon, former director of the Culinary Arts Institute in Mexico City, wrote it more than 40 years ago. In it she says, "Among our oldest and most famous dishes of genuine Mexican origin is *mole de guajolote,* known in the days of the Aztec empire before the Conquest. The word *mole* is derived from *molli* or *mulli,* which meant sauce."

Guajolote—turkey—is only one partner for the sauce. It also associates with many meats and takes innumerable forms—classic and otherwise—with ingredient lists long or short. Some moles begin as thick pastes (in different colors) of blended chilies, masa, and spices. And some moles are even canned. The "secret" recipe for the highly reputed mole in one household I visited in Mexico City long ago actually started with a jar of Doña María mole poblano—in which chocolate is a constituent.

In Las Vegas recently, I came across another mole, almost as simple as the Mexico City one, as I sought refuge from the swarming Strip. It was my second visit to this famous city. I'd come to celebrate the midcentury birthday of a dear friend, Wolfgang Puck. (He was an infant the last time I'd been to Vegas. But since he has become a regular in town,

getting a good meal isn't the gamble it once was.) This richly flavored pork stew, which I enjoyed for lunch before the party, was created by Chef Saul Garcia at Z' Tejas Grill; it was in itself a reason to celebrate.

Mole Pork

PREP AND COOK TIME: About 3¾ hours

NOTES: If making up to 1 day ahead, chill meat with sauce airtight. To reheat, stir often over medium heat until steaming. Serve with hot cooked rice or black beans. Add sour cream flavored to taste with more of the canned chipotle chili, minced or mashed. Garnish with slivered green onions (including tops) or fresh cilantro leaves and lime wedges.

MAKES: 8 to 10 servings

1 **boned, tied pork
   shoulder** or butt
   (about 4 lb.)

1 **onion** (½ lb.), peeled
   and chopped

1 **firm-ripe tomato**
   (½ lb.), rinsed, cored,
   and chopped

2 cups **tomato juice**

1 cup fat-skimmed
   chicken broth

2 tablespoons firmly
   packed **brown sugar**

1 **dried ancho** or
   dried pasilla **chili**
   (about ½ oz.)

1 tablespoon
   chopped **canned
   chipotle chili**

1. Rinse pork and put in a
5- to 6-quart pan. Add
onion, tomato, tomato juice,
broth, and brown sugar.
Rinse dried chili, break off
stem, and shake seeds from
pod. Add dried chili and
chipotle chili to pan.

2. Cover and bring to a boil
over high heat; reduce heat
to low and simmer until meat
is very tender when pierced,
3 to 3½ hours, occasionally
pushing meat aside and stirring sauce to be sure it's not
sticking.

3. Supporting meat with 2
slotted spoons, transfer to an
8- or 9-inch-wide pan, fat up.

4. Bake meat in a 350° oven
until very well browned,
30 to 40 minutes. Cut and
discard string. With 2 forks,
tear meat into large chunks;
keep warm.

5. Meanwhile, skim and discard fat from meat juices.
Boil juices over high heat
until reduced to 3 cups,
about 30 minutes. Whirl, a
portion at a time, in a
blender until smooth.

6. Put pork in a bowl; pour
sauce over meat.

Per serving: 363 cal., 64% (234
cal.) from fat; 24 g protein;
26 g fat (9.6 g sat.); 8.5 g carbo
(1.3 g fiber); 256 mg sodium;
85 mg chol.

Stable as a wok

■ A wok is much too useful to relegate
to a single cuisine. And as the pan has
been adopted in contemporary Western
kitchens, it has been adapted in materials and
shape. A prime example is the Buffalo five-ply
stainless steel wok. This pan has a three-layer core of
aluminum and aluminum alloy sealed between layers of
stainless steel. The aluminum provides good heat distribution, while
the stainless steel functions at high temperatures without wear and tear (unlike many
nonstick-finished woks), won't rust, and doesn't affect the colors or taste of foods—a common
fault of standard cold-rolled-steel woks, which turn artichokes black and impart a metallic flavor to
some foods. • In addition, the Buffalo wok, which comes in 11- to 16-inch diameters, has a slightly
flattened bottom—enough to give stability on a regular burner, but not enough to take away the
advantages of a bowl-shaped pan. • The model I find big enough to be useful but not too large to
maneuver is 15 inches wide (8 qt. to the rim), with two handles for easy lifting, and a domed lid that
provides needed space for steaming foods. Prices are in the fancy-pan range, from $189 to $249.
But if you shop at (888) 833-8833 or www.chinesewok.com, you save about 20 percent.

Of Marco Polo and spinach

■ The epicenter of ancient trade routes,
Venice retains a complex array of fra-
grances and flavors in its cuisine. In my
imagination, this spinach dish, which I
tasted in a little restaurant alongside a relatively quiet canal, just might be able to
trace its heritage to the spice-laden caravans of Marco Polo's time. To make the
journey full circle, use a Chinese wok—
it's the perfect pan for quickly wilting the
voluminous fluff of dark green leaves.

Spinach with Lemon and Currants

PREP AND COOK TIME: About 10 minutes

MAKES: About 1½ cups; 4 servings

1 tablespoon **butter** or olive oil

¼ cup **dried currants**

¼ cup minced **lemon** (including peel)

1 teaspoon **sugar**

1 pound (about 3 qt.) **spinach
   leaves,** rinsed and drained

½ teaspoon fresh-grated or ground
   nutmeg

   Salt

1. In a 14- to 15-inch wok or 6- to 8-quart
pan over high heat, stir butter, currants,
lemon, and sugar until lemon is tinged
with brown, about 3 minutes. Scrape into
a bowl.

2. Add spinach leaves and nutmeg to
wok. Stir often over high heat until
spinach is wilted and browned bits in
pan are released, 2 to 3 minutes. Stir in
currant mixture and salt to taste. Pour
into a bowl.

Per serving: 84 cal., 37% (31 cal.) from fat; 3.8 g
protein; 3.4 g fat (1.9 g sat.); 13 g carbo (3.4 g
fiber); 120 mg sodium; 7.8 mg chol.

Train of thought

■ Great Northern, the railway company, faded away in a merger in 1970. But its name is preserved at Denver's Great Northern Tavern. And clearly, chef Peter Braidman couldn't resist reinforcing the thought of the train. He has Great Northern beans (a variety) on the menu in a warming soup. He starts from scratch with dried beans, then adds them to the seasoned broth and vegetables. But because he's a mile high, dried beans take up to four hours to simmer until tender. Canned beans keep this soup on a tighter schedule—at any altitude.

Great Northern Bean Soup

PREP AND COOK TIME: About 50 minutes
MAKES: 15 cups; 6 to 8 servings

- ½ pound **bacon,** diced
- 1 **onion** (½ lb.), peeled and diced
- ¾ cup diced **celery**
- 1 **carrot** (¼ lb.), peeled and diced
- 2 cloves **garlic,** minced
- 2 tablespoons **dried oregano**
- 1 tablespoon minced **fresh jalapeño chili**
- 2 quarts fat-skimmed **chicken broth**
- 1½ cups **beer** (12 oz.)
- ¾ teaspoon **coarse-ground pepper**
- 2 teaspoons **Worcestershire**
- 6 cups drained **canned** or cooked **Great Northern** or other small white **beans**
- ¼ cup chopped **fresh cilantro**
   Salt

1. In a 5- to 6-quart pan over medium-high heat, frequently stir bacon until almost crisp, 10 to 12 minutes. Discard all but about 2 tablespoons fat. Add onion, celery, carrot, and garlic.

2. Stir often until vegetables are limp, about 15 minutes. Add oregano, chili, broth, beer, pepper, Worcestershire, and beans. Bring to a boil, cover, and simmer to blend flavors, 20 to 30 minutes. Add cilantro, then salt to taste.

Per serving: 370 cal., 18% (6/ cal.) from fat; 26 g protein; 7.4 g fat (2.4 g sat.); 48 g carbo (12 g fiber); 257 mg sodium; 9 mg chol.

His nibs

■ When John Scharffenberger makes chocolate, he starts with the cocoa beans. And my favorite stop when he showed me through his factory was the cocoa bean roaster. Here the beans tumble and toast at just the degree of heat that brings out the flavor we anticipate in chocolate. The aroma was heavenly. John slid open a little door, pulled out a few hot beans, and cracked open their papery shells. Inside, the beans were so brittle they crumbled into tiny chunks—technically nibs. "Taste," ordered John. I did. The nibs were a paradox—crunchy and silken, dark and mellow, slightly bitter but faintly sweet—if

only by way of my mental bridge to chocolate confections. I was hooked.

But not until the past few months have Sharffen Berger Cacao Nibs become available for all to enjoy—for munching, to sprinkle over ice cream or into cookies, to use like nuts in salads, or even, if you follow package instructions, to turn into chocolate (more for fun—especially for curious chil-dren—than for creamy perfection).

Scharffen Berger Cacao Nibs (roasted shelled cocoa beans) are sold in fancy and specialty food stores; a 6-ounce tin costs about $8. You can also order at (800) 930-4528 or www.scharffen-berger.com.

Chocolate Niblets

PREP AND COOK TIME: 5 minutes, plus 15 to 20 minutes to chill

NOTES: In Parisian restaurants where I dined last fall, the petite sweets that accompanied coffee invariably included little rounds of white chocolate sprinkled with cocoa nibs. They are embarrassingly easy to make; start with a white candy bar.

MAKES: 24 pieces

- 1 tablespoon **cocoa nibs** (roasted shelled cocoa beans)
- 3 ounces **white candy with cocoa butter,** chopped

1. Put cocoa nibs in a heavy plastic food bag; coarsely crush with a rolling pin.

2. In a microwave-safe bowl, heat white candy on full power (100%), stirring at 15-second intervals, until soft and smooth, about 45 seconds total.

3. Drop candy in ½-teaspoon portions about 1½ inches apart on a sheet of foil. While candy is still soft, use a small spatula to spread each portion into a 1¼-inch round. Sprinkle crushed cocoa nibs evenly over soft candy. Chill until firm, 15 to 20 minutes.

4. Peel candy from foil. Serve, or store airtight up to 2 weeks.

Per piece: 21 cal., 62% (13 cal.) from fat; 0.2 g protein; 1.4 g fat (0.9 g sat.); 2 g carbo (0 g fiber); 4.2 mg sodium; 0.4 mg chol. ◆

The Wine Guide

BY KAREN MacNEIL-FIFE

RICK MARIANI

How to throw a wine-tasting party

■ At the Culinary Institute of America at Greystone in Napa Valley, I teach a week-long course on wine. It's fun, interactive—and hard. After all, most of us usually concentrate on one or two wines a week. Imagine focusing on 100!

On the last day, my students invariably ask how they can continue to learn about wine. My response: Taste more than one wine at a time, and taste with others.

Think about it: If you taste only a wine or two a week, your knowledge progresses slowly. But if you taste several wines at once, with friends, not only do you get an idea of, say, the differences among California, Australian, and French Chardonnays, but you also expand your thinking about wine by hearing what others have to say.

Here's how to throw a productive wine-tasting party.

Select a group of friends. Six is ideal because everyone can sit around a fairly small table. Choose people who have relatively the same extent of wine knowledge, so no one feels intimidated.

Choose a theme. You could, for example, taste wines from one grape variety such as Merlot, and compare Merlots from around the world. Or choose a type of wine or a wine region you don't yet know very much about. How about Barolo? Rioja? Sancerre? You could also focus on wines from a country you'd like to get to know—maybe New Zealand, Argentina, or South Africa. Finally, you could choose an *idea,* such as "white varieties we've never tasted" or "rosé champagnes for Valentine's Day."

Give everyone an assignment. Ask each friend to bring one bottle of wine that fits the theme. So that everyone will bring wines of similar quality, set a price range: Zinfandels between $12 and $18, for example. If you've chosen a white wine theme, don't forget to have everyone bring their bottles already chilled.

Get ready for the tasting. Have a few good corkscrews on hand. Also, every person will need a napkin, a pencil and paper to take notes, a water glass, and a spit cup (paper or plastic works fine—that's often what professionals use). "Spit cups?" you might be wondering. Yes, in the beginning of the evening, when everyone is forming opinions, it's best not to swallow as you taste. Later on, abandon the cups and just enjoy.

As for wine glasses, each person will need one for each wine. Since few of us have that many glasses, ask tasters to bring their own. Again, even professionals do this—and it saves you from washing 36 wine glasses later! Don't worry about having properly shaped glasses for white wine versus red. Just make sure everyone brings glasses with generous bowls so you can swirl the wines.

Don't worry about food—until later. Wine tasting requires you to use your senses intensely to pick up flavor differences, so it's best not to make the task difficult by distracting your palate with food or cheese. During the tasting itself, all you'll need are some plain crackers or bread (not sourdough), just in case someone wants to nibble something

A THEME TO GET STARTED

Choosing wines for many themes is easy. Each person can simply go to a wine shop and, with the help of the merchant, pick out a wine that fits the theme and price range. Luckily, people seldom bring duplicates. Selecting wines for some unfamiliar themes, however, can be more challenging. Here is a list of wine suggestions for a fairly difficult one: "California's Rhône-style wines." The reds are made primarily from Syrah, Mourvèdre, and Grenache.

WHITES

■ **Kunde Viognier 1998 (Sonoma Valley),** $20. Beautifully aromatic, with lingering light apricot and honeysuckle flavors.

■ **McDowell Valley Viognier 1998 (Mendocino),** $16. Apple-fresh, with light quincelike flavors.

REDS

■ **Beaulieu Vineyards "Ensemble" 1996 (California),** $25. Fairly powerful and structured, with meaty black-fruit flavors.

■ **Jade Mountain "La Provençale" 1997 (California),** $17. Black cherries with game, smoke, and tar.

■ **Joseph Phelps "Le Mistral" 1997 (California),** $25. Woodsy and earthy, with cherry and forest-floor aromas.

■ **Zaca Mesa "Z Cuvee" 1997 (Santa Barbara County),** $17. Rustic, meaty, and spicy, with big fruit flavors.

neutral between wines. Of course, by the end of the tasting, everyone will be starving, so by all means have some cheese or appetizers ready to pull out then.

Set up to pour. Have everyone arrange their glasses in a semicircle in front of them. The glass on each person's far left is glass number one. The glass on the far right is six. Number the wines from one to six, writing each number on the bottle's label with a marker. Then pour each wine into the corresponding glasses.

The fun—and hard—part is talking about the wines. You might be lost for words in the beginning, but by wine six, everyone should be in expansive form. ◆

Wake up to a great breakfast!

B ED-AND-BREAKFAST: THE PHRASE PROMISES MORE than just cozy comfort and peaceful slumber in quaintly elegant lodgings. It implies the irresistible aromas that make waking up a pleasure. • Don't deny yourself the pleasures of a special breakfast. On our travels around the West, we've collected recipes that have garnered praise from approving guests. Enjoy those compliments at home, when you're hosting guests of your own.

— *Linda Lau Anusasananan*

Spice Pancakes with Fresh Lemon Sauce

Honor Mansion, Healdsburg, CA

PREP AND COOK TIME: About 50 minutes

NOTES: Subtle spices and a tart lemon sauce distinguish these tender pancakes by Cathi Fowler (Honor Mansion; 800/554-4667).

MAKES: About 18 pancakes; 4 to 6 servings

- 3 **large eggs,** separated
- 1¾ cups **buttermilk**
  About 3 tablespoons **butter** or margarine, at room temperature
- 1 tablespoon **sugar**
- 2 teaspoons **dark molasses**
- 1½ cups **all-purpose flour**
- 2 teaspoons **ground ginger**
- 1 teaspoon **baking soda**
- 1 teaspoon **baking powder**
- 1 teaspoon **ground cinnamon**
- ½ teaspoon **ground nutmeg**
- ½ teaspoon **salt**
- ¼ teaspoon **ground cloves**
  Fresh lemon sauce (recipe follows)
  Lemon wedges (optional)
  Lemon leaves (optional)

1. In a deep bowl with mixer on high speed, whip egg whites until they hold distinct moist peaks.

2. In another large bowl (with unwashed beaters), beat egg yolks, buttermilk, 3 tablespoons butter, sugar, and molasses until blended. Add flour, ginger, baking soda, baking powder, cinnamon, nutmeg, salt, and cloves. Beat until smooth.

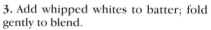

A STACK OF pancakes awaits a shower of tangy fresh lemon sauce.

3. Add whipped whites to batter; fold gently to blend.

4. On a buttered nonstick griddle or 12-inch nonstick frying pan over medium-high heat, pour batter in ¼-cup portions, spacing so pancakes don't touch. Cook until tops are full of bubbles, 2 to 3 minutes. Turn over and cook until bottoms are golden brown, 1 to 2 minutes. Repeat to cook remaining batter. As pancakes are cooked, stack on plates, or arrange slightly overlapping on baking sheets and keep warm in a 150° oven.

5. Serve with warm lemon sauce. If desired, garnish with thin lemon slices and leaves.

Per serving: 266 cal., 37% (99 cal.) from fat; 8.8 g protein; 11 g fat (6 g sat.); 32 g carbo (0.8 g fiber); 672 mg sodium; 130 mg chol.

Fresh Lemon Sauce

PREP AND COOK TIME: About 10 minutes

MAKES: 3 cups

In a 1- to 2-quart pan, mix 1 cup **sugar** and 2 tablespoons **cornstarch.** Stir in 2 cups **water.** Bring to a boil over high heat, stirring, about 4 minutes. Remove from heat. Add ¼ cup (⅛ lb.) **butter** or margarine, 2 tablespoons grated **lemon peel,** and ¼ cup **lemon juice.** Stir until butter melts. Serve warm.

Per tablespoon: 27 cal., 33% (9 cal.) from fat; 0 g protein; 1 g fat (0.6 g sat.); 4.6 g carbo (0 g fiber); 10 mg sodium; 2.7 mg chol.

Spicy Baked Pears with Yogurt

Joshua Grindle Inn, Mendocino, CA

PREP AND COOK TIME: About 35 minutes

NOTES: Arlene Moorehead (Joshua Grindle Inn; 800/474-6353) serves warm baked pears to start breakfast. If making up to 1 day ahead, complete through step 2, then cover and chill; uncover to continue.

MAKES: 10 servings

- ½ cup firmly packed **dark brown sugar**
- 1 teaspoon **ground cinnamon**
- ½ teaspoon **ground mace**
- ⅛ teaspoon **ground cloves**
- 5 **firm-ripe pears** (each 10 oz.)
- ¼ cup (⅛ lb.) **butter** or margarine
- ¾ cup **orange juice**
- 2 cups **vanilla-flavor nonfat yogurt**
  Fresh-grated **nutmeg**

1. In a 9- by 13-inch casserole, mix sugar, cinnamon, mace, and cloves and spread evenly.

2. Rinse pears, cut in half lengthwise, core, and stem. Lay pears, cut side down, in a single layer on sugar mixture. Dot with butter and pour orange juice evenly over fruit.

3. Bake in a 350° oven until sauce is

bubbling and pears are hot, about 20 minutes.

4. Transfer pears to shallow bowls and spoon sauce over them. Top each portion with a dollop of yogurt and a dusting of nutmeg.

Per serving: 210 cal., 23% (48 cal.) from fat; 3.1 g protein; 5.3 g fat (3 g sat.); 40 g carbo (3.2 g fiber); 85 mg sodium; 14 mg chol.

Egg Blossoms with Hollandaise

Castle Marne, Denver

PREP AND COOK TIME: About 1¾ hours

NOTES: Guests at Castle Marne (800/926-2763) might anticipate this elegant version of baked eggs. If filo dough is frozen, thaw overnight in refrigerator.

MAKES: 6 servings

- 3 cups (about 4 oz.) **spinach leaves**, rinsed and crisped
- 6 sheets **filo dough** (about 12 by 18 in.)
- 6 tablespoons melted **butter** or margarine
- ¼ cup **grated parmesan cheese**
- 6 **large eggs**
    Salt and **pepper**
- ¼ cup finely chopped **green onion** (including tops)
- 1 cup **hollandaise sauce** (recipe follows)
    Paprika

1. Stack ½ cup spinach leaves and cut into thin slivers.

2. Lay 1 filo sheet flat and brush lightly with butter; cover remaining dough with plastic wrap to prevent drying. Lay

FILO BASKET cradles an egg.

another filo sheet onto the buttered piece; brush top lightly with butter. Cut stack into 6 equal squares; cover with plastic wrap. Repeat to make a total of 18 filo squares.

3. Butter 6 muffin or custard cups (2½ to 2¾ in. wide; if using a muffin pan, butter alternate cups). Press 3 filo squares into each cup, overlapping, to line the cavity smoothly; filo edges will extend above the rim (in muffin pans, arrange so filo edges don't touch).

4. Sprinkle 2 teaspoons grated parmesan into each filo basket and top with about 1 tablespoon slivered spinach leaves. Break 1 egg into each filo basket, lightly sprinkle with salt and pepper, and sprinkle eggs equally with green onion.

5. Bake in a 350° oven until filo is golden and eggs are softly set when gently shaken, 18 to 20 minutes.

6. Meanwhile, mound remaining spinach equally onto dinner plates. Using a spoon and a small spatula, gently lift egg blossom baskets from baking cups and set 1 on each plate. Add hollandaise to taste. Dust with paprika.

Per serving: 326 cal., 72% (234 cal.) from fat; 11 g protein; 26 g fat (14 g sat.); 12 g carbo (0.6 g fiber); 427 mg sodium; 315 mg chol.

Hollandaise Sauce

PREP AND COOK TIME: About 10 minutes

NOTES: If you need to hold sauce up to 30 minutes, nest pan in hot tap water and stir often; add more hot water to pan to keep warm.

MAKES: About 1⅓ cups

In a 1- to 2-quart pan over low heat, whisk to blend 2 **large egg** yolks and 1 tablespoon **lemon juice**. Add ¼ cup (⅛ lb.) **butter** or margarine, in chunks, and whisk until butter melts and sauce thickens. Use at once.

Per serving: 96 cal., 94% (90 cal.) from fat; 2.2 g protein; 9.6 g fat (5.5 g sat.); 0.4 g carbo (0 g fiber); 103 mg sodium; 92 mg chol.

Decadent French Toast Soufflé

Foothill House, Calistoga, CA

PREP AND COOK TIME: About 1 hour, plus 8 hours to chill

NOTES: Doris Beckert (Foothill House; 800/942-6933) assembles this scrumptious puffy bread pudding the night before. If you don't have 8 soufflé dishes, assemble ingredients in a shallow 2½- to 3-quart baking dish; bake 5 to 15 minutes longer.

MAKES: 8 servings

- ½ pound **croissants** (2 or 3)
    About ½ cup (¼ lb.) **butter** or margarine, at room temperature
- 2 packages (3 oz. each) **cream cheese**, at room temperature
- 1¼ cups **maple syrup**
- 10 **large eggs**
- 3 cups **half-and-half** (light cream)
- 1 teaspoon **ground cinnamon**
- 2 tablespoons **chopped pecans**
    Powdered sugar
    Raspberries or edible flowers, such as rose petals or nasturtiums, rinsed and drained

1. Tear croissants into ½-inch chunks. Whirl in a food processor until coarsely chopped, or chop with a knife. Butter 8 soufflé dishes (1- to 1¼-cup size) and fill equally with croissant pieces.

2. In a food processor, combine cream cheese, ½ cup butter, and ¼ cup maple syrup; whirl until blended. (Or, in a bowl, beat with a mixer until smoothly blended.) Drop equal portions into each soufflé dish.

3. In a bowl, beat eggs to blend with ½ cup maple syrup and the half-and-half. Pour equally into each soufflé dish. Sprinkle with cinnamon. Cover and chill at least 8 hours or up to 1 day. Set dishes slightly apart in a 10- by 15-inch pan.

4. Bake, uncovered, in a 350° oven until pudding-soufflés are richly browned and centers barely jiggle when gently shaken, 45 to 50 minutes.

5. About 5 minutes before pudding-soufflés finish baking, in a 1- to 1½-quart pan over medium-high heat, frequently stir remaining ½ cup maple syrup until hot. Sprinkle pudding-soufflés with pecans, dust with powdered sugar, garnish with berries or flowers, and add hot syrup to taste.

Per serving: 666 cal., 61% (405 cal.) from fat; 15 g protein; 45 g fat (25 g sat.); 54 g carbo (0.9 g fiber); 531 mg sodium; 359 mg chol.

Mildly Decadent French Toast Soufflé

Follow recipe for **decadent French toast soufflé** (preceding), but use **low-fat milk** instead of half-and-half, and **neufchâtel cheese** instead of cream cheese.

Per serving: 566 cal., 51% (288 cal.) from fat; 16 g protein; 32 g fat (17 g sat.); 54 g carbo (0.9 g fiber); 567 mg sodium; 321 mg chol. ◆

The Low-Fat Cook

HEALTHY CHOICES FOR THE ACTIVE LIFESTYLE

BY ELAINE JOHNSON

WOO YOUR VALENTINE with a surprisingly intense—and low-fat—midnight chocolate cake.

JAMES CARRIER

Luscious cakes with no guilt

■ Sometimes, only chocolate will do. But if a slab of really intense chocolate cake seems like forbidden fruit when you're counting fat calories, think again. *Sunset* readers have met the challenge, producing chocolate cakes with deep, dark, rich flavor that comes from unsweetened cocoa, a powdered form of chocolate with most of the fat removed.

So when you want to be kind to your valentine's heart *and* taste buds too, these cakes are the ticket.

Midnight Chocolate Cake

PREP AND COOK TIME: About 1¼ hours

NOTES: Jane Ingraham of Santa Barbara reworked her great-grandmother's recipe to lower the fat. She calls this rich, dark cake "my number one favorite dessert." Mile-high bakers need to add an extra 2 tablespoons all-purpose flour and decrease the sugar by 2 tablespoons.

MAKES: 8 servings

About ¼ cup **salad oil**

About ⅔ cup **unsweetened cocoa**

1⅓ cups **all-purpose flour**

1 teaspoon **baking soda**

¼ teaspoon **salt**

1¼ cups **sugar**

2 **large egg** whites

1 teaspoon **vanilla**

Whipped frosting (recipe follows)

1. Oil a metal 8-inch-square or 8-inch-wide round cake pan, or a 9-inch-wide, 1½- to 2-inch-deep heart-shaped pan. Line pan bottom with waxed paper cut to fit; oil paper. Dust pan with cocoa, shaking out excess.

2. In a bowl, mix ⅔ cup cocoa, flour, soda, and salt.

3. In another bowl with a mixer, beat to blend sugar, ¼ cup salad oil, egg whites, vanilla, and 1 cup water. Add flour mixture; stir to mix, then beat until batter is smooth. Scrape batter into prepared pan.

4. Bake in a 350° oven until cake begins to pull from pan side and springs back when lightly pressed in center, 35 to 40 minutes.

5. Let cool in pan on a rack for 10 min-

utes. Run a thin knife between cake and pan rim, invert cake onto a rack, lift off pan, and gently pull off and discard waxed paper. Let cool about 1 hour. Invert a flat plate onto cake; holding rack and plate together, turn cake over onto plate. Spread cake with whipped frosting, swirling with small spatula. Lightly dust with more cocoa.

Per serving: 336 cal., 23% (77 cal.) from fat; 4.9 g protein; 8.6 g fat (1.6 g sat.); 64 g carbo (2.8 g fiber); 252 mg sodium; 0 mg chol.

Whipped Frosting

PREP AND COOK TIME: About 15 minutes

NOTES: If you are concerned about egg safety, use a thermometer to check frosting temperature as it cooks; it should be between 140° and 150° for 3 minutes. A double boiler is most effective for heating the mixture evenly.

MAKES: 2 cups

1 **large egg** white

½ cup **sugar**

⅛ teaspoon **cream of tartar**

½ teaspoon **vanilla**

1. Use a double boiler, or snugly nest a 2- to 3-quart metal bowl in a 2- to 3-quart pan. Add 1 inch water to base of double boiler or pan. Bring to boiling over high heat.

2. Meanwhile, in double boiler top or bowl, combine egg white, sugar, 2 tablespoons water, and cream of tartar. Beat with a portable mixer until blended. Nest over boiling water; immediately reduce heat to maintain a gentle simmer. With mixer on medium speed, beat icing until it holds peaks that curve slightly, 5 to 7 minutes (overcooked, the icing gets grainy).

3. At once, remove icing from hot water. Mix in vanilla. Use, or if making up to 1 hour ahead, set pan or bowl in cool water to stop cooking, and cover airtight.

Per ¼ cup: 51 cal., 0% (0 cal.) from fat; 0.4 g protein; 0 g fat; 13 g carbo (0 g fiber); 7 mg sodium; 0 mg chol.

Midnight Orange Cake

Follow directions for **midnight chocolate cake** (at left), adding 1 teaspoon grated **orange** peel to the batter in step 3. Follow directions (preceding) for **whipped frosting**, adding ¹⁄₂ teaspoon grated **orange** peel with the vanilla in step 3.

Per serving: 336 cal., 23% (77 cal.) from fat; 4.9 g protein; 8.6 g fat (1.6 g sat.); 64 g carbo (2.8 g fiber); 252 mg sodium; 0 mg chol.

Black Forest Cake

PREP AND COOK TIME: About 1 hour

NOTES: If desired, mound up to 2 tablespoons semisweet chocolate curls on top of the frosted cake.

MAKES: 8 servings

1. In a bowl, combine 1 can (1 lb.) drained **pitted tart pie cherries in water** and ¹⁄₄ cup **kirsch.** Let stand at least 30 minutes, stirring occasionally.

2. Follow directions for **midnight chocolate cake** batter (preceding), using an 8-inch-wide round pan. When cake is cool, use a long serrated knife to cut the cake horizontally into 3 equal layers.

3. Meanwhile, follow directions for **whipped frosting** (preceding), using 2 **large egg** whites, 1 cup **sugar,** ¹⁄₄ cup **water,** ¹⁄₄ teaspoon **cream of tartar,** and 1 teaspoon **vanilla.**

4. Drain cherries, pouring kirsch into a small pitcher.

5. To assemble cake, place bottom layer on a flat plate, cut side up. Spread cut side with about ¹⁄₄ the frosting; dot with ¹⁄₂ the cherries. Set center cake layer on frosting; spread with about ¹⁄₄ the frosting; dot with remaining cherries. Lay top of cake, cut side down, onto cherries. With a small spatula, swirl remaining frosting over cake. Cut cake into wedges; drizzle each portion with reserved kirsch.

Per serving: 428 cal., 18% (77 cal.) from fat; 5.8 g protein; 8.6 g fat (1.6 g sat.); 84 g carbo (2.8 g fiber); 263 mg sodium; 0 mg chol.

Chocolate Pudding Cake

PREP AND COOK TIME: About 50 minutes

NOTES: Dawn Dixon of Tucson accompanies this gooey dessert with vanilla nonfat ice cream.

MAKES: 9 servings

 About 2 tablespoons **salad oil**

 About 1 cup **all-purpose flour**

¾ cup **granulated sugar**

¹⁄₂ cup **semisweet chocolate chips**

6 tablespoons **unsweetened cocoa**

2 teaspoons **baking powder**

¹⁄₄ teaspoon **salt**

1¹⁄₂ cups **low-fat buttermilk**

¾ cup firmly packed **brown sugar**

1. Oil and flour an 8-inch square pan.

2. In a bowl, mix 1 cup all-purpose flour, granulated sugar, ¹⁄₄ cup chocolate chips, 2 tablespoons cocoa, baking powder, and salt. Add 2 tablespoons salad oil and ¹⁄₂ cup buttermilk; stir until the thick batter is evenly moistened. Scrape batter into prepared pan and spread level.

3. In the same bowl (no need to wash), mix brown sugar with remaining ¹⁄₄ cup cocoa and ¹⁄₄ cup chocolate chips. Scatter over batter in pan. Evenly pour remaining 1 cup buttermilk over brown sugar mixture; do not stir.

4. Bake in a 350° oven until edges of cake feel firm and spring back when lightly pressed, about 40 minutes.

5. Let cool in pan on a rack at least 15 minutes. Serve hot, warm, or at room temperature in bowls, scooping under cake to pan bottom to include pudding with each portion.

Per serving: 288 cal., 22% (64 cal.) from fat; 3.9 g protein; 7.1 g fat (2.5 g sat.); 56 g carbo (1.5 g fiber); 224 mg sodium; 1.7 mg chol.

Mocha Angel Food Cake

PREP AND COOK TIME: About 1¹⁄₄ hours

NOTES: Elizabeth Monroe of Seattle shares this recipe. The tube pan must not be buttered or oiled for the cake to maintain its volume while baking.

MAKES: 12 servings

 About ¹⁄₂ cup **cake flour**

1¹⁄₄ cups **sugar**

¹⁄₂ cup **unsweetened cocoa**

1 tablespoon **dried instant espresso coffee**

¹⁄₄ teaspoon **salt**

1¹⁄₂ cups **egg** whites (9 to 11 large egg whites)

1 teaspoon **cream of tartar**

1 teaspoon **vanilla**

 Mocha sauce (recipe follows)

1. Sift cake flour and measure ¹⁄₂ cup. In a bowl, mix flour, ¹⁄₄ cup sugar, cocoa, instant espresso, and salt.

2. In a deep bowl (at least 4-qt.) with a mixer at high speed, whip egg whites and cream of tartar until they form a thick foam. Continue to beat and add remaining 1 cup sugar, 1 tablespoon about every 15 seconds, whipping until whites hold very stiff peaks. Mix in vanilla.

3. Sprinkle about ¹⁄₂ the flour mixture over whipped whites. Gently fold mixture until blended. Sprinkle with remaining flour mixture and gently fold to blend well. Scrape batter into a 10-inch tube cake pan with a removable rim; spread level.

4. Bake in a 350° oven until center of cake springs back when lightly pressed and begins to pull from pan side, 40 to 45 minutes.

5. Invert pan on a rack; let stand at least 1 hour. Run a thin knife between cake and pan rim. Push cake from pan rim. Slide thin knife between cake and pan bottom, and around tube to pan bottom. Invert cake onto a plate and lift out tube section. Drizzle mocha sauce onto top of cake, letting it run down the sides. Use an angel food cake cutter or serrated knife to cut slices.

Per serving plain: 155 cal., 12% (18 cal.) from fat; 4.8 g protein; 2 g fat (1.1 g sat.); 32 g carbo (1.3 g fiber); 105 mg sodium; 0.2 mg chol.

Per serving with sauce: 188 cal., 16% (31 cal.) from fat; 5.4 g protein; 3.4 g fat (2 g sat.); 37 g carbo (1.6 g fiber); 111 mg sodium; 0.4 mg chol.

Mocha Sauce

PREP AND COOK TIME: About 10 minutes

MAKES: About ¹⁄₂ cup

1 tablespoon firmly packed **dark brown sugar**

2 teaspoons **cornstarch**

1 teaspoon **dried instant espresso coffee**

¹⁄₄ teaspoon **ground cinnamon**

2 ounces chopped **semisweet** or bittersweet **chocolate**

 About ¹⁄₂ cup **nonfat milk**

In a 1- to 2-quart pan, whisk sugar, cornstarch, instant espresso, cinnamon, chocolate, and ¹⁄₂ cup milk to blend. Whisking, bring to a boil over medium-high heat, 3 to 4 minutes. If sauce is too thick to drizzle, stir in more milk, 1 tablespoon at a time. Use hot or warm.

Per tablespoon: 49 cal., 39% (19 cal.) from fat; 0.8 g protein; 2.1 g fat (1.3 g sat.); 7.6 g carbo (0.4 g fiber); 9.5 mg sodium; 0.3 mg chol. ◆

BASIL AND CHILIES garnish chicken curry, which seeps into hot rice.

Bowled over by rice

Delicious, easy
dinner solutions

BY LINDA LAU ANUSASANANAN

PHOTOGRAPHS BY
JAMES CARRIER

In my family, we bought Texas long-grain white rice in 50-pound bags and ate some every night. The same is true for many other Asians all over the world—a meal is not complete without rice. One reason: It doesn't take much more to make the meal complete.

Westerners are catching on to this simple concept in the form of the *rice bowl*.

What is a rice bowl? A little protein, some vegetables, and lively seasonings spooned onto hot rice. The result is a supper that's quick, satisfying, nutritious, and very easy to make, particularly when you turn to Asian roots for inspiration.

Start with your choice of rice (see box, page 53) and select toppings from the following favorites from Japan, China, Korea, and Thailand. All ingredients are available in a well-stocked supermarket, but some of them are alternatives for the authentic seasonings that you can find in an Asian food market.

Thai Curry Rice Bowl

PREP AND COOK TIME: About 45 minutes
MAKES: 4 servings

- 1 **red bell pepper** (½ lb.), rinsed
- 1 pound **boned, skinned chicken breast**
- 1 can (14 oz.) **coconut milk**
- 1 tablespoon **Thai red curry paste**
- 1 cup **frozen corn kernels**
- 1 tablespoon packed **brown sugar**
- 1 tablespoon **lemon juice**
  About 1 tablespoon **Asian fish sauce** (*nuoc mam* or *nam pla*)
- 1 recipe's worth (page 53) or 6 cups **hot cooked rice**

1. Stem bell pepper, seed, and cut into ¼-inch-wide strips about 3 inches long.
2. Rinse chicken, pat dry, and cut crosswise into ¼-inch-thick slices.
3. Place a 14-inch wok or 12-inch frying pan over high heat. Measure 1 tablespoon solidified coconut milk from the top of the can and add to wok with pepper and ¼ cup water. Stir often until pepper strips are limp, 3 to 5 minutes.
4. Add remaining coconut milk and curry paste. Stir to blend smoothly. Stir until boiling; add chicken, corn, and sugar. Reduce heat to medium; stir often until chicken is white in center of thickest part (cut to test), about 3 minutes. Add lemon juice and fish sauce to taste.
5. Scoop rice into bowls and top equally with chicken curry mixture.

Per serving: 740 cal., 30% (225 cal.) from fat; 37 g protein; 25 g fat (20 g sat.); 93 g carbo (2.6 g fiber); 460 mg sodium; 66 mg chol.

Japanese Tofu Donburi

PREP AND COOK TIME: About 40 minutes
NOTES: Although shelf-stable tofu doesn't require refrigeration before it is opened, it is often sold alongside fresh tofu in refrigerated cases.

MAKES: 4 servings

- 2 teaspoons **salad oil**
- 1 **onion** (6 oz.), peeled and thinly sliced
- 2 tablespoons minced **fresh ginger**
- 1 cup fat-skimmed **chicken broth**
- ¼ cup **soy sauce**
- 4 teaspoons **sugar**
- 1 package (12.3 oz.) **shelf-stable silken-style firm tofu**
- 6 cups (about 6 oz.) **baby spinach leaves**, rinsed and drained
- 3 **large eggs**
- 1 recipe's worth (page 53) or 6 cups **hot cooked rice**
- ¼ cup diced **Roma tomato**

1. In a deep 10- to 12-inch frying pan over high heat, stir oil, onion, and ginger until onion is lightly browned, about 2 minutes.
2. Add broth, soy sauce, and sugar. Crumble tofu into about 1-inch chunks and add to pan. Bring to a boil.
3. Add spinach, cover, and cook until wilted, about 1 minute. Meanwhile, in a small bowl, beat eggs to blend.
4. Reduce heat to low, evenly distribute mixture in pan, and pour in eggs. With a spatula, push vegetables aside slightly so egg mixture can flow down through sauce. Cover and cook just until eggs are softly set, 2 to 2½ minutes.
5. Meanwhile, spoon rice into bowls. Top equally with egg-spinach mixture, including juices. Sprinkle with tomato.

Per serving: 528 cal., 16% (86 cal.) from fat; 22 g protein; 9.5 g fat (1.9 g sat.); 88 g carbo (2.8 g fiber); 1,166 mg sodium; 159 mg chol.

Japanese Chicken Donburi

Follow directions for **Japanese tofu donburi** (preceding), but omit tofu and use ½ pound **boned, skinned chicken breast**, rinsed and cut into ¼-inch strips.

Per serving: 539 cal., 13% (68 cal.) from fat; 29 g protein; 7.6 g fat (1.8 g sat.); 86 g carbo (2.8 g fiber); 1,172 mg sodium; 192 mg chol.

Chinese Shrimp and Pea Rice Bowl

PREP AND COOK TIME: About 40 minutes
MAKES: 4 servings

- ¾ pound **edible-pod peas**
- 3 tablespoons **oyster** or soy **sauce**
- 2 tablespoons **cornstarch**
- 4 teaspoons **rice vinegar**

2 cups fat-skimmed **chicken broth**

2 teaspoons **salad oil**

2 tablespoons minced **fresh ginger**

4 cloves **garlic,** peeled and minced

2 or 3 **small dried hot chilies**

1 pound thawed **frozen peeled, deveined shrimp** (41 to 50 per lb.), rinsed and drained

1 recipe's worth (see box) or 6 cups **hot cooked rice**

3 tablespoons coarsely chopped **salted roasted peanuts** (optional)

   Salt

1. Rinse peas, drain, and discard stem ends and strings.

2. In a small bowl, blend oyster sauce, cornstarch, vinegar, and broth.

3. Set a 14-inch wok or 12-inch frying pan over high heat. When pan is hot, add 3 tablespoons water and peas. Cover and stir often until peas are bright green and barely tender to bite, 2 to 3 minutes. Drain peas into a bowl.

4. Return wok to high heat. When pan is hot, add oil, ginger, garlic, and chilies; stir until chilies begin to brown, about 1 minute. Add shrimp and stir frequently until they are barely opaque in thickest part (cut to test), 3 to 4 minutes.

5. Add broth mixture; stir until boiling. Mix in peas. Scoop rice into bowls and spoon the shrimp mixture equally onto each portion. Sprinkle with peanuts and salt to taste.

Per serving: 570 cal., 8% (47 cal.) from fat; 38 g protein; 5.2 g fat (0.9 g sat.); 89 g carbo (3.5 g fiber); 751 mg sodium; 173 mg chol.

Korean Beef Rice Bowl

PREP AND COOK TIME: About 50 minutes
NOTES: If you can't find toasted sesame seed, stir regular sesame seed in a frying pan over low heat until golden, 1 minute.
MAKES: 4 servings

1 pound fat-trimmed **beef flank steak**

   Korean marinade (recipe follows)

³⁄₄ pound **green beans,** rinsed

1 **carrot** (¹⁄₄ lb.), peeled

2 tablespoons **rice vinegar**

1 tablespoon **Asian** (toasted) **sesame oil**

2 teaspoons **sugar**

   Salt

1 tablespoon **salad oil**

¹⁄₂ cup fat-skimmed **beef broth**

CRISP SWEET-TART VEGETABLES with Korean beef blanket steaming rice.

1 recipe's worth (see box) or 6 cups **hot cooked rice**

¹⁄₄ cup thinly sliced **green onions**

1 tablespoon **toasted sesame seed** (see notes)

1. Rinse beef, pat dry, and cut across the grain into ¹⁄₈-inch-thick slices about 3 inches long. In a small bowl, mix beef with ¹⁄₄ cup Korean marinade.

2. Remove and discard bean stem ends

and strings. Cut beans diagonally in 3-inch lengths. Cut carrot into matchstick-size pieces about 3 inches long.

3. In a 14-inch wok or 12-inch frying pan over high heat, mix ¹⁄₂ cup water, beans, and carrot. Cover and stir occasionally just until tender to bite, about 3 minutes. Drain; immerse in cold water. Drain when cool. In a bowl, mix with vinegar, sesame oil, sugar, and salt to taste.

4. Place wok over high heat; when hot, add salad oil. Add beef with liquid in bowl; stir until meat is no longer pink, about 2 minutes. Add remaining marinade and broth to pan; stir until boiling.

5. Scoop rice into bowls; add beef and sauce, then vegetables and seasonings. Sprinkle with onions and sesame seed.

Per serving: 664 cal., 24% (162 cal.) from fat; 33 g protein; 18 g fat (5 g sat.); 90 g carbo (3.7 g fiber); 626 mg sodium; 57 mg chol.

Korean Marinade

PREP AND COOK TIME: About 10 minutes
MAKES: About ³⁄₄ cup

In a small bowl, mix 6 tablespoons **soy sauce,** 3 tablespoons **sugar,** 1 tablespoon minced **garlic,** 1 tablespoon minced **fresh ginger,** and 1 tablespoon **Asian** (toasted) **sesame oil.**

Per tablespoon: 28 cal., 35% (9.9 cal.) from fat; 0.5 g protein; 1.1 g fat (0.2 g sat.); 4.2 g carbo (0 g fiber); 515 mg sodium; 0 mg chol.

Suitable foundations for these one-bowl meals are long-grain white or aromatic jasmine rice; sticky short- or medium-grain rice; or chewy brown rice. If rice is tender to bite before all the liquid is absorbed, drain. When using a rice cooker, follow manufacturer's measurements and directions.

Hot Cooked Long-Grain Rice

PREP AND COOK TIME: About 25 minutes
MAKES: About 6 cups; 4 servings

In a 3- to 4-quart pan, combine 2 cups **long-grain** or jasmine **rice** and 3¹⁄₂ cups **water.** Bring to a boil over high heat. Cover and simmer over low heat until rice is tender to bite, about 20 minutes.

Per serving: 337 cal., 1% (5.4 cal.) from fat; 6.6 g protein; 0.6 g fat (0.2 g sat.); 74 g carbo (0.9 g fiber); 4.6 mg sodium; 0 mg chol.

Hot Cooked Short-Grain Rice

Follow directions for **hot cooked long-grain rice** (preceding), but omit long-grain or jasmine rice, and

use 2 cups **short-** or medium-**grain rice** (pearl, calrose) and a total of 2¹⁄₂ cups **water.**

Per serving: 358 cal., 1% (4.5 cal.) from fat; 6.5 g protein; 0.5 g fat (0.1 g sat.); 79 g carbo (1 g fiber); 1 mg sodium; 0 mg chol.

Hot Cooked Brown Rice

PREP AND COOK TIME: About 50 minutes
Follow directions for **hot cooked long-grain rice** (at left), but omit long-grain or jasmine rice, and use 2 cups **long-grain brown rice** and a total of 4 cups **water.** Simmer, covered, over low heat until tender to bite, about 45 minutes.

Per serving: 342 cal., 7% (24 cal.) from fat; 7.3 g protein; 2.7 g fat (0.5 g sat.); 71 g carbo (3.2 g fiber); 6.5 mg sodium; 0 mg chol. ◆

HOT COOKED RICE

The Quick Cook

MEALS IN 30 MINUTES OR LESS
BY ANDREW BAKER

Prime-time portabellas

■ There's a reason so many restaurants offer portabella "burgers" these days—the giant mushrooms taste deceptively meaty, with a rich flavor and succulent texture that mimic tender beef steaks.

Truth is, portabellas are nothing more than common brown (crimini) mushrooms that have been allowed to reach adulthood and picked when their caps are 4 to 5 inches wide. Past their prime, they become too woody.

Portabellas are sold whole (with stems), as caps (with stems trimmed), and sliced. Caps are the most practical choice for these recipes. Oven-roasting is a quick way to cook them, plain or filled.

Warm Lentil Salad with Portabellas

PREP AND COOK TIME: About 30 minutes

NOTES: Chef Daniel Patterson served this dish at Babette's, his former restaurant in Sonoma, California. Currently, he is at Restaurant Elisabeth Daniel in San Francisco. Beluga lentils, a small, black variety, are grown in Montana; hulled Red Chiefs come from the Northwest.

MAKES: 4 servings

- ½ cup minced **shallots** or onion
- 1 teaspoon **olive** or salad **oil**
- 1 cup **beluga** or Red Chief **lentils**
- 3 cups fat-skimmed **chicken broth**
- 2 teaspoons **fresh thyme** leaves or dried thyme
- 4 **portabella mushroom caps** (5 in. wide)
- ¾ cup **mayonnaise**
- ¾ teaspoon minced or pressed **garlic**
- 4 teaspoons **lemon juice**
- ½ teaspoon grated **lemon** peel
- 4 cups (about ¼ lb. total) lightly packed rinsed and crisped **frisée** or salad mix
- **Salt** and **pepper**

1. In a 2- to 3-quart pan over medium-high heat, stir shallots in oil until limp, about 3 minutes. Add lentils, broth, and thyme. Bring to a boil, cover, reduce heat, and simmer just until lentils are tender to bite, about 25 minutes (6 to 8

minutes for red lentils). Drain lentils; save liquid for other uses.

2. Meanwhile, trim off discolored mushroom stem ends; rinse caps well. Oven-roast mushroom caps (recipe follows).

3. In a small bowl, mix mayonnaise, garlic, lemon juice, and lemon peel.

4. Thinly slice mushroom caps. Mound frisée equally on plates; top equally with lentils, then mushroom slices. Spoon about 1 tablespoon garlic-mayonnaise mixture onto each salad. Season salads to taste with remaining garlic mayonnaise, salt, and pepper.

Per serving: 553 cal., 57% (315 cal.) from fat; 24 g protein; 35 g fat (5.2 g sat.); 40 g carbo (8 g fiber); 318 mg sodium; 24 mg chol.

Oven-roasted portabellas. Set mushroom caps, gill side up, in a single layer in a lightly oiled 10- by 15-inch pan. Bake in a 400° oven until caps are flexible enough to bend easily, about 12 minutes (about 9 minutes in a convection oven).

Per cap: 37 cal., 7.3% (2.7 cal.) from fat; 3.5 g protein; 0.3 g fat (0 g sat.); 7.2 g carbo (2.1 g fiber); 8.5 mg sodium; 0 mg chol.

Teriyaki Portabella Steaks with Noodle Slaw

PREP AND COOK TIME: About 30 minutes

MAKES: 4 servings

- 1 package (about 3¾ oz.) **cellophane noodles** (*mai fun*, or rice sticks)
- 4 **portabella mushroom caps** (5 in. wide)
- ½ cup **low-sodium soy sauce**
- ¼ cup **dry sherry**
- 1 tablespoon **Asian** (toasted) **sesame oil**
- 1 tablespoon firmly packed **brown sugar**
- 2 teaspoons minced **fresh ginger**
- 1 teaspoon minced or pressed **garlic**
- 6 tablespoons **seasoned rice vinegar**
- ¾ cup shredded **carrots**
- 2 cups thinly sliced **radicchio**

About ½ cup **fresh cilantro** leaves

1. Place noodles in a large bowl and add 1 quart boiling water. Stir to separate noodles and let stand until tender to bite, about 10 minutes. Drain well. Return noodles to bowl.

2. Meanwhile, trim off discolored mushroom stem ends; rinse caps well. In a

ROASTED MUSHROOMS and black beluga lentils make salad a main dish.

heavy plastic food bag, mix soy sauce, sherry, sesame oil, brown sugar, ginger, and garlic. Add mushrooms, seal bag, and turn over to mix. Let stand 10 to 20 minutes, turning over several times.

3. Lift mushrooms from bag and save marinade. Oven-roast mushroom caps (recipe preceding).

4. To noodles, add rice vinegar, carrots, radicchio, and ½ cup cilantro leaves. Add about 2 tablespoons reserved soy marinade, or to taste. Mix well.

5. Spoon noodle slaw equally into wide bowls. Thinly slice mushroom caps and arrange equally on portions. Garnish with additional cilantro leaves.

Per serving: 194 cal., 10% (20 cal.) from fat; 4.3 g protein; 2.2 g fat (0.3 g sat.); 40 g carbo (2.8 g fiber); 1,039 mg sodium; 0 mg chol.

Shrimp-stuffed Portabellas on Tomato Polenta

PREP AND COOK TIME: About 25 minutes

MAKES: 4 servings

- 4 **portabella mushroom caps** (5 in. wide)

  Salad oil
- ¾ pound **shelled cooked tiny shrimp,** rinsed
- ⅓ cup finely chopped **green onions**
- 2 tablespoons **mayonnaise**
- 1 cup shredded **chili-flavor jack cheese**
- 4½ cups fat-skimmed **chicken broth**
- 1 cup **instant polenta**

¼ cup finely chopped drained **oil-packed dried tomatoes**
Salt

1. Trim off mushroom stems flush with caps. Rinse caps well; place gill side up in a lightly oiled 10- by 15-inch pan.
2. In a bowl, mix shrimp, green onions, mayonnaise, and cheese. Spoon shrimp mixture equally into mushroom caps.
3. Bake in a 400° oven until cheese is melted and mushrooms are flexible when pressed, about 12 minutes.
4. Meanwhile, in a 3- to 4-quart pan, combine broth, polenta, and tomatoes. Stir over high heat until boiling, then re-duce heat to low. Stir often until polenta is very smooth to taste, about 3 minutes.
5. Spoon polenta equally into wide bowls. Set a stuffed mushroom on each portion. Add salt to taste.

Per serving: 605 cal., 27% (162 cal.) from fat; 44 g protein; 18 g fat (6.1 g sat.); 66 g carbo (10 g fiber); 571 mg sodium; 200 mg chol. ◆

The food lover's Napa Valley

Where to shop among the vines for gourmet ingredients and professional cookware

BY LORA J. FINNEGAN

Napa Valley wines and restaurants have become world-class. And so has the food-oriented shopping.

It reached critical mass once the huge Marketplace at the Culinary Institute of America came in, says one chef, and now boasts a whole support system for foodies (and those who buy gifts for them). With food and wine writer and friend Susan French, I roamed from Yountville to Calistoga, bypassing winery shops to avoid the crowds.

Our harvest: this guide to some of Napa Valley's finest food shops—and seven great gifts for foodies. Area code is 707 unless noted.

Barrel Cellar. Specializes in Riedel stemware and exotic corkscrews. *Best bet:* safari picnic tote with wine duffel ($99.95). *6525 Washington St., Yountville; 944-8057 or www.thebarrelcellar. com. Mail order is available.*

Campus Store and Marketplace at the Culinary Institute of America at Greystone. Massive shop in a majestic old stone building, the former Christian Brothers winery. It has cutlery, bakeware, cookware, culinary jewelry, and more than 1,500 cookbook titles. *Best bet:* set of four heat- and stain-resistant Le Creuset spatulas ($33). *2555 Main St., St. Helena; 967-2309 or www. ciachef.edu. Mail order is available: (888) 424-2433.*

Cantinetta Tra Vigne. Want that dipping sauce you tried in the restaurant? It's here, along with flavored olive oils, balsamic vinegars from Italy, cookbooks, and a deli. *Best bet:* homemade vinegars and marinades ($5.95) or the Consorzio roasted garlic olive oil ($9). *1050 Charter Oak Ave., St. Helena; 963-8888. Mail order is available.*

Dean & Deluca. The only Western location for this popular New York gourmet store. A roomful of serious cookware, plus racks of sauces, vinegars, and oils, as well as more than 200 rare cheeses. *Best bet:* prepared picnic baskets ($35–$145). *607 S. St. Helena Hwy., St. Helena; 967-9980 or www. deananddeluca-napa.com.*

Keller's Market. A valley mainstay since 1930, this family-owned market offers picnicking food to keep you going, plus food gifts from lots of small, local companies. *Best bet:* Meyer lemon–pecan pancake mix ($4.99) or smoky chipotle grilling sauce ($5.99). *1320 Main, St. Helena; 963-2114.*

Napa Valley Olive Oil Mfg. Co. Its considerable charm lies in a nearly 100-year-old barn and an Old Country way of doing business: The cash register is a cigar box; your receipt, a tally on the grocery bag. The big draws are the stuffed olives, marinated olives, and house-made olive oils. *Best bet:* first press/cold press (extra-virgin) olive oil ($10.75 for a quart) or Sicilian olives ($2.50). *835 Charter Oak, St. Helena; 963-4173 or www.napavalleyoliveoilmfg.com. Mail order is available.*

Palisades Market. A laid-back store with more than 100 brands of wine, locally produced foods, and a home and garden shop (cookbooks, cooking gadgets, linens, outdoor furniture, birdhouses). *Best bet:* Napa Valley Collection cheese platter ($53.50) or French grape harvest baskets ($93.50). *1506 Lincoln Ave., Calistoga; 942-9549.* ◆

A RUSTIC, CENTURY-OLD BARN houses Napa Valley Olive Oil Mfg. Co., a favored wine country destination.

Ham, eggs, and the sound of surf

Where do you go for the best meal of the day? Southern California's classic beach breakfast joints

BY PETER JENSEN

We hold these truths to be self-evident: Salt air makes us hungry, waitresses who call us "Hon" are the original Best People on Earth, and rumpled locals who wait in lines at cafe doors early in the morning are a sure sign that a fry cook inside wields a pretty mean spatula.

Each morning, as the mist rises from Southern California's beaches, true connoisseurs of great breakfasts come to worship the grill gods near the sandy strands. Bleary-eyed, stomachs rumbling, we go down to the sea in search of hash browns so crisp that the edges crackle and shatter beneath a fork. We want American coffee—none of that weird gourmet, burnt-tasting stuff—served in earthenware mugs heavy enough to bulge the biceps. Eggs in fluffy golden heaps. Rainfalls of Tabasco or homemade salsa. Tributaries of melting butter joining rivers of maple syrup sliding off a mountainside of pancakes.

Why are there so many great breakfast joints near the Southern California seaside? Maybe it's the surfers. Since the '50s, they've been pulling themselves out of the water around 7 or 8 A.M., as hungry as harbor seals. Or maybe we should credit the rough-handed lobstermen down San Diego way, tanking up on coffee and eggs before motoring out to their traps off Point Loma. Or the bodybuilders in Venice, wolfing down mega-carbs after a dawn session of heavy lifting.

Of course, surfers and lobstermen and bodybuilders and the rest of us breakfast fans want more than good food. We want dive-ism—that certain sheen from years of nonstop usage that knocks the edges off even the spiffiest place until it, too, becomes a "joint."

We also want "Hon" culture. We long for ultra-efficient waitresses (and, nowadays, waiters too) who entertain us with

AT KONO'S SURF CLUB CAFE, hungry San Diegans line up for the Pacific Beach restaurant's fabled breakfasts.

their barked orders and plate-balancing ballets. Packed into Uncle Bill's Pancake House in Manhattan Beach, we worship the diminutive waitress who uses a back scratcher to pull the heavy, heaped-high plates across the kitchen pass-through. A back scratcher! The true cafe anthropologist thrills to stuff like this.

It's enough to make us want to eat nothing but breakfast. So here you are, Hon: almost a month of breakfasts at the beach, working down the coast from Santa Barbara to San Diego.

You want cream with that?

Santa Barbara

Esau's Coffee Shop. Surfers love the huge portions of pancakes and Esau's wonderful ham and eggs. One dish gets its name from boardster lingo: Gnarly Scramble is a mishmash of ham, bacon, sausage, and mushrooms. Sink into the lurid yellow vinyl booths and dig in. *Opens at 6 Mon-Thu, 7 Fri-Sun. 403 State St., Santa Barbara; (805) 965-4416.*

Los Angeles County

Marmalade Cafe. A homey joint that does a good eggs Benedict. The chunky roasted potato sides come replete with peppers and onions. *Opens at 7:30 daily. 3894 Cross Creek Rd., Pacific Coast Hwy., Malibu; (310) 317-4242.*

Patrick's Roadhouse. Correctly pronounce this place's most famous dish and you're in the same league with Arnold Schwarzenegger's mom, who was known to do breakfast here. *Bauernfrühstück* means *farmers' breakfast,* and Patrick's fits the bill with a large omelet filled with ham, bacon, sausage, cheeses, and more. *Opens at 8 Mon-Fri, 9 Sat-Sun. 106 Entrada Dr. at Pacific Coast Hwy., Santa Monica; (310) 459-4544.*

Blueberry Coffee Shop. Okay, so it's still too new to be a "joint," but you can't miss the Big Italy omelet (with pesto and goat cheese). Expect a very long wait on weekends, but there's complimentary coffee for sidewalk sipping. *Opens at 8 daily. 510 Santa Monica*

Blvd., Santa Monica; (310) 394-7766.

Ocean Park Omelette Parlor. Early birds love the Parlor's half-price omelets, including the popular Schwarzenegger (yes, another Arnold-worship menu name) full of Swiss cheese, ham, and tomatoes, but the offer holds only between 6 and 7 A.M.! Zeppelin-size creations are still a bargain (about $6) the rest of the day. *Opens at 6 daily. 2732 Main St., Santa Monica; (310) 399-7892.*

Sidewalk Cafe. Famous for spicy bloody Marys and an unobstructed view of the show on Venice's boardwalk. Patio opens to the ocean breeze, and the awning rolls back and forth based on patrons' tanning needs. Bring sunglasses. *Opens at 9 Mon-Thu, 8 Fri-Sun. 1401 Ocean Front Walk, Venice; (310) 399-5547.*

Firehouse. Popular with bodybuilders from Gold's Gym next door. Buckwheat pancakes and scrambled egg whites may seem out of place in a 1902 building (yes, it was a firehouse), but hey, this is Venice. *Opens at 7 Mon-Fri, 8 Sat-Sun. 213 Rose Ave., Venice; (310) 396-6810.*

Edie's Diner. Classic American diner meals served with an *On the Waterfront* '50s feel. Patio seating overlooks marina. *Opens at 7 daily. 4211 Admiralty Way, Marina del Rey; (310) 577-4558.*

Uncle Bill's Pancake House. To feel like a regular customer, opt to sit at the small counter that is way, way off to the right where the waitress uses that back scratcher mentioned earlier. As for the pancakes, every kind is here, with real maple syrup available (for a buck extra, a bargain). Funky ranch house façade. *Opens at 6 Mon-Fri, 7 Sat-Sun. 1305 Highland Ave., Manhattan Beach; (310) 545-5177.*

Martha's 22nd Street Grill. Hard to call this a dive yet—it's way too hip, and everyone is just too darned beautiful. But the food may be the wave of future dive-dom, right down to the cornmeal pancakes, hummus omelet with sun-dried tomatoes, and the killer Asian tofu scramble served with rice. Try eggs scrambled with fresh-off-the-ear white corn (in season) and the many dishes using havarti cheese, obviously the chef's

favorite. *Opens at 7 daily. 25 22nd St., Hermosa Beach; (310) 376-7786.*

Chuck's Coffee Shop. Waitress Dawn has been "coming here since before I was born"—her mom was a regular. Dig into the Weasel, a hefty scramble with homemade chili, cheese, and onions over the top. *Opens at 6 Mon-Fri, 7 Sat-Sun. 4120 E. Ocean Blvd. (by the Belmont Plaza Pool), Long Beach; (562) 433-9317.*

Shore House Cafe. Home of the 11-page menu, huge portions, and some of the best huevos rancheros in Southern California. *Open 24 hours daily. 5271 E. Second St., Long Beach; (562) 433-2266.*

Orange County

Russell's Burgers. Known at lunch for burgers shaped by hand, Russell's also believes in manual labor for breakfast staples like hash browns; they're peeled, steamed, and riced by hand. *Opens at 9 Mon-Thu, 8 Fri, 7 Sat-Sun. 1198 Pacific Coast Hwy., Seal Beach; (562) 596-9556.*

Michelle's Sugar Shack. Inside seating at this local favorite gets plenty busy most mornings. But check out the back patio; new heaters make it comfortable outdoors year-round. And breakfast is served all day. *Opens at 5 daily. 213 Main St., Huntington Beach; (714) 536-0355.*

Beach Cafe. Basic breakfasts, with good chatter and abundant newspapers. Try the famous breakfast burrito (the cafe once sold more than 1,000 in a month). *Opens at 7 daily. 328 11th St., Huntington Beach; (714) 960-7008.*

North San Diego County

Pipes Cafe— A Breakfast Place. Don't let the long line scare you off; order at the counter first, then wait for your paper plate to find you on the open-air patio. A single order, especially the breakfast burrito stuffed with eggs, cilantro, green

chilies, and cheese, is enough for two hungry people—it must contain eight scrambled eggs. The informal service begets incredible prices as well (most meals cost less than $4). *Opens at 7 daily. 121 Liverpool Dr., Cardiff-by-the-Sea; (760) 632-0056.*

San Diego Area

John's Waffle Shop. After 47 years in the same location, John's still makes a Waffle Supreme with strawberries and whipped cream that your grandpa would appreciate. Very busy on weekends, but wintertime brings a blessed lull in the long wait times. *Opens at 7 Mon-Sat, 8 Sun. 7906 Girard St., La Jolla; (619) 454-7371.*

Kono's Surf Club Cafe. Another counter-order joint with lines out the door. The twist here is the hidden ocean-view deck, across the pedestrian walk behind the shell shop. Wangle a table there and you're in breakfast heaven, watching the surfers beside Crystal Pier. *Opens at 7 daily. 704 Garnet Ave., San Diego (Pacific Beach); (858) 483-1669.*

Landing. Hidden on a section of Mission Bay called Quivera Basin, the Landing caters to early-morning fishermen (and -women) about to board party boats or tend their own lobster traps. The grill jockey here works the range in plain view of the counter and tables, turning out plate after plate of crunchy hash browns, good eggs, fluffy pancakes, and crisp, salty bacon. *Opens at 5 daily. 1729 Quivera Rd., San Diego (Mission Bay); (619) 222-3317.* ◆

WHAT MAKES A BREAKFAST CLASSIC? Great food is a must; surfside decor (above, at Kono's) helps.

Kitchen Cabinet

READERS' RECIPES TESTED IN SUNSET'S KITCHENS

BY ANDREW BAKER

SHREDDED CARROTS meld with chicken for flavorful fajitas.

Chicken-Carrot Fajitas

Eleanor Gossett, Laramie, Wyoming

Eleanor Gossett enjoys Southwest flavors, but she wanted a vegetable other than bell peppers in her fajitas. She discovered carrots are the perfect companion for chicken and cumin.

PREP AND COOK TIME: About 30 minutes

MAKES: 4 servings

- 1 pound **boned, skinned chicken breasts**
- 1 teaspoon **olive** or salad **oil**
- 1 cup sliced **onion**
- 1 cup shredded **carrots**
- 2 teaspoons minced or pressed **garlic**
- 1 teaspoon **ground cumin**
- 8 warm **flour tortillas** (10 in.)
  Sour cream
  Shredded jack cheese
  Salsa
  Salt and **pepper**

1. Rinse chicken, pat dry, and cut into $^1/_2$-inch pieces.

2. In a 10- to 12-inch nonstick frying pan over high heat, combine oil, onion, carrots, garlic, and cumin; stir often un-

til onion is lightly browned, about 5 minutes. Pour into a bowl.

3. Add chicken to pan and stir often until no longer pink in center of thickest part (cut to test), about 5 minutes. Pour onion-carrot mixture back into pan and stir until hot, 1 to 2 minutes.

4. Spoon chicken mixture onto tortillas. Add sour cream, cheese, salsa, and salt and pepper to taste. Fold tortillas around filling to eat.

Per serving: 524 cal., 19% (99 cal.) from fat; 37 g protein; 11 g fat (1.7 g sat.); 68 g carbo (5 g fiber); 612 mg sodium; 66 mg chol.

Ginger-Chili Scallops

Al Zangri, Juneau

For her birthday, Al Zangri's wife, Judy, wanted a special meal built around seafood. This dish was Al's gift to her.

PREP AND COOK TIME: About 35 minutes

MAKES: 4 servings

- $^3/_4$ pound **asparagus**
- $1^1/_2$ pounds **sea scallops**
- $^1/_4$ cup **olive oil**
- 1 tablespoon minced **fresh ginger**
- 2 tablespoons minced or pressed **garlic**
- 2 tablespoons minced **fresh jalapeño chilies**
- $^1/_8$ teaspoon **hot chili flakes**
- $^1/_2$ cup **dry white wine**
- $^1/_4$ cup ($^1/_8$ lb.) **butter** or margarine
  Salt and **pepper**

1. Rinse asparagus, snap off and discard tough ends, and cut remaining stalks diagonally into $1^1/_2$-inch pieces. Rinse scallops well and pat dry; if wider than $1^1/_2$ inches, cut in half.

2. In a 12-inch nonstick frying pan or 14- to 15-inch wok over high heat, combine asparagus and $^1/_3$ cup water. Stir often just until asparagus is tender-crisp when pierced, 3 to 4 minutes. Pour asparagus into a bowl.

3. To pan, add oil, ginger, garlic, jalapeño chilies, and chili flakes. Stir until sizzling, about 1 minute. Add scallops and stir often for 1 minute longer. Add wine. Stir until scallops are opaque but still moist-looking in center of thickest part (cut to test), 2 to 3 minutes. With a slotted spoon, transfer scallops to bowl.

4. Boil liquid in pan until reduced to $^1/_2$ cup, 5 to 7 minutes. Reduce heat, add butter, and stir just until melted, about 1 minute. Return asparagus and scallops to pan; stir until hot, about 2 minutes. Pour at once into a serving bowl. Add salt and pepper to taste.

Per serving: 402 cal., 60% (243 cal.) from fat; 31 g protein; 27 g fat (9.4 g sat.); 9.1 g carbo (0.9 g fiber); 400 mg sodium; 88 mg chol.

Apricot-Cheese Loaves

Audrey Thibodeau, Gilbert, Arizona

Audrey Thibodeau prepares loaves of bread as gifts; in this recipe she combines tangy dried apricots with cheddar cheese. Eat slices plain or spread with butter or cream cheese.

PREP AND COOK TIME: About 45 minutes

MAKES: 2 loaves, $1^1/_2$ pounds each

- About $2^1/_2$ cups **all-purpose flour**
- $^3/_4$ cup **granulated sugar**
- 2 teaspoons **baking soda**
- $1^1/_2$ teaspoons **ground cinnamon**
- $^1/_4$ teaspoon **ground nutmeg**
- $^1/_4$ teaspoon **salt**
- $^3/_4$ cup finely chopped **pecans** or walnuts
- 2 cups ($^1/_2$ lb.) **shredded sharp cheddar cheese**
- 1 cup finely chopped **dried apricots**
- 2 **large eggs**
- 1 cup **milk**
  About $^1/_3$ cup melted **butter** or margarine
- 3 tablespoons firmly packed **brown sugar**

1. In a large bowl, mix $2^1/_2$ cups flour, granulated sugar, baking soda, 1 teaspoon cinnamon, nutmeg, and salt. Add nuts, cheese, and apricots and mix well.

2. In a medium bowl, beat eggs, milk, and $^1/_3$ cup melted butter to blend. Add mixture to dry ingredients and stir to moisten evenly.

3. Butter and flour two $4^1/_2$- by $8^1/_2$-inch loaf pans; scrape batter equally into pans. In a small bowl, combine brown sugar, 1 tablespoon melted butter, and $^1/_2$ teaspoon cinnamon. Sprinkle evenly over batter in pans.

4. Bake in a 350° oven until bread is well browned, springs back when lightly pressed in the center, and begins to pull

TUCKER & HOSSLER

from pan sides, 30 to 35 minutes.

5. Let stand in pans on a rack for about 10 minutes. Run a thin-bladed knife between bread and pan sides. Invert loaves onto rack and set upright to cool. Serve warm or cool.

Per oz.: 96 cal., 43% (41 cal.) from fat; 2.5 g protein; 4.5 g fat (2.1 g sat.); 11 g carbo (0.5 g fiber); 114 mg sodium; 18 mg chol.

Angel's Heart Cookies

Louise Ross, Elk Grove, California

After tasting similar cookies at a party, Louise Ross embellished the recipe with lemon. The new name reflects the cookies' delicate texture.

PREP AND COOK TIME: About 50 minutes

MAKES: About 3½ dozen cookies

About ½ cup **butter** or margarine

⅔ cup **granulated sugar**

⅔ cup **ricotta cheese**

1 **large egg**

¾ teaspoon **lemon extract**

1⅓ cups **all-purpose flour**

½ teaspoon **baking powder**

½ teaspoon **baking soda**

¼ teaspoon **salt**

1¼ cups **powdered sugar**

3 tablespoons **milk**

1. In a large bowl, with a mixer, beat 6 tablespoons butter and the granulated sugar until well blended. Add ricotta, egg, and ½ teaspoon lemon extract; beat until well mixed.

2. In a medium bowl, mix flour, baking powder, baking soda, and salt. Add to butter mixture, stir to mix, then beat until well blended.

3. Butter 14- by 17-inch baking sheets.

Drop batter in 1-tablespoon portions about 1½ inches apart on sheets.

4. Bake cookies in a 325° oven until golden brown, 20 to 25 minutes. If baking more than 1 pan at once, switch pan positions every 10 minutes. With a wide spatula, transfer cookies to racks.

5. Melt 2 tablespoons butter. In a deep bowl, mix butter, powdered sugar, ¼ teaspoon lemon extract, and milk until smooth. One at a time, hold cookies by the edges and dip rounded tops into icing; set in a single layer, icing up, on racks and let stand until icing is firm, about 10 minutes. Serve, or store airtight up to 1 day; freeze to store longer.

Per cookie: 52 cal., 16% (8.1 cal.) from fat; 1 g protein; 0.9 g fat (0.5 g sat.); 9.9 g carbo (0.1 g fiber); 42 mg sodium; 7.7 mg chol. ◆

Vancouver Island's gourmet trail

Meet the chefs and enjoy outstanding meals on a tour of five first-class island lodgings

BY JENA MacPHERSON

CATHIE FERGUSON

LOCAL MUSHROOMS: Chris Jones, chef at Aerie Resort, meets with guests to discuss the menu, local produce, and wine.

With chefs commanding the respect usually granted to film and sports stars, more people are taking an active interest in learning what goes into great cuisine. Tour companies offer food-themed tours in regions where local ingredients are in ample supply. Case in point: the gourmet trail on Canada's Vancouver Island.

"There's no better way to get to know an area than to discover it with locals," says third-generation islander Patricia Hatchman. All year long, she runs six-day tours to five British Columbia lodgings—all of which have world-class reputations for cuisine—with side trips to island food producers. Tucked away in remote spots in the midst of farmed and natural island bounty and beauty, the collection of culinary gems (four inns plus the Empress Hotel) has been dubbed Vancouver Island's "gourmet

trail." You can follow the route on one of Hatchman's tours or arrange to visit each place independently.

The route begins at the farthest point, the Wickaninnish Inn and the Pointe Restaurant, a prime storm-watching destination on the wild west coast at Tofino. Chef Jim Garraway uses local oysters, Dungeness crab, and unusual seafoods in imaginative creations, including the inn's signature dish, potlatch stew.

Toward Victoria, at the Aerie Resort, chef Chris Jones gives predinner briefings, identifying seasonal local ingredients. High on Malahat Pass, the inn looks out on stunning water views and thick forest—where, in season, Jones leads guests on foraging expeditions for mushrooms, which are later prepared in the Aerie's kitchen.

At Hastings House on Salt Spring Island (just a 30-minute ferry ride from Vancouver Island), guests meet with chef Marcel Kauer in the kitchen after dinner to discuss the meal. Menus feature local produce, organic fruit from the inn's trees, and grilled leg of Salt Spring Island lamb. Cheesemaker David Wood conducts cheese tastings.

West of Victoria at Sooke Harbour House, Sinclair and Frederique Philip are renowned for unusual native dishes.

The tour ends with the Empress Hotel's legendary afternoon tea, a perfect way to end a delectable journey.

Information on Patricia Hatman's all-inclusive guided tours is available at *(800) 970-7722, (250) 658-5367, or www.firstislandtours.com.* ◆

Great taco hunt: We tracked down the top taquerias in the West and captured their recipes to try at home. Recipe on page 73.

March

The great
taco hunt

Somebody had to do it—find the
best tacos in the West. We volunteered.
Months of research, thousands of
tacos, a list of winners.

The taco is a simple concept with a big reach. Though basically a street snack, it represents an entire culture—that little corn tortilla alone holds centuries of symbol and sustenance for the peoples of Mexico (try reading that much significance into a hamburger bun). • And unlike our large impostor taco chains, which impose one mediocre style nationwide, "real" (that is, authentic Mexican) taquerias are spreading variety and quality throughout the land. The taco may be fast food in the end, but in the beginning, someone took a lot of time to grind the masa, braise the meat, and stem innumerable chilies. • A fresh, sweet, earthy corn tortilla—usually two, in fact—is the earmark of a good soft taco. Wonderful traditional regional Mexican dishes are its heart and soul: simple *carne asada* (grilled meat), spicy pork *al pastor*

REGIONAL STARS:

Lone Star fish tacos

in Salt Lake City

(left); Claire and

Shawna Archibald,

owners of Café Azul

in Portland (above).

(barbecued country-style), deep red *chile colorado* (beef or pork in red chili sauce). • Such tacos are capable of mobilizing more than a dozen *Sunset* scouts on a search for the finest in the West. We got directions first—from you. Last April we asked our readers to tell us about the best places in the West to buy tacos. We got nearly 800 nominations, creating an astonishingly wide taco trail from Missoula, Montana, to Las Cruces, New Mexico;

from Tuba City, Arizona, to Lahaina, Hawaii. Did I mention California? • We were critical, looking for authentic Mexican traditions or truly creative variations. The tortillas could be made of corn (yellow is the most common, but we found white and blue too) or wheat flour (the tortilla material of choice near the northern Mexican border), but they had to be fresh. If a taco was fried, its crunch had to be honestly come by through a recent encounter with sizzling fat. We checked out full-service restaurants with strong taco contingents on their menus, order-at-the-register taquerias, and even a few taco trucks (not nearly enough—there's a world to explore). • After logging many miles and uncinching our belts a few notches, we made a list of favorites (it starts at right; recipes start on page 70). Clearly, the taco deserves respect as a food: It loses no integrity just because it's fast. — *Sara Schneider*

Top of the tacos

Café Azul, Portland, OR

"Tacos are very exotic for something so familiar," says Claire Archibald, chef and co-owner of the elegant Café Azul. "They're a great introduction to this restaurant." Although a plate of tacos at Café Azul is a remarkably different experience than one in the local barrio, it's not to be missed.

A sampling from the ever-changing appetizer selection might include tender, hand-made tortillas wrapped around achiote-marinated pork roasted in banana leaves with sour orange juice—a complex bite of sweet, spicy, earthy, and faintly bitter notes. In another tortilla, silky pillows of black beans get a sprinkling of tangy cotija cheese, cherry tomatoes, and cilantro. (The recipe for Café Azul's rajas con queso is on page 72, for tomatillo-avocado salsa, page 74.)

Café Azul is in the front ranks of new Western restaurants going beyond well-known Tex-Mex food to authentic and sophisticated regional Mexican flavors—in this case, of Oaxaca.

112 N.W. Ninth Ave., Portland; (503) 525-4422.
— *Stacey Philipps*

Lone Star Taqueria, Salt Lake City, UT

So, what's with the beat-up, graffiti-painted station wagon permanently crashed into the rail fence around the colorful patio? And what about the decidedly Texan implications in the name of this taqueria opened six years ago by Susan Harries? Ask Lone Star chef Manuel Valdez, and he'll

the great taco hunt: winners

WE GET GLOWING REPORTS about Salt Lake City's Lone Star Taqueria (above). Filling big, fresh tortillas with a smile at La Taqueria in San Francisco (top right). Pure taco satisfaction at La Super-Rica in Santa Barbara (right). Hanging out at Chope's Bar and Cafe in La Mesa, New Mexico (opposite page).

just smile and shrug. He's from Zacatecas, Mexico, and his only concern is that the tacos streaming out of his cramped Salt Lake City kitchen taste positively south of the border—if not out of this world.

The specialty of the house is a fish taco that needs nothing but dollops of Valdez's special cilantro-jalapeño mayonnaise and pico de gallo to bring the flavors together. (Fish taco recipe is on page 73; for sauces, see page 74.) Step up to the salsa bar for extra heat. Sixteen other tacos on the menu make this a place you can't sample in one sitting, but don't miss the carne adobada.

2265 E. Fort Union Blvd., Salt Lake City; (801) 944-2300. — Jeff Phillips

La Taqueria, San Francisco, CA

On opening day in 1973, a hungry mob shoved its way into La Taqueria on San Francisco's Mission Street. Clearly,

owner Miguel Jara delivered what his customers craved: fresh Mexican-style tacos. "It was overwhelming!" Jara recalls. "We took in $276. In those days that was a lot of money." The food ran out at 2 in the afternoon.

Fueled by memories of eating tacos as a boy in Tijuana, the visionary Jara had spent a year—and much of his life savings—shaping the San Francisco storefront into his taco stand. When he couldn't find an appropriate commercial grill, Jara, a former body shop worker, fabricated one himself. He built the furniture, uncovered the skylights—and learned to cook. In the town of Tepatitlán in Jalisco, Mexico, he discovered the secret to delicious carnitas (recipe is on page 73).

Today, La Taqueria serves as many as 1,200 people a day in two locations (Jara opened a branch in San Jose in 1978). "The Best Tacos in the Whole World," his neon sign boasts. No argument here. Crackling, sweet carnitas and smoky

carne asada are delicious piled over cheese in the soft, fresh corn tortillas.

2889 Mission St., San Francisco (415/285-7117); 15 S. First St., San Jose (408/287-1542). — Alan Phinney

La Super-Rica, Santa Barbara, CA

As a taqueria, Santa Barbara's La Super-Rica is seriously overqualified but underidentified. No large sign announces the goings-on in the low green-and-white hut. "I couldn't afford one at first," explains owner Isidoro Gonzalez. The fact that, after 20 years, he still hasn't invested in that most basic advertising is in itself a sign of Gonzalez's

priorities—which are, in a phrase, *tacos al carbón.*

Tacos al carbón is a concept that derailed Gonzalez from his teaching track in the late '70s. While studying in Mexico City, he was captivated by this very specific style of tacos: top-quality grilled meats, melted cheeses, fresh salsas, and homemade tortillas. Obsessed with the idea of bringing back to Santa Barbara a kind of good, casual Mexican cooking the town didn't have, he set out to learn how to do it, and opened La Super-Rica in May 1980.

The narrow focus stuck—almost all of the menu items chalked on the original board are still there (recipe for the beans is on page 74). The

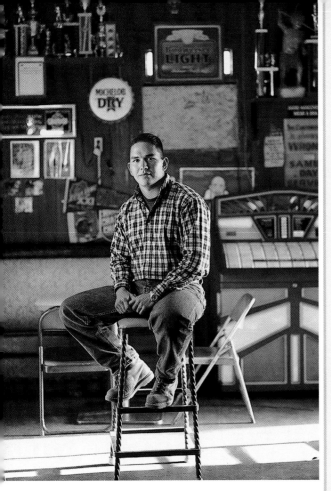

favorites: *taco de bistec* (grilled steak), *taco de adobado* (grilled marinated pork), *alambre de filete o pechuga* (grilled tri-tip or chicken with peppers, onions, and bacon or mushrooms—known elsewhere as fajitas), and the *Super-Rica Especial* (a poblano—Gonzalez's favorite chili—stuffed with cheese).

Gonzalez introduces daily specials to stimulate curiosity about a variety and quality of Mexican food people still can't get in other local restaurants. He wants people to think, "Today is Monday. La Super-Rica is serving chiles rellenos. But what *kind* of chiles rellenos?"

622 N. Milpas St., Santa Barbara; (805) 963-4940.
— S.S.

Chope's Bar and Cafe, La Mesa, NM

To reach Chope's, take a 12-mile drive south of Mesilla, New Mexico, through pecan groves, fields of chilies and cotton, and villages that are older than the border between Old and New Mexico. Expect a line at lunchtime. Inside the plain, half-century-old cafe, families of several generations share what many believe is the best regional food in the state, which prides itself on its cuisine.

Around a yellow table in the kitchen, the staff chops fresh ingredients as if preparing a big family dinner. The tacos are everything classic tacos should be—aromatic ground beef, cooked to crumbly firmness (recipe is on page 73), in a crisp, fried tortilla shell that tastes of roasted corn, served with a truly addictive fresh green chili salsa.

On Friday and Saturday nights, local musicians turn out to play traditional ranchero tunes.

16145 S. State 28, La Mesa; (505) 233-3420.
— *Sharon Niederman*

More winning Northwest taquerias

OREGON
Portland

■ **Chez Grill**, 2229 S.E. Hawthorne Blvd.; (503) 239-4002. In this artsy warehouse space, couples and families alike munch house-made flour tortillas wrapped around tasty, albeit yuppified, fillings. The shredded chicken is second only to the fish—a seasonal catch with baby greens and tomato salsa. — S.P.

■ **La Calaca Comelona**, 1408 S.E. 12th Ave.; (503) 239-9675. The tacos at "the hungry skeleton" are rib-sticking good. Try the pollo—spicy, juicy shredded chicken mixed with potatoes and carrots—and the chorizo sausage, which, along with the tortillas, is made on these hip premises. — S.P.

■ **La Sirenita**, 2817 N.E. Alberta St.; (503) 335-8283. La Sirenita ratchets up the quality and atmosphere slightly over its neighbor, Mi Ranchito (following). Tangy-sweet pork barbacoa and carne asada win top honors. — S.P.

■ **Mi Ranchito Taqueria**, 2829 N.E. Alberta; (503) 331-1774. A simple, booth-lined room yields 10 kinds of tacos in the traditional style. The best are tender lengua and spicy chorizo sausage. Sizzling salsas liven up the fillings. — S.P.

■ **Salvador Molly's**, 1523 S.W. Sunset Blvd.; (503) 293-1790. Grab a smoky shredded pork taco at this popular neighborhood cafe—or the Willapa Bay oyster taco for a Northwest interpretation. Gourmet garnishes abound, but the atmosphere is funky and comfortable. — S.P.

■ **Taqueria Chavez**, 5703 S.E. 82nd Ave.; (503) 777-2282. Ask for tortillas "made inside" at this no-frills taco stand and get thick, hand-patted rounds with expertly seasoned interiors. Cabeza and *puerco* (pork) shine. — S.P.

WASHINGTON
Seattle

■ **Anthony's Pier 66 & Bell Street Diner**, 2201 Alaskan Way; (206) 448-6688. The flagship of a fleet of popular Anthony's eateries serving fish tacos: strips of mahimahi in a colorful nest of cabbage, topped with a famous mayonnaise sauce and wrapped in a thick flour tortilla. — S.S.

■ **El Puerco Llorón**, 1501 Western Ave.; (206) 624-0541. This tiny taqueria, tucked behind Pike Place Market, produces some of the best Mexican food in the city. Fresh corn tortillas, pressed and flipped on the griddle while you move through line, do magic with classic carne asada. — S.S.

■ **Malena's Taco Shop**, 620 W. McGraw Ave.; (206) 284-0304. This plain but pleasant Queen Anne–district shop turns out some compelling carne asada tacos. — S.S.

■ **Tacos Guaymas**, five locations in the Seattle area. Most authentic: White Center, 1622 Roxbury St. S.W.; (206) 767-4026. Impressive quality for a mini-chain. The fillings taste of time spent with spices, and the fresh tomato and dried chili salsas from the bar are downright "head-bangers," in the words of one Sunset reader; try the smoky *salsa quemada*.
— S.S.

Spokane

■ **El Rio Mexican Restaurant**, 2023 W. Northwest Blvd.; (509) 327-7539. Unquestionably, this neighborhood diner–like establishment's forte is tacos—scrumptious and thick enough to require two hands, juicy enough to call for additional napkins.
— *Jeff Halstead*

the great taco hunt

More winning Northern California taquerias

SAN FRANCISCO BAY AREA

Mountain View

■ Ramon's Burrito Real, 580 N. Rengstorff Ave.; (650) 988-6705. The secret here is *taquitacos*—tiny tortillas filled with any of a counterful of regional specialties. — *S.S.*

Palo Alto

■ Andalé Mexican Restaurant, 209 University Ave.; (650) 323-2939. Wonderful mesquite-grilled chicken and beef, rich chile verde, and tangy al pastor are tucked into soft flour tortillas in this lively order-at-the-counter cafe. Other locations in Los Gatos and San Francisco. — *S.S.*

Redwood City

■ Naranjo's Taqueria, 2647 Broadway; (650) 369-9196. *Muy auténtico* tacos are served over the counter of this little storefront shop. The *carne suave* (shredded beef) and chili-seasoned shredded pollo stand out. — *S.S.*

San Francisco

■ Cafe Marimba, 2317 Chestnut St.; (415) 776-1506. Michoacan-style carnitas and meaty grilled swordfish with chunky pineapple-chipotle salsa are both consistently wonderful at this upscale cafe. — *S.S.*

San Jose

■ Las Brasas, 763 E. Julian St.; (408) 971-9639. Las Brasas moves its tacos outside every Friday, Saturday, and Sunday night, giving the place a fiesta flavor. Don't miss the *suadero*—tender, spicy beef; it disappears for the rest of the week. — *S.S.*

San Mateo

■ Taqueria La Cumbre, 28 N. B St.; (650) 344-8989. Anchoring a block of Mexican and Central American shops, La Cumbre grills a mean pollo asado—delicious dressed with the oniony salsa verde. Another location in San Francisco. — *A.P.*

MONTEREY AND SANTA CRUZ COUNTIES

Gonzales

■ Taqueria Valparaiso, 31 Fourth St.; (831) 675-0965. "Not for the Taco Bell crowd," advises one reader. But for others, the slow heat from the tender tacos al pastor is infinitely satisfying. — *S.S.*

Santa Cruz

■ El Palomar Restaurant Taco Bar, Pacific Garden Mall; (831) 425-7575. The best place to eat tacos and watch cable-TV sports in downtown Santa Cruz. The scallop and carne asada versions are especially good. And the guacamole taco is downright delicious. — *Clare Chatfield*

■ Tacos Moreno, 1053 Water St.; (831) 429-6095. This six-table joint doesn't have a lot of ambience—just fantastic tacos. The richly seasoned carnitas and chile verde fillings justify the lines out the door. Also Tacos Moreno 2 in Santa Cruz. — *C.C.*

■ Taqueria Santa Cruz, 2215 Mission St.; (831) 423-0606. A must for adventurous eaters. Why settle for the usual carnitas or pollo asado (both of which are very good here) when you can try birria or *buche* (pork stomach)? Another location in Santa Cruz. — *C.C.*

Seaside

■ Fishwife's Turtle Bay Taqueria, 1301 Fremont Blvd.; (831) 899-1010. Ironically, slow-cooked Yucatán-style pork loin, with a schmear of black beans, shines at this seafood-oriented hut. — *S.S.*

Watsonville

■ El Alteño, 323 Main St.; (831) 768-9876. No "taco joint" this. Creative fillings and a bougain-villea-brightened courtyard make El Alteño a terrific choice. The grilled snapper and pork al pastor are favorites. — *C.C.*

NORTH COAST, SACRAMENTO, AND SIERRA NEVADA

Davis

■ Dos Coyotes Border Café, 1411 W. Covell Blvd., Suite 107; (530) 753-0922. Nine years after the first Dos Coyotes opened, people still flock here. The Tres Tacos Basket, which includes a shrimp version, is an excellent deal. Other locations in Roseville and Sacramento. — *C.C.*

Fort Bragg

■ Purple Rose, 24300 N. State 1; (707) 964-6507. Locals jam the Rose nightly for fresh corn tortillas overflowing with moist fillings like shredded chicken. — *Lora J. Finnegan*

Rancho Cordova

■ Olé Mexico, 2320 Sunrise Blvd.; (916) 851-1868. Choose from 11 varieties of tacos in this bright, sports-themed restaurant. — *Fred Sandsmark*

Sacramento

■ Beto's Mexican Food, 2234 El Camino Ave.; (916) 924-9402. This popular eatery makes one of the best chicken tacos this side of the Rio Grande. — *C.C.*

■ El Mercadito, 3134 Northgate Blvd.; (916) 927-3161. This "little market" isn't much to look at from the outside. But the tacos? Well, you've come to the right place. If you're feeling a little adventurous, try the *chicharron* (pork rind) or tripa. — *C.C.*

■ Ernesto's Mexican Food, 1901 16th St.; (916) 441-5850. This downtown restaurant is known locally as a great place for a first date. The chile verde and carnitas are great. — *C.C.*

■ Pescado's Mexican Restaurant, 2801 P St.; (916) 452-7237. The Pescado Superior at this downtown joint could be habit-forming. Another location at 2610 Fair Oaks Blvd.; (916) 483-3474. — *C.C.*

Santa Rosa

■ El Patio Numero Dos, 901 Fourth St.; (707) 571-2222. Choose either crisp or soft tacos filled with well-seasoned meats (especially satisfying carnitas) to eat at pleasant, awning-covered picnic tables across from a park. — *S.S.*

South Lake Tahoe

■ Hot Pepper Grill, 3490 Lake Tahoe Blvd.; (530) 542-1015. Simple, fresh, traditional tacos just a short hop from the ski slopes or Stateline's casinos. — *F.S.*

GOLD COUNTRY AND SAN JOAQUIN VALLEY

Fresno

■ Al Rico Tacos, 2950 E. Ventura Ave.; (559) 441-8131. For more than 14 years, this bright yellow stand has been serving delicious tacos. Try the carne adobada. — *Cindy Evans*

Mariposa

■ Sal's Taco Wagon, 5038 State 140; (209) 966-7257. Parked behind this hillside town's historical museum, the silver wagon from Sal's Mexican Restaurant serves wonderful, spicy al pastor. — *C.E.*

Oakhurst

■ Castillo's Mexican Restaurant and Cantina, 49271 Golden Oak Loop; (559) 683-8000. Friendly Castillo's offers a welcome break en route to Yosemite—flavorful, meaty tacos and frothy blackberry margaritas. — *C.E.*

Stockton

■ San Felipe Grill, 4601 Pacific Ave.; (209) 952-6261. Stuffed with beans and cheese, San Felipe tacos are practically burritos—hard to handle but worth the work. — *F.S.*

Visalia

■ El Rosal, 3718 S. Mooney Blvd.; (559) 733-7731. Large flour or corn tortillas are filled with tender chicken, beef, or pork. Be sure to try the mild cabbage salsa. Other locations in Fresno, Lodi, Modesto, and Turlock. — *C.E.*

More winning Southern California and Hawaii taquerias

LOS ANGELES COUNTY
Culver City
■ Tito's Tacos, 11222 Washington Place; (310) 391-5780. Long lines at the counters every Saturday night for deep-fried shredded beef tacos qualify Tito's as a phenomenon. You decide. — S.S.

Long Beach
■ Baja Sonora, 2940 Clark Ave.; (562) 421-5120. Bright ocher paint and chili-shaped lights offset the aging strip-mall location. Big, flavorful chunks of grilled beef and generous jumbles of shredded carnitas are wrapped with guacamole and house-made salsa in soft corn tortillas. — S.S.

■ Tequila Jack's, 407 Shoreline Village Dr.; (562) 628-0454. This noisy joint within walking distance of the Queen Mary offers more than 100 tequilas and lots of tasty tacos. Our favorite was blackened swordfish.
— Monica Gullen

Los Angeles
■ Señor Fish, 4803 Eagle Rock Blvd.; (323) 257-7167. This campy landlocked beach shack is famous for its soft tacos filled with delicately breaded and fried lobster, shrimp, or fish. Other locations in the L.A. area. — M.G.

■ Talpa, 11751 W. Pico Blvd.; (310) 478-3353. This unassuming little place, decorated with plastic flowers, offers a variety of soft and crispy tacos, including ground beef and fish. — M.G.

■ Yuca's, 2056 N. Hillhurst Ave.; (323) 662-1214. The richly seasoned Yucatecan shredded pork is worth a fair jaunt across town to this Los Feliz–district parking-lot stand with the blue awning. (Recipe for Yucatán-style chicken is on page 72.) — S.S.

Pasadena
■ Dorados Fish Tacos, 2383 E. Colorado Blvd.; (626) 683-9515. Its name notwithstanding, this sleek mini-mall restaurant serves a better carne asada than fish taco. — M.G.

Santa Monica
■ Holy Guacamole, 2906 Main St.; (310) 314-4850. The most heavenly fillings served under the Michelangelesque painting of God handing Adam a taco are carne asada and juicy carnitas. — M.G.

Tarzana
■ Sharky's Mexican Grill, 5511 Reseda Blvd.; (818) 881-8760. Organic beef, very fresh fish, and hormone-free chicken cater to health-conscious taco lovers. Try the mahimahi. — M.G.

ORANGE COUNTY
Costa Mesa
■ Taco Mesa, 647 W. 19th St.; (949) 642-0629. Painted like a Taco Bell hut off to a fiesta, Taco Mesa fills soft corn tortillas with lively meat mixtures that seem both authentic and healthful. — S.S.

Laguna Beach
■ Javier's Cantina & Grill, 480 S. Coast Hwy.; (949) 494-1239. Great atmosphere, food, and service. Try the tender carnitas, carne asada, or juicy chicken in moist corn tortillas made fresh daily at the local El Metate tortilleria. — Becky Soret

Laguna Niguel
■ Las Golondrinas Mexican Food, 27981 Greenfield Dr., Suite G; (949) 362-1913. Try the mole taco—shredded beef drenched in sauce served over fluffy rice. Takeout or outside seating only. — B.S.

RIVERSIDE AND SAN BERNARDINO COUNTIES
Mentone
■ Casa Maya, 1839 Mentone Blvd.; (909) 794-7458. This full-service restaurant specializes in the cuisine of the Yucatán Peninsula. Homemade corn tortillas are filled with meats marinated in spices and citrus juices. — B.S.

Riverside
■ Josie's Tacos, 9782 Magnolia Ave.; (909) 687-9402. Crisp tacos are filled with wonderfully seasoned beef, chicken, or fish. Soft tacos come with carnitas, carne asada, or al pastor. All are worth a stop. — B.S.

SAN DIEGO COUNTY
Pacific Beach
■ Los Dos Pedros, 723 Turquoise Ave.; (858) 488-3102. Walk up from the beach to this tiny stand for a crisp-fried chicken taco, a tender carne asada taco, or a soft fish taco.
— Jana Ford-Harder

Point Loma
■ Tommy's Tex-Mex, 4145 Voltaire St.; (619) 223-5225. Echoes of the Beach Boys blend well with the extraordinary hand-made tortillas at this small Ocean Beach surfer hangout. — J.F.-H.

San Diego
■ El Cuervo Taco Shop, 110 W. Washington St.; (619) 295-9713. Queue up in this busy uptown location for especially moist and flavorful carnitas. — J.F.-H.

■ Fins Mexican Eatery; five locations in San Diego. A clone of Rubio's (see below): juicy fish tacos with lots of mayo sauce and salsa. — J.F.-H.

■ Rubio's Baja Grill; locations throughout Southern California. Rubio's beer-battered and fried fish tacos epitomize the Southland classic taco: shredded cabbage, tangy mayonnaise sauce, salsa, and a squeeze of lime.
— J.F.-H.

SAN LUIS OBISPO, SANTA BARBARA, AND VENTURA COUNTIES
Atascadero
■ Tia Juana's Mexican Restaurant, 9550 El Camino Real; (805) 466-7592. This little place, just off U.S. 101, fills the fresh corn tortillas with scoops of flavorful carne asada and carnitas. — J.P.

Cayucos
■ Taco Temple, 101 D St.; (805) 995-1814. Seared albacore tuna, dark with spices on the outside, tops a riot of color and flavor: varicolored cabbages and lettuces, tomatoes, carrots, cilantro, and sweet-hot mango salsa. Substitute chunky crab cakes for the albacore, and the taco is to die for. Another location in Morro Bay. — S.S.

Paso Robles
■ Papi's Tacos & Gorditas, 840 13th St.; (805) 239-3720. Felix Rincón's carnitas are unevenly shredded but uncommonly good. Other locations in Atascadero and Paso Robles. — S.S.

Pismo Beach
■ El Mirador Restaurant, 187 Pomeroy Ave.; (805) 773-1972. A real find—authentic soft tacos filled with chile verde, marinated pork in a finger-staining red sauce, or rich carnitas. — S.S.

San Luis Obispo
■ Chili Peppers, 2121 Broad St.; (805) 541-9154. Tangy pork al pastor wrapped with grilled onions, shredded jack, guacamole, and salsa. Good stuff. — S.S.

Ventura
■ El Taco de Mexico, 3114 Telegraph Rd.; (805) 642-9409. Cabeza is one option here, though our tasters gave their loudest vote of approval to the spicy shredded chicken. — Peter Fish

HAWAII
Lahaina, Maui
■ Maui Tacos, 840 Wainee St., Lahaina Square; (808) 661-8883. Fast, convenient, and not the least bit fancy, this great restaurant offers distinctive flavors—bold and spicy but not too hot. Other locations on the Big Island, Maui, and Oahu.
— Garret Seabolt

the great taco hunt

More winning Southwest taquerias

ARIZONA

Chandler

■ Guedo's Taco Shop, 71 E. Chandler Blvd.; (480) 899-7841. Soft corn tortillas, lined with cheese, are filled with pork, beef, or marinated chicken; you customize your tacos at the bar with shredded cabbage, cilantro, radishes, and salsa.
— *Nora Burba Trulsson*

Phoenix

■ El Taquito, 2720 W. Van Buren Ave.; (602) 278-4620. In a distinctly Latino neighborhood, this taqueria specializes in small, spicy tacos filled with chicken and pork or the more adventurous tripa and lengua. **Another location in Phoenix.** — *N.B.T.*

■ Tacos Mexico, 2333 N. 16th St.; (602) 253-5163. This taco bar is packed for lunch and early dinner with office folks who crave the savory potato (mashed, with a Veracruz-style red sauce) or fish tacos, served in soft flour tortillas. — *N.B.T.*

Scottsdale

■ El Guapo's Taco Shop, 3015 N. Scottsdale Rd.; (480) 423-8385. Choose soft corn or flour tortillas filled with marinated and grilled chicken, pork, or carne asada, then head to the salsa bar to top your taco with salsas and shredded greens. — *N.B.T.*

South Tucson

■ Taqueria Pico de Gallo, 2618 S. Sixth Ave.; (520) 623-8775. The Delgado family's tacos have Tucsonans addicted. Petite corn or flour tortillas made on the premises are filled with grilled chicken, beef, and, for vegetarians, guacamole or beans. For the daring, there's lengua or cabeza. Seafood tacos are favorites: fish, shrimp, and (sometimes) ray. — *N.B.T.*

Tucson

■ El Charro Restaurant, 311 N. Court Ave.; (520) 622-1922. The must-try taco in this old-time restaurant (open since 1922) is filled with carne seca. Other winners: shredded beef or chicken. — *N.B.T.*

■ El Minuto Cafe, 354 S. Main Ave.; (520) 882-4145. In one of downtown's oldest neighborhoods, El Minuto serves its tacos two to a plate, with sides of rice and beans. Choose chicken, guacamole, shredded beef, carne seca, or carne asada. — *N.B.T.*

■ St. Mary's Mexican Food, 1030 W. St. Mary's Rd.; (520) 884-1629. A favorite on the west side of town, St. Mary's offers beef, birria, chicken, and carne seca tacos to eat in or take out. They're petite, so you can sample the whole taco menu if you're hungry. — *N.B.T.*

NEW MEXICO

Albuquerque

■ Acapulco Tacos, 840 San Mateo Blvd. S.E.; (505) 268-9865. The paint is faded, but the crowds are thick at this main-drag drive-in that turns out tasty tacos at bargain prices. — *S.N.*

■ Camino Real de Ron, 416 Yale Blvd. S.E.; (505) 255-0973. Ron's supreme creation: a big flour tortilla grilled with cheese, then filled with slow-baked carne adobada, lettuce, and tomato. Voilà—the Santa Fe Taco! — *S.N.*

■ El Norteño, 6416 Zuni Rd. S.E.; (505) 255-2057. A modest spot that brings a northern Mexico interpretation to tacos: homemade corn tortillas wrapped around grilled steak, chicken, or *nopal* (cactus), with piquant fresh salsas. — *S.N.*

■ Fajitaville, 6313 Fourth St. N.W.; (505) 341-9683. The emphasis at this low-key neighborhood eatery is on fresh salsas—apple-jicama, papaya, roasted tomato–chipotle—to top grilled steak and chicken fajitas. — *S.N.*

■ Garcia's Kitchen, 1736 Central S.W.; (505) 842-0273. Unbeatable brisket tacos crowned with guacamole and pico de gallo are the Monday special at this local chain. Decor is "early carnival." — *S.N.*

■ Los Cuates, 5016B Lomas Blvd. N.E.; (505) 268-0974. You can't go wrong with either the soft chicken taco with green chili sauce or the crisp, cumin-scented ground beef taco with crimson house salsa. **Another Los Cuates location in Albuquerque.** — *S.N.*

■ M&J Sanitary Tortilla Factory, 403 Second St. S.W.; (505) 242-4890. This downtown monument to down-home New Mexico food puts an outstanding chicken filling, with an intense salsa—only for the hardy—in crackling-crisp shells. — *S.N.*

Española

■ El Parasol, 602 Santa Cruz Rd.; (505) 753-8852. A classic northern New Mexico takeout restaurant that draws low-riders and movie stars alike with its crisp grilled chicken and guacamole tacos. Always crowded! — *S.N.*

Las Cruces

■ Little Nellie's, 600 E. Amador Ave.; (505) 523-9911. This comfortable hangout dishes up all-around excellent tacos filled with shredded or ground beef, chicken, or shrimp, with a dynamite salsa fresca. — *S.N.*

Mesilla

■ El Comedor, 2190 Avenida de Mesilla; (505) 524-7002. No one who tastes the *tacos rancheros*—homemade corn tortillas filled with shredded beef grilled with onions, jalapeños, and spices—within these cozy adobe walls could possibly remain in a bad mood. — *S.N.*

Ranchos de Taos

■ Rita's Mexican Food, 4133 State 69; (505) 758-8556. English simply isn't spoken in this hole in the wall, where authentic carne asada is dished up on soft white corn tortillas and topped with zingy pico de gallo. Locals love these tacos—eat 'em with a fork! — *S.N.*

Santa Fe

■ Baja Tacos, 2621 Cerrillos Rd.; (505) 471-8762. Generations of locals have headed to this landmark drive-in for a fix of "all natural" tacos bursting with flavorful ground beef, chicken, tofu, or a combo of veggies. — *S.N.*

■ Bert's La Taqueria, 1620 St. Michael's Dr.; (505) 474-0791. Santa Fe's finest tacos are Bert's Mexico City–style, roll-your-own al pastor, with pineapple and cilantro on tender homemade corn tortillas. — *S.N.*

■ Café Pasqual's, 121 Don Gaspar Ave.; (505) 983-9340. Tacos of roasted cabrito are the Sunday *especialidad de la casa* at this colorful spot celebrated for its Southwestern and regional Mexican cooking. (See page 71 for the cafe's beef barbacoa recipe, page 74 for its three-chili salsa recipe.) — *S.N.*

Springer

■ El Taco Café y Cantina, 704 Maxwell Ave.; (505) 483-0402. The salsa is hot and the tacos are *muy delicioso* in this restaurant just off the interstate. The crisp ground beef and soft chicken are packed with flavor. These could be the best tacos between Española and Denver. — *S.N.*

Taos

■ Orlando's New Mexican Cafe, 1114 Juan Valdez Rd.; (505) 751-1450. Spicy shredded beef is tucked into blue corn tortillas and delivered in a warm, bright Mexican-folk-art setting. The patio is a popular place to meet. — *S.N.*

More winning Rocky Mountain taquerias

COLORADO
Denver

■ Benny's Restaurant & Cantina, 301 E. Seventh Ave.; (303) 894-0788. The most popular eatery from longtime Denver restaurateur Benny Armas. Get right to the meat of the matter with the house specialty, *tacos al carbón:* a generous plate of spicy grilled sirloin strips ready to be added to soft corn tortillas, along with hand-mashed guacamole and a fiery pico de gallo.
— *Kyle Wagner*

■ El Taco de Mexico, 714 Santa Fe Dr.; (303) 623-3926. When locals think of el taco de Denver, the tiny El Taco de Mexico is it. In the open kitchen, small tortillas are filled with carefully cooked meats—including cabeza, sesos, and lengua—seasoned with mouth-numbing spices. The place has no liquor license, but you really want to face these powerful suckers sober. — *K.W.*

■ Mexico City Lounge, 2115 Larimer St.; (303) 296-0563. Denverites often plan their workday around the daily steak taco special at Mexico City, a true dive within spittin' distance of Coors Field. About $5 buys three greasy bundles—corn tortillas packed with seasoned strip steak, anointed with oil, and fried crisp. Extra napkins are a must. — *K.W.*

Pueblo

■ Cactus Flower, 2149 Jerry Murphy Rd.; (719) 545-8218. This local favorite spices up its diner atmosphere with Tejano music, smoky salsa, and deep-fried taquitos—hand-rolled tacos stuffed with beef or chicken and served with red or green chili

sauce. — *Brad Cope*

■ Grand Prix Restaurant & Lounge, 615 E. Mesa Ave.; (719) 542-9825. Neon beer signs, comfy booths with plastic laminate tabletops, and "tacos on white." That last item—beef, chicken, beans, or chorizo sausage tucked into flaky flour tortillas and deep-fried—tastes so good, even the glowing St. Pauli Girl won't distract you.
— *B.C.*

■ Mexi-Deli, 215 E. Abriendo Ave.; (719) 583-1275. Despite the fast-food atmosphere, Mexi-Deli serves up sit-down flavor with its *taco azteca*—a flat, crisp-fried flour tortilla loaded with your choice of 10 toppings and smothered in green chili sauce. Dine in or drive through (honk twice at the window for service).
— *B.C.*

IDAHO
Boise

■ Atomic Taco, Fifth Ave. and Main St.; (208) 384-1041. Tucked in the back of Cristina's Bakery & Coffee Bar, this popular lunch-only spot serves a variety of tacos in soft, lightly grilled tortillas. All the fillings are good, but the shredded chicken has a slight edge. — *Nancy Gordon*

■ La Fiesta, 1221 W. Boise Ave.; (208) 343-4334. The freshly fried, crisp tacos at this homey, family-run spot are hard to beat. Ground beef, topped with lettuce, tomato, and thickly shredded cheese, is a definite favorite. House-made salsa is available at the table. — *N.G.*

Ketchum

■ Desperado's Mexican Restaurant, 211 Fourth St.; (208) 726-3068. Even more impressive than the vast array of Mexican specialties here is how much flavor the fresh, healthful

variations deliver. Soft taco fillings include beef, chicken, beans (black or pinto), guacamole, fish, and carne asada, plus four *salsas de la casa*—go for the Burn Your Buddy habanero.
— *N.G.*

■ Ketchum Burritos, 200 Sixth St. E.; (208) 726-2232. Although best known for "healthy" burritos, this small, slightly funky place has great flour tortilla–wrapped tacos too. Our favorite is the chicken, with extra zip from the house Cabo sauce. — *N.G.*

MONTANA
Missoula

■ El Topo Azul, 802 S. Higgins St.; (406) 543-6727. Belly up to the brightly colored tile counter for yellowfin tuna or shredded beef tacos in flour tortillas with fresh sauce. — *Caroline Patterson*

■ Taco del Sol, 422 N. Higgins St.; (406) 327-8929. Under a canopy of tissue-paper skeletons, try tasty fish tacos made with Alaskan cod, shredded cabbage, a creamy white sauce, fresh salsa, and cilantro.
— *C.P.*

NEVADA
Incline Village

■ T's Rotisserie, 901 Tahoe Blvd.; (775) 831-2832. The smoky, churning rotisserie is the tip-off: This meat—tri-tip, pork, and chicken—is freshly cooked. What's more, the tortillas are excellent (good salsa too).
— *Fred Sandsmark*

Reno

■ Beto's Mexican Food, 575 W. Fifth St.; (775) 324-0632. Close to Reno's glitzy casinos but a world away in atmosphere, this rough-around-the-edges place serves nine taco varieties—including tripa and sesos—for only $1 apiece. There's often a line, but the tacos are worth the wait. — *F.S.*

DOUGLAS MERRIAM

DRIED RED CHILIES give rich color—but not too much heat—to chile colorado Fandango (left). Above, Café Pasqual's beef barbacoa evokes the flavors of pit-cooked meat in Old Mexico.

Taco fiesta

Tacos are casual, potentially messy, and fun to assemble—in short, they make great party food. We coaxed recipes for fillings and sauces from our favorite taco stands and restaurants, to mix and match for a colorful fiesta at home. • Ingredients for these traditional Mexican dishes are available throughout the West in many well-stocked supermarkets and in Latino food markets: fresh and dried chilies; achiote paste, packed in cellophane-wrapped blocks; Mexican *crema* and *jocoque* (heavy creams similar to sour cream), in tubs or jars; Mexican cheeses, such as cotija and queso fresco; and dried Mexican oregano, a variety more pungent than regular oregano. • Tender corn tortillas just off the comal make it worth scouring the neighborhood for a *tortillería* (tortilla factory). If you come up short, choose the freshest, most flexible corn tortillas in the market (cracking is a sign of age). • To fit the festivities, offer *aguas frescas* (fresh fruit beverages) and Mexican beers. The only thing our scouting team couldn't agree on was the best match—Corona with achiote roast chicken? Negra Modelo with chile colorado? Pacifico with barbacoa? Better try 'em all. — *Recipes by Sara Schneider*

Taco Bar for a Party

PREP AND COOK TIME: Varies according to fillings and condiments used

NOTES: Allow 3 tacos per serving. Arrange plates and warm tortillas at the head of the line, followed by fillings grouped with the salsas, sauces, condiments, and vegetables that suit each best (see suggestions in notes for each filling; however, all are interchangeable). End with the beans; set bowls and soup spoons alongside. And provide plenty of napkins to help keep drips under control.

MAKES: 18 tacos; 6 servings

36 **corn tortillas** (6 to 8 in.)

    Fillings (choose 3 of the following)

    Salsas and **sauces** (choices follow)

    Condiments and **vegetables** (choices follow)

    La Super-Rica pinto beans (recipe on page 74)

1. Warm tortillas, without crowding, in a single layer on a medium-hot griddle or in a 10- to 12-inch frying pan over medium-high heat, turning once, until hot and flexible, 30 to 60 seconds per tortilla. As they're heated, stack in a basket lined with a thick towel (or in an insulated tortilla warmer); add more tortillas to griddle. Or divide tortillas into 3 equal stacks, seal each stack in foil, and heat in a 350° oven until hot in the center, 12 to 15 minutes; unwrap and stack in a towel-lined basket.

2. Place fillings, salsas, sauces, condiments, vegetables, and beans in separate containers and arrange on buffet (see notes); keep those that need to be warm on an electric warming tray or over a candle (stir occasionally to prevent scorching).

3. To assemble each taco, stack 2 tortillas on a plate and spoon filling down the center; add salsas, sauces, condiments, and vegetables to taste, and fold tortillas over filling to enclose. If desired, wrap with a napkin, and hold to eat.

Per 2 corn tortillas: 111 cal., 9.9% (11 cal.) from fat; 2.8 g protein; 1.2 g fat (0.2 g sat.); 23 g carbo (2.6 g fiber); 81 mg sodium; 0 mg chol.

Fillings (recipes follow): 3 cups **Café Pasqual's barbacoa**, 3 cups **chile colorado Fandango**, 3 cups **La Taqueria carnitas**, **Café Azul rajas con queso**, **Yuca's achiote roast chicken with red onions en escabeche**, **Chope's ground beef with potato**, **Lone Star fish**.

Salsas and sauces (recipes follow; use those suggested in notes with fillings chosen): **Café Pasqual's three-chili salsa**, **Café Azul tomatillo-avocado salsa**, **Lone Star cilantro-jalapeño mayonnaise**, **Lone Star pico de gallo**.

Condiments and vegetables (use those suggested in notes accompanying fillings): 2 cups total (about 10 oz.) **crumbled cotija cheese** and/or shredded **white** or yellow **cheddar cheese** or jack cheese; 1½ cups **Mexican crema**, jocoque, or sour cream; 6 cups total shredded **iceberg lettuce,** a mix of romaine lettuce and red cabbage, or green and red cabbage; 1½ cups chopped **onions** (taquerias typically use those with white skins); 1 cup minced **fresh cilantro**; 2 cups diced **firm-ripe tomatoes**; 2 **firm-ripe avocados** (1 lb. total), peeled and coarsely mashed with 2 tablespoons **lime juice**; and 3 **limes** (¾ lb. total), rinsed and each cut into 6 wedges.

the great taco hunt: winning fillings

Most of these recipes yield enough to fill six tacos; however, for the barbacoa, chile colorado, and carnitas, which involve long cooking, we've increased the yield to justify your labor. Serve the amount you need for the taco bar; the tasty leftovers each make 4 main-dish portions for another meal. They also freeze well.

Café Pasqual's Barbacoa

PREP AND COOK TIME: 4½ to 5½ hours, plus at least 3 hours to marinate

NOTES: Katharine Kagel, owner-chef of Café Pasqual's in Santa Fe, mimics the rich flavor and tender texture of pit-cooked barbacoa (traditionally goat). Garnish tacos with minced cilantro, chopped onions, and Café Pasqual's three-chili salsa (page 74). If cooking meat up to 3 days ahead, chill airtight; freeze to store longer.

MAKES: About 10 cups

- 1 pound **onions,** peeled and diced
- 1 pound **firm-ripe tomatoes,** rinsed, cored, and chopped
- 4 cloves **garlic,** peeled and minced
- 3 ounces **fresh jalapeño chilies** (about 4 total), rinsed, stemmed, seeded, and quartered lengthwise
- 2 **dried bay leaves**
- 1 cup fat-skimmed **chicken broth**
- ½ cup **lime juice**
- 2 tablespoons **white wine vinegar**
- 2 teaspoons **dried thyme**
- 2 teaspoons **ground cumin**
- 1 teaspoon **dried Mexican** or regular **oregano**
  About 1 teaspoon **salt**
- ½ teaspoon **coarse-ground pepper**
- 1 **boned, tied beef chuck** or boned pork shoulder or butt (4 to 5 lb.)

1. In a 9- by 13-inch pan, mix onions, tomatoes, garlic, jalapeños, bay leaves, chicken broth, lime juice, vinegar, thyme, cumin, oregano, 1 teaspoon salt, and pepper. Rinse meat, place in pan, and turn to coat. Cover and chill at least 3 hours or up to 1 day, turning meat occasionally. Seal pan with foil.

2. Bake in a 300° oven until meat is tender enough to pull apart easily, 4 to 5 hours. Supporting with 2 slotted spoons, transfer meat to a platter. Pour pan juices through a strainer into a 12-inch frying pan or a 5- to 6-quart pan (discard bay leaves; reserve remaining vegetable mixture); skim and discard fat. Boil juices over high heat until reduced to 1 cup, 25 to 30 minutes.

3. When meat is cool enough to handle, in about 10 minutes, discard string. Use 2 forks or your fingers to pull meat into shreds; discard fat and connective tissue. Add meat and reserved vegetable mixture to pan with juices. Stir occasionally over medium heat until steaming, about 5 minutes. Season to taste with salt.

Per ½ cup: 231 cal., 62% (144 cal.) from fat; 17 g protein; 16 g fat (6.3 g sat.); 4 g carbo (0.7 g fiber); 164 mg sodium; 64 mg chol.

Chile Colorado Fandango

PREP AND COOK TIME: 4 to 4½ hours

NOTES: This version of chile colorado, which combines beef and pork, is from Christine Keff, chef-owner of Flying Fish restaurant in Seattle. In late spring Keff will open another Seattle restaurant, Fandango, featuring the cuisines of Mexico and South America—head for the bar area for "street foods" like tacos. Garnish chile colorado tacos with minced cilantro, chopped onions, Mexican crema, and Lone Star pico de gallo (page 74). If cooking meat up to 3 days ahead, chill airtight; freeze to store longer.

MAKES: 8 to 9 cups

- 12 **dried New Mexico** or California **chilies** (about 4 oz. total)
- 1 pound **onions,** peeled and chopped
- 5 cloves **garlic,** peeled
- 3 tablespoons **salad oil**
- 2½ to 3 pounds **beef bottom round,** rinsed, dried, and cut into 1-inch chunks
- 1½ to 2 pounds **boned pork shoulder** or butt, rinsed, dried, and cut into 1-inch chunks
- 1 tablespoon **ground cumin**
  About 1 teaspoon **salt**
  About ½ teaspoon **pepper**
- 3 cups **dark beer**

1. Discard chili stems and seeds. Rinse chilies, put in a bowl, and add 2½ cups boiling water. Let stand, mixing occasionally, until chilies are limp, 8 to 10 minutes. Drain chilies, reserving ¾ cup soaking liquid; discard remainder.

2. In a blender or food processor, whirl chilies, reserved soaking liquid, onions, and garlic until smoothly puréed.

the great taco hunt: winning fillings

TACO FILLING TAKES A NEW SHAPE: Whole achiote roast chicken on a bed of red onions. Scoop onions into tortillas then pull off chicken pieces to add to the wrap.

3. Pour oil into a 5- to 6-quart pan over medium-high heat. When oil is hot, add beef and pork, 1 layer at a time; stir often until browned on all sides, 5 to 7 minutes per batch. As meat is browned, transfer with a slotted spoon to a bowl. Discard any fat in pan.

4. Return meat and accumulated juices to pan; add chili mixture, cumin, 1 teaspoon salt, ½ teaspoon pepper, and beer. Bring to a boil over high heat, stirring frequently. Reduce heat, cover, and simmer, stirring occasionally, until meat is very tender when pierced, 3 to 3½ hours. If sauce is thinner than you like, uncover and simmer until reduced to desired consistency, 20 to 30 minutes longer. Season to taste with salt and pepper.

Per ½ cup: 253 cal., 60% (153 cal.) from fat; 18 g protein; 17 g fat (5.6 g sat.); 6.5 g carbo (1.7 g fiber); 173 mg sodium; 64 mg chol.

Café Azul Rajas con Queso

PREP AND COOK TIME: About 45 minutes

NOTES: This tangle of sautéed onions and roasted chilies—*rajas*—has the simple, direct flavors often found in Mexico's tacos. It's from Claire Archibald, chef and co-owner with her sister, Shawna, of Portland's Café Azul. Tuck the cheese into the warm tortillas and top with the rajas.

MAKES: Enough for 6 tacos

1¼ pounds **fresh poblano chilies** (also called pasillas)

1¼ pounds **onions**

1 tablespoon **salad oil**

About 1 teaspoon **salt**

¼ pound **queso fresco** or jack cheese

1. Rinse and dry chilies. Arrange in a

single layer in a 10- by 15-inch pan. Broil 4 to 5 inches from heat, turning to char chilies on all sides, about 10 minutes total. Let stand until cool to touch, 8 to 10 minutes. Pull off and discard chili skins, stems, and seeds. Cut chilies lengthwise into thin strips.

2. Meanwhile, peel onions and cut lengthwise into slivers. In a 12-inch frying pan or a 5- to 6-quart pan over medium-high heat, frequently stir onions, oil, and 1 teaspoon salt until onions are lightly browned, 7 to 8 minutes. Add chilies and stir occasionally to blend flavors, about 5 minutes. Season to taste with salt.

3. Thinly slice cheese. See notes for assembly.

Per serving: 140 cal., 46% (65 cal.) from fat; 5.7 g protein; 7.2 g fat (3.6 g sat.); 14 g carbo (2.4 g fiber); 529 mg sodium; 13 mg chol.

Yuca's Achiote Roast Chicken with Red Onions en Escabeche

PREP AND COOK TIME: About 1½ hours

NOTES: Socorro Herrera and her daughter Dora Herrera, owners of Yuca's in Los Angeles, sometimes serve this traditional Yucatecan dish at the Los Feliz district's yearly street fair in June. Herrera poaches the chicken to make a flavorful broth that she pours over the onions *en escabeche* (pickled), then roasts the bird. We take a simpler tack, serving the roast chicken—colored deep red by the ground annato seeds in the achiote paste—on a bed of the sautéed onions. To eat, scoop the onions into the warm tortillas, then tear chicken into shreds and lay meat on the onions. Top with Mexican crema.

Have your butcher cut the chicken in half. If you can't find achiote paste, add as a substitute 3 more cloves garlic, 1 more tablespoon salad oil, 2 more tablespoons vinegar, 3 tablespoons paprika, 1½ teaspoons dried Mexican or regular oregano, and ½ teaspoon ground cumin in step 1; whirl until smooth.

MAKES: Enough for 6 tacos

4 cloves **garlic,** peeled

3 tablespoons **salad oil**

¾ cup **cider vinegar**

4 ounces (½ cup) **salted red achiote paste**

1 **chicken** (3 to 3½ lb.), cut in half lengthwise through breast and back (see notes)

1¾ pounds **red onions**

1 tablespoon chopped **fresh oregano** leaves

1 tablespoon chopped **fresh mint** leaves

Salt and **pepper**

1. In a blender or a food processor, whirl 2 cloves garlic, 2 tablespoons salad oil, 6 tablespoons vinegar, and achiote paste until smoothly puréed.

2. Rinse chicken, pat dry, and pull off and discard any lumps of fat. Rub both halves on all sides with half the achiote mixture. Set chicken pieces, skin up and side by side, in a 9- by 13-inch pan.

3. Bake in a 375° oven for 30 minutes. Remove from oven and quickly spread skin sides equally with remaining achiote mixture. Continue baking, occasionally basting with pan juices, until skin is richly browned (under paste), 30 to 45 minutes longer.

4. Meanwhile, peel and thinly slice onions; mince remaining 2 cloves garlic. In a 12-inch frying pan or a 5- to 6-quart pan over medium-high heat, combine onions, garlic, and remaining 1 tablespoon salad oil; stir often until vegetables are limp, 8 to 10 minutes. Add remaining 6 tablespoons vinegar and stir occasionally until liquid is evaporated and onions are lightly browned, 10 to 15 minutes longer. Add oregano, mint, and salt and pepper to taste. Spread onion mixture on a platter and keep warm.

5. Set chicken halves on onion mixture. Tear or cut meat from bones.

Per serving: 360 cal., 53% (189 cal.) from fat; 30 g protein; 21 g fat (4.7 g sat.); 15 g carbo (2.2 g fiber); 475 mg sodium; 88 mg chol.

Chope's Ground Beef with Potato

PREP AND COOK TIME: About 40 minutes

NOTES: Chope's Bar and Cafe in La Mesa, New Mexico, serves this ground beef filling with shredded iceberg lettuce, diced tomatoes, and shredded white cheddar cheese.

MAKES: Enough for 6 tacos

1 pound **ground beef chuck**

1½ teaspoons **ground cumin**

¾ teaspoon fresh-ground **pepper**

1 **russet potato** (about ½ lb.)

About 1 teaspoon **salt**

1. In a 10- to 12-inch frying pan over medium-high heat, stir ground beef, cumin, and pepper until beef is crumbled and browned, 10 to 12 minutes.

2. Meanwhile, peel potato. Coarsely shred, immersing shreds in cool water as you go; drain well.

3. Add potato to beef and stir occasionally until potato is tender to bite and beef is very well browned, 10 to 12 minutes longer. Add salt to taste.

Per serving: 230 cal., 63% (144 cal.) from fat; 14 g protein; 16 g fat (6.3 g sat.); 6.5 g carbo (0.7 g fiber); 444 mg sodium; 57 mg chol.

Lone Star Fish

PREP AND COOK TIME: About 20 minutes, plus at least 1 hour to marinate

NOTES: Susan Harries, owner of Lone Star Taqueria in Salt Lake City, makes waves with these tacos (photo on page 62). Manager and chef Manuel Valdez also uses ahi or blue marlin on occasion; he marinates the fish overnight covered with oil, but less time and less oil provide ample flavor. Top cooked fish with shredded cabbage, Lone Star pico de gallo and Lone Star cilantro-jalapeño mayonnaise (recipes on page 74), and a squeeze of lime.

MAKES: Enough for 6 tacos

6 tablespoons **ground dried New Mexico** or California **chilies**

3 tablespoons **salad oil**

½ teaspoon **pepper**

About ½ teaspoon **salt**

½ teaspoon **garlic powder**

½ teaspoon **cayenne**

½ teaspoon **ground cumin**

2 **whole cloves**

1 **dried bay leaf,** broken into pieces

1 pound **boned, skinned firm-flesh fish** such as halibut, mahimahi, or rock fish (see notes)

1. In a large bowl, mix ground dried chilies, oil, pepper, ½ teaspoon salt, garlic powder, cayenne, cumin, cloves, and bay leaf.

2. Rinse fish and pat dry. Add to bowl and turn to coat with marinade; cover and chill at least 1 hour or up to 1 day, mixing several times.

3. Lift fish from marinade and arrange pieces in a single layer in a 9- by 13-inch pan. Discard marinade.

4. Broil fish 4 to 5 inches from heat until opaque but still moist-looking in center of thickest part (cut to test), about 5 minutes for ½-inch-thick pieces. With a slotted spatula, transfer fish to towels to blot oil, then set on a platter. Cut fish along the grain into ½-inch slices, and season to taste with salt.

Per serving: 163 cal., 53% (86 cal.) from fat; 16 g protein; 9.5 g fat (1.3 g sat.); 3.6 g carbo (1.5 g fiber); 236 mg sodium; 24 mg chol.

La Taqueria Carnitas
(photo on page 60)

PREP AND COOK TIME: About 4½ hours

NOTES: At La Taqueria in San Francisco, owner Miguel Jara cooks pork in cauldrons of bubbling lard until tender, then roasts it to make crowd-pleasing carnitas. At home, braise the pork, then roast until tender-crisp. For best results, select meat with the most fat marbling; fat is rendered during roasting, making the carnitas moist and crisp. Garnish tacos with cotija cheese, Café Azul tomatillo-avocado salsa (page 74), and diced tomatoes. If cooking meat up to 3 days ahead, chill airtight; freeze to store longer.

MAKES: 8 to 9 cups

1 **boned, tied pork shoulder** or butt (4 to 5 lb.)

2 **onions** (1 lb. total), peeled and quartered

4 stalks **celery** (including leaves), rinsed and cut into chunks

4 cloves **garlic,** peeled

2 **dried bay leaves**

2 teaspoons **dried thyme**

About 1 teaspoon **salt**

½ cup **milk**

1. Rinse pork and put in a 6- to 8-quart pan. Add onions, celery, garlic, bay leaves, thyme, 1 teaspoon salt, and enough water to cover meat—2½ to 3½ quarts.

2. Bring to a boil over high heat; cover, reduce heat, and simmer until meat is very tender when pierced, 2 to 2½ hours. With slotted spoons, transfer pork to a 9- by 13-inch pan; reserve cooking juices. Discard string, and use 2 forks to pull meat into large chunks. Pour milk over meat.

3. Bake pork in a 325° oven until drippings are browned, about 1 hour, stirring and scraping pan occasionally.

4. Meanwhile, pour reserved juices through a strainer into a bowl; discard residue. Skim and discard fat. Return juices to pan. Boil over high heat until reduced to 2 cups, about 45 minutes.

5. When pork drippings are browned, add 1 cup of the reduced juices; scrape drippings free and stir meat, breaking into smaller pieces. Bake until juices have evaporated and drippings are browned, about 15 minutes, stirring occasionally. Repeat step, using remaining juices, and cook until meat edges are crisp and browned, 15 to 20 minutes longer. Season to taste with salt.

Per ½ cup: 255 cal., 67% (171 cal.) from fat; 17 g protein; 19 g fat (6.9 g sat.); 3 g carbo (0.5 g fiber); 191 mg sodium; 71 mg chol.

the great taco hunt: superlative salsas and beans

FROM FRONT: Onions, tomatillo-avocado salsa, pico de gallo, and Mexican crema.

Café Pasqual's Three-Chili Salsa

PREP AND COOK TIME: 40 to 50 minutes

NOTES: This dark red salsa from Café Pasqual's has significant heat.

MAKES: About 1½ cups

- 3 dried guajillo chilies (about 1 oz. total)
- 3 dried chiles de arbol (¹⁄₁₀ to ¹⁄₅ oz. total)
- ⅓ pound tomatillos, husked, rinsed, and halved
- 1 firm-ripe tomato (½ lb.), rinsed, cored, and quartered
- 1 fresh jalapeño chili (1 oz.), rinsed and stemmed
- 2 tablespoons chopped onion
- 2 cloves garlic, peeled
   About ¾ teaspoon salt
- ¼ teaspoon ground cumin
- ¼ teaspoon ground cloves
- ¼ teaspoon dried Mexican or regular oregano

1. Trim and discard stems from guajillos and chiles de arbol; discard seeds from guajillos. Rinse chilies.

2. In a 2- to 3-quart pan, combine dried chilies, tomatillos, tomato, jalapeño, onion, garlic, ¾ teaspoon salt, and 1 cup water. Cover and bring to a boil over high heat; stir frequently until dried chilies are limp, 10 to 15 minutes. Let cool about 10 minutes.

3. Meanwhile, in an 8- to 10-inch frying pan over low heat, stir cumin, cloves, and oregano until fragrant, about 4 minutes.

4. Combine chili mixture and spices in a blender. Whirl until coarsely puréed. Add salt to taste. Pour into a bowl.

Per tablespoon: 7.3 cal., 25% (1.8 cal.) from fat; 0.3 g protein; 0.2 g fat (0 g sat.); 1.4 g carbo (0.4 g fiber); 74 mg sodium; 0 mg chol.

Café Azul Tomatillo-Avocado Salsa

PREP TIME: About 30 minutes

NOTES: According to chef Claire Archibald, Portlanders travel across town for this sprightly green salsa.

MAKES: About 2½ cups

- ⅓ pound tomatillos, husked, rinsed, and quartered
- ¼ pound fresh jalapeño chilies, rinsed, stemmed, seeded, and halved
- 2 cloves garlic, peeled
- ½ cup lightly packed fresh cilantro
- 1 tablespoon olive oil
- 1 firm-ripe avocado (about ½ lb.), peeled and diced
- ½ cup minced onion
- 1½ to 2 tablespoons lime juice
   Salt

1. In a blender or food processor, whirl tomatillos, chilies, garlic, and cilantro until coarsely puréed. Pour into a bowl.

2. Stir in olive oil, avocado, and onion. Add lime juice and salt to taste.

Per tablespoon: 13 cal., 69% (9 cal.) from fat; 0.2 g protein; 1 g fat (0.1 g sat.); 0.9 g carbo (0.2 g fiber); 0.8 mg sodium; 0 mg chol.

Lone Star Cilantro-Jalapeño Mayonnaise

PREP TIME: About 20 minutes

NOTES: Chef Manuel Valdez of Lone Star makes his mayonnaise from scratch; for food safety at home, this sauce starts with prepared mayonnaise.

MAKES: About 2¼ cups

In a blender or food processor, combine 1¾ cups mayonnaise, 2 tablespoons water, 2 tablespoons distilled white vinegar, 1 rinsed and stemmed fresh jalapeño chili (remove seeds for less heat), 1 peeled garlic clove, ½ cup lightly packed fresh cilantro, and ¼ teaspoon pepper. Whirl until smooth. Add salt to taste.

Per tablespoon: 77 cal., 99% (76 cal.) from fat; 0.1 g protein; 8.4 g fat (1.3 g sat.); 0.4 g carbo (0 g fiber); 61 mg sodium; 6.3 mg chol.

Lone Star Pico de Gallo

PREP TIME: About 20 minutes

MAKES: About 2 cups

In a bowl, mix 2 cups diced tomatoes, ½ cup finely diced onion, 2 tablespoons minced jalapeño chilies, ¼ cup minced fresh cilantro, 2 tablespoons lime juice, and ½ teaspoon garlic powder. Add salt to taste.

Per tablespoon: 3.8 cal., 0% (0 cal.) from fat; 0.1 g protein; 0 g fat ; 0.9 g carbo (0.2 g fiber); 1.3 mg sodium; 0 mg chol.

La Super-Rica Pinto Beans

PREP AND COOK TIME: About 2 hours

NOTES: At Santa Barbara's La Super-Rica, these simple beans have maintained their popularity for almost 20 years, according to owner Isidoro Gonzales. You'll need 6 cups for the party. If making up to 3 days ahead, chill airtight; freeze to store longer.

MAKES: About 10 cups; 8 to 10 servings

- 1 pound dried pinto beans
   About 1 teaspoon salt
- 3 slices bacon (about 2½ oz. total), chopped
- ½ pound chorizo or linguisa (Portuguese) sausage
- 1 poblano chili (also called pasilla; about 3½ oz.), rinsed, stemmed, seeded, and finely chopped

1. Sort beans and discard any debris. Rinse beans and put in a 5- to 6-quart pan. Add 2½ quarts water. Cover and bring to a boil over high heat; reduce heat and simmer, stirring occasionally, until beans are tender to bite, 1¼ to 1½ hours. Add 1 teaspoon salt.

2. Meanwhile, in an 8- to 10-inch frying pan over medium-high heat, stir bacon frequently until browned, about 3 minutes. With a slotted spoon, transfer bacon to a bowl.

3. Remove and discard chorizo casings. Crumble sausage into frying pan. Stir frequently until browned, 4 to 5 minutes. Add chili and stir until limp, 3 to 4 minutes.

4. To sausage mixture, add cooked bacon and ½ cup bean cooking liquid; stir occasionally for 5 minutes. Stir sausage-bacon mixture into beans and simmer to blend flavors, about 5 minutes. Add salt to taste.

Per serving: 300 cal., 39% (117 cal.) from fat; 16 g protein; 13 g fat (4.9 g sat.); 30 g carbo (5.6 g fiber); 567 mg sodium; 25 mg chol. ◆

The Quick Cook

MICHAEL LAMOTTE

SPICE-COATED SALMON, quickly seared, nestles on tender-crisp braised bok choy.

Braisingly fresh

■ Like many cooks, Sam Gugino favors meals that come together quickly. But as a food editor and writer, he's not willing to sacrifice flavor to speed. Armed with the conviction that the two goals aren't diametrically opposed, he wrote *Cooking to Beat the Clock: Delicious, Inspired Meals in 15 Minutes* (Chronicle Books, San Francisco, 1999; $16.95; 800/722-6657 or www. chroniclebooks.com).

Gugino lets big flavors speak in his Asian-spiced salmon with braised bok choy. We liked the results so much that we've added variations on pan-browned, spice-rubbed fish to go with briefly braised greens. Gugino uses two frying pans; the greens get started in one while the fish cooks in the other. If you cook the greens first, then keep them warm while you brown the fish in the same pan, you add about 10 minutes to the cooking process but cut back on cleanup.

Asian-spiced Salmon with Braised Bok Choy

PREP AND COOK TIME: About 15 minutes
NOTES: To make a blend similar to five spice, use equal parts ground cinnamon, ground cloves, ground ginger, and finely crushed anise seed.

MAKES: 4 servings

1½	pounds **bok choy**
2	teaspoons minced **garlic**
4	teaspoons **salad oil**
¾	cup fat-skimmed **chicken broth**
1½	pounds **boned salmon fillet with skin** (maximum 1 in. thick)
2	tablespoons **Chinese five spice** (see notes)
	Salt and **pepper**

1. Rinse bok choy; trim off and discard tough stem ends and any bruised parts. Cut the leafy tops crosswise into 2-inch strips; cut the stems crosswise into 1-inch pieces.

2. In a 10- to 12-inch frying pan over high heat, stir garlic in 2 teaspoons oil until sizzling, 1 to 2 minutes. Add bok choy and broth, cover, and cook until thickest stems are just tender when pierced, 4 to 5 minutes; keep warm.

3. Meanwhile, rinse salmon, pat dry, and cut into 4 equal pieces. Rub fish evenly with five spice. Pour remaining 2 teaspoons oil into a 10- to 12-inch frying pan over high heat. When oil is hot, in about 1 minute, lay salmon, skin down, in pan; cook 3 minutes. With a wide spatula, turn fish and cook until it is opaque but still moist-looking in center of thickest part (cut to test), about 3 minutes more.

4. Place salmon in wide bowls and spoon bok choy and broth equally around fish. Season to taste with salt and pepper.

Per serving: 394 cal., 55% (216 cal.) from fat; 38 g protein; 24 g fat (4.3 g sat.); 6.7 g carbo (2.3 g fiber); 215 mg sodium; 100 mg chol.

Sesame-Ginger Salmon with Braised Bok Choy

PREP AND COOK TIME: About 15 minutes

MAKES: 4 servings

Follow directions for **Asian-spiced salmon with braised bok choy** (preceding), but omit Chinese five spice and use 4 teaspoons **sesame seed** mixed with 1½ teaspoons **ground ginger** to coat fish.

Per serving: 400 cal., 56% (225 cal.) from fat; 38 g protein; 25 g fat (4.5 g sat.); 5 g carbo (1.9 g fiber); 213 mg sodium; 100 mg chol.

Salt and Pepper Bass with Braised Spinach

PREP AND COOK TIME: About 15 minutes

MAKES: 4 servings

Follow directions for **Asian-spiced salmon with braised bok choy** (at left), but instead of bok choy use 2 packages (10 oz. each) **washed spinach leaves** (add in batches) and decrease chicken broth to ¼ cup. Instead of the salmon, use 1½ pounds **boned, skinned bass** (white seabass or grouper bass), cut into 4 equal portions. Instead of Chinese five spice, use 1½ teaspoons **kosher salt** mixed with 2 teaspoons **pepper**. Rub salt mixture on fish.

Per serving: 245 cal., 31% (77 cal.) from fat; 36 g protein; 8.5 g fat (1.5 g sat.); 6.5 g carbo (4.1 g fiber); 1,337 mg sodium; 70 mg chol. ◆

Tropical treats

Take your palate to paradise with the Islands' sweetest flavors

BY ANDREW BAKER • PHOTOGRAPHS BY JAMES CARRIER

■ COCONUTS REALLY DO FALL FROM THE TREES IN HAWAII. AND PAPAYAS GROW ALONG THE roadside. I always thought these were mythical descriptions of a Hawaiian utopia that existed only in travel brochures. But a recent trip to the former Sandwich Islands brought their culinary legacy to life in the form of indigenous tropical ingredients.

Hawaii's luscious produce and products—bright mangoes, juicy pineapples, dark chocolate—are ripe for decadent desserts. Even mainland chefs have fallen under their sway. Here's a collection of recipes from masters on both sides of the water that will bring a piece of paradise to your next dinner party, no matter how far from a coconut tree you live.

Pineapple Cheesecake with Haupia Sauce

PREP AND COOK TIME: About 1¼ hours, plus about 3½ hours to chill

NOTES: Mark Okumura, executive pastry chef at Alan Wong's Hawaii Regional Cuisine Marketplace in Honolulu, as well as the Pineapple Room, gives cheesecake a triple tropical twist with pineapple, coconut (*haupia*), and macadamia nuts.

MAKES: 10 to 12 servings

1	**peeled, cored pineapple** (about 1 lb.)
½	cup firmly packed **brown sugar**
2	tablespoons **rum**
3	packages (8 oz. each) **cream cheese**
½	cup **sour cream**
⅔	cup **granulated sugar**
3	**large eggs**
	Macadamia crust (recipe follows)
½	cup **sweetened shredded dried coconut**
	Haupia sauce (recipe follows)

1. Cut pineapple in half crosswise. Cut 1 portion into 4 equal slices. Finely chop remaining portion.

2. In a 10- to 12-inch frying pan over high heat, stir brown sugar and rum until sugar is dissolved. Add pineapple slices; cook, turning once, until liquid is boiling rapidly and fruit is slightly darker, about 4 minutes. With a slotted spoon, transfer glazed pineapple slices to a rimmed plate. Cover and chill. Add chopped pineapple to frying pan; stir often until fruit is slightly darker, about 3 minutes. Remove from heat.

3. In a large bowl with a mixer on medium speed, beat cream cheese, sour cream, granulated sugar, and eggs until blended. Stir in chopped pineapple–brown sugar mixture. Pour cream cheese filling into cool macadamia crust.

4. Bake in a 350° oven until center barely jiggles when cake is gently shaken, 40 to 50 minutes. Let cake cool to room temperature, about 1½ hours, then cover and chill until cold, at least 2 hours or up to 1 day.

5. Meanwhile, rinse frying pan, wipe dry, add coconut, and stir over medium-high heat until golden, 4 to 6 minutes. Pour into a small bowl; when cool, cover airtight.

6. Arrange glazed pineapple slices on top of the cheesecake; sprinkle with coconut. Cut cheesecake into wedges, transfer to plates, and spoon about 2 tablespoons haupia sauce around each portion.

Per serving: 577 cal., 62% (360 cal.) from fat; 8.5 g protein; 40 g fat (22 g sat.); 48 g carbo (0.9 g fiber); 247 mg sodium; 130 mg chol.

Haupia sauce. In a 1- to 1½-quart pan, combine 1 cup **canned coconut milk,** ½ cup **water,** ¼ cup **sugar,** and 1 tablespoon **cornstarch.** Stir over high heat until boiling. Let cool, then cover and chill until cold, at least 1½ hours or up to 1 day. Stir before serving. Makes 1½ cups.

Per tablespoon: 28 cal., 64% (18 cal.) from fat; 0.2 g protein; 2 g fat (1.8 g sat.); 2.6 g carbo (0 g fiber); 1.3 mg sodium; 0 mg chol.

Macadamia Crust

PREP AND COOK TIME: About 25 minutes, plus 45 minutes to cool

NOTES: To remove salt from salted macadamias, pour nuts onto a towel; enclose and rub, then lift nuts from

towel. If making crust up to 1 day ahead, wrap airtight and store at room temperature.

MAKES: 1 crust; 10 to 12 servings

- 1 cup **unsalted roasted macadamias** (see notes)
- ¾ cup **all-purpose flour**
- 6 tablespoons firmly packed **brown sugar**
- ¼ cup (⅛ lb.) **butter** or margarine, cut into chunks

1. In a food processor, whirl macadamias until finely chopped. Pour into a bowl. In food processor, whirl flour, sugar, and butter until fine crumbs form. Add macadamias and whirl just until dough sticks together. (Or mince nuts with a sharp knife and put in a bowl with flour, sugar, and butter; rub with your fingers until mixture sticks together, then pat into a ball.)

2. Press mixture evenly over bottom and about 1¼ inches up sides of a 9-inch cheesecake pan with a removable rim.

3. Bake crust in a 350° oven until golden brown, 12 to 18 minutes. Set on a rack and cool at least 30 minutes.

Per serving: 168 cal., 64% (108 cal.) from fat; 1.8 g protein; 12 g fat (3.7 g sat.); 14 g carbo (0.2 g fiber); 44 mg sodium; 11 mg chol.

Chocolate Macadamia Torte with Vanilla Port Sauce

PREP AND COOK TIME: About 1 hour, plus at least 4 hours to chill

NOTES: Charlie Paladin/Wayne, executive chef at Justin Vineyards & Winery in Paso Robles, California, uses Hawaiian-grown and -manufactured chocolate in this torte, and the winery's Obtuse port-style wine for the sauce.

MAKES: 10 to 12 servings

- ¾ pound **semisweet chocolate,** chopped
- 1½ teaspoons **ground cinnamon**
- 1½ cups **whipping cream**
- 3 **large egg** yolks

  Macadamia crust (recipe precedes)

  Vanilla port sauce (recipe follows)

1. In the top of a double boiler, combine chocolate, cinnamon, and ¾ cup cream. Stir over simmering water just until chocolate is melted and smooth. Add egg yolks and whisk over simmering water until mixture reaches 140°. Adjust heat to keep mixture between 140° and 150°, and continue to whisk for 3 minutes. Nest pan in ice water and stir often until mixture is cool, about 15 minutes.

2. In a deep bowl with a mixer at high speed, whip remaining cream until it holds distinct peaks. Gently fold whipped cream into chocolate mixture, then pour into cool macadamia crust. Cover airtight (don't let cover touch filling) and chill at least 4 hours or up to 2 days.

3. Remove cheesecake pan rim, cut torte into wedges, and accompany with vanilla port sauce to taste.

Per serving without sauce: 407 cal., 69% (279 cal.) from fat; 4.3 g protein; 31 g fat (15 g sat.); 33 g carbo (1.9 g fiber); 59 mg sodium; 97 mg chol.

Vanilla Port Sauce

PREP AND COOK TIME: About 15 minutes, plus 15 minutes to cool

NOTES: If making up to 2 days ahead, cover and chill; sauce thickens when it's cool.

MAKES: 1 cup

- 1½ cups **port**
- 1 cup **sugar**
- 1 **vanilla bean** (about 7 in.)

1. In a 1½- to 2-quart pan, combine port and sugar. With a small, sharp knife, slit vanilla bean open lengthwise. Scrape seeds from pod; add seeds and pod to the port mixture.

2. Boil over high heat, stirring occasionally, until reduced to 1 cup, 10 to 15 minutes. Let sauce cool at least 15 minutes; discard vanilla pod. Serve warm, cool, or chilled.

Per tablespoon: 59 cal., 0% (0 cal.) from fat; 0 g protein; 0 g fat; 15 g carbo (0 g fiber); 2.1 mg sodium; 0 mg chol.

MANGO INFUSES each creamy layer of tiramisu in a pool of raspberry sauce.

Mango Tiramisu with Raspberry Sauce

PREP AND COOK TIME: About 1½ hours, plus at least 2 hours to chill

NOTES: This creative spin on tiramisu is inspired by a dessert served at Surt's Restaurant in Volcano Village on the Big Island.

MAKES: 9 servings

- 2 **firm-ripe mangoes** (about 1¾ lb. total)
- ½ cup **canned coconut milk**
- 3 **large egg** yolks
- ⅓ cup **granulated sugar**
- 2 tablespoons **brandy**
- 1 cup (½ lb.) **mascarpone cheese**
- 1½ cups **whipping cream**
- ½ cup **powdered sugar**
- 42 **double ladyfingers** (about 2 packages; 3 oz. each), split
- ½ cup **sweetened shredded dried coconut**

   Raspberry sauce (recipe follows)

1. Peel mangoes and cut from pit lengthwise into ¼-inch slices. Measure 1 cup of the smallest pieces; cover and chill remaining large slices. In a blender or food processor, whirl the 1 cup mangoes and the coconut milk to a smooth purée; pour into a bowl.

2. In the top of a double boiler, combine egg yolks, granulated sugar, and brandy. Whisk over simmering water until mixture reaches 140°. Adjust heat to keep mixture between 140° and 150°, and continue to whisk for 3 minutes. Remove from heat and add the mascarpone cheese; stir until mixture is well blended.

3. In a deep bowl with a mixer on high speed, whip cream and powdered sugar until cream holds distinct peaks. Add the mascarpone mixture and fold gently to blend.

4. Separate ladyfinger pieces. With a fork, dip half the pieces, 1 at a time, in mango purée to coat; lift out, drain briefly, and arrange flat side down in a single layer in a 9-inch square pan. Cover ladyfingers in pan with half the mascarpone mixture, spreading it level. Repeat to dip remaining ladyfinger pieces in mango purée and arrange in a single layer over mascarpone mixture in pan. Spread remaining mascarpone mixture smoothly over top layer of ladyfingers. Cover tiramisu airtight and chill at least 2 hours or up to 1 day.

5. In an 8- to 10-inch frying pan over medium-high heat, stir coconut until golden, 4 to 6 minutes; pour into a small bowl. When cool, cover airtight.

6. To serve, cut tiramisu into 9 equal squares. Use a wide spatula to lift out portions and set on plates. Arrange reserved mango slices equally on portions and sprinkle equally with toasted coconut; spoon raspberry sauce equally around desserts.

Per serving: 488 cal., 57% (279 cal.) from fat; 6.3 g protein; 31 g fat (20 g sat.); 47 g carbo (0.9 g fiber); 70 mg sodium; 205 mg chol.

Raspberry sauce. Rub 1½ cups thawed **frozen raspberries** through a fine strainer into a bowl; discard seeds. Add 3 tablespoons **sugar** and stir to blend. Makes about 1 cup.

Per tablespoon: 15 cal., 6% (0.9 cal.) from fat; 0.1 g protein; 0.1 g fat (0 g sat.); 3.9 g carbo (0 g fiber); 0 mg sodium; 0 mg chol.

Tropical Fruit Soup

PREP AND COOK TIME: About 1¼ hours, plus 2 hours to chill

NOTES: Cookbook author David Lebovitz (_Room for Dessert,_ HarperCollins, 1999; $30; 800/242-7737) shows off tropical fruits in this soup. Use a combination of 3 or more kinds: peeled and diced pineapple, mango, papaya, kiwi, or banana; fresh or canned litchis; sliced kumquats or strawberries; passion fruit pulp; orange segments.

MAKES: 4 servings

- 1 **cinnamon stick** (2 in.)
- 1 **star anise**
- 8 **whole cloves**
- 8 **black peppercorns**

2 stalks (about 2 oz.) **fresh lemon grass**

1 cup **sugar**

1½ tablespoons grated **orange** peel

4 thin, quarter-size slices peeled **fresh ginger**

1 piece **vanilla bean** (2 in.)

1 tablespoon **rum**

1 **large egg** white

½ cup **unsweetened shredded dried coconut**

About 2 cups **fruit** (see notes)

1 pint **coconut** or tropical fruit **sorbet**

Mint sprigs, rinsed

1. Put cinnamon, star anise, cloves, and peppercorns in a heavy plastic food bag; coarsely crush with a rolling pin.

2. Trim and discard root ends and coarse outer leaves from lemon grass. Chop tender white part of stalks.

3. In a 1- to 1½-quart pan over high heat, combine 2 cups water, crushed spices, lemon grass, ⅔ cup sugar, orange peel, and ginger. Slit vanilla bean lengthwise; scrape seeds into pan and add pod. Bring to a boil, remove from heat, cover, and let stand at least 1 hour.

4. Pour spice syrup through a fine strainer into a bowl; discard residue. Add rum, cover, and chill until cold, at least 2 hours or up to 2 days.

5. Meanwhile, in a bowl with a mixer on high speed, whip egg white until it holds soft peaks. Gradually add remaining ⅓ cup sugar, and continue to beat until white holds distinct peaks. Fold in coconut.

6. Line a 12- by 15-inch baking sheet with cooking paper or parchment. With a narrow spatula, spread egg white mixture in a 10- by 13-inch rectangle.

7. Bake in a 350° oven until meringue is deep golden brown, about 10 minutes. Let cool on sheet to room temperature. Gently pull off paper, then break meringue into 4 or 8 equal pieces.

8. Spoon fruit equally into wide soup bowls and fill equally with spice syrup. Scoop sorbet into balls and add equally to bowls; insert meringue pieces into sorbet, and garnish with mint sprigs.

Per serving: 438 cal., 15% (66 cal.) from fat; 3 g protein; 7.3 g fat (5.7 g sat.); 93 g carbo (1.4 g fiber); 64 mg sodium; 4.8 mg chol.

Kona Coffee–Chocolate Bread Pudding

PREP AND COOK TIME: 1 to 1¼ hours

NOTES: Lisa Siu, pastry chef for both Kakaako Kitchen and 3660 on the Rise in Honolulu, created this pudding. To brew the coffee, put 3 tablespoons finely ground coffee beans in a paper-lined coffee filter set over a pitcher. Pour 1⅓ cups hot (about 190°) water through ground coffee. Measure; if necessary, add water to make 1 cup.

MAKES: 8 to 10 servings

1 loaf (1 lb.) **French bread**

½ cup (¼ lb.) **butter** or margarine, cut into chunks

¾ cup **sugar**

4 **large eggs**

2 cups **whipping cream**

1 cup cold **Kona** or regular **coffee** (see notes)

2 tablespoons **dried instant espresso coffee**

Crème anglaise (recipe follows)

1 ounce **semisweet chocolate**, finely chopped

1. Cut bread crosswise into ¾-inch slices. Overlap slices in a single layer in a shallow 3-quart casserole (about 9 by 13 in.).

2. In a large bowl with a mixer on high speed, beat butter and sugar until well blended. Add eggs and beat until blended. Add whipping cream, coffee, and instant espresso; stir until mixed. Pour egg mixture over bread. Let stand at least 15 minutes or cover and chill up to 1 day.

3. Bake, covered, in a 350° oven until filling no longer jiggles when casserole is gently shaken, about 30 minutes (about 45 minutes if chilled). Pour crème anglaise over pudding and sprinkle with chocolate.

4. Serve warm. Spoon portions, including sauce, into bowls.

Per serving: 507 cal., 55% (279 cal.) from fat; 9.8 g protein; 31 g fat (18 g sat.); 48 g carbo (1.4 g fiber); 433 mg sodium; 232 mg chol.

Crème anglaise. In a 1½- to 2-quart pan, combine 3 tablespoons **sugar**, 2 teaspoons **cornstarch**, 1½ cups **milk**, 3 **large egg** yolks, and 1½ teaspoons **vanilla**. Whisk over high heat until mixture is boiling, 3 to 4 minutes. At once, nest pan in ice water and stir often until mixture is cool, about 5 minutes. Makes about 2 cups.

Per tablespoon: 18 cal., 45% (8.1 cal.) from fat; 0.6 g protein; 0.9 g fat (0.4 g sat.); 1.9 g carbo (0 g fiber); 6.3 mg sodium; 22 mg chol. ◆

COLORFUL SCOOPS of sorbet and coconut meringue wafers top tropical fruit soup.

foodguide

BY JERRY ANNE DI VECCHIO

PHOTOGRAPHS BY JAMES CARRIER

Classic lobster tales

Hold the bib when you serve this elegant shellfish dish

■ There's no better way to enjoy lobster's pure flavor than to have it boiled and shelled. It's true, though, that the bib your server ties around your neck when you order boiled lobster has a purpose: Eating the creature is a messy operation.

When dinner isn't suited to rolled-up sleeves, I go for Newburg, a shellfish classic. The delicate sauce enhances, without over-whelming, the sweet freshness that makes lobster so appealing. You cook and shell the animals in private, hours ahead—and save the brilliant red hulls for a dramatic presenta-tion. You can even start the sauce in advance. My only break with tradition is to whip the cream; I add part to the sauce and reserve a cool dollop to spoon on last. The pale cloud melts smoothly into every bite.

Lobster Newburg

PREP AND COOK TIME: About 30 minutes

MAKES: 2 servings

½ pound **mushrooms**

  About ¼ cup **dry sherry** or dry madeira

¼ cup finely chopped **shallots**

1 tablespoon **lemon juice**

  About 2 tablespoons **butter** or margarine

¼ cup **whipping cream**

  Salt and **pepper**

½ cup fat-skimmed **chicken broth**

1½ teaspoons **cornstarch**

2 slices **white bread** (about 2 oz. total), toasted and crusts trimmed

2 cooked and shelled **Maine lobsters** (1½ lb. each) or 2 spiny (rock) lobster tails (about 6 oz. each); directions follow

  About 1 cup **watercress sprigs,** rinsed and crisped

1. Rinse and drain mush-rooms; trim and discard dis-colored stem ends. Thinly slice mushrooms and put in a 10- to 12-inch frying pan. Add ¼ cup sherry, shallots, lemon juice, and 2 table-spoons butter. Stir often over high heat until juices evapo-rate, about 10 minutes.

2. Meanwhile, in a small, deep bowl, whip cream until it holds soft peaks. Flavor to taste with salt, pepper, and about 1 tablespoon sherry. If making up to 2 hours ahead, cover and chill.

3. In another small bowl,

mix broth and cornstarch. Add to mushroom mixture and stir until boiling, about 1 minute; if making up to 2 hours ahead, remove from heat and let stand.

4. Butter toast, if desired, and set on dinner plates; lay lobster tail shells, cupped sides up, beside toast (if using Maine lobster, also garnish plates with body shells). Arrange a cluster of watercress sprigs on each plate.

5. Cut lobster tail meat into ½-inch chunks. Add tail and leg meat and about half the flavored whipped cream to mushroom mixture; stir over medium-high heat until boiling, 2 to 3 minutes (3 to 4 minutes if chilled). Quickly spoon mixture into tail shells and onto toast. Spoon remaining whipped cream onto lobster mixture; if available, lay claw meat on cream.

Per serving: 445 cal., 47% (207 cal.) from fat; 31 g protein; 23 g fat (13 g sat.); 28 g carbo (2.6 g fiber); 733 mg sodium; 146 mg chol.

How to cook and shell lobster

■ Maine, or American, lobsters have large, meaty claws; mostly, this shellfish is sold fresh-cooked or live for cooking. Spiny and other rock lobsters have tiny claws; all the meat is in their tails, which are widely available frozen; look for great deals at discount warehouse stores.

PREP AND COOK TIME: 10 to 20 minutes to boil water; 25 to 35 minutes to cook, cool, and shell lobsters

MAKES: A 1½-pound Maine lobster yields about 4 ounces meat, a 6- to 8-ounce spiny lobster tail 4 to 6 ounces meat; each makes 1 serving

1. Bring 6 quarts **water** to a boil in an 8- to 10-quart pan over high heat. Plunge 2 **live Maine lobsters** (about 1½ lb. each) headfirst into boiling water (or add 2 thawed frozen spiny lobster tails, 6 to 8 oz. each, to 3 qt. boiling water in

a 5- to 6-qt. pan). Cover and cook 10 minutes; when boil resumes, reduce heat to a simmer. Drain lobsters and let stand until cool enough to touch.

2. For Maine lobsters, twist off tails (**A**). For both Maine lobsters and spiny lobster tails, use scissors to snip free the flat underside of each tail shell, cutting along inside edges (**B**); discard underside shell and flippers. Lift out meat; pull out and discard vein, if present. Put meat in a bowl. Rinse and save tail shell backs.

3. Twist legs with claws from Maine lobsters. Pull shells from bodies. If desired, scoop

out and save red roe, green tamalley (liver), and white fat for other uses. Discard body shell interiors; rinse and save shells. If desired, reserve small legs to eat later. Break claws from large legs. Crack leg shells and remove meat; add to bowl. Insert scissor tips into open end of each claw (**C**); snip along ridge to tip. Break shell open; carefully remove claw. Discard shells; add meat to bowl.

4. If cooking up to 6 hours ahead, cover meat and seal reserved shells in a plastic bag; chill.

Per ounce: 28 cal., 6% (1.8 cal.) from fat; 5.8 g protein; 0.2 g fat (0 g sat.); 0.4 g carbo (0 g fiber); 108 mg sodium; 20 mg chol.

ILLUSTRATIONS: ERIC LARSEN

New vermouths

■ You've heard the story: The martini—where vermouth joins forces with gin (or vodka)—was invented in Martinez, California. But did you know that vermouth, a fortified wine, was once a common product of the Western wine industry? Alex Ryan, vice president at Duckhorn Vineyards, says those now-forgotten early vermouths had little to distinguish them. But Ryan, as well as Andy Quady of Quady Winery, has decided to give

vermouths another chance, infusing fine fortified wine with herbs, spices, and botanicals.

To my taste, these domestic products are even better than European imports. Duckhorn's golden King Eider dry vermouth (750 ml.; about $20) is the most intensely flavored. Quady's pale gold Vya extra-dry vermouth (750 ml.; about $16) is gentler and very smooth, while the darker Vya sweet

vermouth (750 ml.; about $16) is redolent of a myriad of spices. You'll find all three in well-stocked wine shops.

Both winemakers recommend their vermouths on

Tangerini

PREP TIME: 3 to 5 minutes

MAKES: 1 serving

Put 3 or 4 **ice cubes** in an 8-ounce glass. Pour in ½ cup **tangerine**, tangelo, or blood orange **juice** and 2 to 3 tablespoons **dry** or sweet **vermouth**; fill with **sparkling water**. Add a 2-inch **lemon** peel twist, and stir.

Per serving: 84 cal., 2.1% (1.8 cal.) from fat; 0.6 g protein; 0.2 g fat (0 g sat.); 13 g carbo (0 g fiber); 2.4 mg sodium; 0 mg chol.

ice, with a citrus twist. They're also intriguing with citrus juice. If Martinez provided an honorable handle for a vermouth cocktail, why can't a tangerine?

The wearing of the green

■ Bright green shamrocks, garishly green beer, and now delicately green cream cheese—layered with corned beef for a first course to honor St. Patrick's Day (or any equally entertaining occasion). Parsley provides the color, horseradish the zip, in this quick-to-prepare terrine.

Corned Beef Horseradish Terrine

PREP TIME: 15 minutes to assemble, plus 4 hours to chill

NOTES: For the neatest results, buy wide, thin slices of corned beef cut to order at a deli.

MAKES: 8 to 10 appetizer servings

2 packages (3 oz. each) **cream cheese**

½ cup (¼ lb.) cold **butter** or margarine, cut into chunks

¼ cup chopped **parsley**

2 to 3 tablespoons drained **prepared horseradish**

About ½ pound fat-trimmed **thin-sliced cooked corned beef**

1 **baguette** (about 8 oz.), thinly sliced

1. In a food processor, whirl cream cheese, butter, parsley, and horseradish to taste until smooth and pale green; scrape container sides as needed.

2. Lightly oil a 3- by 5-inch loaf pan (about 2¼ cups to the rim). Line with 1 layer of corned beef slices, neatly overlapped from 1 rim across bottom to the other rim (with ends extending over rim). Line ends of pan with corned beef slices, overlapping the bottom and pan rim.

3. Dot ⅓ cup cheese mixture onto meat in pan bottom; gently spread level. Cut 2 or 3 corned beef slices to fit pan, and lay neatly onto cheese mixture. Repeat to make 3 more layers, ending at the rim with cheese mixture. Cut 2 or 3 corned beef slices to fit pan and lay on cheese mixture to cover. Fold meat at pan rim neatly over filling; pat gently to make level. Wrap airtight.

4. Chill until firm enough to slice, at least 4 hours or up to 2 days. Unwrap terrine; invert a flat plate onto pan. Holding plate and pan together, turn over and lift pan off. Pat loose pieces of corned beef back in place.

5. With a sharp knife, cut terrine into 8 to 10 equal slices. Serve with baguette slices on plates.

Per serving: 265 cal., 71% (189 cal.) from fat; 7.5 g protein; 21 g fat (11 g sat.); 13 g carbo (0.7 g fiber); 543 mg sodium; 66 mg chol.

Push, don't stir

■ If you want velvety scrambled eggs, don't stir them—push instead. And for added security, blend the eggs with a little thickened broth. The broth stabilizes the eggs, keeping them extra-moist and resistant to weeping if cooked firm, even if held on a warming tray up to 45 minutes. You can use a wide metal spatula to scramble eggs, but the ideal tool is one of the new flexible silicone spatulas (see above), which push the eggs smoothly away from the pan bottom and sides. Silicone spatulas can withstand heat up to 450°.

Large eggs	Fat-skimmed chicken broth	Cornstarch and butter (or margarine), each	Frying pan, inches wide
6	5 tablespoons	1½ teaspoons	8 to 10
12	⅔ cup	1 tablespoon	10 to 12
18	1 cup	1½ tablespoons	12 to 14
24	1½ cups	2 tablespoons	12 to 14
30	1¾ cups	2½ tablespoons	12 to 14
36	2 cups	3 tablespoons	14 to 16

Creamy Scrambled Eggs

PREP AND COOK TIME: 5 to 15 minutes to assemble, depending on volume, plus 3 to 20 minutes to cook

MAKES: 6 to 36 servings; 1 to 2 eggs per person

1. In a bowl, beat eggs to blend. In a 1- to 3-quart pan (depending on amount being cooked), blend broth with cornstarch. Stir over high heat until boiling. Let cool slightly (or cover and chill up to 1 day). Whisk broth mixture into eggs.

2. Set a frying pan (see chart for size) over medium heat. Add butter; when melted, pour in the egg mixture. With a heat-resistant flexible spatula, or a wide metal one, push cooked eggs from pan bottom and sides, letting liquid mixture flow against hot pan; for creamiest texture, don't stir. Cook until eggs are firm but still moist and shiny on top (they must be at least 160° for egg safety), 3 to 20 minutes.

Per egg: 87 cal., 62% (54 cal.) from fat; 6.7 g protein; 6 g fat (2.1 g sat.); 1.2 g carbo (0 g fiber); 77 mg sodium; 215 mg chol. ◆

The Wine Guide

BY KAREN MacNEIL-FIFE

JAMES CARRIER

What are you saving it for?

■ Here's one of the biggest myths about wine: It gets better if you age it.

I have some experience with this illusion. Throughout my 20s, I closeted away (literally—wines competed with shoes) a score of gift bottles of champagne on the theory that such wonderful wines shouldn't be "wasted" on a single person. I was waiting to share them with Mr. Right, an idea that (as every woman reading this and smiling to herself understands) made entire sense to me—then. Some 12 or so years later and still unmarried, I decided to splurge and open one of the bottles. It tasted like a cross between rancid cooking sherry and stale bread. Panicked, I opened another bottle, then another. That night hundreds of dollars' worth of now worthless wine went down the drain.

I learned several lessons from that fiasco, but the one that concerns us here is the simple yet insidious fallacy that all wines get better over time. A decade of wine research later, I know it's simply not true. In fact, most of the wines in the world are meant to be aged no longer than it takes to bring them home from the store.

However, the fact that certain wines don't *need* to be aged in order to be enjoyed doesn't mean they *can't* be aged. Take Zinfandel, for example. You can certainly keep a bottle of Zin around for several years. But whether it will actually taste better is a matter of opinion.

As wines age they lose their fresh, forward fruit character. If what you loved about that Zinfandel was its deliciously explosive ripe cherry flavors, aging it would make little sense: The longer you keep it, the more you sacrifice that dramatic cherryness. In place of expressive fruitiness, an aged wine takes on more subtle flavors that often defy description. This happens as a result of molecules recombining and coalescing in unpredictable ways. Sometimes these aged flavors are gorgeous and refined. Sometimes the wine just ends up tasting tired.

Is there any way to know which path a wine will take? Not definitively. What makes a wine develop the exact flavors it does over time remains largely a mystery. Practiced wine drinkers may have an inkling, but even for the most experienced palate, it's still a guess.

That said, certain types of wine are more likely to taste better after they've been aged than others. Three key factors make this possible: sugar, acid, and tannin. Each, in its own way, acts as a preservative.

Sugar is the easiest for most people to understand. Think of that honey you've had in the cabinet for 10 years; it probably still tastes fine. Similarly, sweet wines, like sauternes, can be aged for years, even decades. Very high acid wines, such as the top German Rieslings, can also

BUILT TO LAST

Wines with potential for longevity are by definition great and, therefore, usually expensive. But consider: A decade from now, they may be worth twice as much.

■ **Robert Pecota "Kara's Vineyard" Cabernet Sauvignon 1997 (Napa Valley),** $36. Not quite as concentrated (or pricey) as the other wines here, but still solidly built, with firm, ripe tannins and a core of black fruit. When it reveals itself, it should be a beauty.

■ **Von Strasser Cabernet Sauvignon 1996 (Diamond Mountain, Napa Valley),** $45. Massive and masculine, with powerful, almost syrupy berry flavors. Very long finish.

■ **Beaulieu Vineyards "Georges de Latour" Private Reserve Cabernet Sauvignon 1996 (Napa Valley),** $75. For decades, this wine has been considered one of the greatest Cabs in the United States. Deep, rich, concentrated cassis, tobacco, and eucalyptus flavors. Ravishing.

■ **Beringer Howell Mountain "Bancroft Ranch" Merlot 1996 (Napa Valley),** $75. Sensational. Totally concentrated and refined, with deep, rich fruit, massive structure, and a texture like velvet. Merlot doesn't get better than this.

■ **Joseph Phelps "Backus" Cabernet Sauvignon 1996 (Oakville District, Napa Valley),** $95. Loads of rich, sweet pipe tobacco, cassis, and mint flavors. Gorgeous balance and concentration.

---

taste miraculously fresh even after 10 or more years. And those high in tannin, a compound in grape skins and seeds, are usually built to last. This is why Cabernet Sauvignon, a grape that is genetically high in tannin, is the wine you're most likely to find in people's cellars.

But for a wine to age successfully, the most important character it must possess is greatness. It must be complex, well balanced, rich, and concentrated right from the start. A simple, moderately priced every-night dinner wine is meant for *tonight.* ◆

The Low-Fat Cook

HEALTHY CHOICES FOR THE ACTIVE LIFESTYLE

BY ELAINE JOHNSON

CRUMB-COATED EGGPLANT and fennel bake to crispy perfection.

JAMES CARRIER

Upper-crust ways with vegetables

■ If you've tried oven-frying chicken, you'll find this approach to vegetables very similar, right down to the minimal fat and munchy textures. Dip vegetables such as eggplant, fennel, peppers, and even big portabella mushrooms in oil-enriched egg whites, then in seasoned crumbs, and bake in the oven until crusty. It's neater than frying.

The first dish is a tweaked version of eggplant parmesan with a fennel bonus. To get the most out of the crisp finish on the vegetables, add the sauce just as you serve. In the second recipe, oven-frying adds texture to the ingredients of the great French casserole, ratatouille. And the rendition of meatlike mushroom burgers gives them a crunchy mantle.

Oven-Crusted Eggplant and Fennel Parmesan

PREP AND COOK TIME: About 45 minutes

NOTES: Crush fennel seed in a mortar, or enclose in a plastic bag and crush with a rolling pin.

MAKES: 4 servings

- 3 **large egg** whites
- 1 tablespoon **olive oil**
- 1 cup **Italian-style fine dried bread crumbs**
- 1½ teaspoons **fennel seed,** crushed (see notes)
- 1 **eggplant** (1 lb.)
- 1 head (4 in. wide) **fennel**
- ¾ cup **shredded parmesan cheese**
- 1¾ cups **canned fat-free tomato pasta sauce**
- ¼ cup **dry red wine**
- **Salt** and **pepper**

1. In a bowl, beat egg whites and oil to blend. In another bowl, mix crumbs and fennel seed.
2. Rinse eggplant; trim and discard ends. Cut eggplant crosswise into ⅓-inch-thick slices. Trim stalks from fennel head; rinse and reserve ¼ cup feathery green leaves. Trim and discard fennel root end, bruised areas, and coarse fibers. Rinse fennel and cut crosswise into ¼-inch slices.
3. Dip eggplant in egg mixture, lift out, drain briefly, and coat with crumb mixture. Arrange slices in a single layer on a 12- by 15-inch baking sheet. Mix fennel, ½ at a time, with egg mixture. Lift out with a slotted spoon, drain briefly, then add to crumb mixture. Mix and lift from crumbs. Spread pieces in a single layer on another 12- by 15-inch baking sheet.
4. Bake in a 450° oven until vegetables are well browned and eggplant is soft when pressed, 15 to 20 minutes; if using 1 oven, switch pan positions after 7 to 9 minutes. Remove fennel from oven and discard any scorched crumbs. Sprinkle eggplant with ½ the cheese. Bake until cheese is lightly browned, 3 to 4 minutes more.

5. Meanwhile, in a 1- to 2-quart pan over medium-high heat, stir pasta sauce and wine until boiling, 2 to 4 minutes.
6. Arrange equal amounts of eggplant and fennel on warm dinner plates; garnish with fennel leaves. Sprinkle with remaining cheese. Spoon sauce onto plates; add salt and pepper to taste.

Per serving: 340 cal., 29% (99 cal.) from fat; 20 g protein; 11 g fat (4.7 g sat.); 39 g carbo (4.8 g fiber); 1,656 mg sodium; 17 mg chol.

Crunchy Ratatouille

PREP AND COOK TIME: About 1 hour

MAKES: 6 servings

- 2 **large egg** whites
- 1 tablespoon **olive oil**
- ¾ cup **Italian-style fine dried bread crumbs**
- 1 teaspoon **dried basil**
- 3 teaspoons minced **garlic**
- 1½ cups 1-inch **eggplant** chunks
- 1½ cups ¾-inch **zucchini** slices
- 1½ cups 1½-inch **red bell pepper** chunks
- 2 cups 1½-inch **tomato** chunks
- 3 tablespoons **reduced-fat mayonnaise**
- 1 to 2 teaspoons **lemon juice**
- **Salt** and **pepper**

1. In a bowl, beat egg whites and oil to blend. In another bowl, mix crumbs, basil, and 2 teaspoons garlic.
2. Add 1 kind of vegetable at a time to the egg mixture—eggplant, zucchini, bell pepper, and 1½ cups tomatoes. Lift out with a slotted spoon, draining briefly, and add to crumbs. Mix gently to coat, then lift out. Arrange vegetables in a single layer on a 14- by 17-inch baking sheet.
3. Bake in a 450° oven until vegetables are well browned and eggplant is soft when pressed, 20 to 25 minutes.
4. Meanwhile, in a blender or food processor, purée until smooth the remaining 1 teaspoon garlic, remaining ½ cup tomatoes, mayonnaise, and lemon juice to taste.
5. Spoon vegetables onto warm dinner plates and season to taste with mayonnaise mixture and salt and pepper.

Per serving: 133 cal., 30% (40 cal.) from fat; 4.8 g protein; 4.4 g fat (0.7 g sat.); 20 g carbo (2.3 g fiber); 484 mg sodium; 0 mg chol.

Crusted Portabella Burgers

PREP AND COOK TIME: About 40 minutes

NOTES: Buy portabella mushroom caps. Or buy whole mushrooms, and trim off stems and save them for other uses.

MAKES: 4 servings

- 2 **large egg** whites
- 1 tablespoon **olive oil**
- 1/3 cup **Italian-style fine dried bread crumbs**
- 2 tablespoons **chili powder**
- 4 **portabella mushroom caps** (5 in. wide; 1 to 1 1/4 lb. total)
- 4 **round sandwich buns** (4 in. wide; 3/4 lb. total)
- 1 cup **nonfat sour cream**
- 2 teaspoons minced **canned chipotle chilies** or hot sauce
- 1/4 cup thinly sliced **red onion**
- 1 cup **spinach leaves**, rinsed and crisped
- **Salt** and **pepper**

1. In a bowl, beat egg whites and oil to blend. In another bowl, mix crumbs and chili powder.
2. Rinse mushroom caps; drain. Coat each cap with egg mixture, drain briefly, then coat with crumbs, shaking off excess. Set caps, gill sides down, slightly apart on a 12- by 15-inch baking sheet. Lay bun halves, cut sides up, side by side on another 12- by 15-inch baking sheet.
3. Bake mushroom caps in a 450° oven until browned and flexible when pressed, about 20 minutes. About 3 minutes before mushrooms are done, add buns to oven; bake until lightly toasted.
4. In a small bowl, mix sour cream and chipotle chilies. Spread mixture on cut sides of buns. Layer equal amounts of onion and spinach on each bun bottom, top with a mushroom cap, add salt and pepper to taste, and cover with bun top.

Per serving: 419 cal., 20% (85 cal.) from fat; 16 g protein; 9.4 g fat (1.6 g sat.); 68 g carbo (5.2 g fiber); 695 mg sodium; 4.5 mg chol. ◆

Want kitsch with your fries?

Quirky restaurants abound in Seattle's Green Lake district

BY JENA MacPHERSON

BEN WOOLSEY

It's 6 P.M. on a Tuesday, and **Bizzarro Italian Cafe** is already packed. A half-dozen people wait in a tiny entry filled with a bowling trophy, pink flamingo, beaded curtain, and piano-board decor. Hostess Kathleen combines seating newcomers with singing riddles to diners. Customers squint at the blackboard for daily specials, which always include a risotto and a stuffed pork tenderloin. Some ask right away for the pasta special—you choose the pasta, the sauce, and a soup or salad.

Bizzarro (photo at right) is just one Green Lake neighborhood eatery that attracts loyal followings of diners who like fun with their food. There are more.

The **Luau Polynesian Lounge** nearby is reminiscent of Trader Vic's, with its thatched bar area and funky barware. The exotic menu delights diners with inventive items like an appetizer of yam brûlée with homemade banana crackers, and a Hilo hot pot with clams, mussels, and homemade duck-fig wontons.

An equally whimsical mood prevails at **Mae's Phinney Ridge Cafe**, with its Midwest-dairy-meets-roadside-cafe decor and lip smackin' good food.

Jeanne Mae Barwick's breakfast specialties—homemade corned-beef hash, fresh-baked cinnamon rolls, grits, biscuits with gravy—have packed folks in on weekends for a dozen years. Breakfast is served from 7 A.M. to 3 P.M. daily. Four dining areas include the Mud Room, with its espresso bar (your latte comes with chocolate chips to stir in), and the Moo Room—a former-lounge-turned-soda-fountain decorated with dozens (maybe even hundreds) of images of Holstein milk cows, the cafe's mascot.

The oldest and perhaps most bizarre restaurant is the **Twin Teepees**. A fixture at the northwest end of Green Lake since 1937, the kitschy, two-tepee structure is a slice of roadside Americana—in fact, it still bills itself as a roadside diner. The circular dining room has a gas "campfire" in its center, and the ceiling is hung with a half-dozen carved totem icons. The martinis in the cozy lounge drew customers long before martinis were cool—and they continue to do so. The menu lists a dozen different burgers—the Teepee Burger with crunchy fries is a good choice—plus various

Offbeat eateries

Advance reservations are usually suggested on weekends and for large parties at most restaurants. Area code is 206.

Bizzarro Italian Cafe (1307 N. 46th St.; 545-7327) and **Luau Polynesian Lounge** (2253 N. 56th St.; 633-5828) serve dinner daily; **Mae's Phinney Ridge Cafe** (6412 Phinney Ave. N.; 782-1222), breakfast daily and lunch weekdays; **Twin Teepees** (7201 Aurora Ave. N.; 783-9740), breakfast, lunch, and dinner daily.

steaks and sandwiches. And there's a salad bar. New owners have added a lengthy dessert list, including an Oreo cheesecake that may well sum up what American cuisine is all about. ◆

GLASS ACT: Creamy soda starts with chocolate milk.

Refreshing ideas for milk

Trends and tricks for an old favorite

BY ANDREW BAKER

The milk section in my regular supermarket stopped me cold the other day—33 feet of shelves filled with 27 varieties of this liquid protein. A veritable Milky Way. Obviously, products from Western dairies are evolving, from the outside in.

First off is the packaging. Dairy marketers want to make it just as easy to reach for a container of milk as to grab a soda or bottle of juice when you want a refreshing beverage. Sleek, drinker-friendly, easily transportable, and resealable bottles are appearing everywhere. Made of either translucent or opaque plastic, many have oversize openings with screw-on lids. Ironically, at the other end of the spectrum, producers have revived old-fashioned glass bottles to feed our yen for nostalgia.

Flavored milks, of course, aren't new. But new flavors, both natural and artificial, are cropping up—everything from blueberry to root beer.

Even the way some milks are produced and processed is shifting—and these developments are getting star billing on bottles and cartons. A few traditional dairies now offer organic milks, produced without chemical fertilizers or bovine growth hormones, as part of their regular lineups. Others sell milks produced just without the hormones. And cream is once again rising to the top: More pasteurized but unhomogenized ("cream top") milks are available.

To sort out the merits of the new products, we staged a blind tasting of 18 plain and flavored whole milks, ranging from supermarket brands to organic varieties. No simple preference curve emerged over differences in flavor, sweetness, and richness (although the differences were obvious)—rather, our opinions rode a roller coaster of individual tastes. We surprised ourselves, however, by favoring a common house brand of plain milk over the organic or specialty milks, proving that preference is often a function of familiarity.

Here are four quick recipes that show off milks, both plain and flavored, in all their timeless glory.

Italian-style Milk Soda

PREP TIME: About 5 minutes
MAKES: 1 serving

Place $\frac{1}{2}$ cup **ice cubes** in a tall glass (at least 16 oz.). Add $\frac{1}{2}$ cup chilled **chocolate-** or strawberry-**flavor milk,** then pour in $\frac{3}{4}$ cup chilled **orange soda.** Sprinkle with long, thin **orange** peel strands and finely chopped **semisweet chocolate** to taste. Stir, and sip immediately through a straw (soda loses its fizz quickly).

Per serving: 218 cal., 31% (67 cal.) from fat; 4.4 g protein; 7.4 g fat (4.5 g sat.); 36 g carbo (2.5 g fiber); 89 mg sodium; 15 mg chol.

Spiced Banana Licuado

PREP TIME: About 5 minutes
MAKES: 3 cups; 3 to 4 servings

In a blender, combine 2 cups chilled **milk,** $\frac{1}{4}$ teaspoon **ground cinnamon,** and $\frac{1}{16}$ teaspoon *each* **ground cardamom, ground cloves,** and **ground nutmeg.** Add $\frac{1}{2}$ cup **banana** chunks, $\frac{1}{4}$ cup **ice cubes,** and 1 tablespoon firmly packed **brown sugar.** Whirl until smooth. Pour into glasses.

Per serving: 105 cal., 36% (38 cal.) from fat; 4.2 g protein; 4.2 g fat (2.6 g sat.); 14 g carbo (0.3 g fiber); 61 mg sodium; 17 mg chol.

Frosty Milk Punch

PREP TIME: About 5 minutes
MAKES: 4 cups; 4 to 5 servings

Follow directions for **spiced banana licuado** (preceding), but omit banana and add $\frac{1}{4}$ cup **brandy.**

Per serving: 100 cal., 30% (30 cal.) from fat; 3.2 g protein; 3.3 g fat (2 g sat.); 7.3 g carbo (0 g fiber); 49 mg sodium; 14 mg chol.

Soft Milk Pudding

PREP AND COOK TIME: About 7 minutes, plus at least 2 hours to chill
NOTES: If desired, substitute other flavored milks, omitting rose-flower water and strawberry jam.
MAKES: 6 servings

1. Pour $\frac{1}{4}$ cup **strawberry-flavor milk** into a 1- to $1\frac{1}{2}$-quart pan; sprinkle with 1 package ($\frac{1}{4}$ oz.) **unflavored gelatin.** Stir over medium-low heat until gelatin is dissolved, about 5 minutes.

2. Remove from heat and stir in an additional $2\frac{3}{4}$ cups strawberry-flavor milk and $\frac{3}{4}$ teaspoon **rose-flower water** (optional). Pour equally into 5- to 6-ounce bowls. Cover and chill until set, about 2 hours, or up to 1 day.

3. In a small bowl, stir 1 tablespoon **strawberry jam** to soften, then dot evenly onto puddings.

Per serving: 192 cal., 12% (23 cal.) from fat; 10 g protein; 2.5 g fat (1.5 g sat.); 33 g carbo (0 g fiber); 134 mg sodium; 15 mg chol. ◆

Curry in a hurry

Start with the spice blend as a shortcut to flavorful dishes

BY LINDA LAU ANUSASANANAN

Ordinary curry powder, shaded with a few more spices, moves from the expected into easy taste adventures. And the seasonings that evolve turn these two simple main dishes—a hot salad and a colorful vegetable curry, with condiments—into party fare.

Hot Turkey Curry Salad

PREP AND COOK TIME: About 30 minutes

MAKES: 4 servings

- 1 tablespoon **salad oil**
- 1 cup chopped **onion**
- 1 tablespoon minced **fresh ginger**
- 2 cloves **garlic,** peeled and pressed
- 2 tablespoons **curry powder**
- ½ teaspoon **ground cumin**
- ¼ teaspoon **cayenne**
- 3⅓ cups fat-skimmed **chicken broth**
- **Turkey meatball mixture** (directions follow)
- 3 tablespoons **cornstarch**
- **Salt**
- 4 to 6 cups hot cooked **rice**
- ½ pound (about 2 qt.) **baby spinach leaves,** rinsed and crisped
- **Apricot-lemon chutney** (recipe follows)
- **Plain nonfat yogurt**

1. In a 12-inch frying pan or 5- to 6-quart pan over medium-high heat, stir oil, onion, ginger, and garlic until onion is limp, about 8 minutes. Add curry powder, cumin, and cayenne; stir until spices are fragrant, about 1 minute. Add 3 cups broth and bring to a boil over high heat.

2. Shape turkey meatball mixture into 1-inch balls and drop, as formed, into boiling broth. Cover and simmer over low heat until meatballs are no longer pink in center (cut to test), 6 to 8 minutes.

3. In a small bowl, mix cornstarch and ⅓ cup broth. Add to pan, stirring until sauce boils, about 2 minutes. Add salt to taste.

4. Mound rice on dinner plates; surround with spinach, and spoon meatballs and sauce over rice and spinach. Add chutney and yogurt to taste.

Per serving: 556 cal., 24% (135 cal.) from fat; 36 g protein; 15 g fat (3.3 g sat.); 69 g carbo (6.3 g fiber); 939 mg sodium; 136 mg chol.

Turkey meatball mixture. In a bowl, mix 1 pound **ground lean turkey,** 1 **large egg,** ¼ cup **fine dried bread crumbs,** 1 teaspoon **ground coriander,** ⅓ cup chopped **onion,** and 1 teaspoon **salt** until well blended.

Apricot-lemon chutney. Rinse 1 **lemon** (6 oz.). With a vegetable peeler, pare yellow skin from lemon and finely chop. With a knife, cut off and discard white pith. Coarsely chop lemon, discarding seeds. In a 1- to 2-quart pan over high heat, bring to a boil 1 cup **water,** lemon peel, chopped lemon (with juice), 1 cup **dried apricots,** ½ cup **sugar,** 1 tablespoon *each* minced **fresh ginger, coriander seed, mustard seed,** and ½ teaspoon **hot chili flakes.** Reduce heat, cover, and simmer for 5 minutes. Uncover and boil over medium heat, stirring often, until most of the liquid is absorbed, 10 to 12 minutes. Add **salt** and 1 to 2 tablespoons **lemon juice,** to taste. Cool. Serve or cover and chill up to 3 days. Makes about 1½ cups.

Per tablespoon: 33 cal., 5.5% (1.8 cal.) from fat; 0.4 g protein; 0.2 g fat (0 g sat.); 8.4 g carbo (0.6 g fiber); 1 mg sodium; 0 mg chol.

South African Vegetable Curry

PREP AND COOK TIME: About 1 hour

NOTES: Joan Bacharach shares this curry from the Cape Malay community in South Africa. She serves it with brown rice, shredded coconut, and chutney (see preceding recipe).

MAKES: 6 to 8 servings

- ¾ pound **carrots,** peeled
- ¾ pound **green beans,** rinsed, ends trimmed
- 1 head **cauliflower** (1½ lb.), rinsed
- 1 **green bell pepper** (6 oz.), rinsed, stemmed, and seeded
- ½ pound (1½ cups) **dried peaches**

TURKEY MEATBALLS in curry sauce make a quick, hearty meal.

- 2 tablespoons **salad oil**
- 1 **onion** (½ lb.), peeled and thinly sliced
- 2 tablespoons minced **fresh ginger**
- 2 cloves **garlic,** peeled and chopped
- 2 **cinnamon sticks** (each 2 in.)
- 2 tablespoons **curry powder**
- ½ teaspoon **ground turmeric**
- 1½ cups **vegetable broth** or fat-skimmed chicken broth
- 3 cups (½ lb.) **coarsely shredded cabbage**
- **Salt**

1. Cut carrots into ½-inch-thick slices. Cut beans into 1½-inch pieces. Cut the cauliflower into 1½-inch florets. Cut pepper and peaches into 1-inch pieces.

2. In a 5- to 6-quart pan over medium-high heat, stir oil, onion, ginger, garlic, and cinnamon sticks until onion is limp, 5 to 7 minutes. Add curry powder and turmeric; stir 30 seconds. Add broth, carrots, beans, cauliflower, bell pepper, peaches, and cabbage; bring to a boil over high heat.

3. Cover and simmer over low heat, stirring occasionally, until carrots are tender when pierced, 20 to 25 minutes. Add salt to taste.

Per serving: 170 cal., 22% (38 cal.) from fat; 4 g protein; 4.2 g fat (0.5 g sat.); 33 g carbo (6.9 g fiber); 43 mg sodium; 0 mg chol. ◆

PIZZA ADOPTS AN ASIAN ATTITUDE with ginger, green onions, and soy sauce.

JAMES CARRIER (2)

½ cup **purchased pizza** or marinara **sauce**

1 cup (¼ lb.) **shredded mozzarella cheese**

1. In a 10- to 12-inch nonstick frying pan over medium-high heat, stir garlic, ginger, green onions, and oil just until onions are limp, about 5 minutes.

2. In a bowl, mix soy sauce with chicken. Rinse and core tomatoes; cut crosswise into ⅛- to ¼-inch-thick slices.

3. Place pizza crust in a 12-inch pizza pan or on a 14- by 17-inch baking sheet. Spread crust evenly with sauce, then scatter chicken mixture and onion mixture over sauce. Sprinkle pizza with cheese, and arrange tomato slices evenly over the surface.

4. Bake in a 350° oven until cheese is melted and pizza is hot in center, 12 to 15 minutes. Cut into wedges.

Per serving: 542 cal., 32% (171 cal.) from fat; 25 g protein; 19 g fat (6.4 g sat.); 61 g carbo (6.2 g fiber); 706 mg sodium; 68 mg chol.

Fettuccine with Spinach, Blue Cheese, and Prosciutto

Carolyn Darlington, Bellevue, Washington

A pasta recipe that a friend sent Carolyn Darlington sounded appealing. She decided to try it herself, adding prosciutto, one of her favorite ingredients, to make it even better.

PREP AND COOK TIME: About 30 minutes

MAKES: 4 to 6 servings

1 pound **dried fettuccine**

3 ounces **thin-sliced prosciutto**

1¼ cups (6 oz.) packed chunks **blue cheese** such as gorgonzola or Stilton

¼ cup **milk**

1 package (10 oz.; about 2½ qt.) **washed spinach leaves**, rinsed and drained

Fresh-ground **pepper**

1. In a 5- to 6-quart pan over high heat, bring 3 quarts water to a boil. Add fettuccine and stir often for 10 minutes.

2. Meanwhile, cut prosciutto into ¼-inch-wide strips and rub with your

Ginger Chicken Pizza

Judy Burk, Oakland, California

Sometimes Judy Burk makes the crust for this pizza from scratch; sometimes she saves time by starting with a purchased pizza crust. Either way, it showcases one of her favorite flavor combinations—ginger and garlic.

PREP AND COOK TIME: About 45 minutes

MAKES: 1 pizza; 4 or 5 servings

2 tablespoons minced or pressed **garlic**

2 tablespoons minced **fresh ginger**

1½ cups finely chopped **green onions** (including tops)

1 teaspoon **olive oil**

2 tablespoons **reduced-sodium soy sauce**

2 cups shredded **boned, skinned cooked chicken**

3 **firm-ripe Roma tomatoes** (about 9 oz. total)

1 **baked pizza crust** (12 in. wide; 1 lb.)

fingers to separate pieces.

3. In a 10- to 12-inch frying pan over high heat, stir cheese and milk until cheese is melted and sauce is smooth, about 3 minutes. Add prosciutto, stir, and keep warm over low heat.

4. After pasta has cooked 10 minutes, add spinach to pan and push down to immerse in water. Continue to cook until pasta is tender to bite, about 2 minutes longer. Pour into a colander and drain well. Return pasta and spinach to pan; add sauce. Mix well, lifting with 2 forks. Serve in wide bowls; add pepper to taste.

Per serving: 430 cal., 25% (108 cal.) from fat; 21 g protein; 12 g fat (6.2 g sat.); 59 g carbo (3 g fiber); 705 mg sodium; 34 mg chol.

California Caesar Salad

Patti Garrity, Manhattan Beach, California

This salad—with a dressing that's even livelier than the traditional Caesar—has been popular in Patti Garrity's family for more than 35 years. The recipe makes about 1 cup dressing, enough for this and several additional salads. Chill extra dressing airtight up to 2 weeks.

PREP TIME: About 30 minutes

MAKES: 6 to 8 servings

  1 can (2 oz.) **anchovy fillets in oil,** drained

 ¼ cup **Worcestershire**

 ¼ cup **red wine vinegar**

  2 teaspoons chopped **garlic**

  2 teaspoons **paprika**

 ½ teaspoon **dried oregano**

 ½ teaspoon **pepper**

 ½ cup **salad oil**

  3 quarts rinsed and crisped **romaine lettuce** leaves

  2 hard-cooked **large eggs**

  2 cups **purchased croutons**

 ⅓ cup **shredded parmesan cheese**

     Lemon juice

1. In a blender or food processor, combine anchovy fillets, Worcestershire, vinegar, garlic, paprika, dried oregano, and pepper. Whirl until smoothly puréed, scraping container sides as needed. With motor running at high speed, pour in the oil.

2. Break romaine leaves into bite-size

pieces and put in a wide bowl. Shell eggs, and shred or finely chop and add to lettuce along with croutons and parmesan cheese. Add anchovy dressing (about 6 tablespoons) and lemon juice to taste, and mix well.

Per serving: 132 cal., 57% (75 cal.) from fat; 6 g protein; 8.3 g fat (1.8 g sat.); 8.7 g carbo (1.8 g fiber); 244 mg sodium; 57 mg chol.

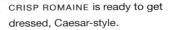

CRISP ROMAINE is ready to get dressed, Caesar-style.

Southwestern Braised Short Ribs

Mickey Strang, McKinleyville, California

When her local market had short ribs on sale, Mickey Strang decided to turn them into an easy Sunday dinner. You'll need to have the ribs sawed into chunks at the market.

PREP AND COOK TIME: About 3½ hours

MAKES: 4 servings

  3 pounds **beef short ribs,** cut through bone into 2½- to 3-inch pieces

  1 tablespoon minced or pressed **garlic**

 ¼ cup **tomato paste**

 ⅓ cup **tequila**

 ¾ cup **tomato juice**

  1 cup thinly sliced **onions**

  1 can (7 oz.) **diced green chilies**

     Salt and **pepper**

1. Rinse ribs and pat dry; trim off and discard excess fat. In a 9- by 13-inch casserole, mix garlic, tomato paste, tequila, and tomato juice; turn ribs over in sauce to coat well. Cover airtight and chill at least 1 hour; if marinating up to 1 day, turn ribs over several times.

2. Uncover ribs, turn over in sauce, and sprinkle with onions and chilies. Seal casserole tightly with foil.

3. Bake in a 350° oven until meat is very tender when pierced, 2¼ to 2½ hours. Skim off and discard fat; season meat to taste with salt and pepper.

Per serving: 591 cal., 67% (396 cal.) from fat; 35 g protein; 44 g fat (19 g sat.); 12 g carbo (2.2 g fiber); 669 mg sodium; 123 mg chol.

Cocoa Puffs

Lori Lerner Gray, Malibu, California

To use up egg whites left from another recipe, Lori Lerner Gray created these cookie-like meringues. Her daughters gave them their name.

PREP AND COOK TIME: About 1 hour

MAKES: About 4 dozen

  4 **large egg** whites

  1 cup **sugar**

  1 teaspoon **vanilla**

 ⅓ cup **unsweetened cocoa**

 1¼ cups **sweetened shredded dried coconut**

  1 cup **chopped pecans** or walnuts

1. In a deep bowl with mixer on high speed, whip egg whites to a thick foam. Continue to beat, adding 1 tablespoon of sugar about every 15 seconds until whites hold very stiff peaks, about 6 minutes total. Mix in vanilla.

2. Sprinkle cocoa over egg whites and fold in gently with a flexible spatula. Add coconut and pecans and fold into mixture (the volume decreases).

3. Drop mixture in 1-tablespoon portions about 1 inch apart on buttered 14- by 17-inch baking sheets.

4. Bake cookies in a 325° oven until firm and dry to touch, about 15 minutes. If baking more than 1 pan at a time, switch positions after 7 or 8 minutes.

5. Slide a wide spatula under cookies and transfer to racks to cool. Serve, or store airtight at room temperature up to 1 week.

Per cookie: 43 cal., 47% (20 cal.) from fat; 0.6 g protein; 2.2 g fat (0.7 g sat.); 5.9 g carbo (0.5 g fiber); 9.7 mg sodium; 0 mg chol. ◆

Blackberry ice cream sundaes with pine nut bonbons add a sweet finish to a feast of Northwest seafood. Recipes on page 95.

April

Northwest

seafood feast

Refreshingly

easy recipes for

shrimp and salmon

showcase the

bounty of

British Columbia

BY LINDA LAU ANUSASANANAN • FOOD PHOTOGRAPHS BY JAMES CARRIER

Joan and Sid Cross have a passion for superlative food and wine. And they indulge frequently by entertaining at their home by English Bay in Vancouver, British Columbia.

The Crosses have ample resources. British Columbia farmers offer a kaleidoscope of produce, local fisheries supply exquisite fresh seafood, and Vancouver's multiethnic population has enriched the variety of foods in local markets. In the middle of such bounty, Joan has a simple cooking philosophy: "You don't need to work hard with good, fresh ingredients." She simply undertakes to bring out their inherent virtues. Uncomplicated dishes, along with strategic planning and many make-ahead steps, result in parties that appear effortless.

Sid, chair of the International Wine and Food Society's Wines Committee, shares his cellar reserves enthusiastically with guests, often pouring several wines with a single course. For our menu he suggests a couple of British Columbia wines, plus more widely available California, Oregon, and Washington labels. Don't feel bound to restrict any to its designated course; follow Sid's lead and experiment with different food and wine combinations. To locate the B.C. wines in your area, call the wineries. *Blue Mountain Vineyard and Cellars; (250) 497-8244. Burrowing Owl Vineyards; (877) 498-0620.*

Dinner starts with prosciutto-wrapped pears (above) and herb-marinated shrimp on toast (right). Joan and Sid Cross (top, right foreground) share their love of good food and wine—and their spectacular view of Vancouver, British Columbia.

Pears with Prosciutto

PREP TIME: About 10 minutes

NOTES: If assembling up to 1 hour ahead, moisten pear slices with lemon juice to prevent darkening.

MAKES: 16 pieces; 8 appetizer servings

  3 ounces **thin-sliced prosciutto**

  1 **firm-ripe Bosc pear** (8 to 10 oz.)

1. Cut prosciutto into strips about 2 inches wide and 3½ inches long.

2. Rinse pear and pat dry; cut in half lengthwise and core. Cut each pear half lengthwise into 8 equal slices.

3. Wrap prosciutto strips equally around pear slices. Arrange on a small platter. Pick up to eat.

Per piece: 20 cal., 36% (7.2 cal.) from fat; 1.6 g protein; 0.8 g fat (0.2 g sat.); 2 g carbo (0.3 g fiber); 98 mg sodium; 4.3 mg chol.

Green beans and baby lettuces sandwich grilled pesto salmon. Roasted tomato-filled red peppers are the colorful accent.

Charlotte's Marinated Prawns

PREP AND COOK TIME: About 1¼ hours

NOTES: When they're in season, Joan (who gave her first name to this recipe) prefers to use British Columbia spot prawns. If time is short, omit the court bouillon and cook the shellfish in 2 quarts water with 1 thin-sliced lemon. If making up to 1 day ahead, cover and chill shellfish in marinade; store cool toast airtight at room temperature.

MAKES: 8 servings

    Court bouillon (recipe follows)

2 pounds (26 to 30 per lb.) **shrimp** or spot prawns (see notes), rinsed

½ cup **extra-virgin olive oil**

2 tablespoons **lemon juice**

1 clove **garlic,** peeled and halved

¼ cup minced **parsley**

3 tablespoons minced **fresh chives** or green onions

1 tablespoon minced **fresh thyme** leaves, dried thyme, or fresh marjoram leaves

1 tablespoon **Dijon mustard**

    Salt and **pepper**

¾ pound **baguettes** (about 1½ loaves) or thin-sliced firm white bread

1. In a 5- to 6-quart pan over high heat, bring court bouillon to a boil. Add shrimp, cover, and cook until opaque but still moist-looking in the center of the thickest part (cut to test), 2 to 3 minutes.

2. Drain shrimp in a colander set over a bowl; reserve court bouillon. Rinse shrimp with cold water; when cool enough to handle, peel and devein.

3. In a large bowl, mix ½ cup court bouillon (reserve remainder for other uses or discard), oil, lemon juice, garlic, parsley, chives, thyme, and mustard. Add shrimp and mix well. Add salt and pepper to taste. Cover and chill at least 2 hours or up to 1 day, stirring occasionally.

4. Cut baguettes into ¼- to ⅜-inch-thick slices (or cut white bread slices diagonally into quarters to make triangles). Put a wire rack on each of 2 baking sheets, 12 by 15 inches, and arrange slices equally on racks. Broil 3 to 4 inches from heat, turning once, until bread is lightly toasted on each side, about 4 minutes total.

5. Remove garlic from shrimp mixture and discard. To eat, spoon chilled shrimp and marinade onto toasted bread.

Per serving: 339 cal., 45% (153 cal.) from fat; 23 g protein; 17 g fat (2.6 g sat.); 24 g carbo (1.3 g fiber); 442 mg sodium; 140 mg chol.

seafood feast

Court Bouillon

PREP AND COOK TIME: About 40 minutes

NOTES: If making up to 1 day ahead, cover and chill. Use for poaching seafood, then strain and save the liquid to use as a base for fish soups; store airtight in the freezer.

MAKES: About 2¼ quarts

In a 5- to 6-quart pan over high heat, combine 2 quarts **water,** 1 cup **dry vermouth,** 6 thin **lemon** slices, 6 thin **onion** slices, 3 rinsed **parsley sprigs** (about 6 in.), 1 rinsed **fresh thyme** sprig (4 in.) or 1 teaspoon dried thyme, 2 **dried whole bay leaves,** and 12 **black peppercorns.** Cover and bring to a boil; reduce heat and simmer for 30 minutes.

Per cup: 6.6 cal., 0% (0 cal.) from fat; 0.1 g protein; 0 g fat; 1.6 g carbo (0.1 g fiber); 2.6 mg sodium; 0 mg chol.

Pesto Salmon

PREP AND COOK TIME: About 20 minutes

NOTES: Up to 1 day ahead, coat salmon with half the pesto (step 3), cover, and chill; cover remaining pesto separately and chill. If serving fish at room temperature, grill up to 2 hours ahead.

MAKES: 8 servings

- 3 pounds **boned salmon fillet** (maximum thickness 1½ in.)
- 2 cups lightly packed **fresh basil** leaves, rinsed
- 2 cloves **garlic,** peeled
- ¼ cup **olive oil**
  Salt and **pepper**

1. Rinse salmon, pat dry, and cut into 8 equal pieces.

2. In a blender or food processor, purée basil, garlic, and oil until smooth. Season pesto to taste with salt and pepper.

3. Spread half the pesto evenly over flesh sides of salmon.

4. Lay salmon, skin down, on a grill over a solid bed of medium-hot coals or medium-high heat on a gas barbecue (you can hold your hand at grill level only 3 to 4 seconds). Cover grill; open vents for charcoal. Cook 4 minutes. Slip a wide spatula between fish and skin, 1 piece at a time; lift fish free, turn over, and set back on skin. Brush remaining pesto equally over pieces. Cover grill. Cook until fish is opaque but still moist-looking in center of thickest part (cut to test), 2 to 3 minutes longer. With spatula, transfer fish to a platter (or serve on baby lettuces with green beans; see notes for recipe, following); discard skin. Serve salmon hot, warm, or at room temperature. Add salt and pepper to taste.

Per serving: 381 cal., 59% (225 cal.) from fat; 35 g protein; 25 g fat (4.6 g sat.); 1.6 g carbo (1.3 g fiber); 102 mg sodium; 100 mg chol.

Mixed Baby Lettuces with Green Beans

PREP AND COOK TIME: About 15 minutes

NOTES: If desired, set warm salmon on portions of salad mix, then sprinkle a few beans over fish and leaves. Up to 1 day ahead, cook beans (through step 2); cool, then chill airtight.

MAKES: 8 servings

- ¾ pound **green beans**
- ¼ cup **olive oil**
- ¼ cup **rice vinegar**
- 1 tablespoon **Dijon mustard**
- 2 tablespoons minced **shallots**
- ¾ pound (about 4 qt.) **baby salad mix,** rinsed and crisped
  Salt and **pepper**

1. Rinse beans; trim and discard ends and any strings. If desired, cut beans into 3-inch lengths.

2. In a 4- to 5-quart pan over high heat, bring 2 quarts water to a boil. Add beans; cook until bright green and barely tender to bite, 3 to 4 minutes. Drain. Immerse in ice water until cool; drain.

3. In a wide bowl, mix oil, vinegar, mustard, and shallots. Add beans and mix to coat. Push beans to 1 side of bowl; add salad mix and stir to coat. With a large spoon, distribute beans over greens. Add salt and pepper to taste.

Per serving: 95 cal., 64% (61 cal.) from fat; 1.7 g protein; 6.8 g fat (0.9 g sat.); 8.1 g carbo (3.2 g fiber); 128 mg sodium; 0 mg chol.

Roasted Tomato-stuffed Peppers

PREP AND COOK TIME: About 50 minutes

NOTES: If regular yellow tomatoes aren't available, use 4 cups unpeeled yellow or red cherry tomatoes, cut in half. If making up to 4 hours ahead, let cooked vegetables stand at room temperature.

MAKES: 8 servings

- 4 **yellow** or red **bell peppers** (6 oz. each)
- 2 **firm-ripe red tomatoes** (6 oz. each)
- 2 **firm-ripe yellow tomatoes** (6 oz. each)
- 2 or 3 cloves **garlic,** peeled and thinly sliced
- 1 tablespoon **fresh thyme** leaves or 1 teaspoon dried thyme
- 2 tablespoons **extra-virgin olive oil**
  Salt and **pepper**

1. Rinse peppers and cut each in half lengthwise through the stem. Remove and discard seeds and veins. Lay peppers in a single layer, cut sides up, in a 9- by 13-inch pan.

2. In a 3- to 4-quart pan over high heat, bring about 2 quarts water to a boil. Drop red and yellow tomatoes into water and boil for about 1 minute. Lift out with a slotted spoon. When cool enough to handle, in 1 to 2 minutes, peel tomatoes, core, and cut into ½-inch wedges. Mix wedges with garlic and thyme.

3. Mound tomato mixture equally in pepper halves. Drizzle evenly with olive oil.

4. Bake peppers in a 400° oven until

Finish on a sweet note with blackberry sundaes and pine nut bonbons.

some of the tomato edges are browned, 45 to 50 minutes (30 to 35 minutes in a convection oven). Add salt and pepper to taste. Serve hot, warm, or at room temperature.

Per serving: 68 cal., 51% (35 cal.) from fat; 1.4 g protein; 3.9 g fat (0.6 g sat.); 8.7 g carbo (2.3 g fiber); 9.2 mg sodium; 0 mg chol.

Blackberry Ice Cream Sundaes

PREP TIME: About 5 minutes

NOTES: Up to 1 day ahead, scoop hard-frozen ice cream onto a baking sheet and freeze; when solid, cover airtight.

MAKES: 8 servings

    1 recipe's worth **blackberry ice cream** (recipe follows)

    About 1 cup **blackberry sauce** (recipe follows)

  2 cups assorted **berries** (blackberries, raspberries, blueberries, and/or hulled strawberries), rinsed and drained

Scoop ice cream into chilled bowls. Drizzle equally with blackberry sauce and sprinkle with berries.

Per serving: 352 cal., 41% (144 cal.) from fat; 2.6 g protein; 16 g fat (9.7 g sat.); 53 g carbo (9.4 g fiber); 18 mg sodium; 55 mg chol.

Blackberry Ice Cream

PREP TIME: About 30 minutes

MAKES: 7 to 8 cups; 8 servings

Mix 5 cups cold **blackberry sauce** (recipe follows) with 1⅔ cups **whipping cream**. Pour into an ice cream maker (2 qt. or larger) and freeze according to manufacturer's directions until mixture is firm enough to scoop, dasher is hard to turn, or machine stops, about 30 minutes. Serve softly frozen or transfer to an airtight container and freeze up to 1 week.

Per serving: 304 cal., 47% (144 cal.) from fat; 2.2 g protein; 16 g fat (9.7 g sat.); 41 g carbo (6.8 g fiber); 17 mg sodium; 55 mg chol.

Blackberry Sauce

PREP AND COOK TIME: About 30 minutes

NOTES: If fresh berries aren't available, use thawed frozen unsweetened ones. If making sauce up to 2 days ahead, cover and chill. Use 5 cups for blackberry ice cream, preceding, and save the remainder to use as sauce for sundaes, also preceding.

MAKES: About 6 cups

1. In a 1- to 1½-quart pan over high heat, bring 1⅔ cups **sugar** and 1 cup **water** to a rolling boil; stir until sugar is dissolved. Let cool about 10 minutes.

2. Rinse and drain 2½ quarts **blackberries.** Purée berries in a blender or food processor, then rub through a fine strainer into a bowl; discard seeds. Mix berry purée and sugar syrup. Taste and add more sugar if desired.

Per cup: 254 cal., 3.2% (8.1 cal.) from fat; 1.7 g protein; 0.9 g fat (0 g sat.); 64 g carbo (11 g fiber); 0.3 mg sodium; 0 mg chol.

Pine Nut Bonbons

PREP AND COOK TIME: About 50 minutes

NOTES: If making up to 1 day ahead, store cool cookies airtight at room temperature; freeze to store longer.

MAKES: 18 cookies

    About ½ cup (¼ lb.) **butter** or margarine, at room temperature

  ⅓ cup firmly packed **brown sugar**

  1 **large egg** yolk

  ½ teaspoon grated **orange** peel

  ½ teaspoon **vanilla**

  1¼ cups **all-purpose flour**

  ¼ cup **pine nuts**

  2 tablespoons **honey**

1. In a bowl with a mixer on high speed, beat butter and sugar until fluffy. Beat in yolk, orange peel, and vanilla. Add flour and stir until well blended.

2. Shape dough into 18 equal balls. Set balls about 2 inches apart on a buttered 12- by 15-inch nonstick baking sheet. Firmly press nuts equally onto tops.

3. Pour honey into a small microwave-safe bowl. Heat in a microwave oven at 50% power just until liquefied, 30 to 60 seconds. Brush honey over cookies.

4. Bake in a 300° oven until cookies are pale golden brown, 15 to 20 minutes. With a spatula, transfer to racks; cool.

Per cookie: 113 cal., 52% (59 cal.) from fat; 1.6 g protein; 6.5 g fat (3.4 g sat.); 13 g carbo (0.5 g fiber); 54 mg sodium; 26 mg chol. ◆

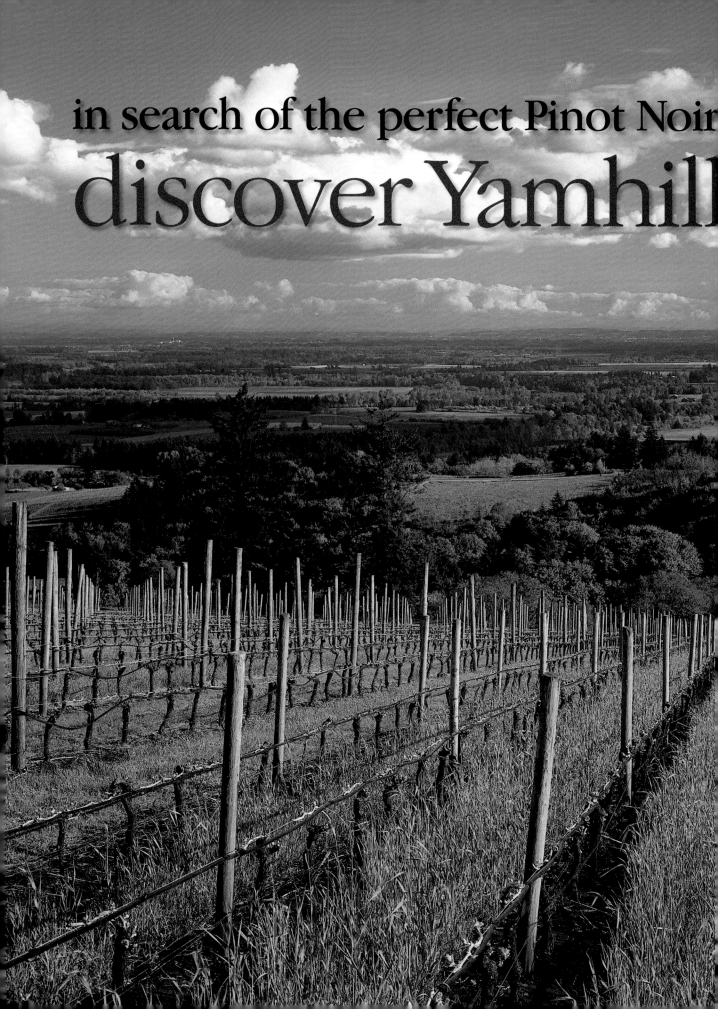

in search of the perfect Pinot Noir

discover Yamhill

County

Not far from Portland, some of the best burgundies in the world are produced. New restaurants and inns make wine touring even more fun

BY PAUL GREGUTT

PHOTOGRAPHS BY WAYNE ALDRIDGE

Driving southwest out of Portland on State 99W, you start seeing winery signs just after you cross the Yamhill County line: Rex Hill, Chehalem, Torii Mor, Argyle, Sokol Blosser. Except for the tasting rooms, the prevailing flavor is rural farm country. There is little to suggest that you have entered a region so intrinsically special that in all the world it has only one superior.

In the competition to make the perfect Pinot Noir—which wine writer Hugh Johnson has called "the world's best red-wine grape, in the right place"—only Burgundy, the French holy of holies, outperforms Yamhill County. And folks around Yamhill County might even argue about that.

Wine touring in Yamhill County has never been easier or more enjoyable. An increasing number of wineries have tasting rooms open to the public. A region that was for years lacking in dining and lodging options has blossomed with adventurous new restaurants and intriguing places to spend the night.

"A wine to dance with, not to wrestle"

Domaine Drouhin brings French inspiration to Oregon vineyards.

Eyrie Vineyards's David Lett, who introduced Pinot Noir grapes to Oregon in the mid-1960s, says, "I'm convinced that there are two climates that produce great burgundy." He doesn't say that one is better, simply that they're different. Lett believes that he couldn't duplicate the conditions in Burgundy if he wanted to. "They plant differently, have different microflora in the cellars, whole dimensions that can't be replicated—and," he grins, "maybe shouldn't be."

Nor is Véronique Drouhin interested in replication. A member of one of Burgundy's most famous families, she now commutes from France to work as winemaker at Domaine Drouhin Oregon, the family's 84-acre salute to Yamhill County. She began by making a single Pinot Noir from purchased grapes; more recently she has incorporated estate-grown fruit into the blend, and made limited quantities of a second, reserve Pinot Noir called Laurene (the name of her young daughter).

"The idea is not to make burgundy, but to make Pinot Noir in the style we think it should be made," she says.

To grasp the significance of what is happening in Yamhill County, one must ask what makes Pinot Noir so special, so challenging, so difficult, and, occasionally, so sublime. Winemakers turn into poets when faced with this question. "It's a wine to dance with, not to wrestle with," says Lett. "It's a woman … complex, fascinating, and changeable."

For consumers it's not always easy, and never cheap, to understand what all the fuss is about. Good burgundies routinely cost $50 or more, and it's common to pay that much for one that's not very good. Pinot Noir from other Western wine regions can be thin and insipid, or ripe and fruity, but almost never is it ethereal, silky, or expressive in the nuanced ways that have created its larger-than-life reputation.

In Yamhill County, Lett, Drouhin, and a few other inspired fanatics are proving that those extra dimensions can be nursed, stressed, and cajoled out of the reluctant grape. Lett has spent three decades trying to figure out exactly where and why and how to make it happen.

Aptly named Brick House Vineyards is typical of Yamhill County's low-key but appealing wineries.

"The idea is to make Pinot Noir in the style we think it should be made."

Lett makes just 2,500 cases of Pinot Noir a year, a third to half of it designated *reserve*. He keeps the crops light, picks when he believes the grapes are ripe, eschews color for flavor, and makes wines that are built to age.

A few miles west of Lett's vineyards, the soil changes from the iron-rich red earth of the Dundee Hills to a sedimentary loam called Willakenzie. Here is where Doug Tunnell, a former foreign correspondent for CBS News, has planted 26 acres of Pinot Noir, Chardonnay, and Gamay Noir for his Brick House Vineyards.

Tunnell believes that the poor soil, undesirable for conventional crops, is perfect for wine grapes. He also believes in doing things as naturally as possible—his vineyard is one of the first in Oregon to be certified organic. He agonizes over the details of pruning and cultivating his vines. "I know that if I don't grow these grapes in particular ways, there's nothing I can do to change them come harvest time," he explains. Brick House made its first wines in 1993. There are just three: Chardonnay, Gamay Noir, and Pinot Noir. So far, all have been wonderful, precocious, and spicy, brimming with ripe fruit flavor.

Tunnell's Pinots are different from Lett's, and Lett's are different from Véronique Drouhin's. Such differences only highlight the growing sophistication of Yamhill County winemakers. If, as Lett says, Pinot is a wine to dance with, then surely there's room for a waltz as well as a mazurka.

travel planner

Area code is 503 unless noted.

wine tasting and wine shopping

Many of the 40 or so wineries west of the Willamette between Portland and Salem are open daily for tasting, at least March through December; some are open weekends only, and a few just on Memorial Day and Thanksgiving Day weekends. Tasting is usually free, though some wineries charge a small fee.

State 99W is the wine route; from the north, take exit 294 off I-5 and follow signs south to Newberg. From Salem, take State 22 west to State 99W at Rickreall. Watch for blue signs leading to the wineries. The "Vintage 2000" guide can help you zero in on the varietals and wineries that most interest you; pick it up (free) at most any winery or get one in advance from the Oregon Wine Advisory Board in Portland (800/242-2363 or www.oregonwine.org).

If you're looking for one place with a broad selection of Yamhill County vintages, try the **Oregon Wine Tasting Room,** 19702 S.W. State 18, McMinnville; 843-3787.

dining

As the number of serious wineries has grown in the north Willamette Valley, the number of serious restaurants has risen as well. Now it takes more than a three-day weekend to do justice to the dinner and lunch options in McMinnville, Dundee, and neighboring burgs.

■ **Caffé Bisbo.** Nothing fancy, but fourth-generation restaurateur Claudio Bisbocci's northern Italian fare is as hearty and genuine as are his personal greetings to his customers. *214 W. Main St., Carlton; 852-7248.*

■ **Dundee Bistro.** Contemporary and casual with a Tuscan flair, the newest addition to Dundee's restaurant row leans toward local produce for its inventive, refined fare. The restaurant-bar-pizzeria-bakery, owned by the Ponzi family, is attached to the Ponzi Vineyards tasting room and wine bar; next to it is a shop featuring Oregon foods. *State 99W at Seventh St., Dundee; 554-1650.*

■ **Joel Palmer House.** A mecca for wild mushroom lovers—and anyone else with an adventuresome palate, thanks to chef Jack Czarnecki's European culinary sensibilities. Extensive wine list includes dozens of local Pinot Noirs; don't even think about asking for Merlot. *600 Ferry St., Dayton; 864-2995.*

■ **Nick's Italian Cafe.** Nick's is a wine country institution—great when it opened in 1977 and still the one to beat. Choose among three entrées for your five-course prix-fixe meal. And yes, the well-lit dining room still looks like the soda fountain it once was. *521 E. Third St., McMinnville; 434-4471.*

■ **Red Hills Provincial Dining.** Dark wood walls in the nearly century-old bungalow make the Red Hills dining room a cozy embrace. Offerings range widely but are mostly French and Italian takes on local specialties, beautifully executed. *276 State 99W, Dundee; 538-8224.*

■ **Tina's.** The dining room at this quietly stylish gem was recently renovated, doubling its size. Now more people can enjoy the French-, Italian-, and Asian-inspired Northwest cuisine served here at lunch and dinner. *760 State 99W, Dundee; 538-8880.*

lodging

■ **McMenamin's Hotel Oregon.** The state's best-known brewmeisters, the McMenamin brothers, have renovated a four-story 1905 hotel in downtown McMinnville in their own quirky, inimitable style. Most rooms share a bath. Beer, wine, and tavern fare—not to mention unforgettable breakfasts, included with room—can be had in the large main-floor pub; check out the diminutive basement and rooftop bars too. *From $75. 310 N.E. Evans St., McMinnville; 472-8427, (888) 472-8427, or www.mcmenamins.com.*

Pinot pioneer: David Lett's Eyrie Vineyards introduced Pinot Noir grapes to Oregon.

■ **Vineyard Suites.** All of the amenities you'd expect of a newish 67-room motel, including indoor pool and movie channels, located just off State 18. *From $85. 2535 Three Mile Lane, McMinnville; 472-1500 or (888) 489-1600.*

■ **Youngberg Hill Vineyard & Inn.** The area's most elegant accommodations are found in a contemporary country-style hilltop inn surrounded by stellar Pinot Noir grapevines and, beyond them, other vineyards and woods. All seven rooms have private baths. *From $130. 10660 Youngberg Hill Rd., McMinnville; 472-2727, (888) 657-8668, or www.youngberghill.com.*

— *Bonnie Henderson* ◆

foodguide

BY JERRY ANNE DI VECCHIO

PHOTOGRAPHS BY JAMES CARRIER

The king of breads

Brioche reigns with ease for a spring brunch

■ Not all breads need to be kneaded in the ordinary way. Take brioche, for instance. This buttery, springy, fragrant dough is best beaten, instead of massaged, to perfection. In olden times, bakers pulled the dough from the bowl and slapped it back until it came free without sticking. But in the age of machines, turn to your electric mixer for a simple execution of this classic French bread—one form of which is a golden ring called a crown.

Brioche Crown

PREP AND COOK TIME: About 1¼ hours, plus about 2½ hours for dough to rise and bread to cool

NOTES: For a plain loaf, good for toasting—and wonderful for French toast—omit pepper and the gruyère and parmesan cheeses.

MAKES: 1 loaf, about 2¼ pounds

- 1 package **active dry yeast**
- 1 tablespoon **sugar**
- 1 cup warm (110°) **milk**
- ½ teaspoon **salt**

  About 3¾ cups **all-purpose flour**

  About ¾ cup (⅜ lb.) **butter** or margarine

- 4 **large eggs**
- ½ pound **gruyère** or Swiss **cheese,** cut into ½-inch cubes
- 1 teaspoon **fresh-ground pepper**
- 1 **large egg** yolk
- 2 to 3 tablespoons **shredded parmesan cheese**

1. In a large bowl, combine yeast, sugar, and milk. Let stand until yeast is softened, about 5 minutes.

2. Add salt and 1 cup flour. Beat with a mixer (rotary or paddle beater) at medium-high speed until smooth, 2 to 3 minutes. Cut ¾ cup butter into thin slices; add to bowl and beat until there are no more lumps, 2 to 3 minutes. Add 4 eggs, stir to mix, then beat until well blended, 2 to 3 minutes. Stir in 2½ cups flour. Mix at medium-high speed with rotary or paddle beater or dough hook until dough pulls from sides of bowl, 8 to 12 minutes (dough is very soft); add up to ¼ cup more flour if necessary. Frequently scrape dough down if it crawls up beater; also scrape bowl sides often. Remove the beater and scrape clean. Sprinkle dough with gruyère cheese and pepper; cover with plastic wrap and let it stand in a warm place until at least doubled, 1½ to 2 hours.

3. With paddle beater, dough hook, or heavy spoon, beat dough to expel air. Rub hands with butter. Scrape dough (it's sticky) onto a floured board; dust lightly with flour. Lifting from the outside, knead gently by folding edges onto center of dough (basically roll it, with almost no pressure) and form a smooth ball, about ½ minute.

4. Set dough, smooth side up, on a buttered 12- by 17-inch baking sheet. If necessary, rinse hands, dry, and butter again. Flatten dough into an 8-inch round. With a finger, poke a hole through center of loaf to pan. Then push fingers of both hands into hole and pull with equal pressure around circle to form a hole 6 inches wide; push any lumps of cheese that pop out back under loaf. With a floured sharp knife, slash dough from center to outside edge, about ½ inch deep, at 2-inch intervals.

5. Lightly drape with plastic wrap and let stand until puffy (dough barely holds an impression when gently pressed), 15 to 20 minutes. Uncover. In a small bowl, beat egg yolk to blend with 1 tablespoon water. Brush yolk mixture gently over dough. Sprinkle with parmesan cheese.

6. Bake in a 400° oven until loaf is well browned, 40 to 45 minutes (30 to 35 minutes in a convection oven). Slide onto a rack to cool at least 10 minutes. Serve warm or cool.

Per ounce: 127 cal., 50% (64 cal.) from fat; 4.5 g protein; 7.1 g fat (4.1 g sat.); 11 g carbo (0.4 g fiber); 111 mg sodium; 48 mg chol.

True grit

■ Polenta, a coarse meal of dried corn, which shows up regularly on fancy menus, is reserved for mid-day and evening meals. Grits, a slightly different-flavored coarse meal of hominy—a hulled, treated dried corn—gets plebeian ranking and is relegated to breakfast. Yet the two have a similar character on the palate and cook the same way. What I see sold as white polenta looks suspiciously like hominy grits, inspiring me to move the latter to the dinner table.

Sour Cream and Green Chili Grits Casserole

PREP AND COOK TIME: 15 to 20 minutes

NOTES: If making casserole through step 2 up to 1 day ahead, increase chicken broth to 2½ cups total; separately, cover casserole and cooked bacon airtight and chill. Reheat casserole on turntable in a microwave oven at full power (100%) until hot in the center, 5 to 8 minutes. Lay crisp bacon slices on casserole.

MAKES: 6 to 8 servings

- 1 **onion** (6 oz.), peeled and diced
- 1 tablespoon **butter** or bacon fat
- 1 can (7 oz.) **diced green chilies**
- 2 cups fat-skimmed **chicken broth**
- 1 cup **quick-cooking hominy grits**
- 1½ cups **sour cream** (regular, reduced-fat, or nonfat)
  Salt
  Oven-fried bacon (recipe follows, optional)

1. In a 4- to 5-quart pan over high heat, stir onion in butter until lightly browned, 3 to 4 minutes. Add chilies, chicken broth, grits, and sour cream.

2. Stir until boiling, then reduce heat and simmer, stirring often until mixture is thick, about 5 minutes. Add salt to taste. Pour into a shallow 2-quart casserole.

3. Arrange bacon on sour cream and grits mixture. Serve hot.

Per serving: 192 cal., 52% (99 cal.) from fat; 5.3 g protein; 11 g fat (6.5 g sat.); 20 g carbo (1.6 g fiber); 208 mg sodium; 23 mg chol.

Oven-fried bacon. Lay ½ pound **sliced bacon** in a single layer in a 12- by 17-inch pan. Bake in a 375° oven until browned and crisp, about 20 minutes. Transfer bacon to towels to drain; discard fat in pan or save for other uses. Use hot or, if making ahead, cool, wrap airtight, and hold at room temperature up to 6 hours or chill up to 1 day; use at room temperature.

Per 1-ounce slice: 46 cal., 76% (35 cal.) from fat; 2.4 g protein; 3.9 g fat (1.4 g sat.); 0 g carbo.; 127 mg sodium; 6.7 mg chol.

An artichoke roast

■ The main California artichoke belt stretches from San Mateo County south into Monterey County. Christie Vogel of El Granada, at the northern end of the region, wrote enthusiastically about her way of cooking the vegetables: She roasts them, to maximize their nutty flavor. The process is so simple, you can tuck it in your head; just choose the number of artichokes to cook, and pick a pan (or pans) into which they will fit.

Roasted Artichokes

PREP AND COOK TIME: About 1 hour

MAKES: 1 or 2 servings from each artichoke

1. Choose **artichokes** that are 3 to 4½ inches wide. Break off and discard small outer leaves. With a knife, slice off artichoke tips. With scissors, snip thorn tips from remaining leaves. Trim dark base from stem ends and, with a knife, peel coarse fibers from stems and artichoke bottoms. Cut artichokes in half lengthwise, rinse well, and drain briefly.

2. Choose a pan in which the artichokes fit close together in a single layer (6 halves fit in a 9- by 13-in. pan); if there are large spaces, the juices will scorch.

3. For each artichoke, pour 1 to 2 tablespoons **olive oil** into pan and add ¼ teaspoon **dried thyme**. Roll artichokes in oil to coat, and turn cut sides down. Slide 1 thin **lemon slice** and 1 peeled **garlic clove** under each artichoke half. Seal pan with foil.

4. Bake in a 375° oven until artichoke bottoms are tender when pierced, 40 to 50 minutes.

5. Transfer artichokes, cut sides up, to a platter; top with lemon and garlic, and sprinkle with **salt** to taste. Drizzle artichokes with pan drippings; or add **butter** and **lemon juice** (about 1 teaspoon each for each artichoke half) to roasting pan, place over high heat (if container is microwave-safe, put in a microwave oven at full power—100%) until butter is melted, and drizzle over artichokes. Serve hot or at room temperature.

Per ½ artichoke with butter and lemon juice: 118 cal., 67% (79 cal.) from fat; 2.8 g protein; 8.8 g fat (2.1 g sat.); 9.3 g carbo (4.2 g fiber); 97 mg sodium; 5.2 mg chol.

Tight pockets

■ When using a gooey mixture to stuff thick chops (lamb or pork), steaks (such as tenderloin), or chicken breasts, the trick to keeping the filling in is to make the opening small. You need to create a large pocket inside the meat, with an opening slit just big enough to push the filling through. These lamb chops are an easy—and flavorful—example, with an aromatic heart of Stilton cheese.

Grilled Stilton-stuffed Lamb Chops

PREP AND COOK TIME: About 25 minutes

MAKES: 4 servings

> 4 **double-bone lamb rib chops** (each about 6 oz. and 2 in. thick), fat trimmed from chop surface and bones
>
> ¼ cup packed **Stilton cheese** or other firm blue cheese
>
> **Salt** and **pepper**

1. Rinse chops and pat dry. To make a pocket, insert a sharp knife, with a blade about ½ inch wide, horizontally into center of each chop from fat side to the bone; don't pierce other side (see photo above). Without enlarging the entry slit, slide knife in an arc through meat to within ½ to ¼ inch of edge—but don't cut through. Remove knife, reverse direction of blade, and reinsert it through entry hole; slide knife in opposite direction to make pocket wider. Push your index finger through the entry hole and widen pocket if it's too narrow.

2. Firmly push 1 tablespoon cheese into each chop; scrape off any cheese that sticks to exterior.

3. To barbecue chops, mound and ignite 70 charcoal briquets on firegrate, with vents open. When coals are dotted with ash, in about 15 minutes, push equal portions to opposite sides of grate; set grill in place. Or turn gas barbecue to high, cover, and heat 10 minutes; adjust burners for indirect heat. When temperature is very hot (you can hold your hand at grill level only 1 to 2 seconds), lay stuffed chops, bones up, on grill, not directly over heat (to avoid flare-ups). Cover grill; open vents for charcoal. Cook until chops are browned, about 3 minutes. Turn chops onto 1 side; cook until browned, about 2 minutes (move directly over heat if browning too slowly). Turn and brown remaining side, about 2 minutes. Turn chops bones down. For rare, cook 3 to 5 minutes longer; for medium-well, 7 to 10 minutes longer. Season to taste with salt and pepper.

Per serving: 183 cal., 59% (108 cal.) from fat; 18 g protein; 12 g fat (5.4 g sat.); 0.4 g carbo (0 g fiber); 263 mg sodium; 61 mg chol.

SWEET SIP

Jack Frost wines

■ *Eiswein*—ice wine in German—is made from grapes harvested and pressed while frozen. In Germany, where most eisweins are produced, freezing conditions at the crucial harvest time are iffy. Limited in supply therefore, the nectar is astronomically priced. However, in Canada, where freezing temperatures at harvest time are more reliable, ice wines are popping up from British Columbia to Quebec. Prices, though still lofty, are more modest; availability, though still spotty, is promising. Leading the pack to

bring ice wine to the West is Inniskillin Wines on the Niagara Peninsula in Ontario. Its Riesling ice wine (375 ml.) costs $65, its oak-aged Vidal ice wine (375 ml.) $80. Light and delectable for sipping, they're both exquisite when splashed over thin-sliced strawberries for a simple dessert. Once open, ice wines keep well up to two weeks if chilled airtight. Look for them in fine wine shops, call (650) 325-2909, or go to www.inniskillin.com. ◆

The Wine Guide

BY KAREN MacNEIL-FIFE

The right glass

■ When Tra Vigne, one of the Napa Valley's most popular restaurants, opened 12 years ago, it served all of its wines in small, chunky tumblers. For a brief instant, there was something charming about that—like being in a Sicilian trattoria. Within about a month, however, the tumblers were history, and in their place were big, long-stemmed wine goblets. The restaurant had been flooded with complaints from winemakers and consumers alike, none of whom seemed to think drinking a $30 Merlot out of a 99-cent tumbler was romantic in the least.

Which brings up an interesting question: Just how much does the glass matter? Is all the fuss about correct wine glasses just a question of aesthetics?

The answer isn't easy. On one hand, how a glass looks and feels in your hand and against your lips does count. On the other hand, does an $80 glass necessarily make a wine taste better than a well-designed $8 glass does? Moreover, is it important to adjust the shape of the glass for the variety of wine—to have different glasses for Merlot and Chardonnay?

After years of buying dozens of kinds of glasses, here's my advice.

• Don't buy glasses you can't afford to break. What's the point of buying $25 burgundy glasses if they sit in the cabinet because you're afraid to use them?

• Buy simple, clear glasses that are not cut, faceted, etched, or colored. You want to be able to see the wine; part of its beauty is how it looks in the glass. Crystal glasses are more elegant than regular glasses, but they're not necessary.

• Choose glasses with generous bowls. One way of maximizing a wine's flavor is by swirling it in the glass to aerate it. If the glass is too small to accommodate swirling, the wine in it

RICK MARIANI

can taste blank and lifeless.

• Don't bother to buy smaller glasses for white wines, larger ones for reds. Since both benefit from aerating, it's perfectly fine to serve both white and red in the same generous-size glasses.

• Always opt for a thin rim. Because liquids flow more easily and evenly over a thin rim than a thick, rolled one, drinking wine from a glass with a thin rim is more pleasurable.

• Be sure the rim of the glass tapers slightly inward. A tapered rim focuses the wine's aroma so you can smell and taste the wine better.

• Avoid small-footed glasses. The foot, or base, of the glass should be wide enough to keep the glass from tottering when it's filled with wine.

• As for the stem, there's no perfect length; you just have to pick up the glass and see how it feels. The stem's purpose is to give you a place to hold the glass easily without cupping the whole bowl in your hand.

A lot of $8 to $10 glasses meet every requirement above. For example, both at home and for the wine classes I teach, I use Riedel's all-

SAUVIGNON BLANCS FOR SPRING

April in Paris—at least in cafes and wine bars—is when warm goat cheese salads begin to replace heartier fare, and white wines, especially Sauvignon Blancs, begin to replace reds. Crisp, fresh-tasting, and herbal, Sauvignon Blanc is the perfect partner for the vegetables and salads of spring. And most are very affordable. (Note: *Fumé blanc* is another term for a wine made from Sauvignon Blanc grapes.)

Cakebread Cellars Sauvignon Blanc 1998 (Napa Valley), $15. Lovely and subtle, with soft lime flavors.

Chateau St. Jean La Petite Etoile Fumé Blanc 1998 (Russian River Valley), $14. Scrumptious flavors exude everything green, from snow peas to sage. This is St. Jean's most famous Sauvignon Blanc.

Husch Sauvignon Blanc 1998 (Mendocino), $12. Zesty and vibrant, with a good, fresh herbal snap.

Lambert Bridge Sauvignon Blanc 1998 (Dry Creek Valley), $14. A softer, creamier style but with fresh green flavors.

Markham Sauvignon Blanc 1998 (Napa Valley), $13. Sassy with lime, along with classic strawlike aromas and herbal flavors.

Mason Sauvignon Blanc 1998 (Napa Valley), $14. Dramatic and exotic, with loads of herbal flavors overlaid with tropical fruits.

purpose red wine glass called "Ouverture" (sold in many good wine shops). It is elegant, costs about $8, and works for every type of wine—red and white—except sparkling, for which I use a flute.

Sure, like many other wine lovers, I also have some specialized, different-shaped glasses for burgundies, Rhône wines, and Cabernets—glasses that come out for special bottles of wine, special occasions, and special friends. But most nights find me perfectly content with my basic Riedels. A good glass won't let you down (which, sadly enough, isn't always true of wine). ◆

Light-hearted casseroles

Magnificent low-fat main dishes that satisfy appetite and good intentions at once

BY ANDREW BAKER • PHOTOGRAPHS BY JAMES CARRIER

■ Childhood food memories, for many Westerners, come in the shape of casseroles—lasagna, enchiladas, baked stew with dumplings. These comfy dishes often fueled growing bodies with a generous helping of fat. Readers tell us they still crave the familiar flavors but—having no desire to keep growing—wish we could come up with recipes for hearty, *low-fat* versions.

Our readers' wish is our command—or challenge, in this case. And it was surprisingly easy to meet. We've shed fat calories and added fresh twists to a cosmopolitan collection of casseroles: The lasagna tiers are layered on potatoes instead of pasta; the meat loaf starts with lamb and conceals a core of seasoned bulgur wheat. Each is hearty enough to serve eight generously. All you need to add is a salad (we've provided a simple one that goes with practically everything) and a fat-shy dessert like crisp meringue cookies or fresh berries.

Cheese-stuffed Chicken with Wild Rice

PREP AND COOK TIME: About 1½ hours

NOTES: Assemble through step 3 up to 1 day ahead; chill airtight.

MAKES: 8 servings

- 3 cups fat-skimmed **chicken broth**
- 1¼ cups **wild rice**
- 1 tablespoon grated **orange** peel
- 2 cups **red pearl onions** (about ¾ in. wide) or coarsely chopped red onions
- 8 **boned, skinned chicken breast halves** (5 to 7 oz. each)
- 1 package (about 5 oz.) **garlic-herb-flavor Boursin** or Alouette **cheese**
- ¾ cup **orange marmalade**

  About 1 teaspoon fresh-ground **pepper**
- 2 tablespoons minced **fresh chives** or green onions

  Salt

1. In a 3- to 4-quart pan over high heat, bring broth, rice, and orange peel to a boil; cover, reduce heat, and simmer until rice is tender to bite, 50 to 60 minutes. As rice cooks, peel onions. Add onions (whole or chopped) to rice for the last 10 minutes of cooking.

2. Rinse chicken and pat dry. With a sharp knife, cut a horizontal slit about 2 inches long on the side of each breast, then wiggle knife back and forth to form a pocket as long and wide as possible without piercing the exterior of chicken. Spoon ⅛ of the cheese deep into each pocket.

3. Spoon rice mixture (including liquid) equally into 2 shallow casseroles (each 3 qt., about 9 by 13 in.). Lay 4 chicken breast halves, smooth side up, on rice in each casserole.

4. Bake, covered, in a 350° oven for 15 minutes.

5. In a bowl, mix marmalade and pep-per. Uncover casseroles, brush chicken evenly with marmalade mixture, and continue to bake until chicken is no longer pink in center of thickest part (cut to test), about 20 minutes.

6. Sprinkle with chives. Spoon rice and chicken breasts onto plates. Add salt and pepper to taste.

Per serving: 421 cal., 21% (87 cal.) from fat; 41 g protein; 9.7 g fat (5.8 g sat.); 43 g carbo (2 g fiber); 249 mg sodium; 103 mg chol.

ORANGE MARMALADE glazes cheese-stuffed chicken on wild rice.

16 **corn tortillas** (6 in.)

2 cups (½ lb.) **shredded jack cheese**

1 cup **tomato salsa**

Salt

1. Rinse peppers and discard stems, seeds, and veins. Cut peppers into ¼- by 2-inch pieces. Peel onions and cut into ¼- by 2-inch pieces.

2. Rinse pork, pat dry, and cut into ¼-inch-thick slices not more than 2 inches long. Set a 10- to 12-inch nonstick frying pan over high heat; add meat and stir just until no longer pink, about 2 minutes. Pour from pan into a bowl. When cool enough to handle, in about 5 minutes, tear meat into strips about ½ inch wide.

3. Meanwhile, add peppers, onions, broth, cumin, and garlic to frying pan. Stir often over high heat until liquid has evaporated and vegetables are lightly browned, about 10 minutes. Pour mixture into bowl with pork; add cilantro.

4. Pour enchilada sauce into frying pan and add juices from meat mixture. In another bowl, blend milk with cornstarch until smooth, and add to enchilada sauce. Bring to a boil over high heat, stirring often. Remove from heat.

5. Stack tortillas and enclose loosely in microwave-safe plastic wrap. Heat in a microwave oven at full power (100%) just until hot, 1 to 2 minutes.

6. Pour about 2 cups enchilada sauce mixture into each of 2 shallow casseroles (each 3 qt., about 9 by 13 in.). Turn 8 tortillas, 1 at a time, in sauce in 1 casserole and stack at 1 end. Distribute ⅟₁₆ of the pork mixture and 1 tablespoon cheese down center of each tortilla, 1 at a time. Roll to enclose filling; set tortillas, seam down and side by side, in sauce. Repeat to fill tortillas in remaining casserole.

7. Pour remaining enchilada sauce over tortillas, coating them evenly.

8. Bake, covered, in a 375° oven until enchiladas are hot (140° to 150°) in the center, 40 to 45 minutes. Uncover, sprinkle remaining cheese evenly over enchiladas, and bake until melted, 2 to 3 minutes longer.

9. Serve with a wide spatula. Add salsa and salt to taste.

Per serving: 466 cal., 25% (117 cal.) from fat; 34 g protein; 13 g fat (6.3 g sat.); 55 g carbo (3.9 g fiber); 1,793 mg sodium; 87 mg chol.

Chile Verde Enchiladas

PREP AND COOK TIME: About 1½ hours

NOTES: Assemble through step 7 up to 1 day ahead; chill airtight.

MAKES: 8 servings

2 **red bell peppers** (¾ lb. total)

2 **onions** (about ¾ lb. total)

1½ pounds fat-trimmed **pork tenderloin**

1 cup fat-skimmed **chicken broth**

1½ teaspoons **cumin seed**

1 tablespoon minced or pressed **garlic**

¼ cup minced **fresh cilantro**

2 cans (19 oz. each; 4 cups total) **green enchilada sauce**

2 cups **nonfat milk**

½ cup **cornstarch**

MEDITERRANEAN FLAVORS—lamb, bulgur, and spices—are layered in a loaf, served with creamy apricot-cucumber sauce.

Bulgur-Lamb Loaf

PREP AND COOK TIME: About 1½ hours

NOTES: Assemble through step 5 up to 1 day ahead; chill airtight.

MAKES: 8 servings

1½ cups **bulgur wheat**

4 cups fat-skimmed **beef broth**

1 **red bell pepper** (½ lb.)

½ cup minced **parsley**

1 cup thinly sliced **green onions** (including tops)

2 pounds **ground lean lamb** or ground lean beef

1 **onion** (about ½ lb.), peeled and finely chopped

1 tablespoon minced or pressed **garlic**

1 cup **fine dried bread crumbs**

¾ teaspoon **ground cinnamon**

1½ teaspoons *each* **ground coriander, ground cumin,** and **pepper**

Yogurt sauce (recipe follows)

Salt

1. Place bulgur in a deep bowl. In a 1½- to 2-quart pan over high heat, bring 2 cups broth to a boil. Add to bulgur, mix, and let stand until liquid is absorbed, about 10 minutes, stirring occasionally.

2. Meanwhile, rinse bell pepper. Slice off relatively flat sides; discard stem and seeds. Cut 6 decorative shapes, each about 1½ inches wide, from bell pepper slabs (use a cookie cutter if desired). Finely chop remaining pepper.

3. Add chopped bell pepper, parsley, and green onions to bulgur; mix well.

4. In a large bowl, combine lamb, onion, garlic, bread crumbs, cinnamon, coriander, cumin, pepper, and remaining 2 cups broth. Mix well.

5. In a shallow 3-quart casserole (about 9 by 13 in.), spread ½ the lamb mixture in an even layer. Cover with bulgur mix-

ture and gently pat level. Spread remaining lamb evenly over bulgur. Press decorative bell pepper pieces, skin side up, firmly onto surface of casserole.

6. Bake, covered, in a 425° oven for 30 minutes. Uncover and continue to bake until lamb is no longer pink in center (cut to test), about 20 minutes longer.

7. Cut into rectangles and use a wide spatula to lift out portions. Add yogurt sauce and salt to taste.

Per serving: 343 cal., 23% (80 cal.) from fat; 31 g protein; 8.9 g fat (3 g sat.); 36 g carbo (6.7 g fiber); 241 mg sodium; 75 mg chol.

Yogurt sauce. In a bowl, mix 1½ cups **plain nonfat yogurt,** 1½ cups finely chopped **cucumber,** ¾ cup finely chopped **dried apricots,** 3 tablespoons *each* minced **fresh mint** leaves and **fresh dill,** and **salt** to taste.

Per serving: 56 cal., 3.2% (1.8 cal.) from fat; 3 g protein; 0.2 g fat (0.1 g sat.); 12 g carbo (1.3 g fiber); 35 mg sodium; 0.9 mg chol.

Ham and Potato Lasagna

PREP AND COOK TIME: About 2¼ hours

NOTES: Assemble through step 5 up to 1 day ahead; chill airtight.

MAKES: 8 servings

- 2 cups fat-skimmed **chicken broth**
- ¼ cup **cornstarch**
- 1 **onion** (about ½ lb.), peeled and finely chopped
  About 1 teaspoon **olive** or salad **oil**
- 2 cups **low-fat (1%) milk**
- ½ teaspoon fresh-grated or ground **nutmeg**
- ½ teaspoon fresh-ground **pepper**
- ½ cup shredded **fontina cheese**
- 2 packages (10 oz. each) **frozen chopped spinach,** thawed
- 2 heads **fennel** (each about 4 in. wide)
- 2 pounds **russet potatoes**
- ½ pound **thin-sliced cooked ham**
- 2 tablespoons **shredded parmesan cheese**
  Salt

1. In a bowl, blend broth and cornstarch until smooth.

2. In a 2- to 3-quart pan over high heat, stir onion in 1 teaspoon oil until limp, about 5 minutes. Add broth mixture, milk, nutmeg, and pepper; stir until mixture boils. Remove from heat, add fontina cheese, and stir until melted.

3. Squeeze liquid from spinach. Rinse fennel. Chop and reserve ½ cup feathery green leaves; trim and discard remaining stalks, root ends, bruised areas, and coarse fibers from fennel heads. Cut heads crosswise into ⅛-inch slices.

4. Scrub and peel potatoes. Cut lengthwise into ⅛-inch slices.

5. Lightly oil a shallow 3-quart casserole (about 9 by 13 in.). Overlap ⅓ of the potatoes in an even layer over casserole bottom. Cover evenly with ½ the fennel, ½ the ham, and ½ the spinach; spoon ⅓ of the fontina cheese sauce over spinach. Repeat layers of potatoes, fennel, ham, spinach, and sauce. Cover sauce with remaining potatoes, then coat potatoes with remaining sauce.

6. Bake, covered, in a 375° oven for 30 minutes; uncover and continue baking until top is richly browned and potatoes are tender when pierced, about 1 hour longer (about 45 minutes longer in a convection oven). Sprinkle parmesan cheese over lasagna and bake 5 minutes more. Let stand 10 minutes.

7. Sprinkle with fennel leaves, cut into rectangles, and, with a wide spatula, lift out portions. Add salt to taste.

Per serving: 289 cal., 30% (86 cal.) from fat; 19 g protein; 9.5 g fat (4.7 g sat.); 32 g carbo (4.2 g fiber); 729 mg sodium; 38 mg chol.

Baked Penne with Double Mushroom Sauce

PREP AND COOK TIME: About 1½ hours

NOTES: Assemble through step 5 up to 1 day ahead; chill airtight.

MAKES: 8 servings

- 2 pounds **common mushrooms** (about 1 in. wide)
- 2 **onions** (about 1 lb. total), peeled and finely chopped
- 2 tablespoons minced or pressed **garlic**
- 4 cups fat-skimmed **beef** or vegetable **broth**
- 1 ounce (¾ cup) **dried porcini mushrooms**
- ¼ cup **cornstarch**
- 1½ cups **dry vermouth**
- 1 teaspoon **fresh thyme** leaves or dried thyme
- ¾ pound **dried penne pasta**
- 1 cup **shredded part-skim mozzarella cheese**
- 2 tablespoons **shredded parmesan cheese**
- 2 tablespoons minced **parsley**
  Salt and **pepper**

1. Rinse and drain common mushrooms. Trim and discard discolored stem ends; cut mushrooms wider than 1 inch in half lengthwise through caps.

2. In a 5- to 6-quart pan, combine mushrooms, onions, garlic, and ½ cup broth. Stir often over high heat until liquid has evaporated and mushrooms begin to brown, about 20 minutes. Add 1½ cups broth and stir often until liquid has evaporated, 12 to 15 minutes longer.

3. Meanwhile, in a bowl, pour 2 cups boiling water over porcini mushrooms; let stand until mushrooms are limp, about 10 minutes. Squeeze porcinis in water to release grit, then lift out, squeeze dry, and chop. Slowly pour out 1¾ cups soaking water, leaving sediment behind, and reserve; discard remainder.

4. In another bowl, blend remaining

POTATOES STAND IN for pasta in a light, luscious lasagna.

2 cups broth with cornstarch. Add chopped porcinis, soaking liquid, vermouth, and thyme to pan with common mushrooms. Mix in cornstarch mixture and stir until boiling. Remove from heat.

5. In another 5- to 6-quart pan over high heat, bring 3 quarts water to a boil. Add pasta and stir occasionally until tender to bite, about 12 minutes. Drain. Mix pasta with mushroom sauce; add mozzarella cheese and stir to blend. Pour pasta mixture into a shallow 3-quart casserole (about 9 by 13 in.).

6. Bake, covered, in a 350° oven until sauce begins to bubble, about 25 minutes (1 to 1¼ hours if chilled). Uncover, sprinkle evenly with parmesan cheese, and bake about 5 minutes longer. Let stand 10 minutes.

7. Sprinkle with parsley. Spoon out portions. Add salt and pepper to taste.

Per serving: 297 cal., 11% (34 cal.) from fat; 16 g protein; 3.8 g fat (1.8 g sat.); 50 g carbo (4.3 g fiber); 138 mg sodium; 9.2 mg chol.

Beef and Chili Stew with Cornbread Dumplings

PREP AND COOK TIME: About 2 hours

NOTES: Assemble through step 3 up to 1 day ahead; chill airtight.

MAKES: 8 servings

- 1 pound **fresh poblano** (often labeled pasilla) **chilies,** rinsed

- 1½ pounds fat-trimmed **beef skirt steak**
- 2 **onions** (1 lb. total), peeled and chopped
- 2 teaspoons minced or pressed **garlic**
- 2 tablespoons **tomato paste**
- 2 cups fat-skimmed **beef broth**
- 1½ teaspoons **dried oregano**
- 1 package (10 oz.) **frozen corn kernels**
- ¼ cup **cornstarch**
- 1¼ cups **yellow cornmeal**
- 1¼ cups **all-purpose flour**
- 2 teaspoons **baking powder**
- 1 tablespoon **sugar**
  About ½ teaspoon **salt**
- ⅓ cup thinly sliced **green onions** (including tops)
- 1 **large egg**
- 1¼ cups **low-fat** (1%) **buttermilk**

1. Place chilies in a 10- by 15-inch pan. Broil 4 to 6 inches from heat, turning as needed, until blackened on all sides, about 15 minutes. When cool enough to handle, in about 10 minutes, pull off and discard chili peels, stems, seeds, and veins. Cut chilies into ½-inch pieces.

2. Meanwhile, rinse meat and pat dry. Cut into ½- by 1-inch pieces.

The casseroles here need only a salad and a simple dessert (frozen yogurt, angel food cake with berries) to make a full meal. Here's a simple recipe for greens that lives up to its name.

Go-with-Everything Salad

PREP TIME: About 15 minutes
MAKES: 8 servings

In a blender or food processor, combine ¼ cup **dried tomatoes** and ¼ cup boiling **water;** let stand 2 to 3 minutes. Add ⅓ cup **seasoned rice vinegar** and ¼ teaspoon **hot chili flakes** (optional), and whirl until smooth. Stir in 2 tablespoons minced **fresh chives** or green onions. Tear 4 quarts rinsed and crisped **butter lettuce** leaves into bite-size pieces and place in a wide bowl. Add tomato dressing, mix, and add **salt** and **pepper** to taste.

Per serving: 28 cal., 6.4% (1.8 cal.) from fat; 1.8 g protein; 0.2 g fat (0 g sat.); 5.8 g carbo (1.5 g fiber); 204 mg sodium; 0 mg chol.

3. In a 5- to 6-quart pan over high heat, stir meat, onions, garlic, tomato paste, and ½ cup broth until liquid evaporates and meat and onions are browned, about 25 minutes. Add chilies, remaining broth, 2 cups water, and oregano. Bring to a boil; cover, reduce heat, and simmer until meat is very tender when pierced, about 1 hour. Stir in corn.

4. In a bowl, blend cornstarch and ½ cup water until smooth. Add to pan and stir over high heat until mixture boils. Pour stew into a 3-quart casserole (about 9 by 13 in.).

5. In a bowl, combine cornmeal, flour, baking powder, sugar, ½ teaspoon salt, and green onions. In another bowl, beat egg to blend; mix in buttermilk. Add egg mixture to cornmeal mixture and stir just until evenly moistened. Drop by ¼-cup portions evenly over stew.

6. Bake in a 400° oven until dumplings are firm and lightly browned, about 20 minutes.

7. Spoon portions into bowls; add salt to taste.

Per serving: 430 cal., 23% (99 cal.) from fat; 27 g protein; 11 g fat (4.4 g sat.); 56 g carbo (4.1 g fiber); 447 mg sodium; 73 mg chol. ◆

BEEF AND CHILI STEW wears a gold crown: a green onion–flecked cornmeal dumpling.

Easy eggs Benedict, from lavish to light

Step-by-step directions to demystify the brunch classic— and add some lighter options

BY ELAINE JOHNSON

ON A SUNNY SUNDAY MORNING, treat yourself to traditional eggs Benedict.

JAMES CARRIER

Crisp English muffins, slices of smoky Canadian bacon, delicate poached eggs, butter-rich hollandaise—the layers of classic eggs Benedict are rather grand. And getting the yolks soft but not too runny, the sauce emulsified without breaking, and all the components hot at the same time can seem intimidating.

Truth is, each step is a simple process, and the serving temperature of the elements is flexible. We've separated the reputedly difficult parts—the eggs and the hollandaise—into individual recipes; make them in the sequence described in the notes for the classic Benedict recipe and you'll get a perfect dish every time.

But feel free to tamper with tradition. Substitute our zesty lemon-caper sauce for the hollandaise, bagels for the English muffins. Or instead of Canadian bacon, add smoked salmon—a grand tradition on its own.

Classic Eggs Benedict

PREP AND COOK TIME: About 1¼ hours
NOTES: First poach the eggs; let stand in cold water. Then make the hollandaise and let it stand at room temperature. When muffins and bacon go in the oven, reheat eggs.
MAKES: 6 servings

  6 **English muffins**

 12 slices (7 oz. total) **Canadian bacon**

 12 warm **perfect poached eggs** (recipe, page 110)

     Foolproof hollandaise (recipe follows)

 2½ cups lightly packed **watercress sprigs**, rinsed

1. Split muffins in half horizontally and arrange in a single layer, cut sides up, on a 14- by 17-inch baking sheet. Lay bacon slices in a single layer in a 10- by 15-inch pan.

2. In a 450° oven, bake muffins and bacon until browned, 5 to 7 minutes.

3. Place 2 muffin halves, cut sides up, on each plate. Lay 1 bacon slice on each muffin half; set 1 egg on each slice of bacon. Spoon hollandaise equally over portions. Arrange watercress next to muffins.

Per serving: 811 cal., 71% (576 cal.) from fat; 27 g protein; 64 g fat (34 g sat.); 29 g carbo (1.5 g fiber); 1,617 mg sodium; 776 mg chol.

Foolproof Hollandaise

PREP AND COOK TIME: About 20 minutes
NOTES: This method produces a bacteria-safe sauce. However, if sauce gets too hot, it may separate. To bring back together, put 2 tablespoons water in a blender or bowl. With motor running or while whisking, add the separated sauce in a slow, steady stream.
MAKES: 2¼ cups; 6 servings

 1½ cups (¾ lb.) **butter** or margarine, cut into chunks

  6 **large egg** yolks

 ¼ cup **lemon juice**

  2 tablespoons **Dijon mustard**

1. In a microwave-safe 2-cup glass measure in a microwave oven at full power (100%), or in a 1- to 2-quart pan over medium-high heat, melt butter until bubbling.

2. Meanwhile, in the bottom of a double boiler or in a 2- to 3-quart pan, bring 1 inch water to a simmer over high heat; adjust heat to maintain simmer.

3. Put yolks, lemon juice, and mustard in the top of the double boiler or in a round-bottomed bowl (about 2 qt.). Nest the container over simmering water and whisk to blend.

4. Whisking, add butter in a slow, steady stream, taking about 1½ minutes. Whisk until sauce reaches 140°; adjust heat to maintain temperature (remove from simmering water if necessary) and continue to whisk for 3 minutes. Immediately remove from simmering water. Serve hollandaise hot, warm, or at room temperature.

Per serving: 473 cal., 97% (459 cal.) from fat;
3.3 g protein; 51 g fat (30 g sat.); 1 g carbo
(0 g fiber); 598 mg sodium; 337 mg chol.

Bagels and Lox Benedict

PREP AND COOK TIME: About 1 hour

NOTES: Ann Beck of Tucson combines two great traditions in this Benedict. First poach the eggs, then make the lemon-caper sauce and keep warm while the eggs reheat.

MAKES: 6 servings

  6 **plain bagels** (1⅓ lb. total)

  9 ounces **thin-sliced smoked salmon** (lox)

 12 slices (¹⁄₁₆ in. thick) **red onion** (6 oz. total)

 12 warm **perfect poached eggs** (recipe below)

     Light lemon-caper sauce (recipe follows)

     Fresh dill sprigs

1. Cut bagels in half horizontally. Place halves in a single layer, cut sides up, on

JAMES CARRIER

Perfect Poached Eggs

PREP AND COOK TIME: Approximately 25 minutes

NOTES: Heating the eggs in the shell first keeps them from sticking together as they poach. You can serve the eggs as soon as they're cooked, but they're easier to manage if you poach them even a few minutes ahead, then reheat.

MAKES: 12 eggs

1. Put about 3 inches **water** in a 5- to 6-quart pan; bring to a boil over high

a 14- by 17-inch baking sheet.

2. Bake in a 450° oven until golden, 5 to 8 minutes.

3. Put 2 bagel halves on each plate; top equally with salmon and onion. Place an egg on each half; spoon lemon-caper sauce equally over portions. Garnish with dill.

Per serving: 556 cal., 28% (153 cal.) from fat;
35 g protein; 17 g fat (5.7 g sat.); 63 g carbo
(2.6 g fiber); 1,827 mg sodium; 443 mg chol.

Light Lemon-Caper Sauce

PREP AND COOK TIME: About 10 minutes

NOTES: If making sauce up to 2 days ahead, cool and chill airtight. To serve, stir over medium-high heat until steaming.

MAKES: 2 cups; 6 servings

  1 cup fat-skimmed **chicken broth**

  2 tablespoons **cornstarch**

 ¾ cup **reduced-fat sour cream**

  2 tablespoons **lemon juice**

  2 tablespoons drained **capers**

     Salt and **pepper**

heat. With a slotted spoon, quickly and gently immerse 12 **large eggs** in the shell, 1 at a time, in water for 8 seconds; lift out.

2. Pour out all but 1 inch water from the pan; reduce heat so bubbles on the pan bottom pop to the surface only occasionally. Crack eggs 1 at a time, holding each shell close to the water surface as you break it open to let egg slide gently into water. If necessary, cook half the eggs at a time to keep from crowding. Cook to desired doneness (poke gently with a spoon to check), 3 to 4 minutes for soft-cooked eggs.

3. With slotted spoon, lift eggs 1 at a time from water and immediately immerse in a bowl of cold water. If making up to 2 days ahead, wrap bowl airtight and chill.

4. To reheat eggs, immerse in hot (about 120°) water until warm to touch, 5 to 10 minutes. Lift out with slotted spoon.

Per egg: 75 cal., 60% (45 cal.) from fat;
6.2 g protein; 5 g fat (1.5 g sat.);
0.6 g carbo (0 g fiber); 140 mg sodium;
212 mg chol.

1. In a 2- to 3-quart pan, whisk broth and cornstarch until smooth. Stir over medium-high heat until boiling, 2 to 3 minutes.

2. Whisk in sour cream, lemon juice, and capers; stir frequently just until steaming, 2 to 3 minutes. Season to taste with salt and pepper.

Per serving: 69 cal., 52% (36 cal.) from fat;
3.4 g protein; 4 g fat (2 g sat.); 5.1 g carbo
(0 g fiber); 156 mg sodium; 10 mg chol.

Monte Cristo Eggs Benedict

PREP AND COOK TIME: About 50 minutes

NOTES: This is a takeoff on the classic Monte Cristo sandwich—turkey and Swiss cheese coated in an egg batter and grilled. The Benedict can be decadent or leaner, depending on the sauce you choose.

MAKES: 6 servings

  1 loaf (1 lb., about 5 in. wide) **sourdough bread**

 ¾ pound **thin-sliced smoked turkey breast**

 ¾ pound **thin-sliced Swiss cheese**

 12 slices (¹⁄₁₆ in. thick) **red onion** (about 6 oz. total)

 12 warm **perfect poached eggs** (recipe at left)

     Foolproof hollandaise (recipe, page 109) or light lemon-caper sauce (recipe at left)

     Chopped **Italian parsley**

1. Trim ends from loaf and save for other uses; cut bread diagonally into 12 equal slices. Arrange slices in a single layer on a 14- by 17-inch baking sheet.

2. Bake in a 450° oven until golden, 4 to 5 minutes. Lay turkey slices equally on bread, then cover equally with cheese. Bake until cheese is melted, 3 to 5 minutes.

3. Set 2 of the open-faced sandwiches on each plate. Top each with a slice of onion and an egg. Spoon sauce equally over portions. Garnish with parsley.

Per serving with hollandaise: 1,122 cal.,
65% (729 cal.) from fat; 51 g protein; 81 g fat
(45 g sat.); 47 g carbo (2.5 g fiber); 2,022 mg
sodium; 836 mg chol.

Per serving with lemon-caper sauce: 717 cal.,
43% (306 cal.) from fat; 51 g protein; 34 g fat
(16 g sat.); 51 g carbo (2.5 g fiber); 1,580 mg
sodium; 509 mg chol. ◆

Great ways with greens

Savory dishes—from homey to elegant—that show off
spring's bright leafy veggies

BY ELAINE JOHNSON • PHOTOGRAPHS BY JAMES CARRIER

MUSTARD GREENS AND RICOTTA fill lasagna circles in a parmesan cheese sauce.

I't's a jungle out there—or at least it
can seem that way in the cooking-
greens section of the produce department. We all know that greens are
nutritional giants, loaded with vitamins
A and C, folic acid, and calcium. But
some look way too unruly to bring
home to dinner.

Taming the wild things, however, is
more fun than it used to be. New, strik-
ingly colorful or rambunctiously shaped
varieties such as rainbow-colored Swiss
chard, purple kale, and Lacinato kale,
once available only in farmers' markets,
perch in supermarket bins. (See our
guide to some of the most interesting

ones on page 114.) And produce companies are domesticating many leafy
greens by selling them stemmed,
washed, and bagged. Spinach has long
been available this way; now Swiss
chard, kale, and collard, mustard, and
turnip greens are following suit.

Though cooking greens are available
year-round, they're sweetest during
cool weather, before summer heat
brings out their stronger flavors. So
grab a bag or a bunch. With a hot pan
and a little olive oil and garlic, the wild
tangle becomes a manageable couple of
cups, delicious on its own or as a base
for other dishes.

Green Lasagna Swirls

PREP AND COOK TIME: About 1¼ hours
NOTES: Use a single kind of greens or a
mix of mustard greens, Swiss chard,
and spinach.
MAKES: 5 to 7 servings

- 1 package (8 oz.) **dried lasagna**
  (1¼ in. wide)
- 2 cups chopped **onions** (about ½ lb.)
- 2 tablespoons **butter** or margarine
- 2 tablespoons **all-purpose flour**
- 1½ cups fat-skimmed **chicken broth**
- 1 cup **low-fat milk**
- 3 cups (about ¾ lb.) **fresh-grated
  parmesan cheese**

  Basic sautéed greens (recipe,
  page 112; see notes)

- 2 tablespoons minced **fresh
  marjoram** leaves or 2 teaspoons
  dried marjoram
- 1 tablespoon minced **fresh sage**
  leaves or 1 teaspoon dried
  rubbed sage
- ¼ teaspoon **ground nutmeg**
- 1 cup **part-skim milk ricotta
  cheese**
- 2 **large eggs**

  Salt and **pepper**

1. In a 5- to 6-quart pan over high heat,
bring 3 quarts water to a boil. Add
lasagna and stir occasionally just until
tender to bite, about 10 minutes. Drain,
immerse in cold water until cool, then
drain again.

2. Meanwhile, in a 2- to 3-quart pan
over medium-high heat, frequently stir
onions in butter until limp, 8 to 10 minutes. Add flour and stir for 1 minute.
Whisk in broth and milk, and continue
whisking until mixture boils. Remove
from heat and stir in 2 cups parmesan.
Spread half the sauce in a shallow
3-quart casserole.

3. Drain greens; save liquid for other
uses. Finely chop greens. In a bowl,
mix greens, marjoram, sage, nutmeg,
ricotta, ¾ cup parmesan, and eggs.

4. One at a time, lay lasagna strips flat;
spread about 2½ tablespoons greens
mixture evenly over each, then roll up
from 1 end. Stand rolls upright, side
by side, on sauce in casserole. Spread
remaining sauce evenly over rolls. Seal
pan with foil.

Basic Sautéed Greens

PREP AND COOK TIME: 15 to 35 minutes

NOTES: For all greens except spinach, you'll need to buy 1 pound in bunches or ¾ pound in bags to yield 2 to 2½ cups cooked. For spinach, buy 2 pounds in bunches, ¾ pound in bags. If beet greens are attached to beets, buy about 2½ pounds; save beets for other uses. To keep greens with red stems or leaves from turning blue during cooking, add 1 tablespoon lemon juice along with greens in step 3.

MAKES: 2 to 2½ cups; 4 servings

- ¾ to 2 pounds **cooking greens** (see notes; choices listed on page 114)
- 1 tablespoon **olive oil**
- 2 cloves **garlic,** peeled and thinly sliced
  Salt and **pepper**

1. Discard yellowed or wilted leaves from greens. If greens aren't washed, immerse in cold water and rinse well; drain.

2. For Swiss chard or beet greens, trim and discard discolored stem ends, then thinly slice stems; trim and discard stems from other greens. Coarsely chop leaves from all greens.

3. Pour oil into a 6- to 8-quart pan over high heat. When hot, add garlic; stir until limp, about 15 seconds. Add greens with the water that clings to leaves (if greens are dry, add ¼ cup water); stir often until greens are wilted, about 2 minutes. For spinach, proceed to step 5.

4. Add ½ cup water, reduce heat to medium, and simmer, covered, until greens are tender to bite, 5 to 12 minutes for medium-textured greens, and up to 25 minutes for firm ones. If all liquid evaporates during cooking, add about ⅓ cup more water.

5. Season to taste with salt and pepper.

Per serving for spinach: 51 cal., 65% (33 cal.) from fat; 2.5 g protein; 3.7 g fat (0.5 g sat.); 3.5 g carbo (2.2 g fiber); 67 mg sodium; 0 mg chol.

SPINACH NEVER TASTED SO GOOD: With gorgonzola cheese in a cornmeal-crust tart.

5. Bake lasagna in a 375° oven until bubbling in center, about 45 minutes (about 30 minutes in a convection oven). Uncover and sprinkle with remaining ¼ cup parmesan. Broil 5 to 6 inches from heat until parmesan begins to brown, about 4 minutes.

6. Season to taste with salt and pepper.

Per serving with mustard greens: 515 cal., 44% (225 cal.) from fat; 35 g protein; 25 g fat (14 g sat.); 37 g carbo (1.6 g fiber); 1,050 mg sodium; 120 mg chol.

Spinach and Blue Cheese Tarts

PREP AND COOK TIME: About 1 hour

NOTES: Prepare sautéed greens using 1¼ pounds (5 quarts) washed spinach. If making crusts up to 1 day ahead, cool, then store airtight at room temperature; reheat in a 350° oven until hot to touch, 8 to 10 minutes.

MAKES: 6 first-course servings

- 1¼ cups **all-purpose flour**
- ⅓ cup **yellow cornmeal**
- ½ teaspoon **baking powder**
- ½ teaspoon **salt**
- ½ cup (¼ lb.) **butter** or margarine, cut into chunks
- 1 **large egg**
- 2 tablespoons **olive oil**
- 1 cup (5 oz.) ½-inch chunks **gorgonzola** or Stilton **cheese**
  Basic sautéed greens (recipe at left; see notes)

1. In a food processor or bowl, combine flour, cornmeal, baking powder, and salt; whirl or stir to blend. Add butter; whirl or rub with your fingers until fine crumbs form. Add egg and oil; whirl or stir with a fork until dough holds together. Divide into 6 equal portions.

2. Press 1 portion of dough evenly over bottom and up sides of each of 6 tart pans (4½ in. wide) with removable rims. Place pans on a 12- by 15-inch baking sheet.

3. Bake in a 300° oven until crusts are golden brown, 35 to 40 minutes. Sprinkle cheese evenly in warm crusts. Return to oven and bake until cheese is melted, about 5 minutes longer.

4. Drain hot cooked greens in a colander, pressing with a spoon to extract liquid (save liquid for other uses). Spoon equally over cheese in crusts.

5. Remove rims from tart pans and set tarts on plates.

Per serving: 436 cal., 64% (279 cal.) from fat; 12 g protein; 31 g fat (16 g sat.); 30 g carbo (3.6 g fiber); 801 mg sodium; 98 mg chol.

Bacon and Vinegar Chard

PREP AND COOK TIME: About 20 minutes
MAKES: 4 servings

Follow directions for **basic sautéed greens** (recipe, facing page), using **Swiss chard.** In step 3 omit olive oil and garlic; instead, in a 6- to 8-quart pan over medium-high heat, stir ½ pound chopped **sliced bacon** often until browned, about 5 minutes. With a slotted spoon, transfer bacon to a towel. Discard all but 1 tablespoon fat from pan. Add greens to pan and proceed. Stir 2 tablespoons **balsamic vinegar** and the cooked bacon into cooked chard in step 4.

Per serving: 137 cal., 72% (99 cal.) from fat; 6.9 g protein; 11 g fat (3.6 g sat.); 4.6 g carbo (1.9 g fiber); 512 mg sodium; 16 mg chol.

Greens and Hominy

PREP AND COOK TIME: About 20 minutes
MAKES: 4 servings

Follow directions for **basic sautéed greens** (recipe, facing page), using **collard, mustard, or turnip greens** or **kale.** Add 1 drained can (15 oz.) **hominy** to cooked greens in step 4, and stir until hominy is hot, about 3 minutes.

Per serving: 135 cal., 30% (41 cal.) from fat; 3 g protein; 4.5 g fat (0.6 g sat.); 22 g carbo (5.4 g fiber); 241 mg sodium; 0 mg chol.

Black Bean Mustard Greens

PREP AND COOK TIME: About 20 minutes
NOTES: Salted fermented black beans are available at Asian markets and well-stocked supermarkets.
MAKES: 4 servings

1. Follow directions for **basic sautéed greens** (recipe, facing page), using **mustard greens.** In step 4 add 1 tablespoon rinsed, drained **salted fermented black beans** and ½ teaspoon **hot chili flakes** to pan along with greens.

2. Meanwhile, stack 10 **won ton skins** (3½ in. square; 2 oz. total). Slice into ¼-inch strips; gently separate with your fingers. Heat 1½ tablespoons **salad oil** in a 6- to 8-quart pan over medium-high heat. Add won ton strips and stir often until golden, 3 to 4 minutes. With a slotted spoon, transfer strips to a towel.

3. In step 5, top greens with won ton strips.

Per serving: 145 cal., 57% (82 cal.) from fat; 4.1 g protein; 9.1 g fat (1.1 g sat.); 13 g carbo (0.9 g fiber); 212 mg sodium; 1.3 mg chol.

Greens, Sausage, and Bean Soup

PREP AND COOK TIME: About 1 hour
NOTES: Use any green variety of kale; collard, turnip, or mustard greens; or Swiss chard.
MAKES: About 3 quarts; 6 to 8 servings

- 1 pound **greens** (see notes)
- 2 cups sliced **onions** (½ lb.)
- 1 cup sliced **carrots**
- 1 cup sliced **celery**
- 1 tablespoon **olive oil**
- 1 tablespoon minced **garlic**
- 2 teaspoons **dried thyme** leaves
- ½ pound **kielbasa** (Polish) **sausage,** thinly sliced
- 1 cup **dry white wine**
- 2 quarts fat-skimmed **chicken broth**
- 2 cans (1 lb. each) **cannellini** (white) **beans,** rinsed and drained

  Pepper

1. Discard any yellowed or wilted leaves

VIVID KALE simmers with sausage, vegetables, and white wine in a hearty soup.

A gallery of greens

■ Supermarkets carry most of these greens. At farmers' markets, you'll find an even wider selection. We've divided the greens according to sturdiness; in the recipes here, use the lower range of cooking times for tender greens, the middle of the range for medium ones, and the top of the range for firm.

TENDER
Spinach. Sweet but slightly astringent.

MEDIUM
Beet greens. Earthy.
Braising mix. Mild to full-flavored, depending on the makeup of the mix; may contain bok choy, kale, escarole, beet greens, and multiple colors of Swiss chard.
Collard greens. Robust, slightly bittersweet.
Mustard greens. Pungent bite mellows with cooking.
Ornamental kale. Nutty, with cabbagelike heads.

Mustard greens

Swiss chard

Ornamental kale

Purple kale

Lacinato kale

Swiss chard. Mild and slightly smoky (green variety) to earthy (red). May be green, red, or rainbow-colored (red, pink, orange, yellow, and green).
Turnip greens. Mellow and slightly sweet.

FIRM
Kale. Robust and herbaceous.
Lacinato kale (also called dinosaur kale or Tuscan cabbage). Robust, grassy.
Purple kale. Very robust and slightly bitter.

---

from greens. If greens aren't washed, immerse in cold water and rinse well; drain. For Swiss chard, trim and discard discolored stem ends; thinly slice stems. Trim and discard stems from other greens. Chop leaves from all greens.

2. In a 6- to 8-quart pan over medium-high heat, frequently stir onions, carrots, celery, oil, garlic, thyme, and kielbasa until sausage is browned, about 10 minutes.

3. Add wine, broth, beans, and greens. Bring to a boil over high heat, then reduce heat and simmer, covered, until greens are tender to bite, 20 to 25 minutes. Season to taste with pepper.

Per serving with kale: 281 cal., 32% (90 cal.) from fat; 20 g protein; 10 g fat (3.1 g sat.); 23 g carbo (6.5 g fiber); 560 mg sodium; 19 mg chol.

Polenta and Greens Gratin

PREP AND COOK TIME: About 1 hour
NOTES: Use mustard greens, spinach, Swiss chard, or a combination. Assemble through step 2 up to 1 day ahead; let cool, then seal with foil and chill. Bake, covered, in a 350° oven for 30 minutes, then uncover, sprinkle with bread crumb mixture (step 3), and proceed.
MAKES: 6 to 8 servings

4½   cups fat-skimmed **chicken broth**
       About 3 tablespoons **butter** or margarine

1   cup **polenta**

1   cup (4 oz.) shredded **fontina cheese**

     Basic sautéed greens (recipe, page 112; see notes)

3   cups fresh coarse **bread** crumbs

     Salt and **pepper**

1. In a 3- to 4-quart pan over high heat, stir broth, 1 tablespoon butter, and polenta until boiling. Reduce heat to medium and simmer, stirring often, until polenta is soft to bite, 8 to 10 minutes. Stir in ½ cup cheese.

2. Scrape polenta into a buttered shallow 2½- to 3-quart casserole, and spread level. Drain greens; spread evenly over polenta.

3. In a bowl, combine remaining ½ cup cheese and the bread crumbs. Melt 2 tablespoons butter and stir into bread crumb mixture. Sprinkle evenly over the greens.

4. Bake in a 350° oven until crumbs are browned, 25 to 30 minutes. Season to taste with salt and pepper.

Per serving with mustard greens: 311 cal., 32% (99 cal.) from fat; 14 g protein; 11 g fat (5.8 g sat.); 38 g carbo (4.1 g fiber); 294 mg sodium; 29 mg chol.

Italian Chard Bundles

PREP AND COOK TIME: About 55 minutes

NOTES: Use rainbow-colored Swiss chard or a single color. If desired, garnish bundles with drained canned anchovies.

MAKES: 8 servings

1½ pounds **Swiss chard** (see notes)

2½ tablespoons **extra-virgin olive oil**

1 tablespoon chopped drained **canned anchovy fillets**

1 tablespoon **lemon juice**

Salt and **pepper**

Lemon wedges

1. Discard any yellowed or wilted leaves from the Swiss chard. Immerse chard in cold water and rinse well; drain. Trim and discard discolored stem ends, then cut off stems flush with the base of the leaves.

2. In a 6- to 8-quart pan over high heat, bring 4 quarts water to a boil. Add the chard stems, cover, and simmer over medium heat until limp, about 10 minutes. Lift out with a slotted spoon and let cool.

3. Push leaves into water and cook, uncovered, until center veins are pliable, 3 to 5 minutes. Lift out with a slotted spoon and immerse in cold water until cool; drain and pat dry.

4. Set aside the 8 most perfect leaves (each about 8 in. long and 5 to 6 in. wide). Chop remaining leaves and the stems; in a bowl, mix chopped chard with 2 tablespoons oil, anchovies, lemon juice, and salt and pepper to taste.

5. Lay reserved leaves flat. Mound an equal amount of chopped chard mixture near base of each leaf. Fold sides over filling, then roll up from base to enclose.

6. Set chard bundles on a platter and brush evenly with remaining ½ tablespoon oil. Serve with lemon wedges to squeeze over bundles to taste.

Per serving: 57 cal., 74% (42 cal.) from fat; 2.1 g protein; 4.7 g fat (0.7 g sat.); 3 g carbo (1.3 g fiber); 250 mg sodium; 1.2 mg chol.

Spinach and Cracked Wheat Pilaf

PREP AND COOK TIME: About 30 minutes

MAKES: 5 cups; 5 to 7 servings

1 tablespoon **olive oil**

½ cup **dried currants**

1 cup **bulgur wheat**

1½ cups fat-skimmed **chicken broth** or vegetable broth

2 teaspoons grated **lemon** peel

½ teaspoon **hot chili flakes**

Basic sautéed greens (recipe, page 112; use spinach)

Salt and **pepper**

1. In a 3- to 4-quart pan over medium-high heat, frequently stir oil, currants, and bulgur until currants are limp, about 4 minutes. Add the broth, lemon peel, and chili flakes. Bring mixture to a boil over high heat, then remove from heat, cover, and let stand until bulgur is tender to bite, about 20 minutes.

2. Stir greens into bulgur mixture. Season to taste with salt and pepper.

Per serving: 152 cal., 26% (39 cal.) from fat; 6 g protein; 4.3 g fat (0.6 g sat.); 25 g carbo (5.5 g fiber); 59 mg sodium; 0 mg chol. ◆

ORANGE SWISS CHARD makes a colorful wrap for first-course bundles of more chard seasoned with anchovies.

all-star San Francisco

A new ballpark. A new waterfront. A boom in SoMa. Everybody's favorite city just got even better

BY JEFF PHILLIPS • PHOTOGRAPHS BY CATHERINE KARNOW

On the waterfront: Attractions of the new San Francisco range from the revived Embarcadero to the baseball stadium and Yerba Buena Gardens (see map). At dusk, the Bay Bridge glitters behind the new Embarcadero promenade, a favorite route of cyclists and strollers (left).

There's no doubt that San Francisco's top ranking in the major leagues of American cities is firmer than ever. A new baseball stadium, PacBell Park, is only the latest step in a complete redevelopment of San Francisco's most prized asset, its waterfront. This transformation began with a disaster: the 1989 Loma Prieta earthquake that shattered the view-blocking, shadow-casting Embarcadero Freeway—and suddenly gave the city a chance to rethink the face it showed to San Francisco Bay.

The new waterfront started becoming visible last year, with the ground-breaking for Harry Bridges Plaza at the foot of Market Street. Next came the new trolley service extending from Market Street north to Fisherman's Wharf and south to the rail-road station. Finishing touches were then applied to the wide public promenade—roomy enough for strollers, bikers, and skaters—that edges the waterfront for 2½ miles from Pier 39 down to the new ballpark.

Combine the resurgent waterfront with the boom of new hotels and restaurants south of Market Street (SoMa), the completion of Yerba Buena Gardens on Mission Street, and the conversion of gritty South Park machine shops and warehouses into the hard drive of Multimedia Gulch, and you can almost feel the city's center of gravity shifting south from Union Square and the financial district.

This is the new San Francisco.

■ Along the Embarcadero

On the bridge of the tugboat *Delta Carey,* captain Steve Ware sips a mug of coffee as we make an early-morning run past the Ferry Building for a waterside view of the new ballpark. We pass Pier 30–32, where the sign on an odd-looking, rusty barge reads, "Allied Cannery Co."

"This is where Don Johnson films his *Nash Bridges* television show," Ware says, nodding at the barge. The owner of Baydelta Maritime, the last tug service based along the Embarcadero, Ware has worked these waters for 35 years. While he misses the days when San Francisco had a true, working waterfront, he's also realistic about the changing nature of the city.

Gunning all 4,400 horses of his powerful tractor tug, Ware swings by PacBell Park. From the water the grandstands, which rise in three angled tiers, are screened by the forest of sailboat masts in South Beach Harbor; the promenade where ferries will unload baseball fans gleams in the morning sun. "This is the future," says Ware as he drops me back on terra firma. "It's already bringing the waterfront back to life."

It's a short walk from the harbor north to the trendy Town's End Restaurant, which serves up the best breakfast along the waterfront. After a heaping plate of potatoes and scrambled eggs with salmon, I continue north up the promenade, admiring viewscapes between the piers. Stopping at the Ferry Building, I meet Port of San Francisco planner Anne Cook, who quickly runs me through the waterfront plan.

The plan, started in 1990 and shaped during six years of complex public review, covers everything from the tips of the piers to the land side of the Embarcadero. "The underlying premise was always to reunite the city with the waterfront," Cook says as we study a map. "We started with identifying the needs of the maritime industry. After that, we looked for ways to encourage commercial development while providing public access and preserving the scale of the piers along

Trolley service skirts the waterfront from Fisherman's Wharf south to PacBell Park and the Caltrain depot.

with their historic bulkheads."

Resuming my northward stroll, I detour out onto Pier 7. This lovely, narrow public walkway out over the bay has benches where anglers can sit while fishing for perch or flounder (although signs warn of potential health hazards from actually eating too many bay fish) and joggers can catch their breath. Both can appreciate the 360° view that includes Treasure Island and Coit Tower.

Across from Pier 17 is the Ferry Plaza Farmers' Market. This time of year, you can shop at stands like Rainbow Orchards and Dirty Girl Produce on a Saturday morning, then plan the rest of your day over an inexpensive brunch from one of the food booths set up by top restaurants like Hayes Street Grill and Rose Pistola. Sometimes my wife and I just hang around and read the newspaper by the waterfall in the green jewel of Levi's Plaza. It's hidden behind tall hedges across the Embarcadero from Pier 23, namesake of another classic waterfront hangout where you can order hearty fare from outdoor tables.

From here to Pier 39, the promenade passes odd-numbered piers fronted with the grandly arching bulkheads that Cook wants to preserve. Built after 1910—part of the "city beautiful"

movement leading up to the 1915 Pan Pacific Exposition—the imposing façades were designed to both secure and hide the gritty warehouses built out on the wharves.

As I walk, I think about the waterfront—what it was and what it is becoming. One of my own earliest memories is of riding with my father on the last of the car ferries from Oakland to San Francisco in the early 1950s. My dad pointed out Treasure Island, where my grandmother was a gypsy fortune-teller during the 1939–'40 Golden Gate International Exposition, and the Ferry Building, which greeted him when he returned from duty in the Pacific after World War II. It wasn't long after our ferry ride that work began on the Embarcadero Freeway—the noisy, double-decked monstrosity that for decades effectively walled off the city from its storied waterfront. Now the waterfront has been reclaimed.

It's an impressive transformation. Hopping aboard one of the trolleys that zip along the Embarcadero on silvery rails in the shade of aristocratic palm trees, I watch joggers trace the route of the new bayfront promenade. Views out over the water, framed by historic pier fronts, reveal the colorful flash of spinnakers on racing sailboats. The trolley passes the yacht harbor, and there are the red brick walls of the new stadium awaiting equipment manager Mike Murphy and his Giants.

San Francisco has done what most cities can only dream of: It has reunited its citizens with their waterfront. In so doing, the city has essentially reinvented itself. As Murphy said as we parted, "We're ready to play ball."

Embarcadero best bets

Area code is 415.

■ Tickets and schedules for **S.F. Giants** games at PacBell Park: 972-2000 or www.sfgiants.com. Details on bus shuttles from the Montgomery St. BART station and limited ferry service to the park: 817-1717, press 7.

■ Another grand San Francisco tradition is the **Ferry Plaza Farmers' Market** (8–1:30 Sat year-round at Embarcadero and Green St.; 10:30–2:30 Tue year-round at Market and Steuart streets; 981-3004).

■ Want to see the waterfront from the water? The **Golden Gate Bay Cruises** of the Blue and Gold Fleet (773-1188) from Pier 39 show you parts of it.

■ Time to eat? For breakfast, don't miss **Town's End Restaurant** (Embarcadero at Townsend St.; 512-0749); sip a latte on the sunny plaza just off the Embarcadero while you wait for a table on weekends.

■ Operated by the estimable nonprofit Delancey Street Foundation, the **Delancey Street Restaurant** (Embarcadero at Brannan St.; 512-5179) is a sure bet for casual all-American dining.

■ **MoMo's** (760 Second St.; 227-8660) is just across the street from the ballpark. Sure, it's loud, but also undeniably fun—it was a hit for lunch and dinner even before the Giants moved in.

■ Very few of the old waterfront dives are left. **Pier 23 Cafe** (Pier 23; 362-5125) serves up a satisfying weekend brunch at outdoor tables with a wharfside view; you're on your own at the bar after dark.

■ Speaking of bars, **Whitehall Tavern** (Pier 33; 788-4343) is the place for a civilized cocktail and friendly banter with Michael McCourt, one of the city's great bartenders; it's also a good bet for lunch or a casual dinner.

■ Yerba Buena Gardens: Art of the new

The gleaming waterfront isn't San Francisco's only news. Another metamorphosis has occurred in the area south of Market now called Yerba Buena Gardens. The $2-billion project—40 years in the making—has taken a neighborhood of auto repair shops and empty lots and turned it into a sensory symphony.

The purple cone of the Zeum children's museum and the ice-skating rink anchor one end of Yerba Buena Gardens. Across Howard Street, the 5½-acre Esplanade Garden is an urban greensward with willow trees, a butterfly garden, and seating in the sun—built atop Moscone Convention Center. Twenty-foot waterfalls dramatize the Martin Luther King Jr. Memorial, with King's words engraved on glass behind the water's roar. Not far away vibrates Sony's hyperactive Metreon: Inside, *blips* and *whirs* escape from video games; you'll find high-tech shopping, dining, a Maurice Sendak–inspired romping area and restaurant for children, and a 15-screen cinema with an Imax theater. For a more sedate ride, board the hand-carved carousel that first spun circles at the city's now-vanished amusement park, Playland-at-the-Beach. Other stellar attractions are nearby, notably architect Mario Botta's San Francisco Museum of Modern Art, a contemporary Sphinx with a striped periscope for a head.

"There's layer on layer of uniqueness here," says Anita Hill, executive director of Yerba Buena Alliance, which promotes the neighborhood. Development of adjacent Jessie Square—including the Mexican Museum and the Jewish Museum San Francisco—is expected to be finished in 2002. But most of Yerba Buena Gardens is complete. At dusk, sip coffee at a table overlooking the reflecting pool and watch red and orange streaks of light appear on the cityscape, turning SFMOMA into the loveliest urban ornament imaginable. Yerba Buena has ornamented the city as well—it's now a neighborhood San Franciscans can be proud of.

Yerba Buena best bets

Area code is 415.

■ For an overview, have a drink at the **View Lounge,** on the 39th floor of the San Francisco Marriott (55 Fourth St.; 896-1600).

■ Exquisite food can be found at **Hawthorne Lane** (22 Hawthorne St.; 777-9779).

■ Admission is free on the first Thursday evening of every month at **Yerba Buena Center for the Arts galleries** (701 Mission St.; 978-2787), and the first Tuesday evening of the month at **SFMOMA** (151 Third St.; 357-4000).

■ At the rooftop **Carousel at Yerba Buena Gardens,** whirl with horses and tigers (Wed-Sun, daily in summer; $1). Nearby, sit in front of Chico McMurtrie's sculpture *Urge,* and the globe-topping figure will wiggle and drop into a crouch.

■ On Wednesdays, enjoy noontime concerts at **St. Patrick's Church** ($5 donation; 756 Mission; 777-3211). — *Lisa Taggart*

■ South Park: The land of buzz

If any one neighborhood exemplifies the metamorphosis of San Francisco from 19th-century seaport to 21st-century cybercity, this is it. Modeled on London crescents, the charming oval park south of Market was

Socializing in South Park.

Newly hot South Park attracts the dot.commed and hip—but some street names mirror long-ago luminaries.

planned, 145 years ago, as an oasis of inherited privilege on Rincon Hill—one of the few spots where 19th-century San Franciscans "could be born respectably," according to memoirist Gertrude Atherton. Now the area is a haven to multimedia whiz kids with stock options, the irreverent privileged of the dot-com world.

Sandwiched between bustling Second and Third streets 2½ blocks from the new ballpark, South Park's tree-lined green feels like a hidden garden in the urban jungle. It's surrounded by architectural firms, small galleries, and a handful of restaurants and stores. Alleys thread to warehouses-turned-offices for multimedia successes such as *Wired* magazine and LookSmart. On a sunny afternoon you're likely to find kids on the oversize play structures, as well as business meetings on the benches.

South Park earned English developer George Gordon little money in the 1850s and '60s: An economic downswing and the ugly leveling of Second Street (which left mansions stranded high above the road) put the neighborhood into a long decline shortly after it was built. Society families fled to Nob Hill, leaving the area to be colonized eventually by machine shops, auto repair services, and warehouses.

But 15 years ago, Kathleen Hagen and Robert Voorhees opened the South Park Cafe, a butter yellow bistro serving French dishes. "Robert has an eye for developing neighborhoods," says Hagen of her partner's inspired choice of a location then evolving into a community of architects, graphic designers, and photographers. More recently, arty software designers have flooded in.

The area has become known as the place to find a great meal or the latest IPO party. The new ballpark will also draw increasing numbers here. This sudden popularity inspires mixed feelings among locals. "South Park used to have a secret quality," says Hagen. "I'm nostalgic for what it was." But turning from busy Second Street into the haven of the keyhole park still feels like a discovery.

Architect Toby Levy, whose firm designed the angular, modern-looking building where she lives and works, says the best thing to do in the neighborhood is hang out. Linger on the poetry-inscribed benches, test the swings, or "eat at one of the cafes and eavesdrop. That's what's most fascinating," she says.

South Park best bets

Area code is 415.

■ **South Park Cafe** (108 South Park Ave.; 495-7275) has tasty French dishes like duck with lavender sauce. Voorhees and Hagen's other neighborhood eatery, **Ristorante Ecco** (101 South Park; 495-3291), specializes in northern Italian meals; try ravioli with asparagus.

■ Soak up a latte and the scene at **Caffe Centro** (102 South Park; 882-1500). For a stiffer drink, sip vodka flavored with grapefruit—or cucumber or red licorice—at **Infusion** (555 Second; 543-2282).

■ Shoppers should check out chic furniture, jewelry, and toiletries at **Maison d'Etre** (92 South Park; 357-1747). **Ma Maison** (592 Third; 777-5370) has French linens and home accessories. **Jeremys** (2 South Park; 882-4929) and **Isda & Co** (29 South Park; 512-0313) feature hip discounted clothing.

■ South Park's numerous tiny galleries have cutting-edge art and often host Thursday-night openings: For architecture-related works, visit Mark Horton's **3A Garage** (27 South Park; 543-3347), through the well-stocked **William Stout Design Books** (27A South Park; 495-6757). **Colorarts** shows new photographs (449 Bryant St.; 543-6717), and **Robert Allen Fine Art** (427 Bryant; 777-0920) exhibits paintings. — *L.T*

■ Forget the car

The difficulty and expense of parking make a car a liability in the new San Francisco—especially when the new trolley service on the Embarcadero is so user-friendly.
Area code is 415.

■ The N-Judah line of the **S.F. Muni** (www. ci.sf.ca.us/muni/) links the **CalTrain** (www.caltrain.com) station and nearby ballpark with Market Street transit. The F-Market-line extension goes up to Fisherman's Wharf. Both trolley lines link up with **BART** (www.bart.org) at the Embarcadero Station on Market.

■ *Visitors:* If you stay in downtown or SoMa hotels, it's city-safe to walk and use public transit during the day and right after a night ball game; call a taxi after dinner.

■ Dining

From justifiably world-famous restaurants to lesser-known, more intimate bistros, the new San Francisco—including the Embarcadero, South of Market, and Yerba Buena districts—explodes with dining adventures. We list our top choices. Note that while dinner for two at many of them can be an expensive (if delicious) proposition, lunch is more reasonably priced. Reservations are strongly suggested for both dinner and lunch.
— *Jerry Anne Di Vecchio*

Dining best bets

Area code is 415 unless noted.

■ **Bizou Restaurant.** This place is invitingly *français* once you walk in the door. No matter how damp the city fog, owner/chef Loretta Keller's soul-warming cassoulet or mustard-crusted beef cheek Sainte-Menehould—along with a blood red glass of Côtes du Rhône—will soon have you humming "La Marseillaise." Menu changes seasonally. *Fourth and Brannan; 543-2222.* — *J.P.*

■ **Boulevard.** Earthy, creative, simple foods perfectly cooked and bountifully served: This is lunch or dinner at Nancy Oakes's Boulevard. The food—coupled with the Pat Kuleto–designed belle epoque interior in a landmark building that survived the 1906 quake—has made this bistro an unquestionable success. Reservations are essential for a table, but walk-ins can enjoy a fine meal at the kitchen counter or at the bar. *1 Mission at Steuart; 543-6084.* — *J.D.V.*

■ **Chaya Brasserie.** Industrial chic meets ballroom sophistication at the third stateside Chaya (the other two are in Southern California) from the Tsunoda family, which has owned teahouses in Japan for more than 300 years (*chaya* is Japanese for *teahouse*). Executive chef Shigefumi Tachibe makes Japanese flavors dance with French techniques—the latter lead-

ing—from smoky sweetbreads, mushrooms, and bacon in a balsamic vinegar sauce to pan-fried oysters with sorel champagne sauce and caviar. All this, and an utterly spectacular Bay Bridge view. *132 Embarcadero; 777-8688* — *Sara Schneider*

■ **Che Bar y Restaurante.** There's no monotone of chilies in this bright SoMa cafe, which executive chef Johnny Alamilla has put on the cutting edge of upscale Latin American cooking. Alamilla uses fascinating ingredients in sophisticated dishes like duck breast on a dried-apricot sauce, with a *camote* (sweet potato) flan and chanterelles. First bites, such as crisp duck confit–filled empanadas, and side dishes, like earthy-sweet corn cakes with caramelized onions and goat cheese, deserve full attention. *320 Third; 546-3131.* — *S.S.*

■ **Fifth Floor.** Chef George Morrone, who has left a trail of success at other San Francisco dining palaces, is flying on the fifth floor of the Hotel Palomar. Dishes bear Morrone's signature complexity and surprise. A complementary *amuse* of egg with curry served in the shell sets the mood for a menu that includes suckling pig presented in five forms, and daily specials such as melting braised oxtails with crisply seared Chilean seabass. *Hotel Palomar, 12 Fourth; 348-1555.* — *J.D.V.*

■ **Flytrap Restaurant.** Great dining traditions die hard in San Francisco. The Flytrap, the stately reincarnation of an old city institution, brings back oysters Rockefeller, celery Victor, petrale sole parma, even calf's brains in brown butter, in renditions that might be even better than their antecedents. *606 Folsom St.; 243-0580.* — *S.S.*

■ **Fringale.** So soothingly intimate is the dining room, so gallantly Gallic the waitstaff, it may take you a while to notice an even more salient point: The food here is perfect. Chef Gerald Hirigoyen has a gift for rendering simple classics—such as rack of lamb accompanied by buttery potatoes gratin—transcendent. His Bayonne (France, not

Boulevard of unbroken dreams: Nancy Oakes–Pat Kuleto landmark is San Francisco dining at its most exalted.

NJ) upbringing reveals itself in a memorable *gâteau basque*. *570 Fourth; 543-0573. — Peter Fish*

■ **One Market Restaurant.** Ground-floor window-walls with views of the action on Market and the Bay Bridge, a spacious setting, and dishes with staying power, like seared day boat scallops with spiced pumpkin ravioli are what keep Bradley Ogden and Michael Dellar's One Market on "best" lists around the country. *1 Market; 777-5577. — J.D.V.*

■ **Red Herring Restaurant & Bait Bar.** The menu is clever ("sea"zer salad and tuna "steak au poivre"); the seafood preparations evince an expert hand (that of executive chef Jeffery Powell); and a seat at the back of the dining room practically makes you part of the waterfront. Dishes like tandoori snapper with tomato-

rajma curry and a banana raita make good on the Polish proverb chalked on the board: "Fish, to taste right, must swim three times—in water, in butter, and in wine in your belly." *155 Steuart; 495-6500. — S.S.*

■ **Shanghai 1930.** Owner George Chen has created a sleek Asian restaurant—with jazz (music, that is). The mood is nightclub swank; the menu is crowded with exotic delights such as pork shanks Wuxi and tofu mixtures flavorful enough to convert the most resistant (but other options keep the timid happy and satisfied). The place is pricey compared with Chinatown, but for a delicious cheap thrill, visit Chen's Longlife Noodle Company & Jook Joint next door. *133 Steuart; 896-5600. — J.D.V.*

■ **Waterfront Restaurant.** The warm, elegant upstairs dining room rises above bayside tourist traps, proving that great views and great food can star together. The Bay Bridge headlines outside; fresh combinations of luxurious seafood and interesting produce carry the show inside—a "fondue" of intense, caramelized sugarplum tomatoes counterbalances sweet Dungeness crab salad. *Pier 7; 391-2696. — S.S.*

■ **XYZ.** Style strikes hard here, through porthole windows, black-and-white-striped chairs, a trendy crowd, and towers of food. Flourishes glam up square meals: a pumpkin seed crust on tender monkfish, peppery ginger beurre blanc with seared ahi. Only the hip get to slip behind the steel beaded curtain into the bar upstairs. *W Hotel, 181 Third; 817-7836. — L.T.* ◆

Peppercorns, herbs, and green onions liven up crackers and flatbread.

Flat-out flavorful

Savory breads and crackers for snacking

BY ANDREW BAKER

My first meal at the legendary Hollywood restaurant Spago was a heady experience, to be sure. The atmosphere buzzed, the menu offered unique flavor combinations, and a movie star held court at the next table. But what really wowed me was the bread.

Standing upright, supported like books between small rolls and thick slices of country breads, were large shards of fresh-baked crisp crackers, flecked with herbs and spices. Served with panache, they were scene-stealers and the inspiration for these easy-to-make breads. Thin and brittle, or slightly thick and chewy, flatbreads use no yeast, require no waiting, and are worthy of celebrity status.

Parmesan-Pepper Crackers

PREP AND COOK TIME: About 30 minutes

NOTES: For an appetizer, serve with a bold, peppery Zinfandel. If making up to 2 days ahead, store cool crackers airtight at room temperature.

MAKES: 8 pieces

2 teaspoons **mixed peppercorns** (black, green, pink, and white)

5 tablespoons **butter** or margarine

1 cup (¼ lb.) **shredded parmesan cheese**

1 cup **all-purpose flour**

1 **large egg**

1. Coarsely crush peppercorns in a mortar, or place in a heavy plastic food bag and coarsely crush with a rolling pin.

2. In a food processor or a bowl, whirl or rub butter, peppercorns, cheese, and flour until very fine crumbs form. Add egg and whirl or stir with a fork until dough holds together; pat dough into a ball.

3. Divide dough in half. Pat each portion into a ½-inch-thick oval and place between 2 sheets of cooking paper or parchment, 12 to 14 inches wide and about 17 inches long. Roll each dough piece ¹⁄₁₆ inch thick. Peel off top paper and set each piece of dough, with paper beneath it, on a 14- by 17-inch baking sheet.

4. Bake in a 350° oven until an even light brown, about 15 minutes; if using 1 oven, switch pan positions after 7 or 8 minutes. Set pans on racks to cool. Carefully peel off paper, breaking each cracker into similar-size pieces. Serve warm or cool.

Per piece: 177 cal., 56% (99 cal.) from fat; 6.7 g protein; 11 g fat (6.6 g sat.); 13 g carbo (0.6 g fiber); 268 mg sodium; 54 mg chol.

Lemon-thyme parmesan crackers. Follow directions for **parmesan-pepper crackers** (preceding), but omit peppercorns. Instead, add 4 teaspoons grated **lemon** peel and 2 teaspoons **fresh thyme** leaves or dried thyme.

Per piece: 176 cal., 56% (99 cal.) from fat; 6.6 g protein; 11 g fat (6.6 g sat.); 13 g carbo (0.4 g fiber); 268 mg sodium; 54 mg chol.

Onion-Herb Rye Flatbread

PREP AND COOK TIME: About 30 minutes

NOTES: Serve with ripe brie cheese and sliced apples. If making up to 1 day ahead, store cool crackers airtight at room temperature.

MAKES: 8 pieces

About 2 tablespoons melted **butter** or margarine

About 1 cup **all-purpose flour**

1 cup **rye flour**

½ teaspoon **salt**

1 tablespoon **baking powder**

⅓ cup thinly sliced **green onions** (including tops)

¼ cup slivered **fresh basil** leaves

1 teaspoon minced **fresh rosemary** leaves or dried rosemary

¾ cup **half-and-half** (light cream)

1. Butter and flour a 14- by 17-inch baking sheet. With your finger or tip of a spoon, draw a 12-inch-wide circle in the flour in the center of the pan.

2. In a bowl, stir together 1 cup all-purpose flour, rye flour, salt, baking powder, green onions, basil, and rosemary. Add 2 tablespoons butter and the half-and-half; stir until dough is moistened. Scrape dough into the center of the circle on baking sheet. Dust dough with about 1 teaspoon flour, then press with fingers until it forms an evenly thick 12-inch-wide round. Prick dough all over with fork tines.

3. Bake in a 400° oven until golden brown, 20 to 25 minutes. Set pan on a rack; let bread cool about 5 minutes, then cut into 8 wedges. Serve hot or cool.

Per piece: 172 cal., 37% (63 cal.) from fat; 3.7 g protein; 6.8 g fat (4 g sat.); 24 g carbo (2.5 g fiber); 377 mg sodium; 19 mg chol.

Seeded rye flatbread. Follow directions for **onion-herb rye flatbread** (preceding), but omit green onions, basil, and rosemary. Instead, add 1 tablespoon *each* **cumin seed** and **fennel seed**.

Per piece: 175 cal., 36% (63 cal.) from fat; 3.8 g protein; 7 g fat (4 g sat.); 25 g carbo (2.7 g fiber); 378 mg sodium; 19 mg chol. ◆

The Quick Cook

MEALS IN 30 MINUTES OR LESS

BY LINDA LAU ANUSASANANAN

PILE CHIPOTLE-charged chicken with onion on a bed of lettuce and tortilla chips for a main-dish salad.

JAMES CARRIER (2)

Easy chicken tinga

■ Good food memories from childhood offer more than pleasant flavor recall. Vicky Rangel of Mountain View, California, remembers *tinga,* a classic slow-braised meat dish from her family home in Michoacán, Mexico. She fits that tasty legacy into her faster-paced life here with a versatile chili- and onion-spiked version that starts with cooked chicken. Pile the quick-cooking mixture on lettuce for a main-dish salad, onto crisp tortillas for tostadas, in soft tortillas for tacos or quesadillas, or on bread for sandwiches—or spoon it onto tortilla chips for a great party appetizer.

Chicken Tinga

PREP AND COOK TIME: About 25 minutes

NOTES: Chorizo sausage and canned chipotle chilies, sold in Mexican groceries and well-stocked supermarkets, give a rich, deep flavor to the tinga mixture. Start with cooked chicken, leftover or purchased. If making up to 1 day ahead, cover and chill; reheat to use.

MAKES: 2 cups

- ¼ pound **chorizo sausage,** casings removed, chopped
- 1 **onion** (10 oz.), peeled and thinly sliced
- 1 or 2 **canned chipotle chilies** (or 1 to 1½ teaspoons hot sauce and ¼ teaspoon liquid smoke)
- 1½ cups shredded skinned **cooked chicken**
- 1 can (8 oz.) **tomato sauce**

  Salt

MENU

Tinga Tostadas*, Tacos*,
or Quesadillas*

Cooked Black or Pinto Beans

Caramel Sundaes
with Strawberries

Beer or Iced Tea

*Recipe provided

1. In a 10- to 12-inch frying pan over medium-high heat, combine sausage, onion, and 3 tablespoons water. Cover and cook 5 minutes, stirring occasionally. Uncover and stir over high heat until onion begins to brown, 3 to 5 minutes longer.

2. If less heat is desired, discard chili seeds. Finely chop chilies.

3. Add chopped chilies, chicken, and tomato sauce to onion mixture. Stir over medium heat until simmering, about 2 minutes. Add salt to taste. Spoon into a bowl.

Per ½ cup: 275 cal., 49% (135 cal.) from fat; 23 g protein; 15 g fat (5.2 g sat.); 11 g carbo (2 g fiber); 782 mg sodium; 72 mg chol.

Tinga Tortilla Salad

PREP TIME: About 20 minutes

NOTES: Look for cotija cheese in Mexican groceries or well-stocked supermarkets.

MAKES: 4 servings

Divide 10 cups (10 oz.) **tortilla chips** equally among 4 dinner plates. Top equally with a total of 2 quarts shredded **iceberg lettuce** and 1 recipe hot **chicken tinga** (recipe precedes).

Garnish each serving with ¼ of each of the following: 1 cup chopped **firm-ripe tomato**, 1 cup diced **firm-ripe avocado**, ½ cup chopped **fresh cilantro**, ½ cup **sour cream**, and ¼ cup crumbled **cotija** or feta **cheese**. Drizzle salads equally with 1 cup **taco sauce**.

Per serving: 823 cal., 51% (423 cal.) from fat; 33 g protein; 47 g fat (14 g sat.); 72 g carbo (9.1 g fiber); 1,717 mg sodium; 88 mg chol.

Build-Your-Own Tinga Tostadas

PREP TIME: About 20 minutes

NOTES: Look for packages of flat, crisp, fried corn tortillas—called tostadas—in Mexican groceries or well-stocked supermarkets. If they're unavailable, purchase crisp taco shells and split each to form a flat base for the toppings.

MAKES: 6 tostadas; 3 servings

In separate serving containers, present 6 **tostadas** (6 in.; see notes), 2 cups finely shredded **iceberg lettuce**, 1 recipe hot **chicken tinga** (recipe, facing page), ¾ cup chopped **firm-ripe tomato**, ¾ cup diced **firm-ripe avocado**, and ½ cup *each* **sour cream**, **red** or green **salsa**, chopped **fresh cilantro**, and crumbled **cotija** or feta **cheese**. To assemble at the table, place 2 tostadas on each dinner plate. Top tostadas equally with lettuce and tinga, then have guests add tomato, avocado, sour cream, salsa, cilantro, and cheese to taste.

Per serving: 705 cal., 55% (387 cal.) from fat; 40 g protein; 43 g fat (16 g sat.); 44 g carbo (6.4 g fiber); 1,778 mg sodium; 123 mg chol.

Tinga Tacos

PREP AND COOK TIME: About 20 minutes

NOTES: Make sure tortillas are fresh; stale ones tend to crack and break.

MAKES: 16 tacos; 4 servings

Follow directions for **build-your-own tinga tostadas** (preceding) but omit tostadas. Instead, use 16 **corn tortillas** (6 in.). Stack tortillas and loosely enclose in microwave-safe plastic wrap. Heat in a microwave oven at 50% power until steaming, about 1½ minutes. Remove plastic and wrap tortillas in a towel to keep warm. Place 4 tortillas on each plate and top as directed for tostadas; fold tortillas around filling and pick up to eat.

Per serving: 661 cal., 42% (279 cal.) from fat; 34 g protein; 31 g fat (12 g sat.); 66 g carbo (8.5 g fiber); 1,352 mg sodium; 92 mg chol.

Tinga Quesadillas

PREP AND COOK TIME: About 30 minutes

MAKES: 4 servings

TINGA QUESADILLAS come together quickly: Fill flour tortillas with versatile chicken mixture and cheese, then bake.

Brush 1 side of each of 4 **flour tortillas** (8 in.) lightly with **salad oil** (about 1 tablespoon total). Turn tortillas oiled sides down. Sprinkle ½ of each tortilla with ¼ of each of the following: 1 cup (¼ lb.) **shredded jack cheese**, 1 recipe **chicken tinga** (recipe, facing page), and ¼ cup chopped **fresh cilantro**. Fold bare half of each tortilla over filling. Lay folded tortillas slightly apart on a 12- by 15-inch baking sheet.

Bake in a 450° oven until browned, 7 to 9 minutes. Transfer quesadillas to plates. If desired, cut in half. Top with **red** or green **salsa** to taste.

Per serving: 525 cal., 51% (270 cal.) from fat; 33 g protein; 30 g fat (11 g sat.); 31 g carbo (3.1 g fiber); 1,102 mg sodium; 102 mg chol.

Tinga Tortas

PREP TIME: About 30 minutes

NOTES: Use sandwich rolls from the supermarket, or *bolillos* or *taleras* (both Mexican sandwich rolls) from a Mexican bakery.

MAKES: 4 servings

Split 4 **crusty sandwich rolls** (about 3 by 6½ in.; see notes) in half horizontally. If desired, toast cut sides. Fill each roll with ¼ of each of the following: 1 recipe hot **chicken tinga** (recipe, facing page), ¾ cup shredded **iceberg lettuce**, and ¼ cup *each* diced **firm-ripe avocado**, chopped **firm-ripe tomato**, chopped **fresh cilantro**, crumbled **cotija** or feta **cheese**, **sour cream**, and **salsa**.

Per serving: 515 cal., 40% (207 cal.) from fat; 31 g protein; 23 g fat (8.6 g sat.); 45 g carbo (4.4 g fiber); 1,347 mg sodium; 82 mg chol.

Tinga Tostaditas

PREP TIME: About 10 minutes

NOTES: Present ingredients separately for guests to assemble by the bite, or make and serve at once on a platter.

MAKES: 6 dozen pieces; 12 to 16 appetizer servings

Spoon about ½ tablespoon hot **chicken tinga** (1 recipe total; facing page) onto each of about 6 dozen **tortilla chips** (7 oz.; about 7 cups). Top each chip with a tiny dollop of **sour cream** (1 cup total) and a sprinkle of chopped **fresh cilantro** (1 cup total).

Per tostadita: 36 cal., 56% (20 cal.) from fat; 1.6 g protein; 2.2 g fat (0.8 g sat.); 2.5 g carbo (0.3 g fiber); 60 mg sodium; 5.4 mg chol. ◆

FINE ART garnishes fare at Picasso (left). Patio dining—not easy to find in Las Vegas—and Latin American specialties star at the Border Grill (above).

Dining in the new Las Vegas

The Las Vegas classic—the all-you-can-eat buffet—is alive and well here, but risen far above its humble beginnings.

BY ELAINE JOHNSON • PHOTOGRAPHS BY TERRENCE McCARTHY

You might ask how a desert town known mainly for the $5.95 buffet got to be an American capital of cutting-edge cuisine. It all started with Wolfgang Puck, who in 1992 opened a branch of his Los Angeles restaurant, Spago, in the Forum Shops at Caesars Palace. Customers came in droves, proving the city was hungry for inventive fare. Resort planners sat up and took notice. By the time Bellagio and Mandalay Bay opened, each with more than a dozen restaurants, resorts were competing with each other to lure the nation's top chefs to open culinary outposts.

Flash is part of the dining fun here. Hope Diamond–size chunks of black truffles, wine lists with 1,000 choices (and prices to match), water shows, aerial acts, live swans, priceless artwork—you'll find them all. Such grandeur doesn't come cheap. But there are still good values among the new restaurants, particularly at lunch (the dinner prices we quote are for a three-course meal for one without wine or tip). Reservations are strongly suggested

(call a week or two in advance), but you should have less trouble getting a table if you dine at off-peak hours.

We present 10 of our favorites. All are inside resorts, most on the Strip, two just off. Loosen your belt and come play.

Aureole. "A bottle of the Opus One," you tell the sommelier. He repeats your request into his tiny headset. Then you watch as Aureole's "wine angel" rises, Peter Pan–like, up the restaurant's 42-foot-tall glass wine tower to retrieve your selection and pop it into her holster.

The wine tower alone is worth a trip to Aureole. But don't pass up chef-owner Charlie Palmer's silky duck mousse, halibut in buttery lobster sauce, and the best warm, oozy chocolate cake in town. Wine service is enthusiastic and knowledgeable, the list long on French bordeaux and California Cabernets. Eat in the main dining room, or in the swan court with views of, yes, live swans and a waterfall. *Mandalay Bay, 3950 Las Vegas Blvd. S.; 632-7401. Dinner ($65, $90 for five-course tasting menu) daily.*

Border Grill. In a land of vast, mall-like interiors, Border Grill boasts a rare commodity: outdoor dining. The setting, overlooking Mandalay Bay's pool, could be a cabana somewhere in Ixtapa; L.A. chefs Mary Sue Milliken and Susan Feniger serve south-of-the-border fare that includes plantain empanadas drizzled with chipotle salsa, and garlic-marinated grilled skirt steak. *Mandalay Bay, 3950 Las Vegas Blvd. S.; 632-7403. Lunch ($25) and dinner ($33) daily.*

Buffet at Bellagio. The Las Vegas classic—the all-you-can-eat buffet—is alive and well here, but risen far above its humble beginnings. Live cooking stations, adroit use of consistently good ingredients, and an international assortment of dishes make this a standout. The weekend champagne brunch offers classic breakfast fare plus surprises such as mu shu pork pizza and seared nori-crusted salmon. *Bellagio, 3600 Las Vegas Blvd. S.; 693-8111. Breakfast ($10), lunch ($13), and dinner ($25) daily; champagne brunch ($18) Sat-Sun.*

Chinois. Wolfgang Puck's spin-off of his

Santa Monica restaurant delivers great value and terrific Hong Kong–inspired flavors. Dishes like shrimp and lobster potstickers and Chinese chicken salad (with candied cashews and a wasabi kick) arrive in generous portions, meant to be shared. *Forum Shops at Caesars Palace, 3500 Las Vegas Blvd. S.; 737-9700. Lunch ($15) and dinner ($25) daily.*

Napa. In the casino below, slot machines chink and aerial acts fly. Up on the second story, chef Jean-Louis Palladin's dining room seems serene—somewhat deceptively, for acrobatics (of a culinary nature) are going on here too.

Our advice: Order the six-course chef's tasting, not listed on the menu but available by special request. Then let the sommelier do his thing, pairing a wine with each course. In one evening, we tried a terrine of black truffles, foie gras, and suckling pig; a cold and briny belon oyster with pork sausage crepinette; rock shrimp and white truffle risotto; pastrami squab cured for 18 hours with molasses and spices ("For this powerful dish, the powerful 1996 Madrigal Petite Syrah," the sommelier explained); and roasted bananas with rum.

After such a dinner, you'll need a walk—stroll to the wine shop downstairs, where the 100,000-bottle inventory includes a $2-million collection of Chateau d'Yquem. *Rio Hotel & Casino, 3700 W. Flamingo Rd.; 252-7777. Dinner ($65, $95 for six-course tasting menu; add $45 for wine by the glass with each course) Tue-Sat.*

Nobu. Chef Nobu Matsuhisa's modern temple to Japanese cuisine is no ordinary sushi joint. You can get impeccably fresh sushi and sashimi, and melt-in-the-mouth black cod with miso. Peruvian influences show up in dishes like yellowtail sashimi served with jalapeño and cilantro. Desserts, such as an espresso bombe topped with a spaceship-shaped chocolate wafer, verge on the extraterrestrial. *Hard Rock Hotel & Casino, 4455 Paradise Rd.; 693-5090. Lunch ($30) Fri-Sun; dinner ($55) daily.*

AIRY, ELEGANT AUREOLE—at Mandalay Bay—is known for winning ways with duck and halibut and for a superlative wine list.

Picasso. The paintings on the walls are indeed original. Floral arrangements are jaw-dropping. Behind it all dance Bellagio's fountains. You'd be hard-pressed to find a more elegant setting for Julian Serrano's understated French fare. The former chef at San Francisco's Masa's produces flawless seafood and meat dishes, often featuring complex sauces and velvety vegetable purées. *Bellagio, 3600 Las Vegas Blvd. S.; 693-7223. Dinner ($75 for four-course prix fixe, $85 for six-course tasting menu; add $38 or $48 for the sommelier wine pairing with each course) Thu-Tue.*

Pinot Brasserie. Every interior detail, from wall sconces to floor tiles, was imported from France to create Joachim Splichal's lovely bistro. The food is equally true to tradition. Some knockouts: caramelized fennel and blue cheese tart, steamed mussels in Muscat broth with garlic frites, and buttery tarte tatin. *Venetian, 3355 Las Vegas Blvd. S.; 414-8888. Lunch ($27) and dinner ($65) daily.*

Prime. Steak houses don't get snazzier: an interior done in chocolate brown and baby blue velvet, with a view of Bellagio's splashing fountains. And steak doesn't get better than chef Jean-Georges Vongerichten's 16-ounce, six-peppercorn New York version. Fish receives equally loving treatment, and side dishes like chickpea "fries" (polenta sticks made from garbanzo flour) are events in themselves. *Bellagio, 3600 Las Vegas Blvd. S.; 693-7223. Dinner ($65) daily.*

Spago. The restaurant that launched high-end Las Vegas dining is still going strong. Pizzas from the cafe out front still have pizzazz; or join the young, noisy crowd in the dining room for eclectic choices like big-eye tuna sashimi with ponzu sauce, and dried fig tart with Sambuca ice cream. *Forum Shops at Caesars Palace, 3500 Las Vegas Blvd. S.; 369-6300. Lunch ($15) and dinner ($30) daily.* ◆

Kitchen Cabinet

READERS' RECIPES TESTED IN SUNSET'S KITCHENS

BY ANDREW BAKER

HUMMUS AND BEEF partner in a hot Mediterranean-style filling for pocket bread.

Hot Hummus Salad

Christine Datian, Las Vegas

Looking for a creative way to use up some leftovers, Christine Datian and her mother put together this attractive platterful of pocket bread filling. "It's unusual to mix hummus with something, rather than use it as a dip," Datian says. This dish is a hit at family get-togethers.

PREP AND COOK TIME: About 50 minutes

MAKES: 8 servings

- 2 **red** or yellow **bell peppers** (or 1 of each; 1 lb. total)
- 1 **onion** (½ lb.), peeled and chopped
- 1 tablespoon minced or pressed **garlic**
- 1 teaspoon **olive** or salad **oil**
- 2 pounds **ground lean beef**
- ½ cup chopped **pitted calamata olives**
- ½ cup minced **parsley**
- 1 teaspoon **dried oregano**
- 2 tablespoons **lemon pepper**
- 2 cups **purchased hummus**
- ½ cup **crumbled feta cheese**
- 2 **firm-ripe tomatoes** (¾ lb. total), rinsed, cored, seeded, and chopped
- ½ cup chopped **cucumber**
- ¼ cup thinly sliced **green onions** (including tops)
- 8 **pocket breads** (6 in.)
  Lemon wedges
  Salt

1. Rinse peppers; trim and discard stems, seeds, and veins. Chop peppers.

2. In a nonstick 12-inch frying pan or 5- to 6-quart pan over high heat, combine bell peppers, onion, garlic, and oil. Stir often until vegetables are lightly browned, about 10 minutes. Add beef; stir, breaking apart, until meat is crumbled and browned, about 15 minutes. Add olives, parsley, oregano, lemon pepper, and hummus. Stir just until mixture is hot, 2 to 3 minutes longer.

3. Spoon mixture onto a wide platter; top with feta. Arrange tomatoes, cucumber, and green onions around meat mixture. Serve hot, warm, or at room temperature.

4. Cut pocket breads in half crosswise. Spoon meat mixture and vegetables equally into pocket bread halves; squeeze lemon wedges over filling and add salt to taste.

Per serving: 673 cal., 48% (324 cal.) from fat; 32 g protein; 36 g fat (12 g sat.); 53 g carbo (4.9 g fiber); 1,329 mg sodium; 93 mg chol.

Garlic Fried Potatoes

Lynn Dutton, Redondo Beach, California

Lynn Dutton loves garlic mashed potatoes. This easy dish delivers that flavor combination but skips the time-consuming steps of roasting the garlic and peeling the potatoes. If desired, start with ½ cup purchased peeled garlic cloves.

PREP AND COOK TIME: About 40 minutes

MAKES: 3 servings

- 1 head **garlic** (about 3 oz.)
- 1 pound **red thin-skinned potatoes,** scrubbed
- 4 teaspoons **olive oil**
  Salt and **pepper**

1. On a flat surface, firmly press garlic head to separate cloves. Peel cloves and slice in half any that are larger than ½ inch.

2. Cut potatoes into ¼-inch-thick slices.

3. In a 10- to 12-inch nonstick frying pan over medium heat, stir oil, potatoes, and garlic often until potatoes and garlic are browned and tender when pierced, about 30 minutes.

4. Pour into a bowl. Add salt and pepper to taste.

Per serving: 212 cal., 27% (58 cal.) from fat; 4.5 g protein; 6.4 g fat (0.8 g sat.); 35 g carbo (3 g fiber); 16 mg sodium; 0 mg chol.

Chocolate-Pear Pie

Margaret Handshoe, Vancouver, Washington

Needing a dessert for unexpected dinner guests, Margaret Handshoe turned to her centerpiece, a pewter bowl full of pears. This pie was the result.

PREP AND COOK TIME: About 1½ hours

JAMES CARRIER

MAKES: 8 servings

- 1 package (15 oz.) **refrigerated pastry for double-crust 9-inch pie,** at room temperature
- ½ cup **chocolate-** or orange-**flavor liqueur**
- 3 tablespoons **cornstarch**
- 2½ pounds **firm-ripe Bosc pears** (4 or 5)
- 1 **orange** (about ½ lb.)
- ½ cup **semisweet chocolate chips,** finely chopped
- 2 teaspoons **sugar**

1. Unfold 1 pastry round and ease into a 9-inch pie pan.

2. In a large bowl, blend liqueur and cornstarch until smooth.

3. Peel pears, cut in half lengthwise, core, and stem. Cut pears lengthwise into ½-inch-thick slices; add to bowl.

4. Grate 2 teaspoons orange peel; add to bowl. Squeeze 2 tablespoons orange juice; add to bowl. Add chocolate chips and stir gently to mix well. Pour mixture into pastry-lined pan.

5. On a lightly floured board, unfold remaining pastry; roll out to make a 12-inch round. Center pastry on pie filling. Pinch pastry at rim to seal, then fold edges under, flush with pan rim; pinch to flute pastry rim. Slash top decoratively. Sprinkle sugar evenly over pastry.

6. Bake in a 350° oven until crust is richly browned, 55 to 60 minutes. Let cool at least 1½ hours; cut into wedges and serve, or cover and chill up to 1 day.

Per serving: 427 cal., 38% (162 cal.) from fat; 2.9 g protein; 18 g fat (7.7 g sat.); 60 g carbo (3.2 g fiber); 267 mg sodium; 14 mg chol.

Raspberry Bars

Elsie Brodjeski, Mentone, California

Elsie Brodjeski's mother-in-law keeps her supplied with jellies made from berries growing in her backyard. Brodjeski makes these bars to take advantage of the homemade raspberry jelly.

PREP AND COOK TIME: About 1 hour
MAKES: About 16 bars (2 in. square)

- 1¼ cups **all-purpose flour**
- ¾ cup **sugar**
- About ½ cup (¼ lb.) **butter** or margarine, cut into chunks
- 1 **large egg**
- 2 **large egg** whites
- ¾ cup **chopped pecans** or walnuts
- ¾ cup **raspberry jelly** or jam

1. In a food processor or bowl, combine flour and ¼ cup sugar. Add butter and whirl or rub with your fingers until fine crumbs form. Add egg; whirl or mix with a fork until dough holds together. Pat into a smooth ball.

2. Firmly press dough evenly over bottom of a buttered 9-inch square pan.

3. Bake in a 350° oven until crust is pale gold, 20 to 25 minutes (about 15 minutes in a convection oven).

4. Meanwhile, in a deep bowl with a mixer on high speed, whip egg whites to a thick foam. Fold in remaining ½ cup sugar and the pecans.

5. Spread jelly evenly over warm crust. Spoon egg white mixture onto jelly; spread level with a spatula.

6. Return pan to oven and bake (at 325° if using a convection oven) until top is brown, about 25 minutes longer. Let cool at least 1 hour, then cut into squares. Lift out portions with a wide spatula.

Per bar: 204 cal., 43% (88 cal.) from fat; 2.3 g protein; 9.8 g fat (4.1 g sat.); 28 g carbo (0.7 g fiber); 77 mg sodium; 29 mg chol.

Capellini with Alfredo Sauce

Jim Ledbetter, Denver

When he was in college, Jim Ledbetter refined his alfredo sauce for a quick, easy meal. His daughter, who's in college now, has made the recipe a staple in her own repertoire.

PREP AND COOK TIME: About 20 minutes
MAKES: 2 servings

- ¼ pound **dried capellini pasta**
- 3 tablespoons **butter** or margarine
- 1 teaspoon minced or pressed **garlic**
- ¾ cup **whipping cream**
- ½ cup fat-skimmed **chicken broth**
- 2 tablespoons minced **fresh basil** leaves or fresh tarragon leaves
- ¾ cup **grated parmesan cheese**
- Fresh-ground **pepper**

1. In a 4- to 5-quart pan over high heat, bring 2 quarts water to a boil. Add pasta; stir occasionally until pasta is tender to bite, about 5 minutes. Drain.

2. Meanwhile, in a 10- to 12-inch frying pan over medium-high heat, stir butter and garlic until garlic is very lightly browned, 2 to 3 minutes. Add cream, ¼ cup broth, and basil. Turn heat to high; when mixture boils, add pasta.

3. Remove pan from heat and mix, lifting with 2 forks. Add remaining broth. Sprinkle cheese over pasta; lift to mix. Serve. Add pepper to taste.

Per serving: 774 cal., 64% (495 cal.) from fat; 24 g protein; 55 g fat (34 g sat.); 47 g carbo (1.6 g fiber); 788 mg sodium; 170 mg chol.

Sesame Spaghetti Squash with Asparagus

Leanne Staley Moore, Jackson, Wyoming

While experimenting with spaghetti squash—the vegetable that looks like pasta—Leanne Staley Moore came up with this colorful dish, which resembles an Asian stir-fry.

PREP AND COOK TIME: About 35 minutes
MAKES: 6 servings

- 1 **spaghetti squash** (2½ to 3½ lb.), rinsed
- 2 teaspoons **sesame seeds**
- 1 pound **asparagus**
- 1 teaspoon **olive** or salad **oil**
- 1 teaspoon minced or pressed **garlic**
- 1 teaspoon minced **fresh ginger**
- ½ cup thinly sliced **green onions** (including tops)
- 1 cup thinly sliced **red bell pepper**
- 2 tablespoons **Asian** (toasted) **sesame oil**
- **Salt** and **pepper**

1. Pierce squash in several places with a sharp knife. Cook in a microwave oven at full power (100%) until soft when pressed, 12 to 14 minutes, turning squash over after 5 minutes. Cut in half lengthwise and discard seeds. Scoop out tender squash strands and reserve; discard peel.

2. Meanwhile, in a 10-inch nonstick frying pan (at least 2 in. deep) or a 12-inch nonstick frying pan, stir sesame seeds over medium-high heat until golden, about 2 minutes. Pour from pan.

3. Rinse asparagus and cut into 2-inch pieces. Combine asparagus with ½ cup water in pan and stir often over high heat just until tender-crisp to bite, 3 to 4 minutes. Pour into a colander to drain.

4. Add olive oil, garlic, ginger, and green onions to pan. Stir over high heat until sizzling, about 30 to 40 seconds. Add asparagus, squash, and bell pepper. Stir gently just until hot, about 3 minutes.

5. Pour into a bowl; drizzle with sesame oil and sprinkle with sesame seeds. Add salt and pepper to taste.

Per serving: 122 cal., 49% (60 cal.) from fat; 3.7 g protein; 6.7 g fat (1 g sat.); 14 g carbo (3.5 g fiber); 26 mg sodium; 0 mg chol. ◆

Savor the flavors of Basque cooking at traditional festivals around the West or create your own meals at home (see page 132).

May

a taste of Basque

An intriguing culture revealed through food and festivals in California, Idaho, and Nevada

SEAN ARBABI (2)

Tradition takes center stage at a Basque festival in Elko, Nevada: Dancers, even little ones, don *abarkaks* (laced leather shoes). Males sport the *txapel* (Basque beret); women swirl in wool skirts (red represents life and love).

See festival listings starting on page 141.

It's a classic emigrant story, of striking out from Europe to find independence and opportunity in the wild lands of the American West. The Basque odyssey began in harsh territory as well—the Pyrenees Mountains of northern Spain and southern France. In the late 1800s, drawn by the Gold Rush, Basques arrived in California, many via South America. Then, turning to their experience as sheepherders, they settled throughout Idaho, Nevada, Oregon, and California and became the backbone of the Western sheep industry. This rangeland life afforded them a measure of the independence they prize as a people. • The story of the Basques has many distinctive elements. For one thing, there's their language, Euskara. It has no known linguistic relatives, and scholars haven't been able to determine its origins. Basque immigrants tended to perpetuate their unique culture here—linguistic and otherwise. In small range towns, Basque boardinghouses popped up, home-away-from-home for new arrivals. Determined and resourceful, they created their own restaurants and social centers. To unite far-flung family members and pass on the complex language, hearty food, and spirited music, dance, and athletic contests, they began to gather in clubs and hold picnics, which turned into festivals. • Today, the ancient traditions are imperiled. "There's very little Basque immigration here now, with the sheep business shrinking—there may not be 50 Basque sheepherders left in the West," says Professor William Douglass, founder of the University of Nevada's Basque studies program. "The festivals give Basques a chance to express their heritage. They help cement the culture and keep the young people from drifting away." You can visit one of these colorful festivals to glimpse the core of an intriguing culture still going strong in the West. — *L.J.F.*

BY LINDA LAU ANUSASANANAN AND LORA J. FINNEGAN

FOOD PHOTOGRAPHS BY JAMES CARRIER

Country

Marinated Pork Loin with Peppers (*Solomo*), the heart of a farmers' supper; page 137.

The Basque table

Food is a cultural safekeeper. Whether you're eating chorizo sandwiches at a festival, sharing a table at a boardinghouse restaurant, or cooking Basque dishes at home, you're keeping the cuisine—and the culture—alive. • Basque food appeals to just about everyone. Timid eaters can take comfort in simply seasoned dishes such as roast lamb, beef stew, and grilled steak. Yet the cuisine intrigues the adventurous palate with the likes of squid in ink sauce, salt cod in pepper sauce, and braised tongue. • Mari Carmen Totorica, an active 67-year-old grandmother in Boise, still cooks the same dishes her mother makes in Guernica, a city in Vizcaya province, which borders the Bay of Biscay in Spain. Her repertoire plays with the bounty of that land and sea: fish, meat, rice, and vegetables. Generous doses of garlic, onions, olive oil, salt, and pepper heighten the natural flavors. • To preserve this culinary heritage, Totorica teaches the next generation to appreciate, and cook, her mother's food. The simplicity of Basque cuisine makes it easy for almost anyone to master. Use one of our menus or build one of your own from our sampler of recipes here, which we've garnered from Basque cooks throughout the West. Follow the traditional course-by-course pattern of restaurants (see page 142) or serve the dishes collectively. — *L.L.A.*

first courses

Potato Omelet
(*Tortilla de Patata*)

PREP AND COOK TIME: 35 to 40 minutes

NOTES: Mari Carmen Totorica, a traditional Basque cook in Boise, serves this potato-dense version of a Basque frittata as a first course or with bread for sandwiches.

MAKES: 8 first-course servings

- 1½ pounds **thin-skinned potatoes**
- ¼ cup **olive** or salad **oil**
- ½ cup thinly sliced **onion**
- ½ cup thinly sliced **green** or red **bell pepper**
- 2 cloves **garlic,** peeled and pressed
- 6 **large eggs**

  About ¾ teaspoon **salt**

1. Rinse potatoes, peel, cut in half lengthwise, and thinly slice.

2. In a 10-inch nonstick frying pan (with sloping sides) over medium heat, combine oil, potatoes, onion, bell pepper, garlic, and 3 tablespoons water; cover. With a wide spatula, turn mixture occasionally until potatoes are tender when pierced, 15 to 20 minutes. Uncover and turn often until onion is lightly browned, about 5 minutes.

3. Meanwhile, in a large bowl, beat eggs to blend with ¾ teaspoon salt. Add vegetable mixture, stir gently, and quickly pour back into pan.

4. Place pan over medium-low heat. As eggs set on the bottom, slide spatula under them and lift to let liquid flow underneath. Also, poke through vegetables with the spatula to let liquid egg seep down to pan bottom. When tortilla is browned on the bottom, in 7 to 9 minutes, invert a baking sheet (with at least 1 rimless side) or wide, flat plate over pan. Holding pans together, invert tortilla onto baking sheet. Slide tortilla, browned side up, back into frying pan. With spatula, push sides of tortilla to form a neat edge. Return to heat and cook until browned on the bottom, about 3 minutes.

5. Slide tortilla from frying pan onto a plate. Serve warm or cool; cut into wedges. Add salt to taste.

Per serving: 183 cal., 54% (99 cal.) from fat; 6.5 g protein; 11 g fat (2.1 g sat.); 16 g carbo (1.5 g fiber); 270 mg sodium; 159 mg chol.

Peppers and Eggs
(*Piperrada Vasca*)

PREP AND COOK TIME: About 40 minutes

NOTES: Marcelino Ugalde teaches Basque cuisine in the Basque studies program at the University of Nevada. One dish he prepares is this version of piperrada from Biarritz and Saint-Jean-de-Luz. Serve it as a first course or for breakfast, lunch, or a light supper; accompany with bread or toast.

MAKES: 6 to 8 first-course servings, 3 or 4 main-dish servings

- 3 **green bell peppers** (1½ lb. total)
- 4 tablespoons **olive oil**
- 6 to 8 thin slices **prosciutto** (4 to 6 oz. total)
- 2 **onions** (1 lb. total), peeled and chopped
- 3 cloves **garlic,** peeled and minced

Grilled Shrimp
(*Langostinos a la Plancha*)

Per first-course serving: 191 cal., 61% (117 cal.) from fat; 10 g protein; 13 g fat (2.6 g sat.); 10 g carbo (1.9 g fiber); 314 mg sodium; 171 mg chol.

Grilled Shrimp
(*Langostinos a la Plancha*)

PREP AND COOK TIME: About 15 minutes, plus at least 4 hours to marinate

MAKES: 6 to 8 first-course servings

- 1 to 1½ pounds (12 to 15 per lb.) **shrimp**
- 2 **lemons** (¼ lb. each)
- 3 or 4 cloves **garlic,** peeled and thinly sliced

  About ½ teaspoon **salt**

  Green-leaf lettuce leaves, rinsed and crisped (optional)

  Pepper

1. To devein shrimp, insert a thin wood or metal skewer perpendicularly through back shell and under vein. Snag vein and gently pull up to remove. Repeat in several places. Rinse and drain shrimp; place in a bowl.

2. Rinse lemons. Cut 1 lemon into wedges and squeeze juice from them over shrimp; add wedges to bowl. Add garlic and ½ teaspoon salt; mix well. Cover and chill at least 4 hours or up to 1 day, stirring occasionally. Discard lemon wedges.

3. Set an 11- to 12-inch nonstick frying pan over high heat. When it's hot, add shrimp and stir often until opaque but still moist-looking in center of thickest part (cut to test), about 5 minutes total. Transfer to lettuce-lined plate. Cut remaining lemon into wedges; arrange around shrimp. To eat, peel shrimp and add juice from lemon wedges, salt, and pepper to taste.

Per serving: 51 cal., 14% (7.2 cal.) from fat; 9.4 g protein; 0.8 g fat (0.2 g sat.); 0.9 g carbo (0 g fiber); 213 mg sodium; 70 mg chol.

Clams and Rice
(*Arroz con Chirlas*)

PREP AND COOK TIME: About 1 hour

NOTES: Mari Carmen Totorica cooks the clams separately to ensure that all the sand is removed; if clams are well scrubbed, however, we find they can be cooked with the rice. Cook and serve from an attractive wide pan or scoop into a wide bowl.

MAKES: 6 to 8 first-course servings, 3 or 4 main-dish servings

- ¼ cup **olive oil**

- 1 jar (4 oz.) **sliced pimientos,** drained

  Salt

- 6 to 8 **large eggs**

  Pepper

1. Rinse peppers, pat dry, and place in a 10- by 15-inch pan. Broil about 4 inches from heat, turning as needed, until charred on all sides, 15 to 20 minutes. Let cool.

2. Set a 12-inch nonstick frying pan over medium-high heat. When it's hot, add 1 tablespoon oil. Lay prosciutto in a single layer in pan; cook, turning once just until prosciutto begins to ripple, about 1 minute total. As it's done, transfer meat to a platter or plates, and keep warm. Repeat to cook remaining prosciutto.

3. To frying pan, add remaining oil and the onions and garlic; stir often until onions begin to brown, 8 to 10 minutes.

Fishermen's Dinner

Grilled Shrimp* or Clams and Rice*

Green Salad with Olive Oil and Sherry Vinegar Dressing

Salt Cod Biscayne*

Crusty Bread

Basque Creamy Rice Pudding*

Albariño (a Spanish white wine variety) or Sauvignon Blanc

*Recipe included

---

4. Meanwhile, pull off and discard pepper skins, stems, and seeds. Cut peppers into ½-inch-wide strips.

5. Add green peppers and pimientos to onion mixture; stir until liquid is evaporated, about 1 minute. Add salt to taste. Reduce heat to medium.

6. In a bowl, beat eggs to blend; pour into frying pan. As eggs set on the bottom, use a wide spatula to push cooked portions aside and let liquid flow under to pan bottom, cooking until eggs are softly set throughout, 3 to 5 minutes total. Spoon piperrada onto prosciutto. Add salt and pepper to taste.

Potato and Asparagus Salad (*Ensalada a la Nicolasa*)

3 to 5 cloves **garlic,** peeled and sliced

2 cups **medium-grain white rice**

5½ cups fat-skimmed **chicken broth**

3 dozen **clams in shells** (1 to 1½ in. wide), suitable for steaming

⅔ cup chopped **parsley**

Salt and **pepper**

1. In a 5- to 6-quart pan over medium heat, stir oil, garlic, and rice until garlic begins to turn golden, about 5 minutes. Add broth; cover and bring to a boil. Reduce heat to low and simmer for 10 minutes.

2. Meanwhile, scrub clams under cool running water.

3. After rice has cooked 10 minutes, stir in ½ cup parsley and distribute clams evenly over the mixture. Cover and simmer until rice is tender to bite and clams have opened, 15 to 20 minutes longer; discard any clams that

haven't opened. Sprinkle with remaining parsley. Add salt and pepper to taste.

Per first-course serving: 313 cal., 22% (69 cal.) from fat; 18 g protein; 7.7 g fat (1 g sat.); 41 g carbo (0.9 g fiber); 92 mg sodium; 23 mg chol.

Potato and Asparagus Salad (*Ensalada a la Nicolasa*)

PREP AND COOK TIME: About 40 minutes

NOTES: Mari Carmen Totorica uses canned asparagus, as is typical in Spain, but fresh-cooked is brighter and more crisp. If assembling salad through step 5 up to 1 day ahead, cover and chill without dressing. Up to 2 hours before serving, drizzle with dressing.

MAKES: 8 first-course servings, 4 main-dish servings

1 pound **asparagus**

7 **thin-skinned white potatoes** (about 6 oz. each), scrubbed

Sheepherders' Barbecue

Potato and Asparagus Salad*

Leg of Lamb "Zikiro"*

Basque Red Beans*

Sheepherders' Bread or Crusty Bread

Wine Fruit Compote*

Red Rioja (from Spain's leading wine region)

*Recipe included

5 **large eggs**

2 **carrots** (6 oz. total)

1 can (12 oz.) **solid, water-packed albacore tuna,** drained

½ cup drained **pimiento-stuffed Spanish-style olives**

½ cup thinly sliced **green onions,** including tops

⅓ cup chopped **green bell pepper**

½ cup **salad oil**

⅓ cup **red wine vinegar**

Salt and **pepper**

1. In a 5- to 6-quart pan over high heat, bring about 2½ quarts water to a boil. Rinse asparagus; snap off and discard tough stem ends. Add asparagus to boiling water and cook just until tender when pierced, 4 to 5 minutes. With tongs, remove asparagus and immerse in a large bowl of ice water until cool; lift from water.

2. Return water in pan to a boil over high heat. Add potatoes and cover; when boil resumes, reduce heat to low, add eggs, and cook 15 minutes. With a slotted spoon, lift eggs from pan and immerse in ice water until cool; drain.

3. Meanwhile, peel carrots and cut diagonally into ¼-inch-thick slices. After removing eggs, add carrots to potatoes in pan. Cover and cook until potatoes and carrots are tender when pierced, 10 to 15 minutes longer. Drain and immerse in cold water until cool, about 5 minutes; drain.

4. Peel potatoes and cut into ¼-inch-thick slices. Shell eggs; cut 3 into quarters and chop remaining 2.

5. In the center of a large platter, invert tuna and lift off can, releasing tuna. Separately, arrange potatoes, carrots, asparagus, and egg wedges attractively around tuna. Sprinkle salad with chopped egg, olives, green onions, and bell pepper.

6. In a small bowl, mix oil and vinegar; drizzle evenly over salad. Sprinkle with salt and pepper to taste.

Per first-course serving: 371 cal., 46% (171 cal.) from fat; 19 g protein; 19 g fat (3.1 g sat.); 32 g carbo (3.5 g fiber); 412 mg sodium; 149 mg chol.

Garlic Soup
(Berakatza Sopa)

PREP AND COOK TIME: About 30 minutes

NOTES: Add more hot broth if you want a thinner soup.

MAKES: 6 to 8 first-course servings

¾ cup thinly sliced **garlic**

¼ cup **olive oil**

4 cups 1-inch chunks day-old **crusty bread**

2 quarts fat-skimmed **chicken broth**

4 **dried California** or New Mexico **chilies** (each about 6 in. long, about 1½ oz. total), rinsed, stemmed, and seeded

---

6 to 8 **large eggs** (optional)

Salt and **pepper**

1. In a 5- to 6-quart pan over medium heat, frequently stir garlic slices in olive oil until they begin to turn golden, 3 to 5 minutes.

2. Add bread, chicken broth, and chilies. Cover and bring to a boil over high heat; reduce heat and simmer until bread is completely saturated and falling apart, and chilies are soft, 10 to 15 minutes.

3. If desired, crack eggs 1 at a time, hold shells close to surface of soup to open, and slip eggs into broth. Cover and cook until eggs are softly set, 3 to 5 minutes. Ladle soup equally into bowls. Add salt and pepper to taste.

Per serving: 182 cal., 41% (75 cal.) from fat; 11 g protein; 8.3 g fat (1.2 g sat.); 17 g carbo (2.2 g fiber); 186 mg sodium; 0 mg chol.

main dishes

Leg of Lamb "Zikiro"

PREP AND COOK TIME: About 45 minutes, plus at least 2 hours to marinate

NOTES: This recipe, adapted to the barbecue, comes from the book *The Basque Kitchen* (Harper Collins Publishers, New York, 1999; $35), by Gerald Hirigoyen, chef-owner of Fringale and Pastis restaurants in San Francisco. Paprika is used as an alternative for a sweet red pepper called *piment d'Espelette,* grown in Basque country.

MAKES: 8 servings

¾ cup **olive oil**

½ cup **sherry vinegar**

⅓ cup chopped **fresh thyme** leaves or 2 tablespoons dried thyme

½ cup thinly sliced **garlic**

1 teaspoon **paprika**

1 tablespoon **kosher salt**

---

1 tablespoon **white pepper**

1 **leg of lamb** (7 lb.), boned, butterflied, and fat-trimmed

1. In a 9- by 13-inch pan, combine oil, vinegar, thyme, garlic, paprika, salt, and pepper.

2. Rinse lamb, pat dry, add to pan, and turn to coat with marinade. Cover and chill, turning lamb occasionally, at least 2 hours or up to 1 day.

3. Lift lamb from pan; reserve marinade. Lay meat, spread flat, on a barbecue grill over a solid bed of medium coals or over medium heat on a gas grill (you can hold your hand at grill level only 4 to 5 seconds). Cover grill; open vents for charcoal. Turn lamb as needed to brown evenly until a thermometer inserted in center of thickest part registers 135° to 140° for rare to medium-rare, 30 to 45 minutes; thin portions will be well-done.

4. Transfer meat to a board or rimmed platter and keep warm; let rest about 15 minutes.

5. Meanwhile, pour remaining marinade into a small microwave-safe bowl. Heat in a microwave oven at full power (100%) until boiling. Or bring to a boil in a 1- to 2-quart pan over high heat.

6. Slice lamb and serve with marinade to add to taste.

Per serving: 565 cal., 56% (315 cal.) from fat; 55 g protein; 35 g fat (8 g sat.); 5.3 g carbo (0.4 g fiber); 684 mg sodium; 170 mg chol.

Marinated Pork Loin with Peppers (*Solomo*)

PREP AND COOK TIME: About 1½ hours, plus at least 1 day to marinate

NOTES: At Bar Gernika in Boise, Dan Ansotegui serves hearty sandwiches of grilled marinated pork loin slices in rolls with roasted red peppers. Chef Alberto Bereziartua of Epi's in Meridian, Idaho, roasts the whole loin with red peppers. This barbecued roast and the sandwich that follows are inspired by their concepts.

MAKES: 8 servings

6 **dried California** or New Mexico **chilies** (each about 5 in. long; 2 oz. total), rinsed, stemmed, and seeded

4 cloves **garlic**

1 **boned, rolled, and tied fat-trimmed pork loin** (3½ to 4 lb.)

6 to 8 **red bell peppers** (½ lb. each), rinsed

2 to 3 tablespoons **mayonnaise**

Salt

1. Tear chilies into ½-inch chunks; soak in 1½ cups hot water until soft, 15 to 20 minutes.

2. Pour chilies and soaking water into a blender or food processor; add garlic and whirl until smooth.

3. Rinse pork, pat dry, and set in a 9- by 13-inch pan; coat with chili purée. Cover and chill at least 1 day or up to 3 days, turning meat over occasionally.

4. If *using charcoal*, ignite 60 briquets on the firegrate of a barbecue with a lid. When coals are dotted with gray ash, in 15 to 20 minutes, push equal amounts to opposite sides of grate. Set a drip pan on grate between mounds of coals. Add 5 briquets to each mound now and every 30 minutes while cooking.

If *using a gas barbecue*, turn heat to high and close lid for 10 minutes. Adjust burners for indirect cooking (no heat down center).

5. Lift pork from marinade and set on grill, not over heat; reserve marinade. Lay bell peppers over direct heat. Cover barbecue; open vents for charcoal. Turn peppers occasionally until charred on all sides, 15 to 25 minutes total; transfer to a rimmed plate. Cook pork until a thermometer inserted in center of thickest part registers 150°, 1 to 1¼ hours total. Transfer to a platter; let rest 5 to 10 minutes.

6. Meanwhile pull skin, stems, and seeds from peppers. Cut peppers in half lengthwise and arrange around pork.

7. Pour reserved marinade into a small microwave-safe bowl; heat in a microwave oven at full power (100%) until boiling. Or bring marinade to a boil in a 1- to 1½-quart pan over high heat. Remove from heat and stir in accumulated juices from pork roast. Add mayonnaise to taste; whisk until smooth. Add salt to taste.

8. Slice meat and serve with peppers, adding salt and chili sauce to taste.

Per serving: 372 cal., 41% (153 cal.) from fat; 42 g protein; 17 g fat (5.7 g sat.); 13 g carbo (3.7 g fiber); 113 mg sodium; 111 mg chol.

Solomo Pork Sandwich

PREP AND COOK TIME: About 10 minutes

NOTES: Use all the roasted marinated pork loin with peppers, or just the leftovers, for these sandwiches.

MAKES: 8 servings

Follow directions for **marinated pork loin with peppers** (preceding), but in step 7, instead of adding 2 to 3 tablespoons mayonnaise to all the boiled marinade, stir 3 to 4 tablespoons boiled marinade into ¾ cup **mayonnaise.** Cut 8 **crusty sandwich rolls** (3 by 6½ in.) in half horizontally; fill with equal portions of sliced pork, roasted peppers, and chili-marinade mayonnaise. Serve with remaining marinade and salt to add to taste.

Per serving: 662 cal., 46% (306 cal.) from fat; 47 g protein; 34 g fat (8 g sat.); 43 g carbo (4.8 g fiber); 521 mg sodium; 122 mg chol.

Salt Cod Biscayne (*Bacalao a la Vizcaina*)

PREP AND COOK TIME: About 45 minutes, plus at least 2 days to soak fish

NOTES: Mari Carmen Totorica makes this classic Basque dish from dried salted cod (bacalao), which you can find whole in seafood, Mexican, Italian, and Mediterranean markets; in supermarkets, dried salt cod is often sold packed in small wood boxes. The fish needs lengthy soaking to be edible. For a simpler version, start with 2 pounds fresh fish, such as boned, skinned rock fish fillets or chunks of halibut, and skip the soaking (step 1). Add fish to sauce and simmer until opaque but still moist-looking in center of thickest part, 5 to 8 minutes.

MAKES: 6 to 8 servings

1 to 1½ pounds **dried, boned, skinned salt cod** (bacalao; see notes)

6 **dried California** or New Mexico **chilies** (each about 5 in. long; about 2 oz. total), rinsed, stemmed, and seeded

2 tablespoons **olive oil**

2 slices **bacon** (2 oz. total), chopped

1 **onion** (6 oz.), peeled and thinly sliced

6 cloves **garlic,** peeled and sliced

1 cup fat-skimmed **beef broth**

Peppers and Eggs (*Piperrada Vasca*); page 134.

1 slice (3 by 4 in.) **crusty bread** (about ³⁄₄ oz.)

1 **large egg,** rinsed

Salt

1. Rinse dried salt cod well under cool running water, rubbing gently to release salt. Put cod in a large bowl and add 2 to 3 quarts water; cover and chill 2 days, changing water 2 or 3 times each day.

2. Tear chilies into ¹⁄₂-inch chunks and soak in 1¹⁄₂ cups hot water.

3. In a 3- to 4-quart pan over medium-high heat, stir 1 tablespoon oil, bacon, onion, and half the garlic until onion is limp, about 5 minutes. Add chilies and soaking liquid, broth, bread, and egg in the shell. Cover and simmer, stirring occasionally, until onion and chilies are soft enough to mash and bread disintegrates, 15 to 18 minutes.

4. With a slotted spoon, lift out egg and immerse in cold water. When cool enough to touch, shell egg; reserve white for other uses.

5. In a blender or food processor, whirl onion-chili mixture and egg yolk until smooth. Rub mixture through a fine strainer set over a bowl.

6. Drain fish, rinse, cut into 6 to 8 equal pieces, and pat dry.

7. Set a 10- to 12-inch nonstick frying pan over medium-high heat; when it's hot, add 1 tablespoon oil and tilt pan to coat. Add fish and cook 3 minutes. Turn fish and add remaining sliced garlic to pan; stir often until garlic is limp and fish is lightly browned, about 3 minutes longer. Reduce heat to low and add onion-chili sauce. Cover and simmer until fish flakes easily, 15 to 20 minutes total; turn fish over halfway through cooking. Transfer to a wide bowl; season with salt to taste.

Per serving: 280 cal., 32% (90 cal.) from fat; 39 g protein; 10 g fat (2.6 g sat.); 6.8 g carbo (1.9 g fiber); sodium not available; 118 mg chol.

companions

Basque Red Beans
(*Babarrun Gorria*)

PREP AND COOK TIME: About 2¹⁄₂ hours

NOTES: If available, use firm, mildly seasoned Basque-style chorizo sausages; however, the spicier Mexican-style chorizos work well too. For best flavor, Jesus Alcelay, chef-owner of Oñati, in Garden City, Idaho, recommends cooking the beans 1 day ahead; cover and chill, then reheat to serve. Offer with lamb or beef steak.

MAKES: 8 servings

1 pound (2 cups) **dried small red beans**

1 **leek** (1¹⁄₂ in. wide, 8 oz.)

1 tablespoon **paprika**

1 tablespoon **olive oil**

1 **onion** (¹⁄₂ lb.), peeled and chopped

¹⁄₂ pound **firm chorizo sausage,** cut into ¹⁄₄-inch-thick slices

1 can (8 oz.) **tomato sauce**

1 tablespoon **instant beef bouillon** or 3 cubes

Salt

1. Sort beans and discard debris; rinse and drain beans.

2. Trim and discard root end, coarse outer layer, and tough dark green tops from leek. Split leek in half lengthwise and rinse well under running water; thinly slice.

3. In a 5- to 6-quart pan over medium-low heat, stir paprika in oil for 1 minute. Add leek, onion, chorizo, beans, and 6¹⁄₂ cups water; cover and bring to a boil over high heat. Reduce heat and simmer for 1 hour.

4. Add tomato sauce and beef bouillon. Cover and simmer, stirring occasionally, until beans are tender to bite, 1 to 1¹⁄₂ hours longer. Add a little more water if beans begin to stick or get thicker than you like. Add salt to taste.

Per serving: 367 cal., 32% (117 cal.) from fat; 21 g protein; 13 g fat (4.4 g sat.); 42 g carbo (6.9 g fiber); 848 mg sodium; 25 mg chol.

Green Beans and Potatoes
(*Leika Patatarekin*)

PREP AND COOK TIME: About 50 minutes

NOTES: As the potatoes fall apart, they thicken the pan juices slightly. Mari Carmen Totorica serves this vegetable medley with meats, poultry, or fish.

MAKES: 8 servings

4 **thin-skinned red potatoes** (3 to 4 oz. each)

1 **carrot** (3 oz.)

1¹⁄₂ pounds **Italian** (romano) or regular **green beans**

¹⁄₂ cup chopped **onion**

4 cloves **garlic,** peeled and sliced

3 tablespoons **olive oil**

Salt and **pepper**

1. Rinse potatoes, peel, and cut into ³⁄₄-inch-thick wedges. Rinse carrot, peel, and cut into ¹⁄₄-inch-thick slices. Trim

and discard ends from beans; rinse beans and cut into 3-inch lengths.

2. In a 5- to 6-quart pan over medium heat, stir onion and garlic in oil until limp and tinged with gold, 8 to 10 minutes. Scrape mixture into a wide bowl.

3. Add 2 cups water to unwashed pan; bring to a boil over high heat. Add potatoes and carrots, cover, and return to a boil; reduce heat and simmer until potatoes are almost tender when pierced, 10 to 12 minutes. Stir in beans, cover, and return to a boil over high heat; reduce heat and simmer until beans are tender to bite, 6 to 8 minutes. Drain vegetables, saving ¹⁄₂ cup of the cooking water.

4. Add hot vegetables to onion mixture in bowl and mix. Stir in enough of the reserved cooking water to moisten vegetables. Add salt and pepper to taste.

Per serving: 112 cal., 43% (48 cal.) from fat; 2.6 g protein; 5.3 g fat (0.7 g sat.); 15 g carbo (2.7 g fiber); 12 mg sodium; 0 mg chol.

desserts

Basque Creamy Rice Pudding
(*Arroza Esnearekin*)

PREP AND COOK TIME: About 40 minutes

NOTES: Dan Ansotegui's grandmother, Epi, made this very creamy rice pudding at her boardinghouse in Hailey, Idaho. If making up to 2 days ahead, cover and chill.

MAKES: 8 servings

6 to 7 cups **milk**

1 cup **medium-grain white rice** (blue rose or pearl)

2 **cinnamon sticks** (3 in. each)

¹⁄₂ to ³⁄₄ cup **sugar**

Ground cinnamon

1. In a 5- to 6-quart pan over medium heat, combine 6 cups milk, rice, and cinnamon sticks. Cover and bring to a simmer over medium heat, stirring occasionally. Adjust heat to maintain a very gentle simmer, cover, and stir often until rice is tender to bite, about 30 minutes.

2. Remove from heat, remove cinnamon sticks if desired, stir in sugar to taste, and spoon into bowls; garnish with a dusting of ground cinnamon. Or to serve cold, cool, discard cinnamon sticks if desired for mild flavor, cover, and chill about 2 hours. If pudding is thicker than you like, stir in milk until it reaches desired consistency.

Per serving: 249 cal., 23% (57 cal.) from fat; 7.6 g protein; 6.3 g fat (3.8 g sat.); 41 g carbo (0.3 g fiber); 90 mg sodium; 26 mg chol.

Wine Fruit Compote (*Konpota*)

Wine Fruit Compote
(*Konpota*)

PREP AND COOK TIME: About 40 minutes, plus at least 3 hours to chill

NOTES: Traditionally, Mari Carmen Totorica serves this compote as a Christmas dessert, but it is a refreshing way to end a meal any time of year.

MAKES: 8 servings

- 3 **Golden Delicious apples** (1½ lb. total)
- 2 **firm-ripe Anjou pears** (1 lb. total)
- 5 cups **dry red wine**
- 2 **cinnamon sticks** (each 3 in.)
- 8 **pitted dried prunes**
- 8 **dried apricots**
- About ¾ cup **sugar**

1. Rinse, peel, and core apples and pears. Cut fruit lengthwise into ½-inch-thick slices.

2. In a 4- to 5-quart pan, combine wine, cinnamon, apples, pears, prunes, and apricots. Cover pan and bring mixture to a boil over high heat; reduce heat and simmer, stirring occasionally, until apples and pears are tender when pierced and prunes and apricots are soft, 10 to 15 minutes.

3. Add sugar to taste; stir until it's dissolved. Cool, cover, and chill until cold, at least 3 hours or up to 1 day.

4. Spoon cold fruit and wine into bowls or glasses.

Per serving: 241 cal., 1.9% (4.5 cal.) from fat; 1.1 g protein; 0.5 g fat (0 g sat.); 50 g carbo (3.8 g fiber); 8.6 mg sodium; 0 mg chol.

— *L.L.A.*

Basque-ing in a festival

■ The red, white, and green Basque flag snaps in the summer breeze over the fairgrounds in Elko, Nevada, as the annual National Basque Festival gets under way to the lively beat of a tambourine. Dancers parade, athletes warm up, and I turn to the former president of the Elko Basque Club, Nicolas Fagoaga, for some insight into it all. At 86, Fagoaga still looks strong, with the deeply tanned face of one who has spent much of his life outdoors. Atop a crown of white hair, he wears a *txapel* (black Basque beret); a red sash and scarf over his white pants and shirt complete the traditional outfit, made famous in the Spanish town of Pamplona by the much-publicized running of the bulls.

According to Fagoaga, the typical festival includes a Catholic mass as well as the dances and tests of strength we've seen contestants preparing for. Festival crowds seem especially to love the last, which grew out of Old Country occupations. Among them are *aizkolariak* (wood chopping) and *astunketa,* which is weightlifting with a twist: Men carry weights for a distance—dragging a ½-ton concrete block, for instance—or, in an exhibition sometimes called the Basque necktie, pick up and roll a beach-ball-size granite ball *around their necks.* Repeatedly. "Men in the Old Country would say that's light," laughs Fagoaga, pointing to a 230-pound granite ball. It seems fitting that these feats are followed by duels of *irrintzi*—the earsplitting howl that is the Basque war cry.

When Basques get together, there's also always a barbecue, and even now the succulent scent of lamb floats from the far end of the park, where a happy mix of festivalgoers and beret-wearing Basques are lining up to sample the grilled dishes.

And there's always music. Fagoaga tells us that we'll see *trikitixa*—two-somes playing the diatonic (button)

Elko, Nevada, kicks off the National Basque Festival with a colorful parade. Festival entertainment gets a mite heavy in a weightlifting contest.

accordion and the *pandareta* (a kind of tambourine). And groups of all ages perform folk dances. "You have to have *oinkari* for our dances—that means fast feet," he grins. One you'll surely see is the *jota* (the traditional Basque dance, similar to the Irish jig). "When I see the dancers doing the jota, it makes me tingle in my heart," Fagoaga says.

CENTERS OF BASQUE CULTURE AND OTHER RESOURCES. At Northern California's **Basque Cultural Center** in South San Francisco, you can watch a game of *pilota* (similar to handball), enjoy a family-style dinner, or sign up for music or dance lessons (55 Railroad Ave.; 650/583-8091). In Idaho, drop in at the **Basque Museum & Cultural Center** in a part of downtown Boise called the Basque block (611 Grove St.; 208/343-2671).

Check out *Amerikanuak! Basques in the High Desert,* by Robert G. Boyd (High Desert Museum, Bend, OR, 1995; $12). Another good source for Basque history, culture, and festivals in the West is *A Travel Guide to Basque America,* by

Nancy Zubiri (University of Nevada, Reno, 1998; $18.95; 877/682-6657). Visit the North American Basque Organization's website, www.naboinc.com, for links to clubs and events.

FESTIVALS. Here is a list of the major festivals throughout the West, but note that events and dates may change; call ahead to confirm. Most of the festivals are free (except for the barbecue). For more information about Nevada's many Basque events, call the Nevada Commission on Tourism at (800) 237-0774 or visit www.travelnevada.com.

May 6. Fresno, California, Basque Club Picnic. A lamb barbecue and traditional Catholic service. *Coombs Riverbend Ranch; (559) 275-6192 or 846-7818.*

June 4. San Francisco Basque Club Picnic in Petaluma, California. Marching band, dance exhibitions, San Francisco Basque Choir performance, barbecue, and mass mark the club's 40th birthday. *Petaluma Fairgrounds; (415) 564-0900 or www.sfbasque.org.*

SEAN ARBABI (2)

June 10–11. Winnemucca, Nevada, Basque Festival. Barbecue, music, games, and dance demonstrations. *Winnemucca Fairgrounds and Convention Center; (800) 962-2638.*

June 30–July 2. Elko, Nevada, 37th National Basque Festival. One of the biggest and best fests opens with a music and dance exhibition and includes an old-fashioned small-town parade, athletic contests, dance contests, barbecue, public dance, and mass. *Elko Fairgrounds and City Park; (775) 738-7135.*

July 22–23. Reno Basque Festival. A parade and barbecue, plus a trikitixa from the Old Country, dance groups from California and Nevada, and a big sports competition. *Wingfield Park; (775) 787-3039.*

July 27–30. Boise, Jaialdi International Basque Cultural Festival. Held every five years, this major event kicks off with extraordinary contests of strength, followed by a block party, music, and dance exhibitions. The final two days see the best competitive dancers, musicians, and athletes. *Western Idaho Fairgrounds; (208) 887-1149 or www.jaialdi.com.*

September 16–17. South San Francisco, Autumn Festival. At the Basque Cultural Center, there'll be a dinner-dance, mass, barbecue, and musicians and dancers from the French Basque country. *55 Railroad Ave.; (650) 583-8091.*

September 17. Carson City, Nevada, Basque Festival. Includes musical entertainment, dancing, and dinner. *Fuji Park; (775) 882-2079. — L.J.F.*

The restaurant tradition

At the appointed hour (7 P.M.), a mixed group of strangers files into the spare dining room and systematically fills the seats at the long tables. Tureens of clam chowder, a simple lettuce salad, and bottles of wine are waiting. Just as we finish our salad, a parade of platters begins: pickled tongue, cottage cheese, beef stew, fried fish, spaghetti, roast lamb, French fries, and blue cheese, then ice cream. My tablemate sums up the appeal of Basque restaurants: "This is the real thing—lots of good food, friendly people."

My dinner at the Noriega Hotel in Bakersfield, California, is typical of meals at Basque restaurants with boardinghouse roots. Although newer establishments may have separate tables, more elaborate service, a choice of entrées, or à la carte selections, Basque menus are remarkably similar: soup and salad, a slew of first courses or what we might call side dishes, followed by a piece of simply cooked meat or fish. Depending on the

restaurant owner's origin, the menu might have French or Spanish accents. Prices for family-style dinners range from $10 to $20 ($7 to $14 for lunch), depending on the entrée; a house wine is sometimes included.

Here is a selected list of restaurants favored by Basques. Some offer single seating only for meals; call for hours.

■ CALIFORNIA
BAKERSFIELD
Noriega Hotel, 525 Sumner St.; (661) 322-8419. The oldest continuously run Basque boardinghouse in the United States (established in 1893). No menu, no credit cards.

Wool Growers, 620 E. 19th St.; (661) 327-9584. A local favorite in a comfortable newer building in the historic eastside district.

CHINO
Centro Basco, 13432 Central Ave.; (909) 628-9014. Family-style meals at communal tables in front dining rooms; dine à la carte in rear dining room.

FRESNO
Basque Hotel, 1102 F St.; (559) 233-2286. Established in 1923, this boardinghouse has no lunch menu but offers a choice of entrées. Sit at separate tables or share. The neighborhood feels safest at lunch.

Santa Fe Basque Restaurant, 935 Santa Fe Ave.; (559) 266-2170. Eat at shared or separate tables in this 1926 boardinghouse next to the train station.

SOUTH SAN FRANCISCO
Basque Cultural Center, 599 Railroad Ave.; (650) 583-8091. Choose the family-style meal or order à la carte from the French-inspired Basque menu at this white-tablecloth restaurant.

■ IDAHO
BOISE
Bar Gernika, 202 S. Capitol Blvd.; (208) 344-2175). Not a traditional restaurant, but it captures the spirit of Basque country bars. Housed in a 1920 building near the Basque Museum & Cultural Center, Bar Gernika

serves tapas and sandwiches.
GARDEN CITY
Oñati, the Basque Restaurant, 3544 Chinden Blvd.; (208) 343-6464. You can't miss this restaurant with a giant palomino on the roof. Spanish-Basque specialties, such as lamb stew or grilled pork loin with pimientos, in generous portions.

MERIDIAN
Epi's, a Basque Restaurant, 1115 E. First St.; (208) 884-0142. Granddaughters of Epi Inchausti, a famous Basque boardinghouse cook in Hailey, continue the family tradition in a fresh style with this new restaurant in a Boise suburb.

■ NEVADA
ELKO
Biltoki, 405 Silver St.; (775) 738-9691. Blackboard menu displays authentic Basque specials such as sweetbreads, bacalao, oxtail soup, beef tongue, pigs' feet, and tripe.

Star Hotel, 246 Silver St.; (775) 738-9925 or 753-8696. Family-style food in a 1910 building.

GARDNERVILLE
Carson Valley Country Club, 1029 Riverview Dr.; (775) 265-3715. Enjoy house-made chorizo under hunters' trophies hanging in the bar. Sit at separate tables or share.

J•T Bar Dining Room, 1426 S. Main St.; (775) 782-2074. This white wood-framed building is more than a century old. The restaurant offers family-style dining at separate tables. A parade of hats decorates the walls of the bar.

RENO
Louis' Basque Corner, 301 E. Fourth St.; (775) 323-7203. Sample sweetbreads, beef tongue, and roast lamb at long communal tables. Start with a picon punch, a traditional bittersweet aperitif with a brandy float.

WINNEMUCCA
Restaurante San Fermin, 485 W. Winnemucca Blvd.; (775) 625-2555. The Mediterranean decor matches a near-gourmet, Spanish-influenced à la carte menu that includes tapas. *— L.L.A.* ◆

The Quick Cook

MEALS IN 30 MINUTES OR LESS

BY ELAINE JOHNSON

Get ahead with ground beef

Ground beef may keep humble company, but it's the kind of company that generations have invited home regularly for weeknight dinner—sloppy Joes, spaghetti Bolognese. Trouble is, you almost always have to brown the meat before adding the other components of these satisfying dishes. If your midweek minutes are more precious than ever, here's a solution: Make a big batch of browned beef with onions and store it in the refrigerator or freezer. The mixture is ready at a moment's notice to pour into sauces, soups, and pilafs.

Make-Ahead Ground Beef

PREP AND COOK TIME: About 30 minutes

NOTES: Use meat hot, at room temperature, chilled, or frozen. Chill airtight up to 3 days; freeze up to 3 months.

MAKES: About 8 cups

- 3 pounds **ground lean beef**
- 1½ pounds **onions**, peeled and chopped
- 1 tablespoon minced **garlic**

1. In a 6- to 8-quart pan over high heat, frequently stir beef, onions, and garlic until onions are limp, juices have evaporated, and meat is browned, about 20 minutes.

2. Use meat, or cool and store (see notes). To freeze, line 2 pans, each 10 by 15 inches, with plastic wrap. Spread cooled beef mixture evenly in pans; cover with plastic wrap and freeze until firm, about 2½ hours. Uncover, invert meat mixture out of pans, break into small chunks, and quickly seal in a gallon-size heavy plastic food bag. As desired, pour out amount needed, reseal bag, and return to freezer.

Per ½ cup: 200 cal., 59% (117 cal.) from fat; 17 g protein; 13 g fat (5.1 g sat.); 3.5 g carbo (0.6 g fiber); 63 mg sodium; 56 mg chol.

Sloppy Joes Olé

PREP AND COOK TIME: About 15 minutes

MAKES: 4 servings

1. Cut 4 **sandwich rolls** (about 3 oz. each) or hamburger buns (about 1½ oz. each) in half horizontally. Brush cut sides lightly with **olive oil** (about 2 tablespoons total). Arrange rolls, cut sides up, in a 10- by 15-inch pan.

2. Bake in a 450° oven until rolls are lightly toasted, 5 to 6 minutes.

3. Meanwhile, in a 3- to 4-quart pan, combine 1 jar (26 oz.) **marinara sauce**, 2 cups **make-ahead ground beef** (recipe precedes), 1 can (4½ oz.) drained **sliced black ripe olives**, ¼ cup sliced **green onions** (including tops), 1½ teaspoons **hot sauce**, and ½ teaspoon **ground cumin**. Stir often over medium-high heat until bubbling, about 6 minutes. Add **salt** to taste.

4. Place bottom half of 1 roll on each plate. Ladle sauce equally onto rolls. Sprinkle with additional sliced green onions (about 2 tablespoons total). Cover sandwiches with roll tops.

Per serving: 666 cal., 47% (315 cal.) from fat; 29 g protein; 35 g fat (9.2 g sat.); 66 g carbo (6.6 g fiber); 1,958 mg sodium; 56 mg chol.

Beef and Cabbage Soup

PREP AND COOK TIME: About 20 minutes

MAKES: 6½ cups; 4 servings

In a 5- to 6-quart pan, mix 2 cups **make-ahead ground beef** (recipe at left); 2 cups **finely shredded green cabbage**; 2 cups fat-skimmed **beef broth**; 1 can (about 1 lb.) **Italian-style sliced stewed tomatoes**; 1 can (about 1 lb.) **small white beans**, rinsed and drained; 2 tablespoons **white wine vinegar**; and 1 teaspoon **caraway seed**. Cover and bring to a boil over high heat; reduce heat and simmer, stirring often, until cabbage is tender to bite, 5 to 8 minutes. Add **salt** and **pepper** to taste.

Per serving: 311 cal., 38% (117 cal.) from fat; 25 g protein; 13 g fat (5.2 g sat.); 23 g carbo (6.5 g fiber); 785 mg sodium; 56 mg chol.

Beef and Pine Nut Pilaf

PREP AND COOK TIME: 25 to 30 minutes

MAKES: 4 servings

1. In a 10- to 12-inch frying pan over medium-high heat, stir 1¼ cups **basmati rice**, ½ cup **pine nuts**, and 1 tablespoon **olive oil** until rice and pine nuts are pale golden, 4 to 5 minutes.

2. Add 2½ cups fat-skimmed **beef broth**,

Sloppy Joe rides again, with lively Southwest seasonings.

2 cups **make-ahead ground beef** (recipe at left), ½ cup chopped **dried apricots**, and 1 teaspoon **ground cinnamon**. Bring to a boil over high heat; reduce heat, cover, and simmer, stirring occasionally, until rice is tender to bite, about 15 minutes. Stir in ¼ cup chopped **parsley** and **salt** to taste.

Per serving: 569 cal., 41% (234 cal.) from fat; 31 g protein; 26 g fat (7 g sat.); 61 g carbo (4.4 g fiber); 135 mg sodium; 56 mg chol.

Penne with Meat Sauce

PREP AND COOK TIME: About 25 minutes

MAKES: 6 servings

1. In a 5- to 6-quart pan over high heat, bring 3 quarts water to a boil. Add 1 pound **dried penne pasta**; cook, stirring occasionally, until tender to bite, 10 to 12 minutes. Drain and pour into a wide, shallow bowl.

2. Meanwhile, in a 3- to 4-quart pan over medium-high heat, frequently stir 1 jar (26 oz.) **marinara sauce**, 2 cups **make-ahead ground beef** (recipe at left), ½ cup **dry red wine**, and 2 teaspoons **fennel seed** until boiling, about 8 minutes.

3. Pour sauce over pasta. Top with ½ cup **shredded parmesan cheese** and 2 tablespoons thinly sliced **fresh basil** leaves or chopped parsley. Add **salt** to taste.

Per serving: 545 cal., 26% (144 cal.) from fat; 26 g protein; 16 g fat (5.4 g sat.); 72 g carbo (4.5 g fiber); 946 mg sodium; 43 mg chol. ◆

Catch a rainbow

Hook your fresh trout in the market and cook up a fast, healthy dinner

BY LINDA LAU ANUSASANANAN • PHOTOGRAPHS BY JAMES CARRIER

■ I'm no angler. My idea of fishing is a trip to the market for the freshest fillets in the seafood case. When I met an avid fly-fisher recently, I was surprised to learn that he fishes the same way I do—even for trout. To him, the sport is catch and release, not catch and consume. The trout he eats, he buys.

Luckily for us, a huge supply of trout—primarily rainbow—is farm-raised for food. About 60 million pounds are grown in the United States each year, in areas—like Idaho, the source of more than 70 percent of U.S. production—that have copious amounts of cold, pure water. Because of the controlled environment, there's a consistent year-round supply.

Think of trout as the ultimate healthy fast food. The fish are sold pan-ready, and they cook in minutes. Relatively low in fat and high in protein and beneficial omega-3 fatty acids, trout deserves a frequent appearance on a healthy table. Compared with many other seafoods, it's also very affordable, usually around $3.75 to $6.25 a pound—less at warehouse outlets.

Most fresh rainbow trout in the market are the perfect size for single servings. A cleaned, bone-in whole trout weighs 12 to 16 ounces; with head and tail removed, about 1½ ounces less. A boned trout weighs in at 8 to 10 ounces. Often, when trout is boned, the fillets are left attached along the back, so the fish opens up flat like a book.

Dress it up, dress it down—trout is equally at home on Limoges china or in a frying pan over a campfire. Its delicate but distinctive flavor adapts to many settings and presentations.

Smoked Trout

PREP AND COOK TIME: About 25 minutes, plus at least 1 hour to cure

NOTES: For the most intense smoky flavor and deepest gold color, use a charcoal barbecue. To present smoked trout as an appetizer, serve on thin triangles of Westphalian-style pumpernickel bread with sour cream, chopped red onion, and lemon wedges. For a salad, combine chunks of smoked trout, hot or cold, with green salad mix and a vinaigrette dressing. As a main dish, serve trout hot with boiled small thin-skinned potatoes, melted butter, and lemon wedges. Chill smoked trout airtight up to 1 week or freeze up to 1 month.

MAKES: 3 main-dish or 9 appetizer servings

- 3 **cleaned, boned whole trout,** heads and tails removed (8 to 10 oz. each)
- ¼ cup **sugar**
- 2 tablespoons **salt**
- 1 teaspoon grated **lemon** peel
- ½ teaspoon **fresh thyme** leaves or dried thyme
- 2 cups **hickory wood chips**
- About 1 tablespoon **salad oil**

Pile quick-smoked trout onto slices of dark pumpernickel for a superb appetizer (below). Chili-spiked tomatillo sauce seasons grilled whole trout and potatoes (right)

1. Rinse trout and pat dry. In a small bowl, mix sugar, salt, lemon peel, and thyme; rub evenly over flesh sides of fish. Stack trout in a 9- by 13-inch baking dish. Cover and chill to cure at least 1 hour or up to 3 hours.

2. In a bowl, soak wood chips in 2 quarts of water for 30 minutes. Drain.

3. *If using a charcoal grill,* ignite 60 charcoal briquets on firegrate. When dotted with gray ash, in 20 to 25 minutes, push half the coals to each side of grate. Sprinkle half the wet wood chips on each mound of coals. Position grill about 6 inches above grate.

If using a gas grill, turn heat to high. Put wet wood chips in smoke box or foil pan directly on heat. Close lid and heat for about 10 minutes. Adjust heat for indirect grilling (no heat down the center).

4. Rinse fish well and pat dry. Coat skin sides of fish with oil and lay fish, skin down, on grill, not over heat source. Cover barbecue; open vents for charcoal. Cook until fish are opaque but still moist-looking in center of thickest part (cut to test), 8 to 10 minutes. With a wide spatula, transfer fish to a platter.

Per main-dish serving: 384 cal., 47% (180 cal.) from fat; 47 g protein; 20 g fat (3.2 g sat.); 2.2 g carbo (0 g fiber); 699 mg sodium; 132 mg chol.

Grilled Trout and Potatoes with Tomatillo Sauce

PREP AND COOK TIME: About 45 minutes

MAKES: 4 servings

12 **red thin-skinned potatoes** (2 in. each)

4 **cleaned, whole bone-in trout** (12 to 16 oz. each)

3 tablespoons **olive** or salad **oil**
   Salt

½ pound **tomatillos**

2 **fresh jalapeño chilies** (1½ oz. total), rinsed

1. Scrub potatoes. In a 3- to 4-quart pan over high heat, bring about 1 quart water to a boil. Add potatoes and return to a boil; reduce heat, cover, and simmer until tender when pierced, 20 to 25 minutes.

2. Meanwhile, rinse trout, pat dry, and coat with about half the oil. Sprinkle fish cavities lightly with salt.

3. Husk and rinse tomatillos. Thread tomatillos onto a metal skewer (8 to 10 in.).

4. Drain potatoes. Coat with remaining oil and thread equally onto 4 metal skewers.

5. Lay potatoes, tomatillos, and chilies on a grill over a solid bed of hot coals or high heat on a gas grill (you can hold your hand at grill level only 2 to 3 seconds). Close lid; open vents for charcoal. Cook 5 minutes; turn vegetables over and lay trout on grill. Cook, turning as needed, until potatoes are lightly browned and tomatillos and chilies are well browned, 6 to 8 minutes longer. Cook fish, turning once, until opaque but still moist-looking in center of thickest part (cut to test), 6 to 8 minutes total. With a wide spatula, transfer potatoes and fish to a platter and keep warm.

6. Cut off chili stems and discard. For less heat, discard seeds. In a food processor or blender, combine tomatillos, 1 chili, and ¼ cup water. Whirl until smooth. Add more chili, if desired, and salt to taste; whirl until smooth. If a thinner sauce is desired, add a little more water. Pour into a bowl.

7. Serve trout and potatoes with tomatillo sauce; add salt to taste.

Per serving: 540 cal., 40% (216 cal.) from fat; 46 g protein; 24 g fat (3.7 g sat.); 34 g carbo (3 g fiber); 118 mg sodium; 116 mg chol.

Trout with Sage

PREP AND COOK TIME: About 30 minutes

NOTES: If desired, buy trout without heads and tails (10 to 12 oz. each).

MAKES: 2 servings

- 1 **lemon** (4 to 5 oz.), rinsed
- 2 **cleaned, bone-in whole trout** (12 to 16 oz. each)

  Salt and **pepper**
- 18 **fresh sage** leaves (each 2 to 3 in. long), rinsed and dried
- 3 tablespoons **all-purpose flour**
- 1½ tablespoons **cornmeal**
- 2 tablespoons **olive oil**
- 2 tablespoons **butter** (or more olive oil)

1. Cut lemon in half lengthwise. From 1 half, cut 4 thin slices crosswise; save rest of half for other uses. Cut remaining half into wedges.

2. Rinse fish, pat dry, and sprinkle lightly, inside and out, with salt and pepper. Tuck 3 sage leaves and 2 lemon slices into the cavity of each fish.

3. On a sheet of waxed paper, mix flour

and cornmeal. Roll fish in mixture to coat; shake off excess and discard remainder.

4. Set a 10- to 12-inch frying pan over medium-high heat. When pan is hot, add oil and tilt pan to coat. Add trout and brown on each side, turning once, until fish are opaque but still moist-looking in center of thickest part (cut to test), 12 to 14 minutes total; reduce heat to medium if fish brown too quickly.

5. With a slotted spatula, transfer fish to plates or a platter. Add butter and remaining sage leaves to pan; shake pan often until butter is melted and sage leaves are darkened and slightly browned, about 1 minute. Spoon butter and leaves over fish. Squeeze lemon wedges over fish and add salt and pepper to taste.

Per serving: 587 cal., 60% (351 cal.) from fat; 44 g protein; 39 g fat (11 g sat.); 15 g carbo (0.7 g fiber); 222 mg sodium; 147 mg chol.

Baked Trout with Lemon-Parsley Butter

PREP AND COOK TIME: About 20 minutes

MAKES: 4 servings

- ⅓ cup **butter** or margarine
- 4 **cleaned, boned whole trout,** heads and tails removed (8 to 10 oz. each)
- 3 tablespoons chopped **parsley**
- 1 tablespoon chopped drained **capers**
- ½ teaspoon grated **lemon** peel
- 2 tablespoons **lemon juice**
- 1 clove **garlic,** peeled and pressed

  Salt and **pepper**

  Lemon wedges

1. Place butter in a small microwave-safe bowl and heat in a microwave oven at full power (100%) until melted, 30 to 60 seconds.

2. Rinse fish, pat dry, and, if fillets are attached, cut apart. Coat fish on all sides with about 1 tablespoon butter total and lay skin side down in a single layer in 2 pans, each 10 by 15 inches.

3. Bake in a 400° oven until fish are opaque but still moist-looking in center of thickest part (cut to test), 8 to 10 minutes, switching pan positions after 4 minutes. With a wide spatula, transfer fish to plates.

4. To remaining butter, add parsley, ca-

Boned and butterflied trout is steamed in the oven with ginger and sherry.

pers, lemon peel, lemon juice, and garlic. Heat in microwave oven at full power until bubbling, about 30 seconds.

5. Drizzle fish with butter mixture. Add salt and pepper to taste. Serve with lemon wedges to squeeze over fish.

Per serving: 475 cal., 57% (270 cal.) from fat; 47 g protein; 30 g fat (12 g sat.); 1.2 g carbo (0.1 g fiber); 370 mg sodium; 173 mg chol.

Oven-Steamed Trout with Ginger

PREP AND COOK TIME: About 30 minutes

NOTES: If they're available, choose fish with fillets attached at the back.

MAKES: 4 servings

- 4 **cleaned, boned whole trout,** heads and tails removed (8 to 10 oz. each)

  About 1 tablespoon **Asian** (toasted) **sesame oil**
- ¼ cup **dry sherry**
- 3 tablespoons finely slivered **fresh ginger**

  About 2 tablespoons **soy sauce**
- ⅓ cup finely slivered **green onions** (including green tops)
- ⅓ cup **fresh cilantro** leaves

1. Rinse trout, pat dry, and coat inside

Wrap trout in cornhusks, then char in a hot oven for a mild, smoky flavor.

and out with oil. Lay fish, spread open, skin side down, in a single layer in 2 baking pans, each 10 by 15 inches. Drizzle sherry evenly over fish and sprinkle with ginger. Cover pan tightly.

2. Bake in a 400° oven until fish are opaque but still moist-looking in center of thickest part (cut to test), 8 to 10 minutes. Supporting with 2 wide spatulas, transfer fish to a platter or plates (if fish start to break up, cut fillets apart and lift 1 piece at a time).

3. Drizzle 2 tablespoons soy sauce evenly over fish; sprinkle equally with onions and cilantro. Add more soy to taste.

Per serving: 395 cal., 41% (162 cal.) from fat; 48 g protein; 18 g fat (3.1 g sat.); 2.7 g carbo (0.3 g fiber); 636 mg sodium; 132 mg chol.

Trout with Tarragon and Leeks

PREP AND COOK TIME: About 40 minutes

MAKES: 4 servings

1½ pounds **leeks**

3 tablespoons **butter** or margarine

⅓ cup **pine nuts**

1 teaspoon **fresh tarragon** leaves or ½ teaspoon dried tarragon

1 tablespoon **white wine vinegar**

Salt and **pepper**

4 **cleaned, boned whole trout,** heads and tails removed (8 to 10 oz. each)

Lemon wedges

1. Trim and discard root ends, tough green tops, and tough outer leaves from leeks. Split leeks in half lengthwise and rinse well under running water; thinly slice crosswise.

2. In a 10- to 12-inch frying pan, melt butter over medium heat. Add nuts and stir until golden, about 3 minutes. With a slotted spoon, transfer nuts to a small bowl. Spoon 1 tablespoon butter into another small bowl. Add leeks and tarragon to remaining butter in pan. Stir often until leeks are limp, 7 to 10 minutes. Stir in vinegar, pine nuts, and salt and pepper to taste.

3. Rinse fish, pat dry, and rub skin sides with reserved butter. Open fish, flesh sides up, and spoon an equal amount of leek mixture down the center of each trout. Fold sides together to enclose filling. Place trout slightly apart in a 10- by 15-inch pan.

4. Bake in a 400° oven until fish are opaque but still moist-looking in center of thickest part (cut to test), 10 to 13 minutes. With a wide spatula, transfer trout to plates or a large platter. Add salt and pepper to taste. Serve with lemon wedges to squeeze over the fish.

Per serving: 520 cal., 52% (270 cal.) from fat; 51 g protein; 30 g fat (8.9 g sat.); 12 g carbo (2.2 g fiber); 221 mg sodium; 155 mg chol.

Cornhusk Trout

PREP AND COOK TIME: About 1¼ hours

NOTES: The charred cornhusks give the trout a distinctive mild, smoky flavor. You can find the cornhusks at well-stocked supermarkets and Latino markets. Wrap the fish (through step 3) up to 2 hours before cooking; cover and chill.

MAKES: 4 servings

4 to 5½ dozen **dried cornhusks** (6 to 8 in. long, 4 to 6 in. wide)

4 **cleaned, bone-in whole trout** (12 to 16 oz. each)

About 1 teaspoon **salt**

Hominy-pepper salsa salad (recipe follows)

1. Remove and discard any silks from cornhusks. Rinse husks, place in a large bowl, cover with very hot tap water, and soak until soft and pliable, about 15 minutes.

2. Meanwhile, rinse the fish and pat dry. If desired, cut off heads and tails. Sprinkle trout inside and out with salt.

3. Tear 3 or 4 of the thicker husks lengthwise into ½-inch-wide strips; tie ends together to make 20 to 24 strips, each 10 to 12 inches long. (Or use 20 to 24 pieces of cotton string, 10 to 12 inches long, soaked in cold water.) For each fish, lay 4 or 5 husk strips or strings parallel 2½ to 3 inches apart. Drain the remaining husks; unfold them and lay them flat on and perpendicular to the strips, overlapping, to make 1 rectangle for each trout, 2 to 3 inches wider and longer than the fish. Cover each rectangle with another layer of husks. Lay 1 fish down the center of each rectangle. Cover fish with 2 layers of husks just the size of the fish, overlapping the edges if needed. Fold bottom rectangles up and over sides of fish and top rectangles to enclose completely. Secure bundles by tying husk strips or string snugly around fish, with 1 at each end cinched tight to close. Lay fish bundles slightly apart in 2 pans, 10 by 15 inches each.

4. Bake in a 500° oven until husks are charred, 30 to 40 minutes. Set a fish on each plate. Snip husk strips, fold back husks, peel off fish skin, and serve trout with hominy-pepper salsa salad and salt to taste.

Per serving: 297 cal., 39% (117 cal.) from fat; 42 g protein; 13 g fat (2.3 g sat.); 0 g carbo (0 g fiber); 687 mg sodium; 6.4 mg chol.

Hominy-Pepper Salsa Salad

PREP TIME: About 20 minutes

MAKES: About 3 cups; 4 servings

Drain 1 can (14½ oz.) **golden hominy;** rinse and drain again. In a bowl, mix hominy, 1 cup chopped **red bell pepper,** ⅓ cup chopped **red onion,** 2 tablespoons **lime juice,** and 2 tablespoons chopped **fresh cilantro.** Add 1 to 2 tablespoons chopped **fresh jalapeño chili** and **salt** to taste.

Per serving: 89 cal., 10% (9 cal.) from fat; 2 g protein; 1 g fat (0.1 g sat.); 18 g carbo (3.2 g fiber); 219 mg sodium; 0 mg chol. ◆

food guide

BY JERRY ANNE DI VECCHIO

PHOTOGRAPHS BY JAMES CARRIER

Weekend chicken

A bird in the oven guarantees great snacks

■ On our first date, David marched into my kitchen, opened the refrigerator, spotted a roasted chicken, and muttered, "You'll do." A quarter of a century later, the cold remains of a chicken, particularly on weekends, still produce cheery mumbling. We whittle away on them for sandwiches and nibbles. It's worth rushing in the door after work on Friday night to pop a chicken and some vegeta-

bles into the oven; then I relax while dinner does its thing. The seasonings and vegetables change from meal to meal, but I almost always slip some herbs under the chicken skin—one of the many interesting uses for herbs suggested by Jerry Traunfeld in *The Herbfarm Cookbook* (see page 150). It's not a new concept, to be sure, but it's one to tuck away—in the next chicken you roast.

Roast Chicken Dinner

PREP AND COOK TIME: About 1¾ hours

NOTES: Use a 6-pound bird if you want leftovers.

MAKES: 4 servings

- 1 **chicken** (4 or 6 lb.)
- 12 **fresh thyme** sprigs (each about 2 in. long)

  About 2 tablespoons **olive oil**

  Salt

  Fresh-ground **pepper**

- 2 **red onions** (½ lb. each)
- 2 tablespoons **lemon juice**
- 4 **Yukon Gold** or other thin-skinned **potatoes** (½ lb. each)

  Lemon-parsley butter (see "Just a Little Shaver," facing page)

1. Pull off and discard lumps of fat from chicken. Rinse chicken, chicken neck, and giblets. Pat chicken dry and fold the wing tips back and under wings. Rinse thyme sprigs.

2. Gently ease your fingers between the meat and skin from the neck side of chicken over breast and down onto thighs, releasing the skin but leaving it in place. Push 8 thyme sprigs under skin and distribute them evenly over breast and thighs. Place remaining thyme sprigs, along with the chicken liver, in the body cavity. Rub chicken all over with about 1 tablespoon olive oil; sprinkle with salt and pepper. Set chicken, breast up, in the highest position on a V-shaped rack (for even browning). Set the rack in a shallow pan (1 to 2 in. deep; 10 to 12 by 15 to 17 in.). Lay the chicken neck and remaining giblets in the pan.

3. Rinse onions and cut in half crosswise (do not peel); rub cut sides with lemon juice. Scrub potatoes and cut in half lengthwise. Rub cut sides of potatoes and onions with oil; set, cut sides up, around the rack in pan; if chicken weighs 6 pounds, add the vegetables 15 minutes after placing the bird in the oven.

4. Bake chicken on the lowest rack in a 400° oven until skin is well browned and a thermometer inserted through the thickest part of the breast to the bone registers 160°, about 1 hour for a 4-pound bird, about 1¼ hours for a 6-pounder. Bake the vegetables until browned and tender when pierced, about 1 hour, occasionally basting with pan drippings.

5. Transfer the vegetables to a platter. Using a carving fork and spatula, tilt the chicken to drain cavity juices into pan. Put chicken on platter and keep warm; let stand 5 to 10 minutes for juices to settle. Discard chicken neck and giblets from pan. Stir pan juices, adding up to ¼ cup hot water to release browned bits; skim and discard fat. Pour juices into a small bowl and keep warm. Carve chicken, setting aside herb sprigs. Serve chicken, potatoes, and onions with pan juices and lemon-parsley butter; add salt and pepper to taste.

Per serving: 921 cal., 50% (459 cal.) from fat; 63 g protein; 51 g fat (17 g sat.); 53 g carbo (5.8 g fiber); 326 mg sodium; 210 mg chol.

Just a little shaver

■ My most effective citrus peel grater is actually intended for spices. It's the smallest in a series of five graters made by Microplane, which manufactures industrial cutting tools. All the graters have razor-sharp edges. I like the little one because it literally shaves the fruit peel to give mixtures like this butter a pure citrus essence. It's a sharp buy, at www. tavolo.com (where it costs $8.95) or in cookware stores.

Lemon-parsley butter. In a bowl or food processor, combine 2 teaspoons grated **lemon** peel, 1 tablespoon **lemon juice,** ¼ cup minced **parsley,** and ¼ cup (⅛ lb.) **butter** or margarine, cut into chunks; mix or whirl until well blended. Scrape into a small bowl. Makes about ⅓ cup.

Per tablespoon: 87 cal., 99% (86 cal.) from fat; 0.2 g protein; 9.6 g fat (6 g sat.); 0.5 g carbo (0.1 g fiber); 99 mg sodium; 26 mg chol.

Salsa sizzle

■ Just when it seems that every possible use for salsa has been conceived, someone comes up with a new surprise. Saul Garcia, chef at Z' Tejas Grill in Las Vegas, boils his fresh salsa, then adds crisp fried tortilla strips and feta cheese, creating almost-traditional *chilaquiles,* a lively, steaming dish that might best be described as a hot salad. For a quick supper or brunch, make scrambled eggs its companion.

Chilaquiles Salad

PREP AND COOK TIME: 25 to 30 minutes

NOTES: To save about 15 minutes, add 2½ cups purchased tomato salsa instead of the salsa ingredients in step 2. Accompany with red radishes, green onions, and lime wedges.

MAKES: 4 servings

- 8 **corn tortillas** (6 in.)
- 3 tablespoons **salad oil**
- 2 cups chopped **tomatoes**
- ½ cup finely chopped **onion**
- ¼ cup minced **fresh cilantro**
- ¼ cup **lime juice**
- 1 tablespoon firmly packed **brown sugar**
- 1 tablespoon chopped stemmed and seeded **fresh jalapeño chili**
- ½ pound **feta cheese,** cut into ¼-inch cubes
  Salt

1. Stack tortillas and cut into ¼-inch-wide strips. Pour oil into an 11- to 12-inch frying pan and set over high heat. When oil is hot, add tortillas and stir until crisp and lightly browned, 7 to 10 minutes. Pour onto towels to drain. Wipe pan clean.

2. Add tomatoes, onion, cilantro, lime juice, sugar, and chili to pan.

3. Stir frequently over high heat until there is no free-flowing liquid when you scrape salsa from pan bottom, 5 to 8 minutes. Add cheese and fried tortilla strips; stir until hot, 1 to 2 minutes. Pour onto a platter. Season to taste with salt.

Per serving: 395 cal., 55% (216 cal.) from fat; 12 g protein; 24 g fat (10 g sat.); 36 g carbo (4.2 g fiber); 727 mg sodium; 51 mg chol.

Refreshing ripple

■ At Water Grill Restaurant in Los Angeles, where fish reigns on the menu, the desserts, created by pastry chef Wonyee Tom, also cause ripples of pleasure. Tom often assembles them in layers of flavors and textures. At the top of one masterpiece I sampled recently, this sophisticated, exceptionally smooth and velvety sour cream sorbet caught my attention. It's very easy to make at home. To enhance the tang of the sour cream, Tom infuses the sweet syrup base with lemon grass; if it's not available, pare the peel from three lemons instead and add to the syrup as it boils.

Sour Cream Sorbet

PREP AND COOK TIME: About 45 minutes using quick-chill option

NOTES: If making up to 1 week ahead, store airtight in the freezer.

MAKES: About 3½ cups; 6 or 7 servings

10 to 12 stalks **fresh lemon grass** (about 1 lb. total)

1½ cups **sugar**

½ cup **lemon juice**

2 cups (1 pt.) **sour cream**

1. Trim and discard root ends, coarse tops, and coarse outer layers from lemon grass. Rinse tender stalks and cut into chunks. Finely chop in a food processor or with a knife.
2. In a 4- to 5-quart pan, combine lemon grass, sugar, and 1 cup water. Bring to a boil over high heat, stirring occasionally. Cover and boil for 8 minutes, stirring occasionally.
3. Pour syrup through a fine strainer into a 1-cup glass measure; discard lemon grass. If there's less than 1 cup syrup, add water. If there's more, rinse pan, return syrup to it, and boil until reduced to 1 cup. Nest glass measure in ice water and stir syrup often until cold, 5 to 10 minutes; or cover and chill until cold, about 1 hour.
4. Pour syrup into a bowl. Add lemon juice and sour

cream; whisk to blend well. Pour mixture into a 1-quart or larger ice cream maker. Freeze according to the manufacturer's directions until dasher is hard to turn and mixture is softly frozen, 15 to 20 minutes. Serve, or cover airtight and store in the freezer. Scoop portions into bowls.

Per ½ cup: 311 cal., 41% (126 cal.) from fat; 2.2 g protein; 14 g fat (8.6 g sat.); 47 g carbo (0 g fiber); 39 mg sodium; 29 mg chol.

Recipes without reservation

■ The Herbfarm Restaurant, set in the Cascade foothills about 17 miles east of Seattle, is so popular that reservations are made available only twice a year. Within hours each time, the restaurant is fully booked for every day. The attraction? Dishes that look deceptively simple but are in fact meticulously prepared, making creative use of the herbs that flourish on the farm and give the restaurant its name. Now, executive chef Jerry Traunfeld presents recipes for 200 of these dishes in *The Herbfarm Cookbook* (Scribner, New York, 2000; $40). In addition to being a skillful culinarian, Traunfeld is an avid gardener, and his knowledge of growing and handling herbs, from bay laurel and basil to angelica and lemon verbena, is part of this handsome 448-page volume. It's available in bookstores and online at sites like www.amazon.com and www.bn.com. ◆

The Wine Guide

BY KAREN MacNEIL-FIFE

RICK MARIANI

Asparagus—wine enemy number 1?

■ Standing in the supermarket the other day, I was about to add a bundle of asparagus from the towering green stacks to my cart for dinner, when I remembered that many people consider the vegetable wine's worst enemy.

To tell you the truth, I've never paid much attention to that old notion. It's a fact that asparagus, a member of the lily family, contains the sulfurous amino acid methionine. This compound, together with the plant's intense grassy flavor, can make many wines taste dank, vegetal, or just plain weird. But I love asparagus, and I love wine. In my dining room, the two do get served together. That day I realized that whenever asparagus is in the picture, I instinctively gravitate to Sauvignon Blanc, and I wondered what the experts in matching food and wine do. I decided to call a few of them.

"Asparagus makes everything you drink with it taste green," said Sid Goldstein, author of *The Wine Lover's Cookbook*. "The worst white wine with asparagus is Chardonnay, which not only tastes vegetal, but also exaggeratedly oaky." However, like me, Goldstein loves both asparagus and wine. His solution? "Steam or microwave the asparagus until almost done, then grill it and serve it with Sauvignon Blanc or Pinot Grigio. The grilling process—maybe it's the flavor of the char—takes the bitter edge off the greenness of the asparagus. Then you can create a harmonious balance by serving it with a wine that also has light green flavors."

Jerry Comfort, culinary director of Beringer Wine Estates in St. Helena, California, called asparagus a "wine-challenged" food. There are two solutions, he said. First, "use seasonings and sauces to bridge the flavors of the asparagus and the wine." Second, "stay away from wines that have a lot of oak and a lot of tannin." As for those flavor bridges, Comfort suggests hollandaise or even mayonnaise. Wines to avoid include oaky Chardonnays and highly tannic Cabernet Sauvignons. The wines Comfort likes with asparagus include Sauvignon Blanc, Pinot Grigio, Riesling, Beaujolais, Dolcetto, and white Zinfandel.

Finally, I called Philippe Jeanty, chef-owner of Bistro Jeanty in Yountville, California. "The best thing to do is grill the asparagus and serve it with a creamy dressing," he said. And having done that, what wine would he drink? "Pinot Noir. The char character from the grilling works wonderfully with Pinot, which is both light-bodied and earthy." Jeanty had perhaps the wisest advice of all: "The French bistro philosophy is 'Enjoy life!' In a three-star restaurant, which is more like

---

SUNSET'S STEAL OF THE MONTH

Fontana Candida Pinot Grigio delle Venezie 1998 (Veneto, Italy), $8. Simple and ultralight, with touches of bitter almond and arugula flavors. Buckets of wine like this are drunk every day in Italian trattorias.

— KAREN MacNEIL-FIFE

PINOT GRIGIO— A SPRING AND SUMMER WINNER

Besides being asparagus-friendly, Pinot Grigio is everything most of us want in a spring and summer quaff—light, crisp, and very refreshing. Pinot Grigio, or Pinot Gris, as it's known in some places, primarily France and Oregon, ranges from ultralight in flavor and body to fairly bold and substantial. The crispest, sassiest, most thirst-quenching versions come from the Alto Adige and Veneto regions of northern Italy. The fullest-bodied and most concentrated come from Alsace, France. Oregon Pinot Gris, when it's good, is between the two. California Pinot Grigios, on the other hand, can be all over the board (many, frankly, are disappointing). Here are some winners.

■ **Alois Lageder Pinot Grigio 1998 (Alto Adige, Italy),** $12. Possibly the best Pinot Grigio in Italy. Bracingly fresh, with gorgeous mineral, ginger, and almond flavors.

■ **Byron Pinot Gris 1998 (Santa Maria Valley, CA),** $17. Creamy and round, with sensational vanilla and apple spice cake flavors.

■ **Chehalem Pinot Gris 1998 (Willamette Valley, OR),** $14. Floral and lemony; simple and satisfying.

■ **Trimbach Reserve "Personelle" Pinot Gris 1996 (Alsace, France),** $34. Possibly the richest and most beautiful Pinot Gris in the world. Minerally and steely, with hints of peaches and cream.

■ **Zenato Pinot Grigio delle Venezie 1998 (Veneto, Italy),** $10. Floral, light, and creamy, with hints of peaches and almonds.

going to church, well, you may need to be more concerned with perfection. But here at Bistro Jeanty, we believe you should eat and drink whatever makes you feel good. Not everything needs to be analyzed." ◆

Present fruit in elegant layers, then mix with a lively mango-ginger sauce to serve.

Fruit salad season

Tropical fruits, spring berries—here are cool dishes for warm days

BY ELAINE JOHNSON • PHOTOGRAPHS BY JAMES CARRIER

The sun—and the barbecue—are out together this time of year. A fruit salad would complete the picture very nicely. Too bad summer's parade of fruit won't show up for another month yet. But wait. It's prime time for strawberries, as well as tropical fruits like pineapples, papayas, and mangoes. Markets also have a sweet selection of kiwi fruit and Asian pears right now. And bananas. There are always bananas. Some spectacular salad combinations lurk in this lineup.

Layer the fruit in a tall, clear bowl to make a spectacular centerpiece for a crowd, or make a grown-up version of a molded salad with sweet Muscat wine. Fruit salad easily becomes the main event for lunch or a light supper too—try it with grilled shrimp or beef.

Mango Velvet Layered Salad

PREP TIME: About 50 minutes
NOTES: If making up to 4 hours ahead, chill airtight; serve chilled or at room temperature.
MAKES: 10 servings

- 2 **firm-ripe mangoes** (1½ lb. total)
- 1 tablespoon minced **fresh ginger**
  About ¼ cup **lime juice**
  About 1 tablespoon **sugar**
- 2 cups **strawberries,** rinsed
- 3 **firm-ripe bananas** (1¼ lb. total)
- 4 **firm-ripe kiwi fruit** (⅔ lb. total)
- 1 **Asian pear** (½ lb.)

1. Pit and peel mangoes. Cut into ½-inch cubes; measure ¼ cup and reserve. In a blender or food processor, whirl remaining mangoes with the ginger, 3 tablespoons lime juice, and 1 tablespoon sugar until smooth. Taste,

and add more lime juice and sugar if desired. Pour mango dressing into a deep 2- to 2½-quart clear glass bowl.

2. Hull strawberries; cut lengthwise into ¼-inch slices. Peel bananas; cut diagonally into ¼-inch slices. In a bowl, gently mix bananas with ½ tablespoon lime juice. Peel kiwi fruit; cut crosswise into ¼-inch slices. Peel, quarter, and core pear; cut into ¼-inch-thick sticks. In another bowl, gently mix pear with ½ tablespoon lime juice.

3. In the deep glass bowl, arrange strawberry slices in an even layer on mango dressing. Arrange banana slices on strawberries, and cover bananas with kiwi fruit. Mound reserved mango and pear on kiwi fruit.

4. To serve, gently mix fruit with mango dressing and spoon onto plates.

Per serving: 105 cal., 5.1% (5.4 cal.) from fat; 1.2 g protein; 0.6 g fat (0.1 g sat.); 27 g carbo (3.5 g fiber); 4 mg sodium; 0 mg chol.

Hot Pineapple-Beef Salad

PREP AND COOK TIME: About 25 minutes
NOTES: If peeled pineapple is unavailable, buy a 5-pound pineapple.
MAKES: 4 servings

- 6 tablespoons **soy sauce**
- 2 tablespoons **sugar**
- 2 tablespoons **Asian** (toasted) **sesame oil**
- 1 tablespoon minced **garlic**
- 1 pound **boneless beef sirloin steak,** fat trimmed
- 4 large **green-leaf lettuce leaves,** rinsed and crisped
- 2 pounds **peeled, cored pineapple**
- ⅓ cup thinly sliced **green onions** (including tops)

1. In a bowl, mix soy sauce, sugar, sesame oil, and garlic. Cut steak across the grain into ⅛-inch-thick slices; add to bowl and mix to coat with marinade. Let stand for 15 minutes or up to 2 hours.

2. Meanwhile, place a lettuce leaf on each plate. Cut pineapple into ½-inch-thick rings. Arrange half the rings equally on lettuce; cut remaining rings into 1-inch chunks.

3. Place a 10- to 12-inch nonstick frying pan over high heat. When it's hot, with a slotted spoon, lift meat from marinade and add to pan. Stir often just until meat is browned on the outside but still slightly pink on the inside (cut to test), 2 to 3 minutes, or as done as you like. With slotted spoon, lift meat to an-other bowl. Add pineapple chunks and ¼ cup marinade to pan; discard remain-ing marinade. Stir pineapple until hot, about 1 minute. Pour meat and juices back into pan, and stir in green onions.

4. Spoon meat mixture and juices equally over pineapple rings and let-tuce leaves.

Per serving: 365 cal., 32% (117 cal.) from fat; 27 g protein; 13 g fat (2.8 g sat.); 38 g carbo (3 g fiber); 1,614 mg sodium; 69 mg chol.

Grilled Papaya and Shrimp Spinach Salad

PREP AND COOK TIME: About 45 minutes

MAKES: 4 servings

- ½ cup **unsweetened shredded dried coconut**
- ½ pound **bacon,** chopped
- 2 **firm-ripe papayas** (1⅔ lb. total)
- 2 **firm-ripe bananas** (1 lb. total)
- ¾ pound (26 to 28 per lb.) **shelled, deveined shrimp,** rinsed
- ¾ cup **orange juice**
- 3 tablespoons **lemon juice**
  About 1½ tablespoons **salad oil**
- 1½ teaspoons **curry powder**
- 2 quarts (½ lb.) lightly packed **baby spinach leaves,** rinsed and drained
  Salt and **pepper**

1. In a 10- to 12-inch frying pan over medium heat, frequently stir coconut un-til golden, 3 to 4 minutes. Pour from pan.
2. Add bacon to pan; stir often over

It's clear—sweet Muscat wine makes a striking fruit mold.

Coconut underscores the tropical flavor in a mixed grill of papayas, bananas, and shrimp.

medium-high heat until browned, 5 to 7 minutes. Transfer bacon to towels; discard fat in pan.

3. Peel papayas, seed, and cut into 1- to 1½-inch chunks. Peel bananas and cut diagonally into 1- to 1½-inch-thick slices. Thread papayas and bananas sep-arately onto 1 or 2 metal skewers (about 14 in.) each. Thread shrimp in a C-shape (through tails and bodies) onto 2 or 3 skewers. Brush shrimp with about ½ tablespoon oil.

4. Lightly oil a barbecue grill over a solid bed of medium-hot coals or a gas grill over medium-high heat (you can hold your hand at grill level only 3 to 4 seconds). Lay skewers on grill; close lid on gas grill. Cook until fruit is hot and shrimp are opaque but still moist-look-ing in center of thickest part (cut to test), turning halfway through cooking, 4 to 6 minutes total.

5. Meanwhile, in a large bowl, mix orange juice, lemon juice, 1 tablespoon oil, and curry powder. Add spinach and bacon to bowl and mix gently. Lift spinach mixture from bowl and mound equally on plates.

6. Slide hot fruit and shrimp from skew-ers into remaining dressing in bowl and mix to coat. Spoon equal portions of fruit and shrimp with dressing onto spinach. Sprinkle coconut equally over salads. Season to taste with salt and pepper.

Per serving: 450 cal., 40% (180 cal.) from fat; 26 g protein; 20 g fat (8.4 g sat.); 45 g carbo (6.6 g fiber); 497 mg sodium; 143 mg chol.

Strawberry–Muscat Wine Terrine

PREP AND COOK TIME: About 25 min-utes, plus at least 3 hours to chill

NOTES: Use a plain sweet Muscat wine such as Bonny Doon Vineyard's Vin de Glacière, or an orange Muscat such as Quady Winery's Essensia. To keep bananas from turning brown, slice

them just before using. If assembling through step 4 up to 1 day ahead, chill airtight. Garnish with fresh mint sprigs.

MAKES: 6 servings

- 2 envelopes **unflavored gelatin**
- ¼ cup **sugar**
- 2½ cups **Muscat dessert wine** (see notes)
- 1 tablespoon **lemon juice**
- 1¼ cups sliced (¼ in.) **strawberries**
- 1¼ cups sliced (¼ in.) **firm-ripe bananas** (see notes)

1. In a 1- to 2-quart pan, mix gelatin, sugar, and ½ cup wine. Stir over medium heat until gelatin and sugar are dissolved, 3 to 4 minutes. Remove from heat.

2. Add remaining wine and 1 table-spoon lemon juice. Pour ⅔ cup into a 2¼-inch-deep, 3½- by 7½-inch loaf pan.

3. Arrange half the sliced strawberries in a single layer in pan. Chill until gelatin mixture is firm to touch, about 45 minutes. Pour another ⅔ cup gelatin mixture over strawberries. Arrange half the banana slices in a single layer in pan. Chill until new gelatin layer is firm to touch, about 45 minutes.

4. Repeat to layer ⅔ cup gelatin and re-maining strawberries, then remaining gelatin and remaining bananas, chilling after each layer of fruit until gelatin mix-ture is firm to touch, about 45 minutes for each layer.

5. Dip pan to rim in very hot tap water until gelatin just begins to soften at edges, 4 to 5 seconds. Lift from water, quickly dry pan, and invert a flat plate onto pan. Holding pan and plate to-gether, invert; lift off pan. If terrine does not slip out, slide a thin metal spatula between pan and dessert to release. Cut terrine crosswise into 6 equal slices; serve with a wide spatula.

Per serving: 260 cal., 1.4% (3.6 cal.) from fat; 2.8 g protein; 0.4 g fat (0.1 g sat.); 37 g carbo (1.8 g fiber); 15 mg sodium; 0 mg chol. ◆

Cakes that rise to the occasion

Two delicious desserts to delight mile-high cooks

BY JERRY ANNE DI VECCHIO

JAMES CARRIER

As a sea-level cook with mile-high grandsons, I've had to adjust my favorite celebration cakes to their altitude. One is an indispensable basic vanilla cake that bakes in tender, even layers to frost; it's ideal for birthdays. To make it work, I reduced the baking powder. Another is a fine-textured pound cake that I've used for events from picnics to weddings. It has no leavening to start with; reducing the sugar did the trick. The recipes here produce beautiful results at 5,000 to 6,000 feet (in a convection oven, use the shorter baking times). To adapt your basic cake formulas to elevated conditions, use the chart below.

Vanilla Layer Cake with Chocolate Frosting

PREP AND COOK TIME: 45 to 50 minutes, plus about 40 minutes to cool

MAKES: 8 to 10 servings

> About ½ cup (¼ lb.) **butter** or margarine, cut into chunks
>
> About 2¼ cups **all-purpose flour**
>
> 1½ cups **sugar**
>
> 3 **large eggs**
>
> 1½ teaspoons **baking powder**
>
> ¼ teaspoon **salt**
>
> 1 cup **milk**
>
> 1 teaspoon **vanilla**
>
> **Chocolate frosting** (recipe follows)

1. Butter 2 round cake pans, each 9 inches wide; line bottoms with waxed paper cut to fit, and butter again. Dust pans with flour.

2. In a bowl with a mixer, beat ½ cup butter and the sugar to blend, then beat on high speed until fluffy, about 3 minutes. Add eggs and stir to mix; beat until well blended, about 3 minutes longer, scraping bowl occasionally.

3. Mix 2¼ cups flour, baking powder, and salt. Add to egg mixture and stir to blend, then beat to mix well. Add milk and vanilla; beat until well blended. Scrape batter equally into cake pans.

4. Bake in a 350° oven until layers are just beginning to pull from pan sides and spring back when lightly pressed in the center, 25 to 35 minutes. Let cool in pan 10 minutes, then invert cake layers onto racks and carefully peel off paper. Let stand until cool, at least 30 minutes.

5. Set 1 layer on a plate, top side down. Spread about ⅓ of the frosting evenly on layer. Set second layer, bottom side down, on frosting. Spread remaining frosting evenly over top and sides of cake, swirling decoratively. Cut into wedges.

Per serving: 594 cal., 32% (189 cal.) from fat; 6.4 g protein; 21 g fat (12 g sat.); 98 g carbo (0.8 g fiber); 315 mg sodium; 108 mg chol.

Chocolate Frosting

PREP AND COOK TIME: About 15 minutes

MAKES: About 2½ cups

> ¼ cup (⅛ lb.) **butter** or margarine, cut into small pieces
>
> ¾ cup **semisweet chocolate chips**
>
> 2 to 4 tablespoons **milk**
>
> About 3 cups **powdered sugar**
>
> ½ teaspoon **vanilla**

1. In a microwave-safe bowl, combine but-

Ups and downs for cake recipes at high altitudes

Change	3,000 feet	5,000 feet	7,000 feet
Baking powder Reduce each teaspoon	by ⅛ to ¼ tsp.	by ⅛ to ¼ tsp.	by ¼ tsp.
Sugar Reduce each cup	by up to 1 tbsp.	by up to 2 tbsp.	by 1 to 3 tbsp.
Liquid Increase each cup	by 1 to 2 tbsp.	by 2 to 4 tbsp.	by 3 to 4 tbsp.
Oven temperature Increase	3° to 5°	15°	21° to 25°

ter, chocolate chips, and 2 table-spoons milk.

2. Heat in a microwave oven at full power (100%), stirring at 15-second intervals, until chocolate is smooth, about 1½ minutes total. Let stand until cool, about 5 minutes.

3. Stir in 3 cups powdered sugar and the vanilla; beat with a mixer on medium speed until smooth. If frosting is too stiff to spread easily, add milk, 1 teaspoon at a time; if too soft to hold swirls, add more powdered sugar, ¼ cup at a time, beating well after each addition.

Per tablespoon: 61 cal., 31% (19 cal.) from fat; 0.2 g protein; 2.1 g fat (1.3 g sat.); 11 g carbo (0 g fiber); 13 mg sodium; 3.4 mg chol.

Pound Cake

PREP AND COOK TIME: About 1¾ hours

MAKES: 16 to 18 servings

About 1½ cups (¾ lb.) **butter** or margarine, cut into chunks

About 2¾ cups sifted **cake flour**

3¼ cups **powdered sugar**

6 **large eggs**

1 teaspoon **vanilla**

1. Butter and flour a 10-cup plain or decorative tube cake pan.

2. In a bowl, mix 1½ cups butter and the sugar; beat with a mixer at high speed until fluffy, about 8 minutes, scraping bowl occasionally.

3. Add eggs, 1 at a time, beating to blend after each addition.

4. Add 2¾ cups flour and the vanilla. Stir to mix, then beat at high speed until well blended. Scrape batter into tube cake pan.

5. Bake in a 325° oven until cake begins to pull from pan sides and springs back when lightly pressed in the center, 1 hour and 10 minutes to 1 hour and 20 minutes. Let cool about 10 minutes. Invert cake onto a plate. Serve warm or cool, cut into thin slices.

Per serving: 305 cal., 53% (162 cal.) from fat; 3.5 g protein; 18 g fat (10 g sat.); 34 g carbo (0 g fiber); 182 mg sodium; 113 mg chol. ◆

Food plus fun

The setting is the show at these San Francisco eateries

BY LISA TAGGART
AND AMY McCONNELL

A special evening out includes more than just a meal. Throw a foreign film into the mix, or perhaps a manicure with your martini. At these four San Francisco hot spots, fab food and drink pairs with entertainment of the quirky kind.

■ **Forbes Island.** Dining on Forbes Island is like spending an evening in a good friend's home—except that the home is floating in the bay. Forbes Thor Kiddoo built his dream home, a 700-ton floating island, in 1975—but it became a restaurant only in February 1999. Kiddoo personally escorts guests on a five-minute cruise to the island, pointing out the 40-foot lighthouse he built. In the underwater dining room, you'll be surrounded by portal windows, where you might see the shadow of a sand shark darting by. The French-inspired food is surprisingly good—as reflected by the prices (entrées average $28). *Dinner Wed–Sun; reservations requested. Pier 39, H Dock (use house phone for pickup); (415) 951-4900 or www.forbesisland.com.*

■ **Foreign Cinema.** Federico Fellini is a regular at this Mission district spin-off of a drive-in theater—it's an "eat-in." The nearly year-old restaurant's spare warehouse-chic style matches the gritty black-and-white international films that are projected onto a neighboring building wall. On our last visit, we watched a surreal drama about a bourgeois dinner party that never ends; one table over was a blonde in a trench coat who looked as though she could have been in the cast. It's tricky to negotiate subtitles and curried mussels ($10) at the patio tables; crank up the volume at your tableside speaker if your Italian or French is good. It's harder to see the movie screen from the indoor tables—but wine-braised lamb shanks ($18) will

At Forbes Island, you dine with the fish.

keep you on the edge of your seat. *Dinner from 5:30 Tue-Sun, films at 7 and 9; reservations recommended. 2534 Mission St.; (415) 648-7600 or www.foreigncinema.com.*

■ **Tonga Room Restaurant & Hurricane Bar.** The other restaurants on this list are relative newcomers. But the Fairmont Hotel's Tonga is a 53-year-old landmark—for good reason. Thunder roars, lightning flashes, and rain pours down around the perimeter of a 7,000-square-foot lagoon. But you'll stay dry as you sip your hurricane cocktail, complete with paper umbrella and keepsake glass. Don't expect haute cuisine; the Chinese-inspired menu features crowd pleasers like sweet-and-sour pork ($14) and assorted dim sum ($12.25). Do expect anything and everything else: a band in a bamboo-roofed boat; a dance floor crowded with couples wearing Hawaiian leis. Why fly to Bora Bora when the Tonga Room is right here? *Dinner (reservations recommended), live band, and dancing nightly. Fairmont Hotel, 950 Mason St.; (415) 772-5278 or www.tongaroom.com.*

■ **Beauty Bar.** Tonics for your head as well as your palate adorn the shelves at this two-year-old Mission district bar, where vinyl chairs are topped with hair dryers and the walls shine with pink glitter. For $10, you can get a sparkle-polish manicure and sip a Perm (vanilla vodka, OJ, and cranberry juice). Don't be intimidated by the severely hip music and super-trendy clientele; with your cosmopolitan in hand, you'll look divine. *Drinks nightly, manicures Wed-Sat. 2299 Mission; (415) 285-0323 or www.beautybarsf.com.* ◆

Freshly picked fruits are these gardeners' rewards. From left: Eunice Messner shows off her cherimoyas, Elva West samples his papayas, and Gary Matsuoka holds his mangoes.

A taste of the tropics

How to grow cherimoyas, mangoes, and papayas in Southern California gardens

BY SHARON COHOON

Your friends back East may envy you your winter days in shirtsleeves while they're bundled up in heavy layers. But to make their envy index really rise, tell them you're harvesting tropical fruit from trees you planted in your garden. If you plant trees now and are willing to wait a couple of years, you'll be able to have fruit to enjoy yourself—and to impress any visitors from colder climates.

Late spring into early summer is ideal for planting tropical and subtropical fruit trees; they'll have maximum time to put out new growth before winter comes. Choices abound—loquat, litchi, white sapote, Surinam cherry. But cherimoya, mango, and papaya have the edge. Not only are their fruits irresistible, but in the right climate, they require no more attention than more familiar fruit trees like plums and apples. Here are tips on growing these tropical trees from three experienced growers.

■ Cherimoya

"Cherimoya is one of the best-tasting fruits in the world," says Eunice Messner of Anaheim Hills. Mark Twain would agree. He described the fruit as "deliciousness itself." The flesh has a creamy, custardlike texture and a flavor that is a mixture of banana and pineapple. "If it didn't have seeds," says Messner, a contributing editor to *The Fruit Gardener*, the bimonthly magazine of the California Rare Fruit Growers, "it would be perfect."

Unpruned trees reach 20 feet, but pruning in March and August keeps trees at an easy-to-harvest 8 to 9 feet.
BEST VARIETY. Messner's choice is 'Pierce', which has "great flavor and doesn't turn dark in the refrigerator like some other varieties."
PREFERRED LOCATION. Cherimoya likes marine influence and does well in coastal and foothill Southern California.
FROST TOLERANCE. Mature trees can endure short periods of temperatures in the low 20s. Young trees need more protection.
POLLINATION. Self-pollinating, so only one tree required. For maximum production and perfectly formed fruit, you'll need to hand-pollinate, as commercial growers do. (There are no known natural cherimoya pollinators in California.) Gardeners such as Messner, however, don't find this necessary. "I get as much fruit as I want without it," she says, "especially if I mist the foliage regularly while they're in flower to help things along." To hand-pollinate, collect pollen from fully open (male) flowers in late afternoon with a slender paintbrush. The next morning, apply pollen to partially open (female) flowers. (Flowers are female in the morning, male by late afternoon.)
YEARS TO HARVEST. Two to three years for grafted trees; five to eight years for seedlings. (Named varieties are always grafted; unnamed ones are seedlings.)
HARVEST TIME. October through May.
CARE. In midwinter, feed trees with compost and well-aged chicken manure. Repeat when the trees leaf out again in May after a brief deciduous period. Messner also gives new leaves a single foliar feeding of kelp and fish emulsion during the growing season ("if I get around to it"). She waters twice a week with drip irrigation for most of the year, less when soil cools and winter rains begin.

■ Mango

"Rich, juicy, spicy, both sweet and tart"—every adjective used to describe a mango's taste is true, says Gary Matsuoka, president of Laguna Hills Nursery in Lake Forest. Mangoes' requirements are very similar to those of avocados: ample summer moisture and excellent winter drainage, which is not the easiest combination to pull off. But the fruit is so delicious, Matsuoka says, the trees are worth the effort. The small stature of the tree, which rarely exceeds 15 feet in our climate, also makes it suitable for home gardens.

BEST VARIETIES. Matsuoka's choices: 'Edward' ("stingy producer but superb flavor"), 'Carrie' ("small-size but rich, spicy fruit"), and 'Glenn' ("large fruit, little fiber, great taste").

PREFERRED LOCATIONS. Ideal are frost-free foothills, away from immediate marine influence: Fallbrook, Tustin, and San Joaquin, for example. But gardeners closer to the coast are reporting success. Matsuoka lives in Mission Viejo, and the fruit can also be grown in the Coachella Valley.

FROST TOLERANCE. Hardy to 26° at maturity. Until it has developed enough wood to give it some protection, it is more frost-sensitive.

POLLINATION. Self-fruiting, so only one tree required.

YEARS TO HARVEST. Two years for grafted tree; 7 to 10 for seedlings. Most people opt for grafted trees, which more quickly bear fruit that's reliable in quality.

HARVEST TIME. August through December.

CARE. Give mangoes your garden's sunniest, best-drained spot—a south-facing slope is ideal. If your soil is heavy, lighten it by digging in pumice or sponge rock. Mangoes like plenty of water, so keep soil consistently moist. Fertilize often with compost during summer and early fall, when trees are actively growing.

The chief problem with mangoes is winter rot, which is why drainage is so critical. Near the coast, powdery mildew can also be a problem. Dust or spray with wettable sulfur.

The first year or two, pinch off developing fruit on grafted plants, or you'll get mango vines instead of trees.

■ Papaya

Papaya is for risk-takers in most of Southern California. But if you live close enough to the coast not to get frost and far enough away not to get ocean breezes, you could succeed. The reward is a melon-textured fruit whose taste transports you to Hawaii. The 12-foot tree is also handsomely ornamental, particularly in subtropical gardens. Elva West lives in Anaheim Hills, which is one of those magic zones. For at least 25 years, he has been growing papayas with 90 to 95 percent success. He's also the papaya specialist for the California Rare Fruit Growers.

BEST VARIETY. 'Florida Jack'.

PREFERRED LOCATIONS. Frost-free foothills.

FROST TOLERANCE. Unknown, but West reports trees surviving 26°.

POLLINATION. Papaya trees have three sexes: male, female, and self-fertile hermaphroditic. Since papayas are grown from seed and you don't know what sex your tree is until it flowers, plant two or three to ensure fruit.

YEARS TO HARVEST. Two.

HARVEST TIME. April through September.

CARE. Keep the soil dry enough in winter to avoid root rot. (Hawaiian 'Solo' is especially vulnerable to this malady.) Plant on a slope, in a raised bed, or in a 15-gallon or larger container. Apply a 3- to 4-inch layer of mulch—leaves, grass clippings, or commercial products—in summer to keep soil moist, then remove mulch in winter so the sun can warm the soil.

Give the trees plenty of water and fertilizer during the growing season, May through September. West foliar-feeds seedlings with a 10-10-10 formula, then switches to a granular form when foliage has grown out of easy reach. He prefers using half the recommended dosage and fertilizing twice as often. Problems with pests and diseases have been minor, West reports.

■ From garden to kitchen

Here's a tasty, refreshing shake that starts with mango or papaya; it's easy to make too.

Mango-Yogurt Shakes

PREP TIME: About 10 minutes
SERVES: 2

1 cup chopped **firm-ripe mango** or papaya

¾ cup **orange juice**

½ cup cooked or canned **sweet potato**

1 cup **vanilla nonfat frozen yogurt**

In a blender, whirl mango, orange juice, and sweet potato until smooth. Add frozen yogurt; whirl until smooth. Pour into tall glasses.

Per serving: 282 cal., 1.6% (4.5 cal.) from fat; 4.4 g protein; 0.5 g fat (0.1 g sat.); 66 g carbo (3.5 g fiber); 58 mg sodium; 0 mg chol. ◆

Where to buy plants

Elva West, (714) 637-4084. West propagates and sells 'Florida Jack' and other papaya varieties.

Laguna Hills Nursery, 25290 Jeronimo Rd., Lake Forest; (949) 830-5653. Always well stocked with tropical fruit in season.

Pacific Tree Farms, 4301 Lynwood Dr., Chula Vista; (619) 422-2400. Walk-in or mail-order nursery; catalog $2.

Papaya Tree Nursery, 12422 El Oro Way, Granada Hills; (818) 363-3680; by appointment only. Specialty nursery for tropical and exotic fruit trees. Sells only fruit trees and other tropical edibles.

For more information on the California Rare Fruit Growers, check out the group's excellent website, www.crfg.org, or write to it in care of Fullerton Arboretum–CSUF, Box 6850, Fullerton, CA 92834.

Kitchen Cabinet

READERS' RECIPES TESTED IN SUNSET'S KITCHENS

BY ANDREW BAKER

Chicken Hollandaise Wraps

Audrey Dennery, Corona del Mar, California

"I created this recipe for my boyfriend, who loves hollandaise," says Audrey Dennery. It incorporates the classic sauce into a quick weeknight meal. Make the hollandaise first, then the other components.

PREP AND COOK TIME: About 35 minutes

MAKES: 4 servings

- 1 pound **boned, skinned chicken breasts**
- ¾ pound **asparagus**
- 1 teaspoon **olive** or salad **oil**
- 2 cups **cooked rice**
- 4 **flour tortillas** (10 in.)
- 2 cups shredded **romaine lettuce**

  Hollandaise sauce (recipe follows)

1. Rinse chicken and pat dry. Cut into ¾-inch pieces. Rinse asparagus; break off and discard tough stem ends. Cut asparagus into 1½-inch pieces.

2. In a 10- to 12-inch nonstick frying pan over high heat, frequently stir chicken in oil until slightly browned, about 5 minutes. Add asparagus and stir until chicken is no longer pink in center of thickest part (cut to test) and asparagus is tender-crisp to bite, about 4 minutes longer. Add rice and stir just until hot. Pour into a bowl.

3. Meanwhile, stack tortillas and enclose loosely in microwave-safe plastic wrap. Heat in a microwave oven at full power (100%) just until hot, 30 seconds to 1 minute. Remove plastic; enclose tortillas in a towel. Put lettuce in a bowl.

4. To assemble each wrap, lay 1 tortilla flat. Spoon ¼ of the chicken mixture down the center, and top with ¼ of the lettuce; spoon ¼ of the hollandaise on top. Roll to enclose.

Per serving: 612 cal., 38% (234 cal.) from fat; 37 g protein; 26 g fat (13 g sat.); 56 g carbo (3.2 g fiber); 521 mg sodium; 192 mg chol.

Hollandaise sauce. Put 2 **large egg yolks** in a blender or food processor. Cut ½ cup (¼ lb.) **butter** or margarine into chunks; melt in a 1- to 2-quart pan over medium-high heat until foam is beginning to brown (butter should be about 230°), 2 to 3 minutes. Turn on blender or food processor and pour ¼ cup boiling **water** into yolks, then add 2 tablespoons **lemon juice.** Immediately pour hot butter into yolks in a steady stream, taking about 10 seconds (sauce will be thin). Sauce should be 160°. If it's not, pour into the top of a double boiler or a metal bowl (about 2 qt.), nest over slightly simmering water in another pan, and whisk until sauce reaches 160°. Pour into a pitcher and let stand at room temperature. Makes about ¾ cup.

Per tablespoon: 59 cal., 98% (58 cal.) from fat; 0.4 g protein; 6.4 g fat (3.8 g sat.); 0.2 g carbo (0 g fiber); 60 mg sodium; 42 mg chol.

Jan's Roasted Red Pepper Soup

Jan Claire, Oakhurst, California

A cooking-show demonstration about roasting peppers inspired Jan Claire to create this soup, which he serves with crusty French bread.

PREP AND COOK TIME: About 40 minutes

MAKES: About 7½ cups; 4 or 5 servings

- 2 **red bell peppers** (about 1 lb. total), rinsed
- 1 **onion** (about ½ lb.), peeled and finely chopped
- ¼ cup (⅛ lb.) **butter** or margarine
- 1 cup grated **carrots**
- ¼ cup **all-purpose flour**
- 2 cups fat-skimmed **beef broth**
- 2 cups **half-and-half** (light cream)
- 1 can (15 oz.) **tomato sauce**

  About ¼ teaspoon **hot chili flakes**

  Salt and **pepper**

1. Rinse the peppers and cut them in half lengthwise. Remove and discard stems, seeds, and veins. Lay peppers, cut sides down, in a 10- by 15-inch pan. Broil 4 to 6 inches from heat until skins are blackened all over, about 12 minutes. When the peppers are cool enough to handle, pull off and discard skins; chop peppers.

Chunks of peppers, carrots, and onion enliven creamy roasted red pepper soup.

2. In a 3- to 4-quart pan over medium-high heat, stir onion in butter until limp, about 3 minutes. Stir in peppers and carrots.

3. Add flour and stir about 1 minute. Add broth, half-and-half, and tomato sauce; stir until mixture boils and is slightly thickened, about 10 minutes.

4. Stir in chili flakes and salt and pepper to taste.

Per serving: 311 cal., 61% (189 cal.) from fat; 8.1 g protein; 21 g fat (13 g sat.); 26 g carbo (4 g fiber); 690 mg sodium; 61 mg chol.

Lemon Grass Orzo

Rofina Wilenchik, San Anselmo, California

To create a jazzy orzo salad, Rofina Wilenchik started with an Asian flavor—lemon grass—then kept adding herbs for fragrance and vegetables for texture.

PREP AND COOK TIME: About 35 minutes

MAKES: 7 to 8 cups; 6 to 8 servings

- 2 stalks **fresh lemon grass** (¼ lb. total)
- 2½ cups fat-skimmed **chicken broth**
- 2 cups **dried orzo pasta**
- 1 cup chopped **English cucumber**
- ½ cup finely chopped **canned roasted red peppers**
- ½ cup thinly sliced **green onions** (including tops)
- ½ cup minced **fresh cilantro**
- ¼ cup minced **fresh mint** leaves
- ¼ cup minced **fresh basil** leaves
- 2 tablespoons minced **fresh marjoram** leaves
- 3 tablespoons **olive oil**
- 2 tablespoons **lemon juice**
   Salt and **pepper**

1. Rinse lemon grass and pull off tough outer layers. Cut off stem ends and coarse leaves. Cut pale, tender stalks into 1-inch pieces.

2. In a 3- to 4-quart pan, combine lemon grass, broth, and 2½ cups water. Bring to a boil over high heat; reduce heat, cover, and simmer for 10 minutes. Add orzo and return to a boil over high heat; cook just until pasta is tender to bite, 6 to 8 minutes.

3. Drain pasta (save liquid for other uses) and pour into a wide bowl; re-

move and discard lemon grass. Add cucumber, roasted peppers, green onions, cilantro, mint, basil, marjoram, olive oil, and lemon juice. Mix well. Add salt and pepper to taste.

Per serving: 229 cal., 23% (52 cal.) from fat; 8.5 g protein; 5.8 g fat (0.8 g sat.); 35 g carbo (1.8 g fiber); 46 mg sodium; 0 mg chol.

Easy Rhubarb Cheesecake

Opal Star, Las Vegas

"When it was on sale, I went wild with rhubarb," says Opal Star. She modified a simple cheesecake recipe to come up with this novel dessert.

PREP AND COOK TIME: About 30 minutes, plus at least 2 hours to chill

MAKES: 6 servings

- ¾ cup (3 oz.) **graham cracker crumbs**
- 2 tablespoons **butter** or margarine, melted
- 2 cups chopped **rhubarb** (about 9 oz.)
- ½ cup **sugar**
- 1 envelope (¼ oz.) **unflavored gelatin**
- 1 package (8 oz.) **cream cheese,** at room temperature, cut into chunks
- ½ cup thinly sliced **strawberries** (about 3 oz.)

1. Pour graham cracker crumbs into an 8-inch cake pan with removable rim. Drizzle butter over crumbs and mix with your fingers until evenly moistened. Press mixture evenly over bottom of pan.

2. Bake crust in a 350° oven until golden brown, 10 to 15 minutes. Let cool about 10 minutes.

3. In a 1½- to 2-quart pan, bring rhubarb, sugar, and ½ cup water to a boil over high heat; reduce heat and simmer until rhubarb is tender when pierced, about 6 minutes.

4. Meanwhile, pour ¼ cup cold water into a blender. Sprinkle gelatin over water and let stand 2 minutes.

5. Pour hot rhubarb mixture into blender. Whirl until rhubarb is smoothly puréed and gelatin is completely dissolved; add cream cheese and whirl until smooth.

6. Pour mixture into crust, and chill until firm, about 2 hours. Remove pan rim. Arrange strawberry slices decoratively on cheesecake. Cut into wedges.

Per serving: 307 cal., 56% (171 cal.) from fat; 5.3 g protein; 19 g fat (11 g sat.); 31 g carbo (0.7 g fiber); 241 mg sodium; 52 mg chol.

Dark and Spicy Gingerbread

Claire Brees, Tucson

Claire Brees often serves this zesty gingerbread with softly whipped cream into which she's folded lemon curd and a dash of ground cardamom.

PREP AND COOK TIME: About 1¼ hours

MAKES: 8 servings

   About 1½ cups **all-purpose flour**
- 2 teaspoons **ground ginger**
- 1 teaspoon **baking soda**
- ¾ teaspoon fresh-ground **pepper**
- ½ teaspoon **ground cardamom**
   About ¼ cup (⅛ lb.) **butter** or margarine, cut into chunks
- ½ cup firmly packed **dark brown sugar**
- 1 large **egg**
- ½ cup **dark molasses**
- ½ cup **buttermilk**
- 2 tablespoons minced **crystallized ginger**

1. Mix 1½ cups flour, ground ginger, baking soda, pepper, and cardamom.

2. In a large bowl, with a mixer on high speed, beat ¼ cup butter and the brown sugar until fluffy. Beat in egg, molasses, and buttermilk. Stir in flour mixture; beat until well blended. Stir in crystallized ginger. Pour batter into a buttered and floured 8-inch round pan.

3. Bake in a 350° oven until gingerbread springs back when pressed in the center, and pulls from pan sides, 40 to 45 minutes. Let cool about 5 minutes.

4. Run a knife between gingerbread and pan sides. Invert onto a rack, and set gingerbread upright. Let cool at least 15 minutes; serve warm or at room temperature. Cut into wedges.

Per serving: 269 cal., 23% (63 cal.) from fat; 3.8 g protein; 7 g fat (4 g sat.); 48 g carbo (0.8 g fiber); 263 mg sodium; 43 mg chol. ◆

Chicken salad spectacular: An versatile favorite steps out on a world tour of flavors. Recipes begin on page 168.

June

this party's really cooking

For a highly entertaining evening, let
your guests team up to chop, mix, grill, and poach

By Linda Lau Anusasananan • Photographs by Just Loomis

Food styling by Basil Friedman

Are you just too busy to entertain? Can't spend an entire Saturday preparing dinner? Or does the whole prospect secretly terrify you? Then this party is for you. • Overworked but clever hosts are discovering how to make entertaining ridiculously easy and prodigiously fun: Let the guests cook. Slicing, dicing, baking, and boiling—in good spirits—become the party mixer, with (usually) delicious results. Your job as the host is to plan the menu; organize the tasks; provide the recipes, ingredients, and tools; and supervise. Hand drinks to your guests, offer appetizers, and let them loose. Within an hour or two, there's a dinner that everyone will be personally proud of. • Standard summer fare—barbecued chicken, potato salad, and strawberry shortcake—will work, of course, but it's more entertaining to choose unexpected dishes. Each recipe in this menu expands guests' cooking repertoires but employs a simple technique. • For an easy-to-manage party, start with eight guest-cooks, divided into teams of two, each producing one or two dishes. Use our countdown on page 166 to bring dinner together on schedule. Teams that finish first can help others, set the table, pass out more drinks, or just snack and anticipate.

Our dining arbor, draped in a cloud of lavender wisteria, resonates with the romance of outdoor living. San Francisco landscape designer Chris Jacobson (www. chrisjacobson.com) designed it for Carol and Gary Olimpia. But whether you have a pergola or a patch of lawn, it's clear that, as these pages show, one of summer's greatest pleasures is a garden gathering to share a meal with friends.

JAY GRAHAM

Get the gang together to cook and eat; with everyone sharing the duties, dinner is easy for you and fun for all.

ABOVE: Weave a long skewer through marinated skirt steak and green onions for a lively dish from the grill.

1 head **garlic** (3 in. wide, 3½ to 4 oz.)

About 2 tablespoons **olive oil**

1 can (15 oz.) **garbanzos**, drained

2 tablespoons **lemon juice**

Salt and **pepper**

1. Cut garlic head in half crosswise. Rub cut surfaces with a little of the oil. Place garlic cut sides down in an 8- or 9-inch pie pan; cover tightly with foil.

2. Bake in a 400° oven until garlic is soft when pressed, about 40 minutes.

3. Pluck or squeeze garlic cloves from skin; discard skin. In a blender or food processor, purée garlic. Add remaining olive oil, the garbanzos, and lemon juice. Whirl until smooth, scraping container sides as needed. Add salt and pepper to taste. Scrape into a bowl.

Per tablespoon: 41 cal., 46% (19 cal.) from fat; 1.3 g protein; 2.1 g fat (0.2 g sat.); 4.5 g carbo (0.8 g fiber); 31 mg sodium; 0 mg chol.

Seeded Breadsticks

PREP AND COOK TIME: About 35 minutes

NOTES: Eat plain or dip into roasted garlic hummus (preceding).

MAKES: About 2 dozen

1 loaf (1 lb.) thawed **frozen bread dough**

2 teaspoons **spice seeds**, such as cumin, dill, fennel, poppy, or sesame (use 1 kind or several)

¼ teaspoon **salt**

1. On a lightly floured board, roll dough into a 6- by 12-inch rectangle and sprinkle evenly with spice seeds and salt. Roll seeds lightly to press into dough, without changing shape of dough. Let stand until dough is slightly puffy, 5 to 10 minutes.

Iced Vegetables

PREP TIME: About 15 minutes

NOTES: This centerpiece appetizer is perfect for guests to nibble as they cook. Assemble up to 4 hours ahead; drape a damp towel over any leafy tops, and chill.

MAKES: 8 servings

Choose an assortment of **vegetables** that won't wilt, such as celery, fresh fennel, radishes, baby carrots, and red bell peppers (or a variety of colors). You'll need about 2 pounds total. For the most attractive presentation, keep vegetables as whole as possible, but rinse and trim or peel as needed: Separate celery and fennel into stalks (cut stalks lengthwise, if desired, to make them easier to eat); leave prettiest leaves on radishes and baby carrots; stem and seed peppers, then cut into strips. In a clear glass bowl or vase, immerse vegetables in **ice water.**

In a small, shallow bowl or rimmed plate, mix 2 tablespoons **balsamic vinegar,** 2 tablespoons **extra-virgin olive oil,** ¼ teaspoon **salt,** and ⅛ teaspoon fresh-ground **pepper.**

To eat, pick vegetables out of water and drain briefly. Dip in balsamic vinegar mixture or scoop into **roasted garlic hummus** (recipe follows).

Per serving vegetables and vinegar mixture: 55 cal., 60% (33 cal.) from fat; 0.9 g protein; 3.7 g fat (0.5 g sat.); 5.5 g carbo (1.2 g fiber); 125 mg sodium; 0 mg chol.

Roasted Garlic Hummus

PREP AND COOK TIME: About 50 minutes

NOTES: If making up to 1 day ahead, cover and chill. Bring to room temperature to serve. Offer with crackers, seeded breadsticks (recipe follows), and iced vegetables (preceding).

MAKES: About 1 cup

The host provides the first nibbles—vegetables in an icy bath. Team 2 makes the first course: Breadsticks and avocado fans. Teams 1 a

2. Oil 2 or 3 baking sheets, each 12 by 15 inches.

3. With a floured knife, cut dough into 5- by ½-inch strips.

4. Pick up both ends of 1 strip, gently stretch until strip is about 15 inches long, and transfer to a baking sheet. Repeat to stretch remaining breadsticks and fill baking sheets, placing strips about ½ inch apart.

5. As each sheet is filled, bake in a 400° oven until breadsticks are browned and crisp, about 12 minutes (about 8 minutes in a convection oven). Transfer to racks to cool.

Per breadstick: 57 cal., 21% (12 cal.) from fat; 1.5 g protein; 1.3 g fat (0.3 g sat.); 9.5 g carbo (0.4 g fiber); 115 mg sodium; 0.9 mg chol.

Avocado Fans with Asian Mint Dressing

PREP TIME: About 30 minutes

NOTES: Choose avocados that are firm but give slightly when gently pressed. You may need to buy them a few days ahead and let them ripen at room temperature. Use a small, sharp knife to cut avocados neatly. Asian fish sauce and hot chili oil can be found in well-stocked supermarkets and in Asian grocery stores.

MAKES: 8 servings

½ cup **rice vinegar**

1 teaspoon **sugar**

2 tablespoons chopped **fresh mint** leaves

1 teaspoon **Asian fish sauce** (*nuoc mam* or *nam pla*) or about ¼ teaspoon **salt**

¼ teaspoon **Asian hot chili oil** (optional)

4 **firm-ripe avocados** (½ lb. each)

Cherry tomatoes, rinsed (optional)

Mint sprigs, rinsed

1. In a small bowl, mix vinegar, sugar, chopped mint, fish sauce (or salt to taste), and chili oil.

2. Cut avocados in half lengthwise; remove and discard pit. Gently peel off skin and discard.

3. Rub avocado halves with a little of the dressing. Set each half, cut side down, on a salad plate. Starting within ½ inch of the stem end of each avocado half, make cuts about ¼ inch apart down length of fruit. With your palm, very gently press rounded side of avocados to fan slices out (see photo below left).

4. Drizzle remaining dressing evenly over avocados. Garnish with tomatoes and mint sprigs.

Per serving: 139 cal., 84% (117 cal.) from fat; 1.8 g protein; 13 g fat (2.1 g sat.); 7 g carbo (1.8 g fiber); 34 mg sodium; 0 mg chol.

Orange-Ginger Skirt Steak with Onions

PREP AND COOK TIME: About 25 minutes, plus at least 30 minutes to marinate

NOTES: For the most flavor, marinate the meat 4 hours ahead; cover and chill. If long metal skewers (18 to 24 in.) are not available, use shorter ones and cut steaks to fit.

MAKES: 8 servings

2½ to 3 pounds **beef skirt steaks** (2 or 3 steaks), fat trimmed

½ cup **reduced-sodium** or regular **soy sauce**

½ cup **dry sherry**

ackle the main course: Grilled steak and onions, figs and lemons, with couscous salad.

COUNTDOWN

TEAM 1 (HOST'S TEAM)

Iced vegetables, roasted garlic hummus, grilled figs and lemons, and couscous and corn salad

Up to 1 day before party: Clean barbecue. Shop for ingredients. Make hummus. Thaw dough for breadsticks.

Up to 4 hours before dinner: Marinate orange-ginger skirt steak (or let guests do it, at least 1 hour before dinner). Gather equipment and set up stations. Assemble iced vegetables in water and chill.

Up to 1½ hours ahead: Set out perishable ingredients at each station.

Up to 1 hour ahead: Prepare couscous and corn salad.

40 minutes ahead: Prepare and assemble figs and lemons on skewers; give to team 3 to grill.

5 minutes ahead: Spoon couscous and corn salad onto spinach.

TEAM 2

Seeded breadsticks and avocado fans with Asian mint dressing

1 hour before dinner: Preheat oven. Roll

Cut corn kernels off the cob for salad.

seeds into dough. Oil pans. Cut dough, stretch, and transfer to pans.

40 minutes ahead: Bake breadsticks.

30 minutes ahead: Make mint dressing. Cut avocados and drizzle with dressing.

TEAM 3

Orange-ginger skirt steak with onions

At least 1 hour before dinner: Make marinade and marinate steaks (unless host has already done it).

45 minutes ahead: Cut onions and oranges.

40 minutes ahead: If using a charcoal barbecue, ignite briquets.

25 minutes ahead: Weave steaks and onions onto skewers. If using a gas barbecue, heat grill.

10 minutes ahead: Grill steaks, along with figs and lemons from team 1. (If grill is too small to accommodate both, grill fruit 5 minutes earlier.)

TEAM 4

Berries in the snow

1 hour before dinner: Cook custard and cool in ice water.

45 minutes ahead: Make and cook meringues.

25 minutes ahead: Arrange custard, meringues, and berries in bowls.

10 minutes ahead: Caramelize sugar and drizzle over desserts (or for crisper caramel, do just before serving dessert).

¼ cup **orange juice**

2 tablespoons minced **fresh ginger**

½ teaspoon **hot pepper flakes**

3 cloves **garlic,** peeled and pressed

8 to 10 **green onions,** rinsed

2 **oranges** (½ lb. each), rinsed and cut into wedges

Salt and **pepper**

1. Rinse steaks and pat dry. Place in a heavy plastic food bag. Add soy sauce, sherry, orange juice, ginger, hot pepper flakes, and garlic. Seal bag, turn to coat meat, and chill at least 30 minutes or up to 4 hours, turning occasionally.

2. Meanwhile, trim and discard root ends and tips from green onions. Cut onions, including tops, into 3-inch lengths.

3. Drain steaks; save marinade. Weave 1 long metal skewer (18 to 24 in.; see notes) down center of each skirt steak, piercing steak at 2- to 3-inch intervals and skewering a piece of green onion each time. Adjust steaks so they lie fairly flat on skewers, rippling only slightly; if they are too bunched up, they won't cook evenly.

4. Lay skewers on a barbecue grill over a solid bed of hot coals or high heat on a gas grill (you can hold your hand at grill

level only 2 to 3 seconds); close lid on gas grill. Cook, turning once, until meat is done to your liking, 7 to 9 minutes for medium-rare in center of thickest part (cut to test). If desired, heat reserved marinade: Pour into a 1- to 1½-quart pan and bring to a boil over high heat, then pour into a small bowl.

5. Transfer steaks and onions to a platter and garnish with orange wedges. To serve, push steaks off skewers and cut meat into serving-size pieces. Accompany with marinade; squeeze orange wedges over meat, and add salt and pepper to taste.

Per serving: 288 cal., 41% (117 cal.) from fat; 29 g protein; 13 g fat (5.5 g sat.); 7.8 g carbo (0.5 g fiber); 689 mg sodium; 71 mg chol.

Grilled Figs and Lemons

PREP AND COOK TIME: About 20 minutes

NOTES: Choose figs that are still slightly firm but give when gently pressed. Serve with steaks and couscous.

MAKES: **8 servings**

2 or 3 **lemons** (¼ lb. each), rinsed

2 tablespoons **honey**

2 teaspoons **olive oil**

16 **firm-ripe figs** (each about 1½ in. wide and 1 oz.), rinsed

1. Trim ends from lemons. Cut center portions crosswise into ⅛-inch-thick slices; you'll need 16. Ream 2 tablespoons juice from ends.

2. In a small bowl, mix lemon juice, honey, and olive oil.

3. Trim and discard stems from figs. Run a flat-bladed skewer through the center of a fig from stem to blossom end, then through a lemon slice, gently folded in half. Repeat with remaining figs and lemon slices, using more skewers as needed.

4. Brush figs and lemon slices with honey mixture.

5. Lay skewers on a barbecue grill over a solid bed of hot coals or high heat on a gas grill (you can hold your hand at grill level only 2 to 3 seconds); close lid on gas grill. Cook, turning once, until fruit is lightly browned and hot, about 5 minutes total. Transfer to a platter. Serve warm or cool. Gently push figs and lemons off skewers.

Per serving: 72 cal., 17% (12 cal.) from fat; 0.6 g protein; 1.3 g fat (0.2 g sat.); 17 g carbo (1.9 g fiber); 1.3 mg sodium; 0 mg chol.

Couscous and Corn Salad

PREP AND COOK TIME: About 20 minutes

NOTES: At least 1 hour or up to 1 day

ahead, rinse spinach; drain, wrap in towels, enclose in a plastic bag, and chill.

MAKES: 8 servings

1½ teaspoons **coriander seed**

1½ cups **couscous**

4 **ears corn** (each 8 in. long)

½ cup chopped **red onion**

½ cup chopped **fresh cilantro**

1 teaspoon grated **orange** peel

¾ cup **orange juice**

¾ cup **rice vinegar**

Salt and **pepper**

½ pound **baby spinach leaves** or arugula, rinsed and crisped (see notes)

1. In a covered 3- to 4-quart pan over high heat, bring 1⅔ cups water and coriander to a boil. Stir in couscous; remove from heat, cover, and let stand until liquid is absorbed, about 10 minutes. Gently fluff couscous with a fork. Let cool.

2. Meanwhile, pull off and discard husks and silks from corn. Stand each cob upright, stem end down, and cut corn kernels off cob (see photo at left).

3. Add corn kernels, onion, cilantro, orange peel, juice, and vinegar to couscous. Gently mix. Add salt and pepper to taste.

4. Arrange spinach on a shallow rimmed platter or in a wide bowl. Spoon couscous salad onto leaves.

Per serving: 221 cal., 4.5% (9.9 cal.) from fat; 7.7 g protein; 1.1 g fat (0.2 g sat.); 47 g carbo (5.4 g fiber); 69 mg sodium; 0 mg chol.

Berries in the Snow

PREP AND COOK TIME: **About 55 minutes**

NOTES: If making dessert up to 1 day ahead, cover custard, meringues, and berries airtight in separate containers and chill.

MAKES: 8 servings

1½ cups **sugar**

2 tablespoons **cornstarch**

2½ cups **milk**

4 **large eggs,** separated

2 tablespoons **kirsch** or 1 teaspoon vanilla

¼ teaspoon **cream of tartar**

2 cups **raspberries,** rinsed and drained

1. In a 2- to 3-quart pan, mix ⅓ cup sugar and the cornstarch. Add milk and egg yolks; whisk until smooth. Whisk

over high heat until mixture boils. At once, nest pan in ice water and stir often until cool, about 9 minutes. Add kirsch and mix.

2. Meanwhile, in a deep bowl with a mixer on high speed, whip egg whites with cream of tartar until foamy. Continue to beat, gradually adding ⅔ cup sugar, 1 tablespoon at a time, until mixture holds stiff, glossy peaks, about 6 minutes total.

3. In a deep 10- to 12-inch frying pan over high heat, bring about 1½ inches water to a boil; reduce heat to medium. Using a large spoon, scoop up about ⅛ of the meringue at a time and push from spoon into simmering water. Add more scoops of meringue to fill pan without letting scoops touch each other (meringues expand slightly). Cook until bottoms of meringues are firm to touch, about 1 minute. Turn over and cook until firm to touch on the other side, about 1

minute longer. With a slotted spoon, lift meringues from water, drain briefly, and set slightly apart in a rimmed pan or dish. Repeat to scoop and cook remaining meringues. They shrink slightly as they cool.

4. To assemble, spoon custard equally into dessert bowls. Add a poached meringue to each bowl and sprinkle with raspberries.

5. Place remaining ½ cup sugar in an 8- to 10-inch frying pan over high heat. Shake pan often until sugar is melted and amber-colored, 3 to 4 minutes. At once, spoon the hot caramel over meringues, but don't let it touch bowls; caramel immediately becomes crisp and brittle, but softens and begins to melt after standing. For crisp caramel, serve immediately; for softer caramel, cover and chill up to 1 hour.

Per serving: 262 cal., 18% (47 cal.) from fat; 5.9 g protein; 5.2 g fat (2.4 g sat.); 48 g carbo (1.5 g fiber); 69 mg sodium; 117 mg chol. ◆

Team 4 prepares dessert: Poached meringues on custard, topped with raspberries and caramel.

Chicken salad spectacular

An all-time favorite steps out on a world tour of flavors

By Linda Lau Anusasananan • Photographs by Tucker & Hossler

■ Chicken salad—once a plain Jane sandwich stuffer—has enormous potential as a sophisticated entrée. It travels the world, absorbing local flavors with amazing versatility.

In Mexico, dressed with a colorful corn salsa, chicken sits atop a crisp tortilla, composing a tostada. In France, it exhibits an affinity for licorice-scented tarragon and peppery watercress. As it passes through India, chicken wears a curry-spiced yogurt-mayonnaise dressing but settles into melon wedges in distinctly Western style. In China, it re-unites with old friends—fried noodles, toasted sesame seeds, and a lemony dressing—to become a salad full of crunchy textures. By the time chicken reaches Southeast Asia, it consorts boldly with sweet, sour, hot, salty, and bitter elements in vivid contrast.

All of these recipes start with shredded cooked chicken. The steeped chicken below is an easy way to cook this essential ingredient. You can also buy a roasted chicken from a delicatessen or the deli department of a supermarket. Then dress the meat with the flavors of your country of choice.

TECHNIQUE: STEEPING

A chicken in every pot makes a great salad

The Chinese technique called *steeping* produces remarkably moist and succulent chicken (recipe follows): Residual heat in poaching water that has been taken off the stove gently penetrates and firms the meat.

An alternative is to purchase a roast chicken from a deli (or roast your own at home). Remove the meat, and reserve the skin and bones for other uses. With your hands, tear the chicken along the grain into strips about ½ inch thick—the shreds will have textured ridges for the salad dressing to cling to. One 2-pound roast chicken yields about 3½ cups shredded meat.

Steeped Chicken

PREP AND COOK TIME: About 30 minutes, plus about 20 minutes to cool

NOTES: If making up to 1 day ahead, cover and chill.

MAKES: 3 to 4 cups shredded cooked chicken

In a covered 5- to 6-quart pan over high heat, bring 2½ to 3 quarts **water** to a boil. Meanwhile, rinse 3 or 4 **boned, skinned chicken breast halves** (about 6 oz. each). Add chicken to boiling water, cover, and return to a boil. Remove from heat and let stand, covered, until chicken is no longer pink in center of thickest part (cut to test), 12 to 18 minutes. If chicken is still pink, return it to the hot water, cover pan, and let steep a few minutes longer. Remove chicken from water and let cool, about 20 minutes. With your hands, tear chicken along the grain into shreds about ½ inch thick.

Per ½ cup: 103 cal., 18% (19 cal.) from fat; 20 g protein; 2.1 g fat (0.6 g sat.); 0 g carbo; 43 mg sodium; 53 mg chol.

Bang-Bang Chicken Salad

PREP AND COOK TIME: About 30 minutes

NOTES: This Southeast Asian salad, an adaptation of one created by Chef John Beardsley at Ponzu in San Francisco, is layered with intense flavors and textures. Roasted rice powder adds an intriguing crunch, but you can omit it if you wish. To simplify assembly, prepare the roasted rice powder, chicken, arugula, candied peel, and dressing up to 1 day ahead; cover elements separately and chill.

MAKES: 4 servings

- ¼ cup **jasmine** or long-grain white **rice** (optional)
- 2 **pink grapefruit** (2½ lb. total)

  Candied grapefruit peel (recipe follows) or 3 tablespoons orange marmalade

  Lemon grass dressing (recipe follows)
- 4 cups shredded **cooked chicken** (see box at left)
- 3 tablespoons finely chopped **lime** (including peel)
- 2 quarts (6 oz.) **baby** or bite-size pieces **arugula** leaves, rinsed and crisped

Flavors pop in an Asian chicken salad laced with fresh grapefruit segments, candied peel, and a spicy lemon grass dressing.

1. If making roasted rice powder, in an 8- to 10-inch frying pan over medium heat, stir rice often until tinged with brown, 5 to 8 minutes. Cool and whirl in a blender to a coarse powder.

2. With a small, sharp knife, cut peel and white membrane from grapefruit. If making candied peel, reserve some; otherwise, discard. Working over a strainer set in a bowl, cut between fruit and inner membranes to release grapefruit segments and drop into strainer. Squeeze juice from membranes into bowl. Discard membranes; reserve juice for other uses.

3. In a large bowl, stir candied grapefruit peel into warm or cool lemon grass dressing, separating pieces. Add chicken, lime, arugula, grapefruit segments, and ground toasted rice; mix gently. Spoon onto plates.

Per serving: 411 cal., 13% (53 cal.) from fat; 44 g protein; 5.9 g fat (1.5 g sat.); 45 g carbo (3 g fiber); 1,318 mg sodium; 105 mg chol.

Candied Grapefruit Peel

PREP AND COOK TIME: About 15 minutes

NOTES: If making up to 1 day ahead, cover and chill. Use peel in bang-bang chicken salad (recipe precedes) to add unexpected bits of sweetness. Candied peel is also delicious sprinkled over vanilla ice cream.

MAKES: About 1/3 cup

1. With a vegetable peeler, pare enough peel (colored part only) from **grapefruit** (see bang-bang chicken salad, preceding) to make 1/3 cup. Stack several pieces and cut into 1/4-inch-wide strips about 1 1/2 inches long. Repeat to cut remaining peel. In a 1- to 2-quart pan over high heat, bring 2 to 3 cups **water** to a boil. Drop peel into water and boil about 1 minute; drain. Repeat with fresh water; boil 1 minute and drain again.

2. Return peel to pan; add 1/2 cup **water** and 1/4 cup **sugar.** Boil over high heat until peel is translucent and all but about 2 tablespoons liquid has evaporated, 5 to 7 minutes. Cool.

Per tablespoon: 32 cal., 0% (0 cal.) from fat; 0 g protein; 0 g fat; 8 g carbo (1.1 g fiber); 0.3 mg sodium; 0 mg chol.

Lemon Grass Dressing

PREP AND COOK TIME: About 15 minutes

NOTES: If making up to 1 day ahead, cover and chill. If lemon grass is not available, substitute 1 teaspoon grated lemon peel. Use this dressing in bang-bang chicken salad (recipe

An oven-crisped tortilla holds refried beans, cabbage, chicken, salsa, and guacamole.

precedes) or other Asian-style salads.

MAKES: About 2/3 cup

1. Trim off and discard root end and tough tops from 1 stalk **fresh lemon grass** (12 in.). Peel off and discard tough outer layer. Chop tender inner portion of stalk and put in a blender or food processor. Add 3 tablespoons *each* **soy sauce, Asian fish sauce** (*nuoc mam* or *nam pla*), and **rice vinegar;** 2 to 3 tablespoons chopped **fresh jalapeño chili;** 2 tablespoons chopped **fresh ginger;** and 1 tablespoon chopped **garlic.** Whirl until fairly smooth.

2. Put 1/3 cup **sugar** in an 8- to 10-inch frying pan over high heat; shake pan often until sugar is melted and amber-colored, 2 to 3 minutes. Add lemon grass mixture (mixture will bubble and sugar will harden). Stir over medium heat until sugar is dissolved. Cool to room temperature.

Per tablespoon: 43 cal., 10% (4.5 cal.) from fat; 1.1 g protein; 0.5 g fat (0.1 g sat.); 8.7 g carbo (0.1 g fiber); 488 mg sodium; 0 mg chol.

Chicken Tostada Salad

PREP AND COOK TIME: About 20 minutes

NOTES: Tortillas can be baked (through step 2) up to 1 day ahead; store airtight at room temperature.

MAKES: 4 servings

    About 2 tablespoons **salad oil**
8 **flour tortillas** (8 in. wide)
    Salt
1 can (16 oz.) **refried beans**
1/4 cup fat-skimmed **chicken broth**

1/2 cup **shredded jack cheese**
4 cups **finely shredded cabbage** or shredded iceberg lettuce
3 cups shredded **cooked chicken** (see box, page 168)
    Tomato-corn salsa (recipe follows)
3/4 to 1 cup homemade or purchased **guacamole** (recipe follows)
1/3 to 1/2 cup **sour cream**
1/3 cup thinly sliced **green onions** (including tops)
4 **radishes,** rinsed (optional)
    Pepper

1. Pour 1 cup water and 2 tablespoons oil into a 9-inch pie pan. Stack 4 tortillas and cut stack into 8 wedges. One at a time, dip tortilla wedges and whole tortillas briefly in water mixture, just to coat. Drain briefly and place in a single layer on 2 oiled 14- by 17-inch baking sheets. Sprinkle lightly with salt.

2. Bake in a 450° oven until wedges and whole tortillas are crisp and lightly browned on both sides, turning once, 6 to 8 minutes total. Cool on sheets.

3. Meanwhile, mix refried beans and broth in a microwave-safe bowl. Cover with microwave-safe plastic wrap and heat in a microwave oven at full power (100%) until hot, about 2 minutes, stirring once about halfway through.

4. Place 1 whole tortilla on each of 4 dinner plates. Spread each with about 1/4 of the bean mixture. Layer 1/4 of each of the following over beans: jack cheese, cabbage, chicken, salsa, guacamole, sour cream, and green onions. Garnish each salad with a radish. Arrange tortilla

wedges evenly around bases of salads. Add salt and pepper to taste.

Per serving: 824 cal., 38% (315 cal.) from fat; 51 g protein; 35 g fat (9.5 g sat.); 80 g carbo (6.8 g fiber); 1,000 mg sodium; 102 mg chol.

Tomato-Corn Salsa

PREP TIME: About 10 minutes

NOTES: If making up to 6 hours ahead, cover and chill. To save time, instead of making the salsa from scratch, you can purchase 1½ cups refrigerated tomato salsa and add ½ cup thawed frozen corn kernels.

MAKES: 2 cups

Mix 1 cup chopped **firm-ripe tomatoes**, ½ cup thawed **frozen corn kernels**, ½ cup chopped **onion**, ¼ cup chopped **fresh cilantro**, 3 tablespoons **lime juice**, 3 to 4 tablespoons minced **fresh jalapeño chilies**, and **salt** and **pepper** to taste.

Per ½ cup: 41 cal., 9% (3.6 cal.) from fat; 1.4 g protein; 0.4 g fat (0 g sat.); 10 g carbo (1.5 g fiber); 7.9 mg sodium; 0 mg chol.

Guacamole

Peel and pit 1 **avocado** (¾ lb.). In a bowl, coarsely mash. Add 1 to 2 tablespoons **lime juice**, 1 clove **garlic** (peeled and pressed or minced), and **salt** to taste. Makes about 1 cup.

Per ¼ cup: 104 cal., 84% (87 cal.) from fat; 1.3 g protein; 9.7 g fat (1.6 g sat.); 5.2 g carbo (1.3 g fiber); 7.1 mg sodium; 0 mg chol.

Chinese Chicken Salad

PREP AND COOK TIME: About 1 hour

NOTES: A classic Chinese chicken salad is a fundraising specialty of the Chinese American Women's Club of Santa Clara County, California. This is an adaptation of the recipe in the club's cookbook, *Chinese Cooking: Our Legacy* (C.I. Printing, San Jose, 1997; $27; Box 5091, San Jose, CA 95150).

The delight in this salad is the mix of crisp textures. Make sure to blot excess water off the vegetables to keep the noodles crisp. Dress the salad lightly and serve immediately after mixing; it gets soggy if it stands. Up to 1 day ahead, cook chicken, shred lettuce and pack in a towel-lined heavy plastic food bag, make dressing, and cut vegetables; cover separately and chill. Fry noodles and store airtight at room temperature.

MAKES: 4 servings

½ cup **slivered almonds**

¼ cup **sesame seed**

Salad oil

2 to 2½ ounces **dried bean thread noodles** (cellophane or *sai fun*)

3 **green onions**, rinsed

2 quarts finely shredded **iceberg lettuce**, rinsed and crisped

2 cups finely shredded **cooked chicken** (see box, page 168)

1 cup chopped **fresh cilantro**

Chinese dressing (recipe follows)

Salt and **pepper**

1. In a 12- to 14-inch wok or deep 10-inch frying pan over medium-low heat, stir almonds occasionally until they begin to turn gold, 3 to 5 minutes. Add sesame seed and stir until almonds and seed are light gold, 2 to 3 minutes longer. Pour from pan.

2. Pour 1 to 1½ inches oil into pan over medium-high heat; when oil reaches 375°, adjust heat to maintain temperature. If you don't have a thermometer, drop 1 noodle strand into oil; if it expands at once, oil is hot enough.

3. Meanwhile, pull noodles apart so they aren't tightly bunched (to avoid a mess, do this in a large paper bag). Drop a small handful of noodles at a time into hot oil; noodles puff and

Crunchy noodles, toasted almonds, and crisp lettuce weave layers of texture into Chinese chicken salad.

expand almost immediately. With a wire strainer or slotted spoon, turn the entire mass over and push down into oil to be sure all noodles are cooked. When noodles stop crackling, in about 15 seconds, lift out with strainer or slotted spoon and drain on towels.

4. Trim and discard root ends and tips from green onions. Cut onions, including tops, into 3-inch lengths, then cut lengthwise into thin shreds.

5. In a large bowl, mix lettuce, chicken, cilantro, green onions, almond–sesame seed mixture, and dressing. Add 8 to 10 cups fried noodles, and salt and pepper to taste. Mix gently. Garnish with remaining noodles. Serve at once.

Per serving: 534 cal., 61% (324 cal.) from fat; 27 g protein; 36 g fat (4.7 g sat.); 28 g carbo (3.8 g fiber); 143 mg sodium; 53 mg chol.

Chinese Dressing

PREP TIME: About 10 minutes

NOTES: If making up to 1 day ahead, cover and chill.

MAKES: About ½ cup

Mix 2 teaspoons grated **lemon peel**, ¼ cup **lemon juice**, 3 tablespoons **salad oil**, 1 tablespoon **Asian** (toasted) **sesame oil**, 1 tablespoon **hoisin** or soy **sauce**, 1 teaspoon **sugar**, 1 teaspoon **dry mustard**, 1 teaspoon **Chinese five spice** (or ¼ teaspoon *each* ground cinnamon, ground cloves, ground ginger, and crushed anise seed), and 1 clove **garlic**, peeled and pressed or minced.

Per tablespoon: 73 cal., 85% (62 cal.) from fat; 0.1 g protein; 6.9 g fat (0.9 g sat.); 2.6 g carbo (0.1 g fiber); 41 mg sodium; 0 mg chol.

Curry-Chutney Chicken Salad

PREP TIME: About 35 minutes

MAKES: 4 servings

1 cup **red** or green **seedless grapes**, rinsed and well drained

3 cups shredded **cooked chicken** (see box, page 168)

1 cup thinly sliced **celery**

½ cup thinly sliced **green onions** (including tops)

Curry-chutney dressing (recipe follows)

Salt and **cayenne**

1 **firm-ripe cantaloupe** or honeydew (3½ to 4 lb.), rinsed

⅓ cup chopped **salted roasted pistachios**

¼ cup chopped **fresh mint** leaves

Chicken and grapes in a curry-spiked dressing tumble out of a juicy wedge of cantaloupe.

1. If grapes are larger than ¾ inch, cut in half.

2. In a bowl, mix grapes, chicken, celery, green onions, and curry-chutney dressing. Add salt and cayenne to taste.

3. Cut melon in half lengthwise; scoop out and discard seeds. Cut halves in half lengthwise. Set each melon quarter on a dinner plate. Spoon ¼ of the chicken salad into each melon cavity, letting it spill over sides. Sprinkle equally with pistachios and mint.

Per serving: 494 cal., 36% (180 cal.) from fat; 37 g protein; 20 g fat (3.2 g sat.); 43 g carbo (3.6 g fiber); 397 mg sodium; 88 mg chol.

Curry-Chutney Dressing

PREP TIME: **About 5 minutes**

NOTES: **If making up to 1 day ahead, cover and chill.**

MAKES: **About 1 cup**

Mix ¾ cup **plain nonfat yogurt**, ¼ cup **mayonnaise**, 3 tablespoons chopped **Major Grey chutney**, 1 teaspoon **curry powder**, ⅛ to ¼ teaspoon **cayenne**, and **salt** to taste.

Per tablespoon: 42 cal., 57% (24 cal.) from fat; 0.6 g protein; 2.7 g fat (0.4 g sat.); 3.6 g carbo (0 g fiber); 60 mg sodium; 2.2 mg chol.

French Country Tarragon Chicken Salad

PREP TIME: **About 40 minutes**

NOTES: **Rinse and crisp watercress up to 1 day ahead.**

MAKES: **4 servings**

About ½ pound **watercress,** rinsed and crisped

Tarragon dressing (recipe follows)

4   cups shredded **cooked chicken** (see box, page 168)

Salt and **pepper**

1   **English cucumber** (1 lb.), rinsed and thinly sliced

1. Discard yellow or wilted leaves from watercress. Trim off tough stems and finely chop enough to make ½ cup; discard remainder. Cut tender sprigs into 3-inch lengths (you should have 7 to 8 cups).

2. Stir chopped stems into dressing.

3. In a bowl, mix ¾ cup of the dressing with chicken and watercress sprigs. Add salt and pepper to taste. In another bowl, mix remaining dressing with cucumber.

4. Arrange ¼ of the cucumber on each of 4 dinner plates. Mound chicken mixture on top. Add salt and pepper to taste.

Per serving: 336 cal., 40% (135 cal.) from fat; 43 g protein; 15 g fat (2.5 g sat.); 5.7 g carbo (2.7 g fiber); 219 mg sodium; 105 mg chol.

Tarragon Dressing

PREP TIME: **About 10 minutes**

MAKES: **About 1¼ cups**

In a bowl, whisk together ½ cup **white wine vinegar**, ⅓ cup **salad oil**, ¼ cup minced **shallots**, 3 tablespoons minced **fresh tarragon** or 1 tablespoon dried tarragon, 2 tablespoons **Dijon mustard**, and ½ teaspoon **sugar**. Add **salt** and **pepper** to taste.

Per tablespoon: 37 cal., 86% (32 cal.) from fat; 0.1 g protein; 3.6 g fat (0.5 g sat.); 0.8 g carbo (0 g fiber); 36 mg sodium; 0 mg chol. ◆

Tarragon, watercress, and cucumber merge in a French-inspired composition.

The Quick Cook

Shrimp and mango chunks cook in a vibrant sauce of puréed fruit and spices.

TUCKER & HOSSLER

Stir-frying, Indian-style

■ If you were to visit a kitchen in India, chances are you'd see a bowl-shaped pan that looks much like a wok. And if you thought it would work for stir-frying, you'd be right—but the Indians call the process *balti*. The flavors that pour forth from the *karahai* (pan) are traditionally Indian, full of spicy surprises. Ranjan Dey, chef-owner of New Delhi Restaurant and owner of New World Spices, both in San Francisco, shares his recipes for stir-fry speed with typical Indian seasonings. If you'd like to explore more complex flavors, Dey sells Indian spice blends for stir-frying; 2-ounce containers are available in six flavors, each $3.99 plus shipping (800/347-7795).

Mango-Cumin Shrimp Stir-Fry

PREP AND COOK TIME: About 30 minutes
MAKES: 4 servings

- 1½ cups 1-inch chunks **mango**
- 2 teaspoons **ground cumin**
- 2 teaspoons **sesame seed**
- 1 teaspoon **ground turmeric**
- 1 pound (26 to 30 per lb.) **shelled, deveined shrimp,** rinsed
- 1 teaspoon **salad oil**
- 1 cup 1-inch chunks **pineapple**
- ½ cup thinly sliced **green onions**
- 2 teaspoons **cornstarch**
- ½ cup fat-skimmed **chicken broth**
- **Lime** wedges
- **Salt**

1. In a blender or food processor, purée ½ cup mango chunks, cumin, sesame seed, and turmeric. Scrape into a bowl; add shrimp and mix.

2. Pour oil into a 10- to 12-inch nonstick frying pan or 14-inch wok over high heat. When hot, add shrimp mixture, remaining mango chunks, pineapple chunks, and green onions. Stir until shrimp are no longer pink in center of thickest part (cut to test), 3 to 4 minutes.

3. Meanwhile, in bowl, blend cornstarch and broth until smooth. Add to pan and stir until boiling. Pour stir-fry into a clean bowl. Serve with lime wedges to squeeze over portions; add salt to taste.

Per serving: 217 cal., 18% (40 cal.) from fat; 25 g protein; 4.4 g fat (0.7 g sat.); 20 g carbo (1.7 g fiber); 183 mg sodium; 173 mg chol.

Lemon-Mustard Chicken Stir-Fry

PREP AND COOK TIME: About 30 minutes
NOTES: Garam masala is found with spices in supermarkets; or use ¼ teaspoon *each* ground coriander and ground cumin and ⅛ teaspoon *each* pepper, ground cardamom, ground cinnamon, and ground ginger.
MAKES: 4 servings

- 2 teaspoons grated **lemon** peel
- 2 teaspoons **mustard seed**
- 1 teaspoon **ground turmeric**
- 1 teaspoon **garam masala** (see notes)
- 1 pound **boned, skinned chicken breasts**
- 2 teaspoons **salad oil**
- 1 cup thinly sliced **carrots**
- ½ pound **edible-pod peas,** rinsed, ends and strings removed
- 1 tablespoon **cornstarch**
- 1 cup fat-skimmed **chicken broth**
- **Salt**

1. In a bowl, mix lemon peel, mustard seed, turmeric, and garam masala.

2. Rinse chicken and pat dry. Cut into bite-size chunks. Add to bowl and mix.

3. Pour oil into a 10- to 12-inch nonstick frying pan or 14-inch wok over high heat. When hot, add chicken and stir until no longer pink on the surface, about 3 minutes. Add carrots and pea pods and stir until vegetables are tender-crisp to bite and chicken is no longer pink in center of thickest part (cut to test), about 3 minutes longer.

4. Meanwhile, in the bowl, smoothly blend cornstarch and broth. Add to pan and stir until boiling. Pour stir-fry into a clean bowl. Add salt to taste.

Per serving: 210 cal., 19% (40 cal.) from fat; 31 g protein; 4.4 g fat (0.7 g sat.); 10 g carbo (2.7 g fiber); 105 mg sodium; 66 mg chol.

Spicy Pepper-Beef Stir-Fry

PREP AND COOK TIME: About 30 minutes
MAKES: 4 servings

- 1 tablespoon minced **garlic**
- ½ teaspoon **cayenne**
- 2 teaspoons **ground coriander**
- 1 teaspoon **ground turmeric**
- 1 pound fat-trimmed **beef sirloin,** rinsed
- 2 teaspoons **salad oil**
- ½ cup *each* diced **green, red,** and **yellow bell peppers** (or 1½ cups of one color)
- 1 cup thinly sliced **onion**
- 1 tablespoon **cornstarch**
- 1 cup fat-skimmed **beef broth**
- **Salt**

1. In a bowl, combine garlic, cayenne, coriander, and turmeric.

2. Rinse meat, pat dry, and cut into ¼-inch-thick bite-size pieces. Add to bowl and mix well.

3. Pour oil into a 10- to 12-inch nonstick frying pan or 14-inch wok over high heat. When hot, add beef mixture, bell peppers, and onion. Stir until meat is no longer pink on surface, about 4 minutes.

4. Meanwhile, in bowl, smoothly blend cornstarch and broth. Add to pan and stir until boiling. Pour stir-fry into a clean bowl. Add salt to taste.

Per serving: 212 cal., 32% (68 cal.) from fat; 26 g protein; 7.5 g fat (2 g sat.); 9.1 g carbo (1.4 g fiber); 87 mg sodium; 69 mg chol. ◆

Living lettuce bowl contains romaine, 'Red Oak Leaf', and butter lettuce. Smaller pots around it hold chives, parsley, rosemary, and basil.

Snip-and-serve greenery

Dress your barbecued burgers with garden-fresh lettuce and herbs from tabletop pots

By Jill Slater
Recipes by Andrew Baker

When summer barbecues call for backyard buffets, why not put crops from your garden on the menu? A pot of salad greens, surrounded by smaller pots filled with herbs such as basil, chives, parsley, and rosemary, makes an attractive garden centerpiece for a patio table. As a bonus, guests can snip bits to garnish grilled burgers (provide cutting tools beside the pots—bonsai clippers work well).

Fragrant basil is always a crowd pleaser, and on a burger topped with chives and melted cheese, it's a taste treat. Maybe you prefer cilantro or Italian parsley. No matter which greens you grow, plant them about three weeks before the barbecue to give them time to fill out. (In hottest weather, grow the lettuce under a lath.) Or stagger planting times, a pot per week, so you always have plants ready for snipping.

To reinforce the garden theme, fill harvest baskets with fresh-picked tomatoes, peppers, corn, and cucumbers, and place them near the barbecue and buffet, with slicing knives and cutting boards at the ready. Many vegetables—such as pattypan squash, peppers, and tomatoes—are delicious when sizzled on the grill; they'll complement garden-fresh salads and barbecue fare (such as the beef burgers recipe on the facing page).

Garden Projects
Lettuce Centerpiece

TIME: About 30 minutes
COST: About $45
MATERIALS

- Large terra-cotta bowl, at least 16 inches in diameter, with drain holes
- Small bag of potting soil
- Lettuces (about five sixpacks)—choose several varieties, such as butter lettuce, romaine, 'Red Oak Leaf', and Swiss chard
- Trowel

PLANTING AND CARE

1. Fill the container halfway with potting soil.

2. Push plants from their sixpacks, then plant them about 2 inches apart. For best effects, group them by kind, with the tallest plants (such as romaine) in the back. Fill in around them with more potting soil.

3. Set the lettuce centerpiece in filtered shade and water it well.

4. Continue to water regularly; fertilize once a week with dilute fish emulsion.

The day of the barbecue, thoroughly mist the leaves with water to clean them before placing the container on the patio table.

Herb Garnishes

TIME: About 15 minutes

COST: About $30 for eight pots

MATERIALS

• Eight 4-inch clay pots with saucers
• Potting soil
• Eight herbs, such as basil, chives, parsley, and rosemary, in small pots

PLANTING

1. Fill each container about one-quarter full with potting soil.

2. Remove plants from nursery pots, loosen the rootballs, then slip them into the 4-inch pots.

3. Fill in around plants with more potting soil.

4. Water thoroughly.

Recipes

Beef Burgers for a Garden Barbecue

PREP AND COOK TIME: About 40 minutes

NOTES: Snip herbs from the table garden to embellish these burgers. If desired, lay herbs on the grilling patties, then top them with cheese; the cheese will help anchor the herbs in place. Before serving, sprinkle additional herbs atop the melted cheese. Accompany the burgers with grilled vegetables, such as peppers, from the garden or market.

To grill bell peppers, rinse them and cut them in half lengthwise; then discard stems and seeds. Lay peppers skin side down beside beef burgers; cook until charred on the bottom, about 6 minutes. Let them cool slightly; if desired, pull off pepper skins and discard.

MAKES: 12 servings

Thinly sliced cheese melts over tender basil laid on burger while it's on the grill. Chives garnish the top.

---

3 **large eggs**

About 1¼ teaspoons **salt**

¾ teaspoon **pepper**

3 pounds **ground lean beef**

¾ cup **fine dried bread crumbs**

12 thin slices **Swiss cheese** (about 5 oz. total; optional)

12 **round sandwich buns** (4 to 4½ in.), cut in half horizontally

Condiments (choices follow)

1. In a large bowl, beat eggs, 1¼ teaspoons salt, and pepper to blend. Add beef and bread crumbs; mix gently to avoid compacting meat. Form 12 equal patties, each ½ inch thick.

2. Lay patties on a barbecue grill over a solid bed of hot coals or high heat on a gas grill (you can hold your hand at grill level only 2 to 3 seconds); close lid on gas grill. Turning once to brown evenly, cook until a thermometer inserted in center of thickest part reads 160° (no pink in the center), 6 to 8 minutes total.

3. When patties are almost done, if desired, top each with a slice of cheese. Also lay buns, cut side down, on grill and toast about 30 seconds.

4. With a wide spatula, transfer patties to bun bottoms. Add condiments and salt to taste. Cover with bun tops.

Per serving: 432 cal., 46% (198 cal.) from fat; 29 g protein; 22 g fat (8.9 g sat.); 27 g carbo (1.1 g fiber); 649 mg sodium; 134 mg chol.

Condiments

BLUE CHEESE AIOLI. In a bowl mash to blend 1 teaspoon minced **garlic,** ¼ cup **crumbled blue cheese,** and 1 cup **mayonnaise.** Makes about 1 cup.

Per tablespoon: 106 cal., 93% (99 cal.) from fat; 0.6 g protein; 11 g fat (2 g sat.); 0.5 g carbo (0 g fiber); 108 mg sodium; 9.7 mg chol.

CHIPOTLE CATSUP. Discard seeds and veins from 1 or 2 **canned chipotle chilies.** In a blender, combine 2 tablespoons of the canned chipotles' sauce, 1 cup **catsup,** and 1 chipotle chili; whirl smooth. Taste, and if desired, add remaining chili and whirl smooth. Makes about 1 cup.

Per tablespoon: 18 cal., 5% (0.9 cal.) from fat; 0.2 g protein; 0.1 g fat (0 g sat.); 4.5 g carbo (0.3 g fiber); 201 mg sodium; 0 mg chol.

MARGARITA MUSTARD. In a bowl stir together 1 cup **Dijon mustard,** ¼ cup **tequila,** 2 teaspoons **lime juice,** and 1 teaspoon grated **orange** peel. Makes about 1¼ cups.

Per tablespoon: 20 cal., 0% (0 cal.) from fat; 0 g protein; 0 g fat; 0.1 g carbo (0 g fiber); 288 mg sodium; 0 mg chol. ◆

food guide

By Jerry Anne Di Vecchio   Photographs by James Carrier

Well bred, Italian-style

Milan's favorite fast food just might be the sandwich

■ In Italy, *pane* is bread, *panino* is a roll, *panini* are sandwiches. And in Milan, from what I have observed, the sandwich reigns. There, panini are assembled with fresh diversity on tender rolls, or popped into sandwich grills to create *tostas,* to satisfy hungry, hurried customers at *paninotecas*—sandwich shops. The package often includes piquant nibbles of pickled onions, mushrooms, artichokes, and other vegetables; a few leaves of some sort; and, with considerable regularity, mayonnaise seasoned as Russian (some would call it Thousand Island) dressing.

Good ideas travel. No doubt you've seen panini on a menu or two. I've spotted them from Seattle to Santa Fe. And at a little Italian restaurant tucked away in a Denver shopping center, I came across this highly evolved focaccia version.

Salmon Panini

PREP AND COOK TIME: About 15 minutes

NOTES: If focaccia is not available, choose rolls that are squat and wide rather than tall and round. Serve with a knife and fork.

MAKES: 4 servings

4   **boned, skinned salmon fillets** (maximum 1 in. thick, 3 to 4 oz. each)

About 1 teaspoon **olive oil**

1   pound **plain focaccia** or 4 tender-crusted rolls (¼ lb. each), cut in half horizontally

Russian dressing (recipe follows)

About 2 cups **arugula,** watercress, or lettuce leaves, rinsed and crisped

Pickled onion (recipe follows)

Salt

Pepperoncini or pickled cherry peppers (optional)

1. Rub your fingers over salmon pieces to locate any bones and pull them out with tweezers. Rinse fish, pat dry, and rub lightly with oil.

2. Set a 10- to 12-inch ovenproof nonstick frying pan over high heat. When hot, lay salmon pieces side by side in pan. Cook until fish is browned on the bottom (lift a corner with a wide spatula to check), 1 to 2 minutes.

3. Transfer pan to a 400° oven and bake until salmon is opaque but still moist-looking in center of thickest part (cut to test), 4 to 5 minutes. When fish goes into the oven, put bread, cut sides together, on rack alongside and bake until hot, 3 to 5 minutes.

4. With halves still together, cut focaccia into 4 equal rectangles. Spread cut sides equally with Russian dressing. Mound ¼ of the arugula on the bottom half of each rectangle and set a piece of salmon on the greens. Top fish equally with pickled onion and cover with top half of bread. Season sandwiches with salt to taste and accompany with pepperoncini.

Per serving: 598 cal., 35% (207 cal.) from fat; 32 g protein; 23 g fat (5 g sat.); 68 g carbo (3 g fiber); 1,078 mg sodium; 56 mg chol.

Russian dressing. In a small bowl, mix ½ cup **reduced-fat** or regular **mayonnaise,** ¼ cup drained **sweet pickle relish,** and 2 tablespoons **tomato-based cocktail sauce** or catsup. Makes ¾ cup.

Per tablespoon: 37 cal., 49% (18 cal.) from fat; 0.1 g protein; 2 g fat (0.3 g sat.); 4.4 g carbo (0 g fiber); 148 mg sodium; 0 mg chol.

Pickled onion. Peel 1 **onion** (½ lb.) and cut lengthwise into slivers. In a 10- to 12-inch frying pan over high heat, bring onion, ¼ cup **water,** and 2 tablespoons **white wine vinegar** to a boil; stir often until liquid has evaporated, 4 to 5 minutes. Pour into a small bowl and add **salt** to taste. Makes 1 cup.

Per ¼ cup: 20 cal., 4.5% (0.9 cal.) from fat; 0.6 g protein; 0.1 g fat (0 g sat.); 4.7 g carbo (0.8 g fiber); 1.5 mg sodium; 0 mg chol.

Turn over a new leaf

■ *Shiso*—also called beefsteak leaf—is a fresh herb with broad, jagged-edged green or purple leaves. Related to mint, shiso blends its delicate minty subtleties with citrus and licorice; the flavor of the purple leaves is more fruity and less minty than the green. The herb is readily found in Japanese and many other Asian markets. In Japanese cuisine, green shiso is added to sushi, soups, salads, sashimi, and tempura. Purple shiso is used most in pickling. Either green or purple shiso leaves show off well in this salad.

Shiso salad. In a bowl, combine 2 cups very thinly sliced peeled **cucumbers** and ⅓ cup **seasoned rice vinegar.** Slightly crush cucumber with your hand, and let stand at least 5 minutes. Rinse and core 1 crisp **green apple** (such as Granny Smith or Newtown Pippin; ½ lb.); thinly slice on a food slicer or mandoline. Add apple at once to cucumbers, and mix. Add ¼ cup finely slivered **fresh shiso** leaves (green or purple); mix. Season to taste with **salt.** With a slotted spoon, mound salad on plates and garnish with fresh shiso leaves. Makes 3 cups, 4 servings.

Per serving: 58 cal., 4.7% (2.7 cal.) from fat; 0.6 g protein; 0.3 g fat (0 g sat.); 14 g carbo (1.7 g fiber); 396 mg sodium; 0 mg chol.

Preserving the times

■ Growing up with a big garden and no freezer, I was stuck with canning. It was a summer ritual that my mother adored and I dreaded. She did the stewing and brewing, the humming and admiring; I did the hulling and peeling, the cleaning and complaining—the volume got me down. For years afterward I avoided canning.

However, with the advent of the microwave oven, I took another look at preserving. Zapped in small quantities in the microwave, jams have merit. Berries or pieces of other fruit, submitted in slow stages to the jostle-free heat, retain their shape and fresh flavor better than when boiled. In a sense, I've returned to the process but not the processing.

Microwave Apricot–Grand Marnier Jam

PREP AND COOK TIME: About 30 minutes, plus about 2½ hours to cool

NOTES: If making ahead, chill airtight for 2 weeks; discard if any signs of mold develop.

MAKES: About 1 cup

- 1 to 1¼ pounds **ripe** to firm-ripe **apricots**
- 2 tablespoons **lemon juice**
- ½ cup **sugar**
- 2 tablespoons **Grand Marnier** or other orange-flavor liqueur

1. Rinse, pit, and quarter apricots; put in a 3- to 4-quart microwave-safe bowl. Add lemon juice and sugar; mix.

2. Heat in a microwave oven at full power (100%) until juices boil, 6 to 8 minutes. Stir gently to turn fruit pieces over; let mixture stand until cool, at least 1 hour or up to 3 hours. Microwave again at full power until boiling, 5 to 6 minutes; let stand at least 1 hour or up to 3 hours.

3. Stir liqueur into apricot mixture, then microwave again at full power until syrup forms big, shiny bubbles, 12 to 15 minutes, stirring gently every 4 to 5 minutes to turn fruit pieces over and prevent browning. The syrup around the apricots will be thinner than jam, but it thickens as it cools. Spoon into a jar or dish and let cool slightly. Serve warm or cool.

Per tablespoon: 39 cal., 2.3% (0.9 cal.) from fat; 0.4 g protein; 0.1 g fat (0 g sat.); 9.9 g carbo (0.3 g fiber); 0.7 mg sodium; 0 mg chol.

A cloud without doubt

■ When eating raw eggs became cause for concern, a number of popular dishes got pushed aside, including cloud-light chiffon pie, which depends on whipped egg whites for its volume and fluffy texture. Now the pie can safely return. Pasteurized dried egg whites—once difficult to find—are available in most supermarkets and do an impressive job. One product (Just Whites) is pure dried egg whites; another (made by Wilton Enterprises) is a meringue powder. Whipped into a plain meringue, either mixture tastes of processing. But with a flavorful dose of berry purée and a little whipped cream to smooth over the issue, this cool summer treat offers pure pleasure—no caution required.

Strawberry-Raspberry Chiffon Pie

PREP AND COOK TIME: About 40 minutes, plus at least 3 hours to chill

NOTES: The proportions in this recipe are based on 2 large egg whites. Although the package directions for both dried egg whites and meringue powder suggest using 2 teaspoons of the mixture as the equivalent of 1 egg white, you need 1 tablespoon dried egg whites or meringue powder and 3 tablespoons water to equal 1 *large* egg white (*Sunset* recipes are tested with large eggs). You can also put the pie filling in a 9-inch graham cracker crust.

MAKES: 8 or 9 servings

- 2 cups **strawberries,** hulled
- 1 cup **raspberries**
- 1 envelope **unflavored gelatin**
- ¾ cup **sugar**
- 1 tablespoon **lemon juice**
- 2 tablespoons **dried egg whites** or meringue powder (see notes)
- ½ cup **whipping cream**
- 1 baked 9-inch **pie crust**

1. Rinse and drain strawberries and raspberries. Set aside several perfect berries. In a blender, whirl remaining berries until smooth.

2. In a 2- to 3-quart pan, mix gelatin with ⅓ cup sugar. Place a fine strainer over pan and rub berry purée through it; discard seeds. Stir mixture over high heat just until boiling, about 2 minutes. Let cool to room temperature, about 20 minutes (or nest pan in ice water and stir frequently until cool but still liquid, 2 to 4 minutes). Stir in lemon juice.

3. In a deep bowl, combine dried egg whites with 6 tablespoons water; dissolve as directed on package. With a mixer on high speed, whip whites to a thick foam. Continue beating, gradually adding remaining sugar, until whites hold distinct peaks.

4. In another bowl, with unwashed beaters, whip cream on high speed until it holds soft peaks. Fold cream into berry mixture, then fold in whipped egg whites until most of the streaks are blended in. If mixture is not thick enough to hold soft mounds, nest bowl in ice water and gently fold occasionally for 2 to 4 minutes. Pour filling into pie crust; cover airtight without touching filling (set pie on a baking sheet and invert a large bowl over it). Chill until firm enough to cut, at least 3 hours or up to 2 days. Garnish with reserved berries.

Per serving: 233 cal., 42% (99 cal.) from fat; 3.5 g protein; 11 g fat (4.3 g sat.); 31 g carbo (1.8 g fiber); 129 mg sodium; 15 mg chol.

PRODUCE TIP

Freshening up

■ The obvious purpose of washing produce is to get rid of dirt and other physical intruders. Run cool water over foods with smooth surfaces, such as apples and melons. But those with nooks and crannies, including lettuce, broccoli, artichokes, herbs, and even mushrooms, should be immersed in plenty of water; give them a good swish to dislodge stubborn boarders. (Caution: Mushrooms are like sponges; lift them out quickly.)

However, when the produce has been treated with pesticides, cleaner is better. To penetrate and remove pesticides effectively, water needs a *surfactant*—a substance that lowers water's surface tension so it can break through films on foods and rinse them away. Make your own surfactant using a nondetergent water softener such as Calgon (2 teaspoons per gallon of water), or you can buy a surfactant cleaner, such as Organiclean. Apply it to foods, then rinse them again with cool water.

But what about microbes like *E. coli* and salmonella? Commercial packers use a chlorine rinse on produce. You can make your own solution with 1 part household chlorine bleach to 10 parts water, plus 1 teaspoon vinegar for each quart of water. Wash foods in it, then rinse them with plain water to get rid of any chlorine odor. ◆

The Wine Guide

By Karen MacNeil-Fife

RICK MARIANI

Asian pairings

■ I generally rely on instinct when pairing wine and food. That's easy enough when the food is roast chicken, which, like many other American dishes—or French or Italian—has not one, but many, delicious wine partners. Bring lemon grass, ginger, and curry into the picture, however, and wine pairing veers off this flexible course.

It's not quite as easy to be instinctive about pairing wine with chili-laced Thai noodles. Even a familiar dish like chicken satay with spicy peanut sauce presents a new challenge in thinking about how flavors work together. Because I love both Asian flavors and wine, I've spent more than a year experimenting with putting them together. Here's what I've discovered so far.

First of all, it's inaccurate to talk about Asian cuisine as a singular entity. The region is immense and, culinarily speaking, includes everything from absolutely subtle dishes to those so vibrantly spiced they make your mouth tingle. Still, what many of us find irresistible are the foods incorporating ingredients that can be hard on wine: soy sauce, fish sauce, chilies and chili paste, ginger, lemon grass, kaffir lime leaves, and hoisin sauce, plus spices and herbs like cardamom, cumin, coriander, five spice, curry powder, and Thai basil. Wonderful as they are in a dish, these flavors can flatten many wines, rob them of their fruity characteristics, and make them taste bitter, oaky, or too high in alcohol.

So what wines do work? Any that meet the following criteria.

• They aren't Chardonnay. Very oaky, toasty Chardonnays taste like 2-by-4s when paired with strong Asian flavors.

• They aren't Cabernet Sauvignon or Merlot. Tannic wines like these fight with Asian flavors, and the wines lose. They end up tasting bitter, lean, and mean.

• They're high in acid. Snappy, clean, high-acid wines are right in sync with Asian flavors. New Zealand Sauvignon Blancs, for instance, with their penetrating acidity and clean tropical flavors, are a sensa-

SUNSET'S STEALS OF THE MONTH

White Ochre 1998 and Red Ochre 1997 (McLaren Vale, Australia), $9 each. These two fabulous wines are made by the Australian producer d'Arenberg, known better for stunning wines that cost several times as much. White Ochre (Riesling, Chenin Blanc, and Sauvignon Blanc) is lightly aromatic and creamy. Red Ochre (Grenache and Shiraz) is packed with deliciously rustic berry, earth, and spice flavors.

— KAREN MACNEIL-FIFE

WINES FOR ASIAN DISHES

■ **Chateau St. Jean Johannisberg Riesling 1998 (Sonoma County),** $9. Beautifully aromatic and flavorful, with orange blossom and apricot notes.

■ **Handley Gewürztraminer 1998 (Anderson Valley, CA),** $14. Dramatic acidity, with an edge of litchi, ginger, and pear.

■ **Wild Horse Malvasia Bianca 1999 (Monterey County),** $13. Almost sorbet-like, with refreshing peach, tangerine, and litchi flavors.

■ **Cambria Tepusquet Vineyard Syrah 1998 (Santa Maria Valley, CA),** $22. Juicy boysenberry pie flavors and a fabulous dense, creamy texture.

■ **Rosemount Estate Shiraz 1999 (McLaren Vale, Australia),** $12. Wonderful berry fruit and a soft, supple texture.

tional match. So are unoaked Pinot Grigios from Italy and California. Or try a Pinot Gris from Oregon.

• They're wildly aromatic, with pronounced fruit flavors. Varieties like Gewürztraminer, Viognier, Riesling, and Malvasia Bianca are superb with Asian dishes. Look for Gewürztraminers from Alsace, Viogniers from California, and Rieslings from Alsace, California, Washington, or Australia.

• If they're red, they're big and jammy. Full-throttled, berry-fruited Zinfandels, Rhône blends, and Syrahs from California, as well as Shirazes from Australia, are all great matches.

And don't forget rosé. This unsung hero of a wine category is just begging to be drunk with Asian dishes. The single best match of all might be a rosé sparkling wine or Champagne.

A FATHER'S DAY IDEA

Yes, you could give him a bottle of wine, but here's something that will last a little longer—*The Oxford Companion to Wine* (Oxford University Press, New York, 1999; $65). The second edition of this book—the single best wine reference written in English—has just been released. With 3,400 entries organized alphabetically, it's easy to look up everything from Alsace to Château Margaux to Zinfandel. Thomas Jefferson and monks even have listings. More to the point, the book explores every wine region, grape variety, famous winemaker, and important time in wine history. And if your father is curious about technology, topics such as tannin maturity, malolactic fermentation, and yeast action should interest him— they are all explained with the lay reader in mind.

The thick *Oxford Companion to Wine* was written by more than 100 wine writers and edited by the highly regarded British wine expert Jancis Robinson. It's available at most bookstores. ◆

Why?

Answers to common cooking questions

By Linda Lau Anusasananan

Makings of teriyaki: sake, soy sauce, sugar, ginger, garlic.

Marinades at work

■ What's the point of marinating meats before cooking them? Anyone who has tasted a marinated steak from the grill knows the answer—it has more flavor. A marinade can pack chicken breasts, beef steak, and pork chops with lively seasonings.

Here's how it works: An effective marinade is a blend of ingredients that includes acid (such as wine, citrus juices, or vinegar), salt (or salty liquids such as soy sauce or fish sauce), and sugar (or other sweetener such as honey or jams and jellies), plus a variety of other flavorings. Each element helps draw the seasoned liquid into the spaces between meat fibers.

In simple terms, acid softens the tissues so the meat fibers can separate and the marinade can enter more easily; in doing so, it slightly tenderizes the meat. Salt transports the liquid into the tissues. Sugar holds the liquid there. The result is

meat that is juicier and a little more tender than nature made it.

Marinades penetrate ⅛ to ¼ inch in two to three hours; thin slices of meat get the maximum benefit of a marinade in as little as 5 to 10 minutes. After the tissues fill with liquid, they can't take in any more. Thicker cuts require more marinating time, but there is a limit, as they can absorb only so much flavor.

One of the most effective marinades is teriyaki. Intensely flavored, it blends the crucial elements—acid (in wine), salt (both acid and salt are in soy sauce), and sugar. Our basic teriyaki formula penetrates boldly; use it, and the flavor variations that follow, on many meats.

Teriyaki Grilled Meats

PREP AND COOK TIME: About 20 minutes, plus 2 hours to marinate

MAKES: 6 to 8 servings

¼ cup **sake** or dry sherry

¼ cup **soy sauce**

2 tablespoons **sugar**

1 tablespoon minced **fresh ginger**

2 cloves **garlic,** peeled and pressed

2½ to 3 pounds 1-inch-thick pieces of fat-trimmed **meat,** such as beef steak (flank, rib-eye, T-bone, porterhouse, top loin, or tenderloin), pork loin chops, or boned, skinned chicken breast halves

1. In a 1-gallon or larger heavy plastic food bag, mix sake, soy sauce, sugar,

ginger, and garlic.

2. Rinse meat, pat dry, and add to marinade. Seal bag and turn over to coat meat. Chill at least 2 hours or up to 1 day, turning bag over occasionally.

3. Lift meat from marinade; reserve marinade if desired. Lay meat on a barbecue grill over a solid bed of hot coals or a gas barbecue on high heat (you can hold your hand at grill level only 2 to 3 seconds). Cook, turning to brown each side, until beef is rare (125°), about 10 minutes total, or medium (135°), about 11 minutes total; or until pork and chicken are no longer pink in center of thickest part (cut to test), 12 to 14 minutes total.

4. Transfer meat to a platter and keep warm; let rest about 5 minutes. If desired, pour reserved marinade into a 1- to 2-quart pan and bring to a boil over high heat. Pour into a bowl and serve with meat, adding to taste.

Per serving pork loin chop: 197 cal., 40% (78 cal.) from fat; 26 g protein; 8.7 g fat (3.2 g sat.); 2.3 g carbo (0 g fiber); 325 mg sodium; 70 mg chol.

Chili Teriyaki

Follow directions for **teriyaki grilled meats** (preceding), adding ½ teaspoon **hot chili flakes** to the marinade in step 1.

Per serving beef flank steak: 244 cal., 48% (117 cal.) from fat; 28 g protein; 13 g fat (5.5 g sat.); 2.2 g carbo (0 g fiber); 352 mg sodium; 71 mg chol.

Teriyaki with Orange

Follow directions for **teriyaki grilled meats** (at left), adding 1 teaspoon grated **orange** peel to the marinade in step 1; instead of sake, use ¼ cup **orange juice.**

Per serving boned, skinned chicken breast: 167 cal., 10% (16 cal.) from fat; 33 g protein; 1.8 g fat (0.5 g sat.); 2.5 g carbo (0 g fiber); 360 mg sodium; 82 mg chol.

Teriyaki with Cumin

Follow directions for **teriyaki grilled meats** (at left), adding 1 teaspoon crushed **cumin seed** to the marinade in step 1.

Per serving beef rib-eye steak: 205 cal., 44% (90 cal.) from fat; 24 g protein; 10 g fat (4.1 g sat.); 2.5 g carbo (0 g fiber); 328 mg sodium; 69 mg chol. ◆

The Low-Fat Cook

Healthy choices for the active lifestyle
By Elaine Johnson

Deceptively creamy chili soup
harbors a hint of smoke—but little fat.

TUCKER & HOSSLER

Vegetable soups from the grill

■ Smoke from mesquite chips in your backyard grill can be a stellar ingredient—even in a bowl of soup. Lay some sweet summer corn, onions, and chilies (or red bell peppers or zucchini) on the barbecue, and they'll pick up intense, complex flavors from the smoldering wood as they cook. Then simply purée the vegetables with broth. From their flavor, you'd never guess that the resulting creamy all-vegetable soups have no extra fat. All of them taste good hot or cold, especially with crusty bread for dunking. Grilled shrimp on the side would complete the meal with style.

Smoked Chili-Corn Soup

PREP AND COOK TIME: About 50 minutes

NOTES: For the smoothest texture, use a blender to purée the soup. Serve at room temperature; stir soup over medium-high heat until steaming, about 6 minutes, and serve hot; or cover and chill until cool, about 1 hour or up to 1 day, and serve cold.

MAKES: About 6 cups; 4 servings

- 1 cup **mesquite wood chips**
- 1 **onion** (½ lb.), peeled and quartered lengthwise
- 1½ pounds **fresh poblano** (also called pasilla) **chilies** (6 or 7), rinsed
- 3 **ears corn** (about 6 in. long), husks and silks removed

- 3 cups fat-skimmed **chicken broth** or vegetable broth
  Salt and **pepper**
- ⅓ cup **nonfat** or reduced-fat **sour cream**

1. In a bowl, soak mesquite wood chips in 2 cups water for 30 minutes. Drain.

2. Lightly oil a barbecue grill over a solid bed of medium-hot coals or a gas grill on medium-high heat (you can hold your hand at grill level only 3 to 4 seconds). If using charcoal, sprinkle chips evenly over coals. If using gas, place chips in a metal smoking box or small, shallow foil pan and set directly on the heat in a corner of the grill. Lay onion, chilies, and corn on grill. Close lid on barbecue, or open vents for charcoal. Turn vegetables occasionally until they're charred in spots, and chilies and onion are soft when pressed, 15 to 25 minutes; transfer to a platter as cooked.

3. Let vegetables stand until cool enough to handle, about 10 minutes. Wearing gloves, pull off and discard chili skins, stems, and seeds. Cut kernels from corn cobs. Trim and discard any burnt edges from vegetables. Tear about half of 1 chili into thin strips and set aside; also set aside about ¼ cup corn kernels.

4. In a blender or food processor, whirl onion and remaining chilies and corn with the broth until very smooth (if desired, rub soup through a fine strainer into a bowl or a 2- to 3-quart pan). Add salt and pepper to taste.

5. Ladle soup into bowls, garnish with reserved chili strips and corn, and add equal portions of sour cream.

Per serving: 188 cal., 5% (11 cal.) from fat; 13 g protein; 1.3 g fat (0.2 g sat.); 36 g carbo (5.2 g fiber); 95 mg sodium; 2 mg chol.

Smoked Red Pepper–Corn Soup

PREP AND COOK TIME: About 40 minutes

MAKES: About 6 cups; 4 servings

Follow directions for **smoked chili-corn soup** (preceding), omitting chilies. Instead, use 4 **red bell peppers** (about ½ lb. each), rinsed. Pull off and discard pepper skins, stems, and seeds. When puréeing vegetables (step 4), add the ⅓ cup nonfat sour cream and 1 to 2 tablespoons **sherry vinegar** or red wine vinegar to taste. Garnish servings with chopped **parsley.**

Per serving: 189 cal., 6% (12 cal.) from fat; 12 g protein; 1.4 g fat (0.2 g sat.); 36 g carbo (6.4 g fiber); 90 mg sodium; 2 mg chol.

Smoked Zucchini-Corn Soup

PREP AND COOK TIME: About 1 hour

MAKES: About 6 cups; 4 servings

Follow directions for **smoked chili-corn soup** (at left), omitting chilies. Instead, use 2¼ pounds **zucchini,** rinsed and ends trimmed. Cut cool zucchini into chunks to purée. Season soup to taste with 2 to 3 tablespoons **lime juice.**

Per serving: 176 cal., 7% (13 cal.) from fat; 13 g protein; 1.4 g fat (0.2 g sat.); 32 g carbo (4.7 g fiber); 96 mg sodium; 2 mg. chol. ◆

Golden, citrus-flavored shortcake flaunts fresh berries and a cloud of whipped cream.

Summer's best shortcakes

One classic dessert shapes up four ways, to mix and match with chocolate, cream, and fresh berries

By Elaine Johnson

A pastry on call in the summer, shortcake sets off the year's most abundant collection of fresh berries—and is a master of metamorphosis. In the first place, shortcakes are really just light, flaky biscuits that have been turned into slightly sweeter and richer cakes with small but significant ingredient shifts.

Drawing on its capacity for personality change, we started with a classic formula, then kept adjusting, just for fun—adding big chocolate chunks to the pastry, mixing the traditional strawberries with boysenberries, raspberries, and other seasonal stars. Then we played with its form: One tweak reshapes the shortcake into an easy cobbler, another produces sconelike wedges. One "berry" flexible concept, four beautiful desserts.

Classic Berry Shortcakes

PREP AND COOK TIME: About 45 minutes
MAKES: 8 servings

About 2 cups **all-purpose flour**
About ²⁄₃ cup **sugar**
2 teaspoons **baking powder**
1 teaspoon grated **lemon** peel
1 teaspoon grated **orange** peel
½ teaspoon **baking soda**
½ teaspoon **salt**
½ cup (¼ lb.) **butter** or margarine, cut into chunks
2 **large egg** yolks
²⁄₃ cup **buttermilk**
2 quarts **berries,** rinsed and drained (use one kind or mix several), such as blueberries, boysenberries, loganberries, olallieberries, raspberries, or hulled strawberries
1 cup **whipping cream**

1. In a bowl, combine 2 cups flour, ⅓ cup sugar, baking powder, lemon peel, orange peel, baking soda, and salt. With a pastry blender or your fingers, cut or rub in butter until coarse crumbs form.

2. In another bowl, mix egg yolks and buttermilk to blend. Add to flour mixture; stir with a fork until evenly moistened.

3. Scrape dough onto a floured board. With floured hands, knead just until smooth, 15 to 20 turns, adding more flour as required to prevent sticking.

4. Pat dough 1 inch thick. With a floured 2½-inch-wide cutter, cut dough into rounds. Transfer each to a 12- by 15-inch baking sheet, spacing evenly. Gather dough scraps into a ball, knead briefly, pat 1 inch thick, cut more rounds, and add to baking sheet.

5. Bake shortcakes in a 400° oven (375° in a convection oven) until browned, 10 to 15 minutes. Transfer to a rack and let cool at least 10 minutes.

6. Meanwhile, slice strawberries, if using. In a bowl, gently mix berries with 2 to 4 tablespoons sugar to taste. Let stand at room temperature up to 1 hour.

7. In a bowl with a mixer on high speed, whip cream until it holds soft peaks; add about 2 tablespoons sugar to taste.

8. Split shortcakes in half horizontally. Place bottoms on plates. Cover equally with berry mixture and whipped cream. Set tops in place.

Per serving: 428 cal., 48% (207 cal.) from fat; 6.5 g protein; 23 g fat (14 g sat.); 51 g carbo (4.8 g fiber); 498 mg sodium; 118 mg chol.

Chocolate Berry Shortcakes

Follow directions for classic berry shortcakes (facing page), but add ⅓ cup coarsely chopped **semisweet chocolate** to egg yolks and buttermilk in step 2. Use only strawberries.

Per serving: 462 cal., 49% (225 cal.) from fat; 6.8 g protein; 25 g fat (15 g sat.); 55 g carbo (5.3 g fiber); 499 mg sodium; 118 mg chol.

Berry Cobbler Shortcake

PREP AND COOK TIME: About 1 hour
NOTES: Priscilla Yee of Concord, California, shares this recipe.
MAKES: 8 servings

- 2 cups **all-purpose flour**
- About 1⅓ cups **sugar**
- 2 teaspoons **baking powder**
- 1 teaspoon grated **lemon** peel
- 1 teaspoon grated **orange** peel
- ½ teaspoon **baking soda**
- ½ teaspoon **salt**
- About ¾ cup (⅜ lb.) **butter** or margarine, cut into chunks
- 2 **large eggs**
- ⅔ cup **buttermilk**
- 2 quarts **berries**, rinsed and drained (use one kind or mix several), such as blueberries, boysenberries, loganberries, olallieberries, raspberries, or hulled strawberries
- 1 cup **whipping cream**

1. In a bowl, combine flour, 1 cup sugar, baking powder, lemon peel, orange peel, baking soda, and salt. With a pastry blender or your fingers, cut or rub in ¾ cup butter until coarse crumbs form.

2. In another bowl, mix eggs and buttermilk to blend. Add to flour mixture; stir with a fork until evenly moistened. Spread batter in a buttered shallow 9- by 13-inch casserole.

3. Slice strawberries, if using. In a bowl, mix berries with ¼ cup sugar. Spoon 3 cups berries evenly over batter. If desired, sweeten remaining berries with more sugar to taste.

4. Bake cobbler in a 350° oven until browned, 30 to 40 minutes.

5. Meanwhile, in a bowl with a mixer on high speed, whip cream until it holds soft peaks; sweeten with about 2 tablespoons sugar to taste.

6. Cut warm or cool cobbler into 8 portions. With a wide spatula, transfer portions to plates. Top equally with remaining berries and whipped cream.

Per serving: 554 cal., 47% (261 cal.) from fat; 7.2 g protein; 29 g fat (18 g sat.); 68 g carbo (4.8 g fiber); 578 mg sodium; 136 mg chol.

Orange Shortcake Wedges

PREP AND COOK TIME: About 40 minutes
MAKES: 8 servings

- About 3 cups **all-purpose flour**
- About ¾ cup **sugar**
- 2 teaspoons grated **orange** peel
- 1 teaspoon **baking soda**
- ½ teaspoon **baking powder**
- ½ cup (¼ lb.) **butter** or margarine, cut into chunks
- ¾ cup **buttermilk**
- 2 quarts sliced **strawberries**, sweetened to taste with sugar
- **Sour cream orange sauce** (recipe follows)

1. In a bowl, combine 3 cups flour, ¾ cup sugar, orange peel, baking soda, and baking powder. With a pastry blender or your fingers, cut or rub in butter until fine crumbs form. Add buttermilk and stir with a fork until dough is evenly moistened.

2. Scrape dough onto a floured board; with floured hands, knead just until dough holds together, 15 to 20 turns, adding more flour as required to prevent sticking.

3. On a buttered 12- by 15-inch baking sheet, pat dough into a neat 9-inch-wide round. With a long floured knife, cut through dough to pan, making 8 equal wedges; leave in place. Sprinkle dough lightly with sugar.

4. Bake in a 375° oven until golden brown, 25 to 35 minutes. Let cool on pan about 10 minutes. Separate wedges, cut shortcakes in half horizontally, and lift off tops. Set bottoms on dessert plates, cover equally with about half the strawberries and their juice; spoon about half the sour cream sauce equally onto fruit. Set shortcake tops in place, mound remaining berries equally on portions; top with remaining sauce.

Per serving: 412 cal., 28% (117 cal.) from fat; 6.8 g protein; 13 g fat (7.7 g sat.); 68 g carbo (5.3 g fiber); 337 mg sodium; 33 mg chol.

Sour cream orange sauce. In a bowl, stir together 3 cups **sour cream**, ¾ cup **powdered sugar**, and 1½ teaspoons grated **orange** peel. Makes 3¼ cups.

Per tablespoon: 35 cal., 71% (25 cal.) from fat; 0.4 g protein; 2.8 g fat (1.7 g sat.); 2.3 g carbo (0 g fiber); 7 mg sodium; 5.8 mg chol. ◆

What's brewing in Forest Grove?

A spiffy new brew pub–hotel comes to this Oregon town

■ What do you do with a retired Masonic convalescent home? If you're McMenamins, a Northwest chain of brew pubs and hotels, you inject a little new blood (make that, new beer) into the old building and reopen it as the **Grand Lodge**. The Forest Grove, Oregon, landmark, built in 1922, now has 77 guest rooms, a brew pub, a wine-tasting room, and lots of colorful murals. *3505 Pacific Ave.; (877) 992-9533 or (503) 992-9533.*

Though the beer-bed-and-breakfast is the biggest news in Forest Grove of late, it isn't the only game in town. Nearby you can drop in at the **SakéOne** rice wine brewery. Unlike the sake familiar to most fans of Japanese food, the fruit-flavored and premium wines produced here are served cold. *Tasting room open 12–5 Sat-Sun. 820 Elm St.; (503) 357-7056.*

If rice wine isn't your cup of tea, head south on State 47 to **Montinore Vineyards**. Here you can sample wines of a more traditional stripe, especially Pinot Noirs—and maybe take in a summertime jazz concert. In 2000, concerts were scheduled for July 16, July 30, and September 3. *3663 S.W. Dilley Rd.; (503) 359-5012.*

— *Karl Samson* ◆

Kitchen Cabinet

Readers' recipes tested in Sunset's kitchens

By Andrew Baker

Cobb salad toys with tradition: Shelled cooked crab and shrimp crown cumin-, cilantro-, and citrus-dressed greens.

JAMES CARRIER (2)

Seafood Cobb Salad

Wendy Nankeville, Novato, California

A big fan of cobb salad, Wendy Nankeville realized she had never tried it with seafood. She found this version to be "a great combination of tastes and textures." Use shelled cooked crab, shelled cooked shrimp, 1-inch-wide scallops, or a combination. To cook scallops, bring 1 quart of water to a boil in a 2- to 3-quart pan. Meanwhile, rinse scallops; add them to boiling water, remove from heat, cover, and let stand until opaque but still moist-looking in center of thickest part (cut to test), about 2 minutes. Drain.

PREP AND COOK TIME: About 40 minutes

MAKES: 4 main-course servings

- ¼ cup **lime juice**
- ¼ cup **olive oil**
- 1 tablespoon **Dijon mustard**
- 1 tablespoon **balsamic vinegar**
- 2 tablespoons minced **fresh cilantro**
- 1 teaspoon minced **garlic**
- 1 teaspoon **sugar**
- ½ teaspoon **ground cumin**
- 2 quarts shredded **romaine lettuce**
- 1 pound (about 3 cups) **cooked shellfish** (see notes)
- ¾ cup diced **tomato**
- ⅔ cup finely diced **red onion**
- 1 **firm-ripe avocado** (6 oz.), peeled, pitted, and diced
- ¾ cup **crumbled blue cheese**
  Salt and fresh-ground **pepper**

1. In a large bowl, mix lime juice, oil, mustard, vinegar, cilantro, garlic, sugar, and cumin.

2. Add romaine and lift with 2 forks to coat with dressing. With a slotted spoon, transfer lettuce equally to individual wide bowls.

3. Add shellfish to dressing in bowl and mix gently. Spoon an equal amount of shellfish and dressing onto lettuce in each bowl, arranging in a 2-inch-wide band across the center.

4. Arrange equal bands of tomato, onion, avocado, and blue cheese on each salad. Season to taste with salt and pepper.

Per serving: 498 cal., 61% (306 cal.) from fat; 37 g protein; 34 g fat (12 g sat.); 13 g carbo (3.4 g fiber); 1,048 mg sodium; 202 mg chol.

Peach Cream Roll

Carlyn Roedell, Burien, Washington

One day Carlyn Roedell's husband requested his favorite cake, a cream roll filled with berries, but she didn't have any berries on hand. She gave peaches a try instead, and liked the result.

PREP AND COOK TIME: About 45 minutes

MAKES: 8 servings

- About 1 cup **all-purpose flour**
- 3 **large eggs**
- 1 cup **granulated sugar**
- 2 teaspoons **vanilla**
- 1 teaspoon **baking powder**
- ¼ teaspoon **salt**
- ¾ pound **firm-ripe peaches**
- 1 tablespoon **lemon juice**
- 1½ cups **whipping cream**
- 1 tablespoon **powdered sugar**

1. Butter a 10- by 15-inch pan. Line with waxed paper cut to fit, then butter again and dust with flour.

2. In a large bowl, with a mixer on high speed, beat eggs until they hold soft mounds, about 5 minutes. Gradually beat in granulated sugar. Stir in 1 teaspoon vanilla and ⅓ cup water, and beat just to blend.

3. In a small bowl, mix 1 cup flour, baking powder, and salt; add to egg mixture and mix until well blended. Pour batter into prepared pan and spread level.

4. Bake in a 375° oven until cake is browned and beginning to pull from pan edges, and center springs back when lightly pressed, 12 to 15 minutes.

5. Let stand 3 to 4 minutes, then run a thin knife between cake and pan edge, and invert cake onto a rack. Gently pull off and discard waxed paper. Let cake cool at least 10 minutes. Lay a clean dish towel on cake. Holding towel and rack together, invert cake onto towel. Trim off firm cake edges to make a neat rectangle.

6. Immerse peaches in boiling water for about 30 seconds; lift out and let cool slightly. Pull off and discard skins; cut fruit in half, cut from pits into ¼- to ½-inch slices, and drop into a bowl. Add lemon juice and mix gently to coat.

7. In a deep bowl with a mixer on high speed, whip cream until it holds soft peaks. Stir in powdered sugar and remaining 1 teaspoon vanilla. Spread about 1 cup whipped cream mixture in an even layer over cake. Lay peach slices on cream.

8. From a long side of the cake, lift towel to guide cake into a smooth, compact roll. Transfer cake, seam down, to a platter. Spread roll with remaining whipped cream mixture. Slice crosswise and serve, or cover (keep cover from touching cream) and chill up to 1 day.

Per serving: 340 cal., 45% (153 cal.) from fat; 5.1 g protein; 17 g fat (9.7 g sat.); 43 g carbo (0.9 g fiber); 180 mg sodium; 131 mg chol.

Serve zesty bean spread on crisp slices of toasted French bread or colorful radicchio leaves.

Italian Bean Spread

Roxanne Chan, Albany, California

Roxanne Chan combined three of her son's favorite ingredients—white beans, olives, and parmesan cheese—with herbs and lemons from her garden for this quick appetizer. Serve on toasted baguette slices or in radicchio cups.

PREP AND COOK TIME: About 20 minutes

NOTES: If making ahead, chill airtight up to 1 day.

MAKES: 3 cups; about 8 servings

- 2 cans (15 oz. each) **small white beans,** rinsed and drained
- 1/2 cup **sour cream**
- 1 jar (2 oz.) **diced pimientos**
- 2 tablespoons finely chopped **black ripe olives**
- 1 tablespoon minced **red onion**
- 1 tablespoon chopped **parsley**
- 1 tablespoon **fresh oregano** leaves or 1 teaspoon dried oregano
- 1 tablespoon **lemon juice**
- 1/2 teaspoon grated **lemon** peel
- 1/2 teaspoon **pepper**
- 1/4 cup **grated parmesan cheese**

1. In a bowl, with a potato masher or mixer, mash beans with sour cream until smooth.

2. Add pimientos, olives, onion, parsley, oregano, lemon juice, lemon peel, pepper, and parmesan cheese. Stir to combine. Scrape into a serving bowl.

Per tablespoon: 18 cal., 35% (6.3 cal.) from fat; 0.9 g protein; 0.7 g fat (0.4 g sat.); 1.9 g carbo (0 5 g fiber); 41 mg sodium; 1.4 mg chol.

Garden Harvest Stuffed Zucchini

Lynne Robinson, Paso Robles, California

When Lynne Robinson's father-in-law brought her an extra-large zucchini from his garden, she wanted to prepare it for him during his stay. She concocted this satisfying filling. Look for larger-than-average zucchini at farmers' markets, or use smaller zucchini as called for in the recipe.

PREP AND COOK TIME: About 1 1/2 hours

MAKES: 6 servings

- 6 **zucchini** (8 oz. each)
- 3/4 pound **ground lean beef**
- 1/3 cup finely chopped **onion**
- 1 teaspoon minced or pressed **garlic**
- 1 can (15 oz.) **stewed tomatoes**
- 3/4 cup fat-skimmed **beef broth**
- 2 tablespoons minced **parsley**
- 1/2 cup **long-grain white rice**
- 2 tablespoons **shredded parmesan cheese**
  Salt and **pepper**

1. Rinse zucchini. Trim and discard ends; cut zucchini in half lengthwise. Scoop out centers, making shells that are about 1/4 inch thick. Finely chop zucchini centers.

2. In a 10- to 12-inch frying pan over high heat, frequently stir beef with onion and garlic until mixture is browned, about 10 minutes. Add chopped zucchini, tomatoes with juice, broth, parsley, and rice. Bring to a boil, cover, reduce heat, and simmer until rice is tender to bite, about 20 minutes; let cool slightly.

3. Spoon meat mixture equally into zucchini shells, patting down firmly.

Place shells in a single layer in an 11- by 17-inch baking pan. Add 1/2 cup water and cover tightly.

4. Bake in a 350° oven until zucchini shells are tender, 40 to 45 minutes (20 to 25 minutes in a convection oven). Uncover, sprinkle with parmesan, and bake 2 to 3 minutes longer.

5. Use a wide spatula to transfer zucchini to dinner plates. Add salt and pepper to taste.

Per serving: 272 cal., 43% (117 cal.) from fat; 16 g protein; 13 g fat (5.1 g sat.); 25 g carbo (2.2 g fiber); 244 mg sodium; 44 mg chol.

Nouvelle Lamb Paprikas

Stephen Nagy, Clancy, Montana

Stephen Nagy updated his mother's favorite lamb recipe with balsamic vinegar and garlic. The complex combination of flavors in the sauce, he says, "worships the richness of the lamb."

PREP AND COOK TIME: About 30 minutes

MAKES: 4 servings

- 3/4 pound **firm-ripe tomatoes,** rinsed, cored, and chopped
- 4 teaspoons **balsamic vinegar**
- 1 teaspoon chopped **garlic**
- 1 tablespoon firmly packed **brown sugar**
  About 1/8 teaspoon **cayenne**
- 8 **lamb rib chops** (about 1 3/4 lb. total) or 4 sirloin (leg) chops (each about 3/4 in. thick; about 2 lb. total), fat trimmed
- 1 tablespoon **paprika**
- 1/2 teaspoon fresh-ground **pepper**
- 1 tablespoon **olive oil**
- 2 tablespoons minced **parsley**
  Salt

1. In blender or food processor, whirl tomatoes, vinegar, garlic, and brown sugar until smooth. Add cayenne to taste.

2. Rinse lamb and pat dry. Rub chops all over with paprika and pepper.

3. Pour oil into a 5- to 6-quart pan over high heat. When hot, add the lamb chops and turn as needed to brown evenly, about 1 minute total.

4. Pour tomato mixture over chops; cover, reduce heat, and simmer, stirring occasionally, until sauce begins to brown and thicken, 15 to 20 minutes.

5. Transfer lamb chops to wide, shallow bowls and spoon sauce evenly over them. Sprinkle with parsley and add salt to taste.

Per serving: 609 cal., 80% (486 cal.) from fat; 22 g protein; 54 g fat (23 g sat.); 9 g carbo (1.3 g fiber); 92 mg sodium; 110 mg chol. ◆

Prizewinning barbecue recipes: Sauceless-in-Seattle Ribs wins top honors in Sunset's Barbecue Cook-off; see page 188.

July

Sunset's
barbecue
cook-off 2000

Prizewinning recipes for ribs, burgers, salmon—even prime rib
and pizza—show off grilling at its Western best

By Elaine Johnson • Food photographs by James Carrier • Portraits by Terrence McCarthy • Food styling by Julie Smith

■ As far as cooking methods go, barbecuing is a blast. That's why, last summer, we invited you to submit your favorite grilling creations for a grand cook-off here at *Sunset* headquarters in Menlo Park, California.

Hundreds of recipes poured in for five categories: steaks, ribs, and chops; burgers; seafood; poultry; and wild cards. There were classic ribs and burgers, some with a twist, and eyebrow-raising Yorkshire pudding (it worked, and won!) and banana splits (intriguing idea—stay tuned for a future story). *Sunset's* food staff narrowed the entries to the most promising 75, all of which we tested in our

kitchens. A tasting panel selected 15 finalists, 3 in each category, to be our guests for a weekend at *Sunset* and prepare their dishes for our judges. Technique, appearance, and flavor were the criteria for the five best-of-category winners and one grand prize (see page 199).

All 15 finalists, however, understand the magical interaction of superb ingredients, a hot grill, and smoke. They also know how to make a mean sauce. Here are their recipes. Instructions for grilling start on page 198. We raise our barbecue tongs to everyone who entered the contest: for your innovation, talent with flavors, and sense of fun.

STEAKS, RIBS, AND CHOPS

Dan Peters
Federal Way, Washington

GRAND PRIZE

Once again, necessity is the mother of invention. "I had friends over for a barbecue," recalls Dan Peters, a veterinary pharmaceuticals sales rep and avid sculptor, rock-and-roll musician, paraglider—and cook. "The ribs were on the grill, and I went to the kitchen for barbecue sauce. The cupboard was bare. But my friends had just returned from picking blackberries. I rummaged around and found ginger, catsup, and a few other things, heated them with the berries in the microwave, and smeared it on the ribs." Voilà.

Peters's friend Carol SinClair liked the sauce so much that after dinner she made him write down the recipe. Then she sent it to us. "I knew Dan wouldn't enter the contest himself," SinClair says.

Our judges gave Peters's ribs top marks for succulence, simplicity, and that addictive sweet-hot blackberry glaze.

Sauceless-in-Seattle Ribs

PREP AND COOK TIME: About 1½ hours
MAKES: 4 servings

- 1 section **pork spareribs** (about 4 lb.)
  Blackberry sauce (recipe follows)
- ¾ cup **blackberries**, rinsed
  Mint sprigs

1. Rinse ribs and pat dry. Trim and discard excess fat.

2. Prepare barbecue for ***indirect heat*** (see page 199). When grill is ***medium-hot,*** lay ribs on it and turn as needed until well browned, 40 to 50 minutes.

3. Baste 1 side of ribs with half the sauce. Turn ribs sauce side down and cook until sauce browns and forms a thick, sticky glaze, about 10 minutes. Baste top of ribs with remaining sauce, turn over, and cook until sauce browns and forms a thick, sticky glaze, about 10 minutes longer.

4. Transfer ribs to a platter and garnish

Succulent spareribs are slathered with a glaze made from blackberries, ginger, and hot sauce, then crowned with more berries.

with blackberries and mint. Cut between bones to separate portions.

Per serving: 878 cal., 55% (486 cal.) from fat; 52 g protein; 54 g fat (20 g sat.); 45 g carbo (3.8 g fiber); 383 mg sodium; 214 mg chol.

Blackberry sauce. In a food processor or blender, combine 1¼ cups rinsed **blackberries**; ¼ cup *each* cat-

sup, **honey,** firmly packed **brown sugar,** and minced **fresh ginger;** 1 teaspoon **pepper;** and ½ teaspoon **salt** (optional). Whirl until berries are puréed. Add 1 to 2 teaspoons **hot sauce** to taste. Pour into a 1-quart glass measure (or combine ingredients in glass measure and mash with a mixer or potato masher). Cover loosely with

microwave-safe plastic wrap, leaving vents for steam. Cook in a microwave oven at full power (100%), stirring occasionally, until berry mixture is reduced to 1⅓ cups, about 8 minutes. Makes 1⅓ cups.

Per serving: 161 cal., 1.7% (2.7 cal.) from fat; 0.8 g protein; 0.3 g fat (0 g sat.); 42 g carbo (2.5 g fiber); 218 mg sodium; 0 mg chol.

Roxanne and Bock Chan
Albany, California

BEST OF CATEGORY

Roxanne Chan's name might be familiar to *Sunset* readers. Since the 1970s we've published scores of her recipes, and she was a winner in our 1998 Centennial Cook-off. But this is the first time she has collaborated with her husband, Bock.

"In our family, I do all the everyday cooking and develop recipes, but I don't start fires or grill. That's Bock's domain," Roxanne explains. For this contest the couple's team efforts were successful enough to win finalist slots in *two* categories. Here, a mellow mixture reminiscent of mole serves as both marinade and sauce for flank steak to wrap with a multicolored pepper relish in tortillas.

Fiesta Fajitas

PREP AND COOK TIME: About 1 hour, plus at least 1 hour to marinate

NOTES: If using charcoal, add 10 briquets after peppers are cooked (step 3).

MAKES: 4 to 6 servings

- 1 **flank steak** (1½ lb.), fat trimmed
  Fiesta sauce (recipe follows)
- 8 to 12 **flour tortillas** (8 in. wide)
- 3 **bell peppers** (1⅓ lb. total; 1 *each* red, green, and yellow, or all 1 color), rinsed
  Sour cream
  Lime wedges
  Salt

1. Rinse steak and pat dry. Place steak and half the fiesta sauce in a 1-gallon plastic food bag. Seal bag; turn to coat meat. Chill at least 1 hour or up to 1 day.

2. Stack tortillas and seal in foil. Pour remaining sauce into a 1- to 1½-quart ovenproof pan.

3. Prepare barbecue for **direct heat** (see page 198). When it is **medium-hot,** lay peppers on grill. Turn as needed until skins are charred on all sides, 15 to 20 minutes. With tongs, transfer peppers to a plate and let stand until cool enough to handle, 10 to 15 minutes.

4. Pull off and discard skins, stems, and seeds from peppers. Chop peppers and place in a bowl.

5. Meanwhile, lift steak from bag; discard marinade. Lay meat on grill and turn as needed until browned on each side and medium-rare in center of thickest part (cut to test), 10 to 15 minutes total. After 5 minutes, set tortilla packet and pan of sauce on grill. Turn tortillas often until hot (open packet to check), about 5 minutes. Stir sauce frequently until bubbling, about 5 minutes. Enclose tortillas in a towel to keep warm; pour sauce into a bowl.

6. Transfer steak to a board. Cut across the grain into thin slices.

7. Fill tortillas equally with meat and peppers. Add sauce, sour cream, juice from lime wedges, and salt to taste. Fold to enclose filling and hold to eat.

Per serving: 435 cal., 29% (126 cal.) from fat; 25 g protein; 14 g fat (3.8 g sat.); 52 g carbo (4 g fiber); 662 mg sodium; 41 mg chol.

Fiesta sauce. In a blender or food processor, combine 1 cup fat-skimmed **beef broth;** ½ cup **chili sauce;** 2 tablespoons *each* **raisins, sliced almonds,** chopped **fresh cilantro,** and chopped **green onions** (including tops); 1 tablespoon *each* **dried instant coffee, unsweetened cocoa, Worcestershire,** and **olive oil;** 2 teaspoons minced **garlic;** and 1 **canned chipotle chili** or 2 teaspoons hot sauce. Whirl until smooth. Makes 1¾ cups.

Per serving: 137 cal., 41% (56 cal.) from fat; 4.1 g protein; 6.2 g fat (0.8 g sat.); 19 g carbo (1.1 g fiber); 641 mg sodium; 0 mg chol.

Lynn Nicholson
Portland

FINALIST

"I'm in the travel business, and for many years I escorted scuba-diving groups throughout the Fiji and Tonga islands," Lynn Nicholson explains. "We enjoyed many impromptu meals featuring coconut milk–marinated pork, barbecued over open fires." Nicholson experimented until she perfected a recipe that captures those fragrant South Pacific flavors.

Steak and peppers are embellished with a complex chili sauce that mixes raisins, nuts, and chocolate.

Bula Barbecued Baby Back Ribs

PREP AND COOK TIME: About 1 hour, plus at least 2 hours to marinate

NOTES: *Bula* means *welcome* in Fijian. Asian chili-garlic sauce and toasted sesame seed are available in Asian food markets and many well-stocked supermarkets. Nicholson serves the ribs with grilled green onions and basmati rice to soak up the extra sauce.

MAKES: 6 to 8 servings

6 pounds **pork back ribs**

South Pacific marinade (recipe follows)

Chopped **fresh cilantro**

Toasted sesame seed (optional)

Salt

1. Rinse ribs and pat dry. Trim and discard excess fat. If needed, cut ribs into sections that will lie flat in a 6- to 8-quart pan. Put ribs and marinade in pan and mix to coat. Cover pan and chill at least 2 hours or up to 1 day, turning ribs occasionally.

2. Prepare barbecue for *indirect heat* (see page 199). When barbecue is *medium-hot*, lift ribs from pan; reserve marinade. Lay meat on grill, cover barbecue (open vents for charcoal), and turn as needed until well browned on each side, about 40 minutes total.

3. Meanwhile, bring reserved marinade to a boil over high heat, stirring occasionally. Pour into a bowl.

4. Transfer ribs to a platter. Sprinkle with cilantro and sesame seed. Add salt and reserved marinade to taste.

Per serving: 817 cal., 68% (558 cal.) from fat; 42 g protein; 62 g fat (28 g sat.); 21 g carbo (0.4 g fiber); 965 mg sodium; 194 mg chol.

South Pacific marinade. Pull off and discard tough outer layers from 2 stalks of **fresh lemon grass.** Trim and discard stem ends and coarse tops. Cut tender stalks into chunks. In a food processor or blender, combine lemon grass, 1 can (14 oz.) **coconut milk,** ½ cup *each* coarsely chopped **fresh cilantro** and firmly packed **brown sugar,** ⅓ cup **soy sauce,** ¼ cup coarsely chopped **shallots,** and 2 tablespoons *each* chopped **garlic,** chopped **fresh ginger, Asian** (toasted) **sesame oil, hoisin sauce,** and **Asian chili-garlic sauce.** Whirl until smooth. Makes 3 cups.

Per serving: 210 cal., 60% (126 cal.) from fat; 1.9 g protein; 14 g fat (9.8 g sat.); 21 g carbo (0.4 g fiber); 800 mg sodium; 0 mg chol.

Juicy lamb burgers with mint and garlic are dressed with creamy avocado sauce.

BURGERS

Meredith Kornfeld
San Rafael, California

BEST OF CATEGORY

"The story behind my burgers is embarrassingly simple," confides Meredith Kornfeld, an aspiring food writer. "I was stirring together a *tsatsiki* sauce of yogurt and mint to go with lamb burgers. But I didn't want to include the texture of cucumber [a typical tsatsiki component]. I happened to have some avocado. It added a nice color and cut the yogurt's tang. I knew I had a keeper."

Mediterranean Lamb Burgers

PREP AND COOK TIME: About 1 hour
MAKES: 4 servings

2 cups thinly sliced **red onions**

1¼ pounds **ground lean lamb**

¼ cup minced **fresh mint** leaves

4 teaspoons minced **garlic**

About ½ teaspoon **salt**

About ½ teaspoon **pepper**

1 **ripe avocado** (½ lb.)

⅔ cup **plain low-fat yogurt**

4 **pocket breads** (6 in. wide), cut in half crosswise

Romaine lettuce leaves, rinsed and crisped

1. Immerse onions in ice water for about 30 minutes; drain.

2. Meanwhile, in a bowl, mix lamb with 3 tablespoons mint, 1 tablespoon garlic, and ½ teaspoon *each* salt and pepper. Divide mixture into 8 equal portions; shape each into a 3½-inch-wide patty and set in a single layer on plastic wrap.

3. Pit and peel avocado. In another bowl, mash avocado with yogurt, remaining 1 tablespoon mint and 1 teaspoon garlic, and salt and pepper to taste.

4. Prepare barbecue for *direct heat* (see page 198). When grill is *very hot,* oil grill and lay lamb patties on it. Brown patties on each side, turning once, until no longer pink in center of thickest part (cut to test), 4 to 5 minutes total, or until done to your taste.

5. With a wide spatula, transfer each burger to a pocket bread half. Add equal portions of onions, lettuce, and avocado sauce. Season to taste with more salt and pepper.

Per serving: 573 cal., 42% (243 cal.) from fat; 34 g protein; 27 g fat (9.4 g sat.); 48 g carbo (3.6 g fiber); 732 mg sodium; 97 mg chol.

Roxanne and Bock Chan

Albany, California

FINALISTS

"Our family loves the Spanish flavors of paella and gazpacho," Roxanne Chan says, "so we decided to combine them." The Chans' ingenious saffron-flavored poultry burgers conceal a surprise—whole shrimp. Gazpacho relish adds more zing.

Paella Burgers with Gazpacho Relish

PREP AND COOK TIME: About 50 minutes

NOTES: Garnish with black ripe olives speared on toothpicks.

MAKES: 4 servings

- $\frac{1}{8}$ teaspoon **saffron threads**
- 1 pound **ground chicken** or turkey
- $\frac{1}{2}$ pound **bulk pork sausage**
- $\frac{1}{2}$ cup **soft white bread crumbs**
- $\frac{1}{2}$ teaspoon grated **lemon** peel
- $\frac{1}{2}$ teaspoon **pepper**
- 4 **shelled, deveined shrimp** (20 to 25 per lb.)
- 4 **sandwich rolls** or hamburger buns (about 3 oz. each), cut in half horizontally
- 2 tablespoons **olive oil**

  Gazpacho relish (recipe follows)

  Red leaf lettuce leaves, rinsed and crisped

1. Crumble saffron into a large bowl. Add 2 tablespoons warm water and let stand until saffron is limp, about 5 minutes. Add ground chicken, sausage, bread crumbs, lemon peel, and pepper; mix well.

2. Divide mixture into 8 equal portions; shape each into a 4$\frac{1}{2}$-inch-wide patty and set in a single layer on plastic wrap. Place 1 shrimp in the center of each of 4 patties. Cover each shrimp with another patty and press patties together to seal.

3. Brush cut sides of rolls equally with olive oil.

4. Prepare barbecue for ***direct heat*** (see page 198). When grill is ***medium-hot,*** oil grill. Lay patties on it and brown on each side, turning once, until no longer pink in center of thickest part (cut to test), about 6 minutes total. One to three minutes before meat is done, place rolls cut side down on grill and toast until golden.

5. Transfer roll bottoms, cut sides up, to a platter. With a wide spatula, set a burger on each bottom. Spoon relish equally over burgers, arrange a lettuce leaf on each, and cover with roll tops.

Per serving: 725 cal., 50% (360 cal.) from fat; 38 g protein; 40 g fat (11 g sat.); 50 g carbo (2.6 g fiber); 958 mg sodium; 199 mg chol.

Gazpacho relish. In a bowl, mix 1 cup chopped **firm-ripe tomato,** $\frac{1}{4}$ cup chopped **English cucumber,** 4 teaspoons minced seeded **fresh jalapeño chili,** 1 tablespoon minced **red onion,** 1 tablespoon chopped **fresh oregano** leaves or 1 teaspoon dried oregano, 1 tablespoon **white wine vinegar,** 1$\frac{1}{2}$ teaspoons **olive oil,** 1 teaspoon minced **garlic,** and $\frac{1}{2}$ teaspoon **Worcestershire.** Season to taste with **salt** and **pepper.** Makes about 1$\frac{1}{4}$ cups.

Per serving: 34 cal., 50% (17 cal.) from fat; 0.8 g protein; 1.9 g fat (0.8 g sat.); 4.1 g carbo (0.9 g fiber); 13 mg sodium; 0.5 mg chol.

Sherlyne Hutchinson

Cornelius, Oregon

FINALIST

Looking for something a little more gourmet than plain grilled hamburgers, Sherlyne Hutchinson came up with the concept of a knife-and-fork cheeseburger stack with taco seasonings. Instead of a bun, she rests each burger on a grilled mushroom cap, then layers green chilies and sliced tomato, onion, and avocado on top.

Portabella Taco Burgers

PREP AND COOK TIME: About 55 minutes

NOTES: Even though these burgers are well done, they are moist. If you want to serve them as sandwiches, enclose the whole burger stack in buns.

MAKES: 4 servings

- 4 **portabella mushrooms** (about 4$\frac{1}{2}$ in. wide, $\frac{3}{4}$ lb. total)
- 1 pound **ground beef chuck**
- $\frac{1}{2}$ cup chopped **spinach**
- $\frac{1}{2}$ cup **soft white bread crumbs**
- 3 tablespoons minced **fresh cilantro**
- 1 **large egg** white
- 1$\frac{1}{2}$ tablespoons **chili powder**
- 1$\frac{1}{2}$ teaspoons **ground cumin**
- 1 teaspoon **dried oregano**

  About $\frac{1}{2}$ teaspoon **salt**

  About $\frac{1}{2}$ teaspoon **pepper**

- 4 slices **red onion** (each $\frac{1}{4}$ in. thick and 4 in. wide)

  About 3 tablespoons **olive oil**

- 4 ounces **jalapeño jack cheese,** cut into $\frac{1}{8}$-inch-thick slices
- 1 can (4 oz.) **whole green chilies,** drained
- 4 slices **firm-ripe tomato** (each $\frac{1}{4}$ in. thick and 4 in. wide)
- 1 **firm-ripe avocado** ($\frac{2}{3}$ lb.), pitted, peeled, and sliced

1. Rinse mushrooms; trim and discard discolored stem ends. Cut off and mince stems.

2. In a bowl, mix mushroom stems, ground beef, spinach, bread crumbs, cilantro, egg white, chili powder, cumin, oregano, and $\frac{1}{2}$ teaspoon *each* salt and pepper. Divide mixture into 4 equal portions; shape each into a 4$\frac{1}{2}$-inch-wide patty and set in a single layer on plastic wrap.

3. Lightly brush onion slices and mushroom caps with olive oil.

4. Prepare barbecue for ***direct heat*** (see page 198). When it is ***medium-hot,*** oil grill. Lay meat patties, onion slices, and mushroom caps, gill sides down, on grill. Cook until patties and onions are browned on the bottom and juices start to drip from mushrooms, about 2 minutes; turn. Cover burgers equally with cheese. Cook until onions are browned on other side and meat is no longer pink in center of thickest part (cut to test), 2 to 3 minutes longer.

5. With a wide spatula, set mushrooms, gill sides up, on a platter. Set a burger on each cap. Tear chilies to split open, and lay equally on burgers. Top equally with tomato, onion, and avocado slices. Season to taste with more salt and pepper.

Per serving: 591 cal., 67% (396 cal.) from fat; 33 g protein; 44 g fat (14 g sat.); 21 g carbo (4.9 g fiber); 808 mg sodium; 100 mg chol.

Cynthia Pederson
Renton, Washington

BEST OF CATEGORY

"Friends brought a jar of home-made marmalade when they came to dinner," Cynthia Pederson recounts. "I wanted to incorporate the marmalade in the menu, so I added some soy sauce and a few other things and spread it on the salmon. Everyone raved about it." Our judges concurred; they especially liked the sweet-salty glaze combined with the smoke the fish picks up from the wood chips.

Marmalade Salmon

PREP AND COOK TIME: About 30 minutes, plus at least 30 minutes to marinate

NOTES: Pederson's favorite salmon is wild King, but we also enjoyed the recipe with farm-raised salmon. For a pronounced smoke flavor, use a charcoal grill; wood chips smolder much less on a gas grill.

MAKES: 6 to 8 servings

- ½ cup **orange** or tangerine **marmalade**
- ½ cup **soy sauce**
- 2 tablespoons minced **fresh ginger**
- 1 tablespoon grated **orange** peel
- 1 tablespoon **rice vinegar**
- 1 teaspoon minced **garlic**
- ¼ teaspoon **cayenne**
- 1 **boned salmon fillet** (maximum 1¼ in. thick, 3 to 3½ lb.)
- 1 cup **cherry** or apple **wood chips**

1. In a bowl, mix marmalade, soy sauce, ginger, orange peel, vinegar, garlic, and cayenne.

2. Rinse salmon and place, skin side down, in a pan large enough for it to lie flat. Pour marmalade mixture evenly over fish. Let stand at least 30 minutes, or chill airtight up to 2 hours. Cut 2 sheets of foil 4 inches longer than fish; stack sheets. Lift fish from marinade and center, skin down, on foil; discard marinade. Trim foil to the outline of the fillet.

3. Meanwhile, in a bowl, soak wood chips in 2 cups hot water for 30 minutes. Drain.

4. Prepare barbecue for **direct heat** (see page 198). When grill is **medium-hot,** sprinkle chips evenly over coals or, for gas, place chips in a metal smoking box or foil pan directly on heat in a corner of grill. Set salmon on foil on grill. Cover barbecue; open vents for charcoal. Cook until fish is opaque but still moist-looking in center of thickest part (cut to test), 15 to 18 minutes.

5. With 2 wide spatulas, transfer fish on foil to a platter. Cut salmon into portions and lift from skin with a spatula.

Per serving: 342 cal., 47% (162 cal.) from fat; 34 g protein; 18 g fat (3.7 g sat.); 7.7 g carbo (0 g fiber); 621 mg sodium; 100 mg chol.

Susan Gutierrez
Fresno, California

FINALIST

Susan Gutierrez melded several techniques to create her winning recipe. "I wanted salmon that was moist but well done, so I combined a ceviche-style citrus cure and a gravlax-style sugar and salt cure [both traditionally applied in lieu of cooking], then barbecued the fish." Gutierrez cures the salmon for only 1 hour, then tops it with a lively mango relish after grilling.

Salmon Tango Mango

PREP AND COOK TIME: About 45 minutes, plus 1 hour to marinate

MAKES: 6 to 8 servings

- ¼ cup **salt**
- ¼ cup firmly packed **brown sugar**
- ⅓ cup **lime juice**
- 1 teaspoon grated **lime** peel
- 3 to 3½ pounds **boned salmon fillet** (6 to 8 equal pieces, maximum 1¼ in. thick), rinsed
- 1 tablespoon **olive oil**

  Tango mango salsa (recipe follows)

1. In a 1-gallon plastic food bag, mix salt, brown sugar, lime juice, and peel. Add salmon, seal bag, and turn to coat fish. Chill for 1 hour, turning bag occasionally.

2. Lift salmon from bag; discard marinade. Rinse fish, pat dry; brush with oil.

3. Prepare barbecue for **direct heat** (see page 198). When it is **medium-hot,** oil grill and lay salmon, skin side up, on it. Cook, turning once with a wide spatula, until fish is opaque but still moist-looking in center of thickest

Smoke from wood chips adds complex layers to simply marinated salmon.

part (cut to test), 7 to 10 minutes total.

4. Transfer fish to plates; top portions equally with salsa.

Per serving: 354 cal., 51% (180 cal.) from fat; 34 g protein; 20 g fat (4 g sat.); 7.2 g carbo (0.5 g fiber); 522 mg sodium; 100 mg chol.

Tango mango salsa. Pit, peel, and chop 1 **firm-ripe mango** (³⁄₄ lb.). In a bowl, mix mango; ¹⁄₂ cup chopped **red bell pepper;** ¹⁄₄ cup chopped **cucumber;** 3 tablespoons *each* **lime juice** and chopped **fresh cilantro;** 1 tablespoon *each* minced **red onion,** seeded and minced **fresh serrano chili,** and minced **fresh ginger;** and 1 teaspoon grated **lime** peel. Season to taste with **salt** and **pepper.** Makes about 2 cups.

Per serving: 24 cal., 3.8% (0.9 cal.) from fat; 0.3 g protein; 0.1 g fat (0 g sat.); 6.3 g carbo (0.5 g fiber); 2.1 mg sodium; 0 mg chol.

Kim Stephens and Ven Kruebbe

Novato, California, and New Orleans

FINALISTS

"When I was growing up in Louisiana, my parents enjoyed taking my sister and me to the various small-town festivals during the summer," Kim Stephens remembers. "At one, bacon-wrapped shrimp were barbecuing on large grills. My mother [Ven Kruebbe] thought they would be even better with something a little more interesting than plain bottled barbecue sauce." Back home, she created a mixture with just enough lemon, smoke, and sherry to set it apart. Now mother and daughter get multicoastal requests for the recipe.

Barbecued Bacon Shrimp

PREP AND COOK TIME: About 45 minutes

NOTES: Hinged grill baskets are sold at barbecue supply stores; choose one with handles that will fit in your barbecue. You can also use a cooking grate (sold at barbecue supply stores as well) with small holes; watch closely and turn shrimp often to brown evenly. Soak wood toothpicks in water for at least 30 minutes before using to keep them from burning. Buy regular—not thick-sliced—bacon.

MAKES: 8 appetizer servings

- 1 pound (32 to 36 per lb.) **peeled, deveined shrimp,** rinsed
- 16 to 18 slices **bacon** (16 to 18 oz.; see notes), cut in half crosswise

  Cooking oil spray or salad oil

  Mom's barbecue sauce (recipe follows)

1. Count shrimp; for each, you need ¹⁄₂ slice bacon and 1 soaked wood toothpick (see notes).

2. Arrange bacon slices in single layers in 2 pans, each 10 by 15 inches.

3. Bake in a 450° oven until bacon begins to brown on the bottom (lift to check), 4 to 8 minutes. As bacon is browned, transfer to towels to drain. Discard fat in pans.

4. Wrap 1 bacon strip around each shrimp; secure with a toothpick. Spritz the inside of an 11- or 12-inch square hinged grill basket with cooking spray (or lightly brush with oil). Arrange wrapped shrimp in a single layer in basket; close basket. Cook in batches, if needed.

5. Prepare barbecue for ***direct heat*** (see page 198). When it is ***medium-hot,*** lay basket on grill and turn as needed to brown bacon lightly, 2 to 3 minutes total. Remove basket from heat, open, and baste bacon-wrapped shrimp with about ¹⁄₄ of Mom's barbecue sauce (proportionately less if cooking in batches). Close basket, flip over, open basket, and baste shrimp with another ¹⁄₄ of the sauce (less if cooking in batches). Close basket, return to grill, and cook, turning once, until shrimp is opaque but still moist-looking in center of thickest part (cut to test) and bacon is well browned, 2 to 3 minutes longer.

6. Transfer bacon-wrapped shrimp to a platter. Pour remaining sauce into a bowl. Dip shrimp into sauce to eat.

Per serving: 215 cal., 37% (80 cal.) from fat; 17 g protein; 8.9 g fat (3 g sat.); 14 g carbo (0.5 g fiber); 1,240 mg sodium; 100 mg chol.

Mom's barbecue sauce. In a 2- to 3-quart pan, combine 1 cup **catsup;** ¹⁄₄ cup *each* **soy sauce** and **cream sherry;** 2 tablespoons *each* **lemon juice** and firmly packed **brown sugar;** 4 teaspoons minced **fresh ginger;** 2 teaspoons **Dijon mustard;** and 1 teaspoon *each* **liquid smoke,** minced **garlic,** and grated **lemon** peel. Stirring occasionally, bring to a boil over high heat; reduce heat and simmer, stirring often, until sauce is slightly thickened and reduced to 1¹⁄₂ cups, about 20 minutes. Makes 1¹⁄₂ cups.

Per serving: 64 cal., 1% (0.9 cal.) from fat; 1 g protein; 0.1 g fat (0 g sat.); 14 g carbo (0.5 g fiber); 903 mg sodium; 0 mg chol.

Bet you can't eat just one: Bacon-wrapped shrimp coated in a smoky-sweet sauce spiked with ginger. To eliminate flare-ups while grilling, cook the bacon first.

POULTRY

Norma Fried
Denver

BEST OF CATEGORY

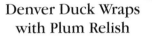

We were tired of skinless chicken breast and realized that barbecued duck breast makes a delicious, quick, meaty meal. It's become a weekly favorite," Norma Fried reports. She serves the duck with a fresh plum relish and wraps the works in thin pancakes as you would mu shu pork.

Denver Duck Wraps with Plum Relish

PREP AND COOK TIME: About 1 hour, plus at least 30 minutes to marinate

NOTES: You may need to order duck breasts ahead from your meat market; thaw if frozen. *Char siu* sauce is available in some well-stocked supermarkets and—along with the thin, pale pancakes called *mu shu* or *moc shoo* wrappers—in Asian markets. Some Chinese restaurants also sell the pancakes.

MAKES: 4 servings

- ⅓ cup **prepared char siu sauce** (Chinese barbecue sauce)
- 2 tablespoons firmly packed **brown sugar**
- 2 tablespoons **dry sherry**
- 1½ tablespoons **rice vinegar**
- 1 tablespoon **Asian** (toasted) **sesame oil**
- 1 tablespoon minced **fresh ginger**
- 4 **boned duck breast halves** (about 7 oz. each; see notes), skinned, fat trimmed, and rinsed
- 12 **green onions,** ends trimmed, rinsed
  Plum relish (recipe follows)
- 12 **mu shu wrappers** (thawed, if frozen) or flour tortillas (8 in. wide)
  Salt

1. In a 1-gallon plastic food bag, combine char siu sauce, brown sugar, sherry, vinegar, sesame oil, ginger, and duck. Seal bag and turn to mix well. Let stand at least 30 minutes, or chill up to 2 hours, turning bag occasionally.

Add onions to bag and turn to mix with sauce.

2. Prepare barbecue for *direct heat* (see page 198). When it is *hot,* oil grill. Lift duck from bag and lay on grill; set bag aside. Turn duck as needed until evenly browned and rare in center of thickest part (cut to test), 5 to 8 minutes total, or until done to your taste. Transfer duck to a platter; let stand 5 minutes. Meanwhile, drain and discard marinade in bag; lay onions on grill and turn as needed to brown lightly, 2 to 3 minutes. Add to platter.

3. Thinly slice duck crosswise; spoon its accumulated juices into plum relish. Set relish and pancakes beside duck.

4. To assemble, spoon relish onto pancakes; top with duck slices, green onions, and salt to taste. Roll to enclose, and hold to eat.

Per serving: 705 cal., 15% (108 cal.) from fat; 48 g protein; 12 g fat (1.6 g sat.); 100 g carbo (6.7 g fiber); 1,367 mg sodium; 193 mg chol.

Plum relish. Rinse, pit, and finely chop 1 pound **ripe red-skinned plums** such as Santa Rosa. In a bowl, mix plums, 2 tablespoons thinly sliced **green onions** (including tops), 1½ tablespoons firmly packed **brown sugar**, 2 teaspoons *each* **rice vinegar** and minced **fresh ginger**, 1½ teaspoons minced **garlic**, and 1 teaspoon **Asian** (toasted) **sesame oil.** Season to taste with **salt** and **pepper.** Makes 2¼ cups.

Per serving: 92 cal., 17% (16 cal.) from fat; 1 g protein; 1.8 g fat (0.2 g sat.); 20 g carbo (2.3 g fiber); 2.8 mg sodium; 0 mg chol.

Denise Neff
Imperial Beach, California

FINALIST

As its name implies, Denise Neff's recipe is an ingredient melting pot. It incorporates her family's favorite flavors. "My husband loves catsup and tends to put it on everything," Neff says. "I love the tang of tamarind, and we both love ginger." She started with these flavors and then added peaches (she also likes the sauce made with mango), rice wine vinegar, maple syrup, and sesame oil to achieve a complex balance.

Glazed duck and fresh plum relish fill mu shu rounds for an Asian-style wrap.

Pacific Rim Chicken with Spitfire Peach Sauce

PREP AND COOK TIME: About 1¼ hours, plus at least 30 minutes to marinate

NOTES: Neff serves the chicken and sauce with steamed white rice and stir-fried vegetables. You can buy tamarind paste at well-stocked supermarkets or Asian food stores.

MAKES: 6 servings

- 2 tablespoons minced **garlic**
- 2 tablespoons **soy sauce**
- 2 tablespoons **maple syrup**
- 2 tablespoons **rice vinegar**
- 1 tablespoon **salad oil**
- 1 tablespoon **Asian** (toasted) **sesame oil**
- 1 tablespoon minced **fresh ginger**
- 1 teaspoon fresh-ground **pepper**
- 6 **boned, skinned chicken breast halves** (about 5 oz. each), fat trimmed, rinsed

  Spitfire peach sauce (recipe follows)

  Mint sprigs

  Salt

1. In a 1-gallon plastic food bag, mix garlic, soy sauce, maple syrup, vinegar, salad oil, sesame oil, ginger, pepper, and chicken. Seal bag and turn to coat meat. Chill at least 30 minutes or up to 2 hours, turning bag occasionally.

2. Prepare barbecue for **direct heat** (see page 198). When it is **medium-hot,** oil grill. Lift chicken from bag, reserving marinade, and lay breasts on grill. Cook, turning chicken occasionally to brown evenly, until no longer pink in center of thickest part (cut to test), 10 to 12 minutes total. Baste chicken often with marinade during the first 5 minutes of cooking. Discard remaining marinade.

3. Spoon peach sauce equally onto plates. Set a chicken breast half in sauce on each plate; garnish with mint. Add salt to taste.

Per serving: 310 cal., 19% (60 cal.) from fat; 35 g protein; 6.7 g fat (1.1 g sat.); 28 g carbo (1.6 g fiber); 1,593 mg sodium; 82 mg chol.

Spitfire peach sauce. Pit, peel, and chop 2 **firm-ripe peaches** (1 lb. total). In a 2- to 3-quart pan, combine peaches; ¾ cup **water;** ½ cup **catsup;** ¼ cup **rice vinegar;** 3 tablespoons **soy sauce;** 2 tablespoons firmly packed **brown sugar;** 1 tablespoon **tamarind paste** or lemon juice; 2 teaspoons *each* **chili powder,** minced **garlic,** and minced **fresh**

ginger; and ½ teaspoon *each* **cayenne** and fresh-ground **pepper.** Bring to a boil over medium-high heat, stirring occasionally; reduce heat and simmer until reduced to 2 cups, about 30 to 40 minutes. Pour mixture into a blender or food processor and whirl until smooth. Serve warm. If making up to 2 days ahead, let cool, then chill airtight; reheat until steaming. Makes 2 cups.

Per ¼ cup: 56 cal., 3% (1.8 cal.) from fat; 1 g protein; 0.2 g fat (0 g sat.); 14 g carbo (1.3 g fiber); 573 mg sodium; 0 mg chol.

Priscilla Yee
Concord, California
FINALIST

"I have always appreciated the flavors of Southeast Asian cooking—sweet, sour, salty, and hot," Yee says.

"When I found gorgeous pomegranates in the store, I tried using their sweet-tart juice to enhance one of my favorite Asian marinades. The combination turned out to be delicious." Yee uses the mixture as both marinade and dressing for her hot grilled chicken salad.

Grilled Pomegranate Chicken and Cantaloupe

PREP AND COOK TIME: About 1½ hours

NOTES: Ream the juice from fresh pomegranates or buy canned unsweetened pomegranate juice at a natural foods store or well-stocked supermarket. Thai curry paste is available at Asian food stores and many supermarkets. As a substitute for the Chinese five spice, you can use equal parts ground cinnamon, ground cloves, ground ginger, and anise seed (1 teaspoon total).

MAKES: 4 servings

- 1½ cups **unsweetened pomegranate juice** (see notes)
- 3 tablespoons **soy sauce**
- 2 tablespoons **prepared hoisin sauce**

- 1½ tablespoons **Asian** (toasted) **sesame oil**
- 2 teaspoons minced **garlic**
- 2 teaspoons minced **fresh ginger**
- 2 teaspoons **Thai red curry paste**
- 1 teaspoon **Chinese five spice** (see notes)
- 4 **boned, skinned chicken breast halves** (about 5 oz. each), fat trimmed
- 1 **cantaloupe** (3⅓ lb.)
- ¾ pound **jicama**
- 2 teaspoons **salad oil**
- 1 tablespoon **lime juice**
- 1 **firm-ripe avocado** (⅔ lb.), pitted, peeled, and sliced
- ½ cup **pomegranate seeds** (optional)

  Lime wedges

  Salt

1. In a 1-quart glass measure, combine pomegranate juice, soy sauce, hoisin sauce, sesame oil, garlic, ginger, curry paste, and five spice. Pour all but ½ cup of the mixture into a 1-gallon plastic food bag; cover and chill remaining mixture. Rinse chicken and add to bag; seal and turn to coat meat. Chill at least 30 minutes or up to 2 hours, turning bag occasionally.

2. Peel cantaloupe, seed, and cut into 2-inch chunks. Thread melon equally onto 4 thin metal skewers, each about 12 inches long. Run a second thin skewer parallel to each first one through melon.

3. Peel jicama, rinse, and coarsely shred. In a bowl, mix jicama with salad oil and lime juice.

4. Prepare barbecue for **direct heat** (see page 198). When it is **medium,** oil grill. Lift chicken from bag and lay on grill. Cook, basting frequently with marinade and turning to brown evenly, for 10 minutes. Add cantaloupe to grill and baste with marinade; discard remaining marinade. Turn foods occasionally until chicken is no longer pink in center of thickest part (cut to test) and melon is slightly browned, 5 to 8 minutes longer.

5. Spoon reserved soy sauce mixture equally onto plates. Mound jicama equally in center, top each portion with a chicken piece, and lay a melon skewer alongside. Garnish with avocado, pomegranate seeds, and lime wedges. Season to taste with juice from wedges and salt.

Per serving: 440 cal., 35% (153 cal.) from fat; 37 g protein; 17 g fat (2.5 g sat.); 38 g carbo (6.6 g fiber); 633 mg sodium; 82 mg chol.

Alison Cappuccio
Leavenworth, Washington

BEST OF CATEGORY

As a wine aficionado (she and her husband have an extensive cellar), Alison Cappuccio often first selects a wine for dinner, then designs a menu to complement it. Her work as a molecular microbiologist at the University of Washington is similar to creating recipes—hands-on inventiveness, massaging protocols until they work for a particular application.

"We were grilling ribs and needed a side dish to go with a big 1997 chianti," she explains. "I had some asparagus and potatoes, and thought a rice wine vinaigrette would be crisp and light without competing with the wine's acidity; parmesan would balance its hearty body."

Grilled Potatoes and Asparagus with Basil and Parmesan

PREP AND COOK TIME: About 45 minutes

NOTES: To cook vegetables concurrently, you need 2 hinged grill baskets or a cooking grate with small holes (see notes for barbecued bacon shrimp, page 194). For flavor, Cappuccio prefers to use imported Italian Parmigiano reggiano cheese; shave the cheese with a vegetable peeler.

MAKES: 4 servings

- ¼ cup **seasoned rice vinegar**
- ¼ cup **extra-virgin olive oil**
- 2 teaspoons fresh-ground **pepper**
  About ½ teaspoon **salt**
- 1 pound **red thin-skin potatoes,** scrubbed
  Cooking oil spray or salad oil
- 1½ pounds **asparagus**
- ½ cup lightly packed **fresh basil leaves,** rinsed
  Basil sprigs, rinsed
- ⅓ cup shaved **parmesan cheese** (see notes)

1. In a 9- by 13-inch pan, mix vinegar, oil, pepper, and ½ teaspoon salt.

2. Cut potatoes into ¼-inch-thick slices; add to pan and mix to coat.

3. Spritz the inside of an 11- or 12-inch square hinged grill basket with cooking oil spray (or lightly brush with oil). Lift potatoes from pan, reserving marinade; arrange in a single layer in basket and close.

4. Snap off and discard tough asparagus ends; add asparagus to marinade in pan and mix to coat. Spritz the inside of another 11- or 12-inch square hinged grill basket with cooking spray (or lightly brush with oil). Lift asparagus from marinade, arrange in a single layer in basket, and close (if you have only 1 basket, cook vegetables in sequence).

5. Prepare barbecue for **direct heat** (see page 198). When it is **hot,** set basket with potatoes on grill; turn often until potatoes are golden brown and tender when pierced, 6 to 8 minutes total. After potatoes have cooked 5 minutes, set basket with asparagus on grill; turn often until tender when pierced, about 5 minutes. Vegetables overlap somewhat when you turn the basket; shake it to spread them out so they cook evenly. Remove cooked vegetables from grill. Dump asparagus onto a board and cut into 2-inch pieces; return to marinade. Add potatoes to marinade.

6. Thinly slice basil leaves; add to vegetables in pan and mix gently.

7. Pour mixture onto a platter. Garnish with basil sprigs. Scatter about half the parmesan over vegetables. Serve warm or at room temperature; add remaining cheese and salt to taste.

Per serving: 276 cal., 52% (144 cal.) from fat; 8.1 g protein; 16 g fat (2.7 g sat.); 30 g carbo (4.2 g fiber); 656 mg sodium; 2.4 mg chol.

Bob House
Scottsdale, Arizona

FINALIST/SPECIAL AWARD OF MERIT

House's unusual recipe caused an in-house stir from the outset. In an attempt to "barbecue the impossible," as he puts it, he came up with a way to simultaneously grill prime rib *and* Yorkshire pudding. For such innovation, the judges honored House with a special award of merit (and dinner for two at the restaurant of his choice) for "adding to the literature of barbecuing."

House rubs the prime rib with an herb-flavored oil, then grills it, catching the drippings below the meat in a pan on the firegrate. Then he pours Yorkshire pudding batter into the drip pan, where it puffs in the hot fat and browns from the heat of the coals.

Enclosed in a grill basket for easy turning, potatoes and asparagus barbecue beautifully.

Why stop with steak? Prime rib with Yorkshire pudding makes a grand grilled feast.

Beef Rib Roast and Yorkshire Pudding from the Grill

PREP AND COOK TIME: About 1½ hours

NOTES: A charcoal grill easily accommodates the Yorkshire pudding; you'll need 1 foil pan to collect drippings from roast for pudding. If using a gas grill, you need a minimum of 2 inches of open space between the heat source and the bottom of the grill to fit drip pan. But since the pudding tends to scorch when cooked on a gas grill, after you pour the batter into the drip pan, transfer it to an oven to bake and put a second pan under the roast.

MAKES: 5 to 7 servings

> 1 **center-cut beef rib roast** (4 to 5 lb.), surface of fat trimmed to no more than ¼ inch thick

Garlic-herb oil (recipe follows)

1 cup **low-fat milk**

1 cup **all-purpose flour**

3 **large eggs**

About ¾ teaspoon **salt**

Melted **butter** or margarine (optional)

Watercress sprigs

Pepper

1. Rinse beef and pat dry. Coat all over with garlic-herb oil.

2. Prepare barbecue for ***indirect heat*** (see page 199). When barbecue is ***medium-hot,*** set an 8-inch square foil pan in center of firegrate or directly on heat source in gas barbecue (see notes); set grill in place. Set roast, bones down, on grill over drip pan.

Cover barbecue; open vents for charcoal. Cook for 45 minutes.

3. Meanwhile, in a blender, whirl milk, flour, eggs, and ¾ teaspoon salt until batter is smooth.

4. Transfer roast to a platter. Protecting your hands, lift grill off and remove drip pan. Pour drippings through a fine strainer into a bowl.

If using a charcoal grill, return 1 tablespoon drippings to pan; discard remainder. Return pan to firegrate and pour batter into pan. Replace grill, set roast back over pan, cover barbecue, and cook until medium-rare (135° in center of thickest part), 30 to 50 minutes longer, or until done to your taste. Cook pudding until well browned, 40 to 50 minutes.

If using a gas grill, return 3 tablespoons drippings (adding melted butter, if needed, to make this amount) to pan and pour in batter. Quickly set another 8-inch square pan on heat source, replace grill, set roast over pan, cover barbecue, and cook until medium-rare (135° in center of thickest part), 30 to 50 minutes longer, or until done to your taste. Meanwhile, bake pudding in a 375° oven until well browned, 30 to 40 minutes.

5. Transfer roast to a platter; let stand in a warm place for juices to settle, at least 10 minutes. If pudding is done before roast is ready to carve, close charcoal barbecue vents and leave pudding in barbecue to keep warm, or turn oven heat off and keep pudding warm in the oven.

6. Scoop pudding in large portions from pan and place around roast. Garnish with watercress. Carve roast and serve with pudding. Season to taste with salt and pepper.

Per serving: 934 cal., 68% (639 cal.) from fat; 53 g protein; 71 g fat (27 g sat.); 18 g carbo (0.8 g fiber); 426 mg sodium; 269 mg chol.

BARBECUE BASICS

For direct heat, the charcoal or gas flame is directly under the food. For indirect heat, the fuel source is balanced on the sides below the food.

DIRECT HEAT

IF USING CHARCOAL BRIQUETS, mound and ignite enough briquets to cover the firegrate in a single, solid layer (you'll need about 75). When the briquets are dotted with gray ash, after 15 to 20 minutes, spread them over the firegrate in a single layer. Let them burn down to the desired heat (see the following tests). Set grill in place.

IF USING A GAS BARBECUE, turn all the burners to high and close the lid for 10 minutes. Adjust the burners to the desired heat (see the following tests).

•**Very hot:** You can hold your hand at grill level only 1 to 2 seconds.

•**Hot:** You can hold your hand at grill level only 2 to 3 seconds.

•**Medium-hot:** You can hold your hand at grill level only 3 to 4 seconds.

•**Medium:** You can hold your hand at grill level only 4 to 5 seconds.

•**Medium-low:** You can hold your hand at grill level only 5 to 6 seconds.

•**Low:** You can hold your hand at grill level only 6 to 7 seconds.

IF RECIPE DIRECTS YOU TO OIL GRILL, brush lightly with salad oil.

LAY FOOD ON GRILL. Cover gas barbecue; do not cover charcoal barbecue unless recipe specifies. Proceed as recipe directs.

Garlic-herb oil. In a food processor, combine ¼ cup peeled **garlic** cloves, 3 tablespoons **olive oil**, and 1½ teaspoons *each* **dried rosemary, dried savory, dried thyme,** and **coarse-ground pepper;** whirl until finely chopped. (Or mince garlic and mix in a bowl with remaining ingredients.) Makes ⅓ cup.

Per serving: 63 cal., 83% (52 cal.) from fat; 0.4 g protein; 5.8 g fat (0.8 g sat.); 2.6 g carbo (0.3 g fiber); 1.5 mg sodium; 0 mg chol.

Renee Scherrer

Vacaville, California

FINALIST

There's not much of a story to my recipe," Renee Scherrer confesses. "My husband and I simply love pesto, we love pizza, and we love to grill year-round here in Northern California." So the Scherrers' barbecue is frequently the focal point for their entertaining. This pizza makes an excellent appetizer or light meal.

Grilled Pesto Pizza

PREP AND COOK TIME: About 2 hours

NOTES: Because the pizza crust cooks quickly, have all the toppings assembled and ready to use beside the grill.

MAKES: 8 appetizer or 4 main-dish servings

  1 package **active dry yeast**

     About 1 tablespoon **olive oil**

  1½ teaspoons **sugar**

  ¾ teaspoon **salt**

     About 1⅓ cups **all-purpose flour**

  ¾ pound **firm-ripe tomatoes**

  1½ ounces **thin-sliced prosciutto**

     Pesto (recipe follows)

  1½ cups (6 oz.) **shredded mozzarella cheese**

     Pepper

1. In a bowl, sprinkle yeast over ½ cup warm (110°) water. Let stand until softened, about 5 minutes. Add 1 tablespoon oil, sugar, salt, and 1⅓ cups flour; stir until evenly moistened. Scrape dough onto a lightly floured board. Knead until smooth and elastic, about 10 minutes, adding flour as required to prevent sticking.

2. Place dough in an oiled bowl, turn over to coat, and cover with plastic wrap. Let stand in a warm place until doubled, about 45 minutes.

3. Meanwhile, rinse tomatoes, core, and cut into ¹⁄₁₆- to ⅛-inch-thick slices.

Tomato-and-pesto-topped pizza, crisp and smoky from the grill.

Cover a 14- by 17-inch baking sheet or tray with towels. Lay slices in a single layer on towels to drain.

4. Cut prosciutto crosswise into ¼-inch-wide strips.

5. Scrape dough onto a lightly floured board and knead to expel air, then roll to make a 12- by 14-inch rectangle. With your hands or 2 wide spatulas, transfer dough to a floured pizza paddle (at least 12 by 15 in.) or 12- by 15-inch baking sheet.

6. Prepare barbecue for **direct heat** (see page 198). When it is **medium-low,** oil grill. Slide dough onto grill and cook until crust is browned on the bottom, about 2 minutes. Slide crust back onto paddle or pan and invert another paddle or pan over it; holding paddles together, invert crust. At once spread pesto evenly over crust, sprinkle with mozzarella, and arrange tomatoes on cheese. Slide pizza back onto grill; cook until cheese is melted and crust is browned on the bottom (lift to check), 2 to 3 minutes longer.

7. Slide paddle or pan under pizza and transfer to a board. Scatter prosciutto strips evenly over pizza. Cut into rectangles. Season to taste with pepper.

Per main-dish serving: 661 cal., 61% (405 cal.) from fat; 24 g protein; 45 g fat (12 g sat.); 45 g carbo (5.6 g fiber); 974 mg sodium; 49 mg chol.

Pesto. In a 350° oven, bake ¼ cup **chopped walnuts** in an 8- or 9-inch-wide pan until lightly browned, 5 to 8 minutes. Meanwhile, in a food processor or blender, combine 1½ cups lightly packed rinsed and drained **fresh basil** leaves, 6 tablespoons fresh-grated **parmesan cheese,** 2 teaspoons minced **garlic,** and 6 tablespoons **extra-virgin olive oil;** add hot nuts. Whirl until coarsely puréed. Makes ¾ cup.

Per serving: 289 cal., 90% (261 cal.) from fat; 6.5 g protein; 29 g fat (5.1 g sat.); 5 g carbo (2.9 g fiber); 174 mg sodium; 7.2 mg chol.

INDIRECT HEAT

IF USING CHARCOAL BRIQUETS, mound and ignite 60 briquets on the firegrate of a barbecue with a lid. When the briquets are hot, after 15 to 20 minutes, push equal amounts to opposite sides of the firegrate. Add 5 more briquets to *each* mound of coals now and every 30 minutes while cooking. Set a drip pan on the firegrate between the coals. Set the grill in place.

IF USING A GAS BARBECUE, turn all the burners to high, close the lid, and heat for 10 minutes. Then adjust the burners for indirect cooking (heat on opposite sides of grill, not down center under food), and keep on high unless recipe specifies otherwise.

IF RECIPE DIRECTS YOU TO OIL GRILL, brush lightly with salad oil.

LAY FOOD ON GRILL, but not over heat source. Cover gas grill. If recipe directs, cover charcoal grill and open vents. Proceed as recipe directs.

What did the winners win?

Grand prize: $2,500. Best of category: a Weber gas or charcoal grill. In addition, all of the finalists received a trip to *Sunset* headquarters, including accommodations; Woodbridge wines by Robert Mondavi; and a copy of last year's *Sunset Recipe Annual.* ◆

the pleasure of pie

A perfect crust and the allure of summer fruit—readers offer their favorite creations

By Elaine Johnson • Photographs by Carin Krasner

■ For a few afternoons every summer, I give myself over to a happy mess of flour, sugar, and juice-dripping fruit. We may be celebrating a birthday or having a little dinner party. Whatever the occasion, the clock stops: I'm making pie.

Out come the rolling pin, the canisters, the oversize mixing bowl (a wedding present from my colleagues). I hear my high school cooking teacher intoning tips on pastry making. And the fuzzy globes on the counter—bound for that pastry—remind me how few foods compare to a perfectly ripe peach. When I push the pie into the oven, it's not long until I wonder, Is there a better smell anywhere on earth?

Our readers often offer concrete proof, in the form of their favorite creations, of the fact that they too love to make pie. These seven recipes from *Sunset* readers, chock-full of peaches, pears, and berries, all reminded us of why we especially love to fill a crust in the summer. Some are classic baked pies; some are simply fresh fruit settled into a pastry.

And about that crust—while a homemade pastry is quite grand (see Perfect Pie Pastry, below; it includes tips distilled from my high school teacher's advice), a purchased pastry serves well, and saves a big step. Either frames one of summer's sweetest pleasures.

Perfect Pie Pastry

PREP TIME: About 20 minutes

MAKES: 8 servings

For a 9-inch single-crust pie

About 1 cup **all-purpose flour**

¼ teaspoon **salt**

3 tablespoons cold **butter** or margarine, cut into chunks

3 tablespoons cold **solid shortening**, cut into chunks

For a 9-inch double-crust pie

About 2 cups **all-purpose flour**

½ teaspoon **salt**

6 tablespoons cold **butter** or margarine, cut into chunks

6 tablespoons cold **solid shortening**, cut into chunks

1. In a bowl, mix 1 cup flour and the salt (for single crust) or 2 cups flour and the salt (for double crust). Add butter and shortening. With a pastry blender or your fingers, cut in the fats or rub in with your fingers until the largest pieces are pea-size.

2. Sprinkle 2 tablespoons water (for single crust) or 4 tablespoons water (for double crust) over flour mixture. Stir with a fork just until evenly moistened. Gently squeeze about ¼ cup of the dough into a ball; if it won't hold together, crumble lump back into bowl and sprinkle with more water, 1 tablespoon at a time; stir with a fork until evenly moistened.

3. With lightly floured hands, gently squeeze dough into a ball. For double crust, divide in half and shape each half into a ball. Pat dough into a 4-inch-wide round (2 rounds for double crust), pressing to make edges smooth.

4. Lay dough (1 round for double crust) on a lightly floured surface. Coat a rolling pin with flour. Roll firmly but gently in short strokes from center of dough outward to form an 11-inch-wide round. If edges split while rolling, push them back toward center to make round relatively smooth. Occasionally lift dough or turn over, dusting flour beneath to prevent sticking.

5. Fold the dough round in half, lift it gently without stretching, and lay the folded edge across the middle of a 9-inch pie pan. Unfold and ease dough into pan without stretching. Trim dough edge evenly ¾ inch beyond pan rim.

6. *For a single-crust pie:* Fold dough edge under itself, flush with pan rim. To flute, press down on dough rim

Pick your pleasure, from the top: Double-crust pineapple-peach pie, raspberry-crowned custard pie in a chocolate crust, or peach-glazed peach pie.

Pineapple-Peach Pie

PREP AND COOK TIME: About 1¾ hours, plus at least 3 hours to cool

NOTES: Andrea Kirsch of Palo Alto shares this delicious fruit pairing. You'll need a 2-pound pineapple or 1¼-pound peeled, cored pineapple. If using a refrigerated pastry, follow steps 5 and 6 of the Perfect Pie Pastry recipe (below left) to line pan, position top crust, and flute.

MAKES: 8 servings

- ¼ cup **quick-cooking tapioca**
- ⅓ cup firmly packed **brown sugar**
- ½ cup **apricot-pineapple jam**
- 1½ tablespoons **lemon juice**
- ½ teaspoon **ground cinnamon**
- ½ teaspoon **ground nutmeg**
  About 2 pounds **firm-ripe peaches**
- 2 cups ½-inch chunks **pineapple** (see notes)
- 1 **perfect pie pastry** for 9-inch double-crust pie (at left) or 1 package (15 oz.) refrigerated pastry for 9-inch double-crust pie (see notes)

1. In a bowl, mix tapioca with sugar. Add jam, lemon juice, cinnamon, and nutmeg; mix. Peel peaches, pit, and slice ½ inch thick (you need 1 qt.); add peaches and their juice to tapioca mixture. Add pineapple and stir gently until evenly mixed. Let stand until tapioca is softened, 15 to 20 minutes.

2. Line a 9-inch pie pan with pastry; scrape in tapioca mixture. Cover with second pastry round and seal (see notes). With a small, sharp knife, cut several 2- to 3-inch slits in top pastry. Line a 10- by 15-inch pan with foil (to catch drips) and set pie on foil.

3. Bake on bottom rack of a 400° oven until fruit is bubbling and pastry is well browned, 50 to 60 minutes.

4. Let pie cool on a rack at least 3 hours; cut into wedges.

Per serving: 445 cal., 38% (171 cal.) from fat; 4.7 g protein; 19 g fat (7.9 g sat.); 67 g carbo (2.7 g fiber); 267 mg sodium; 23 mg chol.

Chocolate–Double Raspberry Cream Pie

PREP AND COOK TIME: About 1¾ hours, plus at least 2 hours to chill

NOTES: Audrey Thibodeau of Gilbert, Arizona, created this pie to showcase her favorite flavors. Use cookies such as Famous Chocolate Wafers.

with your thumb and first finger to make an indentation; at the same time, press against dough edge with 1 finger of your other hand, pushing it between your fingers on the rim. Repeat indentations side by side. Bake or fill crust as recipe directs.

For a double-crust pie: Fill bottom crust as recipe directs. Roll second ball of dough as directed in step 4 into a 10-inch-wide round. Fold as directed in step 5, center on filling, and unfold. Trim edge flush with dough in pan. Fold dough edges under, flush with pan rim. Flute as directed for single-crust pie.

Per serving for a single crust: 148 cal., 57% (84 cal.) from fat; 2 g protein; 9.3 g fat (3.9 g sat.); 14 g carbo (0.5 g fiber); 116 mg sodium; 12 mg chol.

MAKES: **8 servings**

- ½ cup plus 1 tablespoon **sugar**
- ¼ cup **pecans**
- 20 **thin chocolate wafer cookies** (about 2 in. wide, 5 oz. total; see notes)
- 3 tablespoons melted **butter** or margarine
- 3 tablespoons **cornstarch**
- 1½ teaspoons **unflavored gelatin**
- 2 cups **milk**
- 1 **large egg**
- 4 **large egg** yolks
- 1½ teaspoons **vanilla**
- ⅓ cup **whipping cream**
- 2 to 2½ cups **raspberries**, rinsed and drained
- ⅔ cup **seedless raspberry jam**

1. In a food processor, whirl 1 tablespoon sugar, pecans, and cookies until finely ground. Add butter and whirl until blended. (Or in a blender, whirl pecans with sugar until nuts are finely chopped; pour into a bowl. Break cookies into chunks and whirl until finely ground; add to nuts. Add butter and stir to mix.) Press cookie mixture evenly over bottom and up sides of a 9-inch pie pan.

2. Bake in a 350° oven until crust feels slightly firmer and smells lightly toasted, 10 to 15 minutes. Let cool on a rack.

3. In a 2- to 3-quart pan, mix remaining ½ cup sugar, cornstarch, and gelatin. Whisk in milk, egg, and egg yolks. Whisk over medium-high heat until mixture is thick enough to coat a spoon and bubbles begin to form at pan sides, about 5 minutes.

4. At once, nest pan in ice water, add vanilla, and stir often until mixture is cool and holds a mound briefly but is not firm, 6 to 8 minutes.

5. In a deep bowl with a mixer on high speed, whip cream until it holds distinct peaks. Fold into cooked mixture. Scrape into cool chocolate crust and spread level. Arrange enough raspberries, stem end down, over pie filling to cover.

6. In a 1- or 2-cup glass measure, heat jam in a microwave oven at full power (100%) until melted, about 45 seconds. Stir until smooth; spoon evenly over raspberries.

7. Chill pie until filling is firm enough to cut, at least 2 hours; if making up to 1 day ahead, cover airtight with a large inverted bowl (to avoid touching jam) and chill. Cut into wedges.

Per serving: 392 cal., 41% (162 cal.) from fat; 6.7 g protein; 18 g fat (7.6 g sat.); 54 g carbo (2.2 g fiber); 203 mg sodium; 164 mg chol.

Peach-glazed Peach Pie

PREP AND COOK TIME: About 30 minutes, plus at least 3 hours to chill

NOTES: Betty Archibald of Boise prefers fresh, uncooked peaches in a pie. If using a refrigerated pastry, follow steps 5 and 6 of the Perfect Pie Pastry recipe (page 200) to line pan. Serve pie with whipped cream flavored with amaretto.

MAKES: **8 servings**

- 1 **perfect pie pastry** for 9-inch single-crust pie (page 200) or 1 refrigerated pastry (half of a 15-oz. package; see notes)
- ¾ cup **sugar**
- ⅓ cup **cornstarch**
- 1 cup **canned peach juice**
- 1 tablespoon **lemon juice**
- ½ teaspoon **almond extract**
  - About 2 pounds **firm-ripe peaches**

1. With a fork, prick bottom and sides of pastry in pie pan at about 1-inch intervals. Bake in a 375° oven until golden, 20 to 25 minutes.

2. In a 4- to 5-quart pan, mix sugar and cornstarch. Add peach juice and mix. Stir over high heat until boiling, about 3 minutes. Remove from heat and stir in lemon juice and almond extract.

3. Peel and pit peaches; cut ½-inch slices into a bowl (you need 1 qt.). Add hot peach glaze and mix to coat slices.

4. Scrape peaches into baked pastry. Chill until firm enough to cut, at least 3 hours. If making up to 1 day ahead, cover airtight with an inverted bowl (to avoid touching fruit) and chill. Cut into wedges.

Per serving: 296 cal., 29% (85 cal.) from fat; 2.6 g protein; 9.4 g fat (3.9 g sat.); 52 g carbo (2 g fiber); 119 mg sodium; 12 mg chol.

Peach-Brandy Pie

PREP AND COOK TIME: About 1½ hours, plus at least 2 hours to cool

NOTES: Mickey Strang of McKinleyville, California, bakes this pie with tree-ripened peaches from the farmers' market. If using a refrigerated pastry, follow steps 5 and 6 of the Perfect Pie Pastry recipe (page 200) to line pan.

MAKES: **8 servings**

- About 2 pounds **firm-ripe peaches**
- ½ cup **sugar**
- ¼ cup **brandy**
- 2 tablespoons **quick-cooking tapioca**
- 1 teaspoon **vanilla**
- 1 **perfect pie pastry** for 9-inch single-crust pie (page 200) or 1 refrigerated pastry (half of a 15-oz. package; see notes)
- **Streusel topping** (recipe follows)

1. Peel and pit peaches; cut ½-inch slices into a bowl (you need 1 qt.). Add sugar, brandy, tapioca, and vanilla; mix gently. Let stand until tapioca is softened, 15 to 20 minutes.

2. Line a 9-inch pie pan with pastry. Scrape peaches into pastry and spread level. Cover evenly with streusel topping. Line a 10- by 15-inch pan with foil (to catch drips); set pie on foil.

3. Bake on bottom rack of a 350° oven until streusel is deep golden brown, 55 to 60 minutes.

4. Let pie cool on a rack at least 2 hours. Serve warm or cool, cut into wedges.

Per serving: 455 cal., 42% (189 cal.) from fat; 4.3 g protein; 21 g fat (11 g sat.); 64 g carbo (2.3 g fiber); 250 mg sodium; 43 mg chol.

Streusel topping. In a bowl, combine 1 cup **all-purpose flour**, ½ cup firmly packed **brown sugar**, ½ cup (¼ lb.) **butter** or margarine, and ½ teaspoon **ground nutmeg**. Cut with a pastry blender or rub with your fingers until coarse crumbs form. Squeeze until about ⅔ of the mixture is shaped into lumps. Makes 2¼ cups.

Per serving: 211 cal., 51% (108 cal.) from fat; 1.7 g protein; 12 g fat (7.2 g sat.); 25 g carbo (0.4 g fiber); 123 mg sodium; 31 mg chol.

Pear Cream Pie

PREP AND COOK TIME: About 1½ hours, plus at least 1½ hours to cool

NOTES: Fay Barr of Medford, Oregon, uses local pears in this recipe. If using a refrigerated pastry, follow steps 5 and 6 of the Perfect Pie Pastry recipe (page 200) to line pan. Serve with whipped cream flavored with cinnamon.

MAKES: **8 servings**

- About 2 pounds **firm-ripe pears**, such as Bartlett
- 1 **perfect pie pastry** for 9-inch single-crust pie (page 200) or 1 refrigerated pastry (half of a 15-oz. package; see notes)
- ½ cup **sugar**
- 3 tablespoons **all-purpose flour**

1 cup **whipping cream**

¹⁄₂ teaspoon **almond extract**

¹⁄₈ teaspoon **ground cinnamon**

1. Peel, quarter, and core pears; cut crosswise into ¹⁄₄-inch slices (you need 1 qt.). Line a 9-inch pie pan with pastry; put pears and their juice into it.

2. In a bowl, mix sugar and flour. Add cream and almond extract; whisk until smooth. Pour mixture over pears. Sprinkle with cinnamon. Line a 10- by 15-inch pan with foil (to catch drips) and set pie on foil.

3. Bake on bottom rack of a 350° oven until pie filling bubbles in the center, 1 hour and 5 minutes to 1 hour and 15 minutes.

4. Let cool on a rack at least 1¹⁄₂ hours. If making up to 1 day ahead, chill airtight. Cut into wedges.

Per serving: 327 cal., 47% (153 cal.) from fat; 2.3 g protein; 17 g fat (8.8 g sat.); 43 g carbo (2.6 g fiber); 144 mg sodium; 40 mg chol.

Pear Crumble Pie

PREP AND COOK TIME: About 1¹⁄₄ hours, plus as least 1 hour to cool

NOTES: Carmela Meely of Walnut Creek, California, likes spiced pears with a streusel topping. For streusel, follow recipe on the facing page, but omit nutmeg and add ¹⁄₄ teaspoon *each* ground cinnamon, ground ginger, and ground mace. If using a refrigerated pastry, fol-

A pair with pears: one topped with cream (front), one with streusel (back).

Spiced sour cream and blueberries in a buttery brown sugar crust taste like a cross between a cheesecake and a pie.

low steps 5 and 6 of the Perfect Pie Pastry recipe (page 200) to line pan. Serve pie with vanilla ice cream.

MAKES: 8 servings

¹⁄₄ cup **sugar**

2 tablespoons **all-purpose flour**

¹⁄₄ teaspoon **ground nutmeg**

¹⁄₄ teaspoon **ground ginger**

About 2¹⁄₄ pounds **firm-ripe pears** such as Bartlett

3 tablespoons **lemon juice**

1 **perfect pie pastry** for 9-inch single-crust pie (page 200) or 1 refrigerated pastry (half of a 15-oz. package; see notes)

Streusel topping (see notes)

1. In a bowl, mix sugar, flour, nutmeg, and ginger. Peel, quarter, and core pears; cut crosswise into ¹⁄₂-inch slices (you need 1¹⁄₂ qt.). To sugar mixture, add lemon juice and pears; mix gently.

2. Line a 9-inch pie pan with pastry; scrape fruit into it and cover evenly with streusel. Line a 10- by 15-inch pan with foil (to catch drips) and set pie on foil.

3. Bake on bottom rack of a 350° oven until streusel is deep golden brown, about 1 hour.

4. Let pie cool on a rack at least 1 hour. Serve warm or cool, cut into wedges.

Per serving: 432 cal., 42% (180 cal.) from fat; 3.3 g protein; 20 g fat (10 g sat.); 63 g carbo (3.3 g fiber); 257 mg sodium; 38 mg chol.

Mama's Blueberry–Sour Cream Pie

PREP AND COOK TIME: About 1 hour, plus at least 2 hours to cool

NOTES: To create this pie, Marjaana Rinne of Bellevue, Washington, adapted a recipe from her Finnish mother. Top it with sweetened whipped cream and additional blueberries.

MAKES: 8 servings

About ³⁄₄ cup **all-purpose flour**

About ¹⁄₄ cup (¹⁄₈ lb.) **butter** or margarine, cut into chunks

¹⁄₄ cup firmly packed **brown sugar**

¹⁄₄ teaspoon **baking soda**

¹⁄₄ teaspoon **ground cardamom**

1 **large egg** yolk

1 cup **regular** or reduced-fat **sour cream**

1 **large egg**

¹⁄₂ cup **granulated sugar**

2 teaspoons **cornstarch**

1 teaspoon grated **lemon** peel

2 cups **blueberries**, rinsed and drained

1. In a food processor, whirl ³⁄₄ cup flour, ¹⁄₄ cup butter, brown sugar, baking soda, and cardamom until fine crumbs form. Add egg yolk and whirl until dough holds together. (Or in a bowl, mix dry ingredients; add butter and rub in with your fingers until fine crumbs form. Add egg yolk and mix with a fork until dough holds together.)

2. Butter and flour a 9-inch nonstick pie pan. Evenly press dough over bottom and up sides of pan to inside edge of rim.

3. Bake pastry in a 325° oven until golden, 8 to 10 minutes.

4. Meanwhile, in a bowl, mix sour cream, egg, granulated sugar, cornstarch, and lemon peel until well blended. Stir in blueberries. Scrape mixture into hot pastry.

5. Return to oven and bake until center no longer jiggles when pan is gently shaken, 30 to 35 minutes.

6. Let stand on a rack until cool, about 1 hour. Cover and chill until cold, at least 1 hour or up to 1 day. Cut into wedges.

Per serving: 279 cal., 45% (126 cal.) from fat; 3.6 g protein; 14 g fat (8.2 g sat.); 36 g carbo (1.2 g fiber); 134 mg sodium; 83 mg chol. ◆

food *guide*

By Jerry Anne Di Vecchio • Photographs by Leigh Beisch

Stock split

An old-fashioned fountain favorite hits it big

■ From San Francisco's swank Fifth Floor restaurant to New York's cozy Lobster Club, a stock item from drugstores and sweetshops of yesteryear is making a significant comeback: the banana split.

Surprisingly enough, even the most imaginative chefs stick pretty close to the basic ingredients: bananas, ice cream, gooey sauces (chocolate, caramel, butterscotch), crunchy nuts or candies, and whipped cream—even the cherry on top. The presentation may be fancier, the ice cream homemade, the sauces richer and thicker—but that's it in the way of gourmet amendments. It's hard to improve on perfection.

Sweetshop Banana Split

PREP AND COOK TIME: About 20 minutes

NOTES: Finely crush the toffee chips or peanut brittle in a food processor (or crush them in a plastic bag as for malted milk balls in step 1), then measure.

MAKES: 4 banana splits, 1 or 2 servings each

- 1¼ cups **chocolate-coated malted milk balls** (about 7 oz.)
- ¾ cup **whipping cream**
- 1 to 2 tablespoons **powdered sugar**
- ¾ cup finely crushed **toffee chips** or peanut brittle (about ¼ lb.; see notes)
- 4 **firm-ripe bananas** (about ½ lb. each)
- 1 cup **semisweet chocolate chips**
- ⅓ cup **milk**
- 1 quart **vanilla ice cream**
- **Bing cherries** with stems or maraschino cherries with stems

1. Put malted milk balls in a heavy plastic food bag (at least 1 qt.). With a rolling pin or flat mallet, pound candy to break into large chunks.

2. In a bowl with a mixer on high speed, whip cream until it holds soft peaks; sweeten to taste with 1 to 2 tablespoons powdered sugar. Scoop into a small bowl; cover and chill.

3. On a 10- to 12-inch-long sheet of foil, spread ½ cup crushed toffee chips in a thick layer. Peel bananas and carefully cut in half lengthwise (if any break, fit pieces back together in the serving dish). Lay cut sides of bananas in crushed toffee and press gently to coat heavily. Form an oval with 2 banana halves, toffee sides up, in each dessert bowl (oval ones are best, about 8 in. long) or plate. Reserve remaining toffee.

4. In a microwave-safe bowl or 2-cup glass measure, combine chocolate chips and milk. Heat in a microwave oven on full power (100%), stirring at 15-second intervals, until chocolate is melted and sauce is smooth, about 30 seconds total. Scrape into a small bowl.

5. Working quickly, scoop ice cream into balls and place equal portions between banana halves. Sprinkle scoops equally with malted milk ball chunks and the remaining crushed toffee. Ladle the warm chocolate sauce over the top. Spoon whipped cream equally onto ice cream; top each banana split with a cherry. Serve immediately.

Per split: 1,230 cal., 50% (621 cal.) from fat; 14 g protein; 69 g fat (30 g sat.); 156 g carbo (3.1 g fiber); 438 mg sodium; 126 mg chol.

Fabulous salad for the Fourth

■ Going on a picnic? Barbecuing in the backyard? Hot dogs? Hamburgers? Steaks? Salmon? Regardless of how you celebrate our nation's birthday, potato salad belongs in the picture. This particular recipe has roots (pun intended). My great-aunt Nora, the last of the family on the Kansas homestead, made the world's best bread-and-butter pickles, and they were the magical ingredient in her potato salad. By July, she'd already had time to make a batch of the pickles using cucumbers from her garden. Sometimes the potatoes in the garden were big enough to dig for the salad, too. That was long ago, but my appetite for a really great potato salad is still keen. Now, it's bread-and-butter pickles from the store and buttery yellow Yukon gold potatoes that satisfy my taste buds and nourish memories too.

Bread-and-Butter Pickle Potato Salad

PREP AND COOK TIME: About 1 hour

NOTES: Pour the pickle juice out of the jar through a fine strainer into a bowl and save the mustard seed for the salad, or use dried mustard seed soaked in hot water for 5 minutes, then drained. If making salad up to 1 day ahead, cover and chill; mix before serving.

MAKES: 6 servings

2 pounds **Yukon gold potatoes** (about 2¼ in. wide), scrubbed

1 tablespoon **mustard seed** (see notes)

½ cup **bread-and-butter pickle** juice (see notes)

½ cup finely chopped **bread-and-butter pickles**

½ cup **reduced-fat** or regular **mayonnaise**

2 tablespoons **cider** or white wine **vinegar**

1 **red bell pepper** (½ lb.), rinsed, stemmed, seeded, and diced

6 tablespoons minced **parsley**

Salt and **pepper**

1. In a 4- to 5-quart pan, combine potatoes and 1½ quarts water. Cover and bring to a boil over high heat. Reduce heat and simmer until potatoes are tender when pierced, 25 to 30 minutes. Drain and let stand until cool enough to touch, about 10 minutes.

2. Meanwhile, in a large bowl, mix mustard seed, pickle juice, pickles, mayonnaise, and vinegar. Peel warm potatoes, cut into about ¾-inch cubes, and drop into dressing. Add bell pepper; mix gently. Let cool to room temperature, at least 15 minutes. Add 4 tablespoons parsley and salt and pepper to taste; mix. Scrape into a serving bowl and sprinkle with remaining parsley.

Per serving: 207 cal., 21% (44 cal.) from fat; 4 g protein; 4.9 g fat (0.7 g sat.); 37 g carbo (3.4 g fiber); 428 mg sodium; 0 mg chol.

Telescopic campfire fork

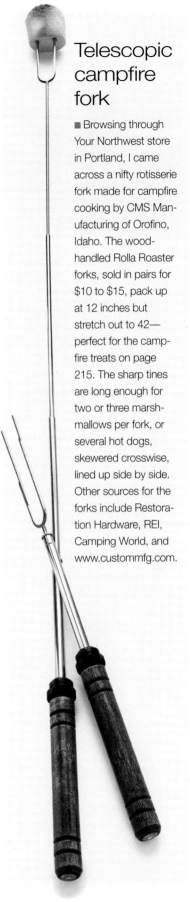

■ Browsing through Your Northwest store in Portland, I came across a nifty rotisserie fork made for campfire cooking by CMS Manufacturing of Orofino, Idaho. The wood-handled Rolla Roaster forks, sold in pairs for $10 to $15, pack up at 12 inches but stretch out to 42—perfect for the campfire treats on page 215. The sharp tines are long enough for two or three marshmallows per fork, or several hot dogs, skewered crosswise, lined up side by side. Other sources for the forks include Restoration Hardware, REI, Camping World, and www.custommfg.com.

Salsa gets fresh

■ Native Kjalii Foods, owned by young entrepreneurs Bret and Julie Jeremy, produces some of the freshest-tasting salsas available, for a logical reason—the ingredients are fresh. Fire-roasted components are highlighted in these refrigerated salsas: avocado-mango, citrus-papaya-chipotle, cucumber, green and red chili–

vegetable blends, guacamole, and papaya-mango. The Jeremys, who began selling their salsas in farmers' markets, now distribute to several Western states; you can also order Native Kjalii Foods salsas from www.greatfood.com (15-oz. containers cost $4 to $6 each).

Bret shares one of the partners' favorite salsa recipes, which they produce when corn is at its sweetest. Try it with grilled shrimp.

Sweet White Corn Salsa

PREP AND COOK TIME: 20 to 25 minutes

NOTES: Cut fresh corn kernels off the cob

MAKES: About 2 cups

- 1 **firm-ripe tomato** (6 oz.)
- 1 **red bell pepper** (½ lb.)
- 2 **fresh jalapeño chilies**
- 1 cup **white corn kernels** (see notes)
- 2 tablespoons **lime juice**
- 2 tablespoons rinsed **canned** or cooked **black beans** (optional)
- ¼ cup chopped **fresh cilantro**
- ¼ cup chopped **green onions** (including tops)

  Salt

1. Rinse tomato, bell pepper, and chilies; lay in a 10- by 15-inch pan. Broil 3 to 4 inches from heat, turning to char vegetables evenly, about 10 minutes; remove from pan as cooked. Let stand until cool enough to touch. Pull skin from tomato, bell pepper, and chilies. Core tomato; discard stems and seeds from pepper and chilies. Chop vegetables and put in a bowl.

2. Add corn, lime juice, beans, cilantro, onions, and salt to taste. Mix and serve, or cover and chill up to 3 days.

Per ¼ cup: 30 cal., 9% (2.7 cal.) from fat; 1.1 g protein; 0.3 g fat (0 g sat.); 6.9 g carbo (1.4 g fiber); 6.6 mg sodium; 0 mg chol.

Shell game

■ Perhaps you have more willpower than I do, but when I'm shelling fresh peas, a fair number tend to disappear as a snack—especially when I perform this peaceful chore with a friend (and a glass or two of dry Sauvignon Blanc). If I end up with enough peas, I put them in this delicate fresh soup. Or sometimes, to avoid temptation, I use frozen petite peas. For the chicken broth foundation, I've discovered a convenient concentrated form in Better Than Bouillon, a moist paste that is less salty than comparable products. The broth base also comes in other flavors,

including beef, vegetable, ham, and lobster; an 8-ounce jar costs about $4. All keep up to one year in the refrigerator after opening. Although widely distributed, Better Than Bouillon isn't available in all markets. Call (800) 300-4210 or go to www.superiortouch.com to find a source in your area.

Summer Pea Soup

PREP AND COOK TIME: About 20 minutes

NOTES: A pound of fresh peas yields about 1 cup shelled peas.

MAKES: 4 to 6 servings

- 1 cup (¼ lb.) grated **parmesan cheese**
- ¼ cup (⅛ lb.) **butter** or margarine
- 1 teaspoon grated **lemon** peel

- About ¼ teaspoon fresh-grated or ground **nutmeg**
- 2 **large egg** yolks
- ½ cup **whipping cream**
- 4 teaspoons **chicken bouillon base paste** or 4 cups chicken broth
- ½ cup **dried rice-** or star-**shaped pasta**
- 4 cups **fresh peas** (see notes) or frozen petite peas

  Salt

1. In a bowl, beat parmesan cheese, butter, lemon peel, ¼ teaspoon nutmeg, and egg yolks until blended. Stir in cream.

2. Meanwhile, in a 4- to 5-quart pan, combine bouillon paste, pasta, and 4 cups water (or use broth and omit bouillon paste and water). Cover and bring to a boil over high heat. Add peas, cover, reduce heat, and simmer until tender to bite, about 1 minute for frozen peas, up to 6 minutes for fresh.

3. Mix about 2 cups hot soup into the cheese mixture, then stir cheese mixture into pan. Remove from heat, ladle into bowls, and sprinkle with nutmeg. Add salt to taste.

Per serving: 361 cal., 52% (189 cal.) from fat; 15 g protein; 21 g fat (13 g sat.); 27 g carbo (4.2 g fiber); 1,094 mg sodium; 127 mg chol. ◆

The Wine Guide

By Karen MacNeil-Fife

Barbecue choices

■ Barbecue—prodigious amounts of which are coming off backyard grills this time of year—is nonnegotiable. It's not that negotiating your way through a plate of it is challenging, exactly (don't even try using anything but your fingers with the sensational blackberry-sauced ribs on page 84). No, what's nonnegotiable about it is its obstinate deliciousness. Barbecue absolutely cannot be resisted. Wise diners simply surrender.

This leaves only one practical issue to resolve: What wine should you drink with barbecue? For me, the answer is as straightforward, lip smacking, and deeply satisfying as barbecue itself: Syrah and Petite Syrah.

Yes, I know, that's two answers, not one. But Syrah and Petite Syrah are connected, not only by similar, sensuous flavors, but also by history and, frankly, by the fact that most of us have never quite known how they are different anyway.

Syrah is a grape indigenous to France's Rhône Valley. From there it was transported to South Africa, Australia (where it was inexplicably rechristened Shiraz), and finally the United States, probably in the 1880s, sometimes under the name Petite Syrah (though now Petite Syrah is a different variety). At the rate Syrah is being planted in California today, it is destined to become the state's next major red grape in terms of quantity. However, because of the sheer number of brand-new Syrahs on the market, the style and quality of the wines vary widely. At its best, Syrah is earthy, powerful, and full of berry flavors.

What we now call Petite Syrah (or Petite Sirah; both spellings are common) has a murkier story. It has also been grown in California since the 1880s, or before, according to professor Carole Meredith of the Department of Viticulture and Enology at the University of California at Davis. In the early days, some of these vines were probably a type of Syrah that had small grapes. (All things being equal, winemakers prefer small grapes for their high ratio of skin to juice. Because color, flavor, and tannin come primarily from the grape skins, small grapes yield the most concentrated and flavorful wines.)

Over the course of many decades, however, different varieties were mixed in vineyards with these "petite Syrah" vines, creating what are known as field blends. As other varieties were interplanted with Petite Syrah, and as new vineyards were started with unidentified cuttings from older vineyards, the true identity of Petite Syrah grew more and more obscure.

Then in the 1990s, Meredith and her colleagues began groundbreaking work profiling the DNA of grapevines. For the first time, this allowed us to really understand what

SYRAHS AND PETITE SYRAHS

■ **Benziger Family Winery Syrah 1997 (Central Coast, CA)**, $20. A big, rich teddy bear of a Syrah with juicy blackberry flavors and a supple texture.

■ **Cambria "Tepusquet Vineyard" Syrah 1998 (Santa Maria Valley, CA)**, $22. A beautifully structured, elegant Syrah packed with ripe blackberry flavors.

■ **Geyser Peak Shiraz 1997 (Sonoma County)**, $17. Thick cassis and black cherry flavors—a Syrah that begs for grilled meat.

■ **Madrigal Petite Sirah 1997 (Napa Valley)**, $25. A fantastic, supersaturated, no-holds-barred Petite Syrah with massive fruit. A bit hard to find but worth the effort.

■ **Stags' Leap Winery Petite Syrah 1996 (Napa Valley)**, $28. Rugged, dense, and perfect with barbecue.

■ **Swanson Syrah 1997 (Napa Valley)**, $40. Pricey but powerful. Delicious menthol, grenadine, black pepper, and black cherry flavors.

had been in our wineglasses all those years. And what did they find when they "fingerprinted" many of California's Petite Syrah vines? They generally fit into one of three categories: a field blend of many varieties, including Syrah, Carignane, Zinfandel, Barbera, and Grenache; Peloursin, an ancient Rhône grape; or Durif, a cross of Peloursin and Syrah developed in France in the 1880s. Most are in fact Durif, a grape that is all but extinct in France today.

Alas, none of this information shows up on wine labels, but maybe that just adds mystery to the wine, giving it cultlike appeal. What is clear is that Petite Syrah—like Syrah—is massive, rich, rustic, and saturated with chocolate and berry flavors. Which is a good thing, all in all, because you *can't* sip something petite with barbecue. And Petite Syrah is anything but little. ◆

Salad on a roll

Wrap up fresh greens with
seafood or chicken
for an appetizer or light lunch

By Linda Lau Anusasananan
Photographs by Craig Maxwell

Rice paper wrappers hold cool salad ingredients: lettuce, cucumber, shrimp,
mint, and noodles. Dip in a spicy sauce to eat.

In Granville Market in Vancouver, British Columbia, stacks of long, skinny white cylinders catch my eye. The sign says "salad rolls," but these stark white tubes look nothing like salad. They're Vietnamese fresh spring rolls, which often appear as appetizers in restaurants.

On closer inspection—and tasting—I find that the name fits. The thin wrappers enclose crisp lettuce, cooked shrimp, fresh mint, and cool rice noodles—elements of a tasty, healthful salad. The rolls would be perfect for a light lunch or as party appetizers.

The key to these packaged salads is the wrapper, a fragile, paper-thin disk made from rice flour, water, and salt. The mixture is dried on shallow bamboo trays, creating a crosshatch pattern. When moistened in warm water, the brittle rounds quickly soften. They can be filled and eaten uncooked at this soft, supple stage (as in the recipes here) or fried to make a delicately crisp casing.

Rice paper wrappers come in several sizes. We use medium ones, which are the easiest for first-timers to handle. If you can't locate the rice paper rounds, nori—the toasted seaweed sheets used for sushi—are a good alternative.

Salad rolls wrapped in rice paper or nori taste best freshly made. You can, however, prepare the elements ahead, then assemble the rolls just before serving. Guests often enjoy helping out with this task.

Rice Paper Salad Rolls with Shrimp

PREP AND COOK TIME: About 1 hour

NOTES: Look for rice paper wrappers in Asian markets near the dried noodles. Labeling is a bit erratic: *Bánh tráng* is the Vietnamese name, but they may be called *spring roll wrappers*. If you can't find them in the size specified, buy smaller or larger ones and adjust the filling proportions accordingly. If making ahead, cover uncut rolls with a damp towel, then plastic wrap; let stand at cool room temperature up to 1 hour or chill up to 1 day (chilling firms and toughens the wrappers and noodles slightly).

MAKES: 12 rolls (12 appetizer or 4 main-dish servings)

12 **shrimp** (21 to 25 per lb.)

¼ pound **dried thin rice noodles** (rice sticks)

1 piece **English cucumber** (5 in. long, 6 oz.), rinsed

12 **dried rice paper wrappers** (*bánh tráng,* about 8½ in. wide; see notes)

⅓ cup **fresh mint** leaves, rinsed and drained

12 pieces rinsed and crisped **red** or green **leaf lettuce** (each 3 by 5 in., about 4 oz. total)

Hoisin-chili sauce
(recipe follows)

1. In a 5- to 6-quart pan over high heat, bring 2 to 3 quarts water to a boil. Add shrimp and noodles; return to a boil and stir to separate noodles. Cover and remove from heat. Let stand until shrimp are opaque in center of thickest part (cut to test) and noodles are barely tender to bite, 3 to 4 minutes. Drain; immerse in cold water until cool, about 5 minutes, and drain again.

2. Remove shrimp from noodles. Peel shrimp and, with a small, sharp knife, split in half lengthwise through back. Remove veins; rinse and drain shrimp.

3. Cut cucumber lengthwise into ¼-inch-thick slices, then cut lengthwise into ¼-inch sticks.

4. Fill a large pan or bowl with hot water. Dip 1 rice paper wrapper into water, lift out, and drain briefly. Set on a flat surface. Repeat with another rice paper round; lay beside first. Let stand until wrappers are soft and pliable, about 30 seconds.

5. Working with 2 wrappers at a time, arrange 2 shrimp halves, cut sides up and end to end, in a horizontal line 2½ inches from bottom of each wrapper, coming to within about 1 inch of each side. Distribute 3 or 4 mint leaves over shrimp on each round. Lay 1 cucumber stick at 1 long edge of each lettuce piece and roll up tightly. Set a lettuce roll over shrimp on each wrapper. Distribute ¼ cup rice noodles evenly over each lettuce roll.

6. Pressing down on filling with your fingers, fold bottom of each wrapper over filling, then fold in sides; roll to enclose filling tightly. Press edges to seal; if rice paper is too dry to seal, moisten unsealed edges with a little more hot water. Set rolls on a platter and cover with a damp towel.

7. Repeat to fill remaining rice paper wrappers, 2 at a time. (If rounds begin to take more than 45 seconds to soften, replace water in bowl with more hot water.)

8. To serve, cut rolls crosswise into 3 or 4 pieces; stand pieces upright. Dip in hoisin-chili sauce to eat.

Per roll: 114 cal., 2% (2.7 cal.) from fat; 4.6 g protein; 0.3 g fat (0.1 g sat.); 23 g carbo (0.8 g fiber); 43 mg sodium; 24 mg chol.

Hoisin-Chili Sauce

PREP AND COOK TIME: About 15 minutes, plus about 30 minutes to cool

NOTES: If making up to 1 day ahead, combine all ingredients except peanuts, then cover and chill; cover peanuts separately airtight and let stand at room temperature. Hoisin sauce and Asian red chili paste are available in well-stocked supermarkets and in Asian food stores.

MAKES: About 1 cup

In a 1- to 1½-quart pan, combine ¾ cup **prepared hoisin sauce,** ¼ cup minced **onion,** 3 tablespoons **rice vinegar,** and 2 tablespoons **water;** stir over medium-high heat until mixture boils, about 3 minutes. Stir in 2 to 3 teaspoons **Asian red chili paste,** to taste. Let cool, about 30 minutes. Just before serving, stir in 2 tablespoons minced **salted roasted peanuts.**

Per tablespoon: 42 cal., 13% (5.4 cal.) from fat; 0.3 g protein; 0.6 g fat (0.1 g sat.); 7.3 g carbo (0.2 g fiber); 247 mg sodium; 0 mg chol.

Nori Salad Rolls with Chicken

PREP AND COOK TIME: About 1 hour

NOTES: The dried rice noodles, nori, pickled ginger, and wasabi are all available in well-stocked supermarkets. If making ahead, cover uncut rolls with plastic wrap and store at cool room temperature up to 1 hour or chill up to 1 day (chilling softens nori and firms noodles slightly).

MAKES: 12 rolls; 12 appetizer or 4 main-dish servings

- 2 **boned, skinned chicken breast halves** (6 oz. each), rinsed
- ½ pound **dried thin rice noodles** (rice sticks)
- 1 piece **English cucumber** (7 in. long, ½ lb.), rinsed
- 12 sheets **roasted** (or toasted) **nori** (about 7 by 9 in.)
- ⅓ cup **thin-sliced pickled ginger,** drained
- 12 pieces rinsed and crisped **red** or green **leaf lettuce** (each 3 by 5 in., about 4 oz. total)
  Soy sauce
  Prepared wasabi

1. In a 5- to 6-quart pan over high heat, bring 2 to 3 quarts water to a boil. Add chicken and return to a boil; cover pan and remove from heat. Let stand until chicken is no longer pink in center of thickest part (cut to test), 12 to 16 minutes. With tongs, lift chicken out; immerse in cold water until cool, about 5 minutes. Lift out and drain.

2. Meanwhile, return water to a boil and add rice noodles; stir to separate. Return to a boil, cover, remove from heat, and let stand just until noodles are tender to bite, 2 to 3 minutes. Drain; immerse in cold water until cool, about 5 minutes, then drain again.

3. Slice chicken crosswise into strips about ¼ inch thick and ½ inch wide. Cut cucumber lengthwise into ¼-inch-thick slices, then cut slices lengthwise into ¼-inch sticks.

4. Set 1 nori sheet on a dry, flat surface. Arrange 3 or 4 chicken slices end to end in a horizontal line 2 inches in from 1 short edge. Top chicken with 2 or 3 slices of ginger. Lay 1 cucumber stick at 1 long edge of a lettuce piece and roll up tightly. Set lettuce roll on ginger. Distribute ⅓ cup rice noodles evenly over lettuce. Pressing filling down with your fingers, fold bottom edge of nori over filling and continue to roll tightly. Moisten free edge of nori with water and press roll over wet edge to seal. Set, seam down, on a platter. Repeat to fill and roll remaining nori sheets.

5. To serve, cut rolls crosswise into 3 or 4 pieces; stand upright. Mix soy sauce and wasabi to taste; offer with nori rolls as a dip.

Per roll: 119 cal., 3% (3.6 cal.) from fat; 7.4 g protein; 0.4 g fat (0.1 g sat.); 21 g carbo (0.3 g fiber); 114 mg sodium; 16 mg chol. ◆

A. Dip brittle dried rice paper rounds into hot water to soften; remove and drain briefly. Lay flat and let stand until soft.

B. Arrange two shrimp halves and three or four mint leaves in a line 2½ inches from the bottom of the softened wrapper.

C. Place a lettuce leaf, with cucumber stick enclosed, on the shrimp, then add cooked rice noodles to the mound.

D. Pressing down on the filling, fold the bottom, then the sides, of the wrapper over the filling and roll tightly to enclose.

Fruit and herbs infuse a liquid lineup to splash over ice.

Iced teas, please

Cool new sippers for your summer comfort

By Andrew Baker

Hot days call for cool drinks. Iced tea is a long-standing favorite; new, creative combinations can make it even more pleasing. Start with tea bags, then add flavors—from floral to fruity. Or, in the case of the lemon-mint infusion here, skip the tea altogether.

Cool tips. For the most intense flavor, chill the beverages, then add ice. To quick-chill, nest the container in ice water and stir often until the tea is cold, about 20 minutes. Cover and chill up to 2 days. If using loose tea, substitute 1 teaspoon leaves for 1 tea bag.

Orange Frost Chai

PREP AND COOK TIME: About 20 minutes, plus about 20 minutes to quick-chill

MAKES: About 2 quarts

1. In a 3- to 4-quart pan over medium-high heat, stir 1 quart **water,** 1 quart **milk,** 1/3 cup firmly packed **brown sugar,** and 2 tablespoons grated **orange** peel until boiling.

2. Add 8 single-serving **orange pekoe tea bags** and 2 tablespoons **vanilla;** reduce heat, stir gently, and simmer 1 to 2 minutes. Cover, remove from heat, and let stand 10 minutes.

3. Pour liquid through a fine strainer into a pitcher (at least 2 qt.). Cool (see "Cool tips," above). Pour into **ice**-filled glasses and garnish with **orange** slices.

Per cup: 122 cal., 30% (37 cal.) from fat; 4 g protein; 4.1 g fat (2.5 g sat.); 16 g carbo (0 g fiber); 71 mg sodium; 17 mg chol.

Lemon-Mint Infusion

PREP AND COOK TIME: About 30 minutes, plus about 20 minutes to quick-chill

NOTES: Erin Quon of San Francisco also serves this blend hot.

MAKES: About 2 quarts

1. With a vegetable peeler or sharp knife, pare peel (colored part only) from 2 rinsed **lemons** (about 5 oz. each).

2. In a deep 3- to 4-quart bowl, combine peel, 1 1/2 cups lightly packed rinsed **fresh mint** leaves, and 1/4 cup coarsely chopped **fresh ginger.** Add 2 quarts boiling **water;** let stand 15 to 20 minutes. Pour liquid through a fine strainer into a pitcher (at least 2 qt.). Cool (see "Cool tips," left).

3. Cut lemons in half, ream juice, and add to pitcher. Sweeten to taste with about 6 tablespoons **honey.** Pour into **ice**-filled glasses.

Per cup: 67 cal., 2.7% (1.8 cal.) from fat; 1 g protein; 0.2 g fat (0 g sat.); 17 g carbo (0 g fiber); 9 mg sodium; 0 mg chol.

Berry-Chamomile Tea

PREP AND COOK TIME: About 15 minutes, plus about 20 minutes to quick-chill

MAKES: About 2 quarts

In a deep 3- to 4-quart bowl, combine 6 single-serving **chamomile tea bags,** 1/2 cup **dried tart cherries** or dried cranberries, and 1/2 cup **dried blueberries.** Add 2 quarts boiling **water;** let stand 10 minutes. Discard tea bags. Cool (see "Cool tips," left). Add 2 tablespoons **sugar,** to taste. Pour into **ice**-filled glasses.

Per cup: 75 cal., 0% (0 cal.) from fat; 0 g protein; 0 g fat; 19 g carbo (1.3 g fiber); 5.6 mg sodium; 0 mg chol.

Lavender-Caramel Tea

PREP AND COOK TIME: About 15 minutes, plus about 20 minutes to quick-chill

MAKES: About 2 quarts

In a deep 3- to 4-quart bowl, combine 6 single-serving **black tea bags** and 1 tablespoon **dried lavender.** Add 2 quarts boiling **water;** let stand 10 minutes. Pour through a fine strainer into a pitcher (at least 2 qt.). Cool (see "Cool tips," left). Sweeten to taste with about 1/2 cup **fat-free caramel sauce.** Pour into **ice**-filled glasses.

Per cup: 57 cal., 0% (0 cal.) from fat; 0 g protein; 0 g fat; 14 g carbo (0 g fiber); 40 mg sodium; 0 mg chol.

Trade Winds Tea

PREP AND COOK TIME: About 15 minutes, plus about 20 minutes to quick-chill

MAKES: About 2 quarts

1. Rinse 6 stalks **fresh lemon grass** (about 1/2 lb.). Trim and discard root ends, tough tops, and coarse outer layers. Finely chop stalks. Put in a 3- to 4-quart pan, add 2 quarts **water,** and bring to a boil over high heat; reduce heat and simmer 10 minutes.

2. Meanwhile, in a deep 3- to 4-quart bowl, combine 4 single-serving **jasmine tea bags** and 4 whole **star anise.** Add lemon-grass mixture; let stand 5 minutes. Pour through a fine strainer into a pitcher (at least 2 qt.). Cool (see "Cool tips," left). Add about 1/4 cup **sugar,** to taste. Pour into **ice**-filled glasses.

Per cup: 26 cal., 0% (0 cal.) from fat; 0 g protein; 0 g fat; 6.7 g carbo (0 g fiber); 3.6 mg sodium; 0 mg chol.

Tarragon-Rose Tea

PREP AND COOK TIME: About 12 minutes, plus 20 minutes to quick-chill

NOTES: Rose flower water is sold in liquor stores and well-stocked supermarkets.

MAKES: About 2 quarts

In a deep 3- to 4-quart bowl, combine 4 single-serving **Earl Grey tea bags** and 2 cups lightly packed **tarragon sprigs** or 1/4 cup dried tarragon. Add 2 quarts boiling **water;** let stand 10 minutes. Pour through a fine strainer into a pitcher (at least 2 qt.). Cool (see "Cool tips," left). Add 1 teaspoon **rose flower water** and about 1/4 cup **sugar,** to taste. Pour into **ice**-filled glasses.

Per cup: 25 cal., 0% (0 cal.) from fat; 0 g protein; 0 g fat; 6.6 g carbo (0 g fiber); 3.6 mg sodium; 0 mg chol. ◆

B.C.'s hot wine country

The search for good wine and history along
the Okanagan's Golden Mile

By Jena MacPherson • Photographs by Graham Osborne

Gold first lured hordes of Americans into the dry and hilly interior of British Columbia. So many California miners came through in the 1858 Gold Rush, the British claimed the region as a colony—no doubt trying to protect it from Yanks with an acquisitive gleam in their eyes. Gold fever hit again in 1895 when Tinhorn Creek Mine and the town of Fairview (now gone) sprang up at the south end of the Okanagan Valley. The short-lived boom fizzled in the early 1900s.

These days, the 130-mile glacier-scoured basin, called simply the Okanagan, is known more for vineyards, fruit-stand bounty, lakes, and proliferating golf courses than for its history. But history has a funny way of repeating itself. After nearly a century, the Tinhorn name is back—on a

winery that is producing treasure of a liquid sort. A winemaking boom that promises to be anything but short-lived is claiming a pocket-size chunk of desert directly north of the border between central Washington and British Columbia. To winemakers, this patch of rocky soil bordering 1 mile of Provincial Highway 97 north and south of Oliver is the Golden Mile.

Canada's desert vineyards

Late on a typical summer afternoon, the terrace of the new Tinhorn Creek Vineyards south of Oliver can be hot. Hot enough to prompt wine columnist and Vancouver radio show host Anthony Gismondi to explain the unique qualities of the Golden Mile microclimate while sipping a glass of velvety Merlot.

Clusters of sun-drenched grapes ripen in front of Tinhorn Creek Vineyards.

It turns out that the Golden Mile is within Canada's only desert. The antelope-brush (greasewood), big sage, and ground-clinging prickly pear cactus growing on the valley's low, flat benches receive less than 10 inches of precipitation a year. Summer temperatures average in the low 90s—about 8° warmer here than in the central and northern parts of the valley—so grapes ripen a couple of weeks earlier. Because it is a desert, there are none of the usual vineyard dis-

Just north of Oliver, vineyards tilt down to Vaseux Lake beneath McIntyre Bluff.

plexity, and lots of depth. The top wines can be exceptional; the second-tier wines vary in quality.

Will winemaking and tourism persevere and lure more Americans than gold once did? Oldfield, a Sonoma

eases here, and Gismondi claims that these are some of the most pristine grapes in the world.

Although he's watched the valley's wine industry for 20 years, Gismondi says the real potential of the entire Okanagan is just beginning to be realized in wines from Golden Mile vineyards. The revolution is only five years old, having begun with the planting of premium varietals such as Cabernet Sauvignon, Chardonnay, and Merlot and continuing with the arrival of talented California winemakers like Tinhorn's Sandra Oldfield and Burrowing Owl Vineyard's Bill Dyer.

Opening wineries

The buzz about the area's grape-growing potential has set off a new kind of gold rush. At impressive new wineries, tastings and other activities draw visitors. Tinhorn Creek, for instance, hosts art shows and offers summer concerts in an outdoor amphitheater. Visitors can also pick up a map to take a 1-mile walk or a 6-mile loop hike leading from the winery to the defunct Tinhorn Creek Mine, where a picnic in the

tree-dotted glade is especially pleasant after climbing the dry hills.

Burrowing Owl's new Tuscan-style winery, tucked into the Golden Mile's eastern hillside, has a handsome viewing terrace perfect for a picnic. Tours explain the winery's state-of-the-art features, which include gravity-flow transfer of grapes from the field into tanks to avoid bruising, and vast underground caves for wine storage.

Just down the valley, Hester Creek Estate Winery's trellis-covered patio and stuccoed tasting room have the intimacy and friendly appeal of a French country house.

While the jury is still out on how the region's grapes will mature, there have been early successes with Merlots. Tinhorn Creek's '97, a big, open wine with chocolate and dried cherry flavors, is an award winner, and Gismondi expects that the '98 will be too. He also likes Burrowing Owl's '98 Chardonnay—another big wine with a fruit bouquet, toasty com-

Okanagan travel planner

The Okanagan, a four-hour drive east of Vancouver, has many attractions. Nicknamed "Palm Springs North" for its 50 golf courses, it also offers houseboating on Okanagan Lake, horseback riding, rail tours, and mountain- and road biking. For travel information, contact **Tourism British Columbia** (800/435-5622 or www.hellobc.com). Prices are quoted in U.S. dollars. Area code is 250 unless noted.

Golden Mile wine touring

Wineries are open for tasting daily in summer; entrances to each are clearly marked along Provincial 97 south of Oliver. **Burrowing Owl Vineyard** (877/498-0620 or www.bovwine.com). **Gehringer Brothers Estate Winery** (498-3537). **Hester Creek Estate Winery** (498-4435 or www.hester-creek.com). **Inniskillin Okanagan Vineyards** (498-6663 or www.inniskillin.com). **Tinhorn Creek Vineyards** (498-3743 or www.tinhorn.com).

You can taste samples and purchase more than 300 wines from 50 British Columbia wineries at the **B.C. Wine Information Centre** (888 Westminster Ave. W., Penticton; 490-2006). On the same site is the **Penticton Chamber of Commerce** (800/663-5052).

Activities

The **Okanagan Fall Wine Festival** (861-6654 or www.owfs.com) is September 29 to October 8.

County transplant, thinks so, noting that the Golden Mile isn't all that far from the Golden State. "Take Provincial 97 north from the California border, drive 10 hours, and don't stop until you see our winery sign."

There are annual festivals in January (eiswein) and May. **Southern Pines Riding Stables** (from $50; 37621 White Lake Rd.; 498-2399), about 5 miles northwest of Oliver, offers trail rides to wineries. At 66-acre **Desert Centre, Osoyoos,** guided tours lead you through the local antelope-brush ecosystem ($3.50, mid-April to mid-October; 146th Ave., off Provincial 97, about 2 miles northwest of Osoyoos; 877/899-0897 or www.desert.org).

Dining
Historic 1912 Restaurant and Country Inn on the lakefront in Kaleden (100 Alder Ave.; 497-6868 or 888/633-1912) has the valley's most extensive wine list.

Lodging
Two contemporary B&Bs on opposite sides of the valley offer views, privacy, and hot tubs. **Wildflower B&B** (from $40; 38950 Fairview–White Lake Rd., Oliver; 498-4326 or www.bbcanada.com/1598.html), on 14 acres, is a great base for biking and has two rooms with private baths. **Villa Blanca B&B** (from $40; 23640 Deerfoot Rd., Osoyoos; 495-5334 or www.bbcanada.com/2681.html), on a dramatic mountaintop perch east of Osoyoos, has two rooms with private baths and one private suite. Reservation services. **Okanagan Reservations** (800/663-1900) provides resort, hotel, golf, and winery tours. The **South Okanagan B&B Association** (497-6721) also offers golf packages. ◆

Tiny black vanilla seeds speckle a tangy custard made from drained yogurt.

Distinctly vanilla

Seeds from very special beans perfume creamy desserts—
and even an entrée

By Linda Lau Anusasananan • Photographs by Rick Mariani

Take one deep whiff of a bouquet of vanilla beans and fall in love. Their intense, sweet aroma is that intoxicating. The compound responsible for this distinctive, complex perfume is vanillin, contained in thousands of pinpoint seeds in the seed pods of a particular orchid plant.

To capture the essence, split the pods open lengthwise and scrape the seeds into sweet or savory dishes, then add the pods for good measure. Afterward, take advantage of the residual fragrance in the pods: Remove them once they've flavored the dish, rinse and dry them, and store them in sugar; they'll impart a sweet, mellow aroma and flavor to the sugar.

Vanilla beans (the seed pods) are expensive—expect to pay $2 to $3 apiece. But stored airtight in a dark place (don't refrigerate), they keep for several years. Look for dark, shiny, pliable, and moist beans in supermarkets, gourmet food stores, and spice shops. Organic vanilla beans and vanilla extract from Mexico are available from Patricia Rain, Box 3206, Santa Cruz, CA 95063; (831) 476-9111 or www.vanilla-queen.com.

Vanilla Yogurt Cheese Custard

PREP AND COOK TIME: About 30 minutes, plus 1 day to drain yogurt and flavor sugar, at least 30 minutes to cool, and 1½ hours to chill
NOTES: At least 1 day ahead, flavor the sugar and drain the yogurt for cheese. The longer you drain the yogurt, the less cheese you get and the firmer it is.
MAKES: 4 servings

Vanilla adds an elusive fragrance to a cream sauce with angel hair pasta, shrimp, and mint.

⅓ cup **sugar**

1 **vanilla bean** (5 to 7 in.)

1 quart **plain nonfat yogurt** (without gelatin)

1 **large egg**

12 **raspberries,** rinsed, drained, and patted dry

1. Put sugar in a small bowl. With a small, sharp knife, split vanilla bean in half lengthwise and scrape seeds from pod into sugar; mix until evenly blended. Add pod to sugar, cover airtight, and let stand at least 24 hours or up to 4 days.

2. Set a strainer or colander over a deep pan or bowl, supporting it so the base of the strainer is at least 2 inches above the pan bottom. Line strainer with 2 layers of cheesecloth or a clean muslin or linen towel.

3. Spoon yogurt into the cloth-lined strainer. Enclose strainer and pan airtight in plastic wrap. Chill at least 24 hours or up to 4 days (see notes), pouring off whey as it accumulates.

4. Scrape yogurt cheese from cloth. Measure 1½ cups; reserve extra for other uses.

5. Remove pod from vanilla sugar and reserve for other uses. In a bowl, mix sugar, 1½ cups yogurt cheese, and egg until well blended.

6. Spoon mixture into 4 soufflé or custard cups (½- to ¾-cup size). Set cups in a 9-inch square baking pan. Pour about 1 inch hot water into pan.

7. Bake in a 325° oven until custard centers jiggle only slightly when cups are gently shaken, 15 to 17 minutes. With a wide slotted spatula, transfer custards to a rack to cool, about 30 minutes, then cover and chill until cold, at least 1½ hours or up to 1 day. Garnish with raspberries just before serving.

Per serving: 165 cal., 7.3% (12 cal.) from fat; 11 g protein; 1.3 g fat (0.4 g sat.); 26 g carbo (0.3 g fiber); 96 mg sodium; 53 mg chol.

Pasta with Peas and Shrimp in Vanilla Cream

PREP AND COOK TIME: About 20 minutes

NOTES: Vanilla is a subtle accent in this pasta course.

MAKES: 3 to 4 servings

½ pound **dried angel hair pasta**

2 cups **frozen petite peas**

1 **onion** (6 oz.), peeled and chopped

2 tablespoons **butter** or margarine

1 **vanilla bean** (5 to 7 in.)

½ cup **chicken broth**

½ cup **whipping cream**

½ pound **shelled cooked tiny shrimp**

Salt and **pepper**

⅓ cup **fresh mint** leaves (1 to 2 in.), rinsed

1. In a 5- to 6-quart pan over high heat, bring 2½ to 3 quarts water to a boil. Add pasta and cook until almost tender to bite, 2 to 3 minutes. Stir in peas. Cook until pasta is barely tender and peas are hot, 1 to 2 minutes longer.

2. Meanwhile, in a 12-inch frying pan or 5- to 6-quart pan over medium-high heat, frequently stir onion in butter until soft, 5 to 7 minutes. With a small, sharp knife, slit vanilla bean in half lengthwise and scrape seeds from pod into broth. Add broth mixture and cream to onion mixture; add pod. Stir until mixture boils, 2 to 3 minutes.

3. Place shrimp in a colander and rinse with cold water. Pour cooked pasta and peas over shrimp in colander to drain. Add to cream sauce and mix gently to coat. Add salt and pepper to taste. If desired, remove vanilla pod.

4. Pour into a serving bowl and sprinkle with mint leaves.

Per serving: 479 cal., 32% (153 cal.) from fat; 25 g protein; 17 g fat (9.7 g sat.); 56 g carbo (5.5 g fiber); 295 mg sodium; 160 mg chol.

Vanilla Strawberry Trifle

PREP AND COOK TIME: About 1 hour, plus at least 4 hours to chill

NOTES: If assembling through step 5 up to 1 day ahead, cover and chill. Add berries up to 4 hours before serving; cover and chill.

MAKES: 8 to 10 servings

- 1 cup **sugar**
- 1 **vanilla bean** (5 to 7 in.)
- 2 cups **milk**
- 2 tablespoons **cornstarch**
- 1 **large egg** yolk
- 1 cup **whipping cream**
- 1 **pound cake** (1 lb.), thawed if frozen
- 2 tablespoons **vanilla extract**
- 1½ to 2 pounds **strawberries,** rinsed, hulled, and patted dry

1. Put ½ cup sugar in a 2- to 3-quart pan. With a small, sharp knife, slit vanilla bean in half lengthwise and scrape seeds from pod into sugar; stir to blend. Add 1¾ cups milk and the vanilla pod. Stir over medium heat until mixture is steaming, 5 to 8 minutes. Remove from heat, cover, and let stand 20 minutes.

2. Meanwhile, in a small bowl, mix remaining ¼ cup milk and the cornstarch; add egg yolk and beat to blend. Pour into warm milk. Stir over medium-high heat until sauce boils, 2 to 3 minutes. Pour through a fine strainer into a bowl; remove vanilla pod from strainer, dry, and reserve for other uses. Nest bowl in ice water and stir sauce often until cold, 10 to 15 minutes.

3. Whip cream until it forms soft peaks. Gently fold cream into sauce.

4. Cut cake into ¼-inch-thick slices. Arrange slices, slightly overlapping, on a 14- to 16-inch platter with sloping sides or a rim, or in a wide, shallow bowl.

5. In a 1½- to 2-quart pan, combine 1 cup water and remaining ½ cup sugar. Bring to a boil over high heat and stir often until reduced to ¾ cup, 7 to 10 minutes. Remove from heat and stir in vanilla extract. Drizzle syrup evenly over cake slices. Spoon cream mixture over cake, leaving uncovered a ½- to 1-inch border around edge. Cover and chill at least 4 hours or up to 1 day.

6. Set berries, stem ends down, in cream mixture. Serve, or cover and chill. Spoon out portions.

Per serving: 391 cal., 44% (171 cal.) from fat; 5.3 g protein; 19 g fat (11 g sat.); 51 g carbo (2.1 g fiber); 214 mg sodium; 155 mg chol. ◆

The Quick Cook

Snacks in 30 minutes or less

By Andrew Baker

Campfire treats

JAMES CARRIER

Crisp tortillas and oozing cheese wrap mini-sausages for an updated rarebit.

▣ If camping, in your book, means ending the day around a fire, swapping stories and toasting tidbits on the end of a stick, these morsels— savory and sweet—are for you. You don't even have to leave home to enjoy the fun—a fireplace, firepit, or barbecue can be the center of the action. Long sticks may not be as available there as they are out in the wilderness, but long skewers with wood handles (or hot mitts to protect your hands) and long forks designed for campfire cooking (see page 205) are ready, reusable alternatives.

Sausage-Tortilla Rarebits

PREP AND COOK TIME: About 25 minutes

MAKES: 18 pieces

- 3 **flour tortillas** (10 in.)
- 2 tablespoons **honey mustard**
- 6 ounces **jack cheese with chilies**
- 18 **cooked mini-sausages** (2 in. long; about ½ lb. total)

1. Stack the tortillas and trim 2 opposite edges off straight to make the center section 6 inches wide; discard the trimmed pieces. Cut the stack lengthwise into 2-inch-wide strips, then cut each strip in half crosswise. Spread mustard evenly onto 1 side of each tortilla piece.

2. Thinly slice cheese; arrange the slices equally on top of the mustard on each tortilla strip, patching the cheese, if needed, to cover the strip (use all the cheese). Lay a sausage across 1 end of each strip and roll the tortilla and cheese to enclose it.

3. Thread 3 tortilla rolls crosswise, through seam, sausage, and opposite side of tortilla, onto the tines of a campfire fork or metal skewer (at least 20 in. long). Repeat for each portion, or reuse fork or skewer.

4. Hold the tortilla rolls about 4 inches above heat source (a campfire or an ignited gas or charcoal barbecue), and turn as needed to cook on all sides until cheese is softened and tortilla is lightly browned, about 1 minute per skewer. Pull rolls off skewers to eat.

Per piece: 89 cal., 52% (46 cal.) from fat; 4.5 g protein; 5.1 g fat (2.2 g sat.); 6.1 g carbo (0.3 g fiber); 194 mg sodium; 18 mg chol.

Anchovy-stuffed Tomatoes

PREP AND COOK TIME: About 15 minutes

MAKES: 18 pieces

- 18 **cherry tomatoes** (1¼ in. wide; about ¾ lb. total)
- 1 can (2 oz.) **anchovy fillets**
- Fresh-ground **pepper**

1. Rinse tomatoes. With a sharp knife, core tomatoes and squeeze gently to remove some of the seeds.

2. Drain anchovies and divide into 18 equal portions. Roll each fillet (or fillet pieces) snugly from a narrow end. Gently push 1 portion into each tomato.

3. Thread 3 tomatoes crosswise onto the tines of a campfire fork or metal skewer (at least 20 in. long). Repeat for each portion, or reuse fork or skewer.

4. Hold tomatoes about 4 inches above heat source (a campfire, or an ignited gas or charcoal barbecue), and turn as needed to cook all sides until tomatoes are very lightly charred and anchovies begin to sizzle, 1 to 2 minutes per skewer. Sprinkle with pepper to taste. Pull from skewers to eat.

Per piece: 9.2 cal., 29% (2.7 cal.) from fat; 0.9 g protein; 0.3 g fat (0.1 g sat.); 0.9 g carbo (0.2 g fiber); 93 mg sodium; 1.4 mg chol.

Prosciutto-wrapped Apricots

PREP AND COOK TIME: About 15 minutes

MAKES: 18 pieces

> 3 ounces **thin-sliced prosciutto**
>
> 18 **dried apricots**

1. Cut prosciutto slices lengthwise into 18 equal strips. Wrap 1 strip snugly around each apricot.

2. Securing the prosciutto ends, thread 3 wrapped apricots onto the tines of a campfire fork or metal skewer (at least 20 in. long). Repeat for each portion, or reuse fork or skewer.

3. Hold fruit about 4 inches above heat source (campfire, or ignited gas or charcoal barbecue) and turn as needed to cook all sides until prosciutto is lightly browned and sizzling, about

2 minutes per skewer. Pull from skewers to eat.

Per piece: 30 cal., 21% (6.3 cal.) from fat; 1.6 g protein; 0.7 g fat (0.2 g sat.); 4.9 g carbo (0.6 g fiber); 88 mg sodium; 3.8 mg chol.

Cinnamon-Hazelnut S'mores

PREP AND COOK TIME: About 15 minutes

NOTES: Cocoa-hazelnut spread, such as Nutella, is sold in well-stocked supermarkets and in specialty food stores.

MAKES: 12 pieces

> 12 **cinnamon graham crackers** (about 2½ by 5 in.)
>
> ¾ cup **cocoa-flavor hazelnut spread**
>
> 24 **marshmallows** (about 1 in. wide)

1. Gently break graham crackers in half to form squares. Cover 1 side of each of the 24 squares equally with the cocoa-flavor hazelnut spread.

2. Thread 2 marshmallows onto a campfire fork or metal skewer (at least 20 in. long). Repeat for each portion, or reuse fork or skewer.

3. Hold marshmallows about 4 inches above heat source (campfire, or ignited gas or charcoal barbecue) and

turn as needed until marshmallows are golden brown on the outside and soft in the center, 1 to 2 minutes.

4. Lay 2 toasted marshmallows on coated side of 1 graham cracker square; top with another square, coated side down. Hold crackers together and pull fork from marshmallows. Repeat to make additional s'mores.

Per piece: 182 cal., 28% (51 cal.) from fat; 2 g protein; 5.7 g fat (0.7 g sat.); 32 g carbo (0.4 g fiber); 106 mg sodium; 0 mg chol.

Ginger-Lemon S'mores

PREP AND COOK TIME: About 15 minutes

MAKES: 12 pieces

Follow directions for **cinnamon-hazelnut s'mores,** preceding, omitting graham crackers and cocoa-hazelnut spread. Instead, use 24 **thin ginger snap cookies** (about 2 in. wide) and coat flat sides equally with **lemon curd** (about ½ cup total). Toast 12 **marshmallows;** for each s'more, sandwich 1 marshmallow between coated sides of 2 cookies.

Per piece: 114 cal., 17% (19 cal.) from fat; 1.6 g protein; 2.1 g fat (0.2 g sat.); 25 g carbo (0.3 g fiber); 105 mg sodium; 0 mg chol. ◆

Viva chile verde

It's the only thing a native New Mexican can't live without

By Sharon Niederman

"**R**ed or green?" That's the official state question, asked and answered thousands of times a day in New Mexico's restaurants and cafes. New Mexicans take the preparation of their state vegetable, the chili pepper, very seriously; they are prone to discussions both lengthy and fierce on the subject. How important is this sauce natives call chile? You can live without sex, many would say, but live without chile? Impossible!

Some people prefer the taste of red chile. It's made from red chili peppers—a riper form of green chilies—which are picked and dried for later use. But many insist on their green. Typically, fresh-picked green chilies are roasted, then cooked

slowly with meat, garlic, onion, oregano, and cumin, although there is no standard recipe. Somewhere between a condiment and a stew, this savory blend is then used to smother burritos, enchiladas, eggs, and burgers, or eaten on its own as a "bowl of green" with the possible addition of beans and potatoes. It's customarily served with a tortilla or sopaipilla.

Trying to describe the chile verde experience to someone who's never tasted it is like trying to describe the ocean to someone who has never seen it. For starters, green chile has a unique earthy, warm, pungent taste. As much a sensation as a flavor, chile ranges in heat from mild to wild, depending on the chili pepper variety,

Red-topped tostada swims in green chile sauce.

the climate where it grew, and the rainfall it received. Most New Mexico green chile has roots in Hatch, where the largest crops of Big Jim and New Mexico 6-4 green chilies are grown.

The chili pepper may be the state

vegetable, but it's not a native. The wild chili originated in South America; Spanish conquistadores carried it north about 400 years ago. Those first Spanish converts were undoubtedly hooked on capsaicin, the chemical that produces the vegetable's heat and the pleasurable, endorphin-induced sensations that keep sweaty-browed aficionados coming back for more.

This heat only partly explains the vegetable's appeal. In the hands of different cooks, the green chile dish takes on distinctly different tastes. From modest holes-in-the-wall to upscale restaurants, New Mexico's eating establishments pride themselves on the originality of their chile recipes.

Red or green? Most of the year it's a tough choice. For those who can't decide, there's always "Christmas"— a portion of each. But by late July, the decision becomes a no-brainer. That's when the harvest begins, and the aromatic perfume of fresh green chilies roasting at roadside stands and open-air markets induces a delirious craving in the local population. This altered state, which lasts through the harvest and into the fall, can only be set straight by sitting down to a good helping of that fresh-roasted green.

A diner's guide to New Mexico's best green chile

■ **ALBUQUERQUE: Barelas Coffee House.** This rowdy chile parlor, beloved of local politicians and old-timers, serves as a neighborhood kitchen for the entire city. The carpet is well-worn, and the waitresses know regulars by name. The blistering green chile is addictive—go for the crisp, green-doused chiles rellenos. *1502 Fourth St. S.W.; (505) 843-7577.*

ALBUQUERQUE: Duran Central Pharmacy. Locals line up at noon for the daily specials at this expanded lunch counter in the back of an Old Town drugstore, where fresh tortillas warm on the grill. Try the blue corn, green

Glasses of water are no match for green chile at Santa Fe's Guadalupe Café.

chile enchiladas smothered in a thick, pungent, sweet-edged green sauce. *1815 Central Ave. N.W.; 247-4141.*

CHIMAYO: Rancho de Chimayo. Taste classic New Mexico green here amid the century-old, foot-thick adobe walls. The nearby Santuario de Chimayo is known as the Lourdes of America because of the reputed healing powers of its "holy dirt." Some would say that Chimayo chile is a religious experience of a different kind. *300 County 98; 351-4444.*

EL RITO: El Farolito. Located on Main Street across from the general store in the village of El Rito, a center of northern New Mexico Rio Grande weaving, this charming cafe with eight picnic tables has taken home International Chile Society trophies for its well-seasoned, piquant green chile. *1212 Main St.; 581-9509.*

GALLUP: Earl's. A Gallup institution, Earl's is a busy landmark for country-western singers traveling coast-to-coast. Here it's customary for Native Americans to sell their jewelry and wares from table to table. Just for fun, try a side of Earl's zinger green chile over mashed potatoes. *1400 E. Historic Rte. 66; 863-4201.*

HATCH: Valley Cafe. Locals here in the "Chili Capital of the World" don't care that this cafe's plates are mismatched or the chairs are solid or-

ange vinyl, because the chile is the real thing. Jesus Robles's green chile stew starts out hot, and the heat waves keep on coming until they warm you clear through and deliver a good kick at the end. You'll need to check your tongue for blisters after eating a bowl. *306 Hall St.; 267-4608.*

LAS CRUCES: My Brother's Place. This downtown hangout with a family atmosphere serves a satisfying, meaty green chile bowl. It's guaranteed to please serious chile eaters as well as those whose palates aren't asbestos-lined. *334 S. Main St.; 523-7681.*

LAS VEGAS: Estella's Cafe. Now run by the second and third generations of the Gonzales family, Estella's Cafe has been around for 50 years. Matriarch Estella Gonzales still presides at a back table, surrounded by family photographs and old friends. Try the combination plate for the warm buzz of a chile kiss. *148 Bridge St.; 454-0048.*

SANTA FE: Guadalupe Cafe. Locals crave the pure chile flavor of the made-from-scratch chicken enchiladas. They're dished up with a generous hand at this friendly 25-year-old cafe tucked into an old adobe. The chef is a purist who refuses to serve your entrée's chile on the side. If your taste buds can't hack a big dose, you can order it "light." *422 Old Santa Fe Trail; 982-9762.*

SANTA FE: Maria's New Mexican Kitchen. As famous for margaritas made with 80 kinds of tequila as for its chile, Maria's is a part of Santa Fe history. A bowl of green is delectably spicy, a rich broth packed with chunks of potato, chili, and meat, with all the nourishing, curative powers of Grandma's chicken soup. *555 W. Cordova Rd.; 983-7929.*

TAOS: Michael's Kitchen. This bakery-cafe is always crammed, but you can still grab a seat at the counter for a taste of creamy, sweet green chile, the deserved winner of numerous Taos awards. The vegetarian version is equally popular. *304 Paseo del Pueblo Norte; 758-4178.* ◆

Kitchen Cabinet

Readers' recipes tested in Sunset's kitchens

By Andrew Baker

Soft chunks of pears encased in eggs make a sweet start in the morning.

Baked Pear Frittata

J Heflin, Woodinville, Washington

This sweet frittata has a tender, almost custardlike texture. It's perfect for brunch and even makes a great dessert.

PREP AND COOK TIME: About 25 minutes

MAKES: 4 servings

2 **firm-ripe pears** (about 1 lb. total)

2 tablespoons **butter** or margarine

6 **large eggs**

⅓ cup **milk**

¼ cup **all-purpose flour**

1 tablespoon **granulated sugar**

1 teaspoon **vanilla**

¼ teaspoon **salt**

¼ cup **mascarpone cheese** or whipped cream cheese

1 to 2 tablespoons firmly packed **brown sugar**

1. Rinse, peel, and core pears. Cut fruit into ½-inch chunks.

2. In a 9- to 10-inch ovenproof nonstick frying pan over medium-high heat, melt butter; add pears and turn occasionally until lightly browned and tender when pierced, 7 to 8 minutes.

3. Meanwhile, in a bowl, whisk to blend eggs, milk, flour, granulated sugar, vanilla, and salt. Remove frying pan from heat and pour egg mixture over pears.

4. Bake in a 425° oven until frittata is golden brown and set in center when pan is gently shaken, 8 to 12 minutes.

5. Cut into wedges to serve. Spoon dollops of cheese onto portions and sprinkle with brown sugar.

Per serving: 358 cal., 53% (189 cal.) from fat; 12 g protein; 21 g fat (11 g sat.); 31 g carbo (2.7 g fiber); 315 mg sodium; 350 mg chol.

Roast Chicken with Bread Salad

Diane Brown, Los Angeles

When Diane Brown entertains, she'd rather be with her guests than in the kitchen. This easy main dish is her solution.

PREP AND COOK TIME: About 45 minutes

MAKES: 4 servings

¼ pound **French bread**

2 tablespoons **balsamic vinegar**

¼ cup **olive oil**

¼ cup **pine nuts**

4 **boned chicken breast halves** (about 7 oz. each)

1 tablespoon **fresh thyme** leaves or 1½ teaspoons dried thyme

4 teaspoons minced or pressed **garlic**

½ cup thinly sliced **green onions** (including tops)

2 cups diced **firm-ripe tomatoes**

2 quarts lightly packed **arugula** (about ½ lb.), rinsed and crisped

Salt and fresh-ground **pepper**

1. Cut bread into 1-inch chunks and spread in a single layer in a shallow 3-quart casserole (about 9 by 13 in.).

2. Bake in a 450° oven, turning occasionally with a wide spatula, until bread is crisp and golden, about 8 minutes. Pour bread into a wide bowl; drizzle with 1 tablespoon balsamic vinegar and 2 tablespoons oil, and mix.

3. Meanwhile, in a 10- to 12-inch frying pan over medium-high heat, stir or shake pine nuts until golden, about 3 minutes. Pour from pan.

4. Rinse chicken and pat dry. Pat thyme and 2 teaspoons garlic onto skin side of chicken. Lay chicken, skin side up, in a single layer in the casserole.

5. Bake in a 450° oven until chicken is no longer pink in center of thickest part (cut to test), 18 to 20 minutes.

6. Add remaining 1 tablespoon balsamic vinegar, 2 tablespoons oil, 2 teaspoons garlic, and green onions to frying pan. Stir over medium-high heat until limp, 2 to 3 minutes. Add tomatoes and stir just until hot, about 2 minutes longer. Put arugula in bowl with bread; pour tomato mixture over arugula. Add pine nuts and mix well.

7. Spoon salad equally onto plates. Lay 1 chicken breast half on each salad. Add salt and pepper to taste.

Per serving: 558 cal., 48% (270 cal.) from fat; 48 g protein; 30 g fat (5.8 g sat.); 26 g carbo (4.6 g fiber); 298 mg sodium; 113 mg chol.

JAMES CARRIER (2)

Sierra's Salad

Sierra Grdeń, Walla Walla, Washington

"I wanted to create the perfect salad," says Sierra Grdeń. This recipe is "a combination of complementary tastes and textures."

PREP AND COOK TIME: About 30 minutes

MAKES: 8 servings

- 1 cup **chopped walnuts**
- 6 tablespoons **balsamic vinegar**
- ¼ cup **olive oil**
- 1½ teaspoons **Asian** (toasted) **sesame oil**
- 2 **firm-ripe avocados** (about 1 lb. total)
- 3 quarts bite-size pieces rinsed, crisped **romaine lettuce**
- 2 cups diced **firm-ripe tomatoes**
- 2 cups thinly sliced **mushrooms**
- 1 cup thinly sliced **red onion**
- 1 can (3.8 oz.) **sliced black ripe olives,** drained
- ½ pound **feta cheese,** crumbled
- ½ cup slivered **fresh basil** leaves
  Salt and **pepper**

1. In an 8- to 10-inch frying pan over medium-high heat, stir or shake walnuts frequently until golden, about 3 minutes. Pour into a large bowl; add vinegar, olive oil, and sesame oil.

2. Pit and peel avocados; cut into ½-inch chunks and add to bowl. Add lettuce, tomatoes, mushrooms, red onion, olives, cheese, and basil. Mix

Kaleidoscopic salad is a medley of fresh vegetables, nuts, and cheese.

and add salt and pepper to taste.

Per serving: 362 cal., 77% (279 cal.) from fat; 9.8 g protein; 31 g fat (7.4 g sat.); 16 g carbo (4.8 g fiber); 455 mg sodium; 25 mg chol.

Sausage and Leek Pies

Carole Thompson Lyon, Malott, Washington

When Carole Thompson Lyon's grandmother lived in England, she came across this dish. Lyon likes it so much, she shared the recipe with us.

PREP AND COOK TIME: About 1 hour

MAKES: 4 servings

- 1 **refrigerated pastry for a single-crust 9-inch pie** (½ of a 15-oz. package), at room temperature
- 1 pound **leeks**
- 2 tablespoons **butter** or margarine
  About 2 tablespoons **all-purpose flour**
- 1 cup **milk**
- ½ cup **half-and-half** (light cream)
  About ⅛ teaspoon **hot sauce**
- ½ cup **shredded Swiss cheese**
- ½ pound **cooked bratwurst** or garlic **sausages,** cut into ½-inch chunks
- 1 to 2 tablespoons minced **parsley**

1. On a floured board, cut pastry into quarters. Roll each quarter into a rounded triangle about 8 inches long on each side. Ease each piece into a round ramekin (about 1½ in. deep and 4 in. wide); fold edges down into ramekin, flush with rim. Press pastry snugly against sides of ramekin to make evenly thick. Prick in several places with the tines of a fork.

2. Bake in a 375° oven until lightly browned, 12 to 15 minutes.

3. Meanwhile, trim root end, coarse tops, and outer layer from each leek; cut leeks in half lengthwise. Hold under running water and flip layers to rinse well. Cut crosswise into ¼-inch pieces.

4. In a 10- to 12-inch frying pan over medium-high heat, frequently stir leeks in butter until

lightly browned, about 10 minutes. Add 2 tablespoons flour and stir until well blended; remove from heat. Smoothly blend in milk and half-and-half; add hot sauce to taste. Return to heat and stir until boiling; stir 1 minute longer. Remove from heat, add cheese, and stir until sauce is smooth.

5. Pile sausage chunks equally into warm pastry-lined ramekins. Pour sauce evenly over sausages.

6. Bake in a 375° oven until sauce bubbles, 18 to 25 minutes. Sprinkle pies with parsley.

Per serving: 640 cal., 63% (405 cal.) from fat; 18 g protein; 45 g fat (21 g sat.); 41 g carbo (0.8 g fiber); 735 mg sodium; 96 mg chol.

Cherry-Berry Pudding

June Gallazin, North Vancouver, British Columbia

The German dessert *rote grütze,* or red pudding, has many variations, depending upon the fruit and the season. June Gallazin creates her own version with cherries and raspberries.

PREP AND COOK TIME: About 15 minutes, plus at least 2 hours to chill

MAKES: 3 servings

- 1½ cups pitted **Bing cherries**
- ¾ cup **sugar**
- 2 cups **raspberries**
- 3 tablespoons **cornstarch**
- 1 tablespoon **lemon juice**
- ⅓ cup **vanilla-flavor low-fat yogurt**

1. In a 1½- to 2-quart pan over high heat, combine cherries and ¼ cup sugar. Stir often until juice boils, about 3 minutes. With a slotted spoon, transfer cherries to a bowl.

2. To pan, add raspberries and remaining ½ cup sugar. Stir often over high heat until mixture is boiling and raspberries fall apart, 2 to 3 minutes. Rub mixture through a fine strainer into another bowl; discard residue. Return raspberry mixture to pan.

3. In the same bowl, blend cornstarch and 6 tablespoons water until smooth. Add to pan and stir over high heat until mixture is boiling. Remove from heat and stir in lemon juice and cherries with accumulated juice.

4. Spoon equally into individual bowls (at least 1 cup); cover without touching pudding and chill until set, at least 2 hours or up to 2 days. Top each serving with a dollop of yogurt.

Per serving: 339 cal., 4% (14 cal.) from fat; 2.9 g protein; 1.5 g fat (0.4 g sat.); 83 g carbo (5 g fiber); 19 mg sodium; 1.2 mg chol. ◆

An easy make-ahead dessert, creamy Peanut butter–Chocolate Pie (page 246) provides a luscious ending to a summer meal.

August

watermelon

Time to enjoy the biggest, juiciest fruit of all—the very symbol of summer

By Andrew Baker • Photographs by James Carrier • Food styling by Basil Friedman

Sassy watermelon-chili glaze jazzes up skewered chunks of swordfish and watermelon from the grill.

weather

Watermelon casts a magical spell on summertime. There's something about a cold slice of the fruit in August that makes you, well, want to sing.

Admittedly, it's the water in watermelon—or, more precisely, its juice—that clinches the fruit's status as the quintessential summer treat. A typical watermelon is 92 percent water. On a hot day, that's a refreshing bite of trivia. An icy glass of watermelon *agua fresca* or bowl of watermelon-tequila sorbet cools like no other food can.

These days, watermelons are available year-round. In the West, farmers in California, Arizona, and Hawaii harvest the fruit from May through September. And from October through April, melons imported from Mexico, and sometimes Central America or the Caribbean, are available in markets.

But summer is the time when the most varieties and colors fill grocery store bins and farmers' market stalls—and at the lowest prices. Large melons— round or oblong, from 16 to 45 pounds—are known as "picnic" types. Markets often cut them up to sell in more manageable pieces. Smaller round "icebox" melons, from 5 to 15 pounds, are usually sold whole. Both categories include seedless varieties, as well as round yellow- and orange-fleshed types in the 10- to 30-pound range (see "Color-blind," page 224).

Red, orange, yellow—combine colorful watermelon juices with citrus and sugar for festive aguas frescas.

Grilled Watermelon and Swordfish Skewers

PREP AND COOK TIME: About 50 minutes
NOTES: Thai sweet chili sauce is sold in some well-stocked supermarkets and in Asian food markets. If it's unavailable, increase watermelon juice to 1½ cups and sugar to 3 tablespoons; add 1 tablespoon minced fresh ginger and ½ teaspoon hot chili flakes to watermelon juice mixture and reduce to ¾ cup as directed in step 1.
MAKES: 4 servings

- 1 cup **watermelon juice** (see recipe, at right)
- ½ cup **Thai sweet chili sauce** (see notes)
- ¼ cup **lime juice**
- 2 tablespoons **sugar**
- About 1¼ pounds **seedless watermelon**
- 1¼ pounds **boned, skinned swordfish** or halibut
- **Salt**

1. In a 1½- to 2-quart pan, bring watermelon juice, chili sauce, lime juice, and sugar to a boil; stir often until reduced to ¾ cup, about 15 minutes.
2. Meanwhile, cut and discard rind from watermelon. Cut fruit into 1-inch cubes.
3. Rinse swordfish and pat dry; cut into 1-inch squares.
4. Thread swordfish and watermelon alternately onto 6 metal skewers (at least 12 in.).
5. Lay skewers on a lightly oiled barbecue grill over a solid bed of very hot coals or a gas grill on high heat (you can hold your hand at grill level only 1 to 2 seconds); close lid on gas grill. Brush frequently with watermelon juice mixture and turn as needed to cook evenly until fish is opaque but still moist-looking in center (cut to test), about 8 minutes.
6. Push watermelon and swordfish chunks from skewers onto plates. Add salt to taste.

Per serving: 276 cal., 21% (58 cal.) from fat; 29 g protein; 6.4 g fat (1.6 g sat.); 26 g carbo (0.9 g fiber); 213 mg sodium; 55 mg chol.

Watermelon Juice

PREP TIME: About 12 minutes
NOTES: If making up to 1 day ahead, cover and chill.
MAKES: 4 to 6 cups

Cut and discard rind from about 6 pounds **seedless watermelon.** Cut melon into 1-inch chunks. In a blender or food processor, whirl a portion at a time until smooth. Pour through a fine strainer into a bowl or pitcher.

Per cup: 76 cal., 12% (9 cal.) from fat; 1.5 g protein; 1 g fat (0 g sat.); 17 g carbo (0.9 g fiber); 4.7 mg sodium; 0 mg chol.

Color-blind

Yellow- and orange-fleshed watermelons are visually startling, to say the least. But are their flavors singular as well? We blindfolded 11 *Sunset* staff members, had them taste red, yellow, and orange seedless watermelons side by side, and asked them to identify which was which. The results—if not the flavors—were surprising: Only one person correctly identified each melon's color. (Later, he admitted it had been pure luck.) Our conclusion? Take full advantage of yellow and orange watermelons for their flashy colors, and interchange them freely with red fruit for that classic watermelon taste.

Watermelon agua fresca. In a pitcher, stir together 1 quart **watermelon juice** (see recipe, page 223), ¼ cup **lime juice,** and 1 teaspoon **sugar.** Pour into **ice**-filled glasses and garnish with **lime** slices. Makes about 1 quart.

Per cup: 83 cal., 11% (9 cal.) from fat; 1.5 g protein; 1 g fat (0 g sat.); 19 g carbo (0.9 g fiber); 7.2 mg sodium; 0 mg chol.

Moroccan watermelon cooler. In a blender or food processor, whirl 2 cups **watermelon juice** (see recipe, page 223), ½ teaspoon **orange flower water** (available in well-stocked grocery stores), and 2 tablespoons lightly packed rinsed **fresh mint** leaves until mint is minced. Pour mixture into a pitcher and stir in 2 additional cups of watermelon juice. Pour cooler into **ice**-filled glasses and garnish with rinsed **mint sprigs.** Makes 1 quart.

— Kitty Morse, Vista, CA

Per cup: 77 cal., 12% (9 cal.) from fat; 1.6 g protein; 1 g fat (0 g sat.); 17 g carbo (1.2 g fiber); 6 mg sodium; 0 mg chol.

Watermelon-Fennel Salad

PREP TIME: **About 20 minutes**

NOTES: Chris Bianco, chef-owner of Pizzeria Bianco in Phoenix, serves this simple, refreshing salad.

MAKES: **4 servings**

- 1 head **fennel** (about 3 in. wide)
- 1 piece **seedless watermelon** (about 6 lb.)
- ¼ cup coarsely chopped **parsley**
- ¼ cup **lemon juice**
  Salt
  Lemon wedges

1. Trim fennel, discarding stalks (reserve feathery green leaves), root end, and any bruised parts. Rinse fennel and feathery green leaves. Using a mandoline or other food slicer, cut fennel into ¹⁄₁₆-inch slices; put in a wide salad bowl. Chop enough feathery greens to make ¼ cup; discard remainder.

2. Cut and discard rind from watermelon. Cut fruit into 1- to 2-inch chunks. Add fruit to bowl.

3. Add parsley and lemon juice. Mix gently and spoon equally onto salad plates. Sprinkle evenly with reserved chopped fennel leaves. Serve with salt and lemon wedges to season portions to taste.

Per serving: 130 cal., 12% (15 cal.) from fat; 3.3 g protein; 1.7 g fat (0 g sat.); 29 g carbo (2.3 g fiber); 88 mg sodium; 0 mg chol.

Watermelon-Tomato Salsa Salad

PREP TIME: **About 30 minutes**

MAKES: **4 servings**

- ½ cup thinly sliced **red onion**
- ⅓ cup **lime juice**
- 2 cups ½-inch cubes **seedless watermelon**

Bright flavors stand out in a quick salad of crisp fennel and juicy watermelon.

- 2 cups ½-inch cubes **tomatoes**
- ½ cup thinly slivered **fresh basil** leaves
- 2 tablespoons thinly slivered **fresh mint** leaves
- ¾ teaspoon **hot chili flakes**
- 4 **butter lettuce** leaves, rinsed and crisped
  Salt

1. In a wide bowl, combine onion and lime juice. Let stand 10 to 15 minutes.

2. Add watermelon, tomatoes, basil, mint, and chili flakes. Mix gently.

3. Arrange lettuce leaves on salad plates and top equally with watermelon mixture. Add salt to taste.

Per serving: 63 cal., 11% (7 cal.) from fat; 2.1 g protein; 0.8 g fat (0.1 g sat.); 14 g carbo (2.6 g fiber); 17 mg sodium; 0 mg chol.

Watermelon-Tequila Sorbet

PREP TIME: **About 10 minutes, plus 20 to 40 minutes to freeze**

NOTES: If making up to 1 week ahead, freeze airtight. If freezing in a machine using a frozen cylinder, chill watermelon mixture before adding to the container.

MAKES: **Makes about 1 quart**

- 4 cups **watermelon juice** (see recipe, page 223)
- ¼ cup **lime juice**
- ¼ cup **tequila**
- ¼ cup **sugar**

1. Pour watermelon juice, lime juice, and tequila into an ice cream maker (1-qt. or larger capacity). Add sugar and stir to dissolve.

2. Freeze according to manufacturer's directions until sorbet is firm enough to scoop, dasher is hard to turn, or machine stops. Serve immediately or freeze airtight.

Per ½ cup: 82 cal., 6% (5 cal.) from fat; 0.7 g protein; 0.5 g fat (0 g sat.); 15 g carbo (0.5 g fiber); 3.7 mg sodium; 0 mg chol.

Indian-spiced Watermelon

PREP AND COOK TIME: **About 15 minutes**

NOTES: Hema Kundargi of Cupertino, California, was inspired by the *chaats* (salads) of her native India to create this recipe.

MAKES: **4 servings**

- 4 cups ½- to ¾-inch cubes **seedless watermelon**
- 3 tablespoons **shredded sweetened dried coconut**
- 1 or 2 **dried hot chilies** (1½ in.)

Colorful pops are nothing more than cubes of seedless watermelon on sticks, frozen for icy fun.

Per pop: 24 cal., 11% (2.7 cal.) from fat; 0.5 g protein; 0.3 g fat (0 g sat.); 5.4 g carbo (0.3 g fiber); 1.5 mg sodium; 0 mg chol.

Dips for Cut Watermelon

Spicy honey-lime. In a bowl, mix ⅓ cup **honey**, 2 tablespoons **lime juice**, and 2 teaspoons *each* minced **fresh ginger** and **fresh jalapeño chili**. Makes about ½ cup.

Per ½ teaspoon: 7.3 cal., 0% (0 cal.) from fat; 0 g protein; 0 g fat; 2 g carbo (0 g fiber); 0.2 mg sodium; 0 mg chol.

Pesto. In a blender or food processor, combine 2 cups lightly packed rinsed **fresh basil** leaves and 2 tablespoons **seasoned rice vinegar**. Whirl until smooth. Makes about ⅓ cup.

Per ½ teaspoon: 2.9 cal., 0% (0 cal.) from fat; 0.2 g protein; 0 g fat; 0.5 g carbo (0.3 g fiber); 19 mg sodium; 0 mg chol.

Black and tan. In a bowl, mix ¼ cup firmly packed **brown sugar**, 2 teaspoons fresh-ground **black pepper**, ¾ teaspoon **ground cumin**, and ¼ teaspoon **salt**. Makes ¼ cup.

Per ¼ teaspoon: 4.6 cal., 0% (0 cal.) from fat; 0 g protein; 0 g fat; 1.2 g carbo (0 g fiber); 12 mg sodium; 0 mg chol.

Coco-mint. In a blender or food processor, whirl ¼ cup lightly packed rinsed **fresh mint** leaves, 1 cup **canned coconut milk**, and 1 tablespoon **lime juice** until smooth. Makes about 1 cup.

Per ½ teaspoon: 4.8 cal., 94% (4.5 cal.) from fat; 0.1 g protein; 0.5 g fat (0.4 g sat.); 0.1 g carbo (0 g fiber); 0.4 mg sodium; 0 mg chol.

Chili salt. Stem and seed 1 **dried chipotle chili**. With a mortar and pestle or in a blender, finely crush chili. In a bowl, mix 1 teaspoon crushed chipotle with 1 tablespoon **salt**. Makes 4 teaspoons.

Per ¼ teaspoon: 0.4 cal., 0% (0 cal.) from fat; 0 g protein; 0 g fat; 0.1 g carbo (0 g fiber); 436 mg sodium; 0 mg chol. ◆

1 tablespoon **olive** or salad **oil**
2 teaspoons **cumin seed**
¼ cup chopped **fresh cilantro**
Salt

1. Place watermelon in a wide bowl.
2. In an 8- to 10-inch frying pan over medium heat, stir coconut until golden, 3 to 4 minutes; pour from pan.
3. Break chilies in half and add to pan, along with oil and cumin. Stir over high heat until mixture is sizzling, 1 to 2 minutes. Pour oil mixture over watermelon and stir to coat well.
4. Sprinkle cilantro and coconut over watermelon; add salt to taste.

Per serving: 106 cal., 47% (50 cal.) from fat; 1.4 g protein; 5.6 g fat (1.5 sat.); 14 g carbo (1.4 g fiber); 14 mg sodium; 0 mg chol.

Watermelon Pops

PREP TIME: About 15 minutes, plus at least 1¾ hours to freeze

NOTES: If using cookie cutters, choose simple shapes so you can make neat cuts through watermelon and remove fruit without breaking the shapes.

MAKES: About 6 pops

1 piece **seedless watermelon** (about 3 lb.)
About 6 **wood juice-pop** (craft) **sticks** or round cardboard sticks
⅓ cup **chocolate chips** (optional)

1. Cut rind from watermelon and discard. Cut fruit into ½-inch-thick slices. With a knife or a cookie cutter, cut decorative shapes about 3 inches wide and 4 inches long, or cut 1-inch squares.
2. Insert a stick horizontally into a narrow edge of each fruit piece or through a row of squares. Cover a 10- by 15-inch baking sheet with plastic wrap and lay pops slightly apart on pan.
3. If desired, decorate pops with piped chocolate: Place chocolate chips in a small, heavy plastic food bag. Heat in a microwave oven at half power (50%) for 30-second intervals until chocolate is soft, about 1 minute total. Push chocolate into corner of bag, then snip ⅛ inch off the tip of the corner. Squeeze chocolate in zigzags or other designs onto watermelon pops.
4. Freeze until watermelon is firm, about 1¾ hours. Serve, or seal airtight up to 1 week.

Quick trick: With a cookie cutter, cut a decorative shape from a watermelon slice; insert a cutout from a contrasting melon. Serve with dips above.

Nancy Silverton and Mark Peel (above right, middle of photo, and far right), both professional cooks, love to spend Sundays cooking for their family and friends. Everyone pitches in—even their 5-year-old son, Oliver (top left), gathers garden herbs.

Simple summer supper

Follow the lead of two Southern California chefs and
let the harvest inspire a feast of fresh flavors

By Linda Lau Anusasananan • Photographs by Just Loomis • Food styling by Christine Masterson

■ What do chefs do on their days off? Mark Peel and Nancy Silverton, chefs and owners of Campanile restaurant and La Brea Bakery in Los Angeles, spend summer Sunday afternoons at home, cooking in the backyard. Here, good food brings family and friends together. Their entertaining style is more casual than in the restaurant, the pace more leisurely. And their guests often help with the cooking.

In this party for eight, Peel and Silverton showcase summer's handsome harvest. Lamb is marinated in ripe plums and fresh herbs; aspara-gus grills on a bed of thyme. Ink black concord grapes infuse an icy granita with intense flavor and color. Vegetables, herbs, and fruits—from the couple's garden and from the market—shine in these remarkably simple and fresh presentations.

Anchovy-marinated Roasted Lipstick Peppers

PREP AND COOK TIME: About 1 hour, plus at least 12 hours to marinate

NOTES: If small peppers or mild chilies aren't available, use red bell peppers (½ lb. each). After peeling in step 4, stem, seed, and quarter lengthwise.

MAKES: 8 servings

8 **red peppers** or fresh mild red chilies such as Lipstick, pimiento, Hungarian, or Anaheim (2 to 4 oz. each; see notes)

About ¼ cup **extra-virgin olive oil**

2 rinsed **salt-packed anchovy fillets** (about ⅓ oz. total) or 3 canned anchovy fillets, drained and chopped

2 cloves **garlic,** peeled and minced

About ⅛ teaspoon **salt**

½ cup minced **Italian parsley**

1 tablespoon **red wine vinegar**

1. Rinse and dry peppers, and rub lightly with about 1 teaspoon olive oil.

2. Lay peppers on a barbecue grill over a solid bed of hot coals or high heat on a gas grill (you can hold your hand at

MENU

Offer a plate full of summer: Rosy lamb, marinated in plums and grilled; black-eyed peas with roasted tomatoes; grilled Lipstick peppers; and thyme-scented asparagus.

---

grill level only 2 to 3 seconds); close lid on gas grill. Cook, turning as needed to char all sides, 12 to 20 minutes total. Transfer to a bowl; let stand until cool, about 15 minutes.

3. Using a mortar and pestle or a food processor, mash or whirl anchovies, garlic, and ⅛ teaspoon salt to a fine paste. Add parsley; mash or whirl until smooth. Stir in vinegar and ¼ cup oil.

4. Pull off and discard pepper skins (leave stem and seeds intact). Layer peppers in a shallow dish, coating each layer with anchovy paste. Cover and chill at least 12 hours. Bring to room temperature to serve. Add salt to taste.

Per serving: 78 cal., 83% (65 cal.) from fat; 1 g protein; 7.2 g fat (1 g sat.); 3.5 g carbo (0.9 g fiber); 94 mg sodium; 0.8 mg chol.

Butter Lettuce and Fresh Herb Salad

PREP TIME: About 45 minutes
NOTES: Up to 1 day ahead, crisp lettuce.
MAKES: 8 servings

- 2 tablespoons **fresh tarragon** leaves
- 2 tablespoons 1-inch pieces **fresh chervil**
- 2 tablespoons 1-inch pieces **chives**
- 2 tablespoons 1-inch pieces **fresh dill** sprigs
- 2 tablespoons **Italian parsley** leaves
- 2 tablespoons 1-inch pieces **fresh basil** leaves
- 2 tablespoons **lemon juice**
- 1 teaspoon **champagne vinegar**
- 6 tablespoons **extra-virgin olive oil**
- 2 tablespoons minced **shallots**
- 2 heads **butter lettuce** (9 oz. each), rinsed and crisped (see notes)

  Salt and fresh-ground **pepper**

1. Rinse and drain tarragon, chervil, chives, dill, parsley, and basil; pat dry. Mix herbs; finely chop half of them.

2. In a wide serving bowl, mix lemon juice, vinegar, oil, and shallots. In a small bowl, mix 2 teaspoons dressing with large herb pieces.

3. Tear lettuce into bite-size pieces. Add lettuce and chopped herbs to wide bowl, and mix, adding salt and pepper to taste. Sprinkle with large herb pieces.

Per serving: 103 cal., 96% (99 cal.) from fat; 1 g protein; 11 g fat (1.5 g sat.); 2.5 g carbo (0.8 g fiber); 5.1 mg sodium; 0 mg chol.

Roasted tomatoes, studded with garlic slivers and drizzled with olive oil, top black-eyed peas.

Grilled Plum-marinated Lamb

PREP AND COOK TIME: About 1 hour, plus at least 8 hours to marinate

NOTES: If using a charcoal grill to cook lamb and corn (facing page), about 10 minutes before lamb is done (when it's 110° in thickest part), add 15 to 18 charcoal briquets to firegrate on each side of grill. When lamb is done, spread briquets evenly over firegrate to cook corn.

MAKES: 8 servings

- 1¾ pounds **firm-ripe red-fleshed plums** such as Santa Rosa, Damson, or Elephant Heart
- 7 cloves **garlic,** peeled and crushed
- 1 cup **dry red wine**
- ¼ cup **red wine vinegar**
- ½ cup chopped **Italian parsley**
- 2 tablespoons chopped **fresh tarragon** leaves
- 2 tablespoons chopped **fresh thyme** leaves
- 1 **leg of lamb** (6 lb.), boned, butterflied, and fat trimmed

  Salt and **pepper**

1. Rinse and pit plums. Whirl fruit in a blender or food processor until smooth; pour into a 9- by 13-inch pan or baking dish. Add garlic, wine, vinegar, parsley, tarragon, and thyme; stir to blend.

2. Rinse lamb and pat dry; add to plum marinade and turn to coat well. Cover and chill at least 8 hours or up to 1 day, turning occasionally.

3. Lift lamb from pan and discard marinade. Lay meat flat (spread out) on a barbecue grill over a solid bed of medium coals or medium heat on a gas

grill (you can hold your hand at grill level only 4 to 5 seconds). Sprinkle lamb with salt and pepper. Close lid on gas grill. Cook, turning as needed to brown meat evenly, until a thermometer inserted in thickest part reaches 135° to 140° for rare, 35 to 50 minutes; thin portions will be well done.

4. Transfer meat to a rimmed platter; keeping warm, let rest about 15 minutes. Slice to serve.

Per serving: 342 cal., 34% (117 cal.) from fat; 47 g protein; 13 g fat (4.5 g sat.); 7 g carbo (1.1 g fiber); 113 mg sodium; 145 mg chol.

Thyme-grilled Asparagus

PREP AND COOK TIME: About 10 minutes, plus at least 30 minutes to soak thyme

NOTES: The thyme sprigs must be soaked before being cooked so they won't be inclined to catch fire. If you can't get a large quantity of fresh thyme, skip the herb bed and season the grilled asparagus with about 2 teaspoons fresh thyme leaves.

MAKES: 8 servings

- About ¼ pound (about 4 cups) **thyme** sprigs, rinsed
- About 2 pounds **asparagus**
- 2 tablespoons **extra-virgin olive oil**

  Salt and **pepper**

1. In a bowl, cover thyme sprigs with cool water and let stand at least 30 minutes or up to 4 hours.

2. Snap off and discard tough stem ends from asparagus. Rinse and drain spears. In a large bowl, mix asparagus with oil.

3. Lift thyme from water, drain, and arrange in a 6- by 18-inch rectangle on a barbecue grill over a solid bed of hot coals or high heat on a gas grill (you can hold your hand at grill level only 2 to 3 seconds). Arrange asparagus in a single layer on thyme; close lid on gas grill. Cook, turning spears once, to brown lightly on two sides, 4 to 6 minutes total.

4. Transfer asparagus to a platter; discard thyme. Add salt and pepper to taste. Serve warm or cool.

Per serving: 50 cal., 66% (33 cal.) from fat; 2.8 g protein; 3.7 g fat (0.5 g sat.); 3.4 g carbo (0.9 g fiber); 1.8 mg sodium; 0 mg chol.

Black-Eyed Pea Stew with Roasted Tomatoes

PREP AND COOK TIME: About 1¼ hours

NOTES: If shelled black-eyed peas are not available, use frozen black-eyed peas; cook 30 to 35 minutes. If making up to 2 hours ahead, cover loosely and keep warm in a 200° oven.

MAKES: 8 servings

- 10 cloves **garlic,** peeled
- 3½ pounds **tomatoes** (2 to 8 oz. each)

  Salt and **pepper**
- 6 tablespoons **extra-virgin olive oil**
- 1 **onion** (¾ lb.), peeled and chopped
- 1 slice **bacon** (about 1½ oz.), chopped
- 4 cups (about 1⅓ lb.) **shelled black-eyed peas**
- 4 cups **fat-skimmed chicken broth** or water
- ½ cup **champagne** or white wine **vinegar**
- 4 **Italian parsley** sprigs (each 8 in. long), rinsed
- 4 **thyme** sprigs (each 4 in. long), rinsed
- 4 **basil** sprigs (each 6 in. long), rinsed
- 2 tablespoons chopped **Italian parsley**

1. Cut 7 garlic cloves into thin slivers; chop remainder.

2. Rinse tomatoes, drain, and cut each in half crosswise. Set, cut sides up and slightly apart, in a 10- by 15-inch pan. Insert 3 or 4 garlic slivers into each tomato half. Sprinkle with salt and pepper. Drizzle with 5 tablespoons olive oil.

3. Bake in a 350° oven until tomatoes are lightly browned at edges and soft when pressed but still retain their shape, 40 to 45 minutes.

4. Meanwhile, in a 3- to 4-quart pan over medium-high heat, stir onion in remaining 1 tablespoon oil until limp, about 5 minutes. Add chopped garlic and bacon; stir often for 2 minutes. Add peas, broth, and vinegar; stir, then turn heat to high.

5. Tie parsley, thyme, and basil sprigs into a bundle with cotton string. Add to peas. When mixture is boiling, reduce heat to low and simmer, stirring occasionally, until peas are tender to bite but still retain their shape, 12 to 15 minutes. Pour peas into a fine strainer over a bowl; discard herb bundle.

6. Put half the tomatoes and half the juices into pan used for peas. Mash with a potato masher or fork. Add drained peas (reserve liquid for other uses). Stir over medium heat until hot. Add salt and pepper to taste.

7. Pour pea mixture into a 2½- to 3-quart shallow casserole. Nestle remaining roasted tomatoes, cut sides up, in peas. Drizzle with remaining roasted tomato juices and sprinkle with chopped parsley.

Per serving: 455 cal., 30% (135 cal.) from fat; 25 g protein; 15 g fat (3 g sat.); 60 g carbo (24 g fiber); 106 mg sodium; 3.6 mg chol.

Grilled Corn with Basil Butter

PREP AND COOK TIME: About 30 minutes

NOTES: Prepare corn to cook up to 6 hours ahead. If cooking on a charcoal grill, after the lamb, see notes for grilled plum-marinated lamb recipe (facing page).

MAKES: 8 servings

- ½ cup (¼ lb.) **butter** or margarine, at room temperature
- ½ cup chopped **fresh basil** leaves
- 8 **ears corn** (each about 8 in. long)
  Salt and **pepper**

1. In a small bowl, mix butter and basil.

2. If stems on corn ears are longer than ½ inch, snap them off. Pull off and discard coarse outer husks, leaving each ear covered with tender inner leaves. Gently pull inner leaves down from ears but leave attached; pull off and discard silks. Smear about 1 tablespoon basil butter over kernels of each ear. Pull leaves back up over kernels; tie with cotton string to secure.

3. Lay corn on a barbecue grill over a solid bed of hot coals or high heat on a gas grill (you can hold your hand at grill level only 2 to 3 seconds). Close lid on gas grill. Cook, turning once, until corn is hot, about 10 minutes total.

4. To eat, snip string and pull down leaves; season to taste with salt and pepper.

Cracked black pepper, mint leaves, and fortified wine add provocative dimensions to melon.

Purple concords give a royal hue to icy granita.

Per serving: 227 cal., 52% (117 cal.) from fat; 4.9 g protein; 13 g fat (7.4 g sat.); 28 g carbo (4.8 g fiber); 139 mg sodium; 31 mg chol.

Charentais Melon with Pineau des Charentes

PREP TIME: About 15 minutes

NOTES: Pineau des Charentes, a cognac-fortified wine, comes from the province in France where Charentais melons are grown. Both Charentais and cantaloupe, a similar melon with a coarser texture, have a rich fragrance when fully ripe. Look for the fortified wine in a well-stocked wine shop or use 3 tablespoons sweet white wine, such as a Sauternes or a late-harvest Riesling, mixed with 1 tablespoon cognac or brandy.

MAKES: 8 servings

- 2 **ripe Charentais melons** or cantaloupes (1 lb. each)
- ¼ cup **fresh mint** leaves, rinsed
- ¼ teaspoon coarse fresh-ground **pepper**
- ¼ cup **Pineau des Charentes**

1. With a sharp knife, cut peel off melons. Cut each melon in half, seed, and slice into thin crescents.

2. Arrange melon on individual plates or a large platter. Tear mint into small pieces and scatter over melon. Sprinkle with pepper, then drizzle evenly with Pineau des Charentes.

Per serving: 33 cal., 5.5% (1.8 cal.) from fat; 0.6 g protein; 0.2 g fat (0 g sat.); 5.9 g carbo (0.7 g fiber); 6.6 mg sodium; 0 mg chol.

- •**Up to 1 week ahead:** Freeze granita.

- •**Up to 1 day ahead:** Marinate peppers, rinse and crisp lettuce for salad, and marinate lamb.

- •**Up to 6 hours ahead:** Prepare corn.

- •**Up to 4 hours ahead:** Soak thyme sprigs. Chill glasses for granita.

- •**2 hours ahead:** Make black-eyed pea stew. Ignite briquets, if using a charcoal grill.

- •**1½ hours ahead:** Grill asparagus.

- •**1 hour ahead:** Bring peppers to room temperature. Grill lamb, then corn.

- •**15 minutes before serving:** Prepare melon.

- •**Just before serving:** Assemble salad.

- •**Just before dessert:** Scrape granita and spoon into glasses.

Concord Grape Granita

PREP AND COOK TIME: About 40 minutes, plus at least 4 hours to freeze

NOTES: If making up to 1 week ahead, freeze airtight. Chill wine glasses or bowls in the freezer. Garnish portions with fresh concord grapes. Serve with homemade or purchased shortbread cookies.

MAKES: 8 servings

- 1¾ pounds **concord grapes**
- 2 cups **Beaujolais** or other light, dry red wine
- ½ cup **sugar**
- ¼ teaspoon **black peppercorns,** cracked or coarsely crushed

1. Pull grapes from stems; discard stems and rinse and drain fruit.

2. In a 3- to 4-quart pan over high heat, bring grapes, wine, sugar, and pepper to a boil. Cover and remove from heat; let stand about 30 minutes.

3. Pour grape mixture into a blender or food processor. Whirl until smooth, then rub through a fine strainer into a 9- by 13-inch metal pan; discard residue.

4. Freeze mixture until solid, at least 4 hours or up to 1 week; cover airtight after 4 hours. Scrape quickly with a fork to break into small clumps.

5. Scoop granita into chilled wine glasses or bowls (see notes).

Per serving: 111 cal., 2.4% (2.7 cal.) from fat; 0.7 g protein; 0.3 g fat (0.1 g sat.); 29 g carbo (0 g fiber); 4.9 mg sodium; 0 mg chol. ◆

Delicate poached salmon becomes a lively summer entrée when paired with a Spanish-style relish of roasted red peppers, calamata olives, red onions, and capers steeped in orange juice and sherry vinegar.

Salmon with a twist

Five classic pairings updated to sauce summer's coolest fish

By Sara Schneider

Salmon, a fish so colorful we've adopted its name as a hue, has flirted with scores of flavor mates through the years. The best of these have become classics. Lemon, of course, and dill. Cucumber. Red onion. Garlic. And even a few noncitrus fruits—fresh berries, for example.

For stunningly simple summer meals, start with poached salmon and serve it with a sauce that expands on one of the classics. With just a few twists, flavors leap to new (but comfortable) heights. Marinated artichokes add compatible texture and taste to a roasted garlic aioli. Orange juice lends a sweet tang to a red pepper relish. Watercress and yogurt revitalize a cucumber sauce. Man-goes take on a rich smoky flavor from dried chipotle chilies. And a creamy mustard-dill sauce gets a jolt from green peppercorns.

All of these sauces—and the salmon—can be prepared hours ahead. Just pull your sauce of choice and the salmon from the refrigerator, and the main course for dinner is ready in minutes.

Lemon-poached Salmon

PREP AND COOK TIME: About 45 minutes, plus at least 30 minutes to cool

NOTES: If poaching salmon up to 1 day ahead, cool, cover, and chill. Serve the fish cold.

MAKES: 4 servings

- 1 **onion** (½ lb.)
- 1 **carrot** (¼ lb.)
- 2 **celery** stalks (including leaves)
- 2 cups **dry white wine**
- ¼ cup **lemon juice**
- 1½ pounds **salmon fillet with skin** (maximum 1 in. thick)
   Sauce (choices follow)

1. Peel onion and carrot, and rinse celery; cut vegetables into ¼-inch slices. In a 4- to 5-quart pan, combine vegetables, wine, lemon juice, and 1 quart water. Cover and bring to a boil over high heat; reduce heat and simmer about 15 minutes.

2. Meanwhile, rub your fingers over salmon to find any bones; pull out and discard. Rinse fish and cut into 4 equal portions. Add to simmering liquid and return to a simmer. Cover pan, remove from heat, and let stand 13 to 15 minutes. With a slotted spoon, lift out 1 salmon piece. It should be opaque but still moist-looking in center of thickest part (cut to test). If not, return to pan, cover, and let stand 3 to 5 minutes longer. If fish still isn't done, set pan over low heat and cook about 3 minutes.

3. With a slotted spoon, gently lift salmon from poaching liquid and arrange in a single layer on a flat plate. Reserve liquid for other uses or discard. Let salmon cool at least 30 minutes. Serve, or cover airtight and chill until cold, at least 2 hours or up to 1 day.

4. Pull off and discard salmon skin. Set 1 piece of salmon on each plate. Serve with sauce and garnish as suggested.

Per serving: 286 cal., 53% (153 cal.) from fat; 31 g protein; 17 g fat (3.3 g sat.); 1.3 g carbo (0.3 g fiber); 95 mg sodium; 90 mg chol.

Sauce choices

Roasted garlic aioli with artichoke hearts. With a sharp knife, cut 1 head **garlic** in half horizontally. Rub cut cloves with **olive oil** (about ¼ teaspoon total). Set garlic, cut sides down, on a sheet of foil about 12 inches square; seal. Bake in a 350° oven until garlic is soft when pressed, about 1 hour. When packet is cool enough to handle, open and squeeze garlic pulp from peel into a food processor; discard peel. To pulp, add ½ cup **mayonnaise**, 1 tablespoon **lemon juice**, ½ tablespoon chopped **fresh rosemary** leaves, and 1 teaspoon grated **lemon** peel. Whirl until smooth. If aioli is thicker than you like, thin with **salmon-poaching liquid** (preceding), 1 teaspoon at a time. Drain and discard liquid from 1 jar (6 oz.) **marinated artichoke crowns** (bottoms) or marinated artichokes; thinly slice artichokes and stir into aioli. Add **salt** and **pepper** to taste. For garnish, use ½ cup rinsed **cherry tomato** halves (red or a variety of colors), **lemon** slices, and **rosemary** sprigs. Makes about 1 cup sauce.

Per ¼ cup: 238 cal., 83% (198 cal.) from fat; 2.2 g protein; 22 g fat (3.3 g sat.); 8.7 g carbo (1.2 g fiber); 282 mg sodium; 16 mg chol.

Roasted red pepper and olive relish. With a sharp knife, cut peel and outer membrane from 1 **orange** (8 oz.). Cut between fruit and inner membranes to release segments and drop into a strainer over a bowl. Squeeze juice from membranes into bowl; discard peel and membranes. To bowl, add ¼ cup **sherry vinegar**, ½ cup thinly slivered **red onion**, 1 cup thinly sliced **canned roasted red peppers**, ½ cup sliced **pitted calamata olives**, and ¼ cup drained **capers**. Mix gently; add **salt** and **pepper** to taste. For garnish, use orange segments and long, thin **orange** peel strands. Makes about 2 cups.

Per ½ cup: 97 cal., 42% (41 cal.) from fat; 0.6 g protein; 4.6 g fat (0.6 g sat.); 14 g carbo (1.6 g fiber); 752 mg sodium; 0 mg chol.

Cucumber-watercress sauce. Place a cheesecloth-lined strainer over a bowl, with at least 2 inches between bottom of strainer and bowl. Spoon 2 cups **plain regular** or low-fat **yogurt** (made without gelatin) into cheesecloth. Cover completely with plastic wrap and chill 2 hours to drain. Measure 1 cup yogurt; save extra for other uses and discard whey. Rinse and dry bowl; in it mix 1 cup drained yogurt with 1 peeled, seeded, and diced (¼ in.) **cucumber** (½ lb.); ¼ cup minced **watercress**; 2 tablespoons **lime juice**; ½ teaspoon **sugar**; and **salt** and **pepper** to taste. For garnish, use thin **lime** slices and rinsed **watercress** sprigs. Makes about 2 cups.

Per ½ cup: 95 cal., 56% (53 cal.) from fat; 5.9 g protein; 5.9 g fat (3.8 g sat.); 5.2 g carbo (0.3 g fiber); 31 mg sodium; 24 mg chol.

Mango-chipotle salsa. Pour 1 cup boiling **water** over 1 **dried chipotle chili** (1½ in. long) in a bowl; let stand until chipotle is soft, about 20 minutes. Wearing gloves, discard stem, seeds, and membrane; mince chili. Peel, pit, and dice (½ in.) 1 **firm-ripe mango** (1 lb.). In a bowl, combine chipotle, mango, ½ cup finely chopped **red bell pepper**, ¼ cup *each* chopped **green onions** and chopped **fresh cilantro**, 3 tablespoons **lime juice**, and 1 tablespoon minced **fresh ginger**. Mix, and season to taste with **salt**. For garnish, use **lime** wedges. Makes about 2 cups.

Per ½ cup: 61 cal., 4.4% (2.7 cal.) from fat; 0.7 g protein; 0.3 g fat (0.1 g sat.); 16 g carbo (1.4 g fiber); 5.3 mg sodium; 0 mg chol.

Dill and green peppercorn sauce. In a bowl, combine ¾ cup **sour cream**; 2 tablespoons *each* Dijon **mustard**, **lemon juice**, and minced **fresh dill**; and ½ to 1 tablespoon rinsed and drained **canned green peppercorns**, to taste. Mix, and add **salt** to taste. For garnish, use rinsed **dill sprigs** and **lemon** wedges. Makes about 1 cup.

Per ¼ cup: 101 cal., 81% (82 cal.) from fat; 1.4 g protein; 9.1 g fat (8.6 g sat.); 2.3 g carbo (0 g fiber); 217 mg sodium; 19 mg chol. ◆

A sauce for any setting (clockwise from top): Smoky sweet mango-chipotle salsa, mustard- and dill-flavored sour cream with green peppercorns, bold roasted garlic aioli with artichoke hearts, and sprightly cucumber and yogurt with watercress.

food guide

By Jerry Anne Di Vecchio
Photographs by James Carrier

Spicing up chicken

Create a rich stew with a blend of familiar flavors

■ Like many people, I grew up believing that aromatic, amber-ocher-colored curry powder was a single spice. And the curry dish I first knew contained meat (usually leftovers) swimming in a white sauce (translation: butter, flour, milk) made exotically golden by a shot of the powder. Rice was the support vehicle. Onto this curry-blanketed rice, my brother, sister, and I daringly scattered toasted coconut, raisins, chopped peanuts, and Major Grey chutney. This simple combination still works lightning-quick wonders on yesterday's cooked chicken or roast.

The fact is, though, curry powder isn't a single spice, but a blend—and there are many. My vision of curry expanded immensely when I visited Thailand. There, coconut isn't the topping; it's usually the milk of the sauce. Potatoes often cook in the sauce, supplanting the rice. And curry comes in many colors, depending on the seasoning blend used.

Another revelation: You can easily make your own blend, as in this one-bowl main-dish stew. Begin the meal with a salad, feast on the stew, then finish with simple mango sorbet or lime sherbet.

Green Curry

PREP AND COOK TIME: About 50 minutes
MAKES: 6 servings

- 1 stalk **fresh lemon grass,** rinsed
- ½ cup chopped **shallots** or onions
- 3 tablespoons chopped **fresh ginger**
- 2 tablespoons chopped seeded **fresh jalapeño chilies**
- 1 teaspoon **cumin seed**
- 1 teaspoon **coriander seed**
- ¼ teaspoon **cardamom seed**
- 1 can (14 oz.) **coconut milk**
- 1½ pounds **boned, skinned chicken thighs**
- 1½ pounds **thin-skinned red potatoes** (about 1½ in. wide), scrubbed
- 1 cup chopped **fresh basil** leaves
- ½ cup chopped **fresh cilantro**
- 1 teaspoon grated **lime** peel
- 1 cup fat-skimmed **chicken broth**

  About ½ teaspoon **salt**
- 3 to 4 tablespoons **lime juice**

  About ¼ cup **fresh basil** leaves, rinsed
- 2 **limes,** rinsed and cut into wedges

1. Trim and discard root end and tough tops from lemon grass; peel off and discard tough outer leaves. Chop peeled stalk. In a 5- to 6-quart pan, combine chopped lemon grass, shallots, ginger, chilies, cumin seed, coriander seed, and cardamom seed. Open coconut milk and scoop about 2 tablespoons of the thick part of the milk into the pan. Stir frequently over high heat until shallots are lightly browned, about **5 minutes.**

2. Meanwhile, rinse chicken and trim off and discard fat; cut meat into 1-inch chunks. Cut potatoes into quarters.

3. Scrape lemon grass–shallot mixture into a blender; add remaining coconut milk, chopped basil, cilantro, and lime peel. Whirl until smooth, scraping container sides as needed. Return mixture to pan.

4. Add chicken, potatoes, broth, and ½ teaspoon salt. Bring to a boil over high heat, stirring often. Reduce heat, cover, and simmer, stirring often, until potatoes are tender when pierced, about **25 minutes.**

5. Add salt and lime juice to taste. Ladle into wide bowls and sprinkle with basil leaves. Accompany with lime wedges to squeeze as desired into curry.

Per serving: 393 cal., 44% (171 cal.) from fat; 28 g protein; 19 g fat (14 g sat.); 30 g carbo (3.0 g fiber); 326 mg sodium; 94 mg chol.

Sunshine from Down Under

■ Kiwi fruit from New Zealand first hit Western markets in the late '50s. The brilliant green flesh, with its exotic flavor hinting of strawberries, bananas, and more, made it a sensation. We couldn't get enough. Kiwi fruit became a Western crop; fortunes here were made and lost. And all the while, New Zealand kept right on sending us fruit. Now they're shipping something new: This summer, through September, you'll find flesh of another color under the brown skin—gold kiwi fruit, distributed by Zespri International. The deep yellow fruit speckled with black seeds is as dazzling as its green counterpart. It has the same texture, but is somewhat sweeter. Slices look like little suns— bright rays to greet the day.

Sun-up Breakfast Fruit

PREP TIME: About 10 minutes

MAKES: 2 servings

2   **kiwi fruit** (¼ lb. each; gold, green, or one of each)

4   peeled **pineapple** slices (each ½ in. thick, about 1 lb. total; fresh-cut or purchased sliced)

1   teaspoon thin strands **orange** peel

2   tablespoons **orange juice**

2   tablespoons **lime juice**

Berry syrup such as boysenberry, blueberry, or raspberry

1. Rinse kiwi, cut off peels, and cut fruit crosswise into ¼-inch slices. On individual plates or in bowls, arrange equal portions of kiwi fruit and pineapple; sprinkle with orange peel.

2. In a small bowl, mix orange juice and lime juice and pour equally over fruit. Add berry syrup to taste.

Per serving: 182 cal., 7% (13 cal.) from fat; 2 g protein; 1.4 g fat (0.1 g sat.); 46 g carbo (6.1 g fiber); 9.8 mg sodium; 0 mg chol.

Square deal

■ Filo dough is incredibly useful when cut down to size. Sinbad Sweets of Fresno, California, has done the deed. Its 5-inch hors d'oeuvre squares—120 in an 8-ounce box—are far easier to handle than large filo sheets that dry and break apart. The frozen filo thaws in minutes (and although the company doesn't suggest it, I refreeze unused squares, airtight). I keep a supply in my freezer for appetizers—particularly for last-minute occasions, when remnants of cheese in the refrigerator can be put to use in the flaky appetizer that follows (allow 3 for a serving).

To find a source for Sinbad filo squares near you, call (800) 350-7933.

Filo cheese sticks. For each stick, lightly brush 3 filo **squares** (5 in.) on 1 side with melted **butter** or margarine (about 1 teaspoon total), then stack. Over the filo stack, evenly sprinkle 1 to 1½ tablespoons **shredded cheese** (a kind that melts well, such as cheddar, fontina, jack, or Swiss), a light dusting of an aromatic **dried herb** (such as dill, thyme, cumin seed, or ground pepper), and about 1 teaspoon minced **onion** (optional). Roll to form a snug tube. Lay tubes, seam down and about 1 inch apart, on a baking sheet. Brush lightly with more butter. Bake in a 350° oven until golden, 8 to 12 minutes. Serve hot.

Per piece: 80 cal., 74% (59 cal.) from fat; 2.3 g protein; 6.5 g fat (3.9 g sat.); 3.2 g carbo (0 g fiber); 111 mg sodium; 18 mg chol.

Off with their heads

One thump of this topper cracks a neat circle around the eggshell; a knife tip lifts off the cap. Sterilized, the shell makes a bowl for a sweet or savory treat.

■ Equipped with this ingenious tool, *Alice in Wonderland's* Red Queen would have sent Humpty Dumpty over the wall in terror. The Toqueur LT, an egg-top cutter, accomplishes its task without a moving part actually touching the egg. Position the cutter's cap-shaped metal base on the narrow end of an egg (resting securely in an eggcup or nested snugly in towels in a small cup). Move your hand up and grasp the stem, then lift the spring-loaded cartridge (sealed in the stem) and release it—"with confidence," as the directions say. The impact at the base snaps a neat ring around the shell. You may have to use the tip of a knife to cut through the membrane or cooked egg.

Use the Toqueur on your soft- or hard-cooked breakfast eggs, or on raw eggs if you want the shells for decorative uses, from tiny vases to containers for the dessert that follows. When you top raw eggs, though, set them and their containers in a pie pan to catch the drips.

To sterilize the fragile shells to hold foods, immerse gently in boiling water, lift out with a slotted spoon, and drain.

The pricey ($47 plus shipping) but practical French-made tool can be ordered from Bridge Kitchenware; (800) 274-3435 or www.bridgekitchenware.com.

Just faux fun

Soft-cooked eggs for dessert? "Citrus eggs from heaven" are a tiny joke: The "yolk" is a smooth citrus curd, the "white," whipped cream, served in eggshell cups created with the cutter at left. If you can't cut the eggshells, serve the dessert in eggcups or small bowls (about ¼-cup size).

Oeufs Citrons du Paradis

PREP AND COOK TIME: About 45 minutes
MAKES: 1 cup filling; 6 servings

- 2 teaspoons grated **lemon** peel
- 1 teaspoon grated **orange** peel
- 6 tablespoons **lemon juice**
- ¼ cup **orange juice**
- 3 **large egg** yolks
  About ¼ cup **sugar**
- ½ cup (¼ lb.) **butter** or margarine
- 6 sterilized **large eggshells** (see directions, left)
  About ¼ cup softly whipped **cream**
  Thin strands shredded **lemon** or orange peel or candied violets

1. In a 10- to 12-inch frying pan, whisk to blend grated lemon peel, grated orange peel, lemon juice, orange juice, egg yolks, and ¼ cup sugar. Cut butter into small pieces and add to pan. Stir over medium heat, scraping pan sides and bottom with a flexible heat-resistant spatula, until 3 or 4 bubbles form on pan bottom about 10 minutes after butter melts; do not boil the mixture.

2. At once, rub citrus curd through a fine strainer into a bowl; discard residue. Nest bowl in ice water and stir curd often until cold, about 15 minutes. If making ahead, cover and chill up to 3 days.

3. Set each sterilized eggshell, open end up, in an eggcup. Spoon citrus curd (or pour it from a measuring cup with a spout) equally into shells. If making ahead, cover and chill up to 4 hours. Sweeten whipped cream to taste with sugar and spoon in mounds onto curd in eggshells. Garnish with peel. Serve with tiny spoons.

Per serving: 221 cal., 77% (171 cal.) from fat; 1.8 g protein; 19 g fat (11 g sat.); 11 g carbo (0.1 g fiber); 162 mg sodium; 153 mg chol. ◆

The Wine Guide

By Karen MacNeil-Fife

RICK MARIANI

A shocking experiment

■ Until about a month ago, whenever I was asked how long an opened bottle of wine would last and which method for keeping it fresh was best, my response was discouraging. Wine, I believed, deteriorated quickly when exposed to oxygen; even after 24 hours, most wines would have lost a lot of their character and charm. As to which preservation system worked best, I was unsure. So I decided to experiment with several methods to find out. And frankly, I was shocked. The outcome was nothing short of startling.

The experiment took 54 bottles of wine. I tested three easy-to-use, widely available systems: Private Preserve (about $10), a canister of harmless inert gases, which you spray into the bottle, supposedly displacing the oxygen; VacuVin Wine Saver (about $10), a small hand-pump and rubber seal—you restop the bottle, then pump out the oxygen, theoretically creating a vacuum; and, finally, simply pouring the remaining wine into a smaller bottle, filling it to the top so there's no air inside, then capping it tightly. I also compared these

methods to using no preservation system at all—that is, just restopping the wine bottle with its original cork.

For each preservation system, I removed the same amount of wine from the original bottle—175 milliliters, or about one quarter of the bottle (one generous glass)—before resealing it. When it came to just recorking the bottle, I experimented with two variations. In one case, I removed one quarter of the wine, in the other case, half the wine.

To make the experiment more meaningful, I included time as a factor. Was it true that the longer a bottle had been open, the worse the wine tasted? To find out, I tested each preservation method on three different bottles—keeping one resealed for one day, one for two days, and one for four days. And so the results would not apply to just one wine or grape variety, I performed the entire experiment on three different wines: Clos du Bois Chardonnay, Geyser Peak Cabernet Sauvignon, and Saintsbury Pinot Noir.

Finally, since I didn't want the experiment to reflect my judgment alone, I asked a winery owner and a wine enthusiast to join me in the tastings, which we did completely blind—none of us knew which wine had been preserved with which system. Nor did we know which was the control wine (from a freshly opened bottle). We ranked the wines in taste from best to worst. My husband (a Stanford Business School graduate) tabulated the results.

The outcome

•No taster consistently rated one preservation system best.
•No preservation system was rated better overall than any other.
•More surprising yet, no preservation

THE TEST WINES

The subjects for this experiment were all delicious—and very good examples of their respective varieties.

■ **Clos du Bois Chardonnay 1998 (Sonoma County),** $14. A nice, all-around Chardonnay, with creamy apple flavors laced with touches of vanilla and oak.

■ **Geyser Peak Cabernet Sauvignon 1997 (Sonoma County),** $17. Beautiful aromas and flavors of cassis, mint, and black raspberry wrapped in a plush texture.

■ **Saintsbury Pinot Noir 1998 (Carneros, CA),** $22. Supple and juicy, with aromas and flavors reminiscent of strawberry jam, mocha, and earth.

system worked better than just recorking the bottle, no matter which variety or whether the wine had been opened for one, two, or four days.
•Wines that had been opened for four days didn't necessarily taste worse than wines that had been opened for only one day.
•And the most stunning revelation of all: In several cases, tasters preferred an opened wine to the control wine! After being opened for a day or more, the Chardonnay sometimes tasted softer and less oaky, the Cabernet rounder and less tannic. Even the Pinot Noir sometimes seemed more mellow, which some tasters liked.

As every scientist knows, conclusive experiments are difficult to design. And so a few caveats are in order. First, the wines were all kept at cool room temperature; at warmer temperatures, the results might be different. Second, after removing some of the wine, I recorked the bottles right away; wine left open during a two-hour dinner and then recorked might not keep as well. And finally, three wines—however interesting the test results—aren't a big sample.

But I'll tell you one thing: This is the last time I'll pour a half-empty bottle of wine down the drain without giving it a second chance. ◆

Anderson Valley, an Eden explored

The secret's out: Mendocino County's wine region has a flavor all its own

By Dale Conour • Photographs by Sean Arbabi

A lone sheep grazes beside Navarro Vineyards. At Greenwood Ridge Vineyards, grapes await the crush (top left).

Most Sunday mornings in the Anderson Valley, it's so quiet you can almost hear the steam rise from your coffee. At the Horn of Zeese Cafe in Boonville, the waiter is likely to be playing a hand of gin rummy with a couple of regulars while keeping tabs on his tables. But this is late summer, and outside there's a certain expectancy sharing the air with the heavy fragrance of apples. The crush is nearing.

Historically, the valley's economy has been dominated by lumber, the raising of sheep, and farming. What has finally put this little area on the cultural map, however, is the rise of its small collection of wineries and vineyards to national prominence.

From woods to wine

The Anderson Valley lies along serpentine State 128, one of the main routes to the Mendocino Coast, and formally consists of some 18 miles of rolling terrain cut by the Navarro River. In rough terms, its limits are marked by the small town of Boonville to the south and the tiny hamlet of Navarro on its north end. In the south, the hills are open and strewn with oaks; farther north, they become dense with mixed evergreens and redwoods.

First populated by Coastal Pomos, the valley was "discovered" in 1851 by one of Walter Anderson's sons while he was trailing an elk on a hunting expedition up the Russian River. The elder Anderson's decision to live in this "Garden of Eden" created the first trickle in what became a stream of white settlers.

Through the early 1900s, about 100 families, mostly subsistence farmers, lived here. Their relative isolation gave rise to a distinct lexicon known as Boontling. *Horn of Zeese,* for instance, translates to cup of coffee—Zachariah Clifton Zeese, the official coffee brewer on hunting expeditions, was known for making strong java.

These days Boontling is rarely if ever spoken, and the Anderson Valley's economy is in a postlumber transition that could very well end with its development into a mini-Napa. Over the past 25 years, blue-collar residents have been joined by progressive, monied back-to-the-landers, most of whom, thus far, have been interested in planting vineyards.

The pioneers

While grape growing has long been pursued by a handful of valley dwellers, the current movement started when Donald Edmeades planted 24 acres in the early 1960s and Tony and Gretchen Husch showed up in '68. Several other would-be wine growers followed on their heels.

The key to success for most of these contemporary wine growers was their introduction of grapes that would thrive in, or at least adapt to, the area's relatively cold climate. Bill Mitchell, who has been working with owners Ted Bennett and Deborah Cahn at Navarro Vineyards since 1984, says the area's climate has more in common with Oregon's Willamette Valley than with Napa or Sonoma county. He says you should "get out of your normal California mind-set when you visit the Anderson Valley"—that is, be open to tasting

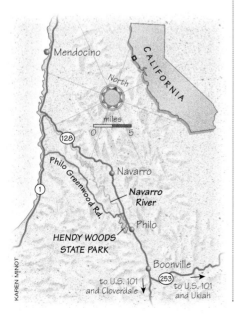

KAREN MINOT

the northern European–style varietals that thrive here, namely, Gewürztraminer, Riesling, and Pinot Noir—in addition to Chardonnays and Cabernet Sauvignons.

These varietals and some fine sparkling wines are now being cultivated and perfected at more than 15 wineries and vineyards in the Anderson Valley—most in and around Philo—as well as a handful in the neighboring Yorkville Highlands. Many of these wineries consist of little more than a modest tasting room up a long dirt drive. But the wines speak for themselves.

Good wine, good beer, good food

Perhaps it's a tribute to the valley's humble origins that the winemakers here are not afraid to help one another. Josh Chandler of Lazy Creek Vineyards often recommends other wineries for people to visit. "We want people to have a good experience here. In the end, that's what will keep people coming back."

That, and a few other things. Good beer, for one. The Anderson Valley Brewing Company, founded in 1987, has twice been ranked among the world's top 10 breweries at the World Beer Championships.

And of course, good food. Just outside Boonville in Philo is the Apple Farm, where Don and Sally Schmitt—former owners of Napa Valley's renowned French Laundry restaurant—revived an old apple orchard and added a now-thriving produce stand and cooking classes. Among the valley's other culinary offerings is the Boonville Hotel, renovated in 1988 by the Schmitts' son John.

The new Anderson Valley

As a result of all this, the Anderson Valley, once simply a pretty place you drove through to get to Mendocino, has become a destination in its own right—a development that some

locals bemoan. There's a fear that the valley may grow from a place where people of modest means can live and work into a tony enclave for wealthy second-home owners.

But it may not. Allan Green, winemaker and owner of Greenwood Ridge Vineyards, says: "There are a lot of people here who object very strongly to what they don't like. Anything controversial will draw a huge amount of attention. Nothing's going to slip by the community."

Nothing but time, perhaps. For now, however, Walter Anderson's Garden of Eden still feels like a discovery, and visitors will enjoy what the valley has always had to offer: an abundance of good food and drink, and the simple pleasures of a few days in the country.

Anderson Valley travel planner

The Anderson Valley is 100 miles north of San Francisco. Take State 128 west from U.S. 101 near Cloverdale. Area code is 707 unless otherwise noted.

Contact

Anderson Valley Chamber of Commerce. *(707) 895-2379 or www.andersonvalleychamber.com.*
Anderson Valley Winegrowers Association. *(707) 895-9463 or www.avwines.com.*

Wineries

Greenwood Ridge Vineyards. Owner Allan Green founded the local wine-tasting championships, acts as a disc jockey for a local radio show, and is an excellent winemaker. *5501 State 128, Philo; 895-2002.*
Handley Cellars. Sample well-crafted wines in a tasting room full of imported arts and crafts (one of the partners also runs the Folk Art International chain). *Tastings 11–6 daily. 3151 State 128, Philo; (800) 733-3151.*
Husch Vineyards. One of the pioneering wineries in the valley. *4400 State 128, Philo; (800) 554-8724 or www.huschvineyards.com.*
Lazy Creek Vineyards. There are just three wines here, but each has been painstakingly perfected since 1974—and the quality shows. *By appointment. 4741 State 128, Philo; 895-3623.*

At Navarro Vineyards, co-owner Ted Bennett has been tending the barrels since 1974.

Row by row: Allan Green takes Cabernet Sauvignon samples at Greenwood Ridge.

Navarro Vineyards. These delicious award-winning wines are available only at the winery. With 16 to taste, you'll want to count on spending some idle time here—and the picnic tables overlooking the vineyards invite you to do just that. *5601 State 128, Philo; (800) 537-9463 or www.navarrowine.com.*

Pacific Echo Cellars. Not long after Mendocino native John Scharffenberger started producing sparkling wines, French champagne maker Pommery took notice and bought him out; ownership has since transferred to Moët Hennessy Louis Vuitton. The winery is still a great place to taste fine bottlings of the bubbly. (Scharffenberger himself has gone on to produce wines in Ukiah and gourmet chocolates in South San Francisco.) *8501 State 128, Philo; (800) 824-7754.*

Roederer Estate. The largest and best known Anderson Valley winery produces sparkling wines that have, on occasion, outranked prestigious French champagnes entered in international competitions. *4501 State 128, Philo; 895-2288.*

Attractions and events

Hendy Woods State Park. Scenic hiking and camping under redwood trees, near the Navarro River (popular with kayakers and canoeists in spring). Ask about their four new rustic cabins with wood-burning stoves. *8 miles northwest of Boonville, ¹/₂ mile west of State 128 on Philo Greenwood Rd.; 895-3141.*

Farmers' Market. Saturday mornings in the Boonville Hotel parking lot. *Anderson Valley Chamber of Commerce; 895-2379.*

Mendocino County Fair & Apple Show. Animal judging, sheepdog trials, midway activities, and valley-grown produce. *September 22–24; Mendocino County Fairgrounds, Boonville; 895-3011.*

Dining and lodging

Anderson Creek Inn. Comfortable lodging in the heart of the valley. *From $110. 12050 Anderson Valley Way, Boonville; (800) 552-6202 or www.andersoncreekinn.com.*

Apple Farm. Buy organic apples and other food products or sign up for the cooking classes. The farm also has three cottages and one guest room, though weekends are usually booked by cooking students. *From $150. 18501 Philo Greenwood Rd., Philo; 895-2461.*

Boonville Hotel. This small hotel has made its reputation with sophisticated cuisine that complements local wines. Rooms and suites have a casual, contemporary style. *Rooms from $75. State 128 at Lambert Lane, Boonville; 895-2210.*

Buckhorn Saloon. The saloon serves Anderson Valley Brewing Company's nationally recognized beers and straightforward food to soak them up. *14081 State 128, Boonville; 895-3369 or www.avbc.com.*

Highland Ranch. A 100-year-old farmhouse and eight guest cottages command a fine perch in the hills above Philo. On-site activities include horseback riding, clay pigeon shooting, swimming, fishing, mountain-biking, and hiking. *$245 per person per day ($175 ages 12 and under), includes all meals, beverages, and activities. Very popular in summer; reserve well ahead. Off Philo Greenwood Rd., Philo; 895-3600 or www.highlandranch.com.*

Horn of Zeese Cafe. Locals come here for coffee and hearty breakfasts. Look for the Boontling word of the day on the chalkboard. *14025 State 128, Boonville; 895-3525.*

Indian Creek Inn. A simple, quiet hideaway on a country road, bordering Indian Creek County Park. *From $110. 9050 State 128, Philo; 895-3861.*

Libby's. A newcomer on the scene—and one of the best values in town. Fresh, authentic Mexican food in a pleasant no-frills atmosphere. *11:30–2:30, 5–8:30 Tue-Thu; 8–11, 12–2:30, 5–8:30 Fri-Sun. 8651 State 128, Philo; 895-2646.*

Philo Pottery Inn. A charming former stagecoach stop (not, however, a pottery kiln) with a lush English country–style garden. *From $100. 8550 State 128, Philo; 895-3069.* ◆

Picnic on the beach

by Andrew Baker

T IS A LAW OF PHYSICS, OR HUMAN BIOLOGY, OR both, that sun, salt air, and salt water inspire ravenous hunger. That's why no picnic is as welcome as the one you assemble at the beach. Here's a hearty seafood stew to cook on-site on a grill or camp stove. Serve it with crisp vegetables (sugar snap peas, baby-cut carrots), French bread, summer-ripe fruits (Asian pears, strawberries, grapes), and sugar cookies. Accompany with wine (see below) for a truly memorable picnic on the sand.

Beach stew checklist

☐ For convenience, chop onions and tomatoes at home and carry in separate plastic food bags.

☐ Pack stew pan with tools and ingredients that don't need to be kept cold.

☐ Bring along a small cutting board (or flexible plastic cutting mat) to provide a work surface, chopping knife, vegetable peeler, cooking spoon, a stiff brush and bowl for scrubbing shellfish, can and bottle openers, towels, hot pads, and a camp stove or small grill (that can be supported on rocks), if there aren't firepits.

☐ If water is not available at the picnic site, bring enough to scrub clams and mussels.

JAMES CARRIER

Chili-Coconut Seafood Stew

PREP AND COOK TIME: About 45 minutes

NOTES: Use a vegetable peeler to cut orange peel.

MAKES: 8 servings

4 or 5 **dried California** (or New Mexico) **chilies** (each about 5 in. long, 1 oz. total), rinsed, stemmed, and seeded

2 **onions** (1 lb. total), peeled and chopped

¼ cup (⅛ lb.) **butter** or margarine

2 strips **orange** peel (colored part only, about 1 by 4 in. each; see notes)

1 can (49½ oz.) fat-skimmed **chicken broth**

1 can (15 oz.) **coconut milk**

2 **Roma tomatoes** (6 oz. total), rinsed, cored, and chopped

32 **clams in shells,** suitable for steaming, and/or **mussels** with beards pulled off, scrubbed

1 **cooked Dungeness crab** (about 1½ lb.), cleaned and cracked

1½ pounds **fish** (boned, skinned salmon or halibut), rinsed and cut into 1-inch chunks, and/or **shelled, deveined shrimp,** rinsed

Lime wedges

1. In a 6- to 8-quart pan over medium-high heat, stir chilies, onions, and butter until onions are lightly browned, 8 to 10 minutes. Add orange peel and stir for 1 minute.

2. Add broth, coconut milk, and tomatoes. Stir occasionally until mixture boils.

3. Add clams and mussels; cover and cook 3 minutes. Add the crab, fish, and shrimp; cover and cook just until clams and mussels open, 3 to 7 minutes longer.

4. Discard chilies. Ladle stew into bowls or mugs. Add juice from lime wedges to taste.

Per serving: 371 cal., 49% (180 cal.) from fat; 37 g protein; 20 g fat (14 g sat.); 11 g carbo (1.8 g fiber); 343 mg sodium; 186 mg chol.

BEACH PICNIC WINES

For wines to accompany our stew (preceding), we selected vintages from the three coasts highlighted in our story—Washington, Northern California, and San Luis Obispo County.

Hogue Pinot Gris (about $10). From one of Washington's top wineries, a peachy, citrusy wine with a good punch—perfectly refreshing, as wine served on the beach should be.

Navarro Vineyards Gewürztraminer (about $15). Anderson Valley slants inward from the Northern California coast like a pocket. One of the valley's top varietals is Gewürztraminer, and one of the best is Navarro's. Fruity and dry, it's only available by calling (or visiting) the winery (800/537-9463).

Alban Vineyards Viognier (about $30). From Edna Valley, inland from Morro Bay, a powerhouse white that's just the ticket for a full-flavored stew.

— *Karen MacNeil-Fife* ◆

Bountiful Brentwood

Pick summer fruit at its tastiest in this Contra Costa County farm town

By Lisa Taggart

After shopping the produce stands in Brentwood last summer, I brought home a feast so delicious, it's become a household legend: apples and Asian pears with wildflower honey, tomato-and-basil salad, chicken tamales with an apricot-pepper sauce, fresh salsa, sweet corn, string beans, and, for dessert, peach pie and strawberries I'd picked that morning. My husband and I had to invite our neighbors over to help us finish it all.

It's easy to overdo it in Brentwood, an eastern Contra Costa County town, where the warm days and cool nights combine to create exceptionally sweet fruit. Here, 33 growers sell edible riches you can gather in baskets or pluck yourself. Apples, apricots, cherries, corn, nectarines, peaches, and tomatoes are specialties, though you'll also find many other fruits and vegetables. August is the ideal time to enjoy Brentwood's bounty, when peaches are at their sweetest and the harvest offers its greatest variety.

It may be surprising to find so many orchards only 60 miles east of San Francisco. "People don't realize there's still farmland out here," says Meredith Nunn, who runs the Farmer's Daughter Produce and Drive-Thru Coffee Bar. Before dawn, SUV-driving commuters cruise through her stand for a caffeine dose; later in the day, visitors from Oakland and Fremont pick apricots and peaches from Nunn's 20-acre orchard.

Tomatoes await your harvesting at Smith Family Farms.

Many growers specialize in heirloom and hard-to-find varieties. You can pick Fay Elberta peaches or Black Friar plums or, later in the season, Mutsu apples. Head over to Smith Family Farms for tomatoes of every color, including heirloom Great White and Flame. Or visit other growers to collect baskets of Fairtime peaches, Santa Rosa plums, nectarines, okra, black-eyed peas, and sweet corn.

Al Courchesne of Frog Hollow Farm says O'Henry and Cal Red peaches are at their best this month. "Those two are really exceptional—they have the quintessential peach quality," says Courchesne, known locally as Farmer Al. He also recommends Sparkling Red nectarines. His organic farm sells produce by mail order and at farmers' markets around the Bay Area, offering 25 varieties of peaches and 15 varieties of nectarines.

Though the region has seen rapid growth—with some of the most affordable housing in the Bay Area, Brentwood has more than tripled in population since 1990—farmers hope to keep the surrounding area agricultural. The Tachella family has been farming here since 1952, and subdivisions recently squeezed out 38 of the farm's acres. But Kathey Tachella says she has no intention of giving up: "The fruit-stand business is good. People who remember the taste of fresh produce come from far away."

Start a Brentwood visit at Walnut Boulevard, south of downtown, where many stands are clustered. The Harvest Time growers' group publishes a map of farms, available at all member stands. After you harvest, you can picnic at one of the orchards or at City Park, at Second and Oak streets. ◆

Brentwood travel planner

WHERE: Brentwood is off State 4, about 60 miles east of San Francisco.
WHEN: Peaches peak this month. While most stands close after Labor Day, some remain open into fall to sell apples, even Halloween pumpkins.
CONTACT: Harvest information, farm phone numbers, and directions are available at www.harvest4u.com. For information on Frog Hollow Farm, call (888) 779-4511 or visit www.froghollow.com.
FYI: Growers recommend that you bring containers for produce and call ahead to check availability.

Fruits of summer

■ These days, a side-salad cherry tomato is all color and no taste, but at Bell Gardens, a 115-acre farm just north of Escondido, a cherry tomato is summer in a red skin, a fruit so sweet you might mistake it for a real cherry.

The Red Cherry, Mountain Gold, Fabulous, and Lemon Boy tomatoes at the Bell Gardens produce stand are just four reasons August is a good time to leave crowded beaches and drive to rural Valley Center, where summer slopes are either corrugated with orange and avocado groves or baked the color of Van Gogh's wheat. Two farms are within 8 miles of each other in this North County town, and both invite you to spend the day—free of charge—among fields, tractors, animals, and blessed shade.

The older of the spreads, where Clifford Bates planted walnut trees in 1921, is home to a menagerie so popular with local children

that some mothers bring their kids here every day to see the goats, pet the sheep, and poke dried corn through the fence for the chickens. Though the walnut groves are long gone, Bates Nut Farm still grows pumpkins and sells roasted nuts from all over the world.

Another bucolic stop is just up the road: the farm started by Taco Bell founder Glen Bell. Although it's immaculately tended and smartly equipped (shiny red and green tractors pull visitors in wagons fitted with canvas-covered hay bales), Bell Gardens isn't a theme park—65 different fruits, vegetables, and cut flowers are grown and sold here.

To see the zinnias, cockscombs, sweet corn, pumpkins,

WHERE: From Escondido, take I-15 north to Old Castle/Gopher Canyon Rd. Drive 9 miles east to Valley Center Rd. To reach Bates Nut Farm (15954 Woods Valley Rd.), turn right on Valley Center Rd., left on Woods Valley Rd., and continue 3 miles. To reach Bell Gardens (30841 Cole Grade Rd.), turn left on Valley Center Rd. and then left on Cole Grade Rd. To see the Pauma Valley from Bell Gardens, drive north on Cole Grade Rd. until it dead-ends at State 76, then turn left and drive 20 miles to I-15.
CONTACT: Bell Gardens; (760) 749-6297. Bates Nut Farm; 749-3333.

At Bell Gardens, kids feast on free watermelon samples while adults peruse the produce stand.

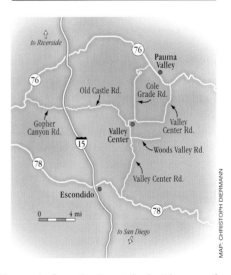

watermelons, and beans before they're picked, ride one of the wagons to the train station, where a miniature train will take you on a breezy trip over a trestle and around Lake Kathleen, revealing not just cultivated beauty but a blue line of mountains to the east.

As you leave Valley Center, there's one more agricultural surprise. Go north on Cole Grade Road to see the California you thought had disappeared 50 years ago. From the pinnacle of Cole Grade Road, the Pauma Valley's immense orange and avocado groves stretch out before you like the scene on the label of an orange crate. This scene, though, you can drive right into. — *Laura McNeal* ◆

The Quick Cook

Meals in 30 minutes or less
By Elaine Johnson

Dark olive tapenade coats bread that tops pungent arugula, roasted red peppers, and goat cheese.

JAMES CARRIER

Sandwiches with the flavors of Provence

■ In the sunny south of France, no tray of hors d'oeuvres is complete without a small pot of tapenade to smear on crisp crackers or baguette slices. This robust spread of olives—black or green—with anchovies, capers, garlic, and olive oil is very easy to prepare. But here in the West, that task is optional because, of late, tapenades flourish on market shelves. Whether you purchase the spread or make your own (following), tapenade can add a delectable provençal flair to hearty sandwiches.

Olive Tapenade

PREP TIME: About 10 minutes

NOTES: Use your favorite salt- (sometimes called oil-) or brine-cured black olives such as calamata or niçoise, or brine-cured green olives such as picholine or Spanish-style. If olives have pits, cut fruit from them. Or place olives on a counter and lay the flat side of a wide knife over one olive at a time. Hit knife with your fist firmly enough to loosen pit; pull olive free and discard pit.

MAKES: 1 cup

In a food processor, whirl 1 clove **garlic** and 1 teaspoon **fresh thyme** leaves or dried thyme until minced. Add 1¼ cups

pitted olives (see notes), 4 drained **canned anchovy fillets,** 2 tablespoons drained **capers,** 5 tablespoons **extra-virgin olive oil,** and 2 teaspoons **lemon juice;** whirl until coarsely puréed; scrape container as needed. Use, or chill airtight up to 1 month.

Per tablespoon: 72 cal., 92% (66 cal.) from fat; 0.3 g protein; 7.3 g fat (1 g sat.); 1.6 g carbo (0 g fiber); 274 mg sodium; 0.6 mg chol.

Goat Cheese–Tapenade Sandwiches

PREP TIME: About 15 minutes

MAKES: 6 servings

1 loaf **herb-flavor** or plain **bread** such as ciabatta or focaccia (1 lb., about 2 in. thick)

¾ cup **fresh chèvre** (goat) **cheese**

1 jar (7¼ oz.; 1 cup) **roasted red peppers,** drained

2 cups lightly packed **arugula,** rinsed and crisped

¾ cup **olive tapenade** (recipe precedes, or purchased)

With a long serrated knife, cut bread in half horizontally. Spread cut side of bread bottom with goat cheese. Cover cheese with red peppers and arugula. Spread cut side of bread top with tapenade and invert onto arugula. Cut in equal portions.

Per serving: 385 cal., 63% (243 cal.) from fat; 11 g protein; 27 g fat (4.4 g sat.); 41 g carbo (2 g fiber); 1,011 mg sodium; 8.9 mg chol.

Roast Beef–Tapenade Sandwiches

PREP TIME: About 15 minutes

MAKES: 6 servings

⅓ cup **mayonnaise**

2 tablespoons drained **dried tomatoes packed in oil**

2 **baguettes** (8 oz. each)

½ cup **olive tapenade** (recipe at left, or purchased)

4 large **romaine lettuce** leaves, rinsed, crisped, and torn in 2-inch pieces

¾ pound **thin-sliced roast beef**

1. In a food processor, whirl mayonnaise and dried tomatoes until coarsely puréed.

2. With a long serrated knife, cut baguettes in half horizontally. Spread cut sides of bread tops equally with mayonnaise. Spread cut sides of bread bottoms equally with tapenade. Cover tapenade with romaine, then beef. Invert cut bread tops onto beef. Cut each sandwich into 3 equal portions.

Per serving: 473 cal., 46% (216 cal.) from fat; 19 g protein; 24 g fat (4 g sat.); 45 g carbo (2.7 g fiber); 1,495 mg sodium; 33 mg chol.

Scrambled Egg–Tapenade Sandwiches

PREP AND COOK TIME: About 15 minutes

MAKES: 4 servings

- 2 **firm-ripe tomatoes** (²⁄₃ lb. total), rinsed
- 4 slices **multigrain bread** (7 oz. total, each ½ in. thick)
- ½ cup **olive tapenade** (recipe on facing page, or purchased)
- 2 cups lightly packed **watercress sprigs**, rinsed and crisped
- 8 **large eggs**
- ½ cup (½ of an 8-oz. package) **neufchâtel** (light cream) **cheese**
- 1 tablespoon chopped **fresh chives** or green onion

  Pepper

1. Core tomatoes and cut crosswise in ¼-inch-thick slices.

2. Lay bread in a single layer on a 12- by 15-inch baking sheet. Bake in a 450° oven until toasted, about 5 minutes. Spread tapenade equally onto 1 side of toast slices, cut slices diagonally in half, and set 2 pieces on each plate. Top equally with tomatoes and watercress.

3. In a bowl, beat eggs to blend. Cut cheese into ½-inch chunks and add with chives to bowl; mix. Place an 10- to 12-inch nonstick frying pan on medium heat; pour egg mixture into pan. As egg mixture cooks, push from pan bottom until softly set, 5 to 7 minutes, or cooked to taste.

4. Spoon eggs equally onto watercress. Season to taste with pepper.

Per serving: 509 cal., 58% (297 cal.) from fat; 23 g protein; 33 g fat (9.8 g sat.); 32 g carbo (5 g fiber); 1,046 mg sodium; 447 mg chol. ◆

Rising to the occasion

Celebrate the renaissance of hearth-baked bread at Portland's Summer Loaf

By Elaine Johnson

Portland's Pearl Bakery shows off hearty multigrain bâtards.

JAMES CARRIER

■ In the early-morning quiet, the farmers' market stands ready. Next to arrays of Red Haven peaches, marionberries, and other products of Oregon's bounty, some of the Northwest's best artisan bakers display just-baked baguettes, bâtards, and boules. They've brought crusty hand-shaped loaves baked on stone hearths, wheat-flecked slicing bread like Mom might have made, and elaborate yeasty sculptures. There are pastries too: cinnamon swirl buns and flaky turnovers oozing with local raspberries.

This mouthwatering scene is Portland's Summer Loaf: A Celebration of Bread. Ten thousand bread lovers are expected to attend in 2000, on August 5 (check date). Lattes in hand, the early birds will catch the worm—or in this case, the loaf. By 2 P.M., only crumbs will be left. Our advice: Come early.

Among food festivals, Summer Loaf is unique. No other city in the country, perhaps the world, devotes an event to bread. The one-day gathering presents an abundance of attractions, including some serious experts, both local and nationally known. At a brick oven on-site, farmers, millers, and bakers will hold court on this year's theme, "From Harvest to Hearth." Baking authors Carol Field and Peter Reinhart, among others, will speak, teach classes, and sign books. There will even be baking classes for kids.

But all this is icing on the cinnamon bun compared to the chance to see, smell, and taste the wares of some two dozen bakeries at once. Generous samples allow attendees to sniff and savor pain au levain, ciabatta, pain de campagne, and more. Then they'll decide which loaves to purchase for home: focaccia or fougasse, pane pugliese or panini?

Despite the international scope of the offerings, Summer Loaf is about a welcome change on the local level: the return of the village bakery, a renaissance that began here in the West. In the 1970s, a cadre of small, dedicated bakeries in Berkeley revived what was by then a dying art. Before long, the phenomenon spread up the coast and to the rest of the country. Now, Summer Loaf provides a singular opportunity to get passionate about crust and crumb and magnificent flavor, to share the pleasures and learn the skills of handmade, locally produced bread.

Portland Summer Loaf: 8–2 August 5 in 2000 (check date); free. Portland Farmers Market, at the Park Blocks on Portland State University campus, corner of S.W. Ninth and S.W. Montgomery streets. Separate classes for children (ages 7–11; $20) and adults (from $30); space is limited. To register for classes or the amateur baking contest, call (503) 241-0032. ◆

The Low-Fat Cook

Healthy choices for the active lifestyle

By Christine Weber Hale

Fancy flavors to sip through a straw: Fresh mango spiced with cardamom.

Great summer smoothies

■ The perennially popular yogurt smoothie—a lively refreshment to begin with—reaches new heights with refined combinations of fruit and spices. Two of our recipes are inspired by Indian *lassi,* sweet or savory yogurt drinks intriguingly spiced with cardamom, cumin, or the like. The tomato *raita,* with its tangy blend of yogurt and cucumber, makes a surprisingly delicious ice-cold drink.

From smoothie to slushy: All of these mixtures—including the raita—go beyond refreshing to addictive when frozen but still soft enough to slurp through a straw. Pour them straight from the blender into an ice cream maker (1½-quart or larger) and freeze according to the manufacturer's directions until they hold soft mounds, 10 to 12 minutes.

Mango Lassi

PREP TIME: About 12 minutes

NOTES: If making mango lassi slushy, add 2 to 4 tablespoons sugar before freezing; omit pistachios.

MAKES: About 5 cups; 3 to 4 servings

- 2 cups **low-fat vanilla yogurt**
- 1 cup **refrigerated mango nectar**
- 2 **firm-ripe mangoes** (about ¾ lb. total), peeled, pitted, and cut into chunks
- ⅛ to ¼ teaspoon **ground cardamom**
- 1 cup **ice cubes**

  Roasted, salted pistachios, coarsely chopped (optional)

In a blender, combine yogurt, mango nectar, mangoes, and cardamom; whirl on high speed until smooth, about 1 minute. Add ice and whirl until puréed, about 1 minute longer. Pour into tall glasses (at least 16-oz. size); sprinkle with pistachios.

Per serving: 172 cal., 8.1% (14 cal.) from fat; 5.9 g protein; 1.6 g fat (1 g sat.); 35 g carbo (0.6 g fiber); 78 mg sodium; 5.7 mg chol.

Cinnamon-Peach Smoothie

PREP TIME: About 8 minutes

MAKES: About 4 cups; 2 to 3 servings

- 2 **ripe peaches** (about ¾ lb. total)
- 2 cups **nonfat plain yogurt**
- 3 tablespoons firmly packed **brown sugar**
- ¼ teaspoon **ground cinnamon**
- 1 cup **ice cubes**

1. In a 2- to 3-quart pan over high heat, bring about 1 quart water to a boil. Immerse peaches in boiling water for 15 seconds; drain. When peaches are cool enough to touch, in 1 to 2 minutes, peel, pit, and cut into chunks. **2.** In a blender, combine peaches, yogurt, brown sugar, and cinnamon; whirl on high speed until smooth, about 1 minute. Add ice and whirl until puréed, about 2 minutes longer. Pour into tall glasses (at least 16-oz. size).

Per serving: 174 cal., 1.6% (2.7 cal.) from fat; 9.3 g protein; 0.3 g fat (0.2 g sat.); 35 g carbo (1.4 g fiber); 120 mg sodium; 3 mg chol.

Honey Almond Plum Smoothie

PREP TIME: About 7 minutes

NOTES: If you don't want bits of plum skin in the smoothie, peel fruit before chopping (see step 1 of the cinnamon-peach smoothie recipe, preceding).

MAKES: About 5½ cups; 3 to 4 servings

- 2 **ripe red-skinned plums** (about ½ lb. total), pitted and cut into chunks
- 2 cups **nonfat plain yogurt**
- 1½ cups **cherry cider** or cherry juice blend
- ¼ cup **honey**
- ¾ teaspoon **almond extract**
- 1 cup **ice cubes**

In a blender, combine plums, yogurt, cherry cider, honey, and almond extract; whirl on high speed until smooth, about 1 minute. Add ice and whirl until puréed, about 2 minutes longer. Pour into tall glasses (at least 16-oz. size).

Per serving: 204 cal., 2.6% (5.4 cal.) from fat; 7 g protein; 0.6 g fat (0.2 sat.); 44 g carbo (1.2 g fiber); 90 mg sodium; 2.3 mg chol.

Savory Tomato Raita Smoothie

PREP TIME: About 15 minutes

NOTES: For a festive touch, garnish glasses with whole green onions. If making savory tomato raita slushy, add salt and hot sauce to taste after freezing.

MAKES: About 3½ cups; 2 servings

- 2 cups **nonfat plain yogurt**
- 2 **Roma tomatoes** (about ¼ lb. total), rinsed, cored, and chopped
- 1 **green onion,** ends trimmed, rinsed, and chopped
- ½ cup peeled, seeded, and chopped **cucumber**
- 3 tablespoons coarsely chopped **fresh cilantro**
- 1 teaspoon **mustard seed**
- ¼ teaspoon **ground cumin**
- 1 cup **ice cubes**

  Salt

  Hot sauce

In a blender, combine yogurt, tomatoes, onion, cucumber, cilantro, mustard seed, and cumin; whirl on high speed until smooth, about 1 minute. Add ice and whirl until puréed, 30 seconds to 1 minute longer. Pour into tall glasses (at least 16-oz. size). Add salt and hot sauce to taste.

Per serving: 155 cal., 7.1% (11 cal.) from fat; 14 g protein; 1.2 g fat (0.4 g sat.); 22 g carbo (1.4 g fiber); 181 mg sodium; 4.5 mg chol. ◆

Holy panettone!

For the nation's best Italian pastries—and more—bring your taste buds to Larkspur

By Lisa Taggart

Temptation, Italian-style: Gary and Jeannie Rulli brought Old World baking expertise to Marin County.

Demurely settled at the base of King Mountain in central Marin County, the town of Larkspur, about 15 miles north of San Francisco, has a culinary sophistication completely out of proportion to its size. Its 12,000 residents can sample English teas, organic greens, bouillabaisse Marseillaise, and Italian pastries without stepping far from the main strip, Magnolia Avenue.

A delectable Larkspur day starts at Emporio Rulli, an authentic pasticceria with house-roasted coffee, gelato, chocolates, and, of course, pastries. Since opening in a tiny storefront 12 years ago, Gary and Jeannie Rulli have expanded their business twice, as acclaim grew for what *Atlantic Monthly* food critic Corby Kummer calls "the closest thing in America to a top-flight Italian pastry shop and cafe."

Entering the store feels like stepping into a Venetian tea room. White-aproned servers stand behind mahogany display cases. A gold espresso machine gleams across the room from a mural of mad Italian pastry chefs. Nearby, tables and shelves are stocked with imported wines, candies, and ceramics.

But the real stars here are the treats. All are made on the premises. You'll find crisp circular almond cookies called *cialde,* dry and sweet *sbrisolona* cake, *pandolce, panforte,* a divine strawberry and chantilly cream–covered sponge cake called Amaretto Fantasia, and both

Milanese and Genovese panettone (the Milan version is cakier, Genoa's has more fruit and pine nuts). Plus tiny shortbread and almond cookies in dozens of shapes and colors, creamy chocolates, and gelato, including the pinnacle of ice cream sophistication—zabaglione.

Eighteen years ago, on a visit to the Old Country with his Italian grandparents, Marin native Gary was inspired to create a real pasticceria in California. He says the secret to stellar desserts is simple: Follow tradition and use the best ingredients. "We only use butter," he says. "Puff pastry to panettone—everything is made from scratch. In Italy, nothing is pre-made."

So good are the cafe's desserts that the shop beat hundreds of other applicants for two spots at the new international terminal at San Francisco International Airport, opening in September. You can also buy their confections online. But a visit to Rulli is a sensory treat and offers the opportunity to sample Larkspur's other delights.

Magnolia Avenue is anchored with top-notch culinary choices. The Lark Creek Inn put the town on the fine-dining map, serving Bradley Ogden and Jeremy Sewall's richly classic American cuisine (pork loin with polenta, organic cauliflower soup with a grilled Vermont cheddar sandwich) in a lovely 19th-century house. This summer, Ogden is opening another

Larkspur dining

Emporio Rulli, 464 Magnolia Ave.; (415) 924-7478 or www.rulli.com. Lark Creek Inn, 234 Magnolia; 924-7766. Left Bank, 507 Magnolia; 927-3331. Chai of Larkspur, 25 Ward St.; 945-7161 or www. chaioflarkspur.com.

Magnolia Avenue restaurant (a "New England–style clam shack," he calls it) that will serve wood-grilled fish, gumbo, and clam chowder.

Left Bank bistro, at the historic downtown's north end, has consistently great French comfort food, including bouillabaisse, lamb sandwiches, and frites. Or put a little English on your meal at Chai of Larkspur, where you can sip tea on the patio while sampling lemon-curd cookies, scones with Devonshire cream, and truffle pâté.

You can enjoy a postprandial stroll through Larkspur's shopping district, which hosts a number of boutiques and antiques stores. One block south of St. Patrick Church are the Arch Street Stairs. Leading to Locust Avenue and a lovely view, the steps are steep enough to work off a piece of panettone. Or plan to climb them twice, and go ahead, eat two. ◆

TERRENCE McCARTHY

Kitchen Cabinet

Readers' recipes tested in Sunset's kitchens

By Andrew Baker

For this easy dessert, creamy peanut butter filling and a ribbon of dark chocolate create a candy bar effect.

Peanut Butter–Chocolate Pie

Mary Vasudeva, San Diego

"Peanut butter is very popular at our house," explains Mary Vasudeva, who took a favorite pie recipe, reduced the butter and chocolate, replaced most of the cream with whipped topping (the peanut butter flavor conceals the secret), and came up with this just-as-luscious version.

PREP AND COOK TIME: About 40 minutes, plus at least 2 hours to chill

MAKES: 8 servings

- 1 **refrigerated pastry for 9-inch single-crust pie** (½ of a 15-oz. package)
- ½ cup **semisweet chocolate chips**
- 3 tablespoons **whipping cream**
- ¾ cup firmly packed **brown sugar**
- 6 tablespoons **butter** or margarine
- ⅓ cup **milk**
- ¾ cup **smooth peanut butter**
- 1 carton (8 oz.) **frozen whipped topping,** thawed

1. Gently fit pastry into a 9-inch pie pan. Fold excess pastry under and flush with pan rim. Pinch pastry rim to flute decoratively. Prick dough all over with a fork.

2. Bake in a 375° oven until golden brown, about 15 minutes. Let cool at least 15 minutes.

3. Meanwhile, in a microwave-safe bowl, combine chocolate chips and whipping cream. Heat in a microwave oven at 50% power, stirring every 30 seconds, until chocolate is soft, about 1 minute total. Stir until mixture is smooth; pour into crust, covering the bottom evenly.

4. Rinse bowl, wipe dry, and add brown sugar and butter (cut into chunks). Heat in a microwave oven at full power (100%), stirring every 30 seconds until butter melts and sugar dissolves, 1 to 2 minutes total. Let mixture cool slightly, about 10 minutes.

5. Add milk and peanut butter to bowl. Beat with a mixer on medium speed to blend well. Add whipped topping, stir to mix, then beat until well blended, scraping bowl often. Scrape peanut butter mixture evenly over chocolate in crust.

6. Cover and chill at least 2 hours or up to 2 days. Cut into wedges.

Per serving: 576 cal., 61% (351 cal.) from fat; 8.8 g protein; 39 g fat (19 g sat.); 50 g carbo (1.5 g fiber); 350 mg sodium; 38 mg chol.

Frank's Grapefruit Appetizer

Karen Degnan, Castaic, California

Karen Degnan came up with this simple, refreshing first course when she was given a bountiful supply of grapefruit as a gift. She named the dish after the fruit's donor.

PREP AND COOK TIME: About 10 minutes

MAKES: 2 first-course servings

- 2 tablespoons **rice vinegar**
- 2 tablespoons **honey**
- 2 **ruby** or pink **grapefruit** (about 2½ lb. total)

  About ⅛ teaspoon fresh-grated **nutmeg** or ground nutmeg

  Watercress sprigs, rinsed

  Salt

1. In a bowl, mix vinegar and honey.

2. With a sharp knife, cut off and discard peel and white membrane from grapefruit. Holding fruit over bowl, cut between inner membranes and fruit to release segments into bowl. Squeeze juice from membrane into bowl; discard membrane. Gently mix grapefruit segments with vinegar and honey.

3. Spoon grapefruit and dressing equally into small bowls. Sprinkle with nutmeg, garnish with watercress, and add salt to taste.

Per serving: 149 cal., 1.8% (2.7 cal.) from fat; 1.6 g protein; 0.3 g fat (0.1 g sat.); 39 g carbo (1.7 g fiber); 0.9 mg sodium; 0 mg chol.

Ensalada Verano

Karin Andersen, Dana Point, California

"We love the combination of chilies, corn, and beans," Karin Andersen says. She mixes them with Caesar dressing, which is part of the recipe, to make a hearty salad. Use a vegetable peeler to shave parmesan cheese into paper-thin slivers.

PREP AND COOK TIME: About 45 minutes

MAKES: 8 first-course or 4 main-dish servings

- ¼ pound **bacon**
- 6 tablespoons **olive oil**
- ⅓ cup **grated parmesan cheese**
- 3 tablespoons **lemon juice**
- 1 clove **garlic,** minced or pressed
- 3 or 4 drained **canned anchovy fillets,** finely chopped
- 1 can (15 oz.) **black beans,** rinsed and drained
- 1 cup thawed **frozen corn kernels**
- 1 cup finely chopped **celery**
- ½ cup finely chopped **red onion**
- 1 pound **firm-ripe tomatoes,** rinsed, cored, and chopped
- 1 **fresh serrano chili,** stemmed, seeded, deveined, and minced
- ¼ cup chopped **fresh cilantro**
- 1 **firm-ripe avocado** (about ½ lb.), peeled, pitted, and diced
- 8 **romaine lettuce** leaves (each 6 to 8 in.), rinsed and crisped
- 2 tablespoons shaved **parmesan cheese** (optional)
- 1 quart **corn tortilla chips**

Black beans, red onions, corn, chilies, and a vibrant dressing blend the flavors, colors, and textures of the Southwest in this hearty salad.

1. Cut bacon crosswise into ¹/₂-inch pieces. In an 8- to 10-inch frying pan over medium-high heat, stir bacon until crisp and brown, 6 to 7 minutes. With a slotted spoon, transfer bacon to towels to drain; discard fat.

2. In a large bowl, combine oil, grated parmesan cheese, lemon juice, garlic, and anchovies; mix well. Add beans, corn, celery, onion, tomatoes, chili, cilantro, avocado, and all but 2 tablespoons of the bacon. Mix gently.

3. Lay lettuce leaves on a wide platter. Mound salad onto lettuce; sprinkle with shaved parmesan cheese and reserved bacon. Accompany with tortilla chips.

Per first-course serving: 349 cal., 59% (207 cal.) from fat; 8.6 g protein; 23 g fat (4.4 g sat.); 30 g carbo (5.1 g fiber); 411 mg sodium; 6.8 mg chol.

Grilled Tuna with Salsa Fresca

Joanne Rasmussen, Oro Valley, Arizona

With a craving for Mexican flavors, Joanne Rasmussen—a fan of meaty fish—seasons ahi tuna with this lively marinade and fresh salsa.

PREP AND COOK TIME: About 40 minutes

MAKES: 4 servings

¹/₂ cup finely chopped **fresh pineapple**

¹/₄ cup finely chopped **red onion**

1 teaspoon minced or pressed **garlic**

1 tablespoon **lime juice**

2 tablespoons minced **fresh cilantro**

1¹/₄ pounds **boned ahi tuna** (1¹/₄ to 1¹/₂ in. thick)

Salsa fresca (recipe follows)

Salt

1. In a bowl, combine pineapple, onion, garlic, lime juice, and cilantro. Rinse tuna, pat dry, and add to bowl, turning to coat with marinade. Let stand at least 15 minutes or cover and chill up to 2 hours, turning fish several times.

2. Lift tuna from bowl; discard marinade. Lay fish on a lightly oiled grill over very hot heat (you can hold your hand at grill level only 1 to 2 seconds). Cook tuna until bottom ¹/₄ inch turns pale in color (cut to test; center should be red), about 2 minutes; turn with a wide spatula. Continue cooking until the bottom is the same color as the top and the center is still red to pale pink, about 1 minute longer.

3. Cut tuna into equal portions, set on plates, top with salsa fresca, and add salt to taste.

Per serving: 161 cal., 8.1% (13 cal.) from fat; 33 g protein; 1.4 g fat (0.3 g sat.); 1.9 g carbo (0.2 g fiber); 54 mg sodium; 64 mg chol.

Salsa fresca. In a blender or food processor, combine 1 can (14 oz.) **stewed tomatoes**; ¹/₂ cup *each* chopped **yellow bell pepper** and **fresh cilantro**; ¹/₄ cup chopped **onion**; 1 tablespoon **lime juice**; and ¹/₂ teaspoon *each* **ground coriander, ground cumin,** and **hot chili flakes.** Whirl until finely chopped. Add **salt** to taste. Serve or cover and chill up to 4 hours. Makes about 2 cups.

Per ¹/₂ cup: 38 cal., 4.7% (1.8 cal.) from fat; 1.2 g protein; 0.2 g fat (0 g sat.); 8.9 g carbo (1.5 g fiber); 222 mg sodium; 0 mg chol.

Pork Chops Sterling

Sterling Hum, Sherman Oaks, California

For an easy weeknight supper, Sterling Hum uses fresh and dried fruit to season pork chops.

PREP AND COOK TIME: About 30 minutes

MAKES: 4 servings

2 **Golden Delicious apples** (1 lb. total), rinsed

1 tablespoon **butter** or margarine

4 **boned center-cut loin pork chops** (each about 1 in. thick, about 1³/₄ pounds total), rinsed and patted dry

1 cup **apple juice**

1 teaspoon **ground ginger**

¹/₄ cup **dried apricots**

2 **oranges** (about 1 lb. total)

Salt

1. Peel apples, core, and cut into quarters. In a 12-inch nonstick frying pan or a 5- to 6-quart nonstick pan over medium-high heat, melt the butter. Add apples and cook, turning occasionally, until flat sides of quarters are browned, about 5 minutes total. Remove from pan.

2. Turn heat to high, add pork chops and lightly brown on each side, about 1 minute total.

3. Meanwhile, in a glass measure, stir together apple juice and ginger.

4. Reduce heat to medium; add apple juice mixture, apple slices, and dried apricots. Cover pan and simmer until pork chops are just barely pink in center (150°, cut to test), about 12 minutes.

5. Meanwhile, with a sharp knife, cut and discard peels and white membranes from oranges. Over a bowl, cut between membranes and fruit to release fruit segments into bowl. Squeeze juice from membranes into bowl.

6. With a slotted spoon, transfer chops and fruit to a rimmed platter; keep warm. Drain orange juice into pan and boil, uncovered, on high heat until reduced to ¹/₃ cup, 5 to 6 minutes. Pour mixture over meat. Garnish with orange segments. Add salt to taste.

Per serving: 566 cal., 46% (261 cal.) from fat; 41 g protein; 29 g fat (11 g sat.); 37 g carbo (4.5 g fiber); 151 mg sodium; 141 mg chol. ◆

Farmers' markets are mushrooming across the West (see page 250). Shop for just-picked produce, then turn it all into a feast.

September

Our Favorite Farmers' Markets

In greater numbers than ever, growers are offering the freshest foods in the West

By Linda Lau Anusasananan

With brilliant colors, intense flavors, and distinctive textures, foods from farmers' markets tempt and delight. They can inspire a lively party too. Visit your favorite market (or discover one of ours; the list begins on page 252) and load up with red greens, yellow tomatoes, and purple peppers to throw a fresh-produce party in your backyard.

From Santa Fe to San Francisco to Boulder, farmers' markets bring produce directly to consumers. Shoppers get vine-ripened fruit, vegetables picked that morning, and heirloom varieties—all treasures hard to find in supermarkets that depend on shipped produce.

PAUL BOUSQUET (LEFT), DOUGLAS MERRIAM (RIGHT)

Under the tent of her favorite vegetable stall at the Westwood Village Farmers' Market in Los Angeles, my friend Nicole picks up a basketball-size head of leaf lettuce, a bunch of leeks, and a bouquet of sorrel. "I shop here every week," she tells me. "They have good, healthy food; it's what I eat." At the flower stand, she chats with the grower like an old friend. He has saved her a spray of her favorite lilies. This is direct marketing at its best, a farmer and customer who know and support each other.

Like Nicole, many Westerners are hooked on farmers' markets. According to USDA agricultural marketing specialist Denny Johnson, there are more than 520 across the West, an increase of 41 percent since 1994. The markets operate on the general principle of offering fresh food that has been grown or produced by the people

selling it (rules vary about the proximity of vendors to markets). The end product is apparently what customers want—just-picked, vine-ripened, often organic produce and good-quality specialty foods such as breads, pastries, seafood, and sausages from small purveyors. Communities win too: Such markets have energized many otherwise untrafficked downtowns.

As a regular shopping resource, the best farmers' market is the one in your neighborhood. To find the market nearest you, check the USDA National Directory of Farmers' Markets at www.ams.usda.gov or call (800) 384-8704. Here is a list of some of our favorites across the West, with their primary days and times of operation. (Many organizations host smaller markets on other days, or even in other locations; call for details.) Use it as a starting point to find your own pick of the crop.

Arizona

■ **Roadrunner Park Farmers' Market.** In a grassy Phoenix park, some 25 vendors set up tents under the shade trees. Look for organically grown squash, eggplant, tomatoes, and greens, as well as grapes, okra, and heat-tolerant melons. Cool-weather crops, such as radishes and spinach, appear in late October. *8–12 Sat, May–September; 9–1 Sat, October–April. 3502 E. Cactus Rd.; (623) 848-1234.* — *Nora Burba Trulsson*

Northern California

■ **Berkeley Farmers' Markets (Certified Farmers' Markets—CFM).** Recycling stations and compost buckets are evidence that this small market is run by the Ecology Center; farmers (60 to 75 percent are registered or certified organic) prominently post their growing and pesticide practices. Pick up heirloom tomatoes, fresh-caught salmon, handmade tortillas, Redwood Hill Farm Camillia (goat cheese)—even raw organic sauerkraut. *10–3 Sat, year-*

round. Center St. at Martin Luther King Jr. Way; (510) 548-3333. — L.L.A.

■ **Davis Farmers' Market (CFM).** The locals hit Central Park's green-roofed shelter en masse for this nearly 30-year-old market with more than 60 vendors. Kids splash in the fountain while parents shop. Try veggies from market founders Jeff and Annie Main, tamales from Pilar's, and dried-apricot jam from Bogdanich Farms. *8–12 Sat, year-round. Fourth and C streets; (530) 756-1695.*

— Lisa Taggart

■ **Downtown Palo Alto Farmers' Market (CFM).** At this volunteer-run 20-year-old nonprofit market, which supports senior services and includes certified organic produce among its offerings, regular customers and vendors greet each other by name. Lines form for crusty loaves and brioche from Bay Bread and wild salmon from F/V Anne B. *8–12 Sat, May 13–early December. Parking lot G on Gilman St.; (650) 328-2827. — L.L.A.*

■ **Ferry Plaza Farmers' Market, San Francisco (CFM).** This waterfront gem carries pristine produce (50 percent organic), such as heirloom tomatoes from Eatwell Farms and Emerald Beaut plums from Honey Crisp. Sample seasonally pressed olive oils from Nick Sciabica & Sons and clabbered cottage cheese from Tomales Bay Foods. Brunch is available at stalls supplied by some of the city's best restaurants. *8–1:30 Sat, year-round. Embarcadero at Green St.; (415) 981-3004. — L.L.A.*

■ **Marin County Farmers' Market (CFM).** Regulars start with a latte and croissant before touring this 17-year-old market. Look for King Flavor pluots from Kashiwase Farms, tangerine raspberries from Sebastapol Berry Farms, and bonsai grapevines from Denise Morgan. You can also sample fresh Italian cheese from Spring Hill. Chef demos regularly. *8–1 Thu and Sun, year-round. Marin Civic Center, N. San Pedro Rd., just off U.S. 101, San Rafael; (800) 897-3276. — L.L.A.*

■ **Pleasanton Certified Farmers' Market.** A tree-lined street off restored, movie set–perfect Main Street provides a backdrop for 45 vendors offering a wide array of seasonal vegetables, from squash blossoms to wavy red heads of Lollo Rosso lettuce. Other temptations include fresh lavash and aged gouda cheese. *9–1 Sat, year-round. W. Angela and Main streets; (800) 949-3276. — L.L.A.*

■ **St. Helena Farmers' Market (CFM).** Beautifully situated in a park with a view of the Mayacamas Mountains, this small, dynamic market is a magnet for food-savvy locals and customers from gourmet shops, restaurants, wineries, and the Culinary Institute of America at Greystone. They highly rate the tomatoes, stone fruit, honey, mushrooms, and flowers.

7:30–11:30 Fri, May-October. Crane Park, just off State 29; (707) 265-8602. — L.L.A.

Southern California

■ **Beverly Hills Farmers' Market (a Certified Farmers' Market—CFM).** In this market just one block from Rodeo Drive, trellised vines from nursery vendors provide walls of brilliant blooms. Try Aunt Polly's pickles, Wong Farm hydroponic tomatoes, and seasonal treasures from the McGrath Family Farms. Local chef demonstrations once a month. *9–1 Sun, year-round. 200 block of N. Canon Dr.; (310) 285-2535. — L.L.A.*

■ **Ocean Beach Farmers' Market (CFM).** At this colorful market on a street lined with antiques and surf shops, homemakers mingle with aging hippies to buy flowers, grapes, stone fruit, sweet corn, and even emu meat. Llama rides for the kids. *4–8 Wed, year-round. 4900 block of Newport Ave. — Peter Jensen*

■ **Santa Barbara Certified Farmers' Market.** Stocked with one of the best selections of local vegetables, fruits, flowers, nuts, eggs, and seafood along this stretch of coast, the 100-stall market offers one of the highest ratios of farmed goods to prepared foods (97-to-3). *8:30–12:30 Sat, year-round. Santa Barbara and Cota streets; (805) 962-5354. — Jim McCausland*

■ **Santa Monica Certified Farmers' Market.** The focus is on farmers here. Ninety vendors strong, the market offers a huge selection of seasonal and unusual produce that draws crowds, including many local chefs. Look for red corn, grapes, plums, Seckel pears, Chinese dates, and lobster mushrooms, as well as line-caught fish, goat cheese, olives, and jams. *9–2 Wed, year-round. Second St. and Arizona Ave.; (310) 458-8712. — L.L.A.*

■ **South Pasadena Farmers' Market (CFM).** This market near the historic downtown area radiates friendly, small-town vibes. Families shop for produce—much of it organic, some of it exotic. There are also free-range eggs, seafood, breads from Bezjian's Grocery, and Bill's Bees honey and beeswax candles. *4–8 Thu, year-round. Meridian Ave. at Mission St.; (213) 244-9190, ext. 18. — L.L.A.*

■ **Vista Certified Farmers' Market.** At 7:45 the whistle blows, signaling the opening of the oldest market in San Diego County; come early for sapotes, figs, Dorsett Golden and Tropical Beauty apples, and subtropical plants from 50 to 60 vendors. *7:45–11 Sat, year-round. Eucalyptus St. and Escondido Ave. — P.J.*

■ **Westwood Village Farmers' Market (CFM).** At this shopping-district market, taste Pink Lady apples from Kosmo Family Ranch and Indian Red peaches from Rosendahl Family Farms. Build dinner around sand dabs, large prawns (with caviar-like eggs), or a tender beef filet. *2–7 Thu, year-round. Weyburn Ave. between Westwood Blvd. and Tiverton Ave., Los Angeles; (310) 208-1034.* — *L.L.A.*

Colorado

■ **Boulder County Farmers' Market.** This vibrant downtown market offers a cornucopia of organic produce. Sample goat cheese from Haystack Mountain Dairy and sprouts from ebullient Karim Amirfathi's Altan Alma Organic Sprout Farm. There are also cooking demonstrations and live entertainment. *8–12 Sat, early April–early November. 13th St. between Canyon and Arapahoe avenues; (303) 444-7325.* — *Claire Walter*

Hawaii

Hilo Farmers' Market. A blaze of anthuriums offers a colorful aloha. Rare tropical fruits such as rambutan, durian, and white pineapples sit alongside staples like papayas and bananas. Look for fresh ahi tuna. If you're lucky, you'll hear a tune from 97-year-old Eddie Castillo, Hilo's oldest mandolin player. *5–5 Wed and Sat, year-round. Mamo St. and Kamehameha Ave.; (808) 933-1000.* — *L.L.A.*

Idaho

■ **Capital City Public Market.** Sidewalk cafes flank downtown Boise's liveliest Saturday attraction. Browse more than 40 stalls for spuds (35 varieties at Eagle Organic Farms), condiments (66 kinds at the Jelly Lady), bridal bouquet–size hydroponic lettuce, sweet red Italian peppers, wild mushrooms, and fresh flowers. Canines stop at Blue Dog Baker's. *9:30–1:30 Sat, May 5–October 28. Eighth and Idaho streets; (208) 345-9287.*
— *Diane Ronayne*

New Mexico

■ **Albuquerque Downtown Growers' Market.** Friends and neighbors meet under the venerable cottonwoods of Robinson Park to select from varieties of produce not available on supermarket shelves. Look for Moriarty sweet corn and pinto beans from Schwebach Farms; all–New Mexico beef, chicken, and lamb from the Organic Meat Coalition; and award-winning goat cheese from Sweetwood Dairy. *7–11 Sat, July 8–October 14. Eighth St. and Central Ave. NW; (505) 243-2230.*
— *N.B.T.*

■ **Santa Fe Farmers' Market.** A trove of northern New Mexico's finest produce, native crafts, and herbal products makes stopping here a must. Tastings, cooking demos, and "Shop with the Chef" events inspire you to buy chilies, melons, corn, apples, and squash. Music and the scent of fresh muffins are in the air. *7–12*

Tue and Sat, May through the first week of November. In the Railyard, 530 S. Guadalupe Ave.; (505) 983-4098. — *N.B.T.*

Oregon

■ **Beaverton Farmers' Market.** The liveliest and largest of the Portland-area markets faces a small park that's perfect for a market picnic. Watch for Unger Farms strawberries. Tomatoes and early apples are also big hits this month. Grab some Paparazzi Pastaficio hand-cut fettuccine for dinner or set your mouth on fire with Rose City Pepperheads jellies. *8–1:30 Sat, May 13–October 28. S.W. Hall Blvd. between Third and Fifth streets; (503) 643-5345.* — *Karl Samson*

■ **Corvallis Wednesday Farmers' Market.** An oak-grove setting gives this the feel of an old English country market. Look for Oregon Coast artichokes, goat cheeses from Alsea Acre Alpines, succulent King oyster mushrooms, and a variety of melons. Don't miss the community table, where early birds can find unusual vegetables brought in by backyard growers. *8–1 Wed, April 19–November 22. Benton County Fairgrounds, 110 S.W. 53rd St.; (541) 752-1510.* — *K.S.*

■ **Portland Farmers' Market.** Under the shade trees on the Portland State University campus, you can shop with Portland's chefs and stock up on artisan breads from Black Bear Organic Bakery, heirloom apples from the Antique Apple Orchard, and plenty of organic produce. Cooking demonstrations provide ideas for what to do with your day's purchases. *8–1 Sat, May 6–October 28. Park Blocks at S.W. Montgomery St.; (503) 241-0032.*
— *K.S.*

Utah

■ **Salt Lake City Downtown Farmers' Market.** Big shade trees surround this festive market at historic Pioneer Park, just west of the center of town. Sample heirloom tomatoes from Borski Organic Farms, crisp apples from Donner Springs, and local honey. *8–12 Sat, July 15–October 14. 300 South and 300 West; (801) 359-5118.*
— *Virginia Rainey*

At farmers' markets, savvy shoppers find the freshest vegetables and fruits, transported direct from grower to consumer. Choose your vine-ripened melons, salad greens picked just hours earlier, and hard-to-find varieties of beans and tomatoes

Washington

■ **Bainbridge Island Farmers' Market.** With about 35 farm and 5 crafts stalls, this downtown Winslow market's strength is in produce and local berry products—but look for great goat cheeses as well. *9–1 Sat, April 15–October. Madison St., half-block north of Winslow Way; (206) 855-1500.* — *Jim McCausland*

■ **Olympia Farmers' Market.** The largest farmers' market in Washington scoffs at rain in its four-year-old permanent waterfront structure. Its offerings are about 75 percent "green" (nursery and farm products, including produce, meat, fish, and shellfish) and 25 percent crafts and food. *10–3 Thu-Sun through October, Sat-Sun only November-December. North end of Capitol Way; (360) 352-9096.* — *J.M.*

■ **University District Farmers' Market.** This time of year, this Seattle open-air market is packed with breads, goat cheeses, flowers, vegetables, plants, early apples, wild mushrooms, and hazelnuts. *9–2 Sat, year-round. University Heights Center, N.E. 50th St. and University Way NE; (206) 547-2278.* — *J.M.*

■ **Yakima Farmers' Market.** At ground zero in the state's most productive farm region, the new Yakima Farmers' Market distributes the valley's best in its 75 stalls. About two-thirds of the vendors are farmers (look for watermelons, tomatoes, squash, and peppers this month), but you can buy Filipino, Mexican, Thai, Bavarian, and soul food as well (sample Mrs. B's sweet potato pie and Miz D's jambalaya). *9:30–2:30 Sun, June 4–October 29. S. Third St. between E. Yakima and E. Chestnut avenues; (509) 457-5765.* — *J.M.*

Farmers' market feast

Shop the beautiful array of fresh foods, take home the pick of the crop, and set out a grand open-air spread

Farmers' markets offer a remarkable array of good-tasting foods these days. Along with produce, many sell farm-raised, fresh-caught, and hand-crafted items of all kinds: wild king salmon, gourmet smoked sausages, fire-roasted chili salsas—the list goes on.

Foray into this open-air fresh-food territory and bring home enough bounty to host a grand harvest party. With cart in tow, stroll through the market, picking the produce that beckons with exceptional freshness or flavor (vendors often set out samples to nibble). The recipes for our menu accommodate a wide range of fruits and vegetables. If you like, expand our plan with artisan cheeses, hearth-baked breads, honey, fruit preserves,

farmers' markets

Turn your market basket into a party for a dozen or more. Start with bruschetta: Spread roasted peppers, sautéed greens, tomatoes (right), roasted grapes, and cheese (far right) on rounds of crusty artisan bread. Then build salads with vegetables, a trio of dressings (bottom left), and fish, lamb, and sausages (bottom center). For a grand finale, layer fruit and honey-yogurt cream on angel food cake (bottom right).

salad dressings, and fresh-pressed olive oils. And while you're at it, pick up some flowers and beeswax candles—your shopping will be just about done.

Set the party up as a garden buffet with three stations: appetizer bruschettas, a main-dish salad bar, and shortcake for dessert. Create a festive market atmosphere by positioning a large umbrella over each table. And for decoration, buy extra produce at the market to display in baskets or pile into mounds; it can go home with guests or freshen your meals all week.

Our party menu is designed to serve 12 people, but it can easily be adjusted to fit any guest list—just choose more or fewer of the options to present at each station.

TOAST AND TOPPINGS

Bruschetta

PREP AND COOK TIME: About 30 minutes

NOTES: At the appetizer station, guests assemble bruschetta, choosing from a variety of toasts and toppings. Allow 3 to 5 toasts (2 to 3 in. wide) and 5 to 7 tablespoons of topping per guest. Buy extra loaves to use as part of the display, then cut to eat later with the rest of the meal.

MAKES: 12 servings

 1 to 1½ pounds **crusty bread** such as baguettes, ciabatta, pain au levain, or walnut (choose 1 kind or several; see notes)

 About ½ cup **extra-virgin olive oil**

 1 to 1½ pounds **cheese** such as fresh chèvre (goat), gouda, or ricotta (choose 1 or several)

 3 or 4 **toppings** (recipes follow)

1. Slice bread about ½ inch thick. Cut large slices into smaller pieces, about 2 inches square. Toast slices lightly in a toaster, or lay slices side by side on an oven rack and broil 3 to 4 inches from heat, turning once, until lightly browned on both sides, 5 to 6 minutes total. Place in a basket.

2. Pour olive oil into a small bowl; accompany with a brush about 1 inch wide. Arrange the firm cheeses on a small board and set a cheese slicer alongside; put soft cheeses in shallow bowls and accompany each with a spreading knife.

3. Set toast, oil, cheese, and toppings close together. Invite guests to assemble their own bruschetta, brushing toast with olive oil, then adding cheese and toppings of choice.

Per serving with oil and fresh chèvre (goat) cheese: 318 cal., 62% (198 cal.) from fat; 11 g protein; 22 g fat (9.4 g sat.); 21 g carbo (1 g fiber); 425 mg sodium; 30 mg chol.

Fresh Tomatoes with Basil

PREP TIME: About 15 minutes

NOTES: For best flavor, use vine-ripened tomatoes.

MAKES: About 1½ cups

Rinse and core ½ pound **firm-ripe tomatoes;** cut in half crosswise and gently squeeze out seeds. Chop tomatoes and put in a small bowl. Add ¼ cup chopped **fresh basil** leaves, 1 tablespoon **balsamic vinegar,** and 1 tablespoon **extra-virgin olive oil.** Mix, and season to taste with **salt** and **pepper.**

Per tablespoon: 7.1 cal., 76% (5.4 cal.) from fat; 0.1 g protein; 0.6 g fat (0.1 g sat.); 0.4 g carbo (0.1 g fiber); 0.8 mg sodium; 0 mg chol.

Sautéed Greens and Garlic

PREP AND COOK TIME: About 10 minutes

NOTES: If making up to 4 hours ahead, cover and let stand at room temperature.

MAKES: 2 to 4 cups, depending on greens used

1. Trim and discard tough stem ends or whole stems from 1 pound **kale,** Swiss chard, or mustard greens. Rinse, drain, and coarsely chop greens.

2. In a 5- to 6-quart pan over high heat, mix 1 tablespoon **olive oil,** 1 to 2 tablespoons chopped **garlic,** and ¼ teaspoon **hot chili flakes.** Add chopped greens and stir until wilted, 3 to 5 minutes. If greens are still chewy when pan is dry, add a few tablespoons water and continue to stir until they are tender to bite. Add 1 to 2 teaspoons **red wine vinegar** and **salt** to taste. For a glossy finish, stir in 1 to 2 tablespoons **extra-virgin olive oil.** With a slotted spoon, transfer greens to a small bowl. Serve warm or at room temperature.

Per tablespoon: 12 cal., 68% (8.1 cal.) from fat; 0.3 g protein; 0.9 g fat (0.1 g sat.); 1 g carbo (0.2 g fiber); 3.8 mg sodium; 0 mg chol.

Pepper Potpourri

PREP AND COOK TIME: About 35 minutes

NOTES: If making up to 1 day ahead, cover and chill. Bring to room temperature to serve.

MAKES: About 1¼ cups

1. Rinse and dry 1 pound **mild peppers** (Hungarian or red, yellow, or green bell) or mild chilies (Anaheim or New Mexico); use 1 kind or a combination of peppers and chilies. Place slightly apart in a 10- by 15-inch pan.

2. Broil about 4 inches from heat, turning as needed, until charred on all sides, 10 to 15 minutes. Let stand in pan until cool, about 20 minutes. Pull off and discard skin, stems, and seeds; thinly slice peppers. Put peppers and any juice in a small bowl. Stir in 1 tablespoon **extra-virgin olive oil** and **salt** and **pepper** to taste.

Per tablespoon: 11 cal., 57% (6.3 cal.) from fat; 0.2 g protein; 0.7 g fat (0.1 g sat.); 1.2 g carbo (0.3 g fiber); 0.4 mg sodium; 0 mg chol.

Roasted Grapes and Onions

PREP AND COOK TIME: About 50 minutes

NOTES: Try this fruit relish on nut toast spread with fresh chèvre (goat) cheese. If making up to 1 day ahead, cover and chill. Bring to room temperature to serve.

MAKES: About 1½ cups

1. Rinse and drain 3 cups stemmed **red seedless grapes** (about 1 lb.). In a 9- by 13-inch pan, mix grapes with 1 cup thinly sliced **red onion** and 1 tablespoon **olive oil.**

2. Bake in a 450° oven, stirring once after 20 minutes, until grapes are browned and begin to collapse, 40 to 45 minutes total (35 minutes in a convection oven). Stir in 1 tablespoon **balsamic vinegar** and **salt** to taste. Scrape into a small bowl. Serve warm or at room temperature.

Per tablespoon: 21 cal., 30% (6.3 cal.) from fat; 0.2 g protein; 0.7 g fat (0.1 g sat.); 4 g carbo (0.4 g fiber); 1.1 mg sodium; 0 mg chol.

Roasted Caponata

PREP AND COOK TIME: About 40 minutes

NOTES: If making up to 1 day ahead,

cover and chill. Bring to room temperature to serve.

MAKES: About 2 cups

1. Rinse 1 **eggplant** (about ½ lb.); trim and discard stem. Cut eggplant into ½-inch cubes. Rinse ¼ pound **yellow zucchini** or Sunburst or crookneck squash; trim and discard stem ends. Cut squash into ½-inch cubes. Rinse 1½ cups (½ lb.) **cherry tomatoes** and discard stems.

2. In a 10- by 15-inch pan, mix eggplant, zucchini, and tomatoes with 2 tablespoons **olive oil** and 2 teaspoons chopped **fresh oregano** leaves or ½ teaspoon dry oregano.

3. Bake the vegetables in a 450° oven, stirring occasionally, until eggplant is very soft when pressed, 30 to 35 minutes (18 to 20 minutes in a convection oven). Add ¼ cup pitted **calamata olives,** 2 tablespoons chopped **parsley,** 1 tablespoon **balsamic vinegar,** and **salt** and **pepper** to taste. Mix well and scrape into a small bowl. Serve the caponata warm or at room temperature.

Per tablespoon: 15 cal., 66% (9.9 cal.) from fat; 0.2 g protein; 1.1 g fat (0.1 g sat.); 1 g carbo (0.2 g fiber); 20 mg sodium; 0 mg chol.

Sautéed Mushroom Mélange

PREP AND COOK TIME: About 25 minutes

NOTES: If making up to 1 day ahead, cover and chill. Bring to room temperature to serve.

MAKES: About 1½ cups

1. Trim and discard discolored stem ends or tough stems and any bits of debris and bruised spots from 1 pound **mushrooms** (chanterelle, common, portabella, oyster, or shiitake; choose 1 or an assortment). Rinse the mushrooms well and drain; slice about ¼ inch thick.

2. In a 10- to 12-inch frying pan over high heat, stir mushrooms, ⅓ cup chopped **shallots,** 2 tablespoons **olive oil,** and 1 teaspoon **fresh thyme** leaves or ½ teaspoon dried thyme until liquid is evaporated and mushrooms are well browned, 10 to 15 minutes. Add **salt** and **pepper** to taste.

3. Pour sautéed mushrooms into a bowl. Serve warm or at room temperature. Shortly before serving, sprinkle mushrooms with 1 tablespoon chopped **parsley.**

Per tablespoon: 16 cal., 69% (11 cal.) from fat; 0.4 g protein; 1.2 g fat (0.2 g sat.); 1.2 g carbo (0.3 g fiber); 1.1 mg sodium; 0 mg chol.

SALAD AND DRESSINGS

Market Basket Salad

PREP AND COOK TIME: About 30 minutes

NOTES: Guests create custom main-dish salads from a handsome array of separate ingredients.

MAKES: 12 servings

> 3 pounds (if boneless) to 4½ pounds (with bones) **meat, chicken, fish,** or **portabella mushroom caps** (choose 1 or a combination; list follows)
>
> About ¼ cup **olive oil**
>
> 6 quarts **salad mix** (about 2¼ lb.), rinsed and crisped
>
> 7 to 9 cups **vegetables** (choose 4 to 6; list follows)
>
> 3 to 4 cups **salad dressings** (2 or more), homemade (recipes follow) or similar purchased versions
>
> **Fresh herb bunches,** rinsed and drained (list follows)
>
> **Salt** and **pepper**

1. Rinse meat, chicken, fish, and mushrooms; pat dry. Brush pieces lightly with olive oil.

2. Place foods on a barbecue grill over hot coals or high heat on a gas grill (you can hold your hand at grill level only 2 to 3 seconds). Cook, turning once, until beef and lamb are done to your liking, 10 to 12 minutes total for rare (still pink in the center; cut to test); pork and chicken are no longer pink in center of thickest part (cut to test), 10 to 12 minutes for pork, 6 to 8 minutes for chicken; fish is barely opaque but still moist-looking in center of thickest part (cut to test), 8 to 10 minutes; sausages are sizzling, 7 to 9 minutes; and portabellas are flexible, 6 to 8 minutes (place gill side down first, then turn when juices start to drip). Transfer grilled foods to a large platter when done and serve hot or warm. Provide sharp knives and, if desired, a rimmed cutting board for cutting pieces into smaller portions.

3. Mound salad mix in a large basket; accompany with tongs. Put vegetables in separate small bowls, with a spoon alongside each. Pour dressings into small bowls or pitchers. Arrange herb bunches in jars of water; provide small scissors to snip leaves.

4. Have each guest mound salad mix on a plate, top it with vegetables and cooked meats and mushrooms, drizzle salad with one or more dressings, scatter with herb leaves, and add salt and pepper to taste.

Per serving with beef: 265 cal., 44% (117 cal.) from fat; 26 g protein; 13 g fat (3.8 g sat.); 9.6 g carbo (2.3 g fiber); 79 mg sodium; 72 mg chol.

Meat, chicken, fish, and portabella mushrooms: 1-inch-thick, fat-trimmed tender beef steak (tenderloin, rib eye, or porterhouse) or beef flank steak; 1-inch-thick lamb or pork chops; 4- to 5-ounce boned, skinned chicken breast halves; 4- to 6-ounce pieces boned, skinned salmon fillet; smoked or cooked sausages; and 3½- to 4-inch-wide portabella mushroom caps (buy caps only, or trim stems of whole portabellas flush with caps and save stems for other uses)

Vegetables: Cherry tomatoes or tomato wedges, sliced cucumbers, diced avocados, raw corn kernels, cold cooked green beans, cold cooked sliced beets, cold cooked asparagus, thinly sliced fresh fennel, and thinly sliced red onion

Fresh herb bunches: Basil, cilantro, dill, parsley, and tarragon

Pesto Dressing

PREP TIME: About 10 minutes

NOTES: If making up to 1 day ahead, cover and chill.

MAKES: About 1⅓ cups

In a blender or food processor, purée 1 cup lightly packed rinsed **fresh basil** leaves, ½ cup **olive oil,** ½ cup **rice vinegar,** 3 tablespoons **pine nuts** or slivered almonds, and 1 or 2 peeled cloves **garlic** until smooth, scraping container sides as needed. Add **salt** and **pepper** to taste. Pour into a small bowl or pitcher.

Per tablespoon: 65 cal., 83% (54 cal.) from fat; 1 g protein; 6 g fat (0.8 g sat.); 3.4 g carbo (0.1 g fiber); 1.8 mg sodium; 0 mg chol.

Cilantro-Yogurt Dressing

PREP TIME: About 15 minutes

NOTES: To reduce the heat level, seed and devein the chili. If making dressing up to 1 day ahead, cover and chill. Stir before serving.

MAKES: About 1¼ cups

In a blender or food processor, purée
½ cup **plain nonfat yogurt**, ½ cup
coarsely chopped **fresh cilantro**, 3
tablespoons coarsely chopped **fresh
mint** leaves, 2 to 4 teaspoons chopped
fresh jalapeño chili (to taste; see
notes), and 1 peeled clove **garlic** until
smooth, scraping container sides as
needed. Add another ½ cup plain
nonfat yogurt and whirl just until
blended. Add **salt** to taste. Pour into a
small bowl or pitcher.

Per tablespoon: 7.1 cal., 0% (0 cal.) from fat;
0.7 g protein; 0 g fat; 1 g carbo (0.1 g fiber);
9 mg sodium; 0.2 mg chol.

Tomato-Herb Dressing

PREP TIME: About 25 minutes

NOTES: For best flavor, use a fully ripe
tomato. If making dressing up to 1 day
ahead, cover and chill.

MAKES: About 1½ cups

In a blender or food processor, purée
1½ cups chopped **ripe tomatoes**,
2 tablespoons **balsamic vinegar**, 2
tablespoons **extra-virgin olive oil**,
and 1 peeled clove **garlic** until
smooth. Add 2 tablespoons coarsely
chopped **fresh basil** leaves, 1 tablespoon **fresh oregano** leaves, and
1 teaspoon **fresh thyme** leaves; whirl
just until herbs are finely chopped.
Add **salt** and **pepper** to taste. Pour
into a small bowl or pitcher.

Per tablespoon: 13 cal., 85% (11 cal.) from fat;
0.1 g protein; 1.2 g fat (0.2 g sat.); 0.6 g carbo
(0.2 g fiber); 1.1 mg sodium; 0 mg chol.

D E S S E R T

Shortcut Shortcake with Honey-Yogurt Cream

PREP TIME: About 50 minutes

NOTES: If none of the suggested cakes
are available among the baked goods
at your farmers' market, simply spoon
the fruit into bowls and eat plain or
with the honey-yogurt cream. Serve
other baked goodies from the market,
such as fruit pies, pastries, or cookies.
Up to 1 hour ahead, slice the fruit and
add sugar and lemon juice (step 1);
cover and chill. Whip the cream and
add yogurt and honey; nestle in a
bowl of ice. As the mixture stands,
some liquid may seep free in the
bottom of the bowl; just before serving, stir gently to blend, and drizzle
surface decoratively with more honey.

Guests create their own main-dish salad: Here grilled salmon rests on a bed of
baby lettuces, onions, beets, green beans, avocado, cucumber, and corn.

Present cake whole, with a knife for
slicing.

MAKES: 12 servings

12 cups **fresh fruit** (sliced figs,
    nectarines, peaches, pears, plums,
    and strawberries, and rinsed
    whole blueberries, grapes, and
    raspberries; choose an
    assortment)

    Sugar and **lemon juice**

1   cup **whipping cream**

1   cup **plain nonfat yogurt**

4   to 6 tablespoons **honey**

    Angel food, chiffon, pound, or
    sponge **cake** (enough to make 12
    slices, each ¾ in. thick)

1. In separate small bowls or combined
in a large bowl, gently mix the fresh
fruit with sugar and lemon juice to
taste.

2. In a deep bowl, with a mixer on high
speed, beat whipping cream until it
holds soft peaks. Fold in yogurt and
add honey to taste. Mound in a bowl
and drizzle more honey decoratively
over the top.

3. Set cake on a platter. For each
portion, cut a ¾-inch slice and transfer
to a plate. Spoon fruit and accumulated juices over cake, and top with
yogurt-cream mixture.

Per serving with angel food cake: 221 cal.,
28% (62 cal.) from fat; 3.7 g protein; 6.9 g fat
(3.9 g sat.); 39 g carbo (3.4 g fiber); 162 mg
sodium; 22 mg chol. ◆

TUCKER & HOSSLER

The Quick Cook

Sweet preserves in 30 minutes or less

By Jerry Anne Di Vecchio

Fresh fruit jamboree

■ Preserving time and energy in the pursuit of fresh flavor is the triumph of these jams and marmalades. For speed, start with commercial preserves; they hold up when heated and reheated. Then add fresh fruit to personalize the results. Boiling the two together gives you homemade taste in minutes. And the product is hot enough to be sterile without any processing. Return the mixtures to the preserves' original jars. If you misjudge the consistency during cooking, a simple step saves the day: Tilt the jars of cool jam or marmalade. If the mixture is runny, return it to the pan, bring it to a rolling boil, stir often, and test again for firmness (see "Fresh jam tips," right) about every minute.

Plum-Apricot Jam

PREP AND COOK TIME: About 30 minutes, plus about 6 hours to cool

MAKES: About 4¾ cups

1. Rinse and thinly slice 1 **orange** (about ½ lb.), discarding end slices and seeds; coarsely chop orange. In a 5- to 6-quart pan, combine pieces and juice with ½ cup **sugar** and ¼ cup **water.** Boil over high heat, stirring often to prevent scorching, until liquid is almost gone, 4 to 5 minutes.

2. Remove from heat and add 2 cups finely chopped **firm-ripe red-skinned plums** and 4 jars (10 oz. each) **apricot jam;** set unwashed empty jars and lids aside. Return pan to high heat and stir until jam is melted. Stirring often to prevent scorching, boil for 10 minutes, then test and boil until jam is firm enough (see test at right), about 5 minutes longer. Seal and store as directed at right.

Per tablespoon: 45 cal., 0% (0 cal.) from fat; 0.2 g protein; 0 g fat; 12 g carbo (0.3 g fiber); 6 mg sodium; 0 mg chol.

Fresh jam tips

TEST FOR FIRMNESS: Lift a spoonful of the boiling jam or marmalade from pan; tilt the spoon and pour jam back into pan. When two distinct drops form on the spoon edge and then flow over together, the mixture will be thick enough to spread when cool.

Fresh plums turn purchased apricot jam into a homemade delicacy.

TO SEAL: When the preserves meet the firmness test, remove from heat and ladle hot mixture into unwashed jars (see recipes) to within ¼ inch of rims; pour any extra preserves into a small bowl or jar. Wipe jar rims clean and screw lids snugly into place. Let stand until cool, about 6 hours.

TO STORE: Serve unsealed preserves warm or cool; chill airtight up to several months or until any mold develops (if it does, spoon it off, but discard jam if moldy flavor is pervasive). Chill sealed jars up to 1 year.

Blueberry-Currant Jam

PREP AND COOK TIME: About 30 minutes, plus about 6 hours to cool

MAKES: About 4 cups

1. Rinse and thinly slice 1 **lemon** (4 to 5 oz.), discarding end slices and seeds; coarsely chop lemon. In a 5- to 6-quart pan, combine pieces and juice with ½ cup **sugar** and ¼ cup **water.** Boil over high heat, stirring often to prevent scorching, until liquid is almost gone, 5 to 8 minutes.

2. Remove from heat and add 2 cups rinsed, drained **blueberries** and 4 jars (10 oz. each) **currant jelly;** set unwashed empty jars and lids aside. Return pan to high heat and stir until jelly is melted. Stirring to prevent scorching, boil until berries begin to fall apart, 8 to 10 minutes, then test and boil until jam is firm enough (see test at left), 4 to 5 minutes longer. Seal and store as directed at left.

Per tablespoon: 57 cal., 0% (0 cal.) from fat; 0.1 g protein; 0 g fat; 15 g carbo (0.3 g fiber); 6.7 mg sodium; 0 mg chol.

Peach-Ginger Marmalade

PREP AND COOK TIME: About 30 minutes, plus about 6 hours to cool

MAKES: About 4 cups

1. Rinse and thinly slice 1 **lemon** (4 to 5 oz.), discarding end slices and seeds; coarsely chop lemon. In a 5- to 6-quart pan, combine pieces and juice with ½ cup **sugar,** ¼ cup **water,** and ¼ cup minced **fresh ginger.** Boil over high heat, stirring often to prevent scorching, until liquid is almost gone, about 5 minutes.

2. Remove from heat and add 2 cups finely chopped peeled **firm-ripe peaches** and 2 jars (18 oz. each) **orange marmalade;** set unwashed empty jars and lids aside. Return pan to high heat and stir until marmalade is melted. Boil, stirring often, until marmalade is firm enough (see test at left), about 15 minutes. Seal and store as directed at left.

Per tablespoon: 48 cal., 0% (0 cal.) from fat; 0.1 g protein; 0 g fat; 13 g carbo (0.2 g fiber); 9 mg sodium; 0 mg chol. ◆

JAMES CARRIER

the flavor of Mexico

Bright and beautiful dishes from Baja to make at home

By Andrew Baker • Photographs by James Carrier • Food styling by Basil Friedman

It's almost 9 P.M. when I sink into a chair at Cien Años restaurant in Tijuana, bone-tired and voracious—a canceled flight has delayed my dinner.

Owner Jose Sparza's welcome instantly dispels the day's stress, and soon the festive fretwork of a strolling guitarist confirms that I've entered a calm and gracious way of life. The food in front of me—oysters with chipotle chilies and melted cheese, and tortilla soup with a zesty cream sauce—is fresh, simple, and very satisfying.

The next few days of exploring the culinary riches of Tijuana and Ensenada in Baja California offer more of the same: ebullient music, a relaxed yet exuberant spirit, and enough good food to inspire me to bring home many a day's worth of recipes.

A leisurely breakfast one morning includes *chilaquiles* (fried tortillas cooked with chili sauce and cheese) and eggs. Another day it's sweet banana waffles with *cajeta* (goat's milk caramel sauce) and tropical fruit.

Such a substantial breakfast calls for a lighter, later lunch—sometime around 2 P.M. I stand at a *carreta* and grab a couple of fish tacos or—when the urge for adventure strikes—a sea urchin tostada drizzled with an avocado sauce hot with habanero chilies. Later I stop for something sweet—carrot-chili ice cream or a coffee-coconut milkshake.

Although most restaurants don't close between lunch and dinner, activity picks up dramatically around 8:00. I sit down to a glass of Château Camou Fumé Blanc, produced in the nearby Valle de Guadalupe, and a bowl of mussels with a creamy cilantro-scented lobster sauce. Quail with tamarind sauce crowns my last delicious day. Mexico has found my heart in the time-honored way.

If you travel to Baja, a similar savory fate is almost sure to be yours (see our list of recommended stops on page 265). But you don't have to leave your kitchen to fall in love with the food. Recipes for many of these dishes and others I enjoyed in Tijuana and Ensenada follow. The Mexican ingredients such as dried chilies, cheeses, crema, and cajeta are widely available throughout the West; look in well-stocked grocery stores or Latino markets. You may also substitute the readily available alternatives that are listed in each recipe. It's easy to put the flavor of Mexico into meals right here at home.

A chili-rich broth floats crisp-fried tortilla strips and avocado chunks; add fresh cheese and seasoned Mexican sour cream. Recipe begins on page 263.

Cornish Hens with Tamarind Sauce

PREP AND COOK TIME: About 45 minutes

NOTES: *Codornices para picar* (loosely, "quail for toothpicks") is a specialty of chef Manuel Brito at Saverio's in Tijuana. We've adapted the recipe to Cornish hens, but you can use 8 quail (about 6 oz. each) instead; bake as directed in step 3 until meat at breastbone is no longer pink, 25 to 30 minutes (15 to 20 minutes in a convection oven). Serve with hot cooked rice sprinkled with fresh cilantro.

MAKES: 4 servings

- 2 teaspoons **sesame seed**
- 4 **Cornish hens** (12 to 15 oz. each; see notes)
- 1 teaspoon **ground cumin**
- 1 teaspoon **ground coriander**
- $1/8$ teaspoon **cayenne**
- 1 **onion** ($1/2$ lb.), peeled and finely chopped
- 1 tablespoon minced **fresh jalapeño chili**
- 1 tablespoon minced **garlic**
- 1 teaspoon **olive** or salad **oil**
- 3 cups **dry red wine**
- 1 tablespoon **sugar**
- 1 tablespoon **balsamic vinegar**
- 2 tablespoons **tamarind paste**
  Cilantro sprigs
  Salt

1. In a 10- to 12-inch frying pan over medium heat, stir or shake sesame seed until lightly browned, about 3 minutes. Pour from pan.

2. Rinse hens and pat dry. In a small bowl, combine cumin, coriander, and cayenne; rub mixture evenly over surface of the birds. Place the hens breast up in a 10- by 15-inch pan.

3. Bake in a 450° oven until birds are lightly browned and meat at breastbone is no longer pink (cut to test), about 35 minutes.

4. Meanwhile, in frying pan over high heat, stir onion, jalapeño, and garlic in oil until lightly browned, 3 to 5 minutes. Add wine, sugar, vinegar, and tamarind paste. Boil, stirring often, until reduced to 2 cups, about 12 minutes. Pour through a fine strainer into a glass measure; discard residue.

5. Transfer hens to a rimmed platter and keep warm. Pour wine mixture into baking pan. Set pan over high heat and stir, scraping up browned bits, until sauce is reduced to $3/4$ cup, 6 to 8 minutes.

Elegant Mexican cuisine: A Cornish hen with tamarind sauce, salad with panela cheese, and oysters with chipotle chilies.

6. Pour sauce over hens and sprinkle with sesame seed. Garnish with cilantro; add salt to taste.

Per serving: 491 cal., 57% (279 cal.) from fat; 37 g protein; 31 g fat (8.3 g sat.); 13 g carbo (1.6 g fiber); 146 mg sodium; 210 mg chol.

Spinach Salad with Mango Dressing and Fried Panela Cheese

PREP AND COOK TIME: About 20 minutes

NOTES: This *ensalada de queso panela frita y vinagreta de mango y chile piquín* makes a delicious first course at Chef Martín San Román's Tijuana restaurant, Rincón San Román. Instead of the panela cheese, you can use part-skim mozzarella cheese; since it melts and spreads more than panela, cook the slices on one side only, then place the hot cheese, browned side up, on salads.

MAKES: 4 servings

- $1/3$ cup **canned mango nectar**
- 2 tablespoons **lime juice**
- 2 tablespoons **olive oil**
  About $1/4$ teaspoon ground **dried chilpequín chilies** or cayenne
- 1 quart **baby spinach leaves** (4 to 5 oz.), rinsed and crisped

- 1 quart bite-size pieces rinsed, crisped inner **romaine lettuce** leaves (about 6 oz.)
- $1/4$ cup **cilantro sprigs**, rinsed
- $1/4$ pound **sliced bacon**, chopped
- 5 to 6 ounces **panela cheese** (see notes)
  Salt

1. In a wide bowl, combine mango nectar, lime juice, olive oil, and ground chilies to taste. Add spinach, romaine lettuce, and cilantro sprigs; mix gently. Spoon salad equally onto plates.

2. In an 8- to 10-inch nonstick frying pan over medium-high heat, stir bacon frequently until crisp and browned, about 5 minutes. With a slotted spoon, transfer to towels to drain. Discard all but about 1 teaspoon of the bacon drippings in pan.

3. Cut cheese into $1/4$-inch-thick slices (about $1\frac{1}{2}$ in. square). Lay without crowding in frying pan over medium-high heat; brown slices lightly on each side, turning once, about 2 minutes total. With a wide spatula, set equal portions of cheese on salads. Sprinkle with bacon; add salt to taste.

Per serving: 247 cal., 80% (198 cal.) from fat; 10 g protein; 22 g fat (8.8 g sat.); 8 g carbo (2.4 g fiber); 416 mg sodium; 20 mg chol.

Chipotle-Cheese Oysters

PREP AND COOK TIME: About 15 minutes

NOTES: Chef Jorge Hernandez at Cien Años restaurant in Tijuana prepares *ostiones chipotle* as a lively appetizer. For convenience, have the oysters shucked at the market, keeping the shells and juice. At home, replace oysters in half-shells and strain juice. Or, to shuck oysters at home, grasp the curved end of each with a towel and, working over a fine strainer set in a bowl to catch juices, push the tip of an oyster knife firmly between the top and bottom shell at the hinge, then twist. Slide the blade into the oyster along the underside of the top shell, cutting the adductor muscle to release oyster. Lift off top shell. Holding the bottom shell steady, slide knife under oyster to cut it free; leave in shell.

MAKES: 4 appetizer servings

1½ teaspoons finely chopped drained **canned chipotle chili**

1 tablespoon **sauce** from **canned chipotle chilies**

12 **shucked oysters** in half-shells (3 to 4 in.; see notes)

2 slices (1 oz. each) **asadero** or jack **cheese**

2 tablespoons minced **fresh cilantro**

1. In a small bowl, combine chili, chili sauce, and 1 tablespoon strained oyster juice from shucked oysters.

2. Set oysters in shells upright in a 10- by 15-inch pan. Spoon chili mixture evenly over oysters. Cut or tear cheese into 12 pieces; lay 1 piece on each oyster.

3. Broil 4 to 6 inches from heat until cheese is melted and juices begin to bubble, about 3 minutes.

4. Sprinkle oysters with cilantro. Pick oysters from shells with forks; sip juice from shells.

Per serving: 80 cal., 53% (42 cal.) from fat; 6.5 g protein; 4.7 g fat (2.5 g sat.); 2.6 g carbo (0.2 g fiber); 197 mg sodium; 36 mg chol.

Chili and Tortilla Soup

PREP AND COOK TIME: About 45 minutes

NOTES: This *sopa Azteca,* from Cien Años, can be served as a first course or a light lunch entrée.

MAKES: 4 servings

4 **flour tortillas** (about 8 in.)
Salad oil

1 **onion** (½ lb.), peeled and chopped

¼ cup **ground dried California** or New Mexico **chilies**

6 cups fat-skimmed **chicken broth**

1 **dried pasilla chili** (4 to 5 in. long, about ¼ oz.)

1 **firm-ripe avocado** (6 to 8 oz.)

¼ pound **queso fresco** or cream cheese, cut into ½-inch chunks
Seasoned crema (recipe follows)
Lime wedges
Salt

1. Stack tortillas; cut stack in half, then cut halves crosswise into ¼- to ½-inch-wide strips.

2. Pour ½ inch of oil into a 10- to 12-inch frying pan over high heat. When oil is hot, add about ⅓ of the tortilla pieces. Stir often until golden and crisp, 1 to 2 minutes. With a slotted spoon, transfer strips to towels to drain. Repeat to cook remaining tortillas. Discard all but 1 teaspoon oil in pan (or reserve for other uses).

3. Pour the 1 teaspoon oil into a 3- to 4-quart pan over high heat. Add onion and stir often until lightly browned, 3 to 5 minutes. Add ground chilies; stir until fragrant, about 30 seconds. Add broth and bring to a boil. Cover, reduce heat, and simmer to blend flavors, about 5 minutes. Pour mixture through a fine strainer into a bowl; discard onion and return broth to pan.

4. Remove and discard stem and seeds from pasilla chili; rinse chili and, with scissors, cut crosswise into ½-inch strips. Add chili strips to broth mixture. Cover and bring to a boil over high heat; reduce heat to low and keep warm.

5. Meanwhile, peel, pit, and chop avocado. Put avocado, queso fresco, seasoned crema, and lime wedges in separate small bowls.

6. Divide tortilla strips evenly among soup bowls (2-cup size). Fill with chili broth. Add avocado, seasoned crema, juice from lime wedges, and salt to taste.

Per serving: 474 cal., 55% (261 cal.) from fat; 23 g protein; 29 g fat (11 g sat.); 32 g carbo (4.5 g fiber); 504 mg sodium; 33 mg chol.

Seasoned crema. In a small bowl, mix ½ cup **Mexican crema** or sour cream, 1 tablespoon **milk**, 1 tablespoon minced **parsley**, ½ teaspoon minced **garlic**, and about ¼ teaspoon fresh-ground **pepper** (to taste). Makes about ½ cup.

Per tablespoon: 33 cal., 85% (28 cal.) from fat; 0.5 g protein; 3.1 g fat (1.9 g sat.); 0.8 g carbo (0 g fiber); 8.8 mg sodium; 6.6 mg chol.

Garlic and Chili Shrimp

PREP AND COOK TIME: About 25 minutes

NOTES: *Camarones al ajillo* is popular as a first course at Pedrin's restaurant in the Real del Mar resort in Tijuana. Chef Humberto Dorantes sometimes adds squid to the dish.

MAKES: 4 servings

½ pound **mushrooms** (caps about 1½ in. wide)

1 pound **peeled, deveined shrimp with tails** (26 to 30 per lb.), rinsed

2 **dried guajillo,** California, or New Mexico **chilies** (5 to 6 in. long, about ¼ oz. total)

3 tablespoons **olive oil**

3 tablespoons **butter** or margarine

2 tablespoons **minced garlic**

2 tablespoons thinly sliced **green onion** (including tops)

1. Rinse mushrooms; trim and discard discolored stem ends. Quarter the mushrooms vertically.

Oceanside living offers fresh seafood in abundance: Shrimp with fresh chilies, garlic, and mushrooms is a Baja classic.

2. Cut shrimp in half lengthwise from head end to—but not through—the tail (see photo at left).

3. Wipe chilies with a damp cloth. Discard stems and seeds. Cut chilies crosswise into ¼-inch slices.

4. In a 10- to 12-inch frying pan over medium-high heat, stir chilies in oil until chilies smell toasted and oil is tinged with red, 2 to 3 minutes. With a slotted spoon, transfer chilies to a small bowl.

5. Add butter and mushrooms to pan. Stir often over high heat until mushrooms begin to brown, about 4 minutes. Add garlic; stir until mushrooms are well browned and garlic is lightly browned, about 1 minute longer. Add shrimp and stir just until opaque but still moist-looking in center of thickest part (cut to test), 4 to 5 minutes. If desired, return chilies to pan.

6. Pour shrimp mixture onto a platter. Sprinkle with green onion.

Per serving: 314 cal., 60% (189 cal.) from fat; 25 g protein; 21 g fat (7.2 g sat.); 6.5 g carbo (1.4 g fiber); 260 mg sodium; 196 mg chol.

Banana Waffles with Cajeta and Tropical Fruit

PREP AND COOK TIME: About 30 minutes
NOTES: Chef Juan Carlos Lozano offers these waffles in the breakfast buffet at the Pueblo Amigo Hotel in Tijuana. You can substitute regular caramel sauce for the *cajeta* (goat's milk caramel sauce). If desired, serve waffles as a dessert, adding scoops of vanilla ice cream or sweetened whipped cream.
MAKES: 12 to 16 waffles, 4 inches square; 4 servings

1⅓ cups **all-purpose flour**
4 teaspoons **sugar**
2 teaspoons **baking powder**
½ teaspoon **salt**
2 **large eggs,** separated
1¼ cups **milk**
1 cup mashed **ripe banana**
3 tablespoons melted **butter** or margarine
   Cooking oil spray or salad oil
¾ cup **cajeta** (see notes)
2 cups diced (½ in.) **papaya** or pineapple (or a combination)

1. In a bowl, combine flour, sugar, baking powder, and salt.

2. In another bowl, with a mixer at high speed, whip egg whites just until they hold distinct, moist peaks.

3. In a third bowl, beat egg yolks to blend with milk, banana, and butter. Pour egg yolk mixture into flour mixture; beat until smooth. Fold in whipped whites until blended.

4. Heat waffle iron to high. Spray grids (or brush lightly) with oil. Spoon batter onto center of each grid, covering about ⅔ of it. Close iron and bake until waffles are evenly browned, about 5 minutes. As waffles are baked, put in a single layer on an 11- by 17-inch baking sheet and keep warm in a 200° oven.

5. Transfer waffles to plates and top equally with cajeta and fruit.

Per serving: 625 cal., 23% (144 cal.) from fat; 14 g protein; 16 g fat (7.9 g sat.); 107 g carbo (2.7 g fiber); 836 mg sodium; 145 mg chol.

Mussels with Tomatillos and Linguisa

PREP AND COOK TIME: About 45 minutes
NOTES: Chefs at La Embotelladora Vieja in Ensenada cook *mejillones a los seis chiles* in a hearty broth flavored with six chilies, as the name promises. We've simplified the dish, but it still delivers rich flavor.
MAKES: **4 servings**

1 pound **tomatillos** (about 1½ in. wide)
1 quart fat-skimmed **chicken broth**
1 cup **dry white wine**
1 teaspoon **ground dried California** or New Mexico **chilies**
1 teaspoon minced **canned chipotle chili** (including sauce)

Banana waffles topped with papaya and cajeta make asweet breakfast.

1 teaspoon minced **fresh serrano chili**
1 teaspoon minced **garlic**
6 dozen **mussels** (beards pulled off), scrubbed
½ pound **cooked linguisa** (Portuguese) **sausage,** cut into ¼-inch slices
2 tablespoons minced **fresh cilantro**

1. Remove and discard tomatillo husks. Rinse tomatillos and quarter vertically.

2. In a 6- to 8-quart pan, combine broth, wine, ground chilies, chipotle chili, serrano chili, and garlic. Bring to a boil over high heat.

3. Discard any gaping mussels that don't close when you tap their shells. Add mussels and linguisa to pan; cover and simmer until mussel shells begin to pop open, 2 to 3 minutes. Stir in tomatillos, cover, and continue to cook until all mussel shells are open, 2 to 3 minutes longer.

4. With a slotted spoon, transfer mussels to wide bowls. Ladle broth mixture over mussels and sprinkle with cilantro.

Per serving: 440 cal., 45% (198 cal.) from fat; 38 g protein; 22 g fat (6.8 g sat.); 12 g carbo (0.2 g fiber); 1,235 mg sodium; 87 mg chol.

Chilaquiles

PREP AND COOK TIME: About 1 hour
NOTES: Chilaquiles is a breakfast staple, often served with eggs cooked any style. Up to 1 day ahead, make sauce through step 6; cover airtight and chill. Also up to one day ahead, fry tortillas (step 7); when cool, store airtight at room temperature.
MAKES: 4 servings

12 **dried California** or New Mexico **chilies** (5 to 6 in. long, about 2½ oz. total)
2 cups fat-skimmed **chicken broth**
1 **onion** (½ lb.), peeled
½ pound **firm-ripe Roma tomatoes**
3 cloves **garlic**
½ teaspoon **ground cumin**
½ teaspoon **dried oregano**
12 **corn tortillas** (6 in.)
   Salad oil
6 ounces **thin-sliced asadero** or jack **cheese**
1 tablespoon minced **fresh cilantro**
   Salt

1. Wipe chilies with a damp cloth. Discard stems and seeds. Lay chilies in a 10- by 15-inch baking pan.

2. Bake in a 250° oven until fragrant, about 3 minutes.

3. In a 3- to 4-quart microwave-safe bowl, combine chilies and broth. Heat in a microwave oven on full power (100%) until boiling, about 3 minutes. Let stand until chilies are soft, 10 to 15 minutes.

4. Meanwhile, cut onion crosswise into ½-inch slices. Rinse tomatoes, core, and cut in half lengthwise. Lay onion slices, tomato halves (cut sides up), and unpeeled garlic cloves slightly apart in a 10- by 15-inch pan. Broil 4 to 6 inches from heat until vegetables are browned, 8 to 10 minutes; remove from pan as they are browned. Peel garlic.

5. In a blender, whirl chilies and liquid until smooth (or whirl chilies in a food processor until smooth, then gradually whirl in liquid). Rub mixture through a fine strainer back into bowl; discard chili residue.

6. Return chili purée to blender or food processor; add onion, tomatoes, garlic, cumin, and oregano. Whirl until smooth; return mixture to bowl.

7. Stack tortillas and cut into ½-inch-wide strips. Pour ½ inch of oil into a 10- to 12-inch frying pan over high heat. When oil is hot, add about ⅓ of the tortilla strips. Stir often until strips are golden and crisp, about 2 minutes. With a slotted spoon, transfer strips to towels to drain. Repeat to cook remaining tortillas.

8. Add tortilla strips to sauce in bowl and mix. Scrape mixture into a shallow 2-quart casserole. Cover evenly with cheese.

9. Bake in a 400° oven until cheese is melted and casserole is hot in the center, 8 to 10 minutes. If desired, broil 4 to 6 inches from heat until cheese is lightly browned, about 4 minutes longer.

10. Sprinkle casserole with cilantro. Spoon portions onto plates and add salt to taste.

Per serving: 581 cal., 56% (324 cal.) from fat; 22 g protein; 36 g fat (10 g sat.); 51 g carbo (9.4 g fiber); 470 mg sodium; 37 mg chol.

Carrot-Chili Ice Cream

PREP AND COOK TIME: About 40 minutes, plus 20 to 40 minutes to freeze

NOTES: This interesting ice cream is one of many exotic blends available at Tepoznieves ice cream parlor in Tijuana. If desired, serve on slices of peeled, cored fresh pineapple.

MAKES: About 1 quart

- 2½ cups **refrigerated carrot juice**
- ½ cup **half-and-half** (light cream)
- ¾ cup **sugar**
- 1 tablespoon **ground dried California** or New Mexico **chilies**

You heard right—carrots put the orange in a delicious ice cream.

- 2 **large eggs**
- ½ teaspoon **vanilla**

1. In a 2- to 3-quart pan over high heat, bring carrot juice to a boil. Remove from heat and add half-and-half, sugar, and ground chilies; stir over high heat until bubbles form at pan edge (scalding, about 180°), about 1 minute. Remove pan from heat.

2. In a small bowl, beat eggs to blend. Stir about ½ cup of the hot carrot juice mixture into eggs. Pour egg mixture into pan and set over medium-low heat. Stir with a flexible spatula, scraping pan sides and bottom for even cooking, until custard coats a metal spoon in a velvety layer, about 10 minutes. Add vanilla.

3. At once, nest pan in ice water and stir often until cold, 10 to 15 minutes.

4. Rub cold custard through a fine strainer into an ice cream maker (1-qt. or larger capacity); discard residue. Freeze as directed until mixture is firm enough to scoop, dasher is hard to turn, or machine stops. Serve, or for firmer ice cream, cover airtight and freeze at least 1 hour or up to 2 weeks.

Per ½ cup: 144 cal., 20% (29 cal.) from fat; 2.8 g protein; 3.2 g fat (1.5 g sat.); 27 g carbo (0.2 g fiber); 45 mg sodium; 59 mg chol.

Coffee-Coco Cooler

PREP TIME: About 5 minutes

NOTES: This rich, creamy *batido* (milkshake) is served as dessert at Restaurante La Costa de Tijuana.

MAKES: 2 cups; 4 servings

- ½ cup **canned coconut milk**
- ¼ cup **canned evaporated milk** (or ¼ cup regular milk and 2 teaspoons sugar)
- ¼ cup **coffee-flavor liqueur**
- 1½ cups **vanilla ice cream**
  Ground cinnamon

1. In a blender or food processor, combine coconut milk, evaporated milk, liqueur, and ice cream. Whirl until smooth.

2. Pour into glasses and sprinkle with cinnamon to taste.

Per serving: 217 cal., 54% (117 cal.) from fat; 3.4 g protein; 13 g fat (9.4 g sat.); 19 g carbo (0 g fiber); 60 mg sodium; 26 mg chol.

IF YOU GO

Tijuana and Ensenada are close enough to San Diego for a day trip, but they are worth a longer sojourn. To find out more, check out www.seetijuana.com and www.enjoyensenada.com. For information on using public transportation to cross the border between San Diego and Tijuana, go to www.sdcommute.com. If calling the following numbers from the United States, dial 011-526 first.

TIJUANA

Restaurants

- **Cien Años.** *José María Velazco 1407, Zona Río; 634-7262.*
- **Rincón San Román.** *Gobernador Ibarra 252, Col. America; 631-2241.*
- **Saverio's Restaurante Mediterráne.** *Carlos Robirosa 250, Col. Aviación; 686-3604.*

- **Tepoznieves.** *Blvd. Sanchez Taboada 4002, Local 14-15 Zona Río; 634-6532.*

Other food stops

- **L.A. Cetto Winery.** Take a tour, sample wines, and visit the gift shop. *Ave. Cañon Johnson 2108; 685-3031.*

- **Mercado Pasaje Anahuac.** Shop for ingredients and cookware. *Calle Segunda 8025.*

ENSENADA

Restaurants

- **La Embotelladora Vieja.** Part of the Bodegas de Santo Tomás winery (Baja's oldest); be sure to check out the adjacent market area, La Esquina de Bodegas. *Ave. Miramar 666, Zona Centro; 178-3557.*

- **Pueblo Cafe.** Have breakfast or a quick snack. *Ave. Ruiz 96, Zona Centro; 178-8055.* ◆

food guide

By Jerry Anne Di Vecchio • Photographs by James Carrier

A steak in the future

Chicken thighs, pounded thin,
lighten up a mixed grill

■ Chicken breasts are today's skinny meat of choice. And the shadow they cast puts the bird's darker meat in a bad light. Thighs in particular are perceived as fatty and slow to cook. But my own experience cries, "Not so!" Well-trimmed thighs offer two genuine bonuses: juicy texture and rich flavor. Much of the fat is on the skin or in pockets that are easy to find and remove.

Start with boned, skinned chicken thighs (most supermarkets carry them) or just pull the skin off boned thighs. Then snip out the lumps of fat in the meat. Pound the meat thin—it only takes seconds—and behold: a chicken-thigh steak. Flipped on a hot grill, it cooks in less than five minutes. Chicken steaks are just fine solo, but teamed with meaty portabella mushrooms, a bit of beef flank, and a few sausages (reduced-fat, if you like), they make a trim mixed grill for the 21st century.

Mixed Grill with Chicken Steaks and Mushrooms

PREP AND COOK TIME: 25 to 35 minutes

NOTES: If you can't find portabella mushroom caps, buy whole portabellas and trim off stems to save for other uses.

MAKES: 6 servings

- 3 **boned, skinned chicken thighs** (³⁄₄ to 1 lb. total)
- 3 **Italian sausages** (about ³⁄₄ lb. total)
- 1 piece **beef flank steak** (about ¹⁄₂ lb.)
- 3 **portabella mushroom caps** (4 to 5 in. wide; see notes)
- 1 tablespoon **Worcestershire**
- 2 to 3 teaspoons **olive oil**

  Pickle relish sauce (recipe follows) or Dijon mustard and prepared horseradish

  Salt

1. Rinse chicken, sausages, beef, and mushrooms; pat dry. Put sausages in a 1¹⁄₂- to 2-quart pan with ¹⁄₂ inch of water; bring to a boil over high heat, cover, reduce heat, and simmer until sausages are no longer pink in the center (cut to test), about 10 minutes; drain.

2. Meanwhile, trim and discard fat from chicken thighs and flank steak. Put thighs between sheets of plastic wrap and pound with a flat mallet until they're an even ¹⁄₄ inch thick. Rub Worcestershire over the flank steak. Lightly rub mushroom caps all over with olive oil.

3. Place mushroom caps, gills down, on a barbecue grill over a solid bed of hot coals or high heat on a gas grill (you can hold your hand at grill level only 2 to 3 seconds); close lid on gas grill. When mushrooms start to drip juice, in about 4 minutes, turn over. Lay flank steak, chicken thigh steaks, and sausages on grill. Cook, turning meats to brown evenly, until beef is rare to medium-rare in the center (cut to test), chicken is no longer pink in the center (cut to test), sausages are lightly browned, and mushrooms are flexible, 3 to 5 minutes longer for all. As foods are cooked, transfer to a platter and keep warm.

4. Thinly slice beef across the grain; cut chicken and mushrooms into thick slices and sausages into chunks. Drain accumulated meat juices into pickle relish sauce, and mix. Serve grilled foods with sauce and salt to add to taste.

Per serving of chicken, steak, and mushrooms: 161 cal., 41% (66 cal.) from fat; 20 g protein; 7.3 g fat (2.3 g sat.); 3.4 g carbo (0.9 g fiber); 102 mg sodium; 66 mg chol.

Per serving of sausages: 134 cal., 74% (99 cal.) from fat; 8.3 g protein; 11 g fat (3.7 g sat.); 0.6 g carbo (0 g fiber); 382 mg sodium; 32 mg chol.

Pickle relish sauce. In a 10- to 12-inch frying pan, combine ³⁄₄ cup **whipping cream,** ¹⁄₄ cup *each* **sweet pickle relish** and **dry vermouth** or dry white wine, 3 tablespoons **Dijon mustard,** and 2 tablespoons **Worcestershire.** Bring to a boil over high heat and stir often until reduced to about 1 cup, about **5** minutes. Remove from heat and add ¹⁄₂ cup chopped **parsley.** Let sauce stand while cooking mixed grill (preceding), then stir over high heat until simmering, about 1 minute. Pour into a small bowl. Makes about 1 cup.

Per tablespoon: 46 cal., 70% (32 cal.) from fat; 0.4 g protein; 3.5 g fat (2.2 g sat.); 2.1 g carbo (0.1 g fiber); 120 mg sodium; 12 mg chol.

Drying foods
the easy way

■ Perhaps the oldest and easiest form of food preservation is sun-drying. But variable weather and bug curiosity make this an iffy proposition. The simple solution is a food dehydrator. The devices function in any season, but it's during the summer, when copious amounts of ripe fruit are available, that I routinely use one—not so much to preserve the harvest bounty as to make healthy snacks.

Even the simplest food dehydrator with a low-temperature heating element, such as the five-tray Ronco at right (about $35), dries many, many foods effectively—the tempting balsamic strawberry crisps that follow, for instance. Fancier dehydrators, with heat regulators and fans to circulate the air, work faster, but the price can zoom to several hundred dollars for serious preserving tools. You'll find food dehydrators in cookware and hardware stores and in cookware sections of department stores. The Ronco is available at Sur La Table; (800/243-0852 or www.surlatable.com).

Crisp berries

Thin chips of sweet-tart dried strawberries turned up recently as the garnish on an opulent dish of foie gras prepared by Tim Kelley at Seattle's Painted Table. I was taken by the tasty bonus. At home, I went one step further, capitalizing on the affinity of strawberries for balsamic vinegar. These chewy-crisp tidbits are every bit as addictive as potato chips but are much more wholesome. They can be dried easily in a convection oven, but if you want to keep your kitchen cool, use a food dehydrator.

Nonstick trick: Cut cooking parchment to fit dehydrator trays.

Balsamic Strawberry Crisps

PREP AND COOK TIME: For ⅛-inch-thick slices, 12 to 18 hours in a dehydrator without a fan, 4 to 5 hours in a convection oven

NOTES: For best results, start with large, sweet red berries without blemishes or soft spots. Rinse, drain, and hull berries. Cut lengthwise across the widest dimension into evenly thick slices that are as large as possible. Save small scraps to eat fresh. Cover dehydrator trays or baking sheets with cooking parchment to keep fruit pieces from sticking or getting intertwined.

MAKES: About 1 cup

- ½ cup **balsamic vinegar**
- 2 tablespoons **sugar**
- 4 cups ⅛- to ¼-inch-thick slices **strawberries** (see notes)

1. In a 3- to 4-quart microwave-safe bowl, combine vinegar and sugar. Heat in a microwave oven on full power (100%), stirring once, until boiling, about 2 minutes total.

2. Add strawberries to bowl and mix gently.

3. Cut cooking parchment to fit flat surface of each dehydrator tray or 2 baking sheets, each 12 by 17 inches.

4. With a slotted spoon, lift strawberry slices from bowl and lay about ½ inch apart on the cooking parchment. Save vinegar mixture for salad dressings.

5. *To dry in a dehydrator,* turn on heat and set fruit-filled trays in place as directed by manufacturer. As strawberries dry, change tray positions as directed. Dehydrate until the tops of the slices look slightly dry, up to 6 hours, depending on heat and air circulation. Turn slices over and lay on unsaturated areas of parchment. Continue to dehydrate until fruit feels dry and leathery, 6 to 12 hours longer; if the fruit is still moist after 4 more hours, turn slices over again and continue. (If you don't want to run the dehydrator untended or overnight, unplug for the interval, then plug in and continue to dry. Time required will be proportionally longer.)

To dry in a 200° convection oven, bake until the tops of the strawberry slices look dry, up to 2 hours. Turn slices over and lay on unsaturated areas of parchment. Continue baking until fruit feels dry and leathery, 2 to 3 hours longer.

To test, remove a few strawberry slices from heat and let cool; the fruit should be dry and slightly crisp to brittle. If it's not, return to dehydrator or oven to dry longer.

6. Transfer fruit from parchment to a flat surface to cool. Eat, or package airtight and store at room temperature up to 6 months (if fruit softens, return to dehydrator or oven to dry more; if mold develops, discard fruit); freeze to store longer.

Per ¼ cup: 53 cal., 6.8% (3.6 cal.) from fat; 0.6 g protein; 0.4 g fat (0 g sat.); 13 g carbo (2.7 g fiber); 2.3 mg sodium; 0 mg chol.

What's in a name?

■ Dark green, broad-shouldered, pudgy poblano chilies have an identity problem: They are often labeled pasillas. But chili experts Manuel Rosas of Seminis Vegetable Seeds and Jean Andrews, the trademarked Pepper Lady, tell me that poblanos and pasillas belong to entirely different groups. Pasillas are part of the slender Anaheim group. Furthermore, true pasillas are dried chilacas, a variety rarely seen fresh north of the Mexican border.

According to Andrews, whose latest book is *The Pepper Trail: History & Recipes from Around the World* (University of North Texas Press, Denton, TX, 1999; $50; 800/826-8911), shape is the distinction between poblanos and Anaheims. Poblano chilies, as a group, are only about twice as long (4 to 6 in. on average) as they are wide, while the members of the Anaheim group (including California and New Mexico chilies) are long and skinny.

For most cooking, you can interchange fresh poblanos and Anaheims—except for stuffing. Here, only plump poblanos can really pack it in. As for dried pasillas, they can stand in for dried poblanos like mulatos and anchos in sauces, completing the circle.

Flying colors for salad

■ At i. Cugini restaurant in Santa Monica, the culinary accent is Italian, as clearly expressed by this salad. It flaunts the colors of Italy's flag—red, white, and green—with three kinds of leaves, each of which has a slightly bitter edge. Italians like to play this edge against creamy pastas and juicy steaks. A number of other countries—including Mexico, Ireland, India, and Madagascar—fly these colors too; the salad could be served with equal patriotic zeal in 10 nations.

i. Cugini Italian Salad

PREP TIME: About 10 minutes, plus at least 15 minutes to chill leaves

NOTES: Use a vegetable peeler to shave the cheese into very thin slices.

MAKES: 6 servings

4 cups **arugula** (4 to 6 oz.)

1 head **radicchio** (about ½ lb.)

1 head **Belgian endive** (about ¼ lb.)

3 tablespoons **balsamic vinegar**

3 tablespoons **extra-virgin olive oil**

¼ teaspoon minced **garlic**

2 ounces **parmesan cheese**

Fresh-ground **pepper**

Salt

1. Rinse and drain arugula; discard coarse stems and discolored leaves. Trim and discard root ends from radicchio and endive, and separate each head into leaves; rinse and drain. Wrap arugula, radicchio, and endive separately in towels and enclose together in a plastic bag. Chill at least 15 minutes or up to 1 day.

2. In a wide bowl, mix vinegar, olive oil, and garlic. Mound arugula in the bowl and top with radicchio (break any very large leaves in half), then endive. Shave parmesan onto salad (see notes) and sprinkle generously with pepper. To serve, lift with 2 forks or spoons to mix; add salt to taste.

Per serving: 112 cal., 77% (86 cal.) from fat; 4.4 g protein; 9.6 g fat (2.6 g sat.); 3.2 g carbo (0.9 g fiber); 164 mg sodium; 6.4 mg chol. ◆

The Wine Guide

By Karen MacNeil-Fife

Beyond beer: Wine with Mexican food

■ Long articles—even books—have been written on pairing wine with French food, but exciting matches for Mexican food have been given short shrift: We drink beer.

This is pretty understandable. Beer tastes good with a lot of Mexican dishes. The fact is, however, what many of us think of as Mexican cuisine is really Tex-Mex food: simple combinations of refried beans and meat smothered in melted cheese, then doused with enough hot sauce to fool your mouth into believing you're eating something more complex. Tex-Mex evolved in the southwestern United States by necessity—the resourceful creation of immigrant ranch workers who had little access to the array of chilies, vegetables, meats, and fish they had enjoyed in Mexico. In all its humbleness, it demanded a no-frills drink—beer, not wine.

But authentic Mexican food is every bit as complex and nuanced as the great cuisines of Europe. Moreover, it's not so much patently hot as it is vividly seasoned.

All of this became clear to me last November at the 1999 Worlds of Flavor Conference devoted to the regional cuisines of Mexico, organized by the Culinary Institute of America at Greystone in Napa Valley. In a tasting session on pairing wine with Mexican dishes, we found some startlingly delicious matches.

"Wine is the human race's most refined beverage," said conference chairman Rick Bayless, acclaimed cookbook author and chef-owner of Frontera Grill and Topolobampo in Chicago. "So I'm committed to pairing it with real Mexican food, which is both sophisticated and elegant."

Bayless's insights, the conference, and my own subsequent experiments have left me with three guiding principles for great pairings.
1. The most successful wines are fresh, sleek, and crisp with acidity. Good white choices include Sauvignon Blanc, Pinot Grigio (also known as Pinot Gris), dry Riesling, and Albariño, a crisp, citrusy knockout from northwestern Spain that's phenomenal with green tomatillo-chili sauces.

Acidity, however, isn't the exclusive domain of white wines. High-acid reds include Spanish Riojas (based on the Tempranillo grape), Italian Chiantis (based on Sangiovese), and Pinot Noir.
2. A second group includes wines with a plush, thick, jammy mouth-feel. Soft, juicy Zinfandels with massive fruit flavors can be sensational with earthy red chile adobo sauces, and supersupple Shirazes and Shiraz blends from Australia, with deep berry flavors, can cushion robust seasonings. If you're not a lover of such powerhouses, try a simple, overtly fruity beaujolais (made from the red grape Gamay); since it's often served chilled, it's re-

GREAT MATCHES

WHITES

■ **Bonny Doon Pacific Rim Dry Riesling,** $10. Sharp and sleek, with light yet bold citrus flavors.

■ **Chateau St. Jean "La Petite Étoile" Fumé Blanc 1998 (Russian River Valley, CA),** $14. A snazzy, snappy Sauvignon Blanc with bright herb and lemon flavors.

■ **J Pinot Gris 1997 (Russian River Valley),** $16. Elegant lemon cream pie flavors. Just right for refined seafood dishes.

■ **Villa Maria Private Bin Sauvignon Blanc 1999 (Marlborough, New Zealand),** $12. Because of their green herb flavors, New Zealand Sauvignon Blancs work beautifully with green chili sauces and guacamole.

REDS

■ **Beringer Zinfandel 1998 (North Coast, CA),** $12. Classic jammy Zinfandel flavors evocative of black cherries.

■ **DuBoeuf Beaujolais Villages 1999 (Beaujolais, France),** $8. Very fruity, with flavors reminiscent of grenadine and blueberry syrup. A great foil for spiciness.

■ **Vinicola del Priorat Ònix 1998 (Priorat, Spain),** $10. With its big, juicy core of cherries, this Spanish wine is a bargain.

■ **Wolf Blass Shiraz 1997 (South Australia),** $12. A terrific, supple Shiraz with the flavor of chocolate-covered cherries. A wonderful match for mole dishes.

freshing with highly seasoned dishes.
3. Avoid Chardonnay. Its typical oaky, toasty character fights with bold, complex Mexican flavors, and the wine ends up tasting coarse and bitter. Cabernet Sauvignon and Merlot don't fare much better. Both have a lot of tannin, and when tannin hits the flavor of chilies, it sets your mouth on fire and you miss all the complexities of the food.

Tuck these guidelines away and experiment without fear. When you try the recipes from Tijuana and Ensenada on page 261, pour a couple of wines. You'll be glad you saved the beer for another time. ◆

Oregon's own red sea: Cranberry bogs dominate the coast near Bandon. BELOW: The Bog Queen and her Bogettes star in the Cranberry Festival parade.

Go west, young cranberry

If you think they grow only in the East, you haven't visited Bandon, Oregon—home to cranberry bogs and a cranberry court

By Bonnie Henderson

Cranberries may be indelibly linked in the public mind to the flinty shores of New England. But they also love Bandon, Oregon, where they thrive in the sandy soil and mild climate. And Bandon in turn loves its favorite fruit, honoring it annually with a Cranberry Festival that includes a high school Cranberry Bowl and the coronation of a teen Cranberry Queen or King. The festivities begin in early September—the warm-up act to the main event, the October-long harvest. If you're any kind of fan of these tart little spheres—not true berries, botanically speaking—Bandon is the place to go.

Cranberries have been grown commercially on the West Coast for a century, and Oregon now ranks fourth among the states in cranberry production and top among Western states. A vast majority of Oregon berries comes from bogs right around Bandon, on the south coast. Most are wet-picked, meaning that growers flood their bogs with water, then use mechanical harvesters to loosen the floating berries from the vines. They are then scooped up to

be used in juice, sauce, candy, and other products that require only good flavor (not physical beauty). A smaller percentage is dry-picked for the fresh produce market, including a small organic crop produced by the Coquille Indians and a handful of other local farmers.

Though harvest time is October, some of those dry-picked berries show up in time for the **Bandon Cranberry Festival** (September 8 to 10 in 2000). There's a parade with the smiling Cranberry Court, craft booths lining Second Street, a barbecue, the big football game, and live music. If you're too early—or

too late—for fresh berries at the **Bandon Little Farmers Market** (10–2 Sat, through mid-September; 350 Second St.), pick up a pound of cranberry fudge or another treat at **Cranberry Sweets & More** (9–6 daily; 280 First St. SE; 541/347-9475) in Old Town.

Faber Farms offers free tours of the bogs from June through the second week in November (10–4 Mon-Sat; 519 Morrison Rd.; 347-1166). There's always something to see, but no time rivals harvest time: The bogs are crimson with ripe berries and turning leaves, and they're a frenzy of activity, with mechanical harvesters and hip-booted helpers cruising the flooded fields. Al Faber supervises the farm's cranberry receiving and shipping facility, while his wife, Ann, oversees the tours and sells gourmet cranberry products from Cranberry Scoop Gift Shop.

Just curious? You'll see some bogs if you drive north or south a few miles out of Bandon on U.S. 101, or explore the backroads east or southeast of town.

Bandon travel planner

The clearest, warmest weather on the southern Oregon coast often comes in the fall. Get trip-planning help from the **Bandon Information Center & Chamber of Commerce;** (541) 347-9616 or www.bandon.com.

Lodging options include a few cozy B&Bs and oceanfront motels. There are luxurious rooms, suites, and a golf course at **Bandon Dunes.** *From $115. 57744 Round Lake Dr.; (888) 345-6008.* ◆

The Low-Fat Cook

Healthy choices for the active lifestyle

By Elaine Johnson

Chicken, almonds, and spices are handsomely wrapped in filo.

ROBERT OLDING

Is it a gift or is it dinner?

■ As health editor for Cooking.com, Cheryl Forberg is nutritionally vigilant in the kitchen. Once a private chef—for notables such as George Lucas of *Star Wars*—she has earned a reputation for entrées that are both light and extravagant. She often makes the Moroccan pie *bastilla*. The individual servings, easily packaged in filo dough, are finished with a twist.

Traditionally, the heart of the pie is pigeon, eggs, nuts, a souk's worth of spices, and butter. Forberg manages a lighter touch by using poached chicken breasts and egg whites. A fine mist of oil, not butter, makes the pastry flaky and crisp. The lean, flavorful poaching broth becomes a smooth, sweet-hot sauce.

Low-Fat Chicken Bastillas

PREP AND COOK TIME: About 1 hour

MAKES: 4 servings

3 cups fat-skimmed **unsalted** or reduced-sodium **chicken broth**

1 cup thickly sliced **onion**

2 cloves **garlic,** peeled and minced

1½ tablespoons minced **fresh ginger**

1½ teaspoons **ground turmeric**

1 teaspoon **ground coriander**

¾ teaspoon **hot chili flakes**

⅛ teaspoon **powdered saffron**

1¼ teaspoons **ground cinnamon**

1 pound **boned, skinned chicken breasts,** cut into ⅓- by 2-inch slices

4 **large egg** whites

¼ cup chopped **fresh cilantro**

   Salt

⅓ cup finely chopped **almonds**

   About 1½ tablespoons **powdered sugar**

6 sheets (12 by 17 in.) **filo dough**

   Cooking oil spray

2 tablespoons **red jalapeño jelly**

1 tablespoon **cornstarch**

1. In a 3- to 4-quart pan over high heat, bring broth, onion, garlic, ginger, turmeric, coriander, chili flakes, saffron, and ¼ teaspoon cinnamon to a boil. Add chicken, cover, remove from heat, and let stand until no longer pink in the center (cut to test), about 2 minutes. With a slotted spoon, transfer chicken, but not onion, to a bowl.

2. In a small bowl, whisk ¼ cup of the cooking broth with egg whites just to blend. Place an 8- to 10-inch nonstick frying pan over medium heat. Pour egg mixture into pan and, with a flexible spatula, scrape from pan bottom just until softly set, 3 to 5 minutes.

3. With spatula, gently combine egg mixture and cilantro with chicken. Season to taste with salt.

4. In another bowl, combine almonds, 1½ tablespoons sugar, and remaining teaspoon cinnamon.

5. Working quickly and keeping unused filo covered, lightly spray filo sheets 1 at a time with oil; stack in pairs, making 3 stacks. Cut each stack of filo dough crosswise into 3 equal parts; you'll have 9 stacks. Lay 1 stack of 2 strips at right angles across another. With 6 more stacks, make 3 more crosses; reserve remaining stack for other uses.

6. Using a slotted spoon, mound ¼ of the chicken mixture onto center of each cross (add any accumulated liquid to the cooking broth). Sprinkle mounds equally with almond mixture. Gather filo strips up over filling and gently squeeze and twist to enclose each bundle. Set filo bundles well apart on an oiled 12- by 15-inch baking sheet.

7. Pull back tips of filo strips on each bundle to make "petals." Lightly spray bundles with oil.

8. Bake bastilla pastries in a 400° oven until golden brown, 15 to 18 minutes (10 to 12 minutes in a convection oven).

9. Meanwhile, boil broth mixture over high heat until reduced to 2 cups, 5 to 10 minutes. Pour through a fine strainer into a bowl; discard residue. Rinse pan; return broth to it. Add jelly. In a small bowl, mix cornstarch with 1 tablespoon water. Set pan over high heat. Add cornstarch mixture; whisk until boiling. Pour into a serving bowl.

10. With a wide spatula, transfer bastillas to plates. Dust with more powdered sugar and accompany with sauce.

Per serving: 385 cal., 28% (108 cal.) from fat; 37 g protein; 12 g fat (1.7 g sat.); 33 g carbo (1.9 g fiber); 352 mg sodium; 69 mg chol. ◆

Kitchen Cabinet

Readers recipes tested in Sunset's kitchens

By Andrew Baker

Roasted potatoes team up with tangy tomato dressing for a zesty side dish.

CRAIG MAXWELL

Baked Potato Chunks with Tomato-Basil Dressing

Helen Martin, Berkeley

Potatoes, splashed with Helen Martin's favorite fresh tomato dressing and baked, make a flavorful summer companion for a steak from the grill.

PREP AND COOK TIME: About 1 hour

MAKES: 4 or 5 servings

- 1½ cups chopped **ripe** or firm-ripe **tomatoes**
- 2 teaspoons chopped or pressed **garlic**
- 3 tablespoons chopped **fresh basil** leaves
- 2 tablespoons **lemon juice**
- ½ cup **olive** or salad **oil**
- 2 pounds **Yukon Gold potatoes**, scrubbed

  Salt and **pepper**

1. In a blender or food processor, combine tomatoes, garlic, 1 tablespoon basil, lemon juice, and oil. Whirl until smooth.

2. Cut potatoes into 1½- to 2-inch chunks and spread level in a shallow 3-quart casserole (9 by 13 in.).

3. Bake in a 425° oven for 20 minutes. Pour tomato mixture over potatoes and continue to bake until potatoes are tender when pierced, 20 to 25 minutes longer; stir several times.

4. Sprinkle remaining 2 tablespoons basil over potatoes; season to taste with salt and pepper.

Per serving: 353 cal., 56% (198 cal.) from fat; 4.1 g protein; 22 g fat (2.9 g sat.); 36 g carbo (3.9 g fiber); 20 mg sodium; 16 mg chol.

Thai Rice Salad

Camilla Saulsbury, Albany, California

When nibbling leftover coconut rice, Camilla Saulsbury realized that a few adjustments could turn the mixture into a colorful salad.

PREP AND COOK TIME: About 50 minutes, plus 45 minutes to cool rice

MAKES: 6 to 8 servings

- 2 cups **white basmati** or long-grain white **rice**
- 1 tablespoon minced or pressed **garlic**
- 1 tablespoon minced **fresh ginger**
- 2 tablespoons **salad oil**
- 1 teaspoon **curry powder**
- 1 can (15 oz.) **reduced-fat coconut milk**
- 1⅓ cups fat-skimmed **chicken broth**
- 1 **red bell pepper** (about 6 oz.)
- 1 cup **Chinese pea pods**
- 1 teaspoon grated **lime** peel
- ¼ cup **lime juice**
- 1 tablespoon **honey**
- ⅓ cup thinly sliced and seeded **kumquats**
- 3 tablespoons minced **fresh cilantro**

  Salt

1. In a large bowl, stir rice in cool water; drain. Repeat several times until water is no longer cloudy. Drain rice.

2. In a 3- to 4-quart pan over medium heat, stir garlic and ginger in oil until lightly browned, about 3 minutes. Add rice and curry powder and stir 1 minute longer.

3. Add coconut milk and broth. Bring to a boil over high heat. Cover pan, turn heat to low, and cook until rice is tender to bite, about 20 minutes. Let cool to room temperature, about 45 minutes; stir occasionally.

4. Meanwhile, rinse, stem, seed, and chop bell pepper. Rinse peas and discard strings and stem ends; cut peas diagonally into ½-inch-wide pieces.

5. In a 2- to 3-quart pan over high heat, bring 2 cups water to a boil. Add peas and bell pepper; cook just until tender-crisp to bite, 1 to 2 minutes. Drain and immerse in ice water until cool, about 1 minute. Drain.

6. In a large bowl, mix lime peel, lime juice, and honey. Add rice, peas, bell pepper, kumquats, and cilantro; mix well. Add salt to taste.

Per serving: 252 cal., 25% (64 cal.) from fat; 7.7 g protein; 7.1 g fat (2.2 g sat.); 45 g carbo (1.3 g fiber); 50 mg sodium; 0 mg chol.

Raisin-Nut Sweet Potato Scones

Cyndy Whitaker, El Cajon, California

When Cyndy Whitaker bakes sweet potatoes or yams, she cooks extras to use in this scone recipe. You can also use drained canned sweet potatoes or yams.

PREP AND COOK TIME: About 35 minutes

MAKES: About 12 scones

- 1¾ cups **whole-wheat flour**
- 1 tablespoon **baking powder**
- ¾ teaspoon **baking soda**
- ½ cup firmly packed **brown sugar**
- 1 teaspoon **ground cinnamon**
- ¼ teaspoon **ground mace** or ground nutmeg
- ¾ cup **raisins**
- ½ cup **chopped walnuts**
- ⅓ cup **low-fat buttermilk**
- ¼ cup **liquid egg substitute** or 2 large eggs
- 1 teaspoon **vanilla**
- 1 cup mashed cooked **sweet potatoes** or yams

1. In a large bowl, stir together flour, baking powder, soda, brown sugar, cinnamon, mace, raisins, and walnuts.

2. In another bowl, beat to blend buttermilk, egg substitute, vanilla, and sweet potatoes.

3. Add buttermilk mixture to flour mixture and stir until evenly moistened.

4. Mound batter in 12 equal portions (about ¼ cup each) on a lightly oiled 14- by 17-inch baking sheet, spacing at least 2 inches apart.

5. Bake in a 375° oven until browned, 12 to 15 minutes. Transfer to a rack and let cool at least 5 minutes; serve hot, warm, or at room temperature.

Per serving: 193 cal., 19% (36 cal.) from fat; 4.6 g protein; 4 g fat (0.4 g sat.); 37 g carbo (3.7 g fiber); 226 mg sodium; 0.3 mg chol.

Hawaiian Luau Pork

Cary Yoshio Mizobe, Gardena, California

Hungry for the *kalua* pork he grew up eating in Hawaii, Cary Yoshio Mizobe developed an easier and quicker version. It's delicious on its own or in quesadillas or chili. If you want the pork to have a more traditional flavor, wrap it in rinsed banana leaves, then seal in foil. You will need 2 banana leaves (fresh or thawed frozen, each about 15 by 24 in.), available in Asian and Latino food markets.

PREP AND COOK TIME: 4½ hours

MAKES: 10 to 12 servings

- 1 **boned pork butt** or shoulder (4 to 4½ lb.)
- 2 tablespoons **kosher** or other coarse **salt**
- 3 tablespoons **liquid smoke**

1. Rinse pork and pat dry. Pierce meat deeply with a fork at about 1-inch intervals and rub all over with salt and liquid smoke.

2. Cut 2 pieces heavy-duty foil, each about 16 by 24 inches. (If using banana leaves [see notes], stack and set on foil.) Set meat in the center of foil (if using banana leaves, fold leaves compactly over meat to enclose). Lift foil around meat (or leaves) to enclose snugly; seal edges. Set packet in a 10- by 15-inch pan.

3. Bake in a 400° oven until meat is very tender when pierced (cut through top of the packet to test), about 4¼ hours (about 3¾ hours in a convection oven).

4. Using mitts to protect your hands, remove and discard foil (and leaves), and put meat with juices in pan. Skim and discard fat from meat juices. Using 2 forks, tear meat into shreds. Serve, or if making ahead, cover and chill up to 2 days. To reheat, cover and bake in a 350° oven until meat is hot, about 20 minutes.

Per serving: 309 cal., 64% (198 cal.) from fat; 27 g protein; 22 g fat (8 g sat.); 0 g carbo; 813 mg sodium; 99 mg chol.

Corn and Pea Shoot Soup

Cindy Wu, Sunnyvale, California

Cindy Wu grows peas in her garden and uses the tender leaves at the end of the shoots as the greenery in this soothing soup. The shoots are sweet-tasting, like fresh peas. You can also use small pea sprouts with tender stems (2 to 3 in. long) or baby spinach leaves.

PREP AND COOK TIME: About 10 minutes

Sweet kernels of corn, delicate strands of cooked egg, and tender pea shoots swim in a light broth.

MAKES: 4 cups, 2 or 3 servings

- 2 cups fat-skimmed **chicken broth**
- 1 cup **corn kernels** (fresh or frozen)
- 1 **large egg**
- 2 cups (about 2 oz.) **pea shoots,** rinsed (see notes)

  Salt

1. In a 2- to 3-quart pan over high heat, combine broth, 1½ cups water, and corn. In a small bowl, beat egg to blend.

2. When corn mixture boils, stir while adding egg to pan; cook until strands are firm, 30 seconds to 1 minute.

3. Add pea shoots to pan and stir just until they are wilted, about 1 minute longer. Add salt to taste. Ladle the soup into bowls.

Per serving: 120 cal., 17% (20 cal.) from fat; 11 g protein; 2.2 g fat (0.6 g sat.); 17 g carbo (1.1 g fiber); 76 mg sodium; 71 mg chol.◆

At our bewitching Halloween feast, decapitated minipumpkins hold creamy parmesan risotto. Party recipes begin on page 294.

October

Vintage
Napa Valley

The ultimate guide to unparalleled inns, restaurants, and bargains—plus recipes for creating your own sublime Wine Country picnic

Napa pleasures, classic and new: Auberge du Soleil's sun-splashed views (above) are available for the price of a glass of wine; Greg Cole presides at Cole's Chop House (above right).

By Andrew Baker and Lora J. Finnegan
Photographs by Terrence McCarthy

FRIDAY NIGHT in downtown Napa, California. Cole's Chop House, to be exact.

A crowd mingles in the bar, the host fields telephone calls, and a waiter hoists a steak the size of home plate to a hungry diner.

"Downtown has been starved for something like this," Greg Cole says, describing his eponymous restaurant. Cole understands one secret of Napa Valley success: pairing perfectly prepared classics, in this case a local Cabernet with an artfully aged steak, to make a sublime marriage of food and wine. Open less than a year, Cole's Chop House is luring visitors to the long-neglected Napa city center, causing people who thought they knew every inch of Napa Valley to realize that it can still surprise them.

Cole's success is only one indication of the revolution that's taken place in the area. Within living memory, after all, this 35-mile-long valley northeast of San Francisco was a lovely but poky rural retreat of interest mainly to Northern Californians. Now Napa Valley has become a five-star destination that ranks with Tuscany or Bordeaux in allure.

La Toque chef-owner Ken Frank calls it "a haven for sophisticated tourists who travel on their stomachs."

The signs are everywhere. Napa Valley restaurants like Thomas Keller's French Laundry and Frank's La Toque are regularly judged among the best in the nation. One can spend the night in some of the most luxurious lodgings this side of Lake Como. Next year, the $70-million American Center for Wine, Food, and the Arts (founded by Robert G. Mondavi) will open in downtown Napa; it will house a wine museum, educational center, and restaurants, where chefs, winemakers, and artists can explore the relationship between gastronomy and art.

Despite its ascent to world renown, Napa Valley holds on to a few secrets—charming, smaller, quieter (and cheaper) gems that are well worth seeking out. The ideal visit to the valley lets you savor both glamour and rusticity: swank spots as heady as sparkling wine, more soothing retreats that invite you to linger and savor the region's many charms.

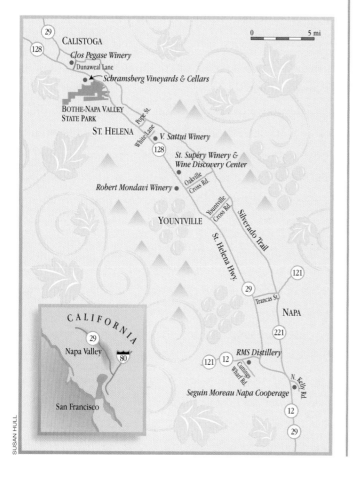

Paris comes to Yountville at Bouchon.

DINING

Choosing a restaurant in Napa Valley can be daunting: Too many good options abound, and trying to snag a last-minute table can bruise nerves and egos. While ordering à la carte provides an affordable meal, some restaurants offer prix fixe and tasting menus (many even have vegetarian versions) that simply can't be missed.

Generally, prices are lower and reservations are easier to come by at lunch than at dinner. Most menus change seasonally and many change daily. For that reason, our descriptions reflect what our staff tasted on scouting trips; specific dishes may have changed. Except as noted in the listings, the prices we quote are averages for a three-course meal without wine or tip. Fixed-price multicourse dinners offer choices for each course. Area code is 707 unless noted.

Elegant La Toque ranks among the valley's finest restaurants.

The hautest of the haute

Gorgeous surroundings, vibrant atmosphere, and imaginative, well-executed cuisine set these restaurants apart from the rest.

French Laundry. Perhaps the most famous restaurant in the valley, French Laundry shows off chef Thomas Keller's artistic creativity—and his technical skills. Where else will you find oysters and caviar in custard or a savory sorbet served with an herb *tuile*? The soothing neutral decor directs your attention to the drama unfolding on the plate before you. The drawback? Getting the required reservation. Put your phone on speed dial and keep hitting the button all day: That's the advice from the restaurant's spokesperson. *Lunch Fri-Sun, dinner daily ($90 five courses, $105 tasting). 6640 Washington St., Yountville; 944-2380.*

La Toque. With one wall dominated by a huge stone fireplace, La Toque's single room looks like the interior of an exquisitely elegant barn. Chef-owner Ken Frank weaves fine ingredients like foie gras, turbot, and rabbit together with intensely flavored sauces to create meals to remember. *Dinner ($72 five courses) Wed-Sun. 1140 Rutherford Rd., Rutherford; 963-9770 or www. latoque.com.*

Pinot Blanc. Purposefully mismatched fabrics add a festive, eclectic touch to Los Angeles restaurateur Joachim Splichal's northernmost outpost. Chef and partner Sean Knight's food is equally surprising: Veal cheeks and planked local salmon make regular appearances on the menu. *Lunch ($32) and dinner ($36)*

daily. 641 Main St., St. Helena; 963-6191 or www.patinagroup.com.

Terra. The decor is massive and rustic—stone walls and exposed redwood beams—as befits a 116-year-old building that has housed a foundry, chicken hatchery, and leather glove factory. The menu consists of "food that we like to eat," says Lissa Doumani, owner and wife of chef Hiro Sone: That includes a sea bass in shiso broth, the lightest, most flavorful dish for miles. Half-bottle amounts of wine are decanted in Erlenmeyer chemistry flasks. "People know exactly what [amount] they're getting," explains Doumani, and "they all of a sudden go back to high school." *Dinner ($40) Wed-Mon. 1345 Railroad Ave., St. Helena; 963-8931.*

Cool and casual

These less formal establishments offer great food at reasonable prices.

Bistro Don Giovanni. Sit outside in the garden and say "hi" to feline BK (Bistro Kitty) while enjoying fare like *pollo alla Napa*, a juicy half-chicken wrapped in grape leaves and baked in a wood-fired oven. Why does everything taste so authentically Italian? Owner Giovanni Scala, whose wife, Donna, is the chef, says, "Donna goes back to Naples and cooks with my mom and sisters every year." *Lunch and dinner ($33) daily. 4110 State 29, Napa; 224-3300.*

Bistro Jeanty. The specials written on the door lead you to hope you've found French cooking at its best. The dishes that pour forth from Philippe Jeanty's kitchen prove that your hopes were not misplaced. You'll encounter things here that you won't find elsewhere: a salad of pigs' feet and *haricots verts,* homemade sausages, oversize crêpes suzette. The interior is wonderfully reminiscent of a French farmhouse, filled with antique cooking implements—even a 1915 Peugeot bicycle once used for delivering bread—from the chef's personal collection. *Lunch and dinner ($33) daily. 6510 Washington, Yountville; 944-0103 or www.bistrojeanty.com.*

Bouchon. One of the few restaurants in the valley open past midnight, Bouchon attracts a fun-loving crowd that spills out through the French doors onto the patio. Inside you'll find a beguiling hideaway—with a dazzling tiled floor, a zinc-plated bar, and antique lighting fixtures—that is the ideal spot to savor classic bistro fare, from *steak frites* to *pots de crème,* while 1930s jazz or Edith Piaf plays in the background. *Lunch and dinner ($30) daily. 6534 Washington, Yountville; 944-8037.*

Cole's Chop House. Chef Greg Cole knew just what he wanted when he opened his chop house: "The kind of thing you see in old black-and-white movies—a place my

At Terra, half-bottle amounts of wine are decanted in Erlenmeyer chemistry flasks.

parents might have walked into in Minneapolis in 1947." He reached his goal. The aged prime steaks are incredible, especially when teamed with all-American dishes like creamed spinach and hash browns, Caesar- and buttermilk-dressed salads, and nostalgic cocktails. Add live jazz on weekend nights and get ready for a retro experience par excellence. *Dinner ($39) Tue-Sun. 1122 Main St., Napa; 224-6328.*

Gordon's Cafe and Wine Bar. Sally Gordon first visited the Napa Valley as a college freshman in 1967. At that time, she "fell in love with the building"—first a stagecoach stop and later a country store—that now houses her namesake restaurant. Gordon's convivial presence adds greatly to the dining pleasure. For the ultimate experience, go for dinner (only on Fridays; reservations recommended), when the kitchen whips up California cuisine with a decidedly Mediterranean emphasis. *Breakfast and lunch ($8) daily, dinner ($38 three courses) Fri. 6770 Washington, Yountville; 944-8246.*

Wine Spectator Greystone Restaurant. Chef Todd Humphries's Temptations menu, a sampling of nibbles served before the meal, is among the most creative in the valley. The lineup might include a spoonful of savory *panna cotta* or a dab of foie gras with cubes of crabapple gelée. "They're very seasonal ingredients," Humphries says. "They come in and we figure out how to make small bites of them." The restaurant is colorful and lively—an open kitchen and high ceilings add to the buzz of activity. *Lunch ($20) and dinner ($37) daily. 2555 Main, St. Helena; 967-1010 or www.ciachef.edu.*

WINERY TOURS

With more than 250 wineries in the valley, it's easy to find a good tour on wine basics. For going beyond the rudiments, these in-depth tours are real corkers. For more information, contact the **Napa Valley Conference & Visitors Bureau.** *226-7459 or www.napavalley.com.*

Robert Mondavi Winery. The mission-style winery—designed by legendary architect Cliff May—is undergoing a face-lift, with new facilities set to open in spring. Meanwhile, you can enjoy Mondavi's fine series of existing tours, including the To Kalon vineyard tour ($10), the vineyard and winery tour ($10), and the guided tasting ($10). Or try an essence tasting and tour ($25), winegrowing tour

beings took a cut for their services when visiting to bless the brandy. Tours are free; reservations are recommended. *10:30–4:30 daily. 1250 Cuttings Wharf Rd., Napa; 253-9055.*

Schramsberg Vineyards & Cellars. You'll see how sparkling wine is made the old-fashioned way, from a tour guide who is energetic—if not downright bubbly. You begin with a briefing on Schramsberg history and on the *méthode champenoise* (the traditional French method). Then you walk into cool, musty, 2-mile-long caves, carved out by Chinese laborers at the turn of the century, now lined with racks filled with bottles on their sides. Hand-riddling (turning the bottles) is still a favored art here—if you've got strong hands you can give it a try at a sample rack. Tours are free and by appointment. *10–4 daily. 1400 Schramsberg Rd., Calistoga; 942-2414.*

Seguin Moreau Napa Cooperage. Hang with the coopers at the only U.S. outpost of the famed French barrel makers, Tonnellerie Seguin Moreau. Watch a small army of barrel makers bend, shave, roast, and toast the oak staves. It's like a workshop in Hades—you feel the heat from barrels set over open fires in the floor and hear the piercing din of hammers on steel as hoops are pounded onto staves. Tours are free; reservations recommended. *8–4 Mon-Fri. 151 Camino Dorado, Napa; 252-3408.*

St. Supéry Winery & Wine Discovery Center. A clever self-guided tour guides you through the process of winemaking; pause at a cutaway of a grapevine or at a SmellaVision station, where you sniff out wine essences. At an outside planting area, you'll see various trellising methods. One-hour guided tours ($5) are also available (at 11, 1, and 3). *9:30–5 daily. 8440 State 29; (800) 942-0809, ext. 44.*

Uncover the mysteries of barrel making at Seguin Moreau (above); educate your palate at Mondavi (right).

and tasting ($25), a vineyard picnic ($48), or the art of wine and food seminar ($65, includes lunch). *10–5 daily. 7801 State 29, Oakville; (888) 766-6328, ext. 2000, or www.robertmondavi.com.*

RMS Distillery. In the Carneros area, this tour covers a process you'll see nowhere else in Napa: brandy making. A scale-model distillery (built by Industrial Light and Magic) begins the tour, then you pass the huge alambic pot stills, shaped like giant peaked caps, where wine becomes brandy (the processing takes place in the fall). Finally, to the accompaniment of Gregorian chants, you enter the barrel, or "angels' share," room: As the brandy ages, small amounts evaporate from the barrels. Early monks dubbed this loss the angels' share, figuring the heavenly

LODGING

Luxury

If you're treating yourself to fabulous tours and four-star dining, it's natural to want the equivalent in lodging. We talked to Wine Country insiders who recommended six of the valley's most luxurious accommodations. Stay at any and you'll get star treatment. Reserve well ahead for weekends. Need more booking help? Try **Accommodation Referral** (800/240-8466), **B&B Style** (942-2888 or 800/995-8884), **Napa Valley Reservations Unlimited** (800/251-6272), or **Wine Country Reservations** (257-7757).

Auberge du Soleil. Perched on the slopes of Rutherford Hill, Auberge du Soleil is like an elegant little Mediterranean hill town, complete with olive grove, vineyard, and 50 rooms and suites, most in separate villas. Most rooms have a private terrace, fireplace, refrigerator, and wet bar. Bathrooms are grand—each has a huge tub (some jetted) surrounded by candles and topped by a skylight. On the grounds there's a pool, new spa and gym, and a sculpture garden. Even if you can't afford to stay here, drop by the bar and drink in the valley view. *From $550; private cottages from $2,500 (ask about packages). 180 Rutherford Hill Rd., Rutherford; 963-1211, (800) 348-5406, or www.aubergedusoleil.com.*

Lavender Bed and Breakfast Inn. For a lower-key yet sybaritic stay, try one of the newest inns. The exterior is tastefully country French; the eight rooms are brightly trendy (eggplant-colored walls in some bathrooms). Rooms have fireplaces, and a winsome teddy bear and a bottle of wine await guests. *From $250. 2020 Webber Ave., Yountville; 944-1388, (800) 522-4140, or www.foursisters.com.*

Meadowood Napa Valley. With its 85 rooms and suites dotting 85 wooded acres, Meadowood specializes in luxurious solitude that's made it a favorite with celebrities. Part of the prestigious Relais & Chateaux group, the resort offers room service around the clock, and a concierge assigned to each guest will work in advance to secure hard-to-get restaurant reservations. Play at the on-site croquet lawn, tennis courts, nine-

Linger luxuriously at Villagio (above left) or the Vintage Inn (above). El Bonita (above right) offers bargain charm.

hole golf course, pools, restaurants, and spa. *From $420. 900 Meadowood Lane, St. Helena; 963-3646, (800) 458-8080, or www.meadowood.com.*

Silverado Country Club & Resort. Built in the 1870s, Silverado's main building is reminiscent of a Southern plantation house. Nearby, Silverado's 280 condominiums are surrounded by 1,200 acres of lush vineyards and rolling hills. This resort is best known for its two championship 18-hole golf courses, but it also has 14 tennis courts, 9 swimming pools, and 3 first-rate restaurants: Royal Oak, Vintners Court, and Bar & Grill. A new spa offers massage therapy, skin-care and body treatments, a

fitness center, salon, and lap pool. *From $165. 1600 Atlas Peak Rd., Napa; 257-0200, (800) 532-0500, or www.silveradoresort.com.*

Villagio Inn & Spa. A sister (and neighboring) property to Vintage Inn (below), Tuscan-inspired Villagio offers garden settings, rooms with fireplaces, and bountiful buffet breakfasts. *From $250. 6481 Washington, Yountville; 944-8877, (800) 351-1133, or www.villagio.com.*

Vintage Inn. The Vintage Inn is more like a château; its 80 rooms, set in clusters, have just undergone a $1.5-million renovation, adding sunken jetted tubs, French country decor, and 18th-century antiques. *From $250. 6541 Washington, Yountville; 944-1112, (800) 351-1133, or www.vintageinn.com.*

Bargain

If you want to save your travel pennies for fine food—or wine—it's good to know you *can* find reasonably priced lodging in Napa Valley. What's considered a bargain? When a night at a top resort can cost the equivalent of a car payment, a room rate of $120 or less per night sounds pretty darn good.

We found eight attractive spots with rooms starting at that price or less (for midweek). You can get better deals in the off-season (November through February). However, some of these lodges are so popular you must book months ahead to get a weekend date.

Calistoga Spa Hot Springs. It combines the comforts of a nice motel (all rooms have kitchenettes) with resort amenities (swimming pool, four mineral hot springs pools, spa treatments, fitness center). *From $100. 1006 Washington St., Calistoga; 942-6269 or www.calistogaspa.com.*

Carlin Cottages. Lovingly remodeled motor court–style cottages, updated with pool, outdoor whirlpool bath, and simple but charming furnishings.

It's sedately set a few blocks off Calistoga's main drag. *From $89. 1623 Lake St., Calistoga; 942-9102, (800) 734-4624, or www.carlincottages.com.*

Comfort Inn Napa Valley North. A quiet location and touches like a mineral springs swimming pool raise this above a chain operation. *From $85. 1865 Lincoln Ave., Calistoga; 942-9400 or (800) 228-5150.*

El Bonita Motel. This 1930s art deco motel has nicely landscaped grounds and seems cozy and tucked away—even though it's right on the highway. *From $119. 195 Main, St. Helena; 963-3216, (800) 541-3284, or www.elbonita.com.*

Golden Haven Hot Springs Spa and Resort. This Calistoga stalwart has had a nip here and a tuck there and has emerged tastefully renovated. (The upstairs rooms are still being refurbished.) Unwind in a big mineral swimming pool or with spa treatments. *From $75. 1713 Lake, Calistoga; 942-6793 or www.goldenhaven.com.*

Hideaway Cottages. Big sycamores, lots of lawn, a large, heated mineral pool, and quaint cottages with kitchenettes make these side-street lodgings great for families—there's cable TV but no room phones. *From $75. 1412 Fairway Ave., Calistoga; 942-4108 or www.hideawaycottages.com.*

Mount View Hotel. The 1917 Mount View is both a national historic landmark and a tasteful spa hotel. Amenities here include mineral hot tub, continental breakfast, and a restaurant. *From $125. 1457 Lincoln, Calistoga; 942-6877, (800) 816-6877, or www.mountviewhotel.com.*

Roman Spa Hot Springs Resort. It's got a basic motel layout, but also a friendly staff, updated decor, palms around the pool, and an on-site spa. *From $86. 1300 Washington, Calistoga; 942-4441, (888) 208-9448, or www.tales.com/romanspa/.*

Napa Valley
picnics

The most memorable Napa Valley meal could be one you assemble yourself. With its oak-studded meadows, rolling hills, and vast stock of first-class foodstuffs, Napa Valley may just be the picnic capital of the world. • Here we offer three picnic menus paired with varietals beyond the tried-and-true Chardonnay and Cabernet Sauvignon. Prepare and pack the heart of the meal at home. (Use insulated containers to keep meat dishes cold; when serving, they should sit at room temperature no longer than two hours.) Stop along the way to pick up the accompaniments. • Among the valley's best places to purchase your picnic necessities—from artisan breads to salads to Napa Valley wines—are the four listed below. We also include two of the valley's best spots to spread out your picnic blanket. You may enjoy yourself so much, you'll decide to replicate this Napa Valley–inspired feast in your own garden. — *Linda Lau Anusasananan*

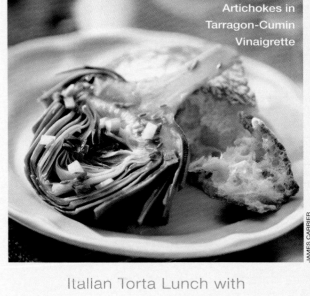

Artichokes in Tarragon-Cumin Vinaigrette

JAMES CARRIER

Italian Torta Lunch with Sauvignon Blanc

Artichokes in Tarragon-Cumin Vinaigrette* Prosciutto and Spinach Torta* • Sliced Tomatoes on Frisée • Ciabatta or Baguettes • Sauvignon Blanc Amaretti and Grapes • Muscat Dessert Wine

*Recipe provided

A cold, dry, herbaceous Sauvignon Blanc goes beautifully with the prosciutto-lined spinach torta—and even the marinated artichokes. An aromatic, chilled Muscat dessert wine with Italian-style almond macaroons and grapes ends the meal decadently.

Picnic supplies

Dean & DeLuca. *9–7 daily. 607 State 29 S., St. Helena; 967-9980.*
Oakville Grocery. *10–6 daily. 7856 State 29, Oakville; 944-8802.*
V. Sattui Winery. *9–6 daily. 1111 White Lane, St. Helena; 963-7774.*
Vallergas Market. *7–10 daily. 301 First St., Napa; 253-1666.*

Picnic sites

Bothe-Napa Valley State Park. Picnic under the redwoods. *Sunrise–sunset daily; $5. 3801 State 29 N.; 942-4575.*
Clos Pegase Winery. Pick up a bottle of wine at the imposing Michael Graves–designed winery, then enjoy a picnic on the tables outside. *10:30–5 daily. 1060 Dunaweal Lane, Calistoga; 942-4981.*

Artichokes in Tarragon-Cumin Vinaigrette

PREP AND COOK TIME: About 25 minutes, plus at least 30 minutes to marinate
NOTES: If making up to 1 day ahead, cover and chill. Bring to room temperature to serve.
MAKES: 6 servings

- 3 tablespoons plus ⅓ cup **rice vinegar**
  About 2 tablespoons **extra-virgin olive oil**
- 1 tablespoon **cumin seed**
- 1 teaspoon **whole black peppercorns**
- 3 **artichokes** (each about 3½ in. wide)
- ¼ cup chopped **red onion**
- 2 tablespoons minced **fresh tarragon** leaves or 1 teaspoon dried tarragon
- 1 tablespoon **Dijon mustard**
- 1 clove **garlic,** peeled and pressed or minced
  Salt

1. Pour about 3 quarts water into a 6- to 8-quart pan. Add 3 tablespoons vinegar, 1 teaspoon olive oil, cumin seed, and peppercorns. Cover and bring to a boil over high heat.

2. Meanwhile, slice off and discard about 1 inch from tops of artichokes. Pull off and discard small outer leaves from bases of artichokes. With scissors, cut off and discard remaining thorny tips from outer leaves. Trim and discard discolored stem ends, and peel stems. Cut artichokes in half lengthwise and rinse well.

3. Add the artichokes to boiling water. Return to a boil, cover, and simmer until the artichoke bottoms are tender when pierced with a fork, 14 to 18 minutes.

4. With a slotted spoon, lift artichokes from pan and set on a rimmed plate. Pour cooking liquid through a strainer into a deep bowl. Reserve spice mixture; discard all but 1⅓ cups of the cooking liquid.

5. Add spice mixture, ⅓ cup vinegar, 2 tablespoons olive oil, onion, tarragon, mustard, and garlic to cooking liquid in bowl.

6. If desired, scoop out and discard fuzzy artichoke centers. Add artichokes to bowl; mix to coat well, and add salt to taste. Turn occasionally for at least 30 minutes, or cover and chill up to 1 day, turning occasionally.

Per serving: 60 cal., 42% (25 cal.) from fat; 2.3 g protein; 2.8 g fat (0.4 g sat.); 7.7 g carbo (2.6 g fiber); 118 mg sodium; 0 mg chol.

Country Pork and Pistachio Terrine

PREP AND COOK TIME: About 1¼ hours, plus at least 5½ hours to cool and chill

NOTES: If making up to 1 day ahead, cover and chill. To serve, cut slices

from terrine and layer on bread with butter, green peppercorn mustard, fig tapenade, and lettuce to make either open-faced or closed sandwiches.

MAKES: 8 servings

- 3 tablespoons **butter** or margarine
- 1 **onion** (¾ lb.), peeled and chopped
- 2 cloves **garlic,** peeled and pressed or minced
- 1 teaspoon **dried thyme**
- 1 teaspoon **ground coriander**
- ¼ teaspoon **ground allspice**
- ¼ teaspoon **white pepper**
- 1½ pounds **ground lean pork**
- 2 **large eggs**

  About 1 teaspoon **salt**
- ¾ cup **all-purpose flour**
- 1 cup **milk**
- ½ cup **shelled salted roasted pistachios**
- 1 can (10 oz.) **condensed beef consommé**
- 1 envelope (about 2½ teaspoons) **unflavored gelatin**
- 2 **fresh** or dried **bay leaves**
- 10 to 15 **black peppercorns**

1. In a 10- to 12-inch frying pan over medium-high heat, stir butter, onion, and garlic often until onion is limp, 5 to 7 minutes. Stir in thyme, coriander, allspice, and white pepper. Remove from heat.

2. In a bowl, with a mixer on medium speed, beat pork, eggs, 1 teaspoon salt, and flour until well blended. Add milk and onion mixture; beat until blended. Stir in pistachios.

3. Spoon the meat mixture into an oiled 8- to 9-cup terrine or deep casserole, or a 5- by 9-inch loaf pan. Spread mixture level; seal with foil or casserole cover.

4. Bake in a 350° oven until a thermometer inserted in center of terrine reaches 155° (or terrine is no longer pink in center; cut to test), about 1 hour. Uncover and let cool at least 1 hour. Cover and chill until cold, at least 3 hours, or up to 1 day. Scrape off and discard any solid fat from meat.

5. Pour ¼ cup consommé into a 1- to 2-quart pan. Add gelatin and stir mixture over medium-low heat until gelatin is dissolved, about 2 minutes,

then stir in remaining consommé. Pour over terrine. Rinse and dry bay leaves and lay on terrine; sprinkle evenly with peppercorns. Cover and chill until consommé is firm, at least 1½ hours.

6. Slice terrine crosswise in casserole; use a wide spatula to lift out slices. Add salt to taste.

Per serving: 424 cal., 64% (270 cal.) from fat; 22 g protein; 30 g fat (11 g sat.); 17 g carbo (1.8 g fiber); 664 mg sodium; 130 mg chol.

Green Peppercorn Mustard

PREP TIME: About 5 minutes

NOTES: If making up to 1 week ahead, cover and chill.

MAKES: About ½ cup

Mix ½ cup **Dijon mustard** with 1 tablespoon coarsely chopped drained **canned green peppercorns.**

Per tablespoon: 15 cal., 0% (0 cal.) from fat; 0 g protein; 0 g fat; 0 g carbo; 398 mg sodium; 0 mg chol.

Fig Tapenade

PREP AND COOK TIME: About 10 minutes

NOTES: Craig Schauffel, chef-owner of Pairs in Napa, adds figs to brighten a traditional olive tapenade. If making up to 1 day ahead, cover and chill.

MAKES: About 1 cup

- ½ pound **ripe black figs**
- 2 tablespoons **sugar**
- ¾ cup drained **pitted calamata olives,** coarsely chopped
- 6 canned **anchovy fillets,** drained
- 2 teaspoons drained **capers**
- 1 teaspoon **dried tarragon**
- 2 tablespoons **extra-virgin olive oil**

1. Rinse the figs, trim off and discard stems, and coarsely chop fruit. In a 1- to 2-quart pan over medium-high heat, combine figs, sugar, and 1 tablespoon water. Stir occasionally until mixture is boiling gently and figs turn shiny and darker, 3 to 5 minutes.

2. In a food processor or a blender, whirl fig mixture, olives, anchovies, capers, tarragon, and olive oil until coarsely puréed, scraping container sides as necessary. Scrape mixture into a small bowl.

Per tablespoon: 54 cal., 59% (32 cal.) from fat; 0.6 g protein; 3.6 g fat (0.5 g sat.); 5.2 g carbo (0.5 g fiber); 185 mg sodium; 0.8 mg chol.

Prosciutto and Spinach Torta

PREP AND COOK TIME: About 1 hour

NOTES: If making up to 1 day ahead, cover and chill. Bring to room temperature to serve. This bright green quiche-like torta was inspired by a creation from Antonia Allegra of St. Helena.

MAKES: About 6 servings

About 2 quarts (6 oz.) **spinach leaves,** rinsed and drained

$^1\!/_2$ cup coarsely chopped **green onions**

5 **large eggs**

1 cup **half-and-half** (light cream)

$^1\!/_3$ cup **grated parmesan cheese**

2 tablespoons **all-purpose flour**

$^1\!/_4$ teaspoon **ground nutmeg**

About $^1\!/_4$ teaspoon **salt**

$^1\!/_8$ teaspoon **pepper**

4 to 5 ounces **thin-sliced prosciutto**

1 **refrigerated pastry for a single-crust 9-inch pie** ($^1\!/_2$ of a 15-oz. package), at room temperature

1. Coarsely chop spinach leaves. In a food processor or blender, whirl

Prosciutto and Spinach Torta

spinach, green onions, eggs, half-and-half, cheese, flour, nutmeg, $^1\!/_4$ teaspoon salt, and pepper until smooth.

2. Line an oiled 9-inch pie pan smoothly with foil, overlapping pan rim; oil foil. Cover foil with prosciutto, slices overlapping so there are no gaps. Slowly pour in spinach mixture. Gently lay pastry round on filling (it's soupy; avoid getting filling on top of pastry). Fold excess pastry under itself flush with pan rim; press around edges with a fork.

3. Bake in a 350° oven until crust is golden brown and a slender wood skewer inserted into center comes out clean, 40 to 45 minutes (30 to 35 minutes in a convection oven). Cool on a rack at least 20 minutes. Invert a plate over torta; holding pan and plate together, invert to release torta onto plate. Peel off foil. Serve warm or at room temperature, cut into wedges.

Per serving: 357 cal., 58% (207 cal.) from fat; 16 g protein; 23 g fat (9.6 g sat.); 22 g carbo (1.3 g fiber); 804 mg sodium; 220 mg chol.

California Vegetable Sandwiches with Rosé

Assortment of Olives

Marinated Grilled Vegetable Sandwiches*

Radishes and Cherry Tomatoes

Dry Rosé

Thin Ginger Cookies with Lemon Curd and Raspberries

Raspberry Eau-de-Vie or Sparkling Wine (Blanc de Noir)

*Recipe provided

A chilled light, dry, fruity rosé suits these sandwich makings perfectly. For a quick, elegant dessert, spoon the lemon curd onto ginger cookies and top each with a few raspberries. Accompany with a fragrant eau-de-vie or chilled sparkling wine.

Marinated Grilled Vegetable Sandwiches

PREP TIME: About 10 minutes

NOTES: If using firm, crusty, coarse-textured bread such as ciabatta or pane francese, you can make the sandwiches at home up to 4 hours ahead; cover and chill. Otherwise, transport bread, arugula, cheese, and marinated vegetables separately, and let everyone assemble their own sandwiches on-site.

MAKES: 4 servings

1 loaf (1 lb.) **herb-flavor** or plain **focaccia,** ciabatta, or pane francese bread (1 to 1$^1\!/_2$ in. thick)

1 to 2 ounces **arugula** or watercress sprigs, rinsed and crisped

1 pound **fresh mozzarella** or fresh chèvre (goat) **cheese,** thinly sliced

Marinated grilled vegetables (recipe follows)

Salt and **pepper**

1. Cut focaccia into 4 equal pieces, then split each piece in half horizontally.

2. Lay arugula evenly over cut sides of focaccia bottoms. Arrange cheese slices evenly over arugula. Top equally with grilled vegetables and moisten with some of the marinade. Add salt and pepper to taste, and cover with focaccia tops.

Per serving: 914 cal., 54% (495 cal.) from fat; 41 g protein; 55 g fat (23 g sat.); 67 g carbo (5.9 g fiber); 1,053 mg sodium; 106 mg chol.

Marinated Grilled Vegetables

PREP AND COOK TIME: About 35 minutes
NOTES: If making up to 2 days ahead, cover and chill. Bring to room temperature to serve.
MAKES: 4 servings

- 1 **eggplant** ($^3/_4$ lb.)
- 2 **red bell peppers** (1 lb. total)
- 1 **red onion** ($^1/_2$ lb.)

  About 6 tablespoons **extra-virgin olive oil**

- 3 tablespoons **balsamic vinegar**
- $^1/_4$ cup chopped **fresh basil** leaves
- 1 clove **garlic**, peeled and pressed or minced

  Salt and **pepper**

1. Rinse eggplant and peppers; pat dry. Trim and discard eggplant stem; cut eggplant crosswise into $^1/_2$-inch-thick slices. Peel onion and cut crosswise into $^1/_2$-inch-thick slices. Brush eggplant slices, peppers, and onion slices with about 2 tablespoons olive oil total.

2. Lay vegetables in a single layer on a barbecue grill over a solid bed of hot coals or high heat on a gas grill (you can hold your hand at grill level only 2 to 3 seconds); close lid on gas grill. Cook, turning as needed to char all sides, 8 to 12 minutes total. Transfer to a bowl; let stand until cool, about 15 minutes.

3. Meanwhile, in a small bowl, mix $^1/_4$ cup olive oil, vinegar, basil, and garlic.

4. Peel, stem, and seed peppers. Quarter lengthwise.

5. In a deep dish (at least 4-cup capacity), layer vegetables with herb marinade (using all the marinade) and salt and pepper to taste. Cover and let stand 30 minutes to 4 hours, or cover and chill up to 2 days.

Per serving: 252 cal., 75% (189 cal.) from fat; 2.8 g protein; 21 g fat (3 g sat.); 17 g carbo (3.8 g fiber); 12 mg sodium; 0 mg chol.

Napa Valley wine guide

The words *Napa Valley* conjure the image of a major wine region. Well, it is and it isn't. Napa Valley is certainly the most prestigious wine region in the United States, but it's nowhere near major when it comes to size. Amazingly, Napa Valley produces only 4 percent of all wine made in California.

But what a delicious 4 percent! From this 35-mile-long, 1- to 5-mile-wide strip of land come many of the most sophisticated and sought-after wines in America. The reasons for this are numerous.

Napa Valley is an ideal place to grow grapes. The climate is neither too warm nor too cold, and the valley is geographically complex (it includes at least 83 major soil types). And Napa Valley winemakers are arguably the most ambitious and well capitalized in the United States. Critics say Napa Valley has an ego, but what it really has is a gargantuan appetite for life. You can taste it in the wines.

Twenty years ago a wide variety of grapes was planted here, but as viticultural research proceeded, certain varieties emerged as the valley's stars—above all, Cabernet Sauvignon. Right on Cabernet's heels are Merlot and, in the cooler, southern end of the valley (known as Carneros, an appellation Napa shares with Sonoma), Pinot Noir and Chardonnay.

Here is one wine lover's very short list of some of the top wines in Napa Valley and the winemakers who make them. Would that it could be three times as long. (The price is what the wine costs at the winery; wine shops may have better deals.) — *Karen MacNeil-Fife*

Beringer Howell Mountain Merlot 1996 ($75). With this wine, winemaker Ed Sbragia proves he's a texture junkie who loves wines with a thick, velvety feel.

Etude Pinot Noir 1998 ($40). Carneros is home to many sumptuous Pinots, but a favorite year in and year out is Etude's elegant, rich example, by owner Tony Soter and aptly named winemaker Scott Rich.

Joseph Phelps Insignia 1997 ($120). This majestic Bordeaux-style wine, made by Craig Williams, remains one of the valley's great classic Cabernet blends.

Markham Merlot 1998 ($21.50). For value, there's no wine I'd rather drink than winemaker Michael Beaulac's bold, supple Merlot.

Paradigm Cabernet Sauvignon 1997 ($48). Overseen by highly respected consulting winemaker Heidi Peterson Barrett (whose other clients include Screaming Eagle Winery and Grace Family Vineyards), Paradigm produces beautifully polished Cabernets.

Saintsbury Carneros Pinot Noir 1998 ($22). This irresistible wine, made by Byron Kosuge, is possibly the Carneros's juiciest Pinot.

Shafer Hillside Select Cabernet Sauvignon 1996 ($110). Winemaker Elias Fernandez is a perfectionist, and this cashmere-soft Cabernet from the valley's tiny Stags Leap District shows it.

Stellar wine shops

For the best selection of Napa Valley wines, try these shops.

Cantinetta Tra Vigne. *11:30–6 daily. 1050 Charter Oak Ave., St. Helena; 963-8888.*

Dean & DeLuca. *9–7 daily. 607 State 29 S., St. Helena; 967-9980.*

St. Helena Wine Center. *10–6 Mon-Sat, 10–5 Sun. 1321 Main, St. Helena; 963-1313 or (800) 331-1311.*

Vintage 1870 Wine Cellar. *9–6 Mon-Fri, 10–6 Sat-Sun. 6525 Washington, Yountville; 944-9070.* ◆

Slow

Let meat and veggies
bubble untended in an
electric slow-cooker;
a very satisfying supper
will be ready at the end
of the day

By Paula Freschet
Photographs by James Carrier
Food styling by Kim Konecny
and Erin Quon

cookin'

LEFT: Wine-braised pot roast
with mashed potatoes. ABOVE:
Lamb shanks with artichoke
hearts and calamata olives
(recipe, page 290) on polenta.

There was a time—30 or so years ago—when a wedding shower would produce a half-dozen Crock-Pots, easy. "A bride's best friend," they were called. And now that all things '70s are cool again, electric slow-cookers are shedding their back-of-the-cupboard spider webs and rejoining the kitchen workforce.

Curiously enough, we need them now more than ever. The two-career, two-child, two-lessons-a-day family has precious little time to produce a wholesome, appealing dinner. And this reliable appliance can save the day. The claims it made three decades ago are true: With minimal effort, you can fill a slow-cooker with vegetables and meat or poultry in the morning, give it almost no attention thereafter, and it will produce a handsome meal in the evening. The cookers require no added fat and need only a small amount of added liquid to do their job because their tight-fitting lids trap the moisture as the foods simmer gently to tenderness.

We've put together a collection of homey dishes—wine-simmered pot roast, lamb shanks with artichokes and olives, five spice pork, and more—that show how versatile slow-cookers can be. Most of the recipes are designed for a 4½- to 6-quart model; if yours is smaller, adjust ingredient amounts proportionally. For best results, the cooker should be at least half full. It must be kept covered

to retain moisture and heat.

Cooking rates vary from model to model. But lack of precision is one of the beauties of this relaxed method—30 minutes to an hour one way or the other won't significantly damage the results; if a dish you've been cooking on high is ready before you want to serve it, just turn the cooker to low to hold the food.

Merlot Pot Roast with Horseradish Smashed Potatoes

PREP AND COOK TIME: 8½ to 9½ hours on low, 5½ to 6½ hours on high

NOTES: Prepare the smashed potatoes as soon as the beef is tender; the meat can continue to cook until they're ready.

MAKES: 6 to 8 servings

- 1 **tied fat-trimmed boned beef chuck roast** (3 to 3½ lb.)
  Fresh-ground **pepper**
- 1 tablespoon **butter** or olive oil
- 3 **carrots** (about ¼ lb. each), rinsed and peeled
- 1 **onion** (½ lb.), peeled and chopped
- ⅔ cup chopped **celery**
- 3 cloves **garlic,** minced or pressed
- ½ teaspoon **dried thyme**
- ¼ teaspoon **black peppercorns**
- 1 **dried bay leaf**
- 1 cup **Merlot** or other dry red wine

⅓ cup **canned tomato paste**

1½ tablespoons **cornstarch**

Horseradish smashed potatoes (recipe follows)

1 tablespoon minced **parsley**

1 to 2 cups **watercress sprigs,** rinsed and crisped (optional)

Salt

1. Rinse beef, pat dry, and sprinkle generously all over with fresh-ground pepper. Melt butter in a 10- to 12-inch nonstick frying pan over high heat. When hot, add beef and brown well on all sides, 6 to 8 minutes total.

2. Meanwhile, cut carrots into sticks about ⅜ inch thick and 2 inches long. In a 4½-quart or larger electric slow-cooker, combine carrots, onion, celery, garlic, thyme, peppercorns, and bay leaf. Set beef on vegetables; add drippings. In a small bowl, mix wine and tomato paste; pour over meat and vegetables.

3. Cover and cook until beef is very tender when pierced, 8 to 9 hours on low, 5 to 6 hours on high. If possible, turn meat over halfway through cooking.

4. With 2 slotted spoons, transfer meat to a platter; keep warm. Skim and discard any fat from cooking liquid. Turn cooker to high. In a small bowl, blend cornstarch with 1½ tablespoons water; pour into cooker and stir often until sauce is bubbling, 10 to 15 minutes.

5. With a slotted spoon, lift vegetables from cooker and arrange beside meat. Spoon horseradish smashed potatoes onto platter; sprinkle with parsley. Garnish platter with watercress. Spoon sauce over meat. Slice meat and serve with vegetables, potatoes, and sauce, adding salt to taste.

Per serving without potatoes: 314 cal., 40% (126 cal.) from fat; 34 g protein; 14 g fat (5.6 g sat.); 11 g carbo (2.3 g fiber); 256 mg sodium; 115 mg chol.

Horseradish smashed potatoes. Scrub and peel 3 to 3½ pounds **russet potatoes;** cut into 1½-inch chunks. Put them in a 4- to 5-quart pan with 2½ quarts **water.** Bring to a boil over high heat; reduce heat, cover, and simmer until potatoes mash easily when pressed, 20 to 25 minutes.

When potatoes are done, heat 1 to 1½ cups **half-and-half** (light cream) or fat-skimmed chicken broth with 2 tablespoons **butter** or margarine in a microwave-safe container in a microwave oven at full power (100%) just until steaming (don't boil), 1 to 3 minutes. Or warm in a 1- to 1½-quart pan over medium heat.

While cream heats, drain potatoes and mash in pan with a mixer or potato masher until almost smooth. Add cream, a portion at a time, and mix until potatoes have the consistency desired. Stir in **salt, pepper,** and 1 to 2 tablespoons **prepared horseradish** to taste. Mound beside **Merlot pot roast** (preceding) or scrape into a bowl. Makes 6 to 7 cups; 6 to 8 servings.

Per serving: 189 cal., 31% (59 cal.) from fat; 3.9 g protein; 6.6 g fat (3.9 g sat.); 29 g carbo (2.6 g fiber); 55 mg sodium; 19 mg chol.

Lamb Shanks with Artichoke Caponata

PREP AND COOK TIME: 6¾ to 7¼ hours on low, 4¾ to 5¼ hours on high

NOTES: Serve with soft polenta or hot cooked orzo (rice-shaped) pasta. For an additional rich touch, sprinkle servings of shanks with toasted pine nuts.

MAKES: 4 servings

4 **lamb shanks** (3¾ to 4¼ lb. total), bones cracked

Fresh-ground pepper

1 **onion** (½ lb.), peeled and chopped

1 **red bell pepper** (½ lb.), rinsed, stemmed, seeded, and thinly sliced

1 cup thinly sliced **celery**

1 box (8 oz.) **frozen artichoke hearts**

1 cup drained **pitted calamata olives**

1 tablespoon drained **capers**

1 teaspoon **dried basil**

1 can (14½ oz.) **diced tomatoes**

1½ tablespoons **red wine vinegar**

1½ tablespoons **cornstarch**

2 tablespoons chopped **parsley**

1. Rinse shanks, pat dry, and arrange slightly apart in a 10- by 15-inch pan; sprinkle all over with pepper.

2. Bake shanks in a 450° oven until well browned, 20 to 30 minutes.

3. Meanwhile, in a 4½-quart or larger electric slow-cooker, combine onion, bell pepper, celery, artichoke hearts, olives, capers, and basil. Set shanks on vegetables in cooker. Add tomatoes with juice, vinegar, and any lamb juices from baking pan.

4. Cover and cook until lamb is very tender when pierced with a fork, 6 to 6½ hours on low, 4 to 4½ hours on high.

5. With a slotted spoon, transfer each shank to a wide, shallow bowl and keep warm. Skim and discard fat from cooking liquid. Turn cooker to high. In a small bowl, mix cornstarch with 1½ tablespoons water; pour into cooker and stir often until sauce is bubbling, about 10 minutes. Spoon sauce and vegetables over lamb, and sprinkle portions with parsley.

Per serving: 834 cal., 56% (468 cal.) from fat; 64 g protein; 52 g fat (20 g sat.); 25 g carbo (6.4 g fiber); 1,155 mg sodium; 229 mg chol.

Drunken Rosemary Chicken with Basmati Rice

PREP AND COOK TIME: About 5½ hours on low, 3½ hours on high

MAKES: 4 to 6 servings

8 **chicken thighs** (2¾ to 3 lb. total)

Salt and fresh-ground **pepper**

6 cloves **garlic,** peeled and thinly sliced

1 teaspoon coarsely chopped **fresh rosemary** leaves or dried rosemary

1 cup **Chardonnay** or other dry white wine

½ cup fat-skimmed **chicken broth**

1½ cups **precooked dried white rice**

¼ cup chopped **green onions** (including tops)

Rosemary sprigs, rinsed

1. Rinse thighs and pat dry. Pull off and discard skin; trim off and discard lumps of fat. Sprinkle thighs lightly with salt and pepper.

2. Place thighs in a 4½-quart or larger electric slow-cooker. Sprinkle with garlic and chopped rosemary; pour wine and broth over chicken.

3. Cover and cook until meat pulls easily from the bone, about 5 hours on low, 3 hours on high.

4. Skim and discard fat from juices. Add rice and mix to moisten evenly. Turn cooker to high; cover and cook, stirring several times, until rice is just tender to bite, about 5 minutes. Spoon chicken and rice onto a platter. Sprinkle with onions and garnish with rosemary sprigs. Add salt and pepper to taste.

Per serving: 242 cal., 17% (42 cal.) from fat; 26 g protein; 4.7 g fat (1.2 g sat.); 21 g carbo (0.6 g fiber); 113 mg sodium; 99 mg chol.

Turkey Thigh and Hominy Chili

PREP AND COOK TIME: 6¾ to 7¾ hours on low, 4¾ to 5¾ hours on high

NOTES: Serve with warm cornbread.

MAKES: 6 to 8 servings

1 **onion** (½ lb.), peeled and chopped

1 **red bell pepper** (½ lb.), rinsed, stemmed, seeded, and chopped

6 cloves **garlic,** peeled and minced or pressed

1 **fresh jalapeño chili,** rinsed, stemmed, seeded, and minced

1 tablespoon **chili powder**

1½ teaspoons **dried oregano**

1½ teaspoons **ground cumin**

2 or 3 **turkey thighs** (about 3 lb. total)

1 can (15 oz.) **hominy** (yellow or white), rinsed and drained

1 can (28 oz.) **crushed tomatoes in purée** or chopped tomatoes

Shredded jack cheese

Canned sliced black ripe olives

Thinly sliced **green onions**

Salt and **pepper**

1. In a 4½-quart or larger electric slow-cooker, mix the onion, bell pepper, garlic, jalapeño, chili powder, oregano, and cumin.

2. Pull off and discard skin from turkey thighs; trim off and discard fat. Rinse thighs and lay on vegetables in cooker. Pour hominy and tomatoes with juice over turkey.

3. Cover and cook until turkey pulls easily from the bone, 6 to 7 hours on low, 4 to 5 hours on high. If possible, turn meat over about halfway through cooking.

4. With a slotted spoon, transfer turkey to a plate. Skim and discard any fat from cooking liquid. When turkey is cool enough to handle, in about 10 minutes, discard bones and tear meat into large chunks. Return meat and juices to cooker; cover and cook until hot, 10 to 15 minutes.

5. Spoon turkey chili into wide bowls. Top portions as desired with cheese, olives, and green onions. Add salt and pepper to taste.

Per serving: 209 cal., 21% (43 cal.) from fat; 22 g protein; 4.8 g fat (1.4 g sat.); 19 g carbo (3 g fiber); 359 mg sodium; 73 mg chol.

Shredded Five Spice Pork

PREP AND COOK TIME: 8 to 9 hours on low, 6 to 7 hours on high

NOTES: The hot meat can also be mounded on plates and accompanied with cooked vegetables, rice, and hoisin or Chinese plum sauce. The five spice blend and hoisin sauce are available in most supermarkets; Chinese black vinegar is available in well-stocked supermarkets and Asian grocery stores.

MAKES: 6 to 8 servings

1 **pork shoulder** or butt (3½ to 4 lb.), fat-trimmed

4 cloves **garlic,** peeled and minced or pressed

1 tablespoon **Chinese five spice**

¼ cup **sugar**

¼ cup **soy sauce**

1 tablespoon **Chinese black vinegar** or balsamic vinegar

12 to 16 **flour tortillas** (7 to 8 in.)

About 3 cups finely shredded **Napa** or green **cabbage**

About 1 cup sliced **green onions** (including tops)

Cilantro sprigs, rinsed

¾ to 1 cup **prepared hoisin** or prepared Chinese plum sauce

1. Rinse pork and cut meat in half. Place halves in a 4½-quart or larger electric slow-cooker. Sprinkle with garlic, five spice, and sugar. Add soy sauce and 1 cup water.

2. Cover and cook until pork is very tender when pierced, 7½ to 8½ hours on low, 5½ to 6½ hours on high. If possible, turn meat over halfway through cooking. With 2 slotted spoons, transfer pork to a 9- by 13-inch pan.

3. Bake in a 450° oven until well browned, 15 to 20 minutes. Using 2 forks, separate pork into shreds; discard bones and fat. Put meat in a bowl, cover, and keep warm.

4. As pork bakes, skim and discard fat from cooking liquid; pour into a 2- to 3-quart pan. Add vinegar. Bring to a boil over high heat; stir often until reduced to 1 cup, about 15 minutes.

5. Stack tortillas and seal in foil. Add to oven and bake until tortillas are warm in the center, 10 to 12 minutes. Place in a towel-lined basket.

6. Pour reduced sauce over shredded pork. Spoon some of the meat onto a warm tortilla; top with cabbage, onions, cilantro, and hoisin to taste. Fold 1 end of tortilla over filling, overlap sides to enclose, and hold shut to eat.

Per serving: 505 cal., 27% (135 cal.) from fat; 34 g protein; 15 g fat (4.5 g sat.); 53 g carbo (2.4 g fiber); 1,354 mg sodium; 97 mg chol.

Turkey thighs and hominy slow-cook with tomatoes for a simple Southwest chili.

Mustard-glazed Corned Beef with Baby Vegetables in Golden Ale Broth

PREP AND COOK TIME: $8\frac{3}{4}$ to $9\frac{3}{4}$ hours on low, $6\frac{3}{4}$ to $7\frac{3}{4}$ hours on high

MAKES: 6 to 8 servings

- 1 piece **center-cut corned beef brisket** ($3\frac{1}{2}$ to 4 lb.)
- 8 **red** or white **onions** (1 in. wide, $\frac{1}{2}$ lb. total), peeled
- 18 to 24 **baby carrots** (about 4 in. long), rinsed and peeled, or baby-cut carrots, rinsed
- 18 to 24 **Yukon Gold potatoes** (1 to $1\frac{1}{2}$ in. wide), scrubbed
- 1 teaspoon **black peppercorns**
- $\frac{1}{2}$ teaspoon **whole allspice**
- 6 **whole cloves**
- 1 **dried bay leaf**
- 2 cups **golden ale** or wheat beer
- 1 head **green cabbage** ($1\frac{1}{2}$ to 2 lb.), cored and cut into 6 or 8 wedges

  About $\frac{1}{2}$ cup **sweet-hot mustard** such as honey-Dijon

1. Trim and discard most of the fat from the surface of the brisket. Rinse meat thoroughly under cool running water, massaging to release the salty brine.

2. In a 5-quart or larger electric slow-cooker, combine onions, carrots, potatoes, peppercorns, allspice, cloves, and bay leaf. Lay meat, fattiest side up, on vegetables. Add the ale. Cover and cook until brisket is very tender when pierced, 8 to 9 hours on low, 6 to 7 hours on high. If possible, turn meat over about halfway through cooking.

3. With 1 or 2 slotted spoons, transfer brisket, fattiest side up, to a 10- by 15-inch pan. Using hot mitts, drain juice from cooker into a 5- to 6-quart pan; turn heat in slow-cooker to low to keep vegetables warm. Add cabbage to juice and bring to a boil over high heat. Cover and cook until cabbage is brighter green and barely tender when pierced, 5 to 7 minutes. Meanwhile, spread fatty side of brisket with $\frac{1}{2}$ cup mustard and broil about 6 inches from heat until surface sizzles, about 3 minutes.

4. Transfer corned beef, mustard side up, to a large platter, spoon vegetable mixture and cabbage around meat. Pour cooking juices into a pitcher. Slice brisket across the grain. Serve meat and vegetables with juices and additional mustard to add to taste.

Per serving: 563 cal., 51% (288 cal.) from fat; 33 g protein; 32 g fat (11 g sat.); 35 g carbo (5.8 g fiber); 2,694 mg sodium; 107 mg chol.

Confit of Duck Breast and Sausage Cassoulet

PREP AND COOK TIME: $6\frac{1}{2}$ to $7\frac{1}{2}$ hours on low, $5\frac{1}{2}$ to $6\frac{1}{2}$ hours on high

NOTES: For best results, boil beans first in water until almost tender to bite; at mile-high or higher altitudes, it may take 2 or more hours for the beans to reach this texture. However, you can cook the beans one day, then assemble the cassoulet and simmer in the slow-cooker the next.

MAKES: 8 servings

- 1 pound **dried Great Northern beans**
- 4 or 5 **boned duck breast halves** (2 to $2\frac{1}{2}$ lb. total)

  About 2 tablespoons **salt**
- 2 tablespoons **sugar**
- $\frac{1}{4}$ pound **thick-sliced bacon,** chopped
- 2 **onions** (about 1 lb. total), peeled and chopped
- 5 cloves **garlic,** peeled and minced or pressed
- 3 cups fat-skimmed **chicken broth**
- $\frac{3}{4}$ cup **dry red wine** such as Beaujolais Nouveau or Zinfandel
- 1 **firm-ripe tomato** (about $\frac{1}{2}$ lb.), rinsed, cored, and chopped
- 1 tablespoon chopped **fresh thyme** leaves or 1 teaspoon dried thyme
- $\frac{1}{2}$ teaspoon **pepper**
- 1 **dried bay leaf**
- $\frac{1}{2}$ pound **garlic sausages,** sliced $\frac{1}{2}$ inch thick

  Duck cracklings (recipe follows)

  Thyme sprigs, rinsed

1. Sort beans and discard debris. Rinse beans, drain, and put into a 5- to 6-quart pan with 4 quarts water. Bring to a boil over high heat, cover, reduce heat, and simmer for 1 hour. Drain beans, discarding liquid; if making up to 1 day ahead, cover and chill. Put beans in a $4\frac{1}{2}$-quart or larger electric slow-cooker.

2. Meanwhile, pull and cut skin from duck breasts; reserve skin for cracklings (cover and chill up to 1 day). Place breasts in a bowl. Add 2 tablespoons salt and the sugar, and mix; cover and chill at least 30 minutes but no longer than 1 hour. Rinse breasts well under cool running water; if making up to 1 day ahead, cover and chill. Cut meat into $\frac{1}{2}$-inch chunks.

3. In a 10- to 12-inch frying pan over medium-high heat, frequently stir ba-con until browned and crisp, about 5 minutes. Discard all but 1 tablespoon bacon drippings. Add onions and garlic to bacon; stir often until onions begin to brown, 8 to 10 minutes. Add broth and wine; bring to a boil over high heat, scraping up browned bits from pan bottom. Pour onion-broth mixture into slow-cooker with beans. Add tomato, chopped thyme, pepper, and bay leaf; mix. Place duck pieces on the beans.

4. Cover and cook until beans and duck are very tender to bite, 5 to 6 hours on low, 4 to 5 hours on high. If there is more liquid than desired, un-cover slow-cooker, turn heat to high, and simmer to concentrate the mixture, up to 30 minutes.

5. Stir sausage slices into cassoulet and cook until hot, 5 to 10 minutes. Ladle cassoulet into bowls, sprinkle equally with duck cracklings, and garnish with thyme sprigs.

Per serving without duck cracklings: 459 cal., 24% (108 cal.) from fat; 41 g protein; 12 g fat (4.1 g sat.); 46 g carbo (24 g fiber); 667 mg sodium; 128 mg chol.

Duck cracklings. Chop **reserved duck skin** (see preceding) into $\frac{1}{4}$-inch pieces. In a 10- to 12-inch frying pan over medium-high heat, frequently stir skin until crisp and golden, 5 to 8 minutes. With a slotted spoon, transfer to towels to drain. Sprinkle with **salt.** When cool, wrap airtight; chill up to 1 day. Makes $\frac{1}{3}$ to $\frac{1}{2}$ cup.

Nutridata not available.

Mushroom and Root Vegetable Potpie

PREP AND COOK TIME: $5\frac{3}{4}$ to $6\frac{1}{4}$ hours on low, $4\frac{3}{4}$ to $5\frac{1}{4}$ hours on high

NOTES: As soon as you stir cream mixture into vegetables, put pastries in the oven to bake.

MAKES: 6 servings

- $\frac{1}{2}$ cup **dried morel mushrooms** ($\frac{1}{2}$ oz.)
- 2 cups **vegetable** or fat-skimmed chicken **broth**
- 1 pound **fresh mushrooms** such as common, chanterelle, oyster, pompon, porcini, portabella, and shiitake (1 to 4 kinds)
- 1 tablespoon **butter** or margarine
- $\frac{1}{2}$ cup chopped **shallots**
- $\frac{1}{2}$ teaspoon **dried thyme**
- $\frac{1}{4}$ teaspoon **dried rubbed sage**
- 1 head **fennel** (about 4 in. wide)

An earthy medley of mushrooms and root vegetables tenderize in a slow-cooker, then join greens under a cheesy puff pastry dome.

grit. Lift out and squeeze dry. Carefully pour morel soaking broth into a glass measure without disturbing sediment; leave sediment behind and discard. Measure soaking liquid; if there's less than 1¾ cup, add enough water to make this amount. Pour into frying pan. Rinse bowl, return morels to it, cover generously with water, and squeeze morels in water to release any remaining grit. Lift out and squeeze dry; discard water. Add morels to frying pan and heat until simmering.

5. Rinse fennel; trim off and discard stalks (reserving feathery green leaves), stem end, and bruised spots. Thinly slice fennel head crosswise. Chop ¼ cup feathery leaves and reserve a few sprigs (discard remainder); cover separately and chill.

6. In a 4½-quart or larger electric slow-cooker, combine fennel, potatoes, and turnips. Pour hot mushroom mixture over vegetables; add wine. Cover and cook until vegetables are very tender when pierced, 5 to 5½ hours on low, 4 to 4½ hours on high.

7. In a small bowl, mix cornstarch and cream. Turn cooker to high. Add cornstarch mixture, reserved chopped fennel leaves, and spinach; stir occasionally until sauce is bubbling, 10 to 12 minutes. Season to taste with salt and pepper.

8. Spoon mushroom-vegetable stew into deep soup bowls (about 2-cup capacity). With a wide spatula, set a hot gruyère pastry on stew in each bowl. Garnish, if desired, with reserved sprigs of green fennel leaves.

Per serving without pastry: 225 cal., 23% (52 cal.) from fat; 6.8 g protein; 5.8 g fat (3.2 g sat.); 38 g carbo (5 g fiber); 178 mg sodium; 16 mg chol.

Gruyère pastry. On a lightly floured board, roll 6 thawed **frozen puff pastry patty shells** (10-oz. package) into 4-inch-wide rounds. Sprinkle each round with 2 tablespoons shredded **gruyère** or Swiss **cheese** (¾ cup total); sprinkle lightly with **cayenne.** With rolling pin, gently press cheese into pastry. Place rounds slightly apart on a 12- by 17-inch baking sheet. Bake in a 400° oven until browned, 8 to 10 minutes.

Per pastry: 327 cal., 63% (207 cal.) from fat; 7.9 g protein; 23 g fat (5.2 g sat.); 23 g carbo (0.8 g fiber); 165 mg sodium; 16 mg chol. ◆

1½ pounds **red thin-skinned potatoes** (1 to 1½ in. wide), scrubbed and cut in half

 3 **turnips** (2½ to 3 in. wide), rinsed, peeled, and cut into eighths

 ½ cup **dry white wine**

1½ tablespoons **cornstarch**

 ¼ cup **whipping cream**

 1 cup chopped **spinach**

 Salt and **pepper**

 Gruyère pastry (recipe follows; optional)

1. Put morels in a microwave-safe bowl; add broth and heat in a microwave oven on full power (100%) until steaming, 6 to 8 minutes. Let stand until morels are pliable, at least 10 minutes.

2. As morels soak, discard any dirt and debris from fresh mushrooms; trim and discard bruised spots and discolored stem ends (including stems from shiitakes). Quickly immerse mushrooms in water and swish to wash, then lift out and drain (avoid saturating them; they are like sponges). Cut mushrooms wider than 1 inch into ¼-inch-thick lengthwise slices; leave smaller ones whole.

3. Melt butter in a 10- to 12-inch frying pan over high heat. Add fresh mushrooms, shallots, thyme, and sage; stir often until liquid is evaporated and mushrooms are browned, 8 to 10 minutes.

4. Meanwhile, with your hand, squeeze morels in broth to release

A ghostly gathering

Bewitch friends with a spread of spellbinding treats

By Linda Lau Anusasananan • Photographs by Tucker & Hossler

fruit with the back of a large spoon several times; the seeds will fall out.

MAKES: **8 servings**

- 3 quarts **salad mix** (about 10 oz.), rinsed and crisped
  About ¾ cup **pomegranate** seeds (see notes)
- 3 tablespoons **rice vinegar**
- 2 tablespoons **orange juice**
- 2 teaspoons **honey**
- 2 teaspoons **Dijon mustard**
  Salt and **pepper**

1. Place salad mix in a wide bowl and sprinkle with pomegranate seeds.
2. In a small bowl, mix rice vinegar, orange juice, honey, and mustard. Pour over salad; mix. Add salt and pepper to taste.

Per serving: 27 cal., 0% (0 cal.) from fat; 0.5 g protein; 0 g fat; 5.6 g carbo (0.5 g fiber); 38 mg sodium; 0 mg chol.

Trick or treat: Meringue ghouls (left) and salad with blood-red "teeth" (above).

Summon the scarlet-clad devils, elegant princesses, ethereal angels, and audacious pirates to a ghoulish Halloween feast, costumed with tricky metaphors.

A green salad sets the scene in gruesome detail, speckled with Dracula's bloodstained teeth (pomegranate seeds). Breadsticks shaped like witches' brooms are an apt partner in first-course dark arts. Succulent chicken encircled by a garland of roast garlic keeps vampires at bay, while decapitated heads (minipumpkins filled with risotto) and bloodshot green eyes (brussels sprouts with chopped tomatoes) revel on the side. Enter the ghosts for dessert, disguised as sweet, crisp meringues, to delight kids of all ages.

Start prepping the salad and make the breadsticks, pumpkin shells, and meringues up to a day ahead so the trick isn't played on you.

Green Salad with Dracula's Teeth

PREP TIME: About 15 minutes
NOTES: Up to 1 day ahead, rinse and crisp greens, seed pomegranate, and make dressing; cover separately and chill. To seed pomegranate (use an 8- to 9-oz. one), cut in half crosswise. Around the cut edge of each half, make 4 equally spaced vertical cuts, ¾ to 1 inch long and deep. Hold 1 half, seeds down, over a deep bowl and pull the fruit open but not apart, using equal pressure from both hands. Holding the pomegranate half, seeds down, in the palm of 1 hand, whack the top of the

Broomstick Breadsticks

PREP AND COOK TIME: About 45 minutes
NOTES: If making up to 1 day ahead, cool, cover airtight, and store at room temperature. To reheat, lay breadsticks on a baking sheet or directly on rack in a 400° oven and bake until hot, about 5 minutes.
MAKES: 10 breadsticks

- 2 loaves (1 lb. each) **frozen bread dough,** thawed to room temperature
- 2 tablespoons **black sesame** or poppy **seed**
- 1½ teaspoons **kosher salt**
- 2 to 3 tablespoons **milk**

1. On a lightly floured board, pat or roll each loaf of dough into a 5- by 10-inch rectangle. With a floured knife, cut each rectangle lengthwise into 5 equal strips. From 1 end of each strip, with floured knife, make lengthwise cuts ¼ inch apart, ⅓ of the length of the strip (to create broom straws; see photo below).

2. Twist uncut portion of each strip 3 to 5 times to make broom handle. Gently lift and transfer breadsticks to an oiled 12- by 15-inch baking sheet, laying them lengthwise and about 2 inches apart. Slightly separate the "straws" at the end of each stick, and twist and pull handles several more times to make each broom about 15 inches long.

3. Mix sesame seed and salt. Brush breadsticks with milk. Sprinkle lightly with seed mixture.

Garlic heads ringing herb-roasted chickens brace trick-or-treaters for their task.

Seed–spotted witches' broomsticks are frozen bread dough in disguise.

4. Bake in a 400° oven until well browned, 12 to 18 minutes. Transfer to racks to cool. Serve warm or cool.

Per breadstick: 272 cal., 22% (59 cal.) from fat; 7.5 g protein; 6.5 g fat (1.4 g sat.); 45 g carbo (2.1 g fiber); 660 mg sodium; 5 mg chol.

Roast Chickens with Vampireproof Garlic Garland

PREP AND COOK TIME: About 1½ hours
NOTES: Eat the roast garlic with the chicken, or spread onto broomstick breadsticks.
MAKES: 8 servings

- 3 tablespoons **olive oil**
- 2 tablespoons **lemon juice**
- 2 teaspoons **dried thyme**
- 1 teaspoon **fresh rosemary** leaves or crumbled dried rosemary
- 1 teaspoon chopped **fresh sage** leaves or dried rubbed sage
  About ½ teaspoon **pepper**
- 2 **chickens** (about 4 lb. each)
- 8 heads **garlic** (each 2 in. wide)
  Rosemary sprigs, rinsed
  Salt

1. In a small bowl, mix 2 tablespoons olive oil, lemon juice, thyme, rosemary leaves, sage, and ½ teaspoon pepper.

2. Rinse chickens and pat dry. Pull off and discard lumps of fat. Rub olive oil mixture all over chickens and set birds breast up and at least 1 inch apart on a rack in a 12- by 17-inch roasting pan. Rub remaining 1 tablespoon olive oil all over garlic. Place garlic heads on rack beside chickens.

3. Roast in a 425° oven until garlic is soft when pressed, about 1 hour, and chickens are well browned and meat is no longer pink at thigh bone (cut to test), 1 to 1¼ hours; if garlic is done before chickens, transfer garlic to a dish and keep warm. Tip juices out of body cavities into roasting pan.

4. Put chickens on a large platter, surround with garlic heads, and garnish with rosemary sprigs. Keeping chickens warm, let rest 5 to 10 minutes.

5. Carve chickens. Separate garlic cloves and squeeze garlic from peels to eat with chicken. Add salt and pepper to taste.

Per serving: 635 cal., 52% (333 cal.) from fat; 59 g protein; 37 g fat (9.5 g sat.); 15 g carbo (1 g fiber); 180 mg sodium; 178 mg chol.

Risotto in Decapitated Pumpkins

PREP AND COOK TIME: About 1 hour
NOTES: Cook and seed pumpkins up to 1 day ahead; cool, cover, and chill. To reheat, set in a single layer on a rack in a pan, add about ¼ inch hot water, cover, and bake in a 350° oven until hot,

Decapitated minipumpkins ooze creamy parmesan risotto.

about 20 minutes; or steam as directed (step 1) until hot, about 6 minutes. If cooking pumpkins up to 40 minutes ahead, keep warm with steam (see step 2). Spoon freshly cooked risotto into pumpkins just before serving.

MAKES: 8 servings

- 8 **miniature pumpkins** (Jack Be Little or Munchkin; each 6 to 8 oz.) with stems
- 2 tablespoons **butter** or margarine
- 1 cup chopped **onion**
- 1½ cups **medium-grain white rice** such as pearl or arborio

   About 4½ cups fat-skimmed **chicken broth**

- ¼ cup **grated parmesan cheese**

   Salt and fresh-ground **pepper**

1. Rinse pumpkins. Pierce tops deeply with a knife or sharp fork several times. Set pumpkins upright on a rack (they can be stacked) at least 1 inch above 1½ inches water in a 14- to 15-inch wok or 6- to 8-quart pan. Cover wok and bring water to a boil over high heat. Keeping water at a boil, steam pumpkins until tender when pierced, 20 to 35 minutes, adding more boiling water to pan as needed. Remove pumpkins from pan.

2. When pumpkins are cool enough to handle, in about 5 minutes, with a small, sharp knife, cut off tops to make lids that will sit in place. Set lids aside. With a small spoon, scoop out and discard seeds without breaking pumpkin skins. To keep warm up to 40 minutes, set lids in place, return pumpkins to

rack over water in pan, cover, and adjust heat so water barely steams.

3. Meanwhile, in a 3- to 4-quart pan over medium-high heat, frequently stir butter and onion until onion is limp, 4 to 5 minutes. Add rice and stir often until it begins to turn opaque, about 3 minutes.

4. Add 4½ cups broth. Bring to a boil over high heat, stirring often. Reduce heat and simmer rice, stirring often, until tender to bite, 15 to 20 minutes. Add a little more broth if a creamier texture is desired. Stir in cheese. Add salt and pepper to taste.

5. At once, spoon risotto into hot pumpkin shells. Top with lids.

Per serving: 227 cal., 16% (36 cal.) from fat; 9.4 g protein; 4 g fat (2.4 g sat.); 39 g carbo (0.8 g fiber); 120 mg sodium; 9.7 mg chol.

Envy Green Brussels Sprout Eyeballs

PREP AND COOK TIME: About 30 minutes
MAKES: 8 servings

- 2 pounds **brussels sprouts**
- 1 tablespoon **olive oil**
- 1 cup chopped **tomatoes**
- 2 tablespoons **balsamic vinegar**

   Salt and **pepper**

1. Trim off and discard stem ends from brussels sprouts; rinse sprouts.

2. In a 10- to 12-inch frying pan, combine olive oil and ¾ cup water; bring to a boil over high heat. Add sprouts, cover, reduce heat to medium, and

Funny—these envy green "eyeballs" taste like brussels sprouts.

shake pan occasionally until sprouts are tender when pierced, 8 to 14 minutes. Uncover and stir in tomatoes and vinegar.

3. Pour into a bowl and add salt and pepper to taste.

Per serving: 64 cal., 30% (19 cal.) from fat; 3.6 g protein; 2.1 g fat (0.3 g sat.); 10 g carbo (6.2 g fiber); 28 mg sodium; 0 mg chol.

Meringue Ghosts

PREP AND COOK TIME: About 2 hours, plus 1 hour to cool in oven
NOTES: If making up to 1 week ahead, cool, then store airtight at room temperature. Handle gently—ghosts are fragile.
MAKES: 8 to 12 ghosts

- 3 **large egg** whites
- ½ teaspoon **cream of tartar**
- ¾ cup **sugar**
- ½ teaspoon **vanilla**
- 16 to 24 **miniature semisweet chocolate chips** or pieces semisweet chocolate

1. Line 2 baking sheets (each 14 by 17 in.) with cooking parchment, or butter sheets and dust with flour.

2. In a deep bowl, with a mixer at high speed, whip egg whites and cream of tartar to a thick foam. Continuing to beat, add sugar, 1 tablespoon every 30 seconds, then whip until meringue holds very stiff peaks.

3. Beat in vanilla. If using cooking parchment, smear a little meringue on the underside of each corner to make it stick to baking sheets.

4. Spoon meringue into a pastry bag fitted with a ½-inch plain tip (or spoon into a gallon-size heavy plastic food bag, then cut off 1 corner to make a ½-inch-wide opening). Pipe meringue onto baking sheets into ghostly shapes about ¼ to ½ inch thick, 2 to 4 inches wide, and 4 to 6 inches long, spacing about 2 inches apart. To make eyes (noses and mouths, if desired) press chocolate chips lightly into meringue.

5. Bake in a 200° oven until meringues begin to turn pale gold and are firm to touch, 1¼ to 1½ hours (1 to 1¼ hours in a convection oven); switch pan positions halfway through baking. Turn off heat and leave meringues in closed oven for 1 hour.

6. Slide a spatula under meringues to release.

Per ghost: 59 cal., 4.6% (2.7 cal.) from fat; 0.9 g protein; 0.3 g fat (0.2 g sat.); 13 g carbo (0 g fiber); 14 mg sodium; 0 mg chol. ◆

The Low-Fat Cook

Healthy choices for the active lifestyle
By Christine Weber Hale

The comforts of polenta

■ They say comfort food is fattening. Well, they're wrong—at least when it comes to polenta. With very few belt-threatening fat calories, polenta cooks into a creamy porridge or bakes into crusty sticks with all the crunch you crave in fried foods. A few fresh green herbs turn it into a pretty casserole or main-dish topper for meaty portabella mushrooms.

Baking, not frying, makes golden polenta sticks extra crisp.

JAMES CARRIER

Creamy Polenta

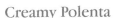

PREP AND COOK TIME: About 20 minutes

MAKES: 4 to 6 servings

In a 5- to 6-quart pan, blend 1 cup **polenta**, 2 cups fat-skimmed **chicken broth**, 1 cup **water**, and ½ cup **evaporated nonfat milk**. Stir over high heat until mixture boils, then reduce heat and simmer, stirring often, until polenta is smooth to taste, about 15 minutes. Stir in ¼ cup **shredded parmesan cheese**, and add **salt** and **pepper** to taste. Scrape polenta into a bowl and sprinkle with another ¼ cup shredded parmesan cheese.

Per serving: 232 cal., 11% (25 cal.) from fat; 12 g protein; 2.8 g fat (1.6 g sat.); 39 g carbo (4.7 g fiber); 201 mg sodium; 7.3 mg chol.

Crusty Polenta Sticks

PREP AND COOK TIME: About 1 hour, plus at least 1 hour to chill

MAKES: 4 to 6 servings

1. Follow directions for **creamy polenta** (preceding), but simmer, stirring often, until mixture is thick enough to hold a trough for about 5 seconds when you draw a spoon across the pan bottom, about 20 minutes total. Stir in all the **shredded parmesan cheese**, and add **salt** and **pepper** to taste.

2. Scrape the polenta into a lightly oiled 8-inch square pan, and spread smooth. Cover loosely and chill until firm, at least 1 hour. If making up to 1

day ahead, cover airtight and chill.

3. Quickly invert pan with polenta onto a cutting board; lift off pan. With a long, sharp knife, cut polenta into 6 or 7 equal strips (wipe knife clean frequently). Cut polenta strips in half crosswise and pull apart.

4. Put ⅓ to ½ cup **seasoned fine dried bread crumbs** on a plate. Gently roll polenta sticks, 1 at a time, in crumbs. Lay slightly apart on a lightly oiled 12- by 15-inch nonstick baking sheet. Mist sticks lightly with **cooking oil** or olive oil **spray.**

5. Bake polenta sticks in a 375° oven until browned and crusty, 45 to 50 minutes. Transfer to a platter or plates with a spatula.

Per serving: 276 cal., 17% (47 cal.) from fat; 13 g protein; 5.2 g fat (1.9 g sat.); 43 g carbo (4.9 g fiber); 376 mg sodium; 7.3 mg chol.

Herbed Polenta Spoon Bread

PREP AND COOK TIME: About 1 hour

MAKES: 6 servings

1. Follow directions for **creamy polenta** (at left), but when smooth to taste, stir in all the **shredded parmesan cheese,** ¼ cup minced **fresh chives** or green onions, 2 teaspoons minced **fresh sage** leaves or ½ teaspoon dried rubbed sage, and **salt** and **pepper** to taste.

2. While polenta cooks, in a deep bowl, with a mixer on high speed, whip 4 **large egg** whites until they hold soft peaks.

3. Remove polenta from heat and stir in 2 **large egg** yolks and about ⅓ of the whipped egg whites, then fold in remaining whites.

4. Scrape mixture into a lightly oiled shallow 1½-quart casserole (8- by 11-in. oval) and spread level.

5. Bake spoon bread in a 375° oven until well browned at the edges and lightly browned on top, about 40 minutes (about 30 minutes in a convection oven). Spoon portions onto plates.

Per serving: 270 cal., 18% (48 cal.) from fat; 15 g protein; 5.3 g fat (2.2 g sat.); 39 g carbo (4.7 g fiber); 240 mg sodium; 78 mg chol.

Polenta Spoon Bread on Portabella Mushrooms

PREP AND COOK TIME: About 1¼ hours

MAKES: 6 servings

1. Prepare **herbed polenta spoon bread** (preceding) through step 3.

2. Meanwhile, rinse 6 **portabella mushroom caps** (4½ to 5 in. wide) and pat dry. Rub tops lightly with **olive** or salad **oil** (about 2 teaspoons total). Lay caps, gill side down and side by side, in a 10- by 15-inch pan. Broil 4 to 6 inches from heat until mushrooms begin to ooze juice; turn them over and broil until flexible when bent, 8 to 10 minutes total.

3. Rinse and core 1 **Roma tomato** (about 3 oz.); cut tomato crosswise into paper-thin slices.

4. Lightly oil a shallow 3-quart (9- by 13-in.) casserole. Arrange mushroom caps, gills up, in a single layer in casserole; pour mushroom juices around caps. Spread spoon bread in an even, solid layer over mushrooms. Arrange tomato slices on spoon bread.

5. Bake in a 375° oven until spoon bread is well browned at the edges and lightly browned on top, about 40 minutes (about 30 minutes in a convection oven). Cut spoon bread and mushrooms into servings. Transfer to plates with a wide spatula.

Per serving: 316 cal., 20% (63 cal.) from fat; 18 g protein; 7 g fat (2.4 g sat.); 46 g carbo (6.6 g fiber); 248 mg sodium; 78 mg chol. ◆

The Wine Guide

By Karen MacNeil-Fife

RETAIL DETAIL
How to shop for wine

■ If you've ever felt overwhelmed in a wine shop, you're not alone. Buying wine can be a little unnerving for almost anyone. A medium-size store might stock 700 or so different wines, a large establishment, 4,000 or more. So how do you thwart intimidation and make shopping for wine a comfortable experience?

•**Choose the right store.** Wine is sold everywhere from small, independent shops to larger discount beverage chains such as Beverages & More! to giant warehouses like Costco. Each has advantages and disadvantages. For example, small shops often—but not always—charge more for their wines, but in my experience, their sales staffs are more helpful and knowledgeable about wine.

For this story, I visited several big discount chains and asked a few general questions about wine. Not only did the clerks know next to nothing about wine, they also gave me blatantly wrong information. One, for instance, told me that no top California Chardonnays are fermented in oak (for the record, about 99 percent are).

If you know exactly what you want, however, discount chains may be a good option since their prices can be considerably lower, especially for wines that are expensive to begin with. But don't take this for granted! The current vintage (1997) of Joseph Phelps Insignia, one of California's

RICK MARIANI

most extraordinary Cabernet blends, costs $120 at the winery; I recently found it for $96 at a well-known discount chain—and for $90 at a small wine shop in San Francisco.

Which brings us to Costco: Insignia costs $80 at the branch near me. The big warehouses often carry dozens of great wines at good prices—but you're definitely on your own, with barely a clerk in sight. There's another concern too: temperature. In the summer, it hovers around 80° inside the Costco near me. And who knows what the temperature is in the storeroom? (By comparison, small wine shops are far more likely to have temperature-controlled back rooms.) A fine wine can be ruined by excessive heat; if I'm springing for Insignia, I want it to be in top condition.

In the end, you have to weigh price, knowledgeable help, and proper storage when deciding where to shop.

•**If you choose a wine shop with an expert staff, make a wine friend there.** Savvy clerks usually can't wait to introduce you to new wines.

•**Don't give in to intimidation,** either external (somebody else makes you feel inadequate) or internal (a little voice in your head says, "You'll never understand this"). They're both complete nonsense. Trying a new wine is really the same thing as tasting an unfamiliar food. (Remember when you didn't know what avocados, sushi, or peach ice cream tasted like?)

•**Think of wine as a way to travel.** You may not be able to trek to Tuscany or the south of France this fall, but you can get a taste of the place through Tuscan or southern French wines. Fascinated by Australia? Ask the shop clerk (your new friend) to point out a couple of classic examples of Australian wines and tell you as much as possible about them.

•**Finally, be endlessly curious.** Wine drinkers who have the courage to be inquisitive have the most fun. Remember, you're not the only one who doesn't know what's inside all those bottles. Most people don't. The best question you can ask in a wine shop is "What does this wine taste like?" Ask it a lot.

SUNSET'S STEAL OF THE MONTH

Rosemount Cabernet Sauvignon 1999 (South Eastern Australia), $11. Unlike many inexpensive Cabernet Sauvignons, this one tastes like a straightforward Cab. It's simple but has a lot of juicy cassis flavors.

— KAREN MacNEIL-FIFE

START WITH ITALY

The Italian sections of wine shops can seem especially daunting with dozens, if not hundreds, of unfamiliar names. Great treasures lurk in these aisles, though, so why not begin exploring? Here are three delicious wines to get you started.

■**Allegrini Valpolicella Classico Superiore 1998 (Veneto),** $10. While most Valpolicella is simple at best, this dramatic, exuberant wine, with complex flavors of licorice, spice, mocha, dried cherries, and vanilla, is in a class by itself.

■**Castello di Ama Chianti Classico 1997 (Tuscany),** $35. The medieval castle of the village of Ama is surrounded by vineyards, the source of this soft, earthy wine with beautiful dried-leaf flavors.

■**Prunotto Barbera d'Asti "Fiulot" 1998 (Piedmont),** $11. Piedmont is famous for expensive Barolo and Barbaresco, but most weeknights winemakers are drinking Barbera, a homey comfort wine. Prunotto's is soft but lively and flavorful. ◆

food guide

By Jerry Anne Di Vecchio • Photographs by James Carrier

A memorable apple cake from Santa Fe

Celebrate autumn with a fruit-full dessert

■ Although Martin Rios was born in Guadalajara, Mexico, where his mother had a restaurant, he grew up in Santa Fe. Here, he followed his mother's path into a food career. Then he moved on to New York and France to study and work. Now Rios is back in Santa Fe, at the Old House restaurant, where his polish shows—particularly when he weaves indigenous ingredients into the menu. He serves a moist apple cake, subtly flavored by browned butter, with a warm caramel sauce commonly known as *dulce de leche* (see "Sweet on milk," page 300) in Latin American countries. Executive chef Rios's presentation of the cake is quite dramatic, but these tender wedges are just as tasty.

Apple-Almond Browned Butter Cake

PREP AND COOK TIME: About 1½ hours

NOTES: Purchased dulce de leche (see page 300) may be too thick to pour onto the cake; warm briefly in a microwave oven to soften. If baking cake up to 2 days ahead, let cool, wrap airtight, and store at room temperature. Freeze to store longer; thaw to room temperature to serve.

MAKES: 8 to 10 servings

About 1½ cups (¾ lb.) **butter** or margarine

1¾ cups **slivered almonds**

3 cups **powdered sugar**

About 1¼ cups **all-purpose flour**

8 **large egg** whites (1⅛ cups)

1 tablespoon grated **lemon** peel

1 tablespoon grated **orange** peel

1¾ cups finely chopped peeled **Golden Delicious apples**

Warm caramel sauce (recipe follows) or purchased dulce de leche (see notes)

Vanilla ice cream

1. In a 12-inch frying pan or 5- to 6-quart pan over high heat, melt 1½ cups butter and stir often until the milk-solid particles turn golden brown, 5 to 7 minutes. Remove at once from heat and let stand until warm, 15 to 20 minutes (or nest

pan in cold water and stir often, 5 to 8 minutes).

2. Meanwhile, in a food processor, whirl ¾ cup slivered almonds to a fine powder (or finely grate with a nut grater); scrape into a large bowl. Spread remaining 1 cup slivered almonds in a 10- by 15-inch pan.

3. Bake in a 350° oven until slivered almonds are golden brown, 6 to 12 minutes. Let cool slightly, then coarsely chop.

4. To bowl with ground almonds, add toasted almonds, sugar, and 1¼ cups flour. Stir to mix well. Scrape melted butter with all browned particles into bowl; mix. Add egg whites, lemon peel, and orange peel. Beat with a mixer on medium speed, scraping bowl often, until batter is well blended. Add chopped apples and stir to mix.

5. Butter and flour a 9-inch cheesecake pan with removable rim. Scrape batter into pan.

6. Bake in a 325° oven (300° convection oven) until cake is golden brown, firm in the center when lightly pressed, and begins to pull from pan sides, 1 hour to 1 hour and 10 minutes. Let cake stand in pan on a rack at least 20 minutes or until cool, about 1 hour. Slide a thin-bladed knife between warm or cool cake and pan rim; remove rim. Set cake on a rimmed plate and, if desired, pour about ½ cup warm

caramel sauce over the top. Cut into wedges; serve with scoops of ice cream and remaining caramel sauce to add to taste.

Per serving: 613 cal., 60% (369 cal.) from fat; 9.5 g protein; 41 g fat (19 g sat.); 57 g carbo (2 g fiber); 334 mg sodium; 76 mg chol.

Warm caramel sauce. In a 3- to 4-quart pan over high heat, stir 3 tablespoons **butter** or margarine and ⅔ cup **sugar** until mixture is caramel-colored, 2 to 4 minutes. Remove from heat and add ⅔ cup **whipping cream**; stir until blended (mixture foams). Return to high heat and stir until caramel sauce comes to a rolling boil, 1 to 2 minutes. Serve hot. If making up to 1 month ahead, cover and chill. Makes 1 cup.

Per tablespoon: 81 cal., 58% (47 cal.) from fat; 0.2 g protein; 5.2 g fat (3.3 g sat.); 8.7 g carbo (0 g fiber); 25 mg sodium; 17 mg chol.

Sweet on milk

■ Folks in Latin countries to our south love caramel sweets (*dulce*) made of milk (*leche* or *arequipe*) boiled and concentrated with sugar. They call them variously *dulce de leche, manjar, dulce de arequipe,* or just *arequipe*. *Cajeta* is similar, but it's traditionally made of goat's milk instead of cow's milk. These sweets range from candy-dense caramel to sauce you can pour. Dulce de leche is spread in and over cakes, slathered onto cookies, ladled over ice cream—in fact, put with anything caramel enhances.

A fine example of Argentina's dulce de leche, made by La Paila, is imported and distributed by Golden Bridge Enterprises (877/423-3663) to well-stocked independent supermarkets, gourmet food stores, and Italian delicatessens. (La Paila makes banana- and coconut-flavored dulce de leche as well.) A 15¾-ounce jar costs about $4. Once opened, dulce de leche keeps indefinitely, if chilled airtight.

Musseling in

■ The flesh of domestic mussels is anywhere from ivory to bright orange; it's the black shells and their iridescent blue interiors that give the mussels their common names: blue and black mussels. There are several species, one of which has been on the West Coast so long that it was considered a native until experts took a closer look and discovered that it is the same as those found in the Mediterranean. (The speculation is that their ancestors fell off the boat bottoms of early explorers and made themselves right at home.) These mussels share a delicate flavor and texture that stand up surprisingly well to the intense black pepper and garlic sauce that chef-proprietor Chris Yeo makes at Straits Cafe (in San Francisco and Palo Alto). This five-ingredient Singaporean dish is as remarkably quick and easy to make as it is bold and beautiful.

Yeo's Garlic Mussels

PREP AND COOK TIME: **25 to 30 minutes**

NOTES: Chef Yeo stirs only the fresh-steamed mussels into the sauce, but I like to add the mussel-cooking juices and boil the sauce briefly to concentrate it. Oyster sauce is sold in well-stocked supermarkets and Asian food stores.

MAKES: **4 servings**

  - 3 pounds **mussels,** beards removed, scrubbed
  - 3 tablespoons **butter** or margarine
  - 3 tablespoons chopped **garlic**
  - 1½ tablespoons **cracked** or coarse-ground **pepper**
  - 6 tablespoons **prepared oyster sauce**
  - **Sourdough bread** (optional)

1. Tap the shells of any mussels that gape; if they don't close, discard. Place mussels in a 5- to 6-quart pan. Add ½ cup water, cover, and bring to a boil over high heat. Reduce heat and simmer until shells pop open, 5 to 10 minutes. Pour juices from pan and save (see notes).

2. In a 14-inch wok, 14-inch frying pan, or 5- to 6-quart pan over high heat, melt butter with garlic and pepper and stir until garlic is golden, 2 to 3 minutes. Add oyster sauce and reserved mussel-cooking liquid. Boil over high heat, stirring often, until sauce is reduced to about 1 cup, 5 to 6 minutes.

3. Pour mussels into wok; stir over high heat until well coated with sauce, 3 to 4 minutes. Ladle mussels and sauce into bowls; pluck mussels from shells and sop up sauce with bread, if desired.

Per serving mussels: 207 cal., 48% (99 cal.) from fat; 15 g protein; 11 g fat (5.8 g sat.); 12 g carbo (0.8 g fiber); 1,444 mg sodium; 51 mg chol.

Breakfast wrap

■ Burritos may not have been around as long as the hauntingly lovely archaeological sites clinging to the canyon walls in Colorado's Mesa Verde National Park, but the breakfast version—filled with scrambled eggs, sausage, onions, green chilies, and melted cheese—in the park's Far View Terrace restaurant is about as popular. The final fortification is a cheese sauce poured over the flour tortilla jacket. It will keep you going most of the day.

Mesa Verde Breakfast Burrito

PREP AND COOK TIME: 35 to 40 minutes

NOTES: Use fresh tortillas; stale ones will crack. You can also heat the burritos 1 at a time on a microwave-safe plate: Cover with microwave-safe plastic wrap and heat in a microwave oven on full power (100%) until hot, about 1½ minutes.

MAKES: 6 servings

- ½ pound **bulk pork sausage**
- 1 **onion** (½ lb.), peeled and finely chopped
- 1 can (4 oz.) **diced green chilies**
- 10 **large eggs**
  About ½ teaspoon **salt**
  About ½ teaspoon **pepper**
- 6 **flour tortillas** (10 in.)
- 2 cups **shredded cheddar cheese** (½ lb.)
  Chili con queso salsa (recipe follows)

1. In a 10- to 12-inch nonstick frying pan over medium-high heat, stir sausage, onion, and chilies until meat is crumbled and browned, about 15 minutes. Drain off and discard fat.

2. In a bowl, beat eggs to blend with ⅓ cup water, ½ teaspoon salt, and ½ teaspoon pepper. Pour eggs into meat mixture in frying pan; with a wide spatula, stir over medium-high heat, scraping pan bottom often, until eggs are set to your taste, about 3 minutes for creamy eggs.

3. Lay flour tortillas flat on a counter. Spoon an equal portion of the meat and egg mixture in a band down the center of each tortilla to within 1 inch of opposite edges. Sprinkle mixture evenly with cheese. To form each burrito, fold the bare 1-inch-wide tortilla edges over filling, then roll snugly

from an open edge to enclose. Set burritos slightly apart, seams down, in a 10- by 15-inch pan; seal pan with foil. If making up to 1 day ahead, chill.

4. Bake in a 200° oven until cheese is melted (cut a slit to test), 15 to 20 minutes; if chilled, bake in a 325° oven until hot in the center, about 15 minutes.

5. Set burritos on plates and ladle about ½ cup hot chili con queso salsa on and around each. Season to taste with salt and pepper.

Per serving: 714 cal., 55% (396 cal.) from fat; 39 g protein; 44 g fat (21 g sat.); 40 g carbo (2.8 g fiber); 1,502 mg sodium; 449 mg chol.

Chili con queso salsa. In a 2- to 3-quart pan over medium-high heat, melt 2 tablespoons **butter** or margarine. Add 2 tablespoons **all-purpose flour** and stir until bubbling. Remove pan from heat and whisk in 2 cups fat-skimmed **chicken broth** and 1 can (4 oz.) **diced green chilies**. Stir over high heat until boiling, 3 to 4 minutes. Add 1½ cups **shredded cheddar cheese** (6 oz.) and stir until melted. Serve hot, or let cool, cover, and chill up to 1 day; if chilled, stir over high heat until steaming. Makes about 3 cups.

Per ½ cup: 174 cal., 67% (117 cal.) from fat; 10 g protein; 13 g fat (8.4 g sat.); 3.5 g carbo (0.3 g fiber); 355 mg sodium; 40 mg chol.

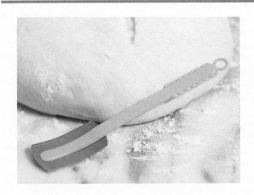

Cutting edge

■ If you bake yeast breads, add this inexpensive ($4 to $7) professional gadget to your tool wardrobe (or treat a baker friend). Best described as a double-edged razor blade with a handle, it's called a baker's blade in some cookware shops; it's a bread blade at Sur la Table (800/243-0852 or www.surlatable.com). Use the blade—hooked, angled, curved, or straight—to make clean cuts through soft, shaped dough so the loaves split neatly while they bake. Most of these tools come with a sheath to protect the blade—and your hands—when not in use. ◆

The capital of Chinese cuisine

For the best, most authentic Chinese food
this side of Beijing, head to the San Gabriel Valley

By Linda Lau Anusasananan

Savory soup steamed in a winter melon is one specialty (be sure to order it a day ahead) at Monterey Park's NBC Seafood Restaurant.

Are you in search of real Chinese food? Want to sample dishes you might encounter in Beijing or Shanghai, untamed by the influence of tourists? There's no need to fly across the Pacific. Some of the best Chinese food in the world can be found right here in our own backyard—in the San Gabriel Valley, the suburban expanse that spreads east of Los Angeles from Monterey Park to Rosemead. Here Chinese restaurants thrive on fierce competition. Prices are low, portions big, and quality high. For adventurous foodies, the valley is a treasure chest of exceptional eating.

Chinese immigrants poured into the San Gabriel Valley in the mid-1970s. At first the newcomers were mostly from Taiwan and Hong Kong; today many come from Mainland China. That's why the area once called Little Taipei now wears the nicknames Little Shanghai and Little Beijing.

Why is the food so superb here? According to Chinese cooking teacher Cynthia Woo, some of the new immigrants were chefs in Asia. But with easier access to quality ingredients in Southern California, they can rival or surpass the cooking of their homelands.

It helps to pretend you're in Asia when exploring the area. Chinese, especially Mandarin, is the prevalent language. Most restaurants have an English menu, but many words get

Chinese restaurants thrive

on fierce competition.

Prices are low, portions big,

and quality high.

lost in translation. Daily specials may be written only in Chinese. Ask a waiter to suggest a few choices or check what's swimming in the fish tanks—specials often include live seafood priced by the pound.

Prices are modest: Eating the same meal in Hong Kong or Taiwan could cost double or triple the tab here. Many restaurants offer bargain-priced lunch specials starting at $2.99. These generously portioned meals almost guarantee enough leftovers for another meal at home. Dinner is also a good buy. Still, if you're on a tight budget, check the prices for live seafood, specials, and rare delicacies before ordering: These can catapult the bill out of the cheap category.

Instead of offering lunch specials, some restaurants serve dim sum— the appetizer-size portions of meat or seafood dumplings, filled buns, and sweets. Servers bring carts and trays of these delicacies to your table. If you don't understand what's being offered, ask to see what's under the lid and point to what you want. Restaurants generally serve this Cantonese meal from midmorning through early afternoon.

Here is *Sunset's* sampling of the San Gabriel Valley's best. All are open daily for lunch and dinner; menus are subject to change. Area code is 626.

888 Seafood Restaurant. Large, spacious marble-trimmed dining room offers Chiu Chiao cuisine (from a county in the southern province of Canton). Try specialties like the spiced goose, house special shrimp with soy sauce and green onions, and crisp-skinned kim-lin special duck. Dim sum draws especially large crowds on weekends. *8450 Valley Blvd. #121, Rosemead; 573-1888.*

Deerfield Garden Restaurant. This eight-table eatery is noteworthy for its homestyle Northern Chinese specialties such as fried lamb with garlic leeks, Mandarin bean curd (a tofu omelet), or mu shu pork. Wheat in the form of noodles or breads is preferred to rice as a starch. Try savory pastries such as the green chive turnover or *jing dong* (lamb) pie. *130 S. Atlantic Blvd. (Deerfield Park Plaza), Monterey Park; 284-3867.*

Happy Family Restaurant III. Meat lovers won't balk at eating at the vegetarian Happy Family. Dishes that mock meat, such as deep fried house chicken (actually mushrooms), truly taste like the real thing. Fried taro becomes pork spareribs in sweet and sour sauce, and vegetables show off in inspired pairings like lotus root with snow peas. *608 N. Atlantic, Monterey Park; 282-8986.*

Juon Yuan Restaurant. This second-floor mall restaurant serves a varied selection of Sichuan dishes. Try five-spice beef rolled in a pan-browned pancake with hoisin sauce. Wonton in red-hot oil isn't as searing as it sounds: Mild red chili oil and tongue-tingling Sichuan peppercorns cloak silky-textured pork won-

tons. For contrast, try the delicate ice fish with yellow chive dumplings. *140 W. Valley Blvd. #210, Focus Plaza (San Gabriel Square), San Gabriel; 288-9955.*

J.Z.Y. Cafe. This charming cafe invites adventurous diners with its jade green and coral red walls, bamboo bird cages, and carved wood

Crispy taro-paste rolls and minced dates soft cake are desserts at Shiang Garden.

furniture. Why adventurous? If you can't read Chinese, you'll be limited to a condensed picture-book menu. Still, the food here is wonderful. When you mix the noodles with fried diced pork and bean catsup, they explode with contrasting textures and vibrant flavors. White gourd stew with scallops is a restorative light broth with chunks of mild winter melon and shreds of dried scallops. Special pastries and sweets, once served only to royalty in the Forbidden City, may be too esoteric for some Western tastes. *1039 E. Valley #102-B (Gold World Plaza), San Gabriel; 288-0588.*

King's Palace. The nondescript menu names belie the complexity of the Shanghai dishes offered here. Order sponge gourd with crabmeat paste—silky pale jade green batons of fresh loofah squash (when dried, it becomes a sponge) topped with a golden crab sauce. "Vegetable deluxe" translates as braised vegetable-filled bean-curd skin rolls nestled with a bed of fava beans in a rich brown sauce. House hot shredded beef is a mound of beef stir-fried with slivers of hot chili. *250 W. Valley #M (Life Palace Center), San Gabriel; 282-9566.*

Lincoln Plaza Garden Restaurant. Bargain prices ($1.50 to $5.00 per dish) for well-seasoned and generous portions of Cantonese dim sum, wheeled to your table on a parade of carts. *Lincoln Plaza Hotel, 123 S. Lincoln Ave., Monterey Park; 288-1312.*

NBC Seafood Restaurant. The best option at this perennial favorite is to select live seafood. The waiter will net your choice and bring it to you for approval. Price is based on weight; you choose the cooking method. On weekends, the extensive variety of dim sum attracts long lines—try to arrive by 11:30 for the best selection. *404-A S. Atlantic, Monterey Park; 282-2323.*

Shiang Garden Restaurant (formerly Charming Garden). An elegant setting for exquisite food that defies the stereotype that all Hunan food is searingly hot. Order fish fillet with supreme broth and watch the tableside show as raw fish and lettuce are melded into a light, refreshing soup. Don't miss the ham in honey sauce or the smoked pomfret. The kitchen takes justifiable pride in its smooth, succulent fried fresh black mushrooms with garlic sauce. *111 N. Atlantic #351 (Atlantic Place Shopping Center), Monterey Park; 458-4508.* ◆

Kitchen Cabinet

Readers' recipes tested in Sunset's kitchens

By Andrew Baker

Maple syrup sweetens French toast toppings of peanut butter and vanilla yogurt.

Apple Crisp French Toast

Lonnie Spin, Sunnyvale, California

Lonnie Spin knew that her experiment of French toast with peanut butter and yogurt was one ingredient shy of a culinary breakthrough. "I kept saying, 'You know what this needs—it needs apple.'" Sure enough, apples, grown by her uncle and thinly sliced, turned the dish into a family hit.

PREP AND COOK TIME: About 35 minutes

MAKES: 6 servings

- 1 cup **low-fat** or nonfat **milk**
- 4 **large eggs**
- 2 teaspoons firmly packed **brown sugar**
- ¼ teaspoon **ground cinnamon**
- ¼ teaspoon **vanilla**
- 1 **Granny Smith apple** (about ½ lb.)

    About 1 tablespoon **lemon juice**

    About 2 tablespoons **butter** or margarine

- 12 slices **egg** or white **bread** (about 1 lb. total)
- ⅔ cup **maple syrup**
- ½ cup **vanilla-flavor nonfat yogurt**
- ½ cup **smooth peanut butter**
- ½ cup **granola**

1. In a shallow pan such as a 8- or 9-inch pie pan, whisk to blend milk, eggs, brown sugar, cinnamon, and vanilla.

2. Rinse apple, core, and cut into ⅛-inch-thick slices. In a small bowl, mix apple slices with lemon juice.

3. In a 10- to 12-inch nonstick frying pan over medium-high heat, melt 1 tablespoon butter. Dip 1 bread slice at a time in milk mixture, turn over, and transfer to frying pan without crowding. Cook each batch, turning to brown both sides, about 6 minutes total. As done, set in a single layer on a 14- by 17-inch baking sheet and keep warm in a 200° oven. Add remaining butter to frying pan as needed to cook successive batches.

4. Meanwhile, in a small bowl, mix ⅓ cup maple syrup with yogurt.

5. Also, in a 1-cup glass measure, mix remaining ⅓ cup maple syrup and peanut butter. Heat in a microwave oven at full power (100%) until warm, about 30 seconds, stirring once or twice.

6. Place 2 slices of French toast on each plate. Drain apple slices and lay fruit equally onto toast; sprinkle with granola. Spoon maple-yogurt and peanut butter sauces equally onto portions.

Per serving: 626 cal., 36% (225 cal.) from fat; 21 g protein; 25 g fat (7.7 g sat.); 82 g carbo (4.5 g fiber); 596 mg sodium; 193 mg chol.

Salmon with Marmalade-Balsamic Sauce

Jenifer-Joan Lauren,
Maple Valley, Washington

"I started experimenting with balsamic vinegar," Jenifer-Joan Lauren says, "and wanted to use it in more things." She often serves salmon, and the vinegar soon became an integral part of a sauce for the fish. If desired, garnish portions with small rosemary sprigs.

PREP AND COOK TIME: About 25 minutes

MAKES: 4 servings

- 1 **boned salmon fillet** (1¼ lb.; maximum 1½ in. thick)

    About ¼ teaspoon fresh-ground **pepper**

- 1 teaspoon minced **fresh rosemary** leaves or crumbled dried rosemary
- ⅓ cup **orange marmalade**
- ⅓ cup **balsamic vinegar**
- ½ cup thin slices **red onion**

    Salt

1. Rinse salmon, pat dry, and lay skin down in a lightly oiled shallow 3-quart casserole (about 9 by 13 in.). Rub ¼ teaspoon pepper over salmon.

2. Bake in a 400° oven until fish is opaque but still moist-looking in center of thickest part (cut to test), about 15 minutes.

3. Meanwhile, in a 1- to 1½-quart pan over high heat, combine rosemary, marmalade, balsamic vinegar, and onion. Boil, stirring often, until reduced to ½ cup.

4. Cut salmon into equal pieces; use a wide spatula to transfer to plates. Spoon onion mixture over and around salmon. Add salt to taste.

Per serving: 336 cal., 40% (135 cal.) from fat; 29 g protein; 15 g fat (3.1 g sat.); 20 g carbo (0.4 g fiber); 102 mg sodium; 84 mg chol.

Melon Salad

Nancee Melin, Tucson

"Living in Arizona, I take advantage of all the fruit," Nancee Melin says, "and I'm a big salad fan." Using her favorites from the produce market, she constructed this wholesome, fresh combination.

PREP AND COOK TIME: About 40 minutes

MAKES: 5 or 6 servings

- ½ teaspoon grated **fresh ginger**
- ½ teaspoon grated **lime** peel
- 2 tablespoons minced **fresh cilantro**
- 3 tablespoons **lime juice**
- ¼ cup **orange juice**
- ½ cup **plain low-fat** or nonfat **yogurt**

    Hot sauce

- 1 **cantaloupe** or honeydew melon (3½ to 4 lb.)
- 2 **oranges** (about 1 lb. total)
- 1 **firm-ripe avocado** (about ½ lb.)
- 1 cup matchstick-size pieces **jicama**
- ⅓ cup **salted roasted pistachios**, coarsely chopped

    Salt

1. In a bowl, whisk to blend fresh ginger, lime peel, cilantro, lime juice, orange juice, and yogurt. Add hot sauce to taste.

2. Rinse melon, cut in quarters, and discard seeds. Cut off and discard melon peel. Thinly slice melon and arrange equally on plates.

3. Rinse oranges; cut off and discard peel and white membrane. Cut between segments and membrane to re-lease fruit. Arrange orange segments equally with melon.

4. Peel and pit avocado. Cut lengthwise into ¼-inch-thick slices. Arrange slices equally on plates. Scatter jicama pieces onto plates, spoon yogurt dressing over salads, and sprinkle with pistachios. Add salt to taste.

Per serving: 186 cal., 42% (78 cal.) from fat; 4.5 g protein; 8.7 g fat (1.3 g sat.); 26 g carbo (4.7 g fiber); 85 mg sodium; 1.1 mg chol.

Heavenly Scones

Judy Burk, Oakland, California

"I like hazelnut and chocolate together," Judy Burk says. Her scones—moist and light—have a tender cake texture.

PREP AND COOK TIME: About 1 hour

MAKES: 8 scones

    About 2¾ cups **all-purpose flour**

- ¾ cup **mini-** or coarsely chopped **semisweet chocolate chips**
- 1 tablespoon **baking powder**
- ½ teaspoon **baking soda**

    About ½ cup (¼ lb.) **butter** or margarine, at room temperature

    About ½ cup **sugar**

- 1 **large egg**
- ¾ cup **buttermilk**
- 3 tablespoons **hazelnut-flavor liqueur,** such as Frangelico

1. In a large bowl, stir together 2¾ cups flour, chocolate chips, baking powder, and baking soda.

2. In another bowl with a mixer on medium-high speed, beat ½ cup butter with ½ cup sugar until fluffy; beat in egg. Stir in buttermilk and liqueur.

3. Scrape butter mixture into dry ingredients; stir just until evenly moistened. Sprinkle 1 teaspoon sugar over bottom of a buttered 9-inch pie pan. Scrape dough into center of pan; sprinkle another 1 to 2 teaspoons sugar onto dough. Pat gently into an 8-inch-wide round. With a floured knife, cut through dough to pan to make 8 equal triangles.

4. Bake in a 350° oven until scones are golden brown and just begin to pull from pan sides, 50 to 55 minutes.

5. Slide a wide spatula under scones, then slip out onto a rack; let cool 10 minutes. Cut wedges apart and serve.

Per serving: 407 cal., 38% (153 cal.) from fat; 6.7 g protein; 17 g fat (10 g sat.); 59 g carbo (1.2 g fiber); 412 mg sodium; 59 mg chol.

Chinese Tacos

Jayne March, Stanford, California

A friend from Thailand, visiting Jayne March and her family, prepared these lettuce rolls, which can also be made with ground chicken.

PREP AND COOK TIME: About 25 minutes

MAKES: 4 servings

    Salad oil

- 1 ounce **dried thin rice noodles** (rice sticks or *mai fun*)
- 1 pound **ground lean beef**
- 1 cup finely chopped **mushrooms**
- ⅓ cup finely chopped **canned water chestnuts**
- ⅓ cup thinly sliced **green onions** (including tops)

    About 2 tablespoons **soy sauce**

- ¼ teaspoon **chili flakes** (optional)
- 1 tablespoon **cornstarch**
- 3 tablespoons **dry sherry**
- 1 pound **iceberg** or butter **lettuce,** rinsed, crisped, and separated into leaves

1. Pour about 1 inch oil into a 14-inch wok or a 5- to 6-quart pan over high heat. When oil reaches 375°, add noodles in 2 equal batches, turning over once until they puff, almost immediately. Lift from pan with a slotted spoon and drain on paper towels.

2. In a 10- to 12-inch frying pan over high heat, stir and crumble beef until small pieces. Add mushrooms, water chestnuts, green onions, 2 tablespoons soy sauce, and chili flakes. Stir often until juices evaporate and mixture is lightly browned, 5 to 7 minutes.

3. Meanwhile, in a small bowl, blend cornstarch and sherry until smooth. Add to pan and stir until mixture boils. Remove from heat and add more soy sauce to taste. Pour into a bowl. Put noodles and lettuce in separate bowls.

4. For each portion, spoon noodles and meat mixture onto a lettuce leaf and roll up to eat.

Per serving: 445 cal., 63% (279 cal.) from fat; 23 g protein; 31 g fat (10 g sat.); 16 g carbo (2 g fiber); 620 mg sodium; 85 mg chol. ◆

Crisp jicama sticks top melon salad with oranges and avocado.

Serve cranberry-poached pears with cheddar cheese as part of a spectacular feast featuring harvest bounty (see page 308).

November

OREGON
HAZELNUTS

PETER McDONALD

High atop a tractor, farmer McDonald emerges from the dense green canopy of his 75-acre hazelnut orchard along the Willamette River near Wilsonville, south of Portland. He hauls a wood tote piled with 1,300 pounds of just-gathered nuts.

"During the harvest in October, we work 12- to 14-hour days—longer if rain is expected," McDonald says. He and his son, James, mechanically sweep the ripe nuts that have fallen to the orchard floor into windrows. Then a giant machine sucks up the nuts and shoots them into the totes. At the processing plant, they're washed and dried, then sent to be shelled if their intended market requires it.

First planted in 1858, hazelnuts from the Willamette Valley account for 99 percent of the U.S. commercial crop. In a good year, McDonald and his fellow farmers together bring in as many as 38,000 tons.

McDonald finds the varying beauty of the orchard through the year irresistible—especially in January, when the trees bloom and pollinate, and brilliant yellow catkins appear on the naked branches. "It looks like someone put up a zillion Christmas tree ornaments," McDonald says. Besides, "it's fun being the brunt of all the nut jokes in the world." No amount of kidding, though, can change his opinion: "When they're roasted, hazelnuts are the best nuts by far!"

A springtime orchard full of blossoms is splendid, and a summertime field rich with grain holds a gentle grandeur. But magic happens when you pick the fruits of your labor in the fall—when the first hazelnuts ripen and drop to the ground, the Hachiya persimmons turn a shiny, bright orange, and the air is pungent with roasting wild rice. • Just listen to the farmers: "On a nice, sunny day, you can't beat the picture—it's gorgeous," Ardell McPhail says. She and her husband, Malcolm, farm 47 acres of cranberries near Ilwaco, Washington. • "We're full golden at harvest time," exults Steve Wilmeth, who tends 4,000 acres of pecan trees at historic Stahmann Farms in the Mesilla Valley near Las Cruces, New Mexico. • There's pride in these voices—personal and regional. For the West produces the majority of the nation's supply of many ingredients vital to Thanksgiving-time dishes: apples, chestnuts, grapes, hazelnuts, pears, persimmons, pomegranates, potatoes, and walnuts, to name a few. • We've combined these foods into imaginative dishes to surround your Thanksgiving turkey with a spectacular feast.

a very western
harvest feast

A glimpse of the growers and a bushel's worth of new recipes for your fall table

By Andrew Baker and Elaine Johnson

Food photographs by James Carrier

WAYNE ALDRIDGE

Sweet-Hot Glazed Nuts

PREP AND COOK TIME: About 40 minutes

NOTES: Use hazelnuts, macadamias, pecans, pistachios, walnuts, blanched almonds, or an assortment.

MAKES: 2 cups; 8 servings

- 3 tablespoons **honey**
- 1½ tablespoons **sugar**
  About 1 tablespoon melted **butter** or margarine
- ½ teaspoon **salt**
- ½ teaspoon **cayenne**
- ½ teaspoon **ground cinnamon**
- 2 cups **shelled, unsalted nuts** (whole or halves; see notes)

1. In a bowl, mix honey, sugar, 1 tablespoon butter, salt, cayenne, and cinnamon. Add nuts and mix well to coat. Scrape nut mixture into a buttered 9- by 13-inch pan and shake to make level.

2. Bake in a 300° oven, shaking pan often, until nuts are golden brown under skins (break to test, if necessary), 20 to 25 minutes.

3. Scrape nuts onto a buttered 10- by 12-inch piece of foil and let cool about 15 minutes, then break apart. Serve, or store airtight up to 3 days.

Per serving: 260 cal., 80% (207 cal.) from fat; 4.4 g protein; 23 g fat (2.4 g sat.); 14 g carbo (2.8 g fiber); 161 mg sodium; 3.9 mg chol.

RIGHT:
Cranberry-
poached
pears with
cheese.
BELOW:
Creamy wild
rice soup with
bacon.

Poached Pears with Cheddar

PREP AND COOK TIME: About 45 minutes

MAKES: 8 first-course servings

- 8 **firm-ripe Seckel** or Forelle **pears** (3 to 4 oz. each) or 4 Bosc pears (6 to 8 oz. each)
- 1½ cups **cranberry juice cocktail**
- ¼ cup **raspberry vinegar**
- ½ cup **sugar**
- 1 **slender baguette** (½ lb.)
- ¼ cup (⅛ lb.) melted **butter** or margarine
- ⅓ pound **sharp cheddar cheese,** thinly sliced
- 2 cups **watercress** sprigs, rinsed and drained

1. Peel pears, leaving stems in place.

2. In a 3- to 4-quart pan over high heat, bring cranberry juice, vinegar, and sugar to a boil; add pears. When mixture resumes boiling, reduce heat, cover, and simmer until fruit is tender when pierced, about 8 minutes (12 minutes for Bosc pears); turn fruit over halfway through cooking.

3. With a slotted spoon, transfer fruit to a rimmed plate. If using Bosc pears, cut

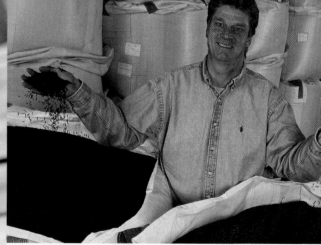

CALIFORNIA WILD RICE

DON KUIKEN "It has a pleasant, tealike smell," says Don Kuiken, operations manager for Indian Harvest Specialtifoods near Colusa, describing the aroma wafting through his processing plant. It's the wild rice roasting.

Back in the days when wild rice was, well, wild, it grew in streams and lakes. Today, all wild rice grown in the West is each in half lengthwise.

4. Boil juice mixture over high heat, stirring occasionally, until reduced to ⅔ cup, about 10 minutes.

5. Meanwhile, cut baguette diagonally into ½-inch-wide slices. Brush both sides of each slice lightly with butter. Arrange slices in a single layer on a 14-by 17-inch baking sheet. Bake in a 375° oven until golden, 10 to 12 minutes.

6. Set each whole pear upright on a plate (lay Bosc halves flat sides down). Spoon syrup equally over or around fruit. Arrange toasted baguette slices, cheese, and watercress next to pears. To eat, cut pieces of pear, dip in sauce, and combine with bites of toast, cheese, and watercress.

Per serving: 329 cal., 36% (117 cal.) from fat; 7.7 g protein; 13 g fat (7.9 g sat.); 46 g carbo (2.8 g fiber); 354 mg sodium; 36 mg chol.

Roasted Potatoes with Grape Mincemeat

PREP AND COOK TIME: About 45 minutes

NOTES: Bake the potatoes (through step 3) up to 1 day ahead; cool, cover pan, and chill. To reheat, bake, uncovered, in a 350° oven until potatoes are hot, about 5 minutes.

MAKES: 8 to 10 servings

cultivated: Farmers drop the seed from airplanes into flooded fields that mimic the natural habitat. (Given that the plant isn't even a member of the rice family—it's an annual aquatic grass—the moniker wild rice is a bit of a misnomer.)

Regardless, after growing for four months, the grain is harvested and trucked to processors. There it's cured and then either parched with dry heat or parboiled under pressure, depending on the processor's preferred technique, to gelatinize the starch. Finally, the rice is dry-roasted, cleaned, hulled, and sorted according to its intended use, in rice blends or even products like wild rice tortilla chips. The wild may have disappeared from the rice (just as it has from the West), but the spirit remains in this cultivated grain.

2 pounds **red thin-skinned potatoes** (each about 1½ in. wide)

About 1 tablespoon **olive oil**

Grape mincemeat (recipe follows)

3 tablespoons minced **parsley**

1. Scrub potatoes and cut each in half. With a melon-baller or a spoon, scoop out a well in each potato half, leaving a shell ¼ to ½ inch thick. Reserve scooped-out potato for other uses.

2. Lightly oil a 10- by 15-inch pan. Arrange potatoes in a single layer, cut sides up, in pan. Brush lightly with 1 tablespoon olive oil total.

3. Bake in a 400° oven for 20 minutes, then turn potatoes over and bake until cut sides are lightly browned, 5 to 10 minutes longer.

4. Meanwhile, heat mincemeat in a microwave-safe bowl in a microwave oven at full power (100%) until hot, about 1 minute, stirring once.

5. Spoon mincemeat equally into potatoes. Sprinkle with parsley. Serve hot, warm, or at room temperature.

Per serving: 121 cal., 38% (46 cal.) from fat; 3.1 g protein; 5.1 g fat (1.5 g sat.); 16 g carbo (1.6 g fiber); 89 mg sodium; 8.6 mg chol.

Grape Mincemeat

PREP AND COOK TIME: About 25 minutes

NOTES: If making up to 2 days ahead, chill airtight.

MAKES: About 1 cup

¼ pound **hot** or mild **Italian sausages**

½ cup finely chopped **onion**

1 cup **seedless red grapes,** rinsed

⅛ teaspoon **ground cloves**

⅛ teaspoon **ground cinnamon**

Fresh-ground **pepper**

1. Squeeze sausages from casings into a 10- to 12-inch frying pan over high heat; add onion. With a spoon, break meat into fine chunks and stir often until meat is well browned, about 10 minutes.

2. Add grapes, ½ cup water, cloves, and cinnamon. Stir often until water is evaporated, 4 to 5 minutes. Add another ¼ cup water and stir, mashing grapes if they don't pop, until liquid is slightly evaporated and mixture is slightly thicker, about 8 minutes. Add pepper to taste.

Per tablespoon: 34 cal., 62% (21 cal.) from fat; 1.1 g protein; 2.3 g fat (0.8 g sat.); 2.3 g carbo (0.2 g fiber); 52 mg sodium; 5.4 mg chol.

Sherried Wild Rice Soup

PREP AND COOK TIME: About 1¾ hours

NOTES: If making up to 1 day ahead, cover soup and bacon separately and chill airtight; to reheat soup, stir occasionally over medium-high heat until steaming.

MAKES: About 9 cups; 8 to 10 servings

¼ pound **bacon,** diced

2 **russet potatoes** (about 1 lb. total)

1 cup **wild rice**

1 cup diced **onion**

6 cups fat-skimmed **chicken broth**

1 teaspoon **fresh thyme** leaves or dried thyme

1 cup **dry sherry**

1 cup **whipping cream**

Salt and **pepper**

1. In a 4- to 5-quart pan over high heat, stir bacon frequently until crisp, about 5 minutes. With a slotted spoon, transfer bacon to paper towels to drain. Discard drippings from pan or save for other uses.

2. Meanwhile, scrub and peel potatoes. Cut into ½-inch chunks.

3. In same pan, combine potatoes, rice, onion, 4 cups broth, and thyme. Bring to a boil over high heat; reduce heat, cover, and simmer until rice is tender to bite, 1 to 1¼ hours.

4. Add remaining 2 cups broth, sherry, and whipping cream. Bring to a boil over high heat, mashing any potato chunks against the side of the pan with a spoon. Reduce heat and simmer to blend flavors, stirring occasionally, about 10 minutes.

5. Ladle soup into bowls. Top equally with cooked bacon. Add salt and pepper to taste.

Per serving: 236 cal., 35% (83 cal.) from fat; 9.6 g protein; 9.2 g fat (5.2 g sat.); 22 g carbo (1.8 g fiber); 111 mg sodium; 29 mg chol.

Chestnut Soup with Pine Nuts and Currants

PREP AND COOK TIME: About 2¼ hours (about 1 hour if using cooked, peeled chestnuts)

NOTES: If using cooked, peeled chestnuts, omit steps 1 and 2. If making soup through step 5 up to 2 days ahead, cover and chill.

MAKES: About 3 quarts; 8 servings

3 pounds **fresh chestnuts** or 5 cups cooked, peeled chestnuts (fresh, frozen, canned, or vacuum-packed; see notes)

1 cup chopped **onion**

1 cup chopped **celery**

2 teaspoons **fennel seed**

1½ tablespoons **olive oil**

7 cups fat-skimmed **chicken broth**

1 cup **half-and-half** (light cream)

¼ cup **dried currants**

¼ cup **pine nuts**

Salt and **pepper**

1. Cut an X about ½ inch long through flat side of each chestnut shell. Place nuts in a 12- by 17-inch pan.

2. Bake in a 400° oven until shells begin to split open and nuts are slightly soft (break 1 open to test), 25 to 30 minutes. Hold 1 hot nut at a time in a soft potholder and squeeze to loosen shell. Pull off shell and brown skin; use a small, sharp knife to pull bits of skin from crevices. Discard any moldy or hard, dried nuts.

3. Meanwhile, in a 5- to 6-quart pan over medium-high heat, frequently stir onion, celery, and fennel seed in 1 tablespoon oil until vegetables are limp, 8 to 10 minutes.

4. Add broth and chestnuts; bring to a boil over high heat. Reduce heat, cover, and simmer until chestnuts mash easily, about 40 minutes.

5. Whirl mixture, a portion at a time, in a blender or food processor until smooth.

6. Return purée to pan and add half-and-half. Stir over medium-high heat until steaming, about 3 minutes (about 8 minutes if chilled).

7. Meanwhile, in a 10- to 12-inch frying pan over medium heat, frequently stir currants and pine nuts in remaining ½ tablespoon oil until nuts are golden, 3 to 5 minutes. Pour into a small bowl.

8. Ladle soup into bowls and top equally with currant–pine nut mixture. Season to taste with salt and pepper.

Per serving: 408 cal., 24% (99 cal.) from fat; 13 g protein; 11 g fat (3.4 g sat.); 65 g carbo (12 g fiber); 96 mg sodium; 11 mg chol.

Creamy Pear and Parsnip Soup

PREP AND COOK TIME: About 45 minutes

NOTES: If making up to 1 day ahead, chill airtight. To reheat, stir occasion-

The salad course highlights autumn colors. BELOW: Bright Fuyu persimmons with fennel and blue cheese. RIGHT: Greens with tangerines, dates, and roasted hazelnuts.

ally over medium-high heat until steaming.

MAKES: About 10 cups; 8 to 10 servings

2 pounds **parsnips**

1 pound **carrots**

About 4 cups fat-skimmed **chicken** or vegetable **broth**

2 pounds **ripe Comice pears**

About ⅓ cup **crème fraîche** or plain low-fat or nonfat yogurt

About ⅓ cup minced **fresh chives**

Salt and **pepper**

1. Peel parsnips and carrots. Cut into ½-inch chunks.

2. In a 4- to 5-quart pan, combine parsnips, carrots, and 4 cups broth. Bring to a boil over high heat; reduce heat, cover, and simmer until vegetables are tender when pierced, 15 to 20 minutes.

3. Meanwhile, peel and core pears. Cut into 1-inch chunks. Add to pan and stir until hot, about 2 minutes.

4. With a slotted spoon, transfer carrots, parsnips, and pears, in batches if necessary, to a blender or food processor. Whirl until smooth, adding enough cooking liquid to purée easily. Return to pan with cooking liquid and stir until steaming. If necessary, add more broth to thin to desired consistency.

5. Ladle soup into bowls. Garnish with

crème fraîche and chives. Add salt and pepper to taste.

Per serving: 178 cal., 18% (32 cal.) from fat; 6.7 g protein; 3.5 g fat (1.9 g sat.); 31 g carbo (7.1 g fiber); 72 mg sodium; 6.6 mg chol.

Persimmon-Fennel Salad

PREP TIME: **About 25 minutes**

MAKES: **8 servings**

  3 heads **fennel** (each 3 to 3½ in. wide)

1¼ pounds **firm-ripe Fuyu persimmons**

  ¼ cup **lemon juice**

1½ tablespoons **extra-virgin olive oil**

  1 cup ½-inch chunks **Stilton** or gorgonzola **cheese**

    Salt and **pepper**

1. Rinse and drain fennel. Trim off tops; discard tough stalks and chop enough feathery greens to make ¼ cup. Save remaining greens for other uses or discard. Trim and discard root ends and bruised areas from fennel heads. Cut fennel crosswise into 1/16- to 1/8-inch-thick slices. Combine sliced fennel and chopped fennel leaves in a wide, shallow bowl.

2. Peel and stem persimmons. Cut fruit crosswise into 1/8-inch-thick slices and put in another bowl. Add lemon juice and oil; mix gently. Holding fruit back, pour liquid over fennel. Mix fennel with dressing.

3. Arrange the persimmon slices over the fennel; sprinkle with cheese. Spoon salad onto plates and add salt and pepper to taste.

Per serving: 174 cal., 44% (77 cal.) from fat; 5.2 g protein; 8.6 g fat (4.1 g sat.); 22 g carbo (0.8 g fiber); 322 mg sodium; 16 mg chol.

Autumn Salad

PREP AND COOK TIME: **About 40 minutes**

NOTES: Up to 1 day ahead, rinse lettuce and radicchio, separate the leaves, and drain. Wrap leaves in a towel, enclose in a plastic bag, and chill to crisp.

MAKES: **8 servings**

  ½ cup **hazelnuts**

  4 **Satsuma tangerines** (1⅓ lb. total)

  6 **Medjool dates** (¼ lb. total)

  1 tablespoon **lemon juice**

  1 tablespoon **extra-virgin olive oil**

  5 cups lightly packed 3-inch pieces rinsed and crisped **butter lettuce** (see notes)

  3 cups lightly packed 3-inch pieces rinsed and crisped **radicchio**

    Salt and **pepper**

1. Put hazelnuts in an 8- or 9-inch pan. Bake in a 350° oven until golden beneath skins, 12 to 15 minutes. Pour onto a towel; let cool. Rub nuts in towel to remove loose skins. Lift nuts from towel and reserve; discard skins.

2. Grate $\frac{1}{2}$ teaspoon peel from 1 tangerine. Cut tangerine in half and ream $\frac{1}{4}$ cup juice; use another tangerine if necessary. Put peel and juice in a wide, shallow bowl. Peel remaining tangerines. Pull each apart into halves. Cut halves crosswise into $\frac{1}{4}$-inch-thick slices. Add to bowl. Pit dates and quarter lengthwise. Add dates, lemon juice, and olive oil to bowl.

3. Add lettuce and radicchio to bowl, mix, and add salt and pepper to taste. Sprinkle with hazelnuts.

Per serving: 133 cal., 44% (59 cal.) from fat; 2.5 g protein; 6.6 g fat (0.6 g sat.); 19 g carbo (2.8 g fiber); 9 mg sodium; 0 mg chol.

Cranberry-Cardamom Chutney

PREP AND COOK TIME: About 40 minutes

NOTES: If making up to 3 days ahead, cover and chill.

harvest feast

Vegetables reign on the sideboard. TOP (front to back): Pomegranate chutney, pickled squash sticks, and cranberry chutney. ABOVE: Curried rice studded with butternut squash. RIGHT: Sweet potatoes baked with chili jelly.

MAKES: About 1⅔ cups; 8 servings

- 1 cup chopped **red onion**
- 1 tablespoon **butter** or margarine
- 2 cups **fresh** or frozen **cranberries**
- ¾ cup **sugar**
- 1 tablespoon **white distilled vinegar**
- ¼ teaspoon **ground cardamom**

1. In a 2- to 3-quart pan over medium heat, frequently stir onion in butter until limp, 8 to 10 minutes.

2. Sort cranberries, discarding any soft or decayed fruit; rinse and drain berries. Add cranberries, sugar, vinegar, and cardamom to pan. Cover, reduce heat to low, and stir occasionally until sugar is dissolved and cranberries are translucent, about 20 minutes. Serve warm or cool.

Per serving: 107 cal., 13% (14 cal.) from fat; 0.4 g protein; 1.5 g fat (0.9 g sat.); 24 g carbo (1.3 g fiber); 17 mg sodium; 3.9 mg chol.

Pickled Squash with Lemon Grass

PREP AND COOK TIME: About 30 minutes

NOTES: Discard tough lemon grass as you eat the pickled squash.

MAKES: 2 cups; 8 to 10 servings

- ¾ pound **butternut squash**
- 6 stalks **fresh lemon grass** (about ½ pound total)
- 2 cups **seasoned rice vinegar**
- 2 tablespoons **sugar**
- 1 teaspoon **black peppercorns**

1. With a vegetable peeler, pare skin from squash and discard; cut squash in half and scoop out and discard seeds. Cut squash into matchstick-size pieces (¼ in. by ¼ in. by 2 in.).

2. Rinse lemon grass and pull off tough outer layers. Cut off stem ends and coarse leaves. Cut stalks into 1-inch pieces.

3. In a 1-quart glass measure, stir together lemon grass, vinegar, sugar, and peppercorns. Heat in a microwave oven at full power (100%) until mixture boils, 3 to 4 minutes total. At once, add squash, and let stand until tender-crisp to bite, about 15 minutes.

4. Serve, or chill airtight up to 1 week.

Per serving: 77 cal., 1.2% (0.9 cal.) from fat; 0.6 g protein; 0.1 g fat (0 g sat.); 19 g carbo (0.5 g fiber); 952 mg sodium; 0 mg chol.

Fresh Pomegranate Chutney

PREP AND COOK TIME: About 30 minutes

NOTES: Remove seeds from pomegranate up to 1 day ahead; chill airtight.

MAKES: About 1¼ cups

- ½ cup **red currant jelly**
- ⅓ cup finely chopped **green onions,** including tops
- 1 cup **pomegranate** seeds (from a 1-lb. pomegranate; see notes)
- 1 tablespoon minced **fresh ginger**
- 1 tablespoon minced **fresh jalapeño chili**
- ½ teaspoon **ground coriander**
- 1 tablespoon **lemon juice**
  Salt and **pepper**

1. Put currant jelly in a 2-cup glass measure. Heat in a microwave oven at full power (100%) until softened, about 20 seconds.

2. Stir in green onions, pomegranate seeds, ginger, chili, coriander, and lemon juice; add salt and pepper to taste. Let stand about 15 minutes before serving.

Per tablespoon: 26 cal., 0% (0 cal.) from fat; 0.1 g protein; 0 g fat; 6.7 g carbo (0.1 g fiber); 3.4 mg sodium; 0 mg chol.

Curried Squash and Basmati Rice

PREP AND COOK TIME: About 1 hour

MAKES: About 7 cups; 8 servings

- 1 pound **butternut squash**
- 2 cups minced **onions**
- 3 tablespoons minced **fresh ginger**
- 1 tablespoon minced **garlic**
- ⅓ cup **butter** or margarine
- 1½ cups **basmati rice,** rinsed and drained
- 1½ tablespoons **curry powder**
  About ½ teaspoon **salt**
- 3 cups fat-skimmed **chicken** or vegetable **broth**
- 2 tablespoons chopped **fresh cilantro**

1. Peel squash and cut in half lengthwise. Remove and discard seeds. Cut squash into ½- to ¾-inch cubes (you should have 2½ cups).

2. In a 5- to 6-quart pan over medium heat, frequently stir onions, ginger, and garlic in butter until onions are very limp, 10 to 15 minutes.

3. Add rice and stir often until opaque, about 5 minutes. Add curry powder and stir for 30 seconds longer.

4. Stir in ½ teaspoon salt, squash, and broth. Bring to a boil over high heat; reduce heat, cover, and simmer, stirring occasionally, until rice and squash are tender to bite, 16 to 18 minutes. Stir in cilantro and salt to taste. Spoon into a bowl.

Per serving: 240 cal., 32% (77 cal.) from fat; 7.9 g protein; 8.5 g fat (4.7 g sat.); 37 g carbo (2.3 g fiber); 270 mg sodium; 20 mg chol.

Chili-glazed Sweet Potatoes

PREP AND COOK TIME: About 1 hour

NOTES: Bake sweet potatoes (through step 2) up to 1 day ahead; cool, combine in 1 pan, cover, and chill. Reheat, covered, in a 450° oven 5 to 10 minutes before combining with jelly mixture in step 4.

MAKES: 8 to 10 servings

- 4½ pounds **sweet potatoes** or yams
- ⅔ cup **red jalapeño jelly**
- ⅓ cup **red wine vinegar**
- ¼ cup minced **fresh cilantro**
  About 3 tablespoons **lime juice**
  Salt

1. Peel sweet potatoes and cut into 1-inch chunks. Divide chunks equally between 2 lightly oiled baking pans (each 10 by 15 in.); cover tightly with foil.

2. Bake in a 450° oven for 15 minutes. Uncover and continue to bake until sweet potatoes are tender when pierced, about 25 minutes longer; switch pan positions halfway through baking.

3. Meanwhile, put jelly in a 2-cup glass measure. Heat in a microwave oven at full power (100%) until softened, about 20 seconds. Add vinegar and stir until well blended.

4. Combine sweet potatoes in 1 pan. Pour jelly mixture evenly over potatoes and turn chunks with a spatula to coat evenly. Continue baking until jelly mixture thickens and sticks to sweet potatoes, about 10 minutes, turning chunks often to prevent scorching.

5. Pour into a wide bowl. Sprinkle with cilantro and add about 3 tablespoons lime juice and salt to taste.

Per serving: 218 cal., 6% (13 cal.) from fat; 2.4 g protein; 1.4 g fat (0.2 g sat.); 49 g carbo (4.4 g fiber); 25 mg sodium; 0 mg chol.

Savory Potato Streusel

PREP AND COOK TIME: About 2 hours

NOTES: Assemble through step 3 up to 1 day ahead; cover and chill, then bake (step 4) about 1 hour and 25 minutes.

MAKES: 8 to 10 servings

- ⅓ cup **hazelnuts**
- 2 cups **sour cream**
- 2 cups fat-skimmed **chicken broth**
- 2 tablespoons minced **fresh marjoram** leaves or 1 tablespoon dried marjoram
- 4 pounds **russet potatoes**
- ½ cup **seasoned fine dried bread crumbs**
- ½ cup **grated parmesan cheese**
- 6 tablespoons **butter** or margarine, cut into chunks

    Salt and **pepper**

1. Put hazelnuts in a shallow 3-quart casserole (about 9 by 13 in.). Bake in a 350° oven until golden under skins, about 15 minutes. Pour onto a towel and let stand until cool enough to touch, about 5 minutes. Rub nuts in towel to remove loose skins. Lift nuts from towel; discard skins. Whirl nuts in a blender or food processor until finely chopped.

2. Meanwhile, in a bowl, blend sour cream, chicken broth, and marjoram until smooth.

3. Scrub and peel potatoes. Cut crosswise into ⅛- to ¼-inch slices. Cover bottom of casserole with about ¼ of the potato slices, overlapping slightly to make an even layer. Pour about ¼ of the sour cream mixture evenly over potatoes to cover. Repeat to layer remaining potatoes and sour cream mixture, ending with sour cream. Cover pan tightly with foil; set in a 10- by 15-inch baking pan.

4. Bake in a 400° oven until potatoes are tender when pierced, 1 to 1¼ hours.

5. While potatoes bake, in a bowl combine chopped hazelnuts, bread crumbs, cheese, and butter. Rub with your fingers until butter is incorporated and mixture forms crumbly chunks. Uncover potatoes and sprinkle evenly with hazelnut streusel. Bake until streusel is browned, 8 to 10 minutes longer. Add salt and pepper to taste.

Per serving: 363 cal., 52% (189 cal.) from fat; 9.3 g protein; 21 g fat (11 g sat.); 36 g carbo (3.3 g fiber); 356 mg sodium; 42 mg chol.

Sourdough, Sausage, and Greens Dressing

PREP AND COOK TIME: About 1 hour

NOTES: Prepare dressing through step 5 up to 1 day ahead; chill.

MAKES: About 2 quarts; 8 servings

- ¾ pound **sourdough bread**, cut into ½-inch cubes (2 qt.)
- ½ pound **Swiss chard**
- ¾ pound **bulk pork sausage**

    About 2½ tablespoons **butter** or margarine

- 1 cup chopped **onion**
- 1 cup sliced **celery**, including tops
- ¼ cup chopped **Italian parsley**
- 2 tablespoons chopped **fresh sage** leaves or 2 teaspoons dried rubbed sage
- 2 teaspoons **poultry seasoning**
- ¾ teaspoon fresh-ground **pepper**
- 1¾ cups fat-skimmed **chicken broth**

1. Put bread cubes in a 9- by 13-inch pan. Bake in a 350° oven, stirring occasionally, until dry and firm to touch, about 20 minutes.

2. Meanwhile, rinse and drain chard. Trim and discard discolored stem ends; thinly slice stems and coarsely chop leaves.

3. In a 5- to 6-quart pan over medium-high heat, stir sausage often until browned and crumbly, 5 to 8 minutes. With a slotted spoon, transfer sausage to pan with bread.

4. Measure fat in the 5- to 6-quart pan; add enough butter to make 3 tablespoons. Add onion and celery. Stir

CALIFORNIA PERSIMMONS

CLIFF SADOIAN "A full-grown persimmon tree can really produce," says Cliff Sadoian, a third-generation farmer in Dinuba. "We can get 1,500 to 2,000 flats per acre." That translates into a lot of persimmons, given his 30-acre orchard.

Sadoian and his family primarily grow the Hachiya persimmon, one of the two chief market varieties. Hachiyas thrive in hot inland parts of the West, such as here in California's Central Valley. They also do well in milder coastal zones. Marked by their pointed tips, they are picked after they've turned bright orange but while they're still firm. Before being eaten they must be allowed to ripen further to lose their puckery astringency and

become as soft and sweet as jelly.

Sadoian also tends a handful of Fuyu persimmon trees, the other main market variety. Flat on the bottom and mild-flavored, Fuyus can be eaten while they're as

crisp as apples or after they've softened a bit. Both varieties ripen slowly at room temperature, which makes them perfect for piling in a huge bowl on your kitchen table—a bright reflection of the season.

LEFT: Mellow and only slightly sweet, chocolate-chestnut torte is similar to a light-textured cheesecake. For an elegant presentation, dust powdered sugar through a stencil onto the torte.

BELOW: Bright tangerine segments layered with citrus-infused cream.

often over medium-high heat until vegetables are limp, about 10 minutes. Add chard and stir often until limp, about 3 minutes.

5. Combine bread mixture, parsley, sage, poultry seasoning, pepper, and chicken broth with chard mixture. Squeeze with your hands until evenly moistened. Return mixture to the 9- by 13-inch pan, spread level, and cover tightly.

6. Bake in a 350° oven until dressing is hot in the center, about 40 minutes (45 to 50 minutes if chilled). For a crusty top, uncover for the last 20 minutes.

Per serving: 351 cal., 56% (198 cal.) from fat; 11 g protein; 22 g fat (8.7 g sat.); 26 g carbo (2.3 g fiber); 666 mg sodium; 39 mg chol.

Italian Chocolate-Chestnut Torte

PREP AND COOK TIME: About 1¾ hours

NOTES: Gary Rulli, chef-owner of Pasticceria Rulli in Larkspur, California, shares this recipe. Purchase chestnuts in syrup, or marrons glacés, and the chestnut flour at a well-stocked supermarket or gourmet food store. Or order from Dean & DeLuca (707/967-9980 or www.deandeluca.com). If making torte up to 1 day ahead, cool, cover airtight, and chill.

MAKES: 8 to 10 servings

2 ounces **bittersweet** or semisweet **chocolate**, chopped

¾ cup **mascarpone cheese**

½ cup **whole-milk** or part-skim **ricotta cheese**

6 tablespoons **granulated sugar**

2 **large eggs,** separated

1 tablespoon **rum** (optional)

¼ cup **chestnut flour** or all-purpose flour

⅓ cup chopped **chestnuts in syrup,** drained, or marrons glacés (see notes)

Cookie crust (recipe follows)

Powdered sugar

8 to 10 whole **chestnuts in syrup**, drained, or marrons glacés (optional)

Coffee ice cream

1. In a large microwave-safe bowl, heat chocolate in a microwave oven on full power (100%) until soft, about 2 minutes, stirring every 30 seconds.

2. To chocolate, add mascarpone, ricotta, $^1/_4$ cup granulated sugar, egg yolks, rum, flour, and chopped chestnuts; stir until well blended.

3. In a bowl, with a mixer on high speed, beat egg whites until foamy. Gradually add remaining 2 tablespoons sugar and continue to beat whites until they hold stiff peaks. Gently fold whites into cheese mixture; scrape into cookie crust and spread level.

4. Bake in a 350° oven until filling is firm when pan is gently shaken and springs back when lightly touched in the center, about 30 minutes (20 minutes in a convection oven).

5. Cool on a rack about 20 minutes. Run a knife between cake and pan rim; remove rim. Let torte cool to room temperature, about 45 minutes; proceed, or chill airtight up to 1 day.

6. Sift powdered sugar over torte. If desired, decorate top with whole chestnuts spaced evenly around rim. Cut into wedges and serve with ice cream.

Per serving: 316 cal., 51% (162 cal.) from fat; 5.5 g protein; 18 g fat (10 g sat.); 34 g carbo (1.5 g fiber); 111 mg sodium; 73 mg chol.

Cookie crust. In a food processor or blender, whirl about 45 **vanilla wafer cookies** (6 oz. total) until finely ground. Pour crumbs into a 9-inch cake pan with removable rim. Add 3 tablespoons melted **butter** or margarine, 1 tablespoon *each* **honey** and **rum**, 1 teaspoon **vanilla**, and $^1/_4$ teaspoon **ground cinnamon**; mix well and press evenly over bottom and 1 inch up sides of pan.

Tangerine Cream Parfaits

PREP AND COOK TIME: About 35 minutes, plus at least $1^1/_2$ hours to chill

NOTES: If using fresh-squeezed tangerine juice, you'll need about $4^1/_2$ pounds tangerines to make 3 cups (including juice from tangerines in step 1). Or buy fresh or frozen tangerine juice (or tangerine juice blend). If making through step 4 up to 1 day ahead, cover tangerine segments and cream mixture separately and chill.

MAKES: 8 to 10 servings

$1^1/_2$ pounds **seedless tangerines**

$^2/_3$ cup **sugar**

2   envelopes **unflavored gelatin** ($^1/_4$ oz. each)

3   cups **tangerine juice** (see notes)

4   **large egg** yolks

3   cups **sour cream**

1. Grate 2 tablespoons peel from tangerines. With a sharp knife, cut off remaining peel and white membrane from tangerines; discard peel and membrane. Working over a strainer set in a bowl, cut between inner membranes and fruit to release segments into strainer. You should have 2 cups segments; cover and chill. Discard membranes; save juice to use in step 2.

2. In a 3- to 4-quart pan, combine sugar, gelatin, grated tangerine peel, and 1 cup tangerine juice. Stir over medium-high heat until simmering. Remove from heat.

3. Beat remaining 2 cups tangerine juice with egg yolks to blend; stir into pan, then stir mixture over medium-low heat for 5 minutes.

4. Remove from heat and whisk in sour cream. Nest pan in ice water and stir often just until mixture begins to thicken, about 10 minutes. Lift pan from ice water, cover, and chill until mixture is firm, at least $1^1/_2$ hours or up to 1 day.

5. Spoon about 2 tablespoons tangerine segments into each glass (at least 12-oz. size). Stir cream mixture, then spoon about $^1/_3$ cup over segments in each glass. Repeat to layer remaining tangerine segments and cream mixture equally in glasses.

Per serving: 283 cal., 54% (153 cal.) from fat; 5.2 g protein; 17 g fat (9.7 g sat.); 30 g carbo (1 g fiber); 44 mg sodium; 115 mg chol.

Baked Persimmon Indian Pudding

PREP AND COOK TIME: About $2^1/_4$ hours, plus at least 1 hour to chill

NOTES: Scoop soft-ripe Hachiya persimmon pulp from skin with a spoon and discard any seeds, or peel Fuyu persimmons, chop, and whirl in a blender to a smooth purée. If making pudding and sauce up to 1 day ahead, cool, cover pudding and sauce separately airtight, and chill.

MAKES: 1 loaf; 12 servings

1   cup **soft-ripe Hachiya** or Fuyu **persimmon** pulp (see notes)

2   teaspoons **baking soda**

$^3/_4$ cup **sugar**

About $^1/_2$ cup ($^1/_4$ lb.) **butter** or margarine, at room temperature

$^1/_4$ cup **dark molasses**

2   **large eggs**

1   teaspoon **vanilla**

1   cup **all-purpose flour**

$^3/_4$ cup **cornmeal**

$^1/_2$ teaspoon **ground cinnamon**

$^1/_2$ teaspoon **ground ginger**

$^1/_4$ teaspoon **ground allspice**

1   cup **raisins**

$^1/_2$ cup chopped **walnuts**

Persimmon-eggnog sauce (recipe follows)

1. In a blender or food processor, whirl persimmon pulp and baking soda until smooth.

2. In a bowl, with a mixer on medium speed, beat sugar, $^1/_2$ cup butter, and molasses until blended. Add eggs and vanilla and beat until smooth. In another bowl, mix flour, cornmeal, cinnamon, ginger, and allspice. Stir dry ingredients and persimmon purée into sugar-butter mixture. Add raisins and walnuts and mix until blended.

3. Pour batter into a buttered and floured 7- to 8-cup loaf pan or ring mold (no deeper than 3 in.); cover tightly with foil. Put pan in a larger pan and place in a 300° oven. Add $^3/_4$ inch boiling water to outer pan around loaf pan or $^1/_2$ inch boiling water around ring mold.

4. Bake until pudding is firm in center when lightly pressed (lift foil to check), about 2 hours (about $1^1/_4$ hours in a convection oven). Carefully lift pan from water and let stand 10 minutes, then uncover. Run a knife between pudding and sides of pan to release. Invert onto a plate. Cut warm or cool pudding into slices, transfer to plates, and top with spoonfuls of persimmon-eggnog sauce.

Per serving: 363 cal., 40% (144 cal.) from fat; 4.8 g protein; 16 g fat (7.7 g sat.); 53 g carbo (1.6 g fiber); 315 mg sodium; 73 mg chol.

Persimmon-eggnog sauce. In a bowl, with a mixer on high speed, beat $^1/_2$ cup **whipping cream** until it holds soft peaks. Gently fold in $^1/_2$ cup **soft-ripe Hachiya persimmon** pulp or Fuyu persimmon purée (see notes for baked persimmon Indian pudding, preceding) and $^1/_2$ cup **purchased eggnog**.

Per serving: 555 cal., 64% (35 cal.) from fat; 0.7 g protein; 3.9 g fat (2.4 g sat.); 4.9 g carbo (0 g fiber); 9.2 mg sodium; 17 mg chol. ◆

The Quick Cook

Meals in 30 minutes or less

By Christine Weber Hale

Second-day turkey

■ Interest in leftover Thanksgiving turkey tends to fade proportionally to the number of days that have passed since the holiday. But this versatile, lean meat will keep its quality for four to five days if refrigerated and well covered, so you can afford to take a short break before coming back to it. Then, any of the following dishes, some of which incorporate other likely Thanksgiving extras, will make a welcome meal. On the other hand, why not freeze the turkey bonus in small, easy-to-thaw packets to have available when a quick meal is in order?

Bow-tie pasta and toasted pecans rejuvenate leftover turkey.

Turkey Pasta with Bacon and Cranberry Sauce

PREP AND COOK TIME: About 30 minutes

MAKES: 4 servings

- 2 teaspoons **cornstarch**
- 1 cup fat-skimmed **chicken broth**
- ½ cup **pecan halves**
- ¼ pound **sliced bacon,** chopped
- 1 **onion** (½ lb.), peeled and chopped
- ¾ pound **dried bow-tie pasta**
- ¾ cup **cranberry sauce** or relish (purchased or homemade)
- 2 cups bite-size pieces skinned **cooked turkey**
- ¼ cup minced **parsley**
  Salt and **pepper**

1. In a 5- to 6-quart pan over high heat, bring 4 quarts of water to a boil. In a small bowl, mix cornstarch with broth.

2. While water heats, pour pecans into a 10- to 12-inch frying pan over medium-high heat. Shake or stir nuts frequently until lightly browned under the skin (break a nut to test), about 5 minutes. Pour from pan and set aside.

3. Return frying pan to medium-high heat; add bacon and onion. Stir often until bacon is brown, about 10 minutes; spoon out fat and discard. Add pasta to boiling water and cook until tender to bite, 10 to 12 minutes.

4. While pasta cooks, add cranberry sauce and broth mixture to bacon and onion; stir over high heat until boiling. Add turkey and parsley, mix, and keep sauce warm.

5. Drain pasta. Return to pan, add turkey sauce, and mix. Spoon onto plates. Sprinkle pasta with toasted pecans and add salt and pepper to taste.

Per serving: 705 cal., 26% (180 cal.) from fat; 38 g protein; 20 g fat (4.2 g sat.); 92 g carbo (3.9 g fiber); 238 mg sodium; 63 mg chol.

Turkey, Mashed Potato, and Jack Cheese Casserole

PREP AND COOK TIME: About 25 minutes

NOTES: For mashed potatoes, use leftovers, purchased, frozen, or a mix.

MAKES: 4 servings

- 3 cups scraps, bite-size pieces, or thin slices skinned **cooked turkey**
- 1 cup **turkey gravy** (see page 329 or purchased)
- 2 cups **mashed potatoes** (see notes)
- 1 cup (¼ lb.) **shredded jack cheese** (plain or with chilies)
  Salt and **pepper**

1. Butter a shallow 1½-quart casserole. Cover bottom evenly with turkey.

Drizzle ¾ cup gravy (hot or cold, stirred to soften) over the meat. Stir potatoes to soften, mound onto turkey, and swirl to cover surface of meat. Drizzle remaining ¼ cup gravy over potatoes, then sprinkle evenly with cheese.

2. Bake in a 450° oven until turkey and potatoes are hot in the center (about 140°), 10 to 15 minutes. If desired, broil 4 to 6 inches from heat until cheese is lightly browned, 2 to 3 minutes. Season portions with salt and pepper to taste.

Per serving: 496 cal., 38% (189 cal.) from fat; 52 g protein; 21 g fat (8.9 g sat.); 24 g carbo (2 g fiber); 627 mg sodium; 184 mg chol.

Turkey and Grape Waldorf Salad

PREP TIME: About 30 minutes

MAKES: 4 servings

- ½ cup **reduced-fat** or regular **mayonnaise**
- 2 tablespoons **white wine vinegar**
- 1 tablespoon **sugar**
- 1 teaspoon **dried tarragon**
- ½ teaspoon **dried thyme**
- 4 cups bite-size pieces skinned **cooked turkey**
- 1 cup thinly sliced **celery**
- 1½ cups **seedless grapes** (red or green), rinsed
- 1 **crisp, tart apple** such as Fuji or Granny Smith (½ lb.), rinsed
  Salt and **pepper**
- 4 or 8 **butter lettuce leaves** (at least 5 in. wide), rinsed and crisped
- ¼ cup **roasted salted almonds,** coarsely chopped

1. In a large bowl, mix mayonnaise, vinegar, sugar, tarragon, and thyme. Add turkey and celery. Cut grapes in half. Core apple and cut into ½-inch chunks. Add grapes and apple to bowl. Mix gently to coat with dressing, adding salt and pepper to taste.

2. Lay lettuce on plates and mound salad equally onto leaves. Sprinkle with chopped almonds.

Per serving: 470 cal., 36% (171 cal.) from fat; 44 g protein; 19 g fat (3.8 g sat.); 31 g carbo (3.8 g fiber); 448 mg sodium; 108 mg chol. ◆

A Thanksgiving to share

Traditions from Italy and America converge for dinner
at a Northern California inn

By Sara Schneider • Photographs by James Carrier

The Zambonis
(above) make
pasta. Nancy
Schultz, Jim Tobin
(right), Patty
Mattson, and
Kathy Tobin
(below) await
dinner (far right).

■ When in Rome ... make Russian
salad. And when in California, ring
Russian salad with gravlax and serve
it with minestrone, pumpkin-stuffed
pasta—and roast turkey.

Into his Thanksgiving dinner, Luciano Zamboni pours a wealth of traditions amassed on his circuitous
journey through life—from Italy to
Sweden to the United States. His In-
diana-born wife, Pauline, supplies the
pure American touches, like cran-
berry-apricot chutney and pumpkin
cheesecake. Now the two continue
their culinary exploits at
Victorian Gardens, a petite
inn set on 92 stunningly
serene coastal acres 20
miles south of Mendocino
in Northern California.

Five years ago Luciano,
a pathologist, and Pauline,
an urban planner, retired
from the University of California at Los Angeles and
transformed the century-old house
on this erstwhile sheep ranch into a
four–guest room country inn. It
could be called a B,B&D because, for
those who reserve a seat, Luciano
cooks his traditional multicourse Italian dinners or his lavish multitrad-
tional Thanksgiving dinners.

Guests compare and swap holiday
memories over hors d'oeuvres and
drinks. By the time everyone claims a

place at the dining table, the spirit of family envelops all. Good Italian wine helps. After dessert and a final sip comes the sweetest treat of all—it's just upstairs to bed.

If you choose to tackle the Zambonis' entire Thanksgiving menu at home, take advantage of the many make-ahead components to reduce last-minute complications. Or turn the meal into a cooperative effort, asking guests to bring some of the foods that transport well. You can also simplify the menu by omitting a few dishes or replacing them with the suggested purchased items. Regardless, you'll achieve the aura of serendipitous celebration that marks Thanksgiving at Victorian Gardens.

Gravlax with Russian Salad

PREP AND COOK TIME: About 2 hours

NOTES: Even though Luciano grew up in Rome, Russian salad was a traditional dish in his family. Up to 2 days ahead, prepare the gravlax, make the dressing, assemble the potato-vegetable salad, and season the beets; chill each separately, airtight. Or instead of making gravlax, purchase 1 pound thin-sliced smoked salmon.

MAKES: 10 to 12 servings

- 2 pounds **Yukon Gold** or other thin-skinned **potatoes** ($^1\!/_2$ lb. each), scrubbed

- 1 pound **cauliflower florets** (4 to $4^1\!/_2$ cups), rinsed

- 2 **carrots** ($^1\!/_4$ lb. each), rinsed and peeled

- $^1\!/_2$ pound **green beans,** ends and strings removed, rinsed

- 3 **gold** or red **beets** (about 3 in. wide), tops trimmed, scrubbed

- $^3\!/_4$ cup **white wine vinegar**

- $1^1\!/_2$ cups **regular** or reduced-fat **mayonnaise**

- $^1\!/_2$ cup finely chopped **cornichons** or sour pickles

- $^1\!/_2$ cup drained **capers**

- $^1\!/_2$ cup chopped **fresh dill** or $^1\!/_4$ cup dried dill

- 1 tablespoon **Dijon mustard**

- 1 tablespoon **dry mustard**

  About $^1\!/_2$ teaspoon **salt**

  Homemade gravlax (recipe follows; see notes)

- 6 to 8 pieces **thin-sliced pumpernickel** or rye **bread** (about $^1\!/_2$ lb. total), cut into quarters

  Pepper

1. In a 5- to 6-quart pan over high heat, bring potatoes and $2^1\!/_2$ quarts water to a boil. Cover, reduce heat, and simmer until potatoes are tender when pierced, about 25 to 30 minutes. With a slotted spoon, lift potatoes out and let stand.

2. Return water to boiling and add cauliflower; cover, reduce heat, and simmer just until tender when pierced, 5 to 6 minutes. With slotted spoon, lift out florets and let stand. Return water to boiling and add carrots; cover, reduce heat, and simmer until tender when pierced, 8 to 10 minutes. With slotted spoon, lift carrots out and let stand. Return water to boiling and add green beans; simmer, uncovered, until

Gold beets surround gravlax filled with Russian salad.

Genoa-style minestrone, full of beans and greens,
is topped with a lively basil-butter pesto.

tender-crisp to bite, 3 to 4 minutes. Drain green beans, immerse in ice water until cool, about 3 minutes, then drain again.

3. Meanwhile, in a 3- to 4-quart pan, bring beets and 1½ quarts water to a boil. Cover, reduce heat, and simmer until beets are tender when pierced, 35 to 40 minutes. Drain and let cool.

4. Peel beets and potatoes; cut into ⅜-inch cubes. In a small bowl, mix beets with 2 tablespoons vinegar. Put potatoes in a large bowl. Cut cauliflower florets into ½-inch-wide pieces. Cut carrots in half lengthwise, then crosswise into ¼-inch slices. Cut green beans into ½-inch pieces. Add cauliflower, carrots, and green beans to potatoes.

5. In another small bowl, combine mayonnaise, 6 tablespoons vinegar, cornichons, capers, ¼ cup dill (or 2 tablespoons dried dill), Dijon mustard, dry mustard, and ½ teaspoon salt. Add 1½ cups of the dressing and remaining ¼ cup vinegar to the potato-vegetable salad; mix gently.

6. Overlap gravlax slices end to end to create an equal-size circle on each plate. Mound potato-vegetable salad equally in the center of the circles, surround with beets, and arrange bread alongside. Sprinkle salads with remaining ¼ cup dill (or 2 tablespoons dried dill). Accompany with remaining dressing and salt and pepper to add to taste.

Per serving: 458 cal., 57% (261 cal.) from fat; 16 g protein; 29 g fat (4.6 g sat.); 34 g carbo (4.3 g fiber); 1,915 mg sodium; 50 mg chol.

Homemade Gravlax

PREP TIME: About 15 minutes, plus 2 days to cure

NOTES: Buy salmon that has been frozen, or freeze fresh salmon for at least 72 hours at -4° or lower to destroy any parasites, then thaw to use.

MAKES: 10 to 12 servings

3 tablespoons **sugar**

3 tablespoons **salt**

1 tablespoon crushed or coarse-ground **black peppercorns**

1½ pounds **salmon fillet** (1 in. thick, 1 or 2 pieces)

1½ cups **dill sprigs**, rinsed, or ¾ cup dried dill

1. In a small bowl, mix sugar, salt, and peppercorns.

2. Rub your fingers over flesh side of salmon to locate any bones; pull them out and discard. Rinse salmon and pat dry. Lay, skin side down, in an 8- or 9-inch pie pan. Sprinkle evenly with sugar-salt mixture and top evenly with dill. Cover pan airtight with plastic wrap.

3. Nest another pie pan of the same size on fish and set 2- to 3-pound weights (such as unopened cans of food) in it. Chill 2 days; every 12 hours, uncover, baste salmon with juices, rewrap, and replace weights.

4. Unwrap salmon, discard dill, and scrape off sugar-salt mixture. Lay

salmon, skin down, on a board; cut into thin diagonal slices and release fish from skin. Discard skin.

Per serving: 112 cal., 50% (56 cal.) from fat; 11 g protein; 6.2 g fat (1.2 g sat.); 2 g carbo (0 g fiber); 1,134 mg sodium; 33 mg chol.

Genovese Vegetable Soup

PREP AND COOK TIME: About 1¼ hours, plus at least 1 hour to soak dried beans

NOTES: If making up to 2 days ahead, cover and chill; reheat to serve. For a quick start, omit dried lima beans and step 1. In step 4, use 2 cans (15 oz. each) butter (lima) beans, rinsed and drained, and add 2½ cups more broth. If making pesto up to 2 days ahead, cover airtight and chill; stir before using. Or buy 1 cup pesto.

MAKES: 10 to 12 servings

¾ pound **dried lima beans** (see notes)

1 **leek** (about 1¼ in. wide)

¼ pound **thin-sliced pancetta,** finely chopped

About 12 tablespoons **extra-virgin olive oil**

1 cup chopped **onion**

1 cup chopped **celery**

⅓ cup finely chopped **Italian parsley**

1 can (49½ oz.) fat-skimmed **chicken broth**

1 can (28 oz.) **diced tomatoes with Italian seasonings**

1 **Yukon Gold** or other thin-skinned **potato** (½ lb.), scrubbed, peeled, and cut into ½-inch chunks

2 **carrots** (6 oz. total), rinsed, peeled, and cut into ½-inch chunks

3 cups finely shredded **cabbage** (7 to 8 oz.)

3 cups thinly sliced **Swiss chard** (7 to 8 oz.)

⅓ pound **green beans,** ends and strings removed, rinsed, and cut into ½-inch pieces

½ pound **zucchini,** ends trimmed, rinsed, and cut into ½-inch chunks

Pesto alla genovese (recipe follows)

Salt and **pepper**

1. Sort lima beans, discarding debris. Rinse beans, put in a 3- to 4-quart pan, and add 1½ quarts water. Bring to a boil over high heat; remove from heat and let stand at least 1 hour or overnight. Drain beans, add 1½ quarts water, and bring to a boil over high heat. Cover, reduce heat, and simmer, stirring occasionally, until beans are tender to bite, about 20 minutes. Drain beans; reserve liquid.

2. Meanwhile, trim and discard stem end and tough green top from leek; peel off and discard tough outer layer. Cut leek in half lengthwise and hold under cold running water, flipping layers to rinse well. Thinly slice crosswise.

3. In an 8- to 10-quart pan over medium heat, frequently stir pancetta in 2 tablespoons olive oil just until limp, about 2 minutes. Add leek, onion, celery, and parsley; stir often over medium-high heat until vegetables begin to brown, 10 to 15 minutes.

4. To pan, add 2½ cups reserved bean-cooking liquid (save remainder for other uses or discard), drained beans, broth, tomatoes with juice, potatoes, and carrots. Bring to a boil over high heat; cover, reduce heat, and simmer, stirring occasionally, about 10 minutes.

5. Add cabbage, Swiss chard, green beans, and zucchini; cover and simmer, stirring occasionally, until all vegetables are very tender to bite, 20 to 25 minutes longer.

6. Ladle soup equally into bowls; spoon 1 tablespoon olive oil and about ½ tablespoon pesto alla genovese into each portion. Serve with remaining pesto and salt and pepper to add to taste.

Per serving: 331 cal., 71% (234 cal.) from fat; 9.2 g protein; 26 g fat (5.4 g sat.); 18 g carbo (3.8 g fiber); 287 mg sodium; 9.6 mg chol.

Pesto alla genovese. In a food processor, combine 4 peeled **garlic** cloves, 4 cups lightly packed rinsed **fresh basil** leaves (about 5 oz.), ½ cup fresh-grated **romano** or parmesan **cheese**, ⅓ cup **extra-virgin olive oil**, and 2 tablespoons **butter** or margarine; whirl until smooth, scraping container sides as needed. Add **salt** and **pepper** to taste. Makes about 1 cup.

Per tablespoon: 65 cal., 94% (61 cal.) from fat; 1.1 g protein; 6.8 g fat (2 g sat.); 0.7 g carbo (0.4 g fiber); 45 mg sodium; 6.5 mg chol.

Pumpkin-filled Pasta

PREP AND COOK TIME: About 1½ hours, plus 30 minutes to dry

NOTES: Cremona fruit in mustard

Thin pasta seals in bright pumpkin filling; fried sage leaves add an earthy accent.

syrup is available at Italian food markets and upscale delicatessens. Instead of making the pasta (steps 2 and 3), you can use 48 to 50 *gyoza* (Japanese equivalent to potstickers) skins; moisten edges with water and press with fingers to seal. Do not dry (step 4); drape with plastic wrap as shaped. Cook filled gyoza only 2 to 3 minutes (step 5). If filling pasta or gyoza skins up to 1 day ahead, chill airtight; freeze up to 6 weeks. Or purchase about 3 pounds cheese-filled ravioli and serve with the sauce.

MAKES: 10 to 12 servings

Filling:

1 cup **canned pumpkin** (about half of a 15-oz. can)

2 tablespoons finely chopped **Cremona fruit in mustard syrup** (see notes; optional)

¼ cup fresh-grated **parmesan cheese**

2 tablespoons finely crushed **amaretti** or other almond macaroon **cookies**

1 tablespoon **fine dried bread crumbs**

⅛ teaspoon fresh-grated **nutmeg**

¼ teaspoon **salt**

1 tablespoon **brandy**

Pasta:

About 2 cups **unbleached** or regular **all-purpose flour**

¼ teaspoon **salt**

3 **large eggs**

2 large **egg yolks**

Sauce:

½ cup (¼ lb.) **butter** or margarine

⅓ cup lightly packed **fresh sage** leaves, rinsed and dried

½ cup fresh-grated **parmesan cheese**

Salt and **pepper**

1. *To make filling:* In a bowl, mix pumpkin, fruit in mustard syrup, parmesan cheese, crushed amaretti cookies, bread crumbs, nutmeg, salt, and brandy.

2. *To make pasta:* In a food processor, whirl 2 cups flour and salt to blend; add eggs and egg yolks, and whirl until dough holds together (or in a bowl, mix ingredients with a fork). Scrape pasta dough onto a lightly floured board and roll to coat with flour. Knead until dough feels smooth, adding flour as required to prevent sticking, about 1 minute if mixed in a food processor, 15 minutes if stirred. Cover dough with plastic wrap and let rest 10 to 15 minutes.

3. Divide dough in half and shape each portion into a smooth ball. Roll each ball through a pasta machine to 1⁄16 inch thick, or roll on a floured board. With a floured 2¾-inch round cutter, cut out 48 to 50 pasta rounds. Reroll dough as needed; discard excess.

4. Spoon an equal portion of filling onto center of each pasta round

(about 1 teaspoon). Moisten pasta rims with water, fold over to enclose filling, and press edges with fork tines to seal. Arrange filled pasta on a floured surface (or 10- by 15-in. baking pans, if making ahead); let dry 10 minutes, turn over, and dry 20 minutes longer (or cover airtight and chill).

5. Bring 4 quarts water to a boil in a 7- to 8-quart pan over high heat; add half the pasta and cook, stirring occasionally, until tender to bite, 8 to 10 minutes. As they are cooked, transfer with a slotted spoon to a rimmed ovenproof platter; cover with foil and keep warm on an electric warming tray or in a 250° oven. Repeat to cook remaining pasta.

6. *To make sauce:* In an 8- to 10-inch nonstick frying pan over high heat, melt butter. Add sage leaves and stir often until darker green, about 30 seconds. Immediately, pour over the filled pasta, sprinkle with ¹/₂ cup parmesan cheese, and add salt and pepper to taste.

Per serving: 221 cal., 49% (108 cal.) from fat; 7.3 g protein; 12 g fat (6.6 g sat.); 20 g carbo (1 g fiber); 311 mg sodium; 114 mg chol.

Salt-and-Pepper Roast Turkey

PREP AND COOK TIME: **2 to 3 hours, 20 minutes to rest, and 12 to 24 hours to cure (optional).** For other turkey sizes, see chart (above right); for larger birds, use a pan large enough that turkey does not overlap rim.

NOTES: Luciano likes to rub the turkey with the salt and pepper the night before roasting to slightly "cure" the meat. He also enhances the menu by roasting a goose along with the turkey. We've settled on 1 turkey large enough to provide leftovers. Garnish the platter with Italian parsley and more thyme and marjoram sprigs.

MAKES: Allow ³/₄ pound uncooked turkey per person

- 1 **turkey** (14 to 23 lb.)
  About ¹/₄ cup **olive oil**
  About 1 tablespoon **salt**
  About 1 tablespoon **pepper**
- 5 or 6 **thyme sprigs** (about 5 in.)
- 5 or 6 **marjoram sprigs** (about 6 in.)

1. Remove and discard leg truss from turkey. Pull off and discard any lumps of fat. Remove giblets and neck; save for rich poultry broth (page 326). Rinse turkey inside and out; pat dry and rub all over with about ¹/₄ cup olive oil. Mix

Oven-roasted whole turkey

See Salt-and-Pepper Roast Turkey (below left) for directions. Follow this chart for oven temperatures and cooking times.

Turkey weight with giblets	Oven temp.	Internal temp.*	Cooking time**
10–13 lb.	350°	160°	1¹/₂–2¹/₄ hr.
14–23 lb.	325°	160°	2–3 hr.
24–27 lb.	325°	160°	3–3³/₄ hr.
28–30 lb.	325°	160°	3¹/₂–4¹/₂ hr.

*To measure the internal temperature of the turkey, insert a thermometer through the thickest part of the breast to the bone.

**Times are for unstuffed birds. A stuffed bird may cook at the same rate as an unstuffed one; however, be prepared to allow 30 to 50 minutes more. While turkeys take about the same time to roast in regular and convection heat, a convection oven does a better job of browning the bird all over.

When you remove the turkey legs, if you find that the meat around the thigh joint is still too pink, cut the drumsticks from the thighs and put thighs in a shallow pan in a 450° oven until no longer pink, 10 to 15 minutes.

One-oven menu note: If you have only one oven, put the sweet potato gratin in with the turkey at 325° one hour before dinner. When you remove the turkey 30 minutes before serving, turn oven temperature to 375° and add the cornbread-chestnut dressing (if chilled, bring to room temperature first); bake sweet potatoes and dressing about 30 minutes longer.

1 tablespoon salt and 1 tablespoon pepper; rub evenly over skin and inside the bird. If desired, wrap airtight and chill 12 to 24 hours.

2. Place turkey, breast up, on a V-shaped rack in a 12- by 17-inch roasting pan; tuck thyme and marjoram sprigs inside body cavity.

3. Roast in a 325° oven until a thermometer inserted through thickest part of breast to bone registers 160°, 2 to 3 hours.

4. Transfer turkey to a platter. Let stand in a warm place to rest at least 30 minutes, then carve. (See chart above for directions if thigh joint is pink.) Serve with salt and pepper to taste.

Per ¹/₄ pound boned cooked turkey with skin, based on percentages of white and dark meat in an average bird: 240 cal., 38% (90 cal.) from fat; 32 g protein; 10 g fat (3 g sat.); 2.9 g carbo (0 g fiber); 376 mg sodium; 93 mg chol.

Cornbread-Chestnut Dressing

PREP AND COOK TIME: About 1¹/₂ hours

NOTES: Bake the polenta cornbread (a variation of the yeast cornbread Luciano makes), or use your favorite cornbread recipe or mix. Instead of roasting the chestnuts, you can use 2 cups peeled cooked chestnuts (canned steamed, water-packed, or vacuum-packed). If making dressing up to 1 day ahead, chill airtight, then bake 50 to 65 minutes.

MAKES: 10 to 12 servings

- 1 pound **chestnuts** (see notes)
- 2 quarts ¹/₂-inch cubes **polenta cornbread** (recipe follows; see notes)
- 6 slices **bacon** (about ¹/₃ lb. total)
- 1 cup finely chopped **onion**
- ³/₄ cup finely chopped **celery**
- ¹/₄ cup finely chopped **green onions**
- 1 tablespoon minced **fresh sage leaves**
- 2 teaspoons minced **fresh thyme leaves**
- ¹/₄ teaspoon fresh-grated **nutmeg**
  Rich poultry broth with meats (recipe follows) or 2 cups fat-skimmed chicken broth
- ¹/₂ cup fat-skimmed **chicken broth** (optional)
  Salt and **pepper**

1. Discard any chestnuts that feel light for their size; they are spoiled or molded. Cut an X about ½ inch long through flat side of each shell. Place nuts in a 10- by 15-inch pan.

2. Bake in a 400° oven until nuts are no longer starchy-tasting (cut 1 open to test), 25 to 30 minutes. Wrap hot nuts in a towel and enclose in a plastic bag; let stand about 15 minutes. Remove 1 warm nut at a time and use a short-bladed knife to pull off shell and as much brown skin as possible; discard shell and skin. Coarsely chop or crumble chestnuts.

3. Meanwhile, in a 350° oven, toast polenta cornbread cubes in a 12- by 17-inch roasting pan, stirring occasionally, until edges begin to brown, 30 to 40 minutes.

4. In a 10- to 12-inch frying pan over medium-high heat, turn bacon occasionally until brown, 4 to 6 minutes; lift from pan and drain on towels. When cool, crumble and add to toasted cornbread.

5. To drippings in frying pan, add onion, celery, and green onions; stir occasionally until limp, 5 to 7 minutes. Add sage, thyme, nutmeg, and chestnuts; stir occasionally until vegetables are lightly browned, about 5 minutes longer. Scrape mixture into pan with cornbread.

6. Add poultry broth and chopped poultry-broth meats and mix gently; for a moister dressing, add ½ cup chicken broth. Season dressing with salt and pepper to taste. Spoon into a shallow 3-quart casserole and cover tightly.

7. Bake in a 350° oven until hot in the center (about 150°), 35 to 40 minutes. For a crusty top, uncover dressing for the last 20 to 25 minutes.

Per serving: 367 cal., 25% (90 cal.) from fat; 22 g protein; 10 g fat (4.5 g sat.); 45 g carbo (6 g fiber); 463 mg sodium; 136 mg chol.

Polenta Cornbread

PREP AND COOK TIME: About 45 minutes

NOTES: You can bake the cornbread 1 day before making the dressing; cool, wrap airtight, and store at room temperature.

MAKES: 9 servings or 2 quarts ½-inch cubes

  1 cup **all-purpose flour**

  1 cup **polenta**

  2 tablespoons **sugar**

2½ teaspoons **baking powder**

¾ teaspoon **salt**

  2 large **eggs**

  1 cup **buttermilk**

    About ¼ cup (⅛ lb.) cool melted **butter** or margarine

1. In a bowl, mix flour, polenta, sugar, baking powder, and salt. In another bowl, beat eggs to blend with buttermilk and ¼ cup butter; pour into flour mixture. Stir batter until evenly moistened.

2. Scrape batter into a buttered 8-inch square pan and spread level.

3. Bake in a 400° oven until cornbread is browned, springs back when lightly pressed in the center, and begins to pull from pan sides, 20 to 25 minutes. Use hot or cool.

Per serving: 251 cal., 27% (67 cal.) from fat; 6.4 g protein; 7.4 g fat (4.1 g sat.); 39 g carbo (3.5 g fiber); 431 mg sodium; 64 mg chol.

Rich Poultry Broth

PREP AND COOK TIME: About 1¾ hours

NOTES: If making up to 2 days ahead, cover and chill broth and meats separately. Or save giblets to make gravy (page 329) and use chicken broth for dressing.

MAKES: 2 cups

    Neck and giblets from 14- to 23-pound **turkey**, rinsed

  1 **chicken breast half** (about ½ lb.), rinsed

  2 stalks **celery** (about ¼ lb.), rinsed and cut into chunks

  1 **carrot** (about ¼ lb.), peeled and cut into chunks

  1 **onion** (about ½ lb.), peeled and quartered

2 or 3 **parsley sprigs**

  1 **fresh** or dried **bay leaf**

5 or 6 **black peppercorns**

  3 **whole cloves**

  1 tablespoon **red wine vinegar**

1. Reserve turkey liver for other uses. In a 5- to 6-quart pan, combine turkey neck, gizzard, and heart with chicken breast, celery, carrot, onion, parsley, bay leaf, peppercorns, cloves, vinegar, and 6 cups water.

2. Bring to a boil over high heat; reduce heat and simmer until gizzard is tender when pierced, about 1½ hours. Pour liquid through a fine strainer into

a bowl; spoon off and discard fat. If you have more than 2 cups broth, return to pan and boil over high heat to reduce; if less, add water to make 2 cups total.

3. When meats are cool enough to touch, discard skin and bones; finely chop meats and reserve for cornbread-chestnut dressing. Discard vegetables.

Per ½ cup: 27 cal., 27% (7.2 cal.) from fat; 1.8 g protein; 0.8 g fat (0.4 g sat.); 3.6 g carbo (0.7 g fiber); 68 mg sodium; 1.9 mg chol.

Cranberry-Apricot Chutney

PREP AND COOK TIME: About 20 minutes, plus at least 1 hour to cool

NOTES: If making ahead, chill airtight up to 3 days; freeze up to 1 month.

MAKES: About 5 cups

  1 package (12 oz.) **fresh** or frozen **cranberries**

  1 cup **sugar**

⅓ cup coarsely chopped **dried apricots**

⅓ cup **dried currants**

⅓ cup **golden raisins**

  2 tablespoons **balsamic vinegar**

  2 **tangerines** (about ¼ lb. each)

½ cup **chopped pecans**

1. Sort cranberries, discarding any bruised or decayed fruit. Rinse berries.

2. In a 3- to 4-quart pan over medium-high heat, bring 1 cup water, cranberries, sugar, apricots, currants, raisins, and vinegar to a boil, stirring often. Reduce heat and simmer, stirring occasionally, until cranberries begin to pop, 5 to 8 minutes.

3. Meanwhile, pull off peel and white membrane fibers from tangerines; discard peel and fibers. Separate segments and coarsely chop, discarding seeds. Add tangerines and juice to pan; simmer to blend flavors, 2 to 3 minutes.

4. Stir in pecans. Serve at room temperature or chilled.

Per ¼ cup: 88 cal., 19% (17 cal.) from fat; 0.6 g protein; 1.9 g fat (0.1 g sat.); 19 g carbo (1.4 g fiber); 1.1 mg sodium; 0 mg chol.

Sweet Potato Gratin

PREP AND COOK TIME: About 1½ hours

MAKES: 10 to 12 servings

  3 cups **whipping cream**

½ cup **sugar**

  1 tablespoon grated **orange** peel

½ teaspoon fresh-grated **nutmeg**

1 teaspoon **salt**

2½ pounds **sweet potatoes**

1 cup **pecan halves**

1. In a 2- to 3-quart pan over medium-high heat, frequently stir whipping cream, sugar, orange peel, nutmeg, and salt just until steaming, about 4 minutes.

2. Meanwhile, scrub sweet potatoes, peel, and slice crosswise very thinly. Spread slices in an even layer in a buttered shallow 3-quart casserole (9 by 13 in.). Pour hot cream mixture evenly over sweet potatoes.

3. Bake in a 350° oven for 30 minutes. Dipping liquid from casserole edge, spoon over sweet potatoes to moisten, then sprinkle evenly with pecans. Return to oven and bake until potatoes are well browned and tender when pierced, about 30 minutes longer.

Per serving: 339 cal., 66% (225 cal.) from fat; 3.1 g protein; 25 g fat (12 g sat.); 28 g carbo (2.6 g fiber); 224 mg sodium; 66 mg chol.

Green Beans with Tomatoes

PREP AND COOK TIME: About 30 minutes

NOTES: Luciano prefers Blue Lake beans for this simple recipe from his grandmother. Up to 1 day ahead, cook beans and make sauce; chill separately airtight. Reheat together.

MAKES: 10 to 12 servings

2 pounds **green beans** (see notes), ends and strings removed, rinsed

2 tablespoons **olive oil**

2 cups thinly sliced **onions**

1 can (28 oz.) **diced tomatoes with Italian seasonings**

Salt and **pepper**

1. In a 5- to 6-quart pan over high heat, bring 3 quarts water to a boil. Add beans and cook until tender to bite, 5 to 6 minutes. Drain beans and immerse in ice water until cool, about 3 minutes; drain again.

2. Pour olive oil into same pan over medium-high heat; add onions and stir often until limp, about 8 minutes. Add tomatoes with liquid; stir occasionally until sauce is reduced to about 2½ cups, about 10 minutes. Add beans and stir occasionally until hot, about 5 minutes. Season to taste with salt and pepper.

Per serving: 64 cal., 34% (22 cal.) from fat; 2.1 g protein; 2.4 g fat (0.3 g sat.); 9.2 g carbo (2.2 g fiber); 109 mg sodium; 0 mg chol.

Salad combines apples, pungent Stilton cheese, and red and white Belgian endive.

Red Onion Confit with Merlot and Balsamic Vinegar

PREP AND COOK TIME: About 45 minutes

NOTES: If making up to 3 days ahead, cover airtight and chill. Reheat in a microwave-safe dish in a microwave oven at full power (100%) for about 4 minutes, stirring halfway through.

MAKES: About 4½ cups; 10 to 12 servings

6 tablespoons **butter** or margarine

3 tablespoons **olive oil**

3 pounds **red onions,** peeled and thinly sliced

About 2 cups **Merlot** or other dry red **wine**

6 tablespoons **sugar**

¼ cup **balsamic vinegar**

Salt

1. In a 5- to 6-quart pan over medium-high heat, melt butter with olive oil. Add onions and stir often until they're limp and liquid has evaporated, 8 to 10 minutes.

2. Add 2 cups wine and the sugar; stir occasionally until liquid has evaporated and onions are sweet to taste and very tender, about 30 minutes. Add balsamic vinegar and salt to taste; stir of-

ten until flavors are blended, about 5 minutes. Serve warm.

Per serving: 155 cal., 54% (84 cal.) from fat; 2 g protein; 9.3 g fat (4 g sat.); 18 g carbo (1.8 g fiber); 73 mg sodium; 16 mg chol.

Belgian Endive Salad with Stilton and Apples

PREP AND COOK TIME: About 1 hour and 10 minutes

NOTES: Up to 1 day ahead, roast and chop shallots (step 1); chill airtight. Trim discolored ends from Belgian endive (or radicchio); rinse leaves, drain, wrap in towels, enclose in a plastic bag, and chill at least 15 minutes or up to 1 day.

MAKES: 10 to 12 servings

6 **shallots** (about 1 oz. each), peeled

About ½ cup **extra-virgin olive oil**

6 tablespoons **red wine vinegar**

1½ tablespoons **Dijon mustard**

½ teaspoon **sugar**

2 **Granny Smith** or Newtown Pippin **apples** (1 lb. total), rinsed

1 pound **white Belgian endive** (see notes)

Savor individual pumpkin cheesecakes with sips of *vin santo,* an Italian dessert wine.

3 tablespoons **brandy** or Cognac

3 tablespoons **maple syrup**

2 **large eggs**

1 can (15 oz.) **pumpkin**

2 tablespoons **whipping cream** or milk

½ teaspoon **ground cinnamon**

½ teaspoon **ground ginger**

¼ teaspoon fresh-grated **nutmeg**

2 tablespoons chopped **crystallized ginger**

2 cups (1 pt.) **sour cream**

1. In a 350° oven, bake pecans in an 8- or 9-inch-wide pan, shaking often until lightly toasted, about 10 minutes. Pour from pan. When cool, whirl in a blender or food processor until finely ground.

2. Brush interiors of 10 tart pans (4½ in. wide with removable rims; see notes) with the melted butter. Sprinkle 2 tablespoons ground toasted pecans over bottom of each pan. Set pans slightly apart on 2 baking sheets (14 by 17 in.).

3. In a bowl, with a mixer on medium-high speed, beat cream cheese to blend with ⅔ cup sugar, 2 tablespoons brandy, and 2 tablespoons maple syrup. Add eggs, pumpkin, cream, cinnamon, ground ginger, and nutmeg; stir to mix, then beat until well blended. Fill tart pans equally with cheesecake mixture.

4. Bake in a 325° oven until centers no longer jiggle when pans are gently shaken, 20 to 25 minutes.

5. Meanwhile, in a small bowl, mix remaining ½ cup chopped pecans and the crystallized ginger.

6. In another bowl, mix sour cream with remaining 2 tablespoons sugar, 1 tablespoon brandy, and 1 tablespoon maple syrup. Spoon mixture equally onto cheesecakes and spread level. Sprinkle pecan-ginger mixture equally over sour cream topping.

7. Return tarts to oven and bake to firm sour cream topping slightly, about 10 minutes. Transfer to a rack and let cool at least 30 minutes. Serve warm; or cool, cover airtight without touching tops, and chill until cold, at least 2 hours or up to 1 day. To serve, remove pan rims and set cheesecakes on plates.

Per serving: 465 cal., 72% (333 cal.) from fat; 6.9 g protein; 37 g fat (16 g sat.); 28 g carbo (1.9 g fiber); 168 mg sodium; 102 mg chol. ◆

1 pound **red Belgian endive** or red radicchio (see notes)

⅔ pound **Stilton cheese,** crumbled

Salt and **pepper**

1. In an 8- or 9-inch-wide pan, mix shallots with about 1 teaspoon olive oil. Bake in a 350° oven, stirring occasionally, until shallots are slightly browned and barely tender when pierced, about 40 minutes (20 to 25 minutes in a convection oven). When cool enough to touch, finely chop.

2. In a wide bowl, mix shallots, ½ cup olive oil, vinegar, mustard, and sugar. Peel apples, quarter, core, and cut lengthwise into ⅛-inch slivers. Add to bowl and mix with dressing.

3. Cut white and red Belgian endive lengthwise into ⅛-inch-wide slices. Add endive and cheese to bowl. Mix gently, and season the salad to taste with salt and pepper.

Per serving: 225 cal., 72% (162 cal.) from fat; 7.4 g protein; 18 g fat (6.7 g sat.); 10 g carbo (2.3 g fiber); 208 mg sodium; 27 mg chol.

Fall Pumpkin Cheesecakes

PREP AND COOK TIME: About 1½ hours, plus at least 2 hours to cool

NOTES: If making individual cheesecakes ahead, chill airtight in pans up to 1 day. Freeze in pans up to 1 week; thaw, wrapped, in the refrigerator for 12 to 18 hours. If desired, reheat in a 325° oven for 10 to 12 minutes. To make a large, single cheesecake (to serve up to 12), use a 9-inch tart pan with removable rim. In step 2 reduce butter to about 1 tablespoon and sprinkle 1½ cups chopped pecans in pan. Bake in a 325° oven as directed in step 4 for 50 to 55 minutes. Cut into wedges.

MAKES: 10 to 12 servings (see notes)

2 cups **pecan halves**

About 2 tablespoons melted **butter** or margarine

2 packages (8 oz. each) **cream cheese**

⅔ cup plus 2 tablespoons **sugar**

Grand gravy

■ Rich taste and caloric richness aren't necessarily synonymous, particularly when it comes to great giblet gravy. At Thanksgiving, when gravy's role is to anoint, moisten, and add an elegant layer of flavor, it can do so lightly, as here. Prepare the gravy base ahead; when the turkey is roasted, skim the drippings judiciously and use them to finish the gravy—dark brown from braising or amber-gold with mushrooms—in minutes.

Braised-brown Giblet Gravy

PREP AND COOK TIME: About 2½ hours

MAKES: 4¼ to 4½ cups

Neck and giblets from a 14- to 23-pound **turkey**

3 **carrots** (about ¾ lb. total), rinsed, peeled, and cut into 2-inch chunks

2 **onions** (about ¾ lb. total), peeled and quartered

4¾ cups fat-skimmed **chicken broth**

2 tablespoons **balsamic vinegar**

1 tablespoon **sugar**

Fat-skimmed **drippings** from a roasted 14- to 23-pound **turkey** (page 325; optional)

⅓ cup **cornstarch**

Salt and **pepper**

1. Rinse turkey neck, heart, gizzard, and liver; wrap liver and chill. Place neck, heart, gizzard, carrots, and onions in a 9-by 13-inch metal pan. Add ½ cup broth.

2. Bake in a 475° oven until liquid is evaporated and vegetables, neck, heart, and gizzard are browned, 40 to 45 minutes (30 to 35 minutes in a convection oven); stir several times. Add ¼ cup broth, vinegar, and sugar to pan; stir to scrape browned bits free. Add liver to pan (or save for other uses). Bake until mixture is richly browned and liver is faintly pink in the center (cut to test), 10 to 15 minutes longer (about 5 minutes in a convection oven); stir several times.

3. Remove from oven; set liver aside. Add 1 more cup broth to pan; let stand until browned bits are soft, about 5

Brown giblet gravy flowing in rivulets over roast turkey and mashed potatoes is a holiday essential.

CRAIG MAXWELL

minutes. Scrape mixture into a 4- to 5-quart pan. Add remaining 3 cups broth. Bring to a boil over high heat; cover and simmer until gizzard is tender when pierced, about 1¼ hours. Pour mixture through a fine strainer into a large bowl. Discard vegetables. Pull meat from neck and chop; discard bones. Finely chop meat and giblets. If making ahead, cover bowl and meat, and chill up to 1 day.

4. Measure broth mixture and, if needed, add water to make 4 cups. Return broth to the 4- to 5-quart pan. Add meat mixture and turkey drippings; bring to a boil over high heat. In a small bowl, blend cornstarch with ¼ cup water. Stir in enough cornstarch mixture to boiling gravy to thicken as desired. Season to taste with salt and pepper.

Per ¼ cup: 98 cal., 17% (17 cal.) from fat; 12 g protein; 1.9 g fat (0.6 g sat.); 6.9 g carbo (0.3 g fiber); 81 mg sodium; 69 mg chol.

Mushroom Essence Giblet Gravy

PREP AND COOK TIME: About 2¼ hours

MAKES: About 4¼ to 4½ cups

1 pound **mushrooms,** finely chopped

½ cup chopped **onion**

½ cup **sherry**

5 cups fat-skimmed **chicken broth**

Neck and giblets from a 14- to 23-pound **turkey**

Fat-skimmed **drippings** from a roasted 14- to 23-pound **turkey** (see page 325; optional)

⅓ cup **cornstarch**

Salt and **pepper**

1. Combine mushrooms, onion, sherry, and 1 cup broth in a 4- to 5-quart nonstick pan over high heat. Bring to a boil and stir often until liquid is evaporated and mushrooms are very well browned, 20 to 25 minutes; add 1 to 2 tablespoons water, if needed, to prevent scorching.

2. Rinse turkey neck, heart, gizzard, and liver; wrap liver and chill. Add neck, heart, gizzard, and 4 cups broth to pan. Cover, bring to a boil over high heat, and simmer until gizzard is tender when pierced, about 1½ hours. Add liver (or save for other uses) and cook until faintly pink in the center (cut to test), 5 to 8 minutes. Pour mixture through a strainer into a bowl. Discard vegetables. Pull meat from neck; discard bones. Finely chop meat and giblets. If making ahead, cover bowl and meat mixture, and chill up to 1 day.

3. Measure broth mixture and, if needed, add water to make 4 cups. Return broth mixture to the 4- to 5-quart pan and add meat mixture and turkey drippings; bring to a boil over high heat. In a small bowl, blend cornstarch with ¼ cup water. Stir in enough cornstarch mixture to thicken boiling gravy as desired. Season to taste with salt and pepper.

Per ¼ cup: 90 cal., 19% (17 cal.) from fat; 12 g protein; 1.9 g fat (0.6 g sat.); 5.5 g carbo (0.2 g fiber); 74 mg sodium; 69 mg chol. ◆

food guide

By Jerry Anne Di Vecchio • Photographs by James Carrier

Salad break

Balance holiday feasting with refreshing greens

■ My job as a food editor includes tasting many dishes—often hourly in our test kitchen. When I'm seriously exploring restaurants on the road, I usually visit five or six a day, sampling my way through each menu. Sure, it's fun, but it's also mighty filling. During some dense dining on a recent whirlwind tour of Seattle eateries, I came across this salad at the Palisade restaurant at the Elliott Bay Marina and was struck by how it refreshed my weary palate. The sweet, smoky combination would be just the thing for a simple supper to break up end-of-the-year holiday excesses.

Butter Lettuce Shrimp Salad with Pears and Blue Cheese

PREP TIME: About 35 minutes

NOTES: Chef John Howie at Palisade smokes the hazelnuts himself, but you can occasionally find smoked hazelnuts in the supermarket. If you can't, use smoked almonds.

MAKES: 4 servings

- 2 heads **butter lettuce** (1¼ to 1⅓ lb. total)
- ½ pound **shelled cooked tiny shrimp**
- ½ cup **cherry tomatoes** (½ in. wide, if available)
- ½ cup **roasted salted smoked hazelnuts** or roasted salted smoked almonds (see notes)
- 2 **firm-ripe Asian,** Comice, or Bosc **pears** (about ½ lb. each)
- 2 tablespoons **lemon juice** or rice vinegar
  Blue cheese dressing (recipe follows)
  Fresh-ground **pepper**

1. Rinse and drain lettuce leaves; wrap in towels, enclose in a plastic bag, and chill at least 15 minutes or up to 2 days.

2. Rinse shrimp with cold water and drain. Rinse and stem tomatoes; if larger than ½ inch, cut into quarters.

3. Coarsely chop nuts. Rinse pears, core, and cut into ¼-inch-thick sticks; in a bowl, mix cut fruit with lemon juice.

4. Mound lettuce on plates or in bowls. Over lettuce, evenly scatter shrimp, tomatoes, and nuts. Top equally with pears. Ladle dressing to taste over salads and sprinkle with pepper.

Per serving: 226 cal., 38% (85 cal.) from fat; 18 g protein; 9.4 g fat (0.8 g sat.); 22 g carbo (5.8 g fiber); 234 mg sodium; 111 mg chol.

Blue cheese dressing. In a bowl, break ½ pound **blue cheese** (1 cup packed) into ½-inch chunks. Add ½ cup **buttermilk,** ½ cup **mayonnaise,** ¼ cup **sour cream,** 1 tablespoon **red wine vinegar,** and 1 teaspoon **dry mustard;** stir until blended. If making up to 4 days ahead, cover and chill; stir before using. Makes 1⅔ cups.

Per tablespoon: 60 cal., 87% (52 cal.) from fat; 1.7 g protein; 5.8 g fat (2 g sat.); 0.6 g carbo (0 g fiber); 121 mg sodium; 8.5 mg chol.

Warming tray

COOL HEAT

■ Evaco's food-warming tray brings a number of assets to elegant dining: no cord to clutter a beautiful table; simple, classic lines; durable materials; and the capacity to keep a casserole or two hot during a long holiday meal. The tray is warmed by candles (it comes with two small votives) and is windproof, so you can use it outdoors in the summer. The heat is distributed by a heavy aluminum plate that nests solidly in the stainless steel base. The warming tray, which costs about $70, makes a gracious and useful gift—but don't deprive yourself. It's available at at Sur La Table (800/243-0852).

The pudding is the proof

■ Dates are the secret ingredient in a very popular, very gooey, very easy English dessert, aptly named sticky pudding. I say secret because the puréed dates are so well integrated in the tender cake—the base of the pudding—that you can't tell the fruit is there. The buttery caramel sauce makes the dish addictive.

Sticky Pudding

PREP AND COOK TIME: About 1¼ hours

NOTES: If making sticky pudding up to 2 days ahead, tip sauced pudding from pan onto a microwave-safe serving plate, cover with a large inverted bowl, and chill. To serve, uncover and heat in a microwave oven on full power (100%) for about 5 minutes.

MAKES: 10 servings

¾ pound **pitted dates**

About ½ cup (¼ lb.) **butter** or margarine

About 1½ cups **all-purpose flour**

1½ teaspoons **baking powder**

½ teaspoon **baking soda**

¾ cup firmly packed **brown sugar**

3 large eggs

Sticky sauce (recipe follows)

Crème fraîche or sour cream

1. In a 3- to 4-quart pan, combine dates and 1½ cups water. Bring to a boil over high heat and stir often until most of the liquid is absorbed, 5 to 7 minutes; watch carefully as liquid reduces to avoid scorching. Let cool at least 15 minutes.

2. Butter and flour a 9-inch square pan. In a bowl, mix 1½ cups flour with baking powder and baking soda.

3. In a food processor, whirl cooked dates until smooth. Add ½ cup butter, sugar, eggs, and flour mixture; whirl until well blended. Scrape batter into pan and spread level.

4. Bake in a 325° oven until cake springs back when lightly pressed in the center and edges begin to pull from pan sides, 30 to 40 minutes. Let cool in pan at least 5 minutes. Invert onto a rack. Cut warm or cool cake in half horizontally.

5. Rinse and dry baking pan. Pour about ½ cup hot sticky sauce into pan. Lay cake bottom, cut side up, in pan. Pour about 2 cups hot sticky sauce evenly over cake. Lay cake top, cut side down, in pan. Pour remaining hot sticky sauce evenly over it. Let stand at least 30 minutes or up to 1 hour. Invert a flat, rimmed plate over pan; holding containers together, turn over, and lift pan off cake. Cut into rectangles and transfer with a spatula to plates. Add crème fraîche to taste.

Per serving: 717 cal., 48% (342 cal.) from fat; 6.2 g protein; 38 g fat (23 g sat.); 94 g carbo (2.2 g fiber); 338 mg sodium; 181 mg chol.

Sticky sauce. In a 5- to 6-quart pan over high heat, boil 1½ cups **whipping cream,** 1½ cups **sugar,** ¼ cup (⅛ lb.) **butter** or margarine, and ¼ cup **light corn syrup,** stirring frequently, until golden brown, 6 to 8 minutes. Remove from heat and immediately stir another 1½ cups whipping cream into pan. Return to high heat and stir until sauce comes to a rolling boil, 1 to 2 minutes. Use hot, or let cool, cover, and chill up to 2 days; stir over high heat until hot. Makes 3½ cups.

A date to celebrate

■ "Fresh" isn't an adjective often applied to dates. Even though technically they aren't dried, by the time these sticky fruits have endured the rigors of maturing on the palm trees in desert heat, most seem dry enough to last forever, whether aboard nomadic caravans in the bleak Sahara or tucked away in your cupboard.

Not all dates are tough, however. Some lesser-known varieties are soft and velvety smooth to the bite. And as you might expect, they're fragile and challenging to ship. The Celebration date, which melts in your mouth, is a notable example. This volunteer variety was discovered in a small grove near Phoenix around 1920. Since then, it has been nurtured for local consumption. You can order Celebration dates from Fruitful Gifts of Arizona (800/575-8597 or www.fruitfulgifts.com). Packed individually like fine chocolates, they are sold in ¾-pound boxes for $17.95, plus shipping.

Count on this Russian

■ Once upon a time, according to the various Russian-authored cookbooks in my library, there was a Count Stroganoff who dabbled in the arts of the table. His legacy is this simple, timeless dish bearing his name. It's recorded that he prepared it before guests, doubtless with an army of servants to lend a hand. Beef stroganoff, however, is uncomplicated enough to execute without a staff. Served in a ring of pasta, it makes a handsome main dish for a party.

Beef Stroganoff

PREP AND COOK TIME: About 45 minutes

NOTES: Make the sauce (through step 2) and slice the meat up to 1 day ahead; cover separately and chill.

MAKES: 5 or 6 servings

- 1 pound **mushrooms**
- 1 **onion** (6 oz.), peeled and chopped
- 3 tablespoons **butter** or margarine
- 2 tablespoons **brandy**
- 2 tablespoons **all-purpose flour**
- 1 tablespoon Dijon **mustard**
- 1 tablespoon **catsup** or tomato paste
- 2 teaspoons **prepared horseradish**
- 1 cup fat-skimmed **beef broth**

  About 1 cup **sour cream**

  Salt and **pepper**
- 1 pound fat-trimmed **tender beef** (such as tenderloin or New York strip)

  Pasta ring (recipe follows), heated
- 2 tablespoons chopped **fresh dill** or 1 teaspoon dried dill weed

1. Rinse mushrooms; trim off and discard discolored stem ends. Cut mushrooms vertically into ⅛- to ¼-inch slices. In a 10- to 12-inch nonstick frying pan, combine mushrooms, onion, and 2 tablespoons butter. Stir often over high heat until juices have evaporated and mushrooms are lightly browned, about 10 minutes. Add brandy and stir until liquid has evaporated, about 1 minute. Remove from heat and stir flour into mushroom mixture. Then stir in mustard, catsup, horseradish, and beef broth.

2. Return pan to high heat and stir until mixture is boiling, about 3 minutes. Add 1 cup sour cream and stir to blend. Add salt and pepper to taste. Pour mushroom sauce into a bowl.

3. Rinse meat and pat dry. Cut across the grain into ⅛-inch-thick slices. Rinse and dry frying pan, place over high heat, and add remaining tablespoon butter. When it just begins to brown, add half the beef; stir until meat is lightly browned in some places and still pink in others, 2 to 3 minutes. With a slotted spoon, transfer cooked meat to mushroom sauce. Add remaining beef to pan and repeat to brown. When all the meat is cooked, return stroganoff mixture to frying pan and stir until bubbling, 2 to 5 minutes.

4. Pour stroganoff into center of pasta ring, sprinkle with dill, and top with a dollop of sour cream. Cut through pasta with a sharp knife and serve stroganoff and pasta with 2 large spoons.

Per serving: 620 cal., 36% (225 cal.) from fat; 30 g protein; 25 g fat (13 g sat.); 68 g carbo (3.3 g fiber); 257 mg sodium; 89 mg chol.

Pasta Ring

PREP AND COOK TIME: About 20 minutes, plus at least 1 hour to stand

NOTES: Shape the pasta in a plain ring mold that holds 6 to 12 cups. If making up to 1 day ahead, cover pasta in mold and chill.

MAKES: 5 or 6 servings

- 1 pound **dried spaghetti**
- 1 tablespoon **butter** or olive oil

1. In a 5- to 6-quart pan over high heat, bring 3 quarts water to a boil. Add spaghetti and cook, stirring occasionally, until tender to bite, 10 to 12 minutes.

2. Drain pasta and immerse in cold water; when cool enough to touch, in about 1 minute, drain again. Mix with butter.

3. Lift pasta, a handful at a time, and let strands shake out until fairly straight; lay neatly around the center of a ring mold (see notes). Repeat, using all the pasta; pat to make level. Let stand at least 1 hour (see notes).

4. Invert a flat, rimmed microwave-safe plate over mold. Holding containers together, flip over and lift off mold.

5. Cover pasta with microwave-safe plastic wrap. Heat in a microwave oven on full power (100%) until pasta is hot, about 5 minutes. Uncover and fill (see beef stroganoff recipe, preceding).

Per serving: 298 cal., 9.3% (28 cal.) from fat; 9.7 g protein; 3.1 g fat (1.4 g sat.); 57 g carbo (1.8 g fiber); 25 mg sodium; 5.2 mg chol. ◆

The Wine Guide

By Karen MacNeil-Fife

THANKSGIVING IN A GLASS:
Wines from Italy

■ Few of us today experience seasonal harvests the way the Pilgrims did. Freshly gathered food is available year-round. Wine, however, is different. It connects us to our past through a well-defined harvest, one monumental period when the entire year's hard work comes to fruition—or doesn't. Maybe more than anyone else, wine-makers understand how the Pilgrims must have felt in the fall when abundant crops were in: thankful.

Because of wine's ineluctable ties to the harvest cycle, I've always thought that, more than any other beverage, it deserves a place on the table at Thanksgiving. I would add only one caveat: Thanksgiving dinner is comfort food at its finest, so the wines must be comforting too.

This year we offer a Thanksgiving menu (page 320) inspired from Italy, a country that produces a myriad of wines worth celebrating. But a trip through the Italian section of a wine shop can leave you reeling from dozens of unfamiliar place-names, grape varieties, and producers. So let me help. Here's a brief Italian-wine primer matched to our menu.

The gravlax, albeit not exactly an Italian beginning, has a perfect Italian partner: sparkling wine. Northern Italy is a vast expanse of vineyards, and much of the wine made there is the sparkler known as *spumante*

RICK MARIANI

(foaming). A good bet for the gravlax would be a top dry spumante such as Bellavista or Ferrari. Or go with my favorite semisparkler: *prosecco*—dry and refreshing but not quite as bubbly as spumante. The Italians call it *frizzante* (lightly fizzy).

The minestrone and pumpkin-stuffed pasta have the rich sweetness that comes out in vegetables when they're cooked slowly, making them perfect foils for a fresh white wine. Italian whites are generally fairly simple, sharp, and lively—easy counterpoints to food. Among my favorites are Pinot Grigio (lemony and

SUNSET'S STEAL OF THE MONTH
Tiziano Chianti 1998 (Tuscany), $7.
This is your basic spaghetti-and-meat-balls Chianti: simple, tart, and cherry-like—a flashback to those bohemian dinners in the '60s. — KAREN MACNEIL-FIFE

crisp); Orvieto (dry and almondy), named after the Umbrian town of Orvieto; and Tocai Friulano (snappy and herbal) from the province of Friuli.

The roast turkey with cornbread and chestnut dressing, the sweet potato gratin, and the onion confit are definitely territory for red wine, an obligatory part of any Italian meal. And there are hundreds of great options. One good plan of attack is to leave yourself in the hands of a wine shop that specializes in Italian wines (such as Traverso's in Santa Rosa, California, near where I live). But I also like the idea of heading straight for a Chianti Classico, made in the province of Tuscany from Sangiovese grapes. A great Chianti is neither powerful nor bold; it has sumptuous, earthy flavors—quiet music compared to Cabernet's rock and roll. Sangiovese has good acidity, so it glides easily around the flavors of all kinds of foods.

Finally, the pumpkin cheesecakes call for something dramatic, something with pizzazz. No problem. One of Italy's best-kept secrets is its dessert wines. For the cheesecakes, I recommend two: *vin santo* (holy wine) from Tuscany and the harder-to-find but glorious Malvasia delle Lipari from the tiny island of Lipari near Sicily. Neither is syrupy sweet, but then a great dessert wine isn't supposed to taste like bad wedding cake. It should be ethereal and a bit seductive—the crescendo of a consummate Italian meal.

A CHOICE LIST FOR THANKSGIVING

■ **Ferrari Brut nonvintage (Trento),** $20. Dry, sassy, and sleek (not unlike the car that shares its name).

■ **Arneri Prosecco nonvintage (Veneto),** $17. Light and frothy, with subtle but delicious hints of lemon and almond.

■ **Zenato Pinot Grigio 1999 (delle Venezie),** $10. Vibrant, lemony, and floral, with light peachy notes.

■ **Zamo & Zamo Tocai Friulano 1999 (Colli Orientali, Friuli),** $24. Dramatically fresh, with a sharp, peppery character.

■ **Ruffino Chianti Classico Riserva Ducale 1996 (Tuscany),** $24. Easy to find, this classic Chianti is a great standby. Supple and earthy, with hints of spice and orange peel.

■ **Castellare "I Sodi di San Niccolo" 1994 (Tuscany),** $40. Though it has a proprietary name, this top wine from Castellare is made in the Chianti region primarily from Sangiovese grapes. Ripe and very earthy, with a long finish. This vintage (the current one) is good; an older one would be even better.

■ **Antinori Vin Santo 1996 (Tuscany),** $33 (500 ml.). This vin santo, with delicate, creamy honey and roasted-nut flavors, isn't overly sweet. ◆

Kitchen Cabinet

Readers' recipes tested in Sunset's kitchens

By Linda Lau Anusasananan

Grand prize: Apple-cranberry-currant pie with a crumbly brown-sugar topping.

PREP AND COOK TIME: About 1½ hours, plus at least 2½ hours to cool

MAKES: 10 to 12 servings

- ¼ cup **brandy**
- ¼ cup **currants**
- 1½ cups **fresh** or thawed frozen **cranberries**
    - About 1¼ cups **granulated sugar**
- 6 tablespoons plus 1 cup **unbleached** or regular **all-purpose flour**
- 1 tablespoon grated **orange** peel
- ¾ teaspoon **ground cinnamon**
- ½ teaspoon **ground nutmeg**
- ¼ teaspoon **salt**
- 6 cups sliced peeled **Granny Smith apples** (about 2¼ lb.)
    - **10-inch pie pastry** for a single-crust pie (recipe, page 337)
- ⅔ cup firmly packed **brown sugar**
- ½ cup (¼ lb.) **butter** or margarine, cut into chunks

1. In a small bowl, combine brandy and currants. Cover and let stand until currants are plump, at least 1 hour or up to 1 day.

2. Sort cranberries and discard any that are bruised or decayed. Rinse and drain berries.

3. In a large bowl, mix 1¼ cups granulated sugar, 6 tablespoons flour, orange peel, cinnamon, nutmeg, and salt. With a slotted spoon, lift currants from brandy; reserve brandy. Add currants, cranberries, and apples to sugar mixture and mix well. Taste and add more granulated sugar if desired. Pour filling into unbaked 10-inch pie pastry in pan. Drizzle evenly with reserved brandy.

4. In another bowl, mix 1 cup flour and the brown sugar. Add butter and cut in with a pastry blender or rub with your fingers until mixture forms small lumps. Sprinkle topping evenly over filling. Set pie in a foil-lined 12-inch pizza pan or 10- by 15-inch baking pan.

5. Bake on the bottom rack of a 375° oven until juices bubble around edges and through topping, 55 to 65 minutes. If pie browns too quickly (check after 30 minutes), cover loosely with foil.

6. Set pie, uncovered, on a rack until cool to touch, 2½ to 3 hours. Cut into wedges.

Per serving: 428 cal., 34% (144 cal.) from fat; 3.6 g protein; 16 g fat (8.3 g sat.); 69 g carbo (2.5 g fiber); 219 mg sodium; 31 mg chol.

Holiday pies: The winners

■ We've long suspected that the best pie recipe in the West isn't expounded in any sleek, award-winning cookbook. It's penned in Aunt Gretel's loose scrawl on a dog-eared sheet tucked into a drawer, or imprinted in Grandma Taylor's mind from years of watching *her* grandmother make it. So last March we sent out a call for your best original pies. Hundreds of you responded, with creations traditional and trendy. Here are the five that our tasting panel gave the highest marks of all. The grand prize winner received a gift certificate for $350 from HomeChef cookware stores and a trip to our headquarters in Menlo Park, California; runners-up received $100 and the *2000 Sunset Recipe Annual*.

Grand Prize

Apple-Cranberry-Currant Pie with French Topping

Beth Secrest, Somers, Montana

Beth Secrest once baked four to eight pies a day at the Northern Lights Saloon on the border of Glacier National Park. Now she puts her baking expertise to use at home, where she created this dressed-up apple pie. If making up to 1 day ahead, cover and chill. To warm cold pie, bake uncovered in a 350° oven 10 to 15 minutes.

Runners-up

Pumpkin Streusel Pie

Sharon L. Klein, Portland

Sharon Klein embellishes a classic pumpkin pie with a streusel topping, then overlaps pastry leaves around the edge and sets a few on top. If making the leaves, double the pastry recipe. Roll out half as directed for crust; roll other half into a ⅛-inch-thick round and use a cookie cutter to make shapes, or place a leaf on dough and cut around it with a small, sharp knife. If making pie up to 1 day ahead, cover and chill.

PREP AND COOK TIME: About 1 hour, plus at least 2 hours to cool

MAKES: 10 to 12 servings

- ½ cup **granulated sugar**
- ½ cup firmly packed **dark brown sugar**
- 1 tablespoon **all-purpose flour**
- 1½ teaspoons **ground cinnamon**
- ½ teaspoon **ground nutmeg**
- ½ teaspoon **salt**
- ¼ teaspoon **ground ginger**
- 1 can (15 oz.) **pumpkin**
- 1 can (12 oz.) **evaporated milk**
- 2 **large eggs**, beaten to blend

  10-inch pie pastry for a single-crust pie (recipe, page 337; for leaves, see notes above)

  Walnut streusel (recipe follows)

1. In a bowl, mix granulated sugar, brown sugar, flour, cinnamon, nutmeg, salt, and ginger. Add pumpkin, milk, and eggs; whisk until well blended.

2. Pour mixture into unbaked 10-inch pie pastry in pan. Sprinkle walnut streusel evenly over filling.

3. Bake on the bottom rack of a 375° oven until center barely jiggles when pan is gently shaken, 35 to 40 minutes.

4. Set on a rack until cool to touch, about 2 hours. Cut into wedges.

Per serving: 395 cal., 43% (171 cal.) from fat; 7 g protein; 19 g fat (8 g sat.); 51 g carbo (1.7 g fiber); 278 mg sodium; 66 mg chol.

Walnut streusel. In a bowl, combine ½ cup firmly packed **brown sugar,** ½ cup **rolled oats,** ½ cup chopped **walnuts,** ¼ cup **all-purpose flour,** ¼ cup (⅛ lb.) **butter** or margarine, and ½ teaspoon *each* **ground cinnamon** and **ground nutmeg.** Mix until crumbly. Makes about 2 cups.

Per serving: 125 cal., 53% (66 cal.) from fat; 1.6 g protein; 7.3 g fat (2.8 g sat.); 14 g carbo (0.7 g fiber); 45 mg sodium; 11 mg chol.

Crunchy walnut-oat streusel tops pumpkin custard. Pastry leaves herald the fall.

Citrus-Almond Pie

Phyllis Ciardo, Albany, California

This pie contains the flavors of the Italian confection *panforte:* honey, nuts, and candied citrus. It's slightly reminiscent of holiday fruitcake. Use the 9-inch pie pastry on page 337 (double the recipe), or buy a refrigerated pastry (15-oz. package; use at room temperature). Follow steps 4 and 5 of pastry recipe to roll half the dough for bottom crust and to line pan (don't fold or flute edge). If making pie up to 2 days ahead, cover airtight and store at room temperature.

PREP AND COOK TIME: About 1¼ hours, plus at least 2½ hours to cool

MAKES: 8 to 10 servings

- 1½ cups (½ lb.) **almonds**
- 3 tablespoons **all-purpose flour**
- 1 tablespoon **ground cinnamon**
- 1 teaspoon **ground allspice**
- ¾ teaspoon **ground coriander**
- ¼ teaspoon **salt**
- 2 cups **orange juice**
- 1 cup **raisins**
- 1 cup (6 oz.) **candied** (glacé) **orange peel**
- 1 cup (6 oz.) **candied** (glacé) **citron**
- ½ cup **honey**

  9-inch pie pastry for a double-crust pie (see notes above)
- 1 **large egg** yolk

1. Place almonds in a 9-inch square baking pan. Bake in a 375° oven until golden under skins, about 10 minutes. Cool about 10 minutes; chop.

2. Meanwhile, in a 2- to 3-quart pan, mix flour, cinnamon, allspice, coriander, and salt. Gradually add orange juice, stirring until smooth. Stir in raisins, orange peel, and citron. Cover and bring to a boil over high heat, stirring occasionally; reduce heat to medium-low and simmer until peel is tender when pierced, about 5 minutes. Remove from heat and stir in honey and almonds.

3. Scrape nut mixture into bottom crust of 9-inch pie pastry in pan.

4. On a lightly floured surface, with a lightly floured rolling pin, roll remaining pastry into a ⅛-inch-thick round about 11 inches wide; center over nut mixture. Fold edge of top pastry under edge of bottom one flush with pan rim, and crimp together to seal. Flute edge decoratively. With a small, sharp knife, cut several slits in top pastry. Set pie in a foil-lined 12-inch pizza pan or 10- by 15-inch baking pan.

Kitchen Cabinet

Double-crusted spiced Asian pear pie wears a cap of caramel and pecans.

JAMES CARRIER

Beat egg yolk to blend with 2 teaspoons cold water; brush lightly over top crust.

5. Bake pie on the bottom rack of a 375° oven until browned, 50 to 55 minutes (30 to 35 minutes in a convection oven). If pie browns too quickly (check after 20 minutes), cover top loosely with foil. Transfer to a rack and let stand, uncovered, until cool to touch, 2½ to 3 hours. Cut into wedges.

Per serving: 603 cal., 40% (243 cal.) from fat; 8.9 g protein; 27 g fat (7.5 g sat.); 86 g carbo (4.2 g fiber); 298 mg sodium; 40 mg chol.

Kathy's Peerless Pear Pie

Kathy Hill, Siletz, Oregon

A caramelized nut topping glazes the top of this spiced Asian pear pie. Use the 9-inch pie pastry on the facing page (double the recipe), or buy a refrigerated pastry (15-oz. package; use at room temperature). Follow steps 4 and 5 of pastry recipe to roll half the dough for bottom crust and to line pan (don't fold or flute edge). If making pie up to 1 day ahead, cover and chill. To warm cold pie, bake uncovered in a 350° oven, 10 to 15 minutes.

PREP AND COOK TIME: About 1 hour and 20 minutes, plus about 3 hours to cool

MAKES: **8 servings**

¾ cup **granulated sugar**

About 6 tablespoons **all-purpose flour**

2 teaspoons **ground cinnamon**

½ teaspoon **ground nutmeg**

½ teaspoon **ground allspice**

6 cups thinly sliced peeled **firm-ripe Asian pears** (about 3 lbs.)

2 tablespoons **lemon juice**

9-inch pie pastry for a double-crust pie (see notes above)

5 tablespoons **butter** or margarine

¾ cup firmly packed **brown sugar**

⅓ cup **honey**

½ cup coarsely chopped **pecans**

1. In a large bowl, mix granulated sugar, flour, 1 teaspoon cinnamon, nutmeg, and allspice. Add pears and lemon juice; mix.

2. Mound fruit in bottom crust of pie pastry in pan so that it's higher in the center than at the edges. Cut 2 tablespoons butter into small pieces and dot over pear mixture.

3. On a lightly floured surface, with a lightly floured rolling pin, roll remaining pastry into a ⅛-inch-thick round about 12 inches wide. Center over fruit. Fold edge of top pastry under edge of bottom one flush with pan rim; crimp together to seal. Flute edge decoratively. With a small, sharp knife, cut several slits in top pastry. Set pie in a foil-lined 12-inch pizza pan or 10- by 15-inch baking pan.

4. Bake on the bottom rack of a 375° oven until juices bubble under slits near center of pie, 50 to 55 minutes (40 to 45 minutes in a convection oven).

5. In a 1- to 1½-quart pan over medium heat, stir 3 tablespoons butter until melted. Stir in brown sugar, honey, and 1 teaspoon cinnamon; cook, stirring often, until mixture bubbles all over, 2 to 4 minutes. At once, stir in nuts and spoon mixture evenly over hot pie. Let cool on a rack about 3 hours. Cut into wedges.

Per serving: 542 cal., 37% (198 cal.) from fat; 3.5 g protein; 22 g fat (8.8 g sat.); 89 g carbo (4 g fiber); 199 mg sodium; 31 mg chol.

Lemon Custard Mincemeat Pie

Ruth Womac, Port Angeles, Washington

A layer of lemon custard brings a fresh touch to mincemeat in this holiday pie. If making up to 1 day ahead, cover and chill.

PREP AND COOK TIME: About 1 hour, plus about 2 hours to cool

MAKES: 10 to 12 servings

1 jar (29 oz.) **prepared mincemeat**

10-inch pie pastry for single-crust pie (recipe, facing page)

1 **lemon** (5 oz.), rinsed

⅔ cup **sugar**

2 tablespoons **all-purpose flour**

1 cup **milk**

3 tablespoons melted **butter** or margarine

2 **large eggs**

1. Spread mincemeat evenly over bottom of unbaked 10-inch pastry in pan. Set pan in a foil-lined 12-inch pizza pan or 10- by 15-inch baking pan.

2. Grate 1 tablespoon of peel (yellow part only) from the lemon. Ream 3 tablespoons juice.

3. In a bowl, mix sugar and flour. Whisk in milk, butter, eggs, lemon peel, and lemon juice. Carefully pour mixture over mincemeat.

4. Bake in a 375° oven until custard barely jiggles when pan is gently shaken, 45 to 55 minutes (35 to 45 minutes in a convection oven). If pie browns too quickly (check after 15 minutes), cover loosely with foil. Let cool on a rack, uncovered, about 2 hours. Cut into wedges.

Per serving: 385 cal., 33% (126 cal.) from fat; 4.3 g protein; 14 g fat (5.9 g sat.); 60 g carbo (0.5 g fiber); 320 mg sodium; 56 mg chol.

perfect pastry

10-inch Pie Pastry

PREP TIME: About 20 minutes

MAKES: 10-inch single crust

1. In a bowl, mix 1½ cups **unbleached** or regular **all-purpose flour** and ¼ teaspoon **salt.** Add ¼ cup (2 oz.) cold **butter** or margarine, cut into chunks, and ¼ cup cold **solid shortening,** cut into chunks (or omit butter and use ½ cup shortening). With a pastry blender or your fingers, cut in the fats or rub with your fingers until mixture forms pea-size crumbs.

2. Sprinkle 3 tablespoons **cold water** over crumbs and mix with your hands until evenly moistened. Gently squeeze about ¼ cup of the dough into a ball; if it won't hold together, crumble lump back into bowl, sprinkle with 1 more tablespoon water, and mix again until evenly moistened.

3. With lightly floured hands, form dough into a ball. Dust ball lightly with flour; flatten into a round about ¾ inch thick, pressing edges to make smooth.

4. On a lightly floured surface, with a lightly floured rolling pin, roll dough firmly but gently in short strokes from the center outward to form a round ⅛ inch thick and about 14 inches wide; lift and turn dough occasionally, dusting underneath with more flour. If edges split while rolling, press them back toward the center to make smooth.

5. Fold dough round in half, lift gently without stretching, and lay folded edge across the center of a 10-inch pie pan. Unfold and ease dough into pan. Trim edge evenly 1 inch beyond pan rim; reserve scraps for other uses or discard. Fold edge under itself flush with rim; flute decoratively. Cover crust and chill until ready to use.

Per serving: 133 cal., 56% (75 cal.) from fat; 1.8 g protein; 8.3 g fat (3.5 g sat.); 13 g carbo (0.5 g fiber); 87 mg sodium; 10 mg chol.

9-inch Pie Pastry

PREP TIME: About 20 minutes

MAKES: 9-inch single crust

Follow recipe for **10-inch pie pastry** (preceding), decreasing **all-purpose flour** to 1 cup and **butter** and **solid shortening** to 3 tablespoons *each* (or omit butter and use 6 tablespoons shortening). Roll dough in step 4 into a 12-inch round.

Per serving: 143 cal., 59% (84 cal.) from fat; 1.8 g protein; 9.3 g fat (3.9 g sat.); 13 g carbo (0.5 g fiber); 116 mg sodium; 12 mg chol. ◆

Fall color at Bartholomew Park.

A wine lover's walk in Sonoma

■ Want a little wine, a lovely walk, and a history lesson full of intrigue? Look no farther than Sonoma's Bartholomew Memorial Park. Easy to reach from the town plaza but hidden from the masses, the 400-acre "Bart Park," as it's known to locals, encompasses vineyards that blaze with autumn color, oak groves, forests of manzanita and madrone, a babbling brook, and, on clear days, views that stretch all the way to San Francisco. What's more, the hike starts and ends at a winery, so you'll never go thirsty.

The first time we hiked the 3-mile loop, we had six children in tow. The kids had a ball climbing the gentle hills (and sliding down them), crossing a brook, and studying the fanciful signage, which uses painted symbols to indicate key features.

The kids even enjoyed poking around at the tiny Bartholomew Park Winery, whose tasting room adjoins a small museum chronicling the park's storied past. While they examined an old wine press, we learned that in 1857, Hungarian nobleman Agoston Haraszthy, the man widely known as the father of the California wine industry, purchased this very patch of land and transformed it into the second-largest vineyard in California.

Haraszthy vanished into the jungles of Nicaragua around 1869, about 10 years before economic depression and phylloxera brought his original winemaking operation to a halt. The property then hosted a series of ill-fated enterprises until United Press director Frank Bartholomew and his wife, Antonia, rededicated it to winemaking in the mid-1900s. In 1994 the vineyards and building became the Bartholomew Park Winery.

Back in the tasting room, we bought wine, juice, and cheese to enjoy at the park's picnic tables. Looking out at the vineyards, the villa, and the view, we toasted Haraszthy for providing us with so much lore and such good wine. — *Amy McConnell* ◆

WHERE: From the Sonoma Plaza, take E. Napa St. to Seventh St. E. Go north on Seventh St. E. to Castle Rd., then follow Castle Rd. to Vineyard Lane (look for signs for the winery).

WHEN: Trails, tasting room, and museum 10–4:30 daily; villa 10–4.

COST: Free tasting.

FYI: Pick up a hand-drawn map of the loop trail in the tasting room.

CONTACT: Bartholomew Park Winery; (707) 935-9511.

Scandinavian Julfest (page 348) features fruit-filled roast pork and vegetables. Our festive holiday buffets begin on page 340.

December

the holiday buffet

A trio of festive dinners—from three rich traditions—to spread on a sideboard for your Christmas gathering

Count them up—there are the two of you, the kids (and their kids), Aunt Sylvia…. Before you know it, your guest list for Christmas dinner numbers a dozen or more, and you're faced with the age-old holiday dilemma: how to serve a profusion of food to a multitude of people. The solution? A buffet. The easiest way to serve a crowd is not to serve them at all—let them help themselves.

The beauty of it is, many holiday foods, from every part of the world, fit naturally into this serving pattern. Here we bring you three menus: an elegant din-ner with classic Northwest accents from Oregon, a unique Mexican–Middle Eastern feast from Arizona, and a Scandinavian smörgåsbord from Washington. Much of each can be made ahead; use the count-downs to plan your preparation schedule. Each menu serves 10 to 12 people. To expand the meal for more guests, make two or three batches of the recipes or add some of your favorite dishes to the spread.

Holiday traditions, after all, are from the people. It stands to reason you should share one of the most traditional meals of the year with a crowd.

By Linda Lau Anusasananan • Photographs by James Carrier • Food styling by Valerie Aikman-Smith

dinner at the White House

At Portland's White House Bed & Breakfast, a stately Greek revival inn that somewhat resembles the more famous White House in Washington, D.C., Lanning Blanks serves this festive meal to raise money for Our House of Port-land, a nonprofit AIDS care facility. The menu, which works beautifully for holiday buffets at home as well, adds Northwest touches to tradi-tional American foods. Little prepara-tion—much of it done ahead of time—delivers a lot of elegance.

Smoked Salmon and Caper Crostini

PREP AND COOK TIME: About 50 minutes
NOTES: Reserve baguette ends and ex-tra pieces for the sage stuffing for grilled beef tenderloin (page 342). Toast slices for crostini up to 1 day ahead; cool and store airtight at room temperature. Make salmon mixture up to 8 hours ahead; cover and chill. Spoon onto toast up to 1 hour ahead. Or present salmon mixture, garnished with remaining tomatoes and dill sprigs, and toast separately so guests can assemble crostini.
MAKES: 36 crostini; 10 to 12 appetizer servings

- 3 dozen **baguette** slices (³/₈ in. thick and 2 in. wide, about 5 oz.)

- 9 ounces **smoked salmon,** chopped

- ³/₄ cup finely chopped **Roma tomatoes**

- ¹/₃ cup finely chopped **red onion**

- 1½ tablespoons chopped **fresh dill**

- 1 tablespoon drained **capers,** finely chopped

- ¹/₄ cup **lemon juice**
  Fresh dill sprigs

Table laden with temptations from Portland's White House Bed & Breakfast (front to back): Beef tenderloin filled with a sage-and-hazelnut stuffing, served with mushroom sauce and roasted garlic and potatoes; cracked Dungeness crab with plain wasabi, pickled ginger, and a wasabi-soy sauce; madeira-glazed carrots; and spinach salad with goat cheese.

1. Arrange baguette slices in a single layer on racks on 2 baking sheets (14 by 17 in. each). Bake in a 425° oven until golden, 6 to 8 minutes; switch pan positions halfway through baking.

2. Meanwhile, in a bowl, mix salmon, ½ cup tomatoes, onion, chopped dill, capers, and lemon juice.

3. Spoon equal portions of salmon mixture onto toast slices. Sprinkle equally with remaining tomatoes and garnish with dill sprigs.

Per piece: 27 cal., 17% (4.5 cal.) from fat; 1.9 g protein; 0.5 g fat (0.1 g sat.); 3.6 g carbo (0.2 g fiber); 190 mg sodium; 1.6 mg chol.

Dungeness Crab with Wasabi Soy and Pickled Ginger

PREP TIME: About 10 minutes

NOTES: Have crabs cleaned and cracked at the seafood market. Look for wasabi and pickled ginger in a well-stocked supermarket or an Asian food market. Offer extra wasabi for those who want their dipping sauce a little hotter.

MAKES: 10 to 12 appetizer servings

- 4 or 5 **cooked Dungeness crabs** (2 lb. each), cleaned and cracked (see notes)
- ¾ cup **soy sauce**
- 3 to 4 teaspoons **prepared wasabi**
- ½ cup **sliced pickled ginger**

1. Arrange crab on a platter, with small forks alongside.

2. In a small bowl, mix soy sauce with 3 to 4 teaspoons wasabi to taste. Mound ginger in another small bowl.

3. Have guests arrange portions of crab and spoonfuls of wasabi soy and pickled ginger on their plates, then extract bites of the crab with small forks, dip in wasabi soy, and eat with pickled ginger.

Per serving: 104 cal., 12% (12 cal.) from fat; 16 g protein; 1.3 g fat (0.2 g sat.); 6.4 g carbo (0 g fiber); 1,274 mg sodium; 72 mg chol.

Baby Spinach Salad with Goat Cheese

PREP TIME: About 20 minutes

NOTES: The fragrant dressing for this salad comes from Justin Petersen of Portland. Make it (step 1) up to 1 day ahead; cover and chill. Also rinse spinach; wrap in towels, enclose in a plastic bag, and chill.

MAKES: 8 servings

- 2 cloves **garlic,** peeled and pressed or coarsely chopped
- ⅓ cup **extra-virgin olive oil**
- 2 tablespoons **balsamic vinegar**

- 1 tablespoon **red wine vinegar**
- 1½ teaspoons **Dijon mustard**
- 1½ teaspoons firmly packed **dark brown sugar**
- ½ teaspoon **pepper**
- ¼ teaspoon **vanilla**
  About ½ teaspoon **salt**
- 6 quarts **baby spinach leaves** (1¼ lb.), rinsed and crisped (see notes)
- 1 cup crumbled **chèvre** (goat) **cheese** (4 oz.)

1. In a food processor or blender, whirl garlic, olive oil, balsamic vinegar, red wine vinegar, mustard, brown sugar, pepper, and vanilla until smooth. Add ½ teaspoon salt, and whirl just until blended. Pour into a wide bowl.

2. Add spinach to bowl and sprinkle with cheese; mix gently to coat with dressing. Season to taste with more salt.

Per serving: 169 cal., 69% (117 cal.) from fat; 4.8 g protein; 13 g fat (4.2 g sat.); 10 g carbo (4.2 g fiber); 374 mg sodium; 11 mg chol.

Grilled Beef Tenderloin with Sage Stuffing and Mushroom Sauce

PREP AND COOK TIME: About 1½ hours

NOTES: Use baguette pieces left over from crostini (page 340) to make the stuffing. Complete through step 3 up to 1 day ahead; cover stuffing and chill.

MAKES: 10 to 12 servings

- 1 cup ½-inch chunks **baguette** (see notes)
- 3 tablespoons chopped **hazelnuts**
- ½ cup chopped **onion**
- 1 clove **garlic,** peeled and pressed or minced
- ¼ cup (⅛ lb.) **butter** or margarine, at room temperature
- 2 tablespoons minced **fresh sage** leaves
  Salt and **pepper**
- 1 **center-cut beef tenderloin** (about 4 lb.)
- ¾ pound **mushrooms** (chanterelles, common, oyster, portabella, or shiitake; 1 kind or an assortment)
- ½ cup chopped **shallots**
- 1 cup **dry red wine**
- 4 teaspoons **cornstarch**
- 1½ cups fat-skimmed **beef broth**
  Fresh sage leaves

1. In a blender or food processor, whirl baguette chunks to coarse crumbs; pour into a 9-inch-wide pan. Place hazelnuts in another 9-inch-wide pan.

2. Bake in a 350° oven, shaking pans occasionally, until bread crumbs and

nuts are lightly browned, 10 to 15 minutes (8 to 10 minutes in a convection oven).

3. Meanwhile, in a 10- to 12-inch frying pan over medium heat, stir onion and garlic in 1 tablespoon butter until onion is beginning to brown, 3 to 4 minutes. Stir in bread crumbs and nuts, 1 tablespoon minced sage leaves, and salt and pepper to taste. Remove from heat.

4. Prepare barbecue: If using charcoal, mound and ignite 60 briquets on the firegrate of a barbecue with a lid. When dotted with gray ash, in 15 to 20 minutes, push equal amounts to opposite sides of firegrate. Add 5 more briquets to each mound of coals now and every 30 minutes during cooking. If using a gas barbecue, turn heat to high and close lid for 10 minutes. Adjust burners for indirect cooking (no heat down center), and keep on high. Set a drip pan on firegrate between mounds (for charcoal) or between burners (for gas). Set grill in place.

5. Rinse meat and pat dry. Trim off any excess fat and discard. Make a lengthwise cut down center of tenderloin to within ½ inch of bottom side. Spread halves open and lay meat flat.

6. Spread cut surfaces evenly with 2 tablespoons butter, then bread crumb mixture, pressing lightly to make it adhere. Bring the two sides of meat together and tie tenderloin securely with cotton string at about 1-inch intervals.

7. Lay tenderloin, seam to the side, on grill, not directly over heat. Cover barbecue; open vents for charcoal. Cook until a thermometer inserted in center of thickest part reaches 120° to 125° for rare, 40 to 45 minutes, or until beef is as done as you like. Transfer to a board or platter. Keeping roast warm, let rest 10 to 15 minutes.

8. Meanwhile, trim and discard bits of debris, bruised spots, and discolored stem ends or tough stems from mushrooms. Rinse mushrooms well, drain, and chop.

9. In a 10- to 12-inch frying pan over medium-high heat, stir mushrooms and shallots often in remaining 1 tablespoon butter until liquid has evaporated and mushrooms are lightly browned, about 12 minutes. Add wine; bring to a boil over high heat, stirring often and scraping browned bits free.

10. In a bowl, mix cornstarch and broth until smooth. Add to pan and stir until mixture boils. Add salt and pepper to taste. Pour sauce into a bowl.

11. Remove strings from roast. Sprinkle remaining chopped sage leaves over beef. Garnish with whole sage leaves.

With a whole pound of chocolate, this truffle tart makes chocolate lovers swoon.

Cut meat crosswise into ¹⁄₂-inch slices. Serve with sauce to add to taste.

Per serving: 269 cal., 47% (126 cal.) from fat; 26 g protein; 14 g fat (5.8 g sat.); 6 g carbo (0.7 g fiber); 124 mg sodium; 82 mg chol.

Roasted Garlic-Potato Medley with Gorgonzola

PREP AND COOK TIME: About 50 minutes

MAKES: 10 to 12 servings

- 3 pounds **thin-skinned potatoes** (a combination of Yukon gold, red, and purple; 1¹⁄₂ in. wide)
- 3 tablespoons **olive oil**
- 3 cloves **garlic,** peeled and minced

  About ¹⁄₂ teaspoon **salt**

  About ¹⁄₄ teaspoon **coarse-ground black pepper**
- ³⁄₄ cup crumbled **gorgonzola cheese** (3 oz.)

1. Scrub potatoes and pat dry. In a 10-by 15-inch baking pan, mix potatoes, oil, garlic, ¹⁄₂ teaspoon salt, and ¹⁄₄ teaspoon pepper.

2. Roast potatoes in a 400° oven, turning occasionally, until tender when pierced, 35 to 45 minutes.

3. Pour potatoes into a bowl and sprinkle with cheese. Add more salt and pepper to taste.

Per serving: 148 cal., 35% (52 cal.) from fat; 3.7 g protein; 5.8 g fat (1.9 g sat.); 21 g carbo (1.9 g fiber); 203 mg sodium; 6.2 mg chol.

Madeira Carrots

PREP AND COOK TIME: About 45 minutes

NOTES: Many supermarkets sell whole baby carrots; if these are unavailable, use baby-cut carrots.

MAKES: 10 to 12 servings

- 2¹⁄₂ pounds **carrots** (¹⁄₂ to ³⁄₄ in. thick, 3 to 5 in. long; see notes)
- 1 cup **chicken broth**
- 1 cup **madeira**
- ¹⁄₄ cup (¹⁄₈ lb.) **butter** or margarine
- 2 tablespoons **sugar**
- 1 teaspoon **cumin seed**

  Salt

1. Trim ends from whole baby carrots and discard; peel or scrub carrots.

2. In a 12-inch frying pan at least 2¹⁄₂ inches deep, or a 6-quart pan, combine carrots, broth, madeira, butter, sugar, and cumin seed. Bring to a boil over high heat, then reduce heat, cover, and simmer, stirring occasionally, until carrots are barely tender when pierced, 8 to 12 minutes.

3. Uncover and boil over high heat, stirring often, until liquid has evaporated and carrots begin to brown, 15 to 20 minutes. Add salt to taste.

Per serving: 92 cal., 42% (39 cal.) from fat; 1.2 g protein; 4.3 g fat (2.6 g sat.); 13 g carbo (2.7 g fiber); 81 mg sodium; 11 mg chol.

Chocolate Truffle Tart

PREP AND COOK TIME: About 1 hour

NOTES: Karen Utz of Portland shared this intense, brownielike tart with Blanks. If making through step 5 up to 1 day ahead, cover and chill. Bring to room temperature to serve.

MAKES: 12 to 16 servings

  About 1 cup (¹⁄₂ lb.) **butter**

  About ³⁄₄ cup **all-purpose flour**
- ¹⁄₂ cup **powdered sugar**

  About 3 tablespoons **unsweetened cocoa**
- ¹⁄₄ teaspoon **ground cinnamon**
- ¹⁄₄ teaspoon **salt**
- 1 pound **bittersweet** or semisweet **chocolate,** chopped
- ¹⁄₂ cup **granulated sugar**
- 4 **large eggs**
- 1 teaspoon **vanilla**

  Slightly sweetened softly **whipped cream** or vanilla ice cream

  Caramel ice cream topping (optional)

1. Butter and flour a 10¹⁄₂-inch tart pan with removable rim.

2. In a food processor or a bowl, whirl or mix ³⁄₄ cup flour, powdered sugar, 3 tablespoons cocoa, cinnamon, and salt until blended. Add ¹⁄₂ cup butter, cut into chunks; whirl or beat with a mixer on high speed until well blended. With well-floured hands, press mixture evenly over bottom of pan.

3. Bake in a 350° oven until crust begins to pull from pan sides, 15 to 18 minutes (13 to 15 minutes in a convection oven).

4. Meanwhile, place half the chopped chocolate and ¹⁄₂ cup butter in a microwave-safe bowl; cook in a microwave oven at half power (50%), stirring occasionally, until chocolate is melted and mixture is smooth, 1 to 1¹⁄₂ minutes. Stir in granulated sugar. Add eggs and mix well. Stir in vanilla and remaining chopped chocolate. Pour mixture into warm crust.

5. Bake in a 350° oven until filling barely jiggles when pan is gently shaken, about 20 minutes. Let cool on a rack at least 1¹⁄₂ hours.

6. Remove pan rim. Dust tart lightly with cocoa. Cut into wedges to serve. Top portions with whipped cream and drizzle with caramel topping.

Per serving: 322 cal., 64% (207 cal.) from fat; 4.5 g protein; 23 g fat (13 g sat.); 31 g carbo (1.1 g fiber); 169 mg sodium; 84 mg chol.

countdown

Up to 1 day ahead: Toast bread for crostini. Make dressing, and rinse and crisp spinach for salad. Make stuffing for beef tenderloin. Bake chocolate tart.

Up to 8 hours ahead: Make salmon mixture for crostini.

1³⁄₄ hours ahead: Fill beef with stuffing.

1¹⁄₄ hours ahead: Prepare grill.

1 hour ahead: Grill beef. Remove tart from refrigerator. Spoon salmon mixture onto toast.

45 minutes ahead: Prepare carrots. Bake potatoes.

30 minutes ahead: Make mushroom sauce for beef. Whip cream for tart; chill.

15 minutes ahead: Arrange crab on platter and prepare wasabi soy.

5 minutes ahead: Assemble salad.

East-Mex in Phoenix

Good food unites the Johnson family. This passion took shape in 1946 when Woodrow (Woody), who is part Swedish and part Mexican, and Victoria, who has Lebanese roots, opened the first Macayo's Mexican restaurant in Phoenix. Woody's mother's Mexican recipes were the foundation of its menu. Now the Johnsons' three children manage the family's 10 Arizona restaurants as well as their chili farms and Fiesta Canning Company. When this large, close-knit clan gathers for the holidays, all the elements of their food-oriented world merge in a unique cross-cultural feast.

To save time, you can purchase stuffed grape leaves at a delicatessen. For the jalapeño hummus, make or buy your favorite hummus, then stir in minced fresh jalapeño chilies to taste. Mound in a bowl, drizzle with extra-virgin olive oil, and sprinkle with chopped parsley and paprika.

Mom's Stuffed Grape Leaves

PREP AND COOK TIME: About 2 hours
NOTES: If making through step 5 up to 2 days ahead, cool, cover, and chill; freeze to store longer. Thaw, if frozen. To reheat, arrange about half the grape leaves with tomato sauce in a single layer on a microwave-safe plate. Drizzle with 1 tablespoon water, cover with microwave-safe plastic wrap, and cook in a microwave oven at half power (50%) until warm in the center (slit 1 open to test), 6 to 7 minutes. Repeat to heat remaining grape leaves.
MAKES: 3½ to 4 dozen

- 1¼ cups **long-grain white rice**
- 1 pound **ground lean lamb**
- 23 ounces **tomato sauce** (a 15-oz. can and an 8-oz. can)
- ½ cup chopped **fresh mint** leaves
  About 1 teaspoon **salt**
- ⅛ teaspoon **dried thyme**
- 1 teaspoon **olive oil**
- 1 jar (8 oz.) **grape leaves**, drained
  Thin **lemon** slices

1. Put rice in a fine strainer and rinse well under cold water; drain. In a bowl, mix rice, lamb, 15 ounces tomato sauce, mint, 1 teaspoon salt, and thyme.
2. Rub olive oil evenly over bottom of a 9- by 13-inch baking dish.
3. Rinse grape leaves well; drain and pat dry. One at a time, lay each leaf flat, underside up and stem end toward you. Shape about 1 tablespoon rice filling into a 2-inch-long log and place across stem end of leaf. Fold sides of leaf over filling and roll snugly to enclose. Arrange filled leaves, seams down, in dish, layering as needed.
4. Mix 8 ounces of tomato sauce with 1 cup water. Pour evenly over grape leaves. Cover dish tightly with foil.

5. Bake in a 350° oven until rice is tender (cut 1 grape leaf open to test), 50 to 60 minutes.
6. Transfer stuffed grape leaves to a platter and serve hot or warm. Garnish with lemon slices. Add salt to taste.

Per piece: 55 cal., 40% (22 cal.) from fat; 2.1 g protein; 2.4 g fat (1 g sat.); 4.9 g carbo (0.3 g fiber); 337 mg sodium; 6.9 mg chol.

Johnsons' Spinach-Artichoke Dip

PREP AND COOK TIME: About 15 minutes
NOTES: If making up to 1 day ahead, cover and chill. Bring to room temperature or reheat, covered, in a microwave oven on full power (100%), stirring occasionally, until warm, 3 to 4 minutes. Serve dip with toasted baguette slices.
MAKES: About 12 appetizer servings

- ¼ cup (⅛ lb.) **butter** or margarine
- 1 **onion** (½ lb.), peeled and chopped
- 1 tablespoon minced **garlic**
- ¼ cup **all-purpose flour**
- 1 **fresh** or dried **bay leaf**
- 1 cup **milk**
- ¾ cup fat-skimmed **chicken broth**
- 1 package (10 oz.) **frozen chopped spinach**, thawed
- 1 can (13¾ to 16 oz.) **artichoke hearts**, drained and chopped
- ⅓ cup thinly sliced **green onions** (including tops)
  Salt and **pepper**

1. In a 2- to 3-quart pan over medium-high heat, melt butter. Add chopped onion and minced garlic and stir often until onion is soft, about 5 minutes. Add flour and stir to coat onion. Add bay leaf. Gradually whisk in milk and broth, and stir until mixture boils,

3 to 4 minutes. Remove bay leaf.
2. Squeeze liquid from spinach. Stir spinach, artichoke hearts, and green onions into white sauce. Add salt and pepper to taste. Serve warm or at room temperature.

Per serving: 81 cal., 53% (43 cal.) from fat; 2.9 g protein; 4.8 g fat (2.9 g sat.); 7.3 g carbo (1.1 g fiber); 74 mg sodium; 14 mg chol.

Fattoush Salad

PREP AND COOK TIME: About 50 minutes
NOTES: Toast pocket bread up to 1 day ahead; cool and store airtight at room temperature. Also rinse lettuce, wrap in towels, enclose in a plastic bag, and chill. Up to 4 hours ahead, mix dressing in bowl and layer vegetables on top (do not mix); cover and chill. Just before serving, add toasted bread and mix; bread softens as it stands in salad.
MAKES: 12 servings

- 6 **pocket breads** (7 in.)
- ⅓ cup **lemon juice**
- ⅓ cup **extra-virgin olive oil**
- 1 or 2 cloves **garlic**, peeled and minced or pressed
- 1½ pounds **firm-ripe tomatoes**
- 2 pounds **cucumbers**
- 6 cups bite-size pieces rinsed and crisped **iceberg lettuce** (¾ lb.; see notes)
- 3 cups chopped **parsley**
- ½ cup chopped **fresh mint** leaves
  About ¾ teaspoon **salt**
  About ½ teaspoon **pepper**

1. Tear pocket breads into 1-inch pieces and spread equally in two 10- by 15-inch baking pans.
2. Bake in a 350° oven, stirring occasionally, until bread is lightly browned and crisp, about 15 minutes (12 minutes in a convection oven). Let cool.

Lobster and shrimp enchiladas with fattoush salad set an ethnically eclectic tone.

3. In a large bowl, mix lemon juice, olive oil, and garlic.

4. Rinse tomatoes; core and chop. Peel cucumbers and chop. Add tomatoes, cucumbers, lettuce, parsley, mint, and bread to bowl. Mix well. Add about ³⁄₄ teaspoon salt and ½ teaspoon pepper to taste.

Per serving: 169 cal., 37% (62 cal.) from fat; 4.4 g protein; 6.9 g fat (1 g sat.); 24 g carbo (2.7 g fiber); 326 mg sodium; 0 mg chol.

Seafood Enchiladas

PREP AND COOK TIME: About 1¼ hours

NOTES: For a less extravagant version, omit the lobster tails and add 1 more pound shrimp. If desired, omit brandy and add ⅓ cup more seafood-cooking broth in step 4. Buy tortillas that are as fresh as possible (cracking is a sign of age). Assemble enchiladas through step 7 up to 1 day ahead; cover and chill. Bake, covered, in a 350° oven for 20 minutes; uncover and continue baking until hot in the center, about 10 minutes longer.

MAKES: 12 enchiladas; 12 first-course or side-dish servings

- 3 cups fat-skimmed **chicken broth**
- 2 **lobster tails** (½ lb. each), thawed if frozen
- ³⁄₄ pound **peeled, deveined raw shrimp** (31 to 40 per lb.), thawed if frozen
- 3 tablespoons **butter** or margarine
- 1 **onion** (½ lb.), peeled and chopped
- 1 clove **garlic**, peeled and minced or pressed
- ¼ pound **mushrooms**, rinsed, drained, and thinly sliced
- ¼ cup **all-purpose flour**
- ⅓ cup **brandy** (optional; see notes)
  Salt and **pepper**
- 1 can (19 oz.) **green enchilada sauce**
- 1 can (7 oz.) **diced green chilies**
- 12 **corn tortillas** (6 in.; see notes)
- 3 cups (³⁄₄ lb.) **shredded jack cheese**

- 1 cup diced **tomatoes**
- ²⁄₃ cup thinly sliced **green onions** (including tops)

1. In a 3- to 4-quart pan over high heat, bring chicken broth to a boil. Add lobster tails and return to a boil; cover, reduce heat, and simmer until lobster is opaque but still moist-looking in center of thickest part (cut through shell to test), 8 to 10 minutes. Lift tails from broth and let cool.

2. Return broth to a boil over high heat. Cut shrimp into 1-inch lengths. Add shrimp to pan, cover, reduce heat, and simmer just until shrimp is opaque but still moist-looking in center of thickest part (cut to test), 1½ to 2 minutes. With a slotted spoon, lift shrimp from broth and let cool. Reserve broth.

3. With kitchen shears, cut through tops of lobster shells lengthwise down the center. Set tails, cut sides up, on a board. With a large knife, slice tails in half lengthwise through cuts. Pull out meat; cut into 1-inch chunks.

4. In a 10- to 12-inch frying pan over medium-high heat, melt butter. Add chopped onion, garlic, and mushrooms; stir often until onion is limp and mushrooms are lightly browned, about 10 minutes. Sprinkle flour over vegetables and stir until evenly coated. Whisk in 2 cups reserved broth (reserve remainder) and the brandy, and stir until mixture boils. Add lobster and shrimp. Season to taste with salt and pepper.

5. In a blender or food processor, whirl 1 more cup reserved broth (save remainder for other uses or discard) with enchilada sauce and chilies. Pour 1½ cups of the mixture into a 9-inch pie pan.

6. Stack 6 tortillas and put in a microwave-safe plastic bag but do not seal. Heat in a microwave oven on full power (100%) until tortillas are warm and pliable, 1 to 1½ minutes. Dip tortillas, 1 at a time, in sauce mixture to coat. Lay each tortilla flat and spread about ⅓ cup seafood filling down the center; roll to enclose. Set filled tortillas, seam down, in a single layer in a shallow 2½- to 3-quart baking dish.

7. Heat remaining 6 tortillas, dip in sauce, fill, and roll. Arrange in another shallow 2½- to 3-quart baking dish. Pour remaining sauce mixture evenly over enchiladas. Sprinkle cheese evenly over each dish.

8. Bake in a 350° oven until enchiladas are hot in the center, about 30 minutes (about 20 minutes in a convection oven). Sprinkle a band of tomatoes, then green onions, down center of each

Roasted Cornish hen rests on chili-chorizo dressing studded with roasted chilies and pine nuts. Mole is ready to pour.

dish. Add more salt and pepper to taste.

Per serving: 307 cal., 38% (117 cal.) from fat; 22 g protein; 13 g fat (7 g sat.); 23 g carbo (2.3 g fiber); 897 mg sodium; 96 mg chol.

Cornish Hens with Mole

PREP AND COOK TIME: About 1¼ hours
NOTES: The simplified mole for these hens has surprising layers of flavor. If making sauce (step 3) up to 1 day ahead, cover and chill. To reheat, stir over low heat until hot, or warm in a microwave oven on full power (100%), stirring occasionally, until hot, 4 to 5 minutes.

MAKES: 12 servings

- 6 **Cornish hens** (1½ lb. each)
- 3 tablespoons **olive oil**
- ¾ teaspoon **chili powder**
- ⅓ cup **slivered almonds**
- ⅓ cup **raisins**
- ½ teaspoon **ground cinnamon**
- ¼ teaspoon **ground cumin**
- 1 can (28 oz.) **red enchilada sauce**
  Salt and **pepper**

1. Remove necks and giblets from hens; reserve for another use or discard. With poultry shears or kitchen

scissors, split birds in half lengthwise through breastbones and backbones. Rinse and pat dry. In a small bowl, mix oil and chili powder. Coat hens all over with chili oil. Set halves slightly apart, skin up, on racks in two 12- by 17-inch baking pans.

2. Bake in a 400° oven until meat at thigh bone is no longer pink (cut to test), about 50 minutes (40 minutes in a convection oven).

3. Meanwhile, in a 10- to 12-inch frying pan over medium-low heat, stir almonds until pale gold, about 5 minutes. Add raisins and stir until plump, about 2 minutes. Add cinnamon and cumin; stir until fragrant, about 30 seconds. Scrape into a blender or food processor and add enchilada sauce; whirl until smooth. Pour mixture into frying pan and stir over medium heat until hot, about 5 minutes. Pour into a bowl.

4. Transfer hens to a platter. Serve with mole. Add salt and pepper to taste.

Per serving: 463 cal., 62% (288 cal.) from fat; 33 g protein; 31 g fat (7.9 g sat.); 10 g carbo (0.4 g fiber); 729 mg sodium; 187 mg chol.

Chili-Chorizo Dressing with Tamales

PREP AND COOK TIME: About 1¼ hours

NOTES: If assembling through step 6 up to 1 day ahead, cover and chill; bake for about 30 minutes in step 7 before uncovering. If your oven space is limited, assemble dressing in a microwave-safe dish and heat, covered, in a microwave oven at full power (100%), stirring occasionally, until hot, 8 to 9 minutes.

MAKES: 12 servings

- ¾ pound **green onions**
- ¾ pound **fresh Anaheim chilies**
- 2 **fresh jalapeño chilies** (2 oz. total)
- 2 tablespoons **olive oil**
- ¾ pound **frozen** or 1 can (15 oz.) **beef tamales**
- ½ cup **pine nuts**
- 1 tablespoon **butter** or margarine
- ⅓ pound **firm chorizo sausage**
- ½ cup chopped **celery**
- ½ teaspoon **dried rubbed sage**
- 1 package (14 oz.) **herb stuffing mix**
- 1½ cups fat-skimmed **chicken broth**
- 1 cup chopped **fresh cilantro**
- 1 can (4¼ oz.) **chopped black ripe olives**
  Salt

1. Rinse onions and chilies. In a 12- by 17-inch baking pan, mix vegetables with olive oil to coat, then spread into a single layer.

2. Bake in a 400° oven for 10 minutes; with a wide spatula, turn vegetables, and continue baking until browned, 10 to 15 minutes longer. When cool enough to handle, trim and discard root ends from onions. Pull loose portions of skin from chilies and discard; stem and seed chilies. Chop vegetables.

3. If frozen tamales are uncooked, cook according to package directions; cool, peel, and chop. Or peel and chop canned tamales.

4. In an 8- to 10-inch frying pan over medium heat, stir pine nuts in butter until golden, 3 to 4 minutes. Lift nuts out with a slotted spoon.

5. Remove casings from chorizo and discard; chop sausage. Add chorizo, celery, and sage to pan and stir often over medium-high heat until celery is soft, about 5 minutes.

6. In a large bowl, mix roasted onions and chilies, tamales, pine nuts, chorizo mixture, stuffing mix, broth, cilantro, and olives. Pour into a shallow 3- to 3½-quart casserole and cover tightly.

7. Bake in a 400° oven for 20 minutes. Uncover and continue baking until dressing is hot (about 150°) in the center, about 10 minutes longer. Add salt to taste.

Per serving: 323 cal., 45% (144 cal.) from fat; 12 g protein; 16 g fat (3.6 g sat.); 36 g carbo (5.6 g fiber); 859 mg sodium; 17 mg chol.

Flan with Berries

PREP AND COOK TIME: About 1¼ hours

NOTES: Bake flan (through step 4) 1 day ahead; cover airtight and chill. If fresh raspberries are not available, use individually quick-frozen (IQF) unsweetened berries such as raspberries or blueberries, or a combination. If desired, serve flan from 9- by 13-inch baking dish: Cut pieces, lift out with a wide spatula, and invert onto plates. Spoon caramel sauce over each portion and garnish with berries.

MAKES: 12 servings

- 1 cup **sugar**
- 2 cans (12 oz. each) **evaporated milk**
- 1 can (14 oz.) **sweetened condensed milk**
- 6 **large eggs**
- 1 teaspoon **vanilla**
- 1 cup **raspberries**, rinsed (see notes)

1. In a 10- to 12-inch frying pan over medium-high heat, shake and tilt sugar until melted and amber-colored, 8 to 9

Raspberries add a festive note to smooth flan in a pool of caramel sauce.

countdown

Up to 2 days ahead: Bake stuffed grape leaves.

Up to 1 day ahead: Make spinach-artichoke dip and toast baguette slices. Toast pocket bread for fattoush salad; rinse and crisp lettuce. Assemble enchiladas. Make mole sauce, chili-chorizo dressing, and flan.

Up to 4 hours before dinner: Cut vegetables for salad.

1 hour before dinner: Roast Cornish hens.

15 minutes before appetizers: Reheat grape leaves. Prepare hummus.

5 minutes before appetizers: Reheat spinach-artichoke dip.

30 minutes before main course (while guests are having appetizers): Bake enchiladas.

10 minutes before main course: Reheat dressing.

5 minutes before main course: Mix salad. Reheat mole. Warm tortillas.

Just before dessert: Unmold and garnish flan.

minutes. Immediately, pour caramelized sugar into a 9- by 13-inch baking dish and tilt pan quickly to let syrup flow over bottom (it doesn't need to cover surface completely).

2. In a bowl, whisk evaporated milk, condensed milk, eggs, and vanilla until well blended. Pour mixture into caramel-lined dish. Nest dish in a 12- by 17-inch roasting pan.

3. Set dish in pan in a 350° oven. Pour about 1 inch boiling water into outer pan. Bake until custard barely jiggles in the center when dish is gently shaken, 60 to 70 minutes (50 to 60 minutes in a convection oven).

4. Remove 9- by 13-inch baking dish from hot water and set on a rack to cool flan completely. Cover and chill at least 24 hours.

5. Invert a rimmed platter or 12- by 17-inch pan over flan. Holding platter and flan dish tightly together, quickly invert. Hold in place until flan slips free and caramel sauce flows over flan. Garnish with berries. Cut into rectangles and transfer to dessert plates.

Per serving: 298 cal., 30% (90 cal.) from fat; 10 g protein; 10 g fat (5.5 g sat.); 42 g carbo (0.5 g fiber); 140 mg sodium; 136 mg chol.

Julfest main course is apricot-and-pear-filled roast pork, marinated cucumbers, red cabbage, and potatoes.

Scandinavian Julfest

A s a small boy, Chuck Fowler loved the yearly Swedish Christmas celebration (*Julfest*) at his grandparents' big house. They would feast on a traditional smörgåsbord, sing sacred and silly songs, and thoroughly enjoy each other's company. In 1976, Chuck and his wife, Karla, restored this cherished holiday tradition at their home in Olympia, Washington. With recipes out of Karla's Danish and Norwegian ancestry, their Julfest now encompasses all of Scandinavia.

The Fowlers' lavish buffet starts with a series of smörgåsbord courses: cheeses, salads and relishes, fish and meat, and breads. These are cleared, and a hot entrée is brought out—in their case usually a fruit-filled pork loin with red cabbage and boiled potatoes rather than the more traditional lutefisk. Many of the foods are purchased; look in a Scandinavian delicatessen or well-stocked supermarket for the cold and hot specialties without an asterisk on our menu. Various family members bring the other dishes, making this a remarkably easy feast.

For 10 to 12 people, choose one to three items each from the cheese, salad and relish, fish and meat, and bread categories. Allow at least 2 ounces of cheese, 2 ounces of bread, and ¼ pound of fish and/or meat per person.

Cucumbers with Dill

PREP TIME: About 15 minutes, plus at least 1¼ hours to marinate and chill
NOTES: Prepare through step 2 up to 1 day ahead; cover and chill.
MAKES: 10 to 12 servings

3 **cucumbers** (¾ lb. each)
1½ tablespoons **salt**
1 cup **white wine vinegar**
1½ tablespoons **sugar**
3 tablespoons chopped **fresh dill**

1. Rinse cucumbers; with a sharp-tined fork, score sides of cucumbers lengthwise. Trim and discard ends; thinly slice cucumbers crosswise and place in a bowl. Add salt and mix. Cover and chill at least 30 minutes or up to 2 hours. Put cucumbers in a colander and rinse well under cold running water; drain. Return to bowl.

2. Add vinegar and sugar; mix. Cover and chill, stirring occasionally, until cold, at least 45 minutes or up to 1 day.

3. Just before serving, drain cucumbers and put in a bowl. Add half the dill and mix; sprinkle with remaining dill.

Per serving: 19 cal., 4.7% (0.9 cal.) from fat; 0.4 g protein; 0.1 g fat (0 g sat.); 4.6 g carbo (0.8 g fiber); 98 mg sodium; 0 mg chol.

Roast Pork with Apricots and Pear

PREP AND COOK TIME: About 1½ hours

NOTES: Pork loin roast may also be labeled top loin.

MAKES: 10 to 12 servings

- ½ cup **dried apricots**
- 1 **firm-ripe pear**
- 1 tablespoon **lemon juice**
- 1 **boned center-cut pork loin roast** (4 lb.; see notes), fat trimmed

  Salt and **pepper**
- 3 tablespoons **red currant jelly**
- ¾ cup **dry vermouth** or dry white wine
- ¾ cup fat-skimmed **chicken broth**
- 1 tablespoon **cornstarch**
- 1 cup **whipping cream**

1. In a small bowl, mix apricots with ½ cup hot water and let stand until soft, about 10 minutes; drain.

2. Meanwhile, peel and core pear; cut into 1-inch cubes and put in another small bowl. Add lemon juice and mix to coat.

3. Trim excess fat from meat and discard. Cut through loin lengthwise to within ½ inch of bottom side. Spread halves open like a book and lay meat flat. Scatter apricots and pear cubes evenly over cut surfaces. Gently press halves back together and tie loin with cotton string at 1- to 1½-inch intervals to secure.

4. Set roast, cut to the side, in a 10- by 15-inch pan. Sprinkle lightly with salt and pepper.

5. Bake in a 375° oven until a thermometer inserted in center of loin (not in fruit) reaches 140°, about 45 minutes (30 minutes in a convection oven). Meanwhile, heat 2 tablespoons red currant jelly in a small microwave-safe bowl in a microwave oven at full power (100%) just until melted, about 15 seconds. Brush loin with melted jelly and continue roasting until a thermometer inserted in center (not in fruit) reaches 150°, 10 to 15 minutes longer. Transfer

pork to a board or platter and, keeping warm, let rest 15 to 20 minutes.

6. Spoon fat from pan drippings and discard. Add vermouth and broth to pan, set over high heat, and stir, scraping up browned bits, until reduced to 1 cup, 6 to 10 minutes.

7. In a small bowl, mix cornstarch and cream until smooth. Add cornstarch-cream mixture and remaining 1 tablespoon jelly to broth mixture and stir until jelly is melted and mixture is boiling, 3 to 4 minutes. Add salt and pepper to taste. Pour sauce into a bowl.

8. Remove strings from pork roast and cut into ½-inch-thick slices. Serve with sauce. Add salt and pepper to taste.

Per serving: 340 cal., 45% (153 cal.) from fat; 34 g protein; 17 g fat (7.9 g sat.); 11 g carbo (0.8 g fiber); 75 mg sodium; 115 mg chol.

Sweet-and-Sour Red Cabbage

PREP AND COOK TIME: About 1¾ hours

NOTES: Cook through step 2 up to 1 day ahead; cover and chill. Reheat, covered, over low heat, stirring occasionally, then continue with step 3.

MAKES: 10 to 12 servings

- 1 head **red cabbage** (3 lb.)
- 1 **red onion** (½ lb.)
- 1 cup shredded peeled **apple**
- ½ cup **red wine vinegar**
- ⅓ cup **red currant jelly**
- 2 tablespoons **butter** or margarine

  About 1 teaspoon **salt**

1. Rinse cabbage. Cut head in half through core; trim off core and discard. In a food processor or with a sharp knife, shred cabbage (you should have about 14 cups). Peel onion and thinly slice.

2. In a 6- to 8-quart pan, combine 3½ cups water, cabbage, onion, apple, vinegar, jelly, butter, and 1 teaspoon salt. Cover and cook over medium heat, stirring occasionally, until cabbage is very limp, about 1 hour. If mixture begins to stick, add more water as needed, ½ cup at a time.

3. If any liquid remains, uncover and cook until evaporated. Add salt to taste. Pour into a bowl.

Per serving: 78 cal., 26% (20 cal.) from fat; 1.6 g protein; 2.2 g fat (1.2 g sat.); 15 g carbo (2.3 g fiber); 228 mg sodium; 5.2 mg chol.

Wreaths, tarts, and twists

The Fowlers' Julfest smörgåsbord ends with a selection of traditional Scandinavian cookies displayed on a 50-year-old handmade wooden cookie tree.

countdown

Up to 3 days ahead: Bake cookies. Purchase foods for smörgåsbord.

Up to 1 day ahead: Prepare cucumbers. Cook cabbage.

Up to 30 minutes before smörgåsbord: Finish cucumbers. Set out cheeses, salads and relishes, fish and meat, and breads.

1½ hours before main course: Roast pork loin.

30 minutes before main course: Boil potatoes.

10 minutes before main course: Reheat cabbage. Make sauce for pork.

Spritsar
(Spritz, or Wreath, Cookies)

PREP AND COOK TIME: About 1 hour

NOTES: This recipe for Swedish spritz cookies comes from the late Rhoda Johnson Laffaw of Gig Harbor, Washington. Use a cookie press to shape them. If making up to 3 days ahead, cool and store airtight at room temperature; freeze to store longer.

MAKES: About 32

- 1 cup (½ lb.) **butter** (or ½ cup *each* butter and margarine), at room temperature
- ¾ cup **sugar**
- 3 **large egg** yolks
- 1 teaspoon **vanilla**
- 2½ cups **all-purpose flour**

  About ½ cup **green candied** (glacé) **cherries** (optional)

  About ¼ cup **red candied** (glacé) **cherries** (optional)

1. In a bowl, with a mixer on high speed, beat butter and sugar until fluffy. Add egg yolks and vanilla; beat until blended. Stir in flour, then beat until well blended.

2. Scrape dough, a portion at a time, into a cookie press fitted with a rosette or star-shaped tip. Press dough through tip onto 12- by 15-inch baking sheets (you'll need 3) into 2-inch rings, spacing about 1½ inches apart. If desired, decorate seams where ends meet with cherries: Cut each green cherry lengthwise into 8 wedges and each red cherry lengthwise into 4 wedges, then cut wedges in half crosswise. Arrange on wreaths to simulate holly sprigs.

A sweet selection of traditional, buttery Scandinavian Christmas cookies ends the Julfest: Wreath-shaped spritsar (top left), jam-filled sandbakelser (top right), and sugar-crusted kringlor (bottom front).

Or for simpler cookies, choose any shape extrusion plate and press dough through it into solid mounds about 1½ inches apart on baking sheets.

3. Bake in a 350° oven until spritz cookies are golden brown, about 16 minutes (about 19 minutes in a 325° convection oven). If using 1 oven, switch pan positions after 8 minutes. With a wide spatula, transfer cookies to racks to cool. Serve warm or cool.

Per cookie: 111 cal., 51% (57 cal.) from fat; 1.3 g protein; 6.3 g fat (3.7 g sat.); 12 g carbo (0.3 g fiber); 59 mg sodium; 35 mg chol.

Sandbakelser (Sand Tarts)

PREP AND COOK TIME: About 1¼ hours
NOTES: These cookies come from Chuck Fowler's Swedish grandmother, Florence Erickson Burrows Fowler. They're traditionally baked in small tart pans with fluted edges, which you can find in stores that sell specialty or Scandinavian bakeware. But you can also shape the cookies into balls by hand, then indent them with your finger. For crisper cookies, bake unfilled, then add jam shortly before serving. If making up to 3 days ahead, cool and store airtight at room temperature; freeze to store longer.
MAKES: About 5 dozen

- ¾ cup **almonds**
- 1 cup (½ lb.) **butter** or margarine, at room temperature
- ½ cup **sugar**
- 1 **large egg**
- ½ teaspoon **almond extract**
- 2½ cups **all-purpose flour**
  About 5 tablespoons **raspberry jam**

1. Whirl almonds in a blender or food processor until finely ground.

2. In a bowl, with a mixer on high speed, beat butter and sugar until fluffy. Add egg and almond extract; beat until blended. Add ground almonds and flour; beat until blended.

3. If using tart pans (about 2 in. wide and ¾ in. deep; you'll need about 5 dozen pans total—bake in sequence if necessary), press a 1½-teaspoon portion of dough over bottom and up sides to rim of each pan (dough should be ¼ inch thick). Set tart pans slightly apart on 10- by 15-inch baking pans (recipe makes 5 panfuls; if baking in sequence, cover unused dough lightly with plastic wrap). Fill each tart with ¼ teaspoon jam.

If not using tart pans, shape 1½-teaspoon portions of dough into balls and set about 2 inches apart on 12- by 15-inch baking sheets (recipe fills 3 sheets). With the tip of your finger or the handle end of a wood spoon, make a ½-inch-wide, ½-inch-deep indentation in the center of each ball; fill each with about ¼ teaspoon jam.

4. Bake in a 350° oven until tarts are golden brown, 16 to 18 minutes (12 to 14 minutes in a 325° convection oven); if using 1 oven, switch pan positions after 8 to 9 minutes. Cool about 7 minutes on pans or sheets, then invert tart pans 1 at a time to release tarts, and set upright on racks; or, with a wide spatula, transfer jam-filled cookies from baking sheets to racks to cool. Serve warm or cool.

Per tart: 68 cal., 53% (36 cal.) from fat; 1 g protein; 4 g fat (2 g sat.); 7.3 g carbo (0.3 g fiber); 33 mg sodium; 12 mg chol.

Kringlor (Twists)

PREP AND COOK TIME: About 1½ hours
NOTES: This recipe was handed down by Mary Johnson and Anna Erickson, early Scandinavian immigrants. Look for pearl sugar in stores that sell specialty or Scandinavian foods. If making twists up to 3 days ahead, cool and store airtight at room temperature; freeze to store longer.
MAKES: About 5 dozen

- 1 cup (½ lb.) **butter** or margarine, at room temperature
- 1 cup **granulated sugar**
- 2 hard-cooked **large egg** yolks
- 1 **large egg**, separated
- 1 **large egg**
- ¼ teaspoon **salt**
- 3 cups **all-purpose flour**
- ⅓ cup **pearl** or coarse decorating **sugar**

1. In a bowl, with a mixer on high speed, beat butter and granulated sugar until fluffy. Add hard-cooked egg yolks, uncooked egg yolk, uncooked whole egg, and salt; beat on medium speed until blended. Stir in flour, then beat until well blended.

2. Shape dough into 1-inch balls; cover with plastic wrap. On a lightly floured board, roll each ball under your palm into a 6-inch-long rope. On a 12- by 15-inch baking sheet (you'll need 3 total), twist each rope into a figure 8 and press ends lightly together to seal; space twists about 1 inch apart. With a fork, beat remaining egg white to blend; lightly brush over twists. Sprinkle with pearl sugar.

3. Bake in a 350° oven until twists are golden brown, about 20 minutes (16 to 18 minutes in a 325° convection oven). If using 1 oven, switch pan positions after 10 minutes. With a wide spatula, transfer twists to racks to cool. Serve warm or cool.

Per twist: 73 cal., 44% (32 cal.) from fat; 1 g protein; 3.6 g fat (2.1 g sat.); 9.2 g carbo (0.2 g fiber); 45 mg sodium; 23 mg chol. ◆

Salad of greens, fruit, and nuts complements succulent sweet-and-sour beef.

Easy twice-baked beef brisket

Jewish family favorite for a traditional holiday meal

By Linda Lau Anusasananan

Nashville native Ruth Silvian became a Jewish cook through marriage. In 1940, touring the country as a dancer in musical revues, she met a nice young man who happened to be the son of a rabbi. Some culinary realignment was in order. After a self-directed tutorial on the Jewish kitchen—studying cookbooks and collecting recipes from neighbors—Silvian struck upon her own blend of Southern style and kosher traditions.

One of her specialties is twice-baked beef brisket topped with slow-cooked onions. When she visits her daughter, Mary Beth Taggart, in Novato, California, the entire family requests this mildly sweet-and-sour dish, along with the accompaniments she typically gives it: boiled red potatoes, candied carrots, and asparagus. If they're celebrating Hanukkah, they start with latkes, and Taggart adds a light salad of greens with fruit and an apple pie for dessert.

Silvian advocates braising the brisket at least one day before serving it, then chilling the meat and sauce separately. When the cold meat is sliced, then reunited with its onion sauce for reheating, it soaks up the pan juices and becomes amazingly moist and succulent. Double baking also gets a lot of the prep work for a large dinner party out of the way ahead of time.

Twice-baked Beef Brisket with Onions

PREP AND COOK TIME: About 5 hours, plus about 2 hours to cool
NOTES: Purchase a whole fresh beef brisket (not corned) or 2 center-cut pieces. Oven-braise the brisket up to 2 days ahead; chill meat and pan juices separately. To serve, slice meat and reheat in sauce. If desired, divide pan juices and meat evenly between 2 casseroles (9 by 13 in. each) in step 3.
MAKES: 16 to 18 servings

- 1 **beef brisket** (7 to 8 lb.; see notes)
- 2 envelopes **onion soup mix** (1 oz. each)
- ⅔ cup firmly packed **brown sugar**

- 2 **onions** (½ lb. each), peeled and thinly sliced
- 1½ cups **dry red wine**
  Salt

1. Trim and discard fat from brisket; rinse meat. Lay brisket, fattiest side up, in a 12- by 17-inch roasting pan. Sprinkle onion soup mix, brown sugar, and onions evenly over meat. Pour wine evenly over onions. Cover pan tightly.

2. Bake in a 325° oven until brisket is very tender when pierced, 3½ to 4 hours. With 2 wide spatulas, transfer meat to a platter. Let meat and juices cool about 2 hours. Cover separately and chill until meat is cold, at least 4 hours or up to 2 days.

3. Lift off and discard solid fat from pan juices. Thinly slice brisket across the grain, leaving slices in place; with a wide spatula, transfer neatly to pan with juices. Cover pan tightly with foil.

4. Bake in a 350° oven until meat is hot, 40 to 50 minutes. Serve with pan juices. Add salt to taste.

Per serving: 268 cal., 40% (108 cal.) from fat; 27 g protein; 12 g fat (4.1 g sat.); 12 g carbo (0.4 g fiber); 350 mg sodium; 84 mg chol.

Salad with Cranberries, Pears, and Cashews

PREP TIME: About 30 minutes
NOTES: Instead of salad mix, you can use bite-size pieces rinsed and crisped iceberg lettuce; you'll need about 2 heads (3 to 3½ lb. total). The recipe can be halved to serve a smaller crowd.
MAKES: 16 to 18 servings

- 1½ teaspoons grated **orange** peel
- ⅓ cup **orange juice**
- ½ cup **raspberry vinegar**
- ¼ cup **salad oil**
- 2 tablespoons **honey**
- 1 cup **sweetened dried cranberries**
- 3 **firm-ripe Bosc pears** (7 oz. each)
- 12 quarts **salad mix** (1⅓ lb.), rinsed and crisped (see notes)
- 1 cup **roasted salted cashews**
  Salt and **pepper**

1. In a wide 10- to 12-quart bowl, mix orange peel, orange juice, vinegar, oil, and honey. Add cranberries.

2. Rinse, dry, quarter, and core pears; cut lengthwise into ¼-inch-thick slices and put in bowl. Mix gently.

3. Add salad mix and cashews; mix gently to coat with dressing. Add salt and pepper to taste.

Per serving: 126 cal., 48% (60 cal.) from fat; 1.7 g protein; 6.7 g fat (1.1 g sat.); 16 g carbo (1.9 g fiber); 53 mg sodium; 0 mg chol. ◆

Celebrating bread traditions

Sweet loaves and shapely rolls for the holidays

By Andrew Baker and Elaine Johnson • Photographs by Leo Gong

■ If the aroma of sweet loaves baking in a warm kitchen during the holidays stirs happy memories in you, you aren't alone. The tradition of baking is one that many families revive at this time of year. Maybe you watched yeast dough swelling as it proofed to become a magnificent wreath, a braid, or coiled buns. Or perhaps you were permitted to lick the spoon after a sweet, quick bread batter was scraped into the baking pan. And while the bread was in the oven, no doubt you were barely able to wait for it to emerge golden brown, fragrant, and tantalizing.

Such memories yield recipes, and here we share favorites from Western families. In addition, we offer new breads from *Sunset's* test kitchens worthy of consideration for special events. Each bread makes a memorable addition to a Christmas breakfast, a festive brunch, a grand open house, an afternoon with the family, or a visit with drop-in guests.

Almond-Apricot Holiday Wreath

PREP AND COOK TIME: About 1½ hours, plus at least 3 hours to rise and cool

NOTES: If making wreath 1 day ahead, complete through step 8, cool, wrap airtight, and store at room temperature; freeze to store longer. To reheat wreath, sealed in foil and thawed, bake in a 325° oven until warm, about 15 minutes. Then glaze and garnish (step 9).

MAKES: 1 loaf (about 4 lb.); 15 or 16 servings

- 1 envelope **active dry yeast**
- ½ cup **milk**
- 3 **large eggs**
- 1 tablespoon **vanilla**
- 1 teaspoon **almond extract**
- About 5 cups **all-purpose flour**
- ½ cup **sugar**
- ¾ teaspoon **salt**
- About ¾ cup (⅜ lb.) **butter** or margarine, cut into chunks
- 1½ cups chopped **dried apricots** (about 9 oz.)
- 10 ounces **almond paste** (1 cup packed), broken into chunks
- ⅔ cup **raisins**
- **Orange glaze** (recipe follows)

1. In a small bowl, sprinkle yeast over ½ cup warm (110°) water. Let stand until yeast is soft, about 5 minutes. Add milk, 2 eggs, vanilla, and almond extract; beat to blend.

2. In a large bowl, combine 5 cups flour, sugar, and salt. Add ¾ cup butter and rub with your fingers or beat with a mixer on slow speed until fine crumbs form. Add milk-egg mixture and stir until well moistened.

3. *To knead with a dough hook,* beat on medium speed until dough no longer feels sticky and pulls cleanly from bowl, 8 to 10 minutes. If dough is still sticky, beat in more flour, 1 tablespoon at a time.

To knead by hand, scrape dough onto a lightly floured board. Knead until smooth and no longer sticky, 10 to 15 minutes; add more flour as required to prevent sticking. Return dough to bowl.

4. Cover bowl with plastic wrap and let dough rise in a warm place until at least doubled in volume, 2 to 2½ hours. Mix with dough hook or knead briefly on a lightly floured board to expel air.

5. Set aside 2 tablespoons chopped dried apricots. On a lightly floured board, roll dough into a 10- by 36-inch rectangle. Scatter remaining apricots, the almond paste chunks, and raisins evenly over dough to within ½ inch of each long side. Starting from 1 long side, roll dough snugly to form a rope.

Brush long outer edge with water; pinch firmly against rope to seal.

6. On a buttered 14- by 17-inch baking sheet, shape dough, placing seam down and butting ends together to form a ring with a 6-inch-wide opening in center. With a floured sharp knife, make a cut every 2 inches that goes ¾ of the way through dough from outside edge toward the center. Lift each cut section, 1 at a time, and twist to the right to lay on a cut side (see at right).

7. Cover wreath loosely with plastic wrap and let rise in a warm place until slightly puffy, 30 to 40 minutes. In a small bowl, beat remaining egg to blend. Uncover wreath and brush lightly with egg; save extra for other uses or discard.

8. Bake in a 325° oven (300° in a convection oven) until bread is deep golden brown, 40 to 45 minutes. Let cool on pan about 1 hour. Slide 2 wide metal spatulas under wreath to release and transfer to a platter or board.

9. Spoon orange glaze evenly over warm bread. Sprinkle reserved chopped apricots onto moist glaze. Serve warm or cool. Tear or cut into sections.

Per serving: 460 cal., 29% (135 cal.) from fat; 8.7 g protein; 15 g fat (6.5 g sat.); 73 g carbo (2.8 g fiber); 221 mg sodium; 65 mg chol.

Orange glaze. In a bowl, mix 1¾ cups **powdered sugar** and 3 tablespoons **orange juice** until smooth.

Icing-glazed wreath is filled with dried apricots, raisins, and almond paste.

Gram's Pecan Rolls

PREP AND COOK TIME: About 1 hour, plus at least 2 hours to rise and cool

NOTES: Ruth Silvian's recipe for *schnecken,* Yiddish for "little snails," is shared by her granddaughter Lisa Taggart of Mountain View, California. If making up to 1 day ahead (through step 6), let cool, cover airtight, and store at room temperature; freeze to store longer. To reheat rolls in pan, sealed in foil and thawed, bake in a 325° oven until warm in the center, about 15 minutes; remove from pan (step 7).

MAKES: 24 rolls

1. Follow directions for **almond-apricot holiday wreath** (page 352) through step 4. Omit vanilla, almond extract, almond paste, apricots, raisins, 1 egg (for brushing on dough), and orange glaze.

2. While dough rises, in a 1- to 2-quart pan combine ⅔ cup *each* firmly packed **brown sugar** and **light corn syrup** with ⅓ cup (⅙ lb.) **butter** or margarine. Stir over medium-high heat until boiling. Pour into a 12- by 17-inch pan and tilt to coat evenly. Sprinkle evenly with 2 cups **pecan halves.** In the unwashed pan used for the sugar mixture, melt ½ cup (¼ lb.) butter or margarine over medium heat.

3. In a small bowl, mix 1 cup firmly packed **brown sugar** and 1 tablespoon **ground cinnamon.**

4. On a lightly floured board, roll dough to form a 10- by 36-inch rectangle. Brush evenly with half the melted butter. Pat brown sugar–cinnamon mixture evenly over dough to within ½ inch of each long side. Starting from 1 long edge, roll dough snugly to form a rope. Pinch long outer edge tightly against rope to seal. With a floured sharp knife, cut rope crosswise into 24 equal slices (about 1½ in. wide). Lay slices, a cut side down and evenly spaced apart, in syrup-coated pan. Brush roll tops with remaining melted butter.

5. Cover loosely with plastic wrap and let rise in a warm place until slightly puffy, about 25 minutes. Uncover.

6. Bake in a 350° oven (325° in a convection oven) until rolls are well browned, about 30 minutes (25 minutes in a convection oven). Run a knife between pan sides and rolls.

7. Invert a large rimmed platter onto pan. Holding pan and platter together with pot holders, invert and let stand 1 or 2 minutes. Lift off pan and scrape any sauce and nuts onto rolls. Serve rolls hot, warm, or cool.

Golden, sugar-speckled braid pulls apart to reveal a tender, spice-flecked interior.

Per roll: 377 cal., 45% (171 cal.) from fat; 4.4 g protein; 19 g fat (8.4 g sat.); 49 g carbo (1.4 g fiber); 224 mg sodium; 52 mg chol.

Six-Braid Cardamom Bread

PREP AND COOK TIME: About 50 minutes, plus at least 3¼ hours to rise and cool

NOTES: For many generations, bread baking has been a passion in Greg Mistell's family. He grew up making yeast breads with his father. In fact, he enjoyed the craft so much, he turned it into a career. He is owner, and frequently the head baker, of Delphina's and Pearl bakeries in Portland. This rich cardamom loaf, sold at Delphina's, is also a favorite that Mistell makes at home with his 10-year-old daughter, Alisen. "Shaping a six-strand braid is fun, and the results are prettier than a standard braid," Mistell notes.

Candied orange peel can be ordered from King Arthur Flour ($3.50 for 6 oz.; 800/827-6836 or www. kingarthurflour.com). Look for coarse sugar with baking ingredients in supermarkets or specialty food stores.

If making up to 1 day ahead, cool loaf, wrap airtight, and store at room temperature; freeze to store longer. Reheat, sealed in foil and thawed, in a 325° oven until warm, 10 to 15 minutes.

MAKES: 1 loaf (3 lb.); 16 servings

  1 envelope **active dry yeast**

1½ teaspoons **cardamom seed**

  ¾ teaspoon **salt**

  ½ cup granulated **sugar**

  ¾ cup chopped **candied orange peel** (5 oz.)

  1 cup **milk**

    About ⅓ cup (⅙ lb.) cool melted **butter** or margarine

  2 **large egg** yolks

  5 to 5¼ cups **all-purpose flour**

  1 **large egg**

  1 tablespoon **coarse sugar** (optional, see notes) or granulated sugar

1. In a large bowl, sprinkle yeast over ½ cup warm (110°) water. Let stand until yeast is soft, about **5 minutes.** Crush cardamom seed on a hard surface with a flat-bottom glass. Add cardamom to bowl along with salt, granulated sugar, orange peel, milk, ⅓ cup melted butter, and egg yolks; mix to blend. Add 5 cups flour and stir until well moistened.

2. *To knead with a dough hook,* beat on medium speed until dough no longer feels sticky and pulls cleanly from bowl, 8 to 10 minutes. If dough is still sticky, beat in more flour, 1 tablespoon at a time.

To knead by hand, scrape dough onto a lightly floured board and knead until smooth and no longer sticky, 10 to 15 minutes; add flour as required to prevent sticking. Return dough to bowl.

3. Cover bowl with plastic wrap and let dough rise in a warm place until at least doubled in volume, 2 to 2½ hours. Mix with dough hook or knead briefly on a lightly floured board to expel air.

4. Divide dough into 6 equal pieces. Shape each piece into a smooth ball, set slightly apart on a floured board, and cover loosely with plastic wrap. Let rest 15 minutes.

5. On an unfloured board, roll each ball under your palms to form a 16-inch rope. Place ropes parallel and slightly apart on a buttered 14- by 17-inch baking sheet. At 1 end, pinch ropes together. Gently lift each rope up and off the center of the baking sheet, laying ends parallel and over pan edges to make an inverted V with 3 legs on each side.

6. To form braid, cross your right arm over your left, then pick up the 2 outer dough ropes. Uncross arms, and in doing so, cross the dough ropes over each other near the pinched ends, and lay ropes parallel to the inner part of the V. Repeat to lift the next 2 outer ropes, cross them just below the preceding ropes, and lay parallel to the inner part of the V. Continue braiding to the ends of the ropes. Pinch braid ends together.

7. Cover braid loosely with plastic wrap and let rise in a warm place until slightly puffy, 35 to 45 minutes. In a small bowl, beat egg to blend. Uncover braid and brush lightly with egg; save extra for other uses or discard. Sprinkle braid evenly with coarse sugar.

8. Bake in a 325° oven (300° in a convection oven) until bread is deep golden brown, 45 to 50 minutes.

9. Slide a wide spatula under bread to release from pan, then gently slide loaf onto a rack. Let cool at least 45 minutes. Slice to serve warm or cool.

Per serving: 260 cal., 20% (53 cal.) from fat; 5.6 g protein; 5.9 g fat (3.2 g sat.); 46 g carbo (1.2 g fiber); 163 mg sodium; 53 mg chol.

Lucia Buns

PREP AND COOK TIME: **About 40 minutes, plus at least 2 hours to rise**

NOTES: Though the Scandinavian tradition is to serve these buns on St. Lucia Day, December 13, the Fowler family of Olympia, Washington, also presents them at its own holiday buffet (page 348). The girl in the family who has most recently turned 12 or 13 years old, wearing a white dress and a crown with candles, offers the buns to guests. The buns are good at breakfast with raspberry jam.

If making buns up to 1 day ahead, cool, wrap airtight, and store at room temperature; freeze to store longer. Reheat, sealed in foil and thawed, in a 350° oven until warm, about 10 minutes.

MAKES: **20 buns**

1. In a blender or food processor, whirl ⅓ cup **slivered almonds** until finely ground. Follow directions for **six-braid cardamom bread** (preceding) through step 3, but omit candied orange peel and add the ground almonds. Also omit coarse sugar.

2. Divide dough into 20 equal pieces (about ¼-cup size) and shape each into a smooth ball. On an unfloured board, roll 1 ball at a time under your palm to make a 16-inch rope. Cut the rope in half crosswise. On a buttered 14- by 17-inch baking sheet (you'll need 2), lay 1 cut rope across the other to form an X. Roll each cut end to the center, forming a bun composed of 4 coils. Repeat to shape other buns, spacing them about 1½ inches apart. Firmly press 1 **raisin** deep into the center of each coil (you'll need 4 raisins for each bun, about ¼ cup total).

3. Cover buns loosely with plastic wrap and let rise in a warm place until slightly puffy, 20 to 25 minutes; the first pan will be ready to bake before the second. In a small bowl, beat 1 **large egg** to blend. Uncover buns and brush lightly with the egg; save extra for other uses or discard.

4. Bake in a 350° oven (325° in a convection oven) until buns are medium golden brown, about 15 minutes. If using 1 oven, switch pan positions when the first buns have baked 7 or 8 minutes. With a wide spatula, transfer buns to a rack. Serve hot, warm, or cool.

Per bun: 205 cal., 27% (55 cal.) from fat; 5.3 g protein; 6.1 g fat (2.7 g sat.); 32 g carbo (1.1 g fiber); 134 mg sodium; 53 mg chol.

Sheridan School Nut Bread

PREP AND COOK TIME: **About 1 hour**

NOTES: "In 1939, we made this nut bread in cooking class at Sheridan Junior High School in Minneapolis," says Amelia Lubansky of Ventura, California. "It was one of the very simple recipes the teacher started with." The bread was an immediate—and lasting—hit: Four generations of Lubansky's family have made it. To make up to 1 day ahead, let cool, wrap airtight, and store at room temperature. If baking at mile-high, increase all-purpose flour to 1¾ cups, reduce brown sugar to ¾ cup, and also reduce baking soda to ¾ teaspoon.

MAKES: **1 loaf (about 1½ lb.) or 2 loaves (about ¾ lb. each); 8 to 10 servings**

- ¾ cup **walnut halves**
- 1 **large egg**
- 1 cup **buttermilk**
- About 2 tablespoons melted **butter** or margarine
- 1½ cups **all-purpose flour**
- 1 cup firmly packed **brown sugar**
- 1 teaspoon **baking soda**
- ¼ teaspoon **salt**

1. Coarsely chop ½ cup walnuts.

2. In a large bowl with a mixer on medium-high speed, beat to blend egg, buttermilk, and 2 tablespoons butter. Add chopped walnuts, flour, brown sugar, baking soda, and salt; stir just until evenly moistened.

3. Scrape batter into a buttered 4½- by 8½-inch loaf pan (about 6½-cup capacity) or equally into 2 buttered loaf pans, each 3½ by 7¼ inches (about 3-cup capacity). Arrange remaining ¼ cup walnut halves evenly on top of batter.

4. Bake in a 350° oven until bread is darker brown and begins to pull from pan sides, 45 to 50 minutes for 6½-cup pan (35 to 40 minutes in a convection oven) and 30 to 35 minutes for 3-cup pans. Let bread cool in pan on a rack, about 10 minutes. Run a thin-bladed knife between bread and pan sides, then invert to release bread. Turn loaf rounded side up on rack. Let cool about 10 minutes. Slice to serve warm or at room temperature.

Per serving: 240 cal., 31% (74 cal.) from fat; 4.5 g protein; 8.2 g fat (2.4 g sat.); 38 g carbo (0.9 g fiber); 252 mg sodium; 29 mg chol.

Bishops' Bread

PREP AND COOK TIME: About 1½ hours

NOTES: Bishops' bread, a Western classic, is said to have been served to traveling clergy in the 19th century, hence the name. This version comes from Flo Braker of Palo Alto. If making up to 1 day ahead, cool, wrap airtight, and store at room temperature; freeze to store longer.

MAKES: 1 loaf (about 2 lb.) or 2 loaves (about 1 lb. each); 8 to 10 servings

About 1 cup (½ lb.) **butter** or margarine, at room temperature

1 cup **sugar**

4 **large eggs**

1 teaspoon **vanilla**

1½ cups **all-purpose flour**

¼ teaspoon **salt**

⅓ cup **candied** (glacé) **whole cherries,** cut into quarters

⅓ cup **sliced almonds**

⅓ cup **semisweet mini chocolate chips** or coarsely chopped chocolate chips

⅓ cup **golden raisins**

1. In a large bowl with a mixer on medium-high speed, beat 1 cup butter and sugar until fluffy, scraping bowl occasionally. Add eggs and vanilla and beat until blended. Stir in flour and salt, then beat until well blended. Add candied cherries, sliced almonds, semisweet chocolate chips, and golden raisins; stir to mix.

2. Scrape batter into a buttered 4½- by 8½-inch loaf pan (about 6½-cup capacity) or equally into 2 buttered loaf pans, each 3½ by 7¼ inches (about 3-cup capacity).

3. Bake in a 325° oven until bread is well browned, cracks on top, and just begins to pull from pan sides, and a wood skewer inserted into center comes out clean, about 1 hour and 25 minutes for 6½-cup pan (about 1 hour and 15 minutes in a 300° convection oven) and about 55 minutes for 3-cup pans (about 45 minutes in a 325° convection oven). Let bread cool in pan on a rack about 10 minutes. Run a thin-bladed knife between bread and pan sides, then invert to release bread. Turn loaf rounded side up on rack. Let cool about 10 minutes. Slice to serve warm or at room temperature.

Per serving: 419 cal., 52% (216 cal.) from fat; 5.6 g protein; 24 g fat (13 g sat.); 47 g carbo (0.9 g fiber); 275 mg sodium; 136 mg chol.

Slices of holiday quick breads are ready to be slathered with butter. Counterclockwise from front: Caramel-apple bread with coconut topping, bishops' bread studded with cherries and chocolate chips, and walnut-buttermilk bread.

Caramel-Apple Bread with Coconut Topping

PREP AND COOK TIME: About 1½ hours

NOTES: As the bread bakes, the caramel chunks in the batter soften to form sweet lumps throughout. If making up to 1 day ahead, cool, wrap airtight, and store at room temperature; freeze to store longer.

MAKES: 1 loaf (about 1¾ lb.) or 2 loaves (about ¾ lb. each); 8 to 10 servings

¾ cup **granulated sugar**

1 **large egg**

1 cup **applesauce**

About ½ cup (¼ lb.) melted **butter** or margarine

1 tablespoon **vanilla**

¼ cup firmly packed **brown sugar**

2 cups **all-purpose flour**

2 teaspoons **baking powder**

½ teaspoon **baking soda**

¼ teaspoon **salt**

¼ teaspoon **ground cinnamon**

¼ cup **sweetened shredded dried coconut**

1. In an 8- to 10-inch nonstick frying pan over high heat, shake and tilt ½ cup granulated sugar until melted and amber-colored, about 4 minutes; be careful not to burn. At once, pour hot caramel onto a 12-inch foil square on a flat surface. When caramel is cool enough to handle, peel off foil. Break caramel into chunks and put in a heavy plastic food bag. With a rolling pin or mallet, crush until largest chunks are about ¼ inch.

2. In a large bowl, combine egg, applesauce, ¼ cup butter, vanilla, and brown sugar. With a mixer on medium-high speed, beat until well blended. Stir in flour, baking powder, baking soda, salt, and cinnamon; beat just until evenly moistened. Stir in caramel.

3. Scrape batter into a buttered 4½- by 8½-inch loaf pan (about 6½-cup capacity) or equally into 2 buttered loaf pans, each 3½ by 7¼ inches (about 3-cup capacity).

4. Set pan on a sheet of foil placed on oven rack (to catch topping drips). Bake in a 350° oven until bread is firm when pressed in the center, about 40 minutes for 6½-cup pan and 30 minutes for 3-cup pans.

5. Meanwhile, in a small bowl, mix coconut with remaining ¼ cup granulated sugar and ¼ cup butter. When bread is firm to touch, spread mixture evenly over hot loaf or loaves. Continue to bake until coconut topping is evenly brown, 15 to 20 minutes. Run a thin-bladed knife between bread and pan sides. Let bread cool in pan on a rack for about 10 minutes, then invert to release bread. Turn loaf rounded side up on rack. Let cool about 10 minutes. Slice to serve warm or at room temperature.

Per serving: 294 cal., 34% (99 cal.) from fat; 3.4 g protein; 11 g fat (6.7 g sat.); 46 g carbo (1.1 g fiber); 330 mg sodium; 47 mg chol. ◆

For wintry eves

Beverages that warm

By Betsy Reynolds Bateson

For parties, drop-in guests, or even the carolers who pause while serenading, a mug of warm holiday cheer is a fitting refreshment for the season. And recipes such as these, which can be made by the bowl or by the mug, with or without alcohol, and from ingredients you can keep on hand, will suit any occasion.

Mulled Cranberry Wine Punch

PREP AND COOK TIME: About 30 minutes
NOTES: For a nonalcoholic punch, replace red wine with apple juice and omit liqueur.
MAKES: 12 to 14 servings

- 1 cup **fresh** or frozen **cranberries**
- 1 bottle (48 oz., 6 cups) **cranberry juice cocktail**
- ½ cup **raisins**
- 4 to 6 **cinnamon sticks** (about 3 in.)
- 2 bottles (750 ml.) **fruity dry red wine** such as Gamay Beaujolais, or 6 cups apple juice and 2 to 4 tablespoons lemon juice, to taste
- ¼ to ½ cup **sugar**
- 1 teaspoon **almond extract**
  About ¾ cup **orange-flavor liqueur** such as Cointreau or triple sec (optional)

1. Sort cranberries, discarding bruised and decayed fruit. Rinse berries and put in a 5- to 6-quart pan; add cranberry juice cocktail, raisins, and cinnamon sticks. Bring to a boil over high heat; cover and simmer on low heat to blend flavors, about 20 minutes.
2. Add wine and ¼ to ½ cup sugar, to taste. Heat until steaming, 5 to 8 minutes; do not boil.
3. Add almond extract and orange liqueur; keep punch warm over lowest heat and ladle into cups or stemmed glasses.

Per serving: 174 cal., 0.5% (0.9 cal.) from fat; 0.4 g protein; 0.1 g fat (0 g sat.); 26 g carbo (0.6 g fiber); 8.3 mg sodium; 0 mg chol.

Steaming and hospitable, stemmed glasses are filled with hot cranberry-and-wine punch.

Mulled Pineapple Wine Punch

PREP AND COOK TIME: About 25 minutes
NOTES: For a nonalcoholic punch, omit wines and add 4½ cups white grape juice.
MAKES: 12 servings

- 2 **oranges** (½ lb. each), rinsed
- 6 cups **refrigerated,** canned, or frozen reconstituted **pineapple juice**
- 2 tablespoons minced **fresh ginger**
- ¼ cup **sugar**
- 1 bottle (750 ml.) **dry white wine** such as Fumé Blanc or Sauvignon Blanc
- 1 bottle (375 ml.) **Muscat dessert wine** such as Moscato d'Asti, Moscato Canelli, Essencia, or Electra

1. Trim and discard ends from oranges. Cut fruit crosswise into ¼-inch-thick slices, discarding seeds. Put fruit in a 5- to 6-quart pan. Add pineapple juice, ginger, and sugar. Bring to a boil on high heat; cover and simmer on low heat to blend flavors, about 15 minutes.
2. Add dry white wine and Muscat wine; heat until steaming, about 5 minutes. Do not boil.
3. Keep punch warm over lowest heat; ladle into cups.

Per serving: 185 cal., 0.5% (0.9 cal.) from fat; 0.8 g protein; 0.1 g fat (0 g sat.); 28 g carbo (0.7 g fiber); 7.4 mg sodium; 0 mg chol.

Hot Berry Lemon Toddy

PREP AND COOK TIME: About 5 minutes
NOTES: To make more than a single serving, combine ingredients in a pan and heat until steaming, then add brandy and ladle into mugs.
MAKES: 1 serving

- 4 **whole cloves**
- 1 **lemon** slice, about ¼ inch thick
- ¼ cup thawed **frozen raspberry-lemonade concentrate**
- 1 teaspoon **honey**
- 1 teaspoon **raspberry-flavor syrup**
- 2 tablespoons **brandy** or rum (optional)

Stick cloves into peel of lemon slice. Put raspberry-lemonade concentrate in a microwave-safe mug (8 to 10 oz.); add ⅔ cup water, lemon slice, honey, and raspberry syrup. Heat in a microwave oven on full power (100%) until steaming, about 1 minute. Add brandy, stir, and serve.

Per serving: 151 cal., 0.6% (0.9 cal.) from fat; 0.2 g protein; 0.1 g fat (0 g sat.); 42 g carbo (0.7 g fiber); 1 mg sodium; 0 mg chol.

Totally Decadent Hot Chocolate

PREP AND COOK TIME: About 30 minutes
NOTES: After using the vanilla bean, rinse it, let dry, and store airtight to use again. Use a vegetable peeler to pare orange peel and make chocolate curls.
MAKES: 4 servings

- 2 cups **milk**
- 1 **vanilla bean** (6 or 7 in.)
- 4 strips **orange** peel (orange part only), each about 2 inches long
- ¾ cup chopped **semisweet chocolate**
- 2 tablespoons **purchased caramel,** butterscotch, or fudge **sauce** (or 1 tablespoon each of any 2)
  About ½ cup **whipped cream**
  Semisweet chocolate curls

1. In a 1- to 2-quart pan, combine milk, vanilla bean, and orange peel. Warm over low heat to blend flavors, about 15 minutes, stirring often; do not boil. Discard orange peel; remove vanilla bean and save (see notes).
2. Add chopped chocolate and caramel sauce to hot milk; stir over low heat until chocolate melts.
3. Pour hot chocolate into mugs (about 8 oz.), top with equal portions of whipped cream, and sprinkle with chocolate curls. Serve with spoons.

Per serving: 296 cal., 55% (162 cal.) from fat; 5.8 g protein; 18 g fat (11 g sat.); 33 g carbo (1.9 g fiber); 104 mg sodium; 34 mg chol. ◆

food guide

By Jerry Anne Di Vecchio • Photographs by James Carrier

Where there's smoke

You don't need fire for flavor

■ When I taste a delicious dish, I can't resist asking how it's made. However, if the source is a professional chef, converting his or her process for the home kitchen can be tricky, often demanding a modified game plan.

For example, John Howie, executive chef at Seattle's Palisade Waterfront Restaurant, turns out delicately flavored smoked scallops and smoked hazelnuts for this mellow and—except for the smoking—very easy pasta. But then he has the advantage of a commercial smoker.

Where there's a trick, there's a trickster: I set out to "smoke" the handful of shellfish and nuts this dish requires without buying a smoker or ever firing up the barbecue. Modifying Howie's initial step a bit, I brined the scallops and hazelnuts in water, salt, sugar, and liquid smoke (made from real smoke— a little goes a long way). Voilà! Smoke flavor that delicately permeates the scallops and hazelnuts.

Smoked Scallop and Hazelnut Fettuccine

PREP AND COOK TIME: About 30 minutes, plus 30 minutes to brine

NOTES: If you can find salted, roasted smoked hazelnuts (see "A Nutty Idea," at right), chop, and omit steps 2 and 3.

MAKES: 3 or 4 servings

- 3 tablespoons firmly packed **brown sugar**

  About 2 tablespoons **kosher** or coarse **salt**
- 1 teaspoon **liquid smoke**
- ½ pound **bay scallops**, rinsed
- ½ cup **hazelnuts**
- 5 tablespoons **butter** or margarine
- 2 teaspoons minced **garlic**
- 1½ cups **whipping cream**

  About ½ cup fat-skimmed **chicken broth**
- 9 to 10 ounces **fresh fettuccine**
- ¾ cup **shredded parmesan cheese**
- ¼ cup thinly sliced **green onions** (including tops)
- 1 tablespoon chopped **fresh dill** or 1 teaspoon dried dill weed

  Fresh-ground **pepper**

1. In a bowl, mix 1 cup water with 1½ tablespoons brown sugar, 1 tablespoon salt, and ½ teaspoon liquid smoke. Add scallops, mix, cover, and chill 30 minutes. Drain scallops. If making up to 1 day ahead, cover and chill.

2. In a 1- to 2-quart pan, mix 1 cup water with remaining 1½ tablespoons brown sugar, 1 tablespoon salt, and ½ teaspoon liquid smoke. Bring to a boil over high heat; add hazelnuts, remove from heat,

A nutty idea

■ The hazelnut harvest in Oregon's Willamette Valley, where more than 99 percent of the domestic crop grows, is over for the year. The nuts are available in the shell and out, salted and seasoned, candy-coated, and roasted (with some or all of the skin removed). For cooking, roasted hazelnuts are a shortcut treasure, but they can be hard to find, unless you order from a producer listed by the Hazelnut Marketing Board (800/503-6887 or www.teleport.com/~hazelnut) or from Your Northwest store (888/252-0699 or www.yournw.com).

and let stand 30 minutes. Drain nuts, pat dry, and very coarsely chop. Spread nuts in an 8- or 9-inch pan.

3. Bake in a 325° oven, shaking pan occasionally, until nuts are golden brown, about 10 minutes. Pour from pan. If making up to 1 day ahead, cover airtight and store at room temperature.

4. In a 12- to 14-inch nonstick frying pan over high heat, combine 4 tablespoons butter and the garlic; stir often until butter is melted and garlic is pale gold, about 1 minute. Add cream and

½ cup broth, and bring to a boil over high heat; stir often 2 to 3 minutes. Pour cream mixture into a bowl. Rinse pan and wipe dry. Return it to high heat and add remaining butter. As butter melts, pour scallops onto a towel; pat dry. Add to pan and shake or turn scallops until juices have evaporated and shellfish is browned, 6 to 7 minutes. Return cream mixture to pan, and stir to release browned bits; keep warm.

5. In a 5- to 6-quart pan over high heat, bring about 3 quarts water to a boil.

While scallops are browning, add pasta to boiling water and cook until tender to bite, 3 to 4 minutes. Drain well and pour into scallop sauce; add hazelnuts. Sprinkle with ½ cup of the cheese; lift with 2 forks to mix. If sauce is thicker than you like, add more broth, 2 tablespoons at a time, and mix. Mound pasta on warm plates, sprinkle equally with green onions, dill, remaining cheese, and pepper to taste.

Per serving: 821 cal., 62% (513 cal.) from fat; 28 g protein; 57 g fat (30 g sat.); 50 g carbo (2.7 g fiber); 2,236 mg sodium; 215 mg chol.

Super squash

■ Successful synergy among ingredients in a dish can lift those foods to a new plateau of taste. Sometimes the magical combination is obvious; other times it's very subtle. It takes a discerning palate, for instance, to credit chestnuts for the depth and richness of this golden squash dish. At the Water Grill in Los Angeles, the mixture is the foundation for pan-browned Atlantic char. But because the squash goes so well with other fish, as well as poultry and meats, I've turned it into a casserole for party and holiday dinners.

Butternut Squash with Chestnuts

PREP AND COOK TIME: 45 to 50 minutes

NOTES: Instead of roasting fresh chestnuts (directions follow), you can use peeled cooked chestnuts, which are available frozen, vacuum-packed and shelf-stable, and packed in water and canned. If making casserole up to 1 day ahead, cool, cover airtight, and chill; to reheat, uncover and cook in a microwave oven on full power (100%) until hot, about 4 minutes.

MAKES: 6 to 8 servings

  2 pounds **butternut squash** (1 whole or a piece), rinsed

  4 cups fat-skimmed **chicken broth**

  ⅓ cup peeled **garlic** cloves

  ¼ cup **sherry vinegar**

  ½ teaspoon **dried rosemary**

  ½ pound **fresh shiitake mushrooms,** stems discarded

  ¼ cup (⅛ lb.) **butter** or margarine

  2 cups **peeled cooked chestnuts** or 1 can (10 oz.) chestnuts packed in water (see notes), drained

     Salt and **pepper**

1. With a vegetable peeler, pare skin from squash and discard. Cut squash in half lengthwise, and scoop out and discard seeds. Cut squash into ¼-inch-thick slices, then cut enough into neat ¼-inch cubes to make 2 cups; chop remainder.

2. In a 3- to 4-quart pan over high heat, bring broth to a boil. Add squash cubes and cook until barely tender when pierced, 3 to 4 minutes. With a slotted spoon, transfer cubes to a bowl.

3. To pan, add chopped squash, garlic, vinegar, and rosemary. Boil, stirring occasionally, until most of the liquid is

evaporated and squash mashes easily when pressed, about 30 minutes.

4. Meanwhile, rinse, drain, and quarter shiitake mushroom caps. In a 10- to 12-inch frying pan over high heat, combine 2 tablespoons butter and shiittakes; stir often until mushrooms are lightly browned, 5 to 6 minutes.

5. In a blender or food processor, combine chopped squash mixture, chestnuts, and 2 tablespoons butter; whirl until smooth. Scrape into a shallow 1½-quart casserole (microwave-safe if making ahead). Scatter cooked cubed squash and mushrooms over puréed squash mixture. Add salt and pepper to taste.

Per serving: 218 cal., 28% (62 cal.) from fat; 7.1 g protein; 6.9 g fat (3.9 g sat.); 34 g carbo (6.3 g fiber); 104 mg sodium; 16 mg chol.

Roasted chestnuts. Sort **chestnuts,** discarding those that feel very light (they are apt to be moldy), to make 1 pound (about 4 cups) nuts. Cut an X through the flat side of each shell. Spread chestnuts in a single layer in a 10- by 15-inch baking pan. Bake in a 400° oven until nuts are no longer starchy-tasting (taste to test), about 30 minutes. Wrap hot nuts in a towel and enclose in a plastic bag; let stand until cool enough to touch, about 10 minutes. Take out 1 nut at a time and, with a short-bladed knife, pull off and discard shell and as much of the brown skin as you can. Use warm or cold. Makes 2 cups.

Party plank

■ The Northwest Coast Indians have a long tradition of putting the aromatic imprint of cedar on foods. At *Sunset,* we've adapted this regional approach through the years by grilling salmon on untreated cedar boards. But Seattle chef John Howie, who also likes to smoke foods (see "Where There's Smoke," page 358), takes cedar cooking a step further: He bakes and serves foods on a thick, rimmed cedar plank. The plank would be inclined to split or warp if not reinforced by long metal screws that can be tightened as needed. Howie reports that with a little care—washing the boards by hand, coating them with salad oil before and after use, baking on them at 350° or lower, and occasionally rubbing them with fine sandpaper to restore the wood's fragrance—planks can survive five or more years of restaurant use.

Made by Pacific Northwest Fine Wood Products, a 9- by 12-inch plank costs $29.95, a 9½- by 16-inch, $37.95. Call (800) 881-1747 or go to Howie's website, www.plankcooking.com.

Mushrooms Lolling on Cedar

PREP AND COOK TIME: About 30 minutes

NOTES: If you use cedar, keep an eye on the plank while cooking; if it begins to char, brush it with water.

MAKES: 6 servings

½ pound **mushrooms** (about 1-in. caps)

About 2 tablespoons **salad oil**

½ teaspoon grated **lemon** peel

2 tablespoons **lemon juice**

½ teaspoon minced **garlic**

¼ teaspoon **pepper**

2 tablespoons minced **parsley**

Salt

1. Rinse mushrooms; trim and discard discolored stem ends. In a bowl, mix 2 tablespoons oil, lemon peel, lemon juice, garlic, and pepper. Add mushrooms and mix.

2. Rinse cedar plank (see "Party Plank," preceding), wipe dry, and rub with oil, then wipe off excess oil with a towel (or oil a 9- by 13-in. pan). Pour mushroom mixture onto plank (or into pan).

3. Bake in a 350° oven on a rack in the middle to upper third of the oven (upper third if oven has electric coils on the bottom) until mushrooms are moist-looking in the center (cut to test), 20 to 25 minutes; stir several times. Sprinkle with parsley and salt to taste, and mix. Serve mushrooms from the board (or pour from pan into a bowl) to spear with small skewers.

Per serving: 52 cal., 81% (42 cal.) from fat; 0.8 g protein; 4.7 g fat (0.6 g sat.); 2.3 g carbo (0.6 g fiber); 3.1 mg sodium; 0 mg chol.

Morning fast food

■ My dad, who rarely strayed from eggs, bacon, and toast to start the day, conceded to simpler fare on Christmas morning when we opened our gifts. After several experimental forays, he pronounced breakfast pizzas his favorite deviation, and this slightly goofy snack became part of our holiday ritual.

Breakfast Pizzas

PREP AND COOK TIME: About 25 minutes

NOTES: For a chewier texture, toast the muffins before adding the toppings.

MAKES: 4 servings

½ pound **bulk pork sausage** or Italian sausage (casings removed)

¼ teaspoon **dried oregano**

¼ teaspoon **pepper**

1 can (8 oz.) **crushed pineapple,** drained

4 **English muffins**

1 can (6 oz.) **tomato paste**

2 cups **shredded cheddar cheese** (½ lb.)

½ cup **shredded parmesan cheese**

1. In a 10- to 12-inch frying pan over high heat, crumble sausage with a spoon; add oregano and pepper, and stir until meat is lightly browned, 5 to 7 minutes. Spoon out and discard fat. Add pineapple and mix.

2. Split English muffins in half horizontally. Spread tomato paste equally on cut sides and set halves slightly apart in a 10- by 15-inch baking pan. Top each half equally with sausage mixture, cheddar cheese, then parmesan cheese.

3. Bake in a 400° oven until cheddar cheese is melted, about 10 minutes.

Per serving: 575 cal., 49% (279 cal.) from fat; 30 g protein; 31 g fat (17 g sat.); 45 g carbo (3.3 g fiber); 1,477 mg sodium; 89 mg chol. ◆

The Wine Guide

By Karen MacNeil-Fife

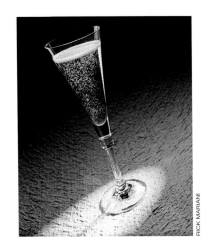

RICK MARIANI

Go for broke

■ I was 24 when I bought my first case of real French Champagne, as a holiday gift to myself. It was the most expensive purchase I had ever made, and on its face illogical. How could I—a struggling writer living in a New York City tenement—justify Champagne?

The answer was embedded in the question itself. Champagne became the pleasure, the indulgence, the bright spot that made hardship more bearable. Though I didn't know it at the time, my case of Champagne—which lasted me a full two years—was a small argument for the thesis put forth by anthropologist Lionel Tiger in his book *The Pursuit of Pleasure* (Little, Brown, Boston, 1992). According to Tiger, pleasure is a legitimate, even imperative component of normal life. Were it not for what he calls "accessible pleasures," we could not have survived the dark nights and bright days of our own evolution.

Exactly what constitutes an accessible pleasure varies, of course, from person to person. But on Christmas Eve or New Year's Eve, I, for one, wouldn't choose to celebrate in a suite at the Four Seasons or on a 30-foot sailboat in the Caribbean. I'd rather be in my living room with one husband, two dogs, and a great bottle of Champagne.

So what are the great Champagnes? Or maybe I should rephrase that: What are the great sparklers—for Champagne, extraordinary as it is, is not the only stunning wine with bubbles in it. In the last decade or so, California sparkling wine companies, many of them owned by Champagne firms, have begun producing simply stellar wines.

What separates Champagne from sparkling wine is not quality per se, but place. Champagne comes from the Champagne region of France, about 1½ hours' drive northeast of Paris. Sixty-five million years ago, this cool inland part of northern France was under a vast prehistoric sea. As the waters receded, they left behind a great crescent of chalk, rich with minerals and sea fossils. From this geologic legacy eventually emerged the vineyards—and, ultimately, the personality—of Champagne.

California has no chalk (not much anyway), and no sea fossils to speak of in its soil. But the state's very tumultuous geologic past, driven by volcanic cataclysms, has made California a unique sparkling wine–producing region on its own.

There's one more big difference between these two places: sun. Champagne has little; California has a lot. As a result, the flavor profiles of their respective sparkling wines are different. California's, not surprisingly, tastes of fruit on its way to ripeness. Champagne tastes less of fruit and more subtly of the earth from which it came.

So how do you judge a great Champagne or sparkling wine? Imagine a sphere, and then add an arrow shooting up through the middle. A bubbly should be like that. On the one hand, you feel and taste its creamy round-

GREAT BUBBLES

There are scores of sparkling wines I love to drink. That said, here is a sampling of my favorites, especially if I'm in the mood to splurge. Prices are approximate.

■ **Schramsberg Blanc de Blancs 1996 (Napa Valley)**, $26.50. Rich, elegant, and supple, with long, creamy brioche and apple pie flavors. *Blanc de Blancs* means that the wine is made solely from Chardonnay grapes.

■ **Domaine Carneros "Le Rêve" 1994 (Carneros, CA)**, $55. *Le rêve* is French for "the dream." And this is dreamy—sleek and dramatic on the one hand, but also beautifully creamy, with caramelized apple flavors.

■ **Billecart-Salmon Brut Rosé nonvintage (Champagne)**, $50. Light-bodied, vibrant, and sassy. Fabulous as an aperitif or with appetizers.

■ **Veuve Clicquot Vintage Reserve 1995 (Champagne)**, $70. Veuve Clicquot always has impeccable balance. The creamy brioche flavors are long and refined.

■ **Pol Roger "Cuvée Sir Winston Churchill" 1990 (Champagne)**, $125. Pol Roger was Winston Churchill's favorite Champagne—and he reportedly drank prodigious amounts of it. This prestigious cuvée, named after the statesman himself, is utterly gorgeous, with irresistible creaminess and zestiness.

■ **Krug Grande Cuvée nonvintage (Champagne)**, $120. Deep and complex with nutty, yeasty flavors and marzipan. The classic among full-bodied Champagnes.

ness, but in the same split second, you also feel and taste a sleek dagger of refreshing acidity that almost seems to vibrate through the center of the wine. I think of it as the contrapuntal tension of opposites. That's what makes great sparklers fascinating.

Not to mention the bubbles, which add textural excitement that makes a sparkler even more intriguing. I can't think of a better way to end one year and begin another than to sip a little intrigue. ◆

Bakers will appreciate a tube pan containing items with which to make and serve our one-step orange pound cake (recipe follows; include a copy with gift).

- 10- to 12-cup fluted tube cake pan
- Citrus zester
- Ice cream scoop

- Candied orange peel (recipe follows)

Additions: Cooking parchment, vanilla beans, colorful decorating sugars

Tasteful gifts

A pretty pan, the perfect platter—serve up your presents in style

By Andrew Baker • Photographs by James Carrier

The dilemma this time of year is not what to buy for the avid griller on your gift list—it's how to wrap the gigantic platter, along with the skewers, the barbecue sauce … .

Look to the gift for a solution: Serve your goodies on the platter and leave behind the cumbersome packaging. All your culinary bundle needs is a sheath of cellophane—clear, colored, or printed—and a festive ribbon.

Based on this packing principle, we've assembled three gift assortments that would delight a barbecuer, a baker, and a seafood lover.

Each includes a theme-appropriate condiment that you can make to personalize the gift and inspire the recipient to use the new tools. Finally, we've included a list of suggestions for expanding each package if your resources allow it. The cost of each collection is entirely up to you: It can be modest or affectionately extravagant, since every item here has an enormous price range, depending on its quality and vendor.

Chipotle Barbecue Sauce

PREP AND COOK TIME: About 35 minutes

NOTES: Use this sweet-hot sauce as a marinade or basting sauce for steaks, chops, or poultry, and as a dip for grilled meats or vegetables. Sauce keeps 6 to 8 weeks if chilled airtight.

MAKES: About 2 cups

4 to 6 **dried chipotle chilies** (each 2 to 2½ in. long, about ½ oz. total)

⅓ cup **red wine vinegar**

1⅓ cups **catsup**

⅓ cup firmly packed **brown sugar**

1½ tablespoons **unsweetened cocoa**

1½ teaspoons **paprika**

1½ teaspoons minced or pressed **garlic**

If grilling is what fires up the person you're shopping for, this collection will fuel the passion.

- Large rimmed platter for grilled meats and roasts (big enough to accommodate skewers)
- Decorative skewers
- Basting brush
- Bottle of chipotle barbecue sauce (see recipe, above)

Additions: Probe thermometer with timer, tongs, dried chipotle chilies

Seafood fans will savor a platter decked with elegant or playful shellfish accoutrements.

- Large rimmed crystal or glass platter
- Decorative cocktail forks
- Oyster knife
- Bottle of tomato–lemon grass cocktail sauce (recipe follows)

Additions: Shrimp deveiner, lobster/crab cracker

1. Wipe chilies with a damp cloth. Combine with $\frac{1}{2}$ cup boiling water in a small bowl and let stand until soft, about 15 minutes.

2. Lift chilies from bowl; reserve soaking liquid. Cut off and discard chili stems; cut chilies in half lengthwise and scrape out and discard seeds and veins.

3. In a blender or food processor, whirl chilies, soaking liquid, and vinegar until smooth. Pour into a 2- to 3-quart pan.

4. Add catsup, brown sugar, cocoa, paprika, and garlic. Stir over high heat until boiling; reduce heat and simmer, stirring often, until reduced to 2 cups, about 5 minutes. Cool, pour into a clean 1-pint jar, cover airtight, and chill.

Per tablespoon: 22 cal., 4.1% (0.9 cal.) from fat; 0.3 g protein; 0.1 g fat (0 g sat.); 5.5 g carbo (0.3 g fiber); 119 mg sodium; 0 mg chol.

Spiced Candied Orange Peel

PREP AND COOK TIME: About $1\frac{1}{2}$ hours

NOTES: You can pare orange peel (colored part only) with a vegetable peeler; stack pieces and cut into $\frac{1}{16}$- to $\frac{1}{8}$-inch-wide slivers. Serve candied peel with one-step orange pound cake (recipe follows) and vanilla ice cream. Peel keeps 6 to 8 weeks if chilled airtight.

MAKES: About $1\frac{1}{2}$ cups

- 5 to 6 pounds **oranges**
- 1 cup **sugar**
- $\frac{1}{2}$ teaspoon **ground cinnamon**
- $\frac{1}{4}$ teaspoon *each* **ground allspice, ground cardamom, ground cloves, ground coriander,** and **ground nutmeg**

1. Rinse and dry oranges. Using a citrus zester, remove 1 cup loosely packed strands of peel from oranges (see notes). Ream 3 cups juice from pared fruit.

2. In a 3- to 4-quart pan over high heat, bring 2 cups water and orange peel to a boil; cook 1 minute. Drain. Add 2 more cups water to peel in pan, bring to a boil, and cook 1 minute. Drain.

3. In pan, combine peel, 2 cups orange juice, 2 cups water, and sugar. Bring to a boil over high heat; cook, stirring often, until liquid has almost evaporated and peel is translucent and slightly darker (to check, remove pan from heat and let bubbles subside), about 30 minutes. Watch carefully to avoid scorching.

4. Stir in remaining 1 cup orange juice, cinnamon, allspice, cardamom, cloves, coriander, and nutmeg; boil just until mixture thickens, about 5 minutes longer. Cool, pour into a clean 1-pint jar, cover airtight, and chill.

Per tablespoon: 32 cal., 0% (0 cal.) from fat; 0 g protein; 0 g fat; 8.1 g carbo (0 g fiber); 0 mg sodium; 0 mg chol.

One-Step Orange Pound Cake

PREP AND COOK TIME: About $1\frac{1}{2}$ hours

NOTES: Dixie Tingley of Shingle Springs, California, makes this easy cake. If making up to 1 day ahead, cover airtight and store at room temperature (sprinkle with powdered sugar just before serving). Serve wedges with vanilla ice cream and spiced candied orange peel (recipe precedes). For mile-high baking, increase flour to 3 cups and reduce sugar to $1\frac{1}{2}$ cups.

MAKES: 10 to 12 servings

- About 1 cup ($\frac{1}{2}$ lb.) **butter** or margarine, at room temperature
- About $2\frac{1}{4}$ cups **all-purpose flour**
- 2 cups **granulated sugar**
- 1 cup **sour cream**
- 2 tablespoons grated **orange** peel
- 3 **large eggs**
- 1 teaspoon **vanilla**
- $\frac{1}{2}$ teaspoon **baking soda**
- $\frac{1}{2}$ teaspoon **salt**
- **Powdered sugar**

1. Butter a 10- to 12-cup fluted tube cake pan; dust with flour.

2. In a large bowl, combine $2\frac{1}{4}$ cups flour, granulated sugar, sour cream, 1 cup butter, orange peel, eggs, vanilla, baking soda, and salt. With a mixer on medium speed, beat until well blended, 1 to 2 minutes.

3. Pour batter into prepared tube cake pan. Spread level with a spatula.

4. Bake in a 325° oven until cake begins to pull from pan sides and springs back when lightly pressed in the center, about $1\frac{1}{4}$ hours (about 55 minutes in a convection oven). Let cake cool in pan for 15 minutes, then invert onto a rack. Sprinkle cake with powdered sugar. Serve warm or at room temperature. Cut into wedges.

Per serving: 420 cal., 45% (189 cal.) from fat; 4.8 g protein; 21 g fat (13 g sat.); 53 g carbo (0.6 g fiber); 338 mg sodium; 105 mg chol.

Tomato–Lemon Grass Cocktail Sauce

PREP AND COOK TIME: About 1 hour

NOTES: Use as a dip for cooked shrimp, a condiment for shucked oysters on the half-shell, or a sauce for crab or shrimp cocktails. Sauce keeps 6 to 8 weeks if chilled airtight.

MAKES: About 2 cups

- $\frac{1}{2}$ pound **lemon grass**
- $1\frac{1}{2}$ cups **seasoned rice vinegar**
- 1 can (15 oz.) **tomato sauce**
- 1 teaspoon **sugar**

1. Rinse lemon grass. Trim off and discard root ends and tough tops. Peel off and discard tough outer layers. Chop tender inner stalks.

2. In a blender or food processor, whirl lemon grass with vinegar until puréed.

3. Pour mixture into a 2- to 3-quart pan. Bring to a boil over high heat, then reduce heat and simmer, stirring often, to blend flavors, about 10 minutes.

4. Pour mixture into a fine strainer set over a bowl. Press with a spatula or spoon to extract as much liquid as possible (you should have about 1 cup). Discard residue in strainer.

5. Combine lemon grass vinegar, tomato sauce, and sugar in pan. Bring to a boil over high heat; reduce heat and simmer, stirring often, until mixture is reduced to 2 cups, about 20 minutes. Cool, pour into a clean 1-pint jar, cover airtight, and chill.

Per tablespoon: 16 cal., 0% (0 cal.) from fat; 0.2 g protein; 0 g fat; 4 g carbo (0 g fiber); 303 mg sodium; 0 mg chol. ◆

Tart ginger-glazed shrimp and grapefruit wedges contrast with the sweetness of rice with coconut milk.

Swinging shrimp

■ Given a choice, would you prefer dinner's main course be quick, low-fat, easy, or exciting? Why choose? These shrimp dishes offer it all, especially if you use pour-from-the-bag individually frozen shrimp—just rinse with hot tap water to thaw almost at once. The first is sticky-glazed shrimp on rice cooked in reduced-fat coconut milk. The other two are one-pan performers; both the couscous and the pasta cook in distinctly seasoned broths along with the shrimp.

Thai Sticky Shrimp with Coconut Rice

PREP AND COOK TIME: About 25 minutes
MAKES: 4 servings

- 1 can (14 oz.) **reduced-fat coconut milk**
- 1¼ cups **short-grain white rice** such as pearl
- 2 **ruby grapefruit** (about 2 lb. total)
- ½ cup firmly packed **brown sugar**
- 1 tablespoon **cornstarch**
- ¼ cup **soy sauce**
- 2 tablespoons **rice vinegar**
- 2 tablespoons minced **fresh ginger**
- 1 pound thawed **frozen uncooked, shelled, deveined shrimp** (38 to 50 per lb.), rinsed and drained
- ½ pound **Belgian endive**, leaves separated, rinsed, and drained
- ½ cup finely slivered **fresh basil** leaves

1. In a 3- to 4-quart pan over high heat, combine coconut milk, rice, and ¾ cup water. Bring to a boil, reduce heat, cover, and simmer until rice is tender to bite, about 15 minutes.

2. Meanwhile, cut peel and membrane from grapefruit. Cut between fruit and membrane to release segments into a bowl.

3. In a 10- to 12-inch frying pan, mix sugar and cornstarch. Add soy sauce, vinegar, and ginger. Stir on high heat until boiling, about 1 minute. Add shrimp and stir often until opaque but still moist-looking in center of thickest part (cut to test), 3 to 4 minutes.

4. Mound rice equally on warm plates, spoon shrimp mixture equally onto rice, and garnish with grapefruit segments, endive leaves, and basil.

Per serving: 569 cal., 12% (68 cal.) from fat; 31 g protein; 7.5 g fat (3.6 g sat.); 96 g carbo (3 g fiber); 1,238 mg sodium; 173 mg chol.

Shrimp Couscous

PREP AND COOK TIME: About 25 minutes
NOTES: Garam masala can be found in the dried herbs and spices section at most supermarkets; if not available, use curry powder.
MAKES: 4 servings

- 3 cups fat-skimmed **chicken broth**
- ¼ cup **catsup**
- 1 tablespoon minced **fresh ginger**
- 2 teaspoons **mustard seed**
- 1 teaspoon **chili powder**
- ½ teaspoon **garam masala**
- ½ teaspoon **dried dill weed**
- 1 pound thawed **frozen uncooked, shelled, deveined shrimp** (38 to 50 per lb.), rinsed and drained
- 2 cups **couscous**
- 2 tablespoons finely slivered **fresh mint** leaves
- **Plain nonfat yogurt**
- **Salt**
- **Lime** wedges

1. In a 3- to 4-quart pan, combine broth, catsup, ginger, mustard seed, chili powder, garam masala, and dill weed. Bring to a boil over high heat; when boiling add shrimp and cook until opaque but still moist-looking in center of thickest part (cut to test), 3 to 4 minutes.

2. At once, stir couscous into pan, cover, and remove from heat. Let stand 5 minutes. Stir mixture with a fork; there should be some liquid. Spoon shrimp couscous onto plates; sprinkle with mint and add to taste yogurt, salt, and juice from lime wedges.

Per serving: 521 cal., 5.8% (30 cal.) from fat; 42 g protein; 3.3 g fat (0.5 g sat.); 78 g carbo (3.9 g fiber); 419 mg sodium; 173 mg chol.

Lemon and Shrimp Capellini

PREP AND COOK TIME: About 30 minutes
MAKES: 4 servings

- 1 **lemon**
- 2 teaspoons **coriander seed**
- 1 teaspoon **fennel seed**
- ½ teaspoon fresh-ground **pepper**
- 6 cups fat-skimmed **chicken broth**
- ½ cup **dry white wine**
- ¾ pound **dried capellini** (angel hair) **pasta**
- 1 pound thawed **frozen uncooked, shelled, deveined shrimp** (38 to 50 per lb.), rinsed and drained
- ½ cup minced **fresh chives** or green onions
- **Lemon** wedges
- **Salt**

1. Rinse lemon; trim and discard thin slices from each end. Thinly slice lemon, saving the juice; discard seeds and finely chop fruit. Put fruit and juice in a 5- to 6-quart pan. Add coriander seed, fennel seed, pepper, broth, and wine. Bring to a boil over high heat. Add pasta, stir, then add shrimp; stir often until pasta is tender to bite and shrimp are opaque but still moist-looking in center of thickest part (cut to test), about 5 minutes.

2. Add chives. Using 2 forks, lift pasta mixture to mix, then transfer equally to wide bowls, adding any remaining broth. Garnish with lemon wedges to squeeze over portions; add salt to taste.

Per serving: 520 cal., 6.2% (32 cal.) from fat; 47 g protein; 3.6 g fat (0.6 g sat.); 69 g carbo (4.1 g fiber); 290 mg sodium; 173 mg chol. ◆

The Quick Cook

Appetizers in 30 minutes or less
By Betsy Reynolds Bateson

Nibbling trio: Tortilla rolls, falafel squares, and red lentil spread.

■ Easy appetizers that come together quickly make good sense this time of year, whether you want to get a head start on a party or just be ready to put out the welcome mat on short notice. And if the appetizers just happen to be all-vegetable, but don't show it— as in this trio of choices—concerns about tending to the needs of vegetarian guests simply disappear.

Red and Green Roll-ups

PREP AND COOK TIME: About 20 minutes
NOTES: For holiday color, choose flour tortillas made with spinach or chili; they must be fresh to roll without cracking.
MAKES: 24 pieces; 12 servings

- 2 cups **broccoli florets** (about 6 oz. total), rinsed
- 1 **red bell pepper** (8 oz.), rinsed, stemmed, and seeded
- 4 **green onions,** rinsed and ends trimmed
- 1 package (8 oz.) **cream cheese**
- 1 tablespoon **prepared horseradish**
- 1 tablespoon **lemon juice**
- 4 **flour tortillas** (10 in.), regular or flavored (see notes)

- ¾ cup packed **feta cheese,** finely crumbled
- ½ cup chopped **fresh cilantro**
- ½ cup chopped **salted roasted almonds**

1. Cut broccoli, bell pepper, and onions into chunks. Whirl in a food processor until coarsely chopped. Cut cream cheese in chunks and add to processor along with horseradish and lemon juice. Whirl, until ingredients are mixed but not puréed; scrape container often.

2. Spread 1 side of each flour tortilla equally, to the edge, with the cheese mixture. Sprinkle each tortilla equally with feta, cilantro, and almonds. Roll tortilla snugly around filling; set seam down. If making up to 1 day ahead, wrap airtight and chill.

3. Cut each roll crosswise into 6 equal pieces and set, cut edge down, on a platter.

Per serving: 217 cal., 62% (135 cal.) from fat; 7.2 g protein; 15 g fat (7 g sat.); 14 g carbo (2.1 g fiber); 376 mg sodium; 35 mg chol.

Falafel Nibbles

PREP AND COOK TIME: About 30 minutes
NOTES: To garnish, cut 12 pitted calamata olives vertically into 3 equal pieces (or slice crosswise); set pieces smooth side up (or lay slices flat), evenly apart, on falafel mixture before baking. If you want a dip for falafel nibbles, mix curry powder to taste with plain yogurt.
MAKES: 36 pieces; 12 servings

- 3 **large eggs**
- 1 cup **dried falafel mix**
- ½ cup chopped **parsley**
- ½ cup chopped **green onions**
- ¼ cup grated **carrot**
- ¼ cup **lemon juice**
  - About 2 tablespoons **olive oil**
- 1 can (4 oz.) **diced green chilies**
- 2 cups (½ lb.) **shredded jack cheese**

1. In a bowl, beat to blend eggs and ¼ cup water. Add falafel mix, parsley, onions, carrot, lemon juice, and 2 tablespoons olive oil; beat to blend. Stir in chilies and cheese. Scrape mixture into an oiled 9- by 13-inch pan; spread level.

2. Bake in a 375° oven until edges are darker brown and center is firm when lightly pressed, about 20 minutes. Let cool at least 5 minutes, or let cool, cover, and chill up to 1 day.

3. Cut falafel into 36 equal pieces and arrange on a platter.

Per serving: 156 cal., 57% (89 cal.) from fat; 8.8 g protein; 9.9 g fat (4 g sat.); 8.9 g carbo (2.4 g fiber); 302 mg sodium; 73 mg chol.

Red Lentil Hummus

PREP AND COOK TIME: About 25 minutes
NOTES: Spread hummus on toasted baguette slices or pocket bread triangles, or serve as a dip for crisp vegetables.
MAKES: About 2 cups; 12 servings

- ½ cup **hulled** (decorticated) **red lentils** such as Red Chief or Crimson
- 2 tablespoons **sesame seed**
- 2 tablespoons **olive oil**
- ¾ cup fat-skimmed **chicken** or vegetable **broth**
- ½ cup chopped **canned roasted red peppers**
- ¼ cup chopped **shallots**
- 1 teaspoon grated **orange** peel
- ½ teaspoon **dried oregano**
- ¼ teaspoon ground **dried turmeric**
  Salt
- 2 tablespoons drained, chopped **dried tomatoes packed in oil**

1. Sort lentils, discard debris, and rinse. In a 1½- to 2-quart pan over high heat, stir sesame seed and olive oil until seed is golden, 1 to 1½ minutes. At once add lentils, broth, red peppers, shallots, orange peel, oregano, and turmeric. Bring to a boil over high heat; cover and simmer until lentils mash when pressed, 15 to 20 minutes.

2. Pour mixture into a blender or food processor; whirl until smooth, scraping sides as needed. Add salt to taste. Scrape into a bowl; scatter tomatoes over hummus. Serve warm or cool, or cover and chill up to 1 day.

Per serving: 68 cal., 46% (31 cal.) from fat; 3.2 g protein; 3.4 g fat (0.4 g sat.); 6.8 g carbo (1.3 g fiber); 27 mg sodium; 0 mg chol. ◆

Kitchen Cabinet

Readers' recipes tested in Sunset's kitchens

By Andrew Baker

This tangy tart is filled with tangerine flavor; the crust is more like a cookie than a pastry.

JAMES CARRIER (2)

■ A year ago we asked you to tell us about your favorite holiday food traditions. For this special edition of Kitchen Cabinet, we culled some wonderful recipes from the unique responses we received.

Tangerine Tart with Cookie Crust

Liz Strongman, Seattle

Liz Strongman likes to end a rich holiday meal (for her family, it's often prime rib and garlic mashed potatoes) with this not-too-sweet citrus tart. Bake the tart (through step 2) up to 1 day ahead; chill airtight.

PREP AND COOK TIME: About 1½ hours, plus at least 1 hour to cool

MAKES: 8 to 10 servings

2 **large eggs**

⅔ cup **granulated sugar**

½ cup **fresh** or bottled **tangerine** juice

1 tablespoon grated **tangerine** peel

1½ tablespoons **lemon juice**

¼ cup **half-and-half** (light cream)

Cookie crust (recipe follows)

¾ cup **whipping cream**

2 tablespoons **powdered sugar**

1 teaspoon **vanilla**

1. In a bowl, with a mixer on high speed, beat eggs and granulated sugar until well blended, about 1 minute. Add tangerine juice, 2 teaspoons tangerine peel, lemon juice, and half-and-half. Beat until blended. Pour into baked cookie crust.

2. Bake in a 325° oven until filling no longer jiggles in the center when pan is gently shaken, 30 to 40 minutes. Let cool completely on a rack, about 1 hour.

3. In a bowl, combine whipping cream, remaining 1 teaspoon tangerine peel, powdered sugar, and vanilla. Beat with a mixer on high speed just until cream holds soft mounds.

4. Cut tart into wedges. With a wide spatula, transfer to plates. Spoon flavored whipped cream evenly onto portions.

Per serving: 409 cal., 53% (216 cal.) from fat; 4.6 g protein; 24 g fat (14 g sat.); 45 g carbo (0.7 g fiber); 186 mg sodium; 108 mg chol.

Cookie crust. In a food processor (or a bowl), combine 2 cups **all-purpose flour,** ¾ cup **powdered sugar,** and 2 teaspoons grated **tangerine** peel. Whirl (or stir) to blend. Add 14 tablespoons (¾ cup plus 2 tablespoons) **butter** or margarine, in chunks, and whirl (or rub in with your fingers) just until dough holds together. Press over bottom and up sides of a 10-inch tart pan with removable rim. Bake in a 325° oven until crust is lightly browned, 25 to 35 minutes.

Per serving: 269 cal., 54% (144 cal.) from fat; 2.7 g protein; 16 g fat (10 g sat.); 28 g carbo (0.7 g fiber); 165 mg sodium; 43 mg chol.

Curried Butternut Squash Soup with Crab

Janet Romero, San Jose

"It's become a special tradition for us," Janet Romero says of the progressive dinner seven or eight couples in her neighborhood stage each year for the holidays. This soup is one of the group's favorite dishes for the occasion.

PREP AND COOK TIME: About 1¼ hours

MAKES: About 16 cups; 8 servings

2 **onions** (1 lb. total), peeled and chopped

1 cup chopped **celery**

2 tablespoons **butter** or margarine

¼ cup **tomato paste**

3 tablespoons **curry powder**

2 pounds **butternut squash,** peeled and cut into 1-inch chunks

2 **Granny Smith apples** (1 lb. total), peeled and coarsely chopped

6 cups fat-skimmed **chicken broth**

2 tablespoons minced **fresh ginger**

1 **dried bay leaf**

2 **whole cloves**

½ teaspoon **pepper**

Sweet crab chunks and red bell pepper slivers top a golden squash soup.

½ cup **dry sherry**

½ pound **shelled cooked crab**

Thinly sliced **red bell pepper** (optional)

Salt

1. In a 5- to 6-quart pan over high heat, stir onions and celery in butter until limp, about 5 minutes. Add tomato paste and curry powder, and stir 1 minute longer.

2. Add squash, apples, broth, 4 cups water, ginger, bay leaf, cloves, and pepper. Stirring often, bring to a boil; cover, reduce heat, and simmer, stirring occasionally, until squash mashes easily, 30 to 40 minutes.

3. Remove and discard bay leaf and cloves. In a blender or food processor, whirl squash mixture, a portion at a time, until smooth.

4. Pour purée through a fine strainer back into pan. Add sherry and stir over medium heat just until steaming, about 2 minutes.

5. Meanwhile, remove any bits of shell from crab.

6. Ladle soup into wide bowls. Mound equal portions of crab in the center of each bowl. Garnish with bell pepper, if desired. Add salt to taste.

Per serving: 208 cal., 18% (37 cal.) from fat; 14 g protein; 4.1 g fat (1.9 g sat.); 27 g carbo (4.9 g fiber); 251 mg sodium; 36 mg chol.

Polish Hunters' Stew

A.J. Diehl, Encino, California

"As a child, I didn't know this was hunters' stew—it was just one of my favorite things," says A.J. Diehl. Her Polish parents always prepared *bigos* for the holidays. Diehl is now quick to point out that the stew is a treasured Polish dish—poetry and other literature have been written in its praise.

A Fresno Armenian Christmas

At Christmas, Christine Vartanian-Datian of Las Vegas always comes home to Fresno, California, where she grew up and where her mother, Alice Vartanian, still lives. The meal is a feast of Armenian specialties, including leeks with lemon dressing and a stuffed leg of lamb. "The house smells wonderful because my mother has baked for a month," says Vartanian-Datian.

Lemon Leeks with Olive Oil

PREP AND COOK TIME: About 25 minutes

MAKES: 10 to 12 servings

3 pounds **leeks**

4 cloves **garlic**, peeled and minced or pressed

½ cup **olive oil**

2 **onions** (1 lb. total), peeled and thinly sliced

1 teaspoon **sugar**

About ¼ cup **lemon juice**

Salt and **pepper**

1. Trim root ends, coarse tops, and outer layers from leeks; cut leeks in half lengthwise. Hold under running water and flip layers to rinse out grit. Cut leeks into 2-inch lengths.

2. In a 12-inch frying pan or 5- to 6-quart pan over medium-high heat, stir garlic in 2 teaspoons oil until lightly browned, about 1 minute. Add leeks, onions, and ½ cup water; cover and simmer until leeks are tender when pierced, about 15 minutes.

3. Add remaining olive oil and sugar to pan, and stir until sugar is dissolved. Add lemon juice to taste.

4. Spoon leeks into a bowl. Add salt and pepper to taste.

Per serving: 127 cal., 65% (83 cal.) from fat; 1.2 g protein; 9.2 g fat (1.2 g sat.); 11 g carbo (1.2 g fiber); 12 mg sodium; 0 mg chol.

Wine-marinated Stuffed Leg of Lamb

PREP AND COOK TIME: About 1½ hours, plus at least 2 hours to marinate

MAKES: 10 to 12 servings

1 bottle (750 ml.) **dry red wine**

¾ teaspoon **ground allspice**

¾ teaspoon **ground nutmeg**

1 **dried bay leaf**

1 **boned leg of lamb** (4 to 4½ lb.)

⅓ cup **pine nuts**

½ pound **mushrooms**, rinsed

2 tablespoons **butter** or olive oil

½ cup finely chopped **onion**

½ cup finely chopped **red bell pepper**

⅓ cup finely chopped **pitted dates**

2 tablespoons minced **fresh chives**

2 tablespoons minced **parsley**

1½ cups fat-skimmed **beef broth**

1 tablespoon **sugar**

Salt and fresh-ground **pepper**

1. In an 11- by 17-inch roasting pan, combine wine, allspice, nutmeg, and bay leaf.

2. Trim excess fat from lamb. Rinse meat and lay flat, boned side up. Make cuts about halfway through all the thickest parts of meat. Push cuts open to make meat as evenly thick as possible. Lay lamb flat in pan. Cover and chill at least 2 hours or up to 1 day, turning meat occasionally.

3. Meanwhile, in a 10- to 12-inch frying pan over medium-high heat, stir pine nuts until golden brown, 3 to 4 minutes; pour into a small bowl.

4. Trim and discard discolored stem ends from mushrooms; finely chop mushrooms. Add mushrooms, butter, onion, and bell pepper to frying pan. Stir often over high heat until vegetables are well browned, 8 to 10 minutes. Remove from heat and stir in pine nuts, dates, chives, and parsley.

5. Lift lamb from roasting pan and lay flat, boned side up. Reserve 1½ cups marinade; discard remaining marinade and bay leaf. Spread mushroom mixture over lamb to within 1 inch of edges. Starting at a narrow edge, roll lamb into a tight log (about 5 by 11 in.). Tie at 2-inch intervals with cotton string. Set in roasting pan.

6. Bake lamb in a 375° oven until a thermometer inserted in center of thickest part reaches 145°, 1¼ to 1½ hours. Transfer lamb to a rimmed platter and, keeping it warm, let rest 10 minutes. Add reserved marinade, broth, and sugar to pan. Stir over high heat, scraping browned bits free, until reduced to 2 cups, about 10 minutes. Add accumulated lamb juices and pour into a bowl.

7. Cut lamb crosswise into 1-inch-thick slices. Serve with sauce. Add salt and pepper to taste.

Per serving: 208 cal., 42% (87 cal.) from fat; 23 g protein; 9.7 g fat (3.5 g sat.); 7.7 g carbo (1.1 g fiber); 81 mg sodium; 70 mg chol.

Santa Fe appetizer party

Nancy Gerlach of Albuquerque prepares a yearly holiday buffet that includes these chili- and raisin-speckled meatballs (a recipe from a friend) and jicama-fruit salad (her own creation) plus blue-corn pozole and chicken tamales.

Party food in Santa Fe: Fruit salad and chili balls (background).

Feast Day Chili Balls

PREP AND COOK TIME: About 45 minutes

MAKES: About 50 meatballs; 8 to 10 servings

- ¼ cup finely chopped **onion**
- 1 tablespoon minced **fresh jalapeño chilies**
- 1 pound **ground lean pork**
- 1 can (7 oz.) **diced green chilies**
- ½ cup **raisins**
- 1 tablespoon **sugar**
  About ½ teaspoon **salt**
- 4 **large eggs**
  About ¾ cup **all-purpose flour**
  Salad oil
- 1 cup **tomato** or green chili **salsa** (or ½ cup of each)

1. In a 10- to 12-inch nonstick frying pan over high heat, stir onion, jalapeño chilies, and ½ pound ground pork until pork is browned, about 5 minutes. Spoon off and discard any fat, then stir in diced green chilies, raisins, sugar, and ½ teaspoon salt. When mixture is cool enough to handle, stir in remaining ½ pound pork and 1 egg.

2. Put about ½ cup flour on a rimmed plate. Shape pork mixture, about 2 teaspoons at a time, into smooth 1-inch balls; 1 at a time, roll balls in flour to coat, shake off excess, and place slightly apart in a waxed paper–lined 10- by 15-inch pan.

3. Pour 1 inch of oil into a 14-inch flat-bottomed wok or a 5- to 6-quart pan over high heat. When oil reaches 360°, adjust heat to maintain temperature.

4. Meanwhile, separate remaining 3 eggs, putting whites in 1 bowl, yolks in another. With a mixer on high speed, beat whites until they hold stiff peaks, then beat yolks and ¼ cup flour (no need to wash beaters) until well blended. Beat ⅓ of the egg whites into the egg yolk mixture until well blended, then gradually fold in remaining whites.

5. With a fork, dip chili balls 1 at a time into egg mixture; lift out and let drain briefly, then slide into hot oil, without crowding, frying in batches. Turn balls occasionally until golden brown all over, 4 to 6 minutes total. Lift out with a slotted spoon when cooked; transfer to a paper towel–lined 10- by 15-inch baking pan in a 200° oven to keep warm. Add more balls to oil as there's room.

6. When all the chili balls are cooked, transfer to a platter. Season to taste with salt. Serve with salsa for dipping.

Per serving: 223 cal., 44% (99 cal.) from fat; 13 g protein; 11 g fat (2.6 g sat.); 18 g carbo (0.9 g fiber); 466 mg sodium; 115 mg chol.

PREP AND COOK TIME: About 2¼ hours

MAKES: About 10 cups; 5 to 6 servings

- 1 ounce **dried porcini mushrooms**
- ¼ pound **bacon,** chopped
- ¾ pound fat-trimmed **beef sirloin**
- ¾ pound **smoked sausages** such as kielbasa (Polish)
- 1 **onion** (½ lb.), peeled and chopped
- 2 cups drained **sauerkraut**
- 1 pound **cooked ham,** cut into ½-inch chunks
- 2 **firm-ripe tomatoes** (about ¾ lb. total), rinsed, cored, and chopped
- ¼ cup **dry red wine**
- 2 cloves **garlic,** peeled and minced or pressed
- 1 tablespoon minced **fresh rosemary** leaves or crumbled dried rosemary
- 2 teaspoons **fresh thyme** leaves or dried thyme
- ½ teaspoon **coriander seed**
- 1 **dried bay leaf**
  Salt and **pepper**

1. In a small bowl, pour 1 cup boiling water over mushrooms and let stand until soft, 10 to 15 minutes. Lift mushrooms from water and squeeze out moisture; reserve soaking liquid. Coarsely chop mushrooms.

2. In a 5- to 6-quart pan over high heat, stir bacon frequently until lightly browned, about 3 minutes. With a slotted spoon, transfer to towels to drain. Discard all but 1 teaspoon drippings in pan.

3. Meanwhile, rinse beef and pat dry. Cut beef and sausages into 1-inch chunks. Add beef and sausages to pan and stir until browned, about 5 minutes. Remove from pan with a slotted spoon and set aside. Add onion to pan and stir until browned, 3 to 4 minutes. Return bacon, beef, and sausages to pan. Carefully pour in reserved mushroom soaking liquid, leaving grit behind, then add 2 cups water, sauerkraut, ham, tomatoes, wine, garlic, rosemary, thyme, coriander seed, and bay leaf. Stirring often, bring to a boil; reduce heat and simmer, stirring occasionally, until beef is tender when pierced, about 1½ hours.

4. Ladle stew into wide bowls, discarding bay leaf. Add salt and pepper to taste.

Per serving: 473 cal., 53% (252 cal.) from fat; 41 g protein; 28 g fat (10 g sat.); 11 g carbo (3.5 g fiber); 2,054 mg sodium; 122 mg chol.

Quick Tortoni Ice Cream

Marge Terhar, Northridge, California

During the holiday season, Marge Terhar keeps these single-serving treats on hand as an impromptu dessert for drop-in guests.

PREP TIME: About 20 minutes, plus at least 1 hour to freeze

MAKES: 18 servings

- 1 quart **vanilla ice cream**
- 18 **paper baking cups** (2½ in. wide)

Jicama-Fruit Salad

PREP AND COOK TIME: About 40 minutes
MAKES: 8 to 10 servings

- ⅓ cup **pine nuts**
- 2 tablespoons **orange juice**
- 2 tablespoons **lime juice**
- 1 teaspoon **sugar**
  About ¼ teaspoon **cayenne**
- 3 cups sliced **strawberries**
- 2 cups matchstick-size strips **jicama**
- 4 **oranges** (about 2 lb. total)
  Butter lettuce leaves
  Salt

1. In an 8- to 10-inch frying pan over medium-high heat, stir or shake nuts frequently until golden, 2 to 3 minutes.

2. In a bowl, whisk to blend orange juice, lime juice, sugar, and cayenne to taste. Add strawberries and jicama; mix gently.

3. With a sharp knife, cut peel and white membrane from oranges; discard. Cut oranges crosswise into ¼- to ½-inch slices. Discard any seeds.

4. Arrange lettuce on a wide rimmed platter and top with oranges. Spoon strawberry mixture on top; sprinkle with pine nuts. Add salt to taste.

Per serving: 82 cal., 29% (24 cal.) from fat; 2.1 g protein; 2.7 g fat (0.4 g sat.); 15 g carbo (4.5 g fiber); 2.1 mg sodium; 0 mg chol.

- ¼ cup diced **candied** (glacé) **cherries**
- ¾ cup crumbled **crisp almond macaroons** (about 3 oz. total)
- ½ cup chopped **salted roasted almonds**
- 3 tablespoons **almond-**, cherry-, or hazelnut-**flavor liqueur** (optional)

1. Let ice cream stand at room temperature until slightly softened, about 10 minutes; scoop into a bowl.

2. Meanwhile, place 1 paper baking cup in each of 18 muffin-pan cups (for 2½- to 2¾-in. muffins).

3. Add cherries, macaroons, almonds, and liqueur to ice cream; mix well. Quickly spoon about ¼ cup ice cream mixture into each paper baking cup. Freeze until firm, at least 1 hour without liqueur, 3 hours with liqueur. Serve, or cover airtight and freeze up to 2 weeks.

Per serving: 113 cal., 50% (56 cal.) from fat; 2.2 g protein; 6.2 g fat (2.2 g sat.); 13 g carbo (0.5 g fiber); 60 mg sodium; 13 mg chol. ◆

Wineries in the woods

Oregon's south Willamette Valley has gorgeous scenery and great wines

■ The wine country south and west of Eugene doesn't look much like wine country. Two-lane Territorial Highway twists and dips over densely forested hills, past rusting tin-roof sheds and crumbling wood barns engulfed in blackberries. But follow a little blue sign down a gravel road and suddenly you'll come upon a neat vineyard carved from the forest, a collection of winery buildings, and the destination you seek: "Tasting Room."

From Eugene, a 70-mile loop takes you to five great wineries. Pack lunch before you go, since these wineries have picnic tables in memorable settings (and wine sold by the glass). Each of the five is a short drive off Territorial Highway, about 12 miles west of Eugene via State 126; look for blue signs pointing the way.

Tasting rooms are normally open from noon to 5 daily through September and on weekends in winter. Pick up a free "Vintage 2000" brochure at any of the wineries or, in advance, from the Oregon Wine

Visit the tasting room at Hinman Vineyards/Silvan Ridge (above); relax at Château Lorane (below).

Advisory Board (503/228-8336 or www.oregonwine.org). The properties below are listed from north to south.

LaVelle Vineyards. Picnic under the cherry trees and browse the art gallery above the tasting bar. *89697 Sheffler Rd., near Elmira; 541/ 935-9406.*

Secret House Winery. Produces méthode Champenoise sparkling wine in addition to Pinot Noir, Chardonnay, and Riesling. *88324 Vineyard Lane, near Veneta; 935-3774.*

Hinman Vineyards/Silvan Ridge. This is closest to Eugene and the oldest of the bunch; be sure to taste its Silvan Ridge reserve wines. *27012 Briggs Hill Rd., near Crow; 345-1945.*

King Estate Winery. Opened in 1992 and definitely worth the drive, the sprawling hilltop estate boasts celebrated wines and a knockout view. *80854 Territorial Hwy., near Lorane; (800) 884-4441.*

Château Lorane. Sip a glass on the deck, looking out at the winery's lake. Its repertoire includes some unusual varietals. *27415 Siuslaw River Rd., near Lorane; 942-8028.*
— *Bonnie Henderson* ◆

Articles Index

Index of Recipe Titles

Low-Fat Recipes

General Index